ZINN & THE ART OF ROAD BIKE MAINTENANCE

By Lennard Zinn

Foreword by Jonathan Vaughters

Illustrated by Todd Telander

VeloPress • Boulder, Colorado USA

Zinn & the Art of Road Bike Maintenance

International Standard Book Number: 1-884737-70-6

Library of Congress Cataloging-in Publication Data

Zinn, Lennard.
Zinn & the art of road bike maintenance / Lennard Zinn;
foreward by Jonathan Vaughters; illustrated by Todd Telander.
p. cm.
Includes bibliographical references and index.
ISBN 1-884737-70-6 (pbk.)
1. Bicycles—Maintenance and repair. I. Title

TL430 .Z56 2000
629.28'772—dc21 99-086767

VeloPress
1830 North 55th Street
Boulder, Colorado 80301-2700 USA
303/440-0601; fax 303/444-6788; e-mail velopress@7dogs.com

To purchase additional copies of this book or other VeloPress books, call 800/234-8356 or visit us on the Web at www.velogear.com.

Designed by Paula Megenhardt
Cover designed by Chas Chamberlin
Edited by Ted Costantino
Cover photography by Galen Nathanson

Printed in the USA
Distributed in the United States and Canada by Publishers Group West

To Chamba La Bamba and Lulupah

ZINN & THE ART OF ROAD BIKE MAINTENANCE

contents

a tip of the helmet to...

Todd Telander. A picture is worth a thousand words, adding up to hundreds of thousands of illustrative "words" from Todd's capable hand. His drawings make my written words more intelligible and this book more useful and beautiful.

My everlasting appreciation goes to the late Bill Woodul for teaching me much of what I know about working on road bikes. And thanks to Scott Adlfinger of Louisville Cyclery (CO) for all of his assistance and insight.

Thanks to Ted Costantino for his fine editing, Lori Hobkirk for keeping this and all VeloPress books moving smoothly through the editorial process, and Charles Pelkey for his editing contributions and content suggestions. My appreciation to Amy Sorrells, Pete Hammond and Rick Rundall for keeping the fires burning under this book, and for making VeloPress such a fine organization for which to work.

Thanks to designers Paula Megenhardt and Chas Chamberlin for putting the pieces into a great-looking package.

And thanks to Felix Magowan and John Wilcockson for creating VeloPress in the first place.

And, finally, thanks to my family for providing support and such a nice working environment for me at home.

Foreword

The guy Colby worked for

Growing up as a teenager along Colorado's Front Range is about as good as it gets for a bike racer. Amazingly, in this part of the great U.S., there were other teenagers who also shaved their legs for this strange sport of cycling. This small social circle led me to meeting Colby Pearce, who has been my best friend ever since. He was a Boulder weirdo completely taken by the same sport. We were both drawn to this cult for the same reasons: it was something few others did—so we were rebels; it didn't involve body size or a ball; it was fast and dangerous; and we weren't good at any other sport anyway—although Colby still maintains he would have made the high school varsity wrestling squad had he not started college so soon. The one thing that set this sport apart, however, was that it involved a machine.

Colby and I were diehard *Star Trek* nerds. We had always taken apart old lawnmower engines, and we were the first to try and make a rocket out of toilet paper rolls and hairspray. Both of us loved to tinker with our bicycles, too. We would tape cellophane over our wheels to make them more aerodynamic, file to a nub every part on the components to make them weigh less, and spend hours arguing as to whether Colby won the Glenwood Springs time trial because he had sealed bearing pulleys and I did not.

Colby was one year older than I, so he was always the first to reach milestones in his life: the first to kiss a girl, the first to race a pro-am race, the first to drive, and, most importantly, the first to enslave himself to labor. In fact, as soon as Colby turned 16, he went out and found a job. Of course, the most logical choice for him was to work in a bike shop, but in a bold move he found a job working for a framebuilder. His new employer's name was Lennard Zinn. Lennard was a strange, cryptic man who worked in a dark laboratory-like shop. He was a guru, one who seemed to have all the knowledge we were seeking.

Instead of studying or training after school, I often stopped by Colby's new workplace and asked questions until I was kicked out. This Lennard fellow knew everything, from Greg LeMond's drag coefficient to how much time you could save in a 40km time trial by taping your ears back. He told us of studies about seat tube angles relating to femur length, tales of long crankarms and heart rate, riddles of meters per second and Newtons, and why steel was always real. We learned of tensile strength, pitted headsets, why belt drives never caught on, and how Laurent Fignon lost the Tour de France because of his ponytail. Soon, Colby and I were armed with something few bike racers have: knowledge. We knew the latest wind tunnel data, we knew how to grease a bottom bracket, we knew which hubs were fast and which ones weren't, we knew how every piece of equipment on our bike functioned, and we knew how we could make it function better.

At first, this knowledge seemed to come back at us, such as the time I broke a carbon seat on the slopes of Mount Evans while on record time, or the time before pursuit nationals when Colby cut off his thumb while cleaning his chain for the 50th time.

Despite these setbacks, experimenting with and knowing the ins and outs of the machine that I now call my trade tool is what has continued to make this sport fascinating to me. The bicycle binds human prowess and power with the intellectual qualities of design and engineering, and it makes our sport very different from most others. Bike knowledge gives me an advantage in what is now a very competitive profession, but I can't tell you exactly how. Lennard's book will, though. I am sure of it.

—Jonathan Vaughters

"Outside of a dog,
a book is man's best friend.
Inside of a dog it's too dark to read." —Groucho Marx

Exploded road bike

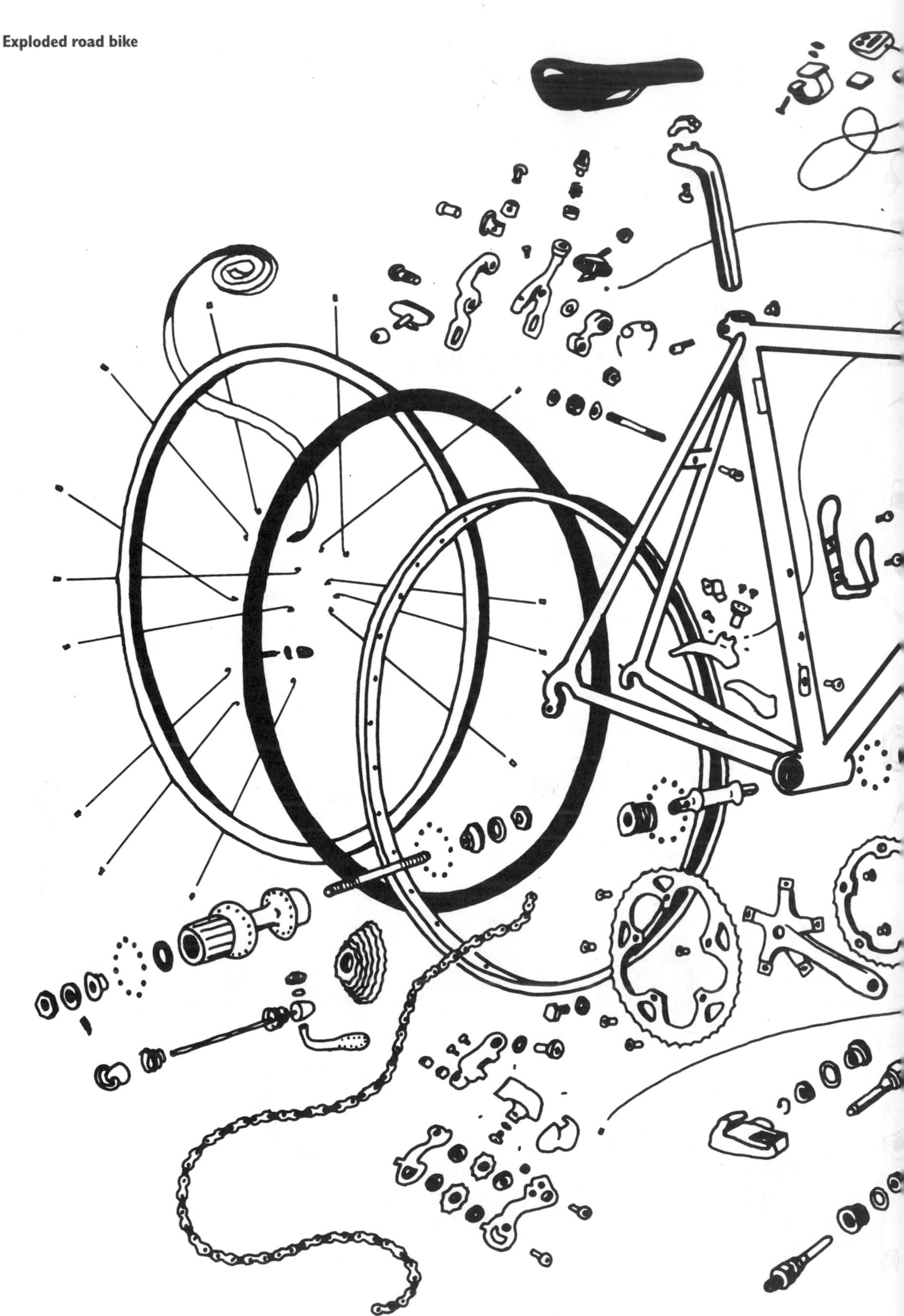

Introduction

"First things first,
but not necessarily in that order."—Doctor Who

ABOUT THIS BOOK

So, you want to maintain your road bike? Congratulations. You will be glad to have taken this step. While it is nice to learn from the input of friends or shop employees who know more about bikes than you do, it is also important to not be dependent on them whenever anything happens. And the romance of riding with the wind in your hair is enhanced by understanding the classical structure of the mechanical system upon which you are sitting and to which you are trusting your life.

Even the pure romantic can follow the simple step-by-step procedures and exploded diagrams in this book and discover a passion for spreading new grease on old parts. And, I hope, everyone will develop an appreciation for how infusing love into the work will guarantee more success at bike maintenance. If not, frustration will take over, you will use less care, and riding enjoyment will be compromised.

Zinn & the Art of Road Bike Maintenance is organized in such a way that you can pick maintenance tasks appropriate for you. Anyone can perform the repairs illustrated on these pages. It takes only a willingness to learn, as well as the appropriate tools.

This book is intended to be valuable for everyone from shop mechanics to those who only want to know about the most minimal maintenance their bike requires. Chapter 2 is for those only interested in the latter; the rest of the book is for those who choose to go to greater lengths to make everything work optimally and look clean and beautiful.

i.1 **the object of our attention (and affection), racing version**

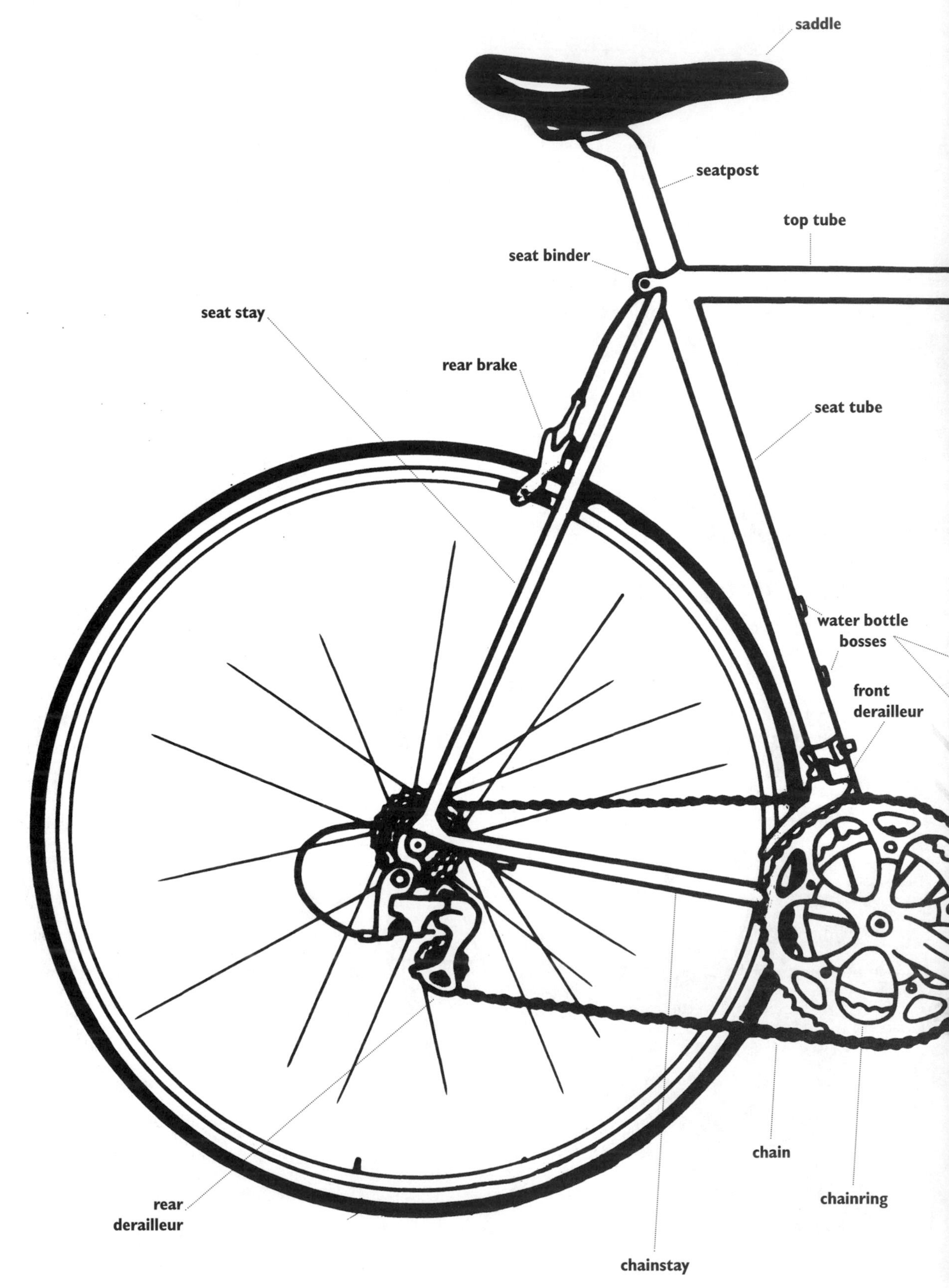

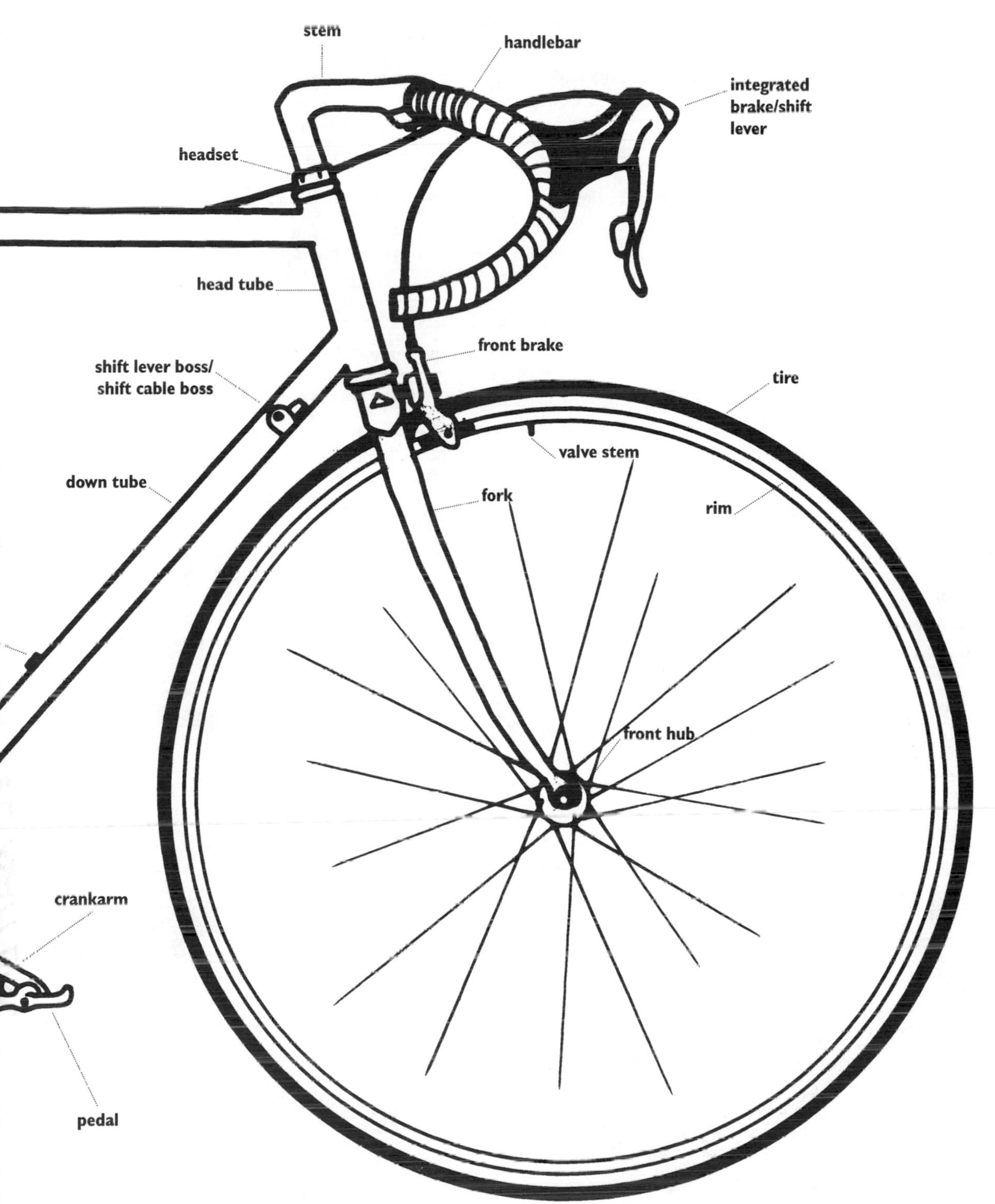
stem
handlebar
integrated brake/shift lever
headset
head tube
front brake
shift lever boss/ shift cable boss
tire
valve stem
down tube
fork
rim
front hub
crankarm
pedal

intro

WHY DO IT YOURSELF?

There are a number of reasons why you would want to learn to maintain your bike. Obviously, if done correctly, it is a lot cheaper to fix a bike yourself than to pay someone else to do it. And home-maintenance is a necessity for most racers and others who live to ride and have no visible means of support.

As your income increases, economic necessity ceases to be a significant issue. However, you may find that you enjoy working on your bike for reasons other than just saving money. Unless you have a trusted mechanic to whom you regularly bring your bike, you are not likely to find anyone else who cares as much about your bicycle's smooth operation and cleanliness as you do. Furthermore, if you have only limited time to ride, you probably can't afford not to be practiced in fixing mechanical breakdowns that may occur on the road. It may also be hard to find the time to drop off your bike and pick it up from the shop. Nor will you like missing a ride during beautiful weather while your bike sits in a shop backed up with repairs. Once you have finally taken your ailing machine to the shop, finding out that you can't just drop it off during high season and expect anything faster than a three-week turnaround on a minor repair can ruin your day. Even scheduling and adhering to a repair appointment can be a hassle. And sometimes, a shop slammed with summer work will return your bike in less-than-optimal condition, having devoted either little time to it or the time of an inexperienced mechanic. But you are not about to go through the wringer again and wait for them to fix it correctly. You decide to save the aggravation and do it yourself.

Working on your bike can be fun. Bicycles are the manifestation of elegant simplicity. Bicycle parts, par-

i.2 **triathlon or time-trial bike**

ticularly high-end components, are meant to work well and last a long time. With the proper attention, they can shine in appearance and performance for years to come. Satisfaction can be found in dismantling and cleaning a filthy, barely functional part, lubricating it with fresh grease, and reassembling it so that it works like new. Knowing that you made those parts work so smoothly, and that you can do it again when they next need it, is rewarding. You will be eager to ride hard and long to see how your work holds up, rather than being reluctant to get far from home for fear of breaking something.

There is also something very liberating about going on a long ride and knowing that you can fix just about anything that may go wrong. Armed with this knowledge and the tools to put it into action, you will have more confidence to explore new areas and go farther than you may otherwise. You may also find yourself more willing to share your love of the sport with other, less-experienced, riders. You will enjoy riding with them more if you know that you can fix their questionably-maintained bikes, and you will revel in their adoration of you after you have removed an annoying squeak or mis-shift from their bike.

HOW TO USE THIS BOOK

Skim through the entire book. Skip the detailed steps, but look at the table of contents and the exploded diagrams, and get the general flavor of the book and what's inside. When it's time to perform a particular task, you will know where to find it, and you will have a general idea of how to approach it.

Illustrator Todd Telander and I have done our best to make these pages as understandable as possible. Exploded diagrams are purposefully used instead of photographs to show more clearly how

i.3 **touring bike**

each part goes together. The first time you go through a procedure, you may find it easier to have a friend read the instructions out loud as you perform the steps.

Obviously, some maintenance tasks are more complicated than others. I am convinced that anyone with an opposable thumb can perform any repair on a bike. Still, it pays to spend some time getting familiar with the really simple tasks, such as fixing a flat, before throwing yourself into complex jobs, such as building a wheel.

Tasks and tools required are divided into three levels indicating their complexity or your proficiency. Level 1 tasks need Level 1 tools and require of you only an eagerness to learn. Level 2 and Level 3 also have corresponding tool sets and are progressively more difficult. All tools are shown in Chapter 1, and all repairs are classified as Level 1 unless otherwise indicated. At the end of Chapter 2 (Section 2-16, page 29) is a "General Guide to Performing Mechanical Work," which is a must-read; it states general policies and approaches that apply to all mechanical work.

Each chapter starts with a list of required tools in the margin. If a section involves more than basic experience and tools there will be an icon designating the difficulty. Tasks and illustrations are numbered for easy reference.

A troubleshooting section is included at the end of some chapters. This is the place to go to identify the source of a certain noise or particular malfunction in the bike. There is also a comprehensive troubleshooting guide in Appendix A.

The appendices contain other valuable information as well. Many tasks will be simplified or improved by using them. Appendix B is a complete gear chart and includes instructions on how to calculate your gear with non-standard-size wheels.

i.4 **track bike**

LEVEL 1 LEVEL 2 LEVEL 3

Appendix C is an extensive section on selecting the proper size bike and positioning it to fit you. It includes information about setting up your bike for triathlons or time trials. The glossary—Appendix D—is an inclusive dictionary of bicycle technical terminology. Appendix E lists the tightening specifications of almost every bolt on the bike. I can't emphasize enough how useful it is to use a torque wrench and tighten bolts as tightly as the component manufacturer intended. Flag Appendix E so you can flip to it easily whenever you work on your bike.

The Internet can be a useful supplement to this book. For instance, www.bikeschool.com, www.dtswiss.com and other sites have spoke-length calculators to use when you are building wheels. And exploded views of some parts can be found on component-company Web sites, such as www.campagnolo.com, www.shimano.com and www.mavic.com.

THE ROAD BIKE

This is the creature (Fig. i.1) to whom this book is devoted. All of its parts are illustrated and labeled. Take a minute to familiarize yourself with these, and now and then refer back to this diagram.

The road bike comes in a variety of forms, from road racing (Fig. i.1) to triathlon (Fig. i.2) to time trial to touring models, which are rigged for carrying luggage (Fig. i.3), to models with front—and even rear—suspension. Some distant cousins are track (Fig. i.4) and cyclo-cross bikes (Fig. i.5).

i.5 **cyclo-cross bike**

THIS MEANS YOU!

By clearly spelling out the steps necessary to properly maintain and repair a bicycle, even those who see themselves as having no mechanical skills will be able to tackle problems as they arise. With a little bit of practice and a willingness to learn, your bike will suddenly transform itself from a mysterious black box, too complicated to tamper with, to a simple, understandable machine that is a delight to work on. Just allow yourself the opportunity and the dignity to follow along, rather than deciding in advance that you can't. All you have to do is follow the instructions and trust yourself.

So, if you think you are not mechanically inclined set that aside—along with any other factors that may stand in the way of rolling up your sleeves in the interest of improving your bike's performance.

1

Tools

"If the only tool you have is a hammer,
you tend to see every problem as a nail." —Abraham Maslow

You can't do much useful work on a bike without a basic assortment of tools. And bicycles, like other evolved machines such as automobiles and watches, have specific fasteners and threads that require specific tools to fit them. This chapter will clarify which tools you should consider owning, based on your level of mechanical experience and interest.

As I mentioned in the introduction, the maintenance and repair procedures in this book are classified by their degree of difficulty. Nearly all repairs are classified as Level 1, because most bicycle repair jobs are pretty easy to complete once you understand the principles involved. The tools for Levels 1, 2 and 3 are pictured and described on the following pages. In addition, the tools you may need for a specific repair are listed in the margin at the beginning of each chapter.

For the uninitiated, there is no need to rush out and buy a large number of bike-specific tools. With few exceptions, the "Level 1 Tool Kit" consists of standard metric tools, many of which you may already own. (In a more compact and lightweight form, this is the same collection of tools I recommend carrying on long rides.)

The "Level 2 Tool Kit" contains several bike-specific tools, allowing you to do more complex work on the bike. "Level 3" tools are extensive (and sometimes expensive), and ensure that your riding buddies will show up not only to ask your sage advice, but to borrow your tools as well. And if you are one to loan tools, you may consider marking your collection, so as to help recover those items that may otherwise take a long time finding their way back to your workshop.

1-1: LEVEL 1 TOOL KIT

Level 1 repairs are the simplest and do not require a workshop, although it is nice to have a well-lit and comfortable work space. For easy repairs, you will need the following tools (Fig. 1.2):

- **Tire pump** with a gauge and a valve head to match your tubes (either Presta or Schrader valves; see Fig. 1.1).
- **Standard slot-head screwdrivers**: small, medium and large.
- **Phillips-head screwdrivers**: one small and one medium.
- Set of three plastic **tire levers**—assuming you have clincher tires.
- At least two **spare tubes**—or tubulars—of the same size and valve type as those on your bike.
- Container of regular **baby powder** for coating tubes and the inner casings of tires.
  Note: *Do not inhale this stuff; it is bad for your lungs.*
- **Patch kit.** Choose one that comes with sandpaper instead of a metal scratcher. Every year, check that the glue has not dried up.
- One **6-inch adjustable wrench** (a.k.a., "Crescent wrench," which is a name brand).
- **Pliers**: regular and needle-nose.
- Set of **metric Allen wrenches** (or "hex keys") that includes 2.5mm, 3mm, 4mm, 5mm, 6mm and 8mm sizes. Folding sets are available and work nicely to keep wrenches organized. I also recommend buying extras of the 4mm, 5mm and 6mm sizes.
- Set of **metric open-end wrenches** that includes 7mm, 8mm, 9mm, 10mm, 13mm, 14mm, 15mm and 17mm sizes.
- **15mm pedal wrench.** This is thinner and longer than a standard 15mm wrench and thicker than a cone wrench, to fit into the space between the pedal and crank.
- **Chain tool** for breaking and reassembling chains. If you have a nine-speed system, you may need a narrower chain tool to avoid bending the center prongs of the tool. Shimano's TL-CN22 and TL-

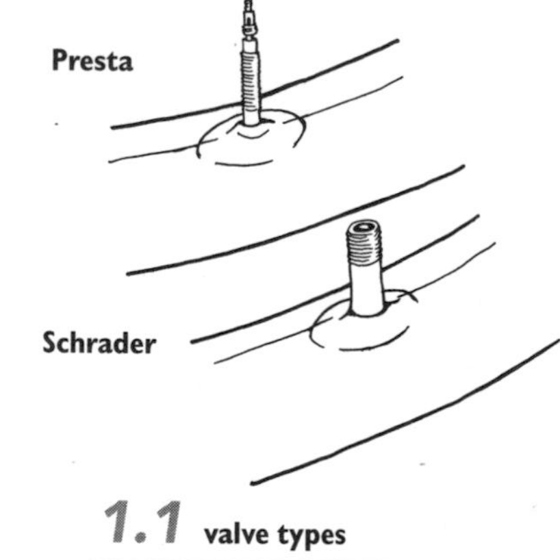

1.1 valve types

LEVEL 1
tool kit

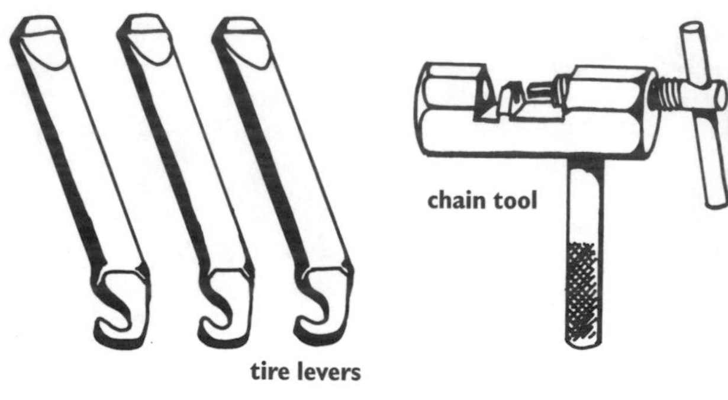

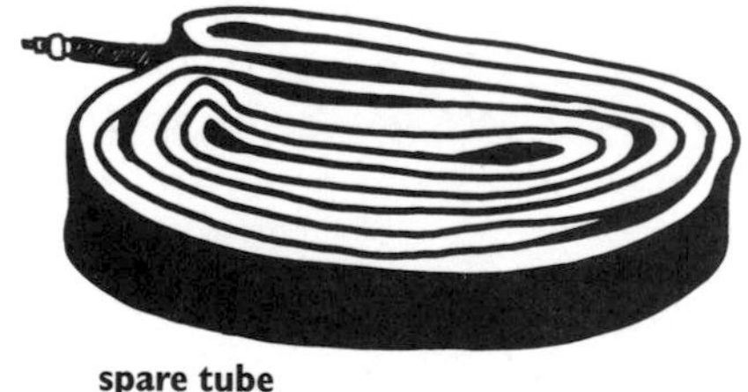

1.2 level I tool kit

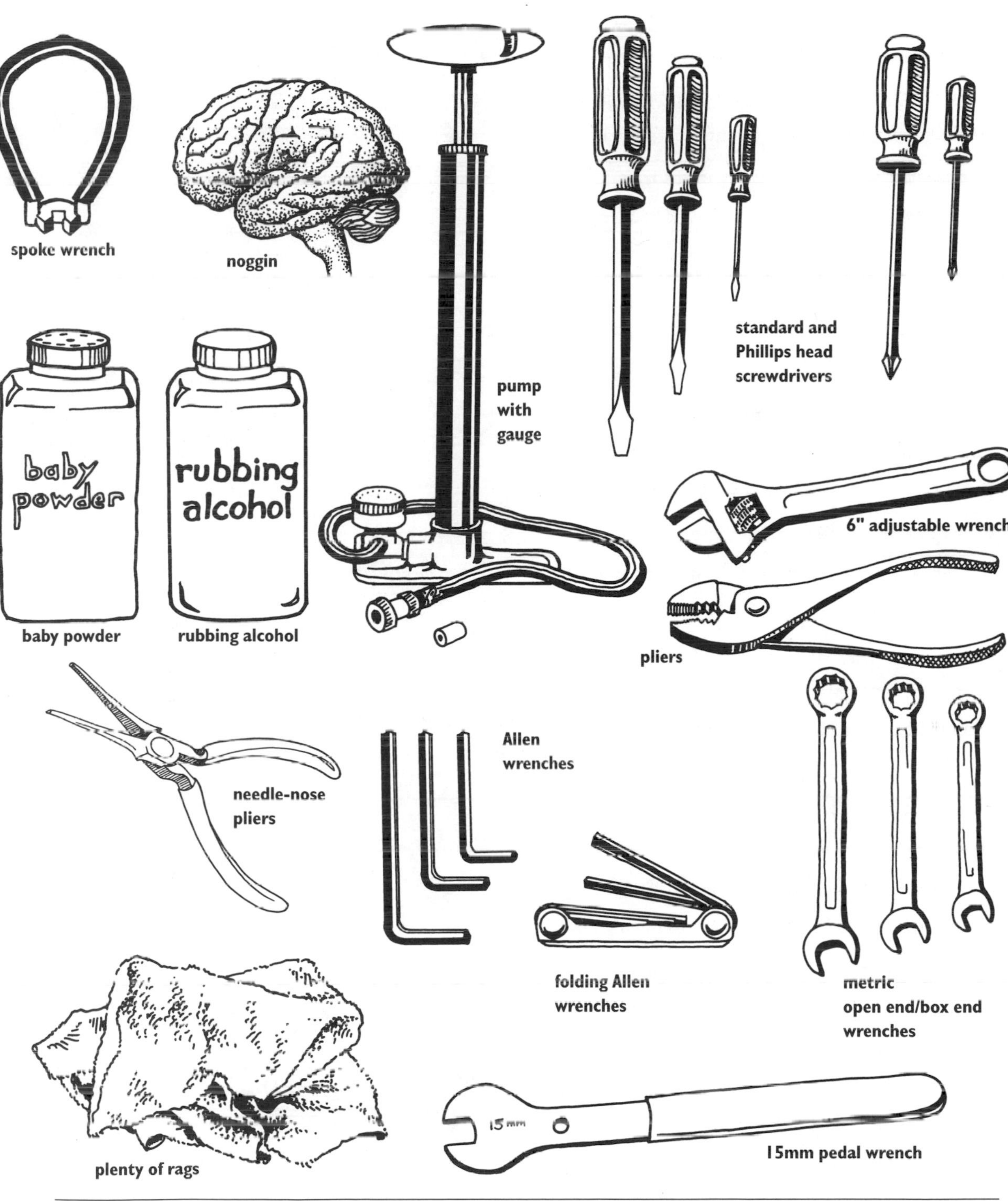

tools

LEVEL 1
tool kit

CN31 work for seven-, eight- and nine-speed chains. Many other chain tools work as well.

- **Spoke wrench** to match the size of nipples used on your wheels.
- **Tube or jar of grease.** I recommend using grease designed specifically for bicycles, but standard automotive grease is okay.
- Drip bottle or can of **chain lubricant**. Please choose a non-aerosol; it is easier to control, uses less packaging, and wastes less in overspray.
- **Rubbing alcohol** for light cleaning, and for removing and installing handlebar grips, if you have them instead of handlebar tape.
- A lot of **rags**! Old T-shirts work fine, by the way.

LEVEL 2

I-2: LEVEL 2 TOOL KIT

Level 2 repairs are a bit more complex, and I recommend that you attack them with specific tools and a well-organized workspace with a shop bench. Keeping your workspace well organized is probably the best way to make maintenance and repair easy and quick. You will need the entire Level 1 Tool Kit (Fig. 1.2) plus the following tools (Fig. 1.3):

- **Portable bike stand.** Be sure that the stand is sturdy enough to remain stable when you're really cranking on the wrenches.
- **Shop apron** (this is to keep your nice duds nice).
- **Hacksaw** with a fine-toothed blade.
- Set of **razor blades** or a sharp shop knife.
- **Files**: one round and one flat, with medium-fine teeth.
- **Cable cutter** for cutting brake and shifter cables without fraying the ends.
- **Cable-housing cutter** for cutting coaxial-indexed cable housing. If you purchase a Shimano, Park or Wrench Force housing cutter, you won't need to buy a separate cable cutter, since all of these cleanly cut cables as well as housings.
- Set of **metric socket wrenches** that includes 7mm, 8mm, 9mm, 10mm, 13mm, 14mm and 15mm sizes.
- **Crank puller** for removing crank arms.
- Medium **ball-peen hammer**.
- Two **headset wrenches**. Be sure to check the size of the headset on your bike before buying these. This purchase is unnecessary if you have a threadless headset and plan to work on your own bike only.
- Medium-size **bench vise** (bolted to a sturdy bench).
- **Cassette-cog lockring tool** for removing cogs from the rear hub.

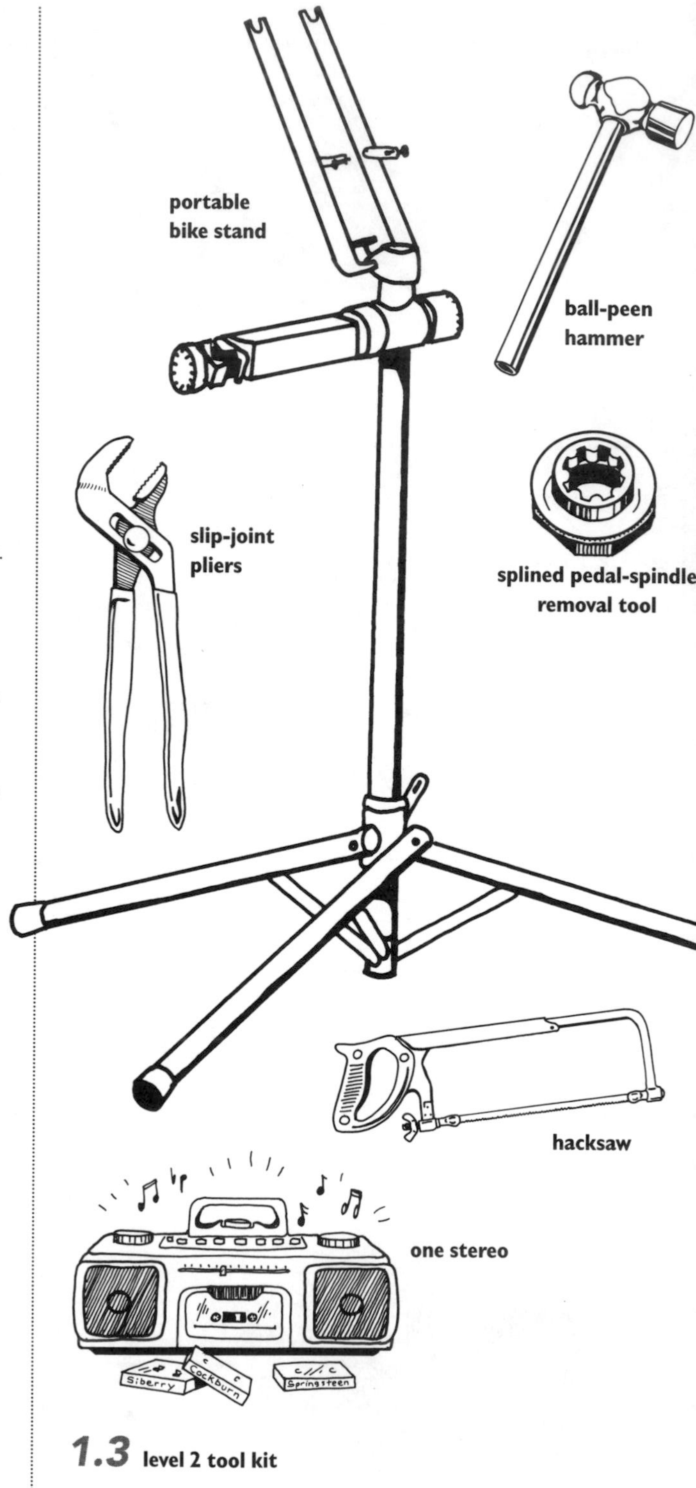

1.3 level 2 tool kit

- **Chain whip** for holding cogs while loosening the cassette lockring.
- **Bottom bracket tools.** For Shimano or Campagnolo cartridge bottom brackets and clones of them, you'll need the splined tool specifically made for this type of bottom brack-

LEVEL 2 tool kit

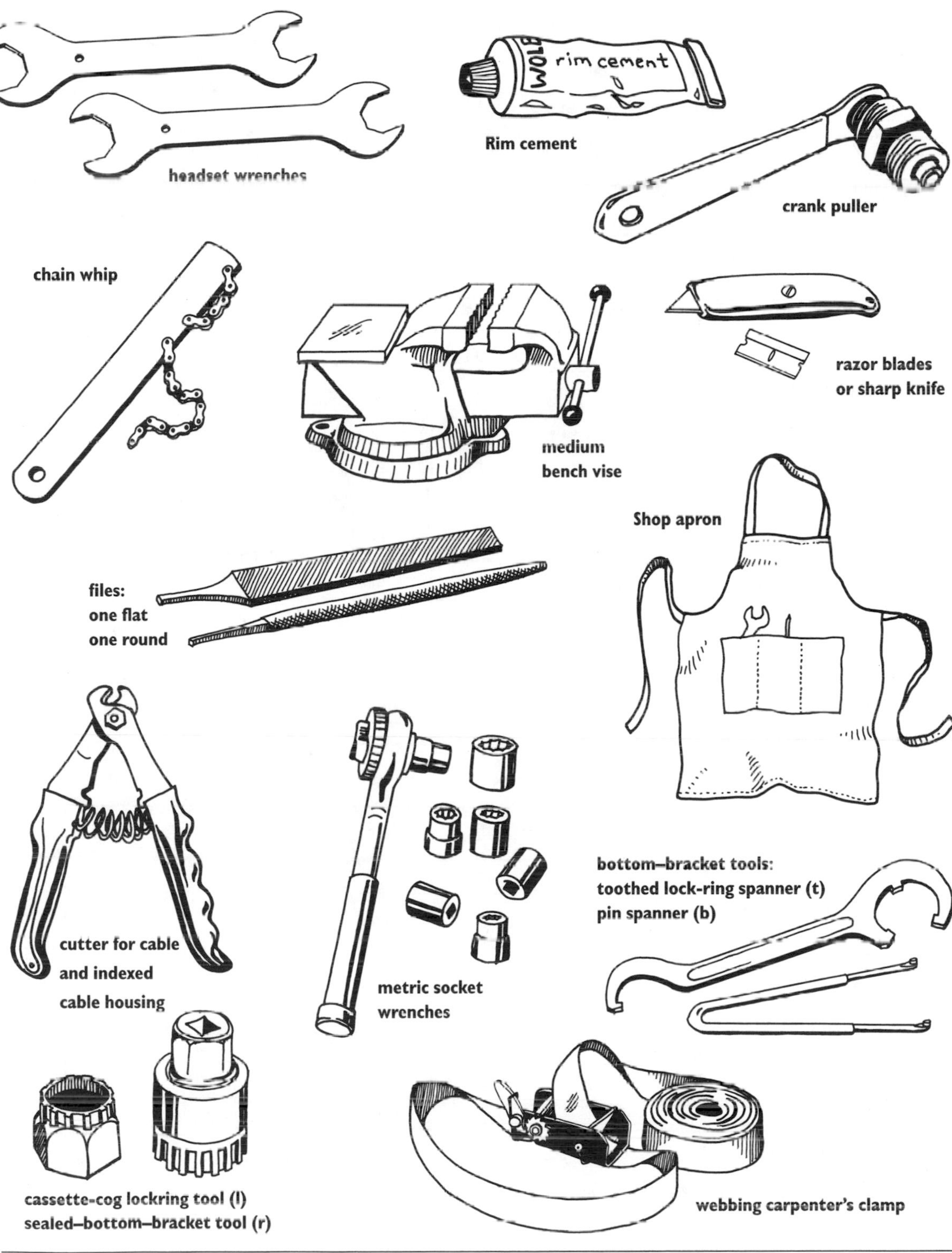

LEVEL 2
tool kit

et. For cup-and-cone bottom brackets, you'll need a lockring spanner and a pin spanner to fit your bottom bracket.

- **Slip-joint** ("Channel-lock") **pliers**.
- **Splined pedal-spindle removal tool.**
- **Rim cement** for tubular tires, if you have them.
- **Webbing carpenter's clamp** for gluing tubulars (optional).
- One **stereo** with good tunes. This is especially important if you plan on spending a lot of time working on your bike.

LEVEL 3

I-3: LEVEL 3 TOOL KIT

If you are an accomplished Level 3 mechanic, you are now completely independent of your local bike shop's service department. This even includes building up brand-new frames. By now, you have a well-organized separate space intended just for working on your bike. Some elements of the Level 3 kit (Fig. 1.4) are obviously heavier-duty replacements for parts of the Level 2 kit.

- **Parts washing tank.** Please use an environmentally safe degreaser. Dispose of used solvent responsibly; check with your local environmental safety office.
- **Fixed bike stand.** Be sure it comes with a clamp designed to fit any size frame tube.
- Large **bench-mounted vise** to free stuck parts.
- **Headset press** used to install headset bearing cups. The press should fit all three cup sizes. Chris King and some other cartridge-bearing headsets need a press that does not contact the pressed-in bearing. King sells inserts for regular headset presses to install his headsets.
- **Fork-crown-race punch** (a.k.a., slide hammer) for installing the fork-crown headset race. (Thin Shimano or Chris King crown races require a second support tool to protect the crown race during installation.)
- **Headset-cup remover.**
- **Star-nut installation tool** for threadless headsets.
- An **additional chain whip**. A second whip is handy for disassembling freewheels or old-style cassettes.
- **Freewheel removers.** If you will be working on retro stuff, you should get removers for Shimano, Sachs and Suntour freewheels.
- **Large ball-peen hammer.**
- **Soft hammer**. Choose a rubber, plastic or wooden mallet to prevent damage to parts.

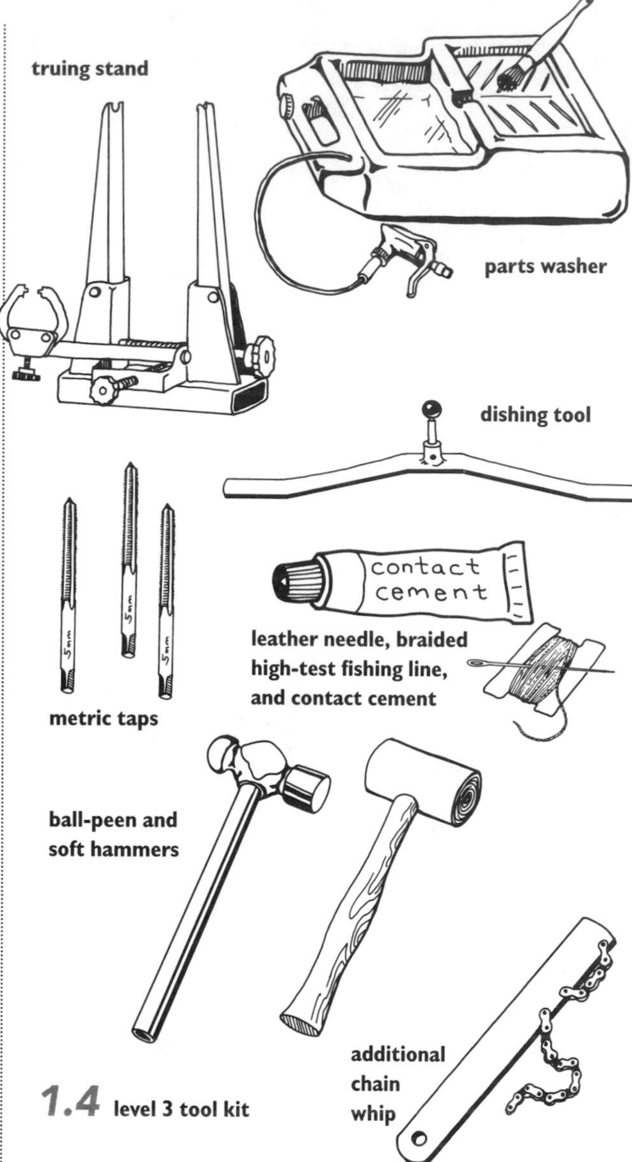

1.4 level 3 tool kit

- **Torque wrench.** Torque wrenches are great for checking proper bolt tightness. Most component manufacturers recommend using one and provide torque specs. There is a complete torque specification list in Appendix E of this book.
- Set of **metric taps** that includes 5mm x 0.8, 6mm x 1 and 10mm x 1. These work for threading bottle bosses, seat binder clamps, derailleur hangers and cantilever bosses (on touring or cyclo-cross frames).
- Pair of **snap-ring pliers** for removing snap rings from suspension forks and other parts.
- **Fine-tip grease gun** for parts with grease fittings.

LEVEL 3 tool kit

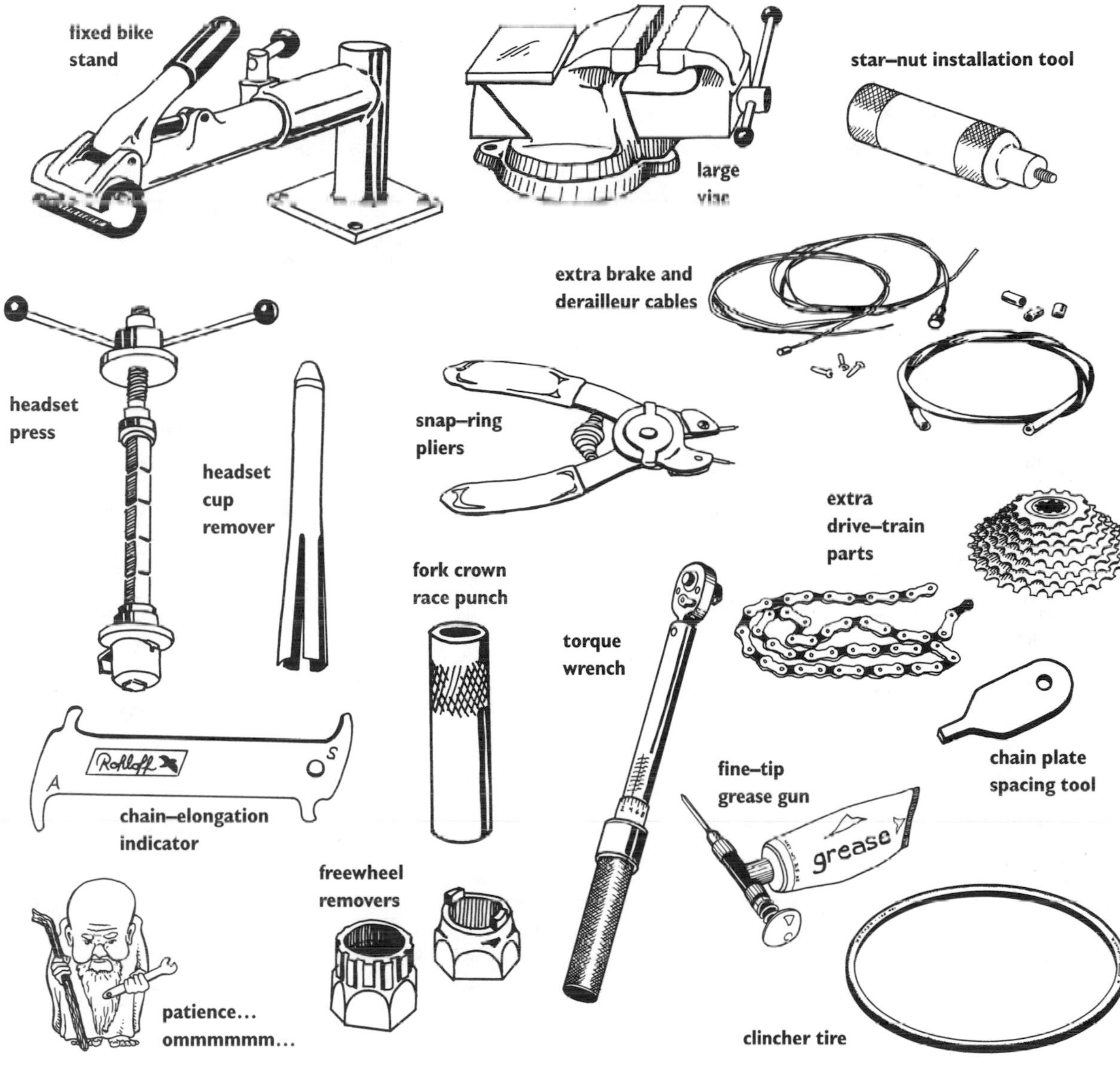

tools

LEVEL 3 tool kit

- ✧ **Morningstar Freehub Buddy tool** for lubricating Shimano freehubs.
- ✧ **Chain elongation gauge.** This handy little plastic item helps you quickly determine if a chain needs replacing. An accurate 12-inch ruler will substitute adequately.
- ✧ Shimano TL-CN24 **chain-plate spacing tool**; assures chain plates are at least 2.38mm apart.
- ✧ **Truing stand** for truing and building wheels.
- ✧ **Dishing tool** for checking if that set of wheels you just built is properly centered.
- ✧ **Leather needle, braided high-test fishing line, and contact cement** for patching tubular tires.
- ✧ One healthy dose of **patience**, and an equal willingness to work and re-work jobs until they have been properly finished.

OTHER

- ✧ **Spare parts.** This will save you from having to make a lot of last-minute runs to the bike shop for commonly used spare parts. Any well-equipped shop really requires several sizes of ball bearings, bolts, spare cables, cable housing, and a life-time supply of those little housing ferrules and cable-end caps. You should also have a good supply of spare tires, tubes, chains and cogsets.

1-4: NOW, IF YOU REALLY WANT A WELL-STOCKED SHOP...

The following tools (Fig. 1.5) are not even part of the Level 3 kit, and are rarely needed for bike repairs. That said, they sure do come in handy when you need them.

- **Bottom-bracket tap set.** This cuts threads in both ends of the bottom bracket while keeping the threads in proper alignment. English-threaded taps are required for most modern road frames. Most Italian frames, however, have Italian threads, and will require appropriate taps. French threading and Swiss threading are different yet, but these threads are fortunately rare in modern road bikes.
- **Head-tube reamer/facer.** This tool keeps both ends of the head tube perfectly parallel and bored out to the right size.
- **Bottom-bracket-shell facer.** Like a bottom bracket tap, this tool cuts the faces of the bottom bracket shell so they are parallel to each other.
- **Electric drill with drill-bit set** for customizing.
- **Dropout alignment tools** (a.k.a., tip adjusters).
- **Derailleur-hanger alignment tool** to straighten the derailleur hanger after you shift the derailleur into the spokes or crash on it.
- **Cog-wear indicator gauge** to determine if cogs are worn out.
- A full collection of **spoke wrenches**, not forgetting Spline Drive nipples.

1-5: SETTING UP YOUR HOME SHOP

Make your shop clean, well-organized and comfortable and you'll find that the speed and quality of your work will improve. Hanging tools on peg-board or slat-board, or placing them in bins or trays, are all effective ways to maintain an organized work area. Being able to lay your hand immediately on the tool

1.5 tools for the well-stocked shop

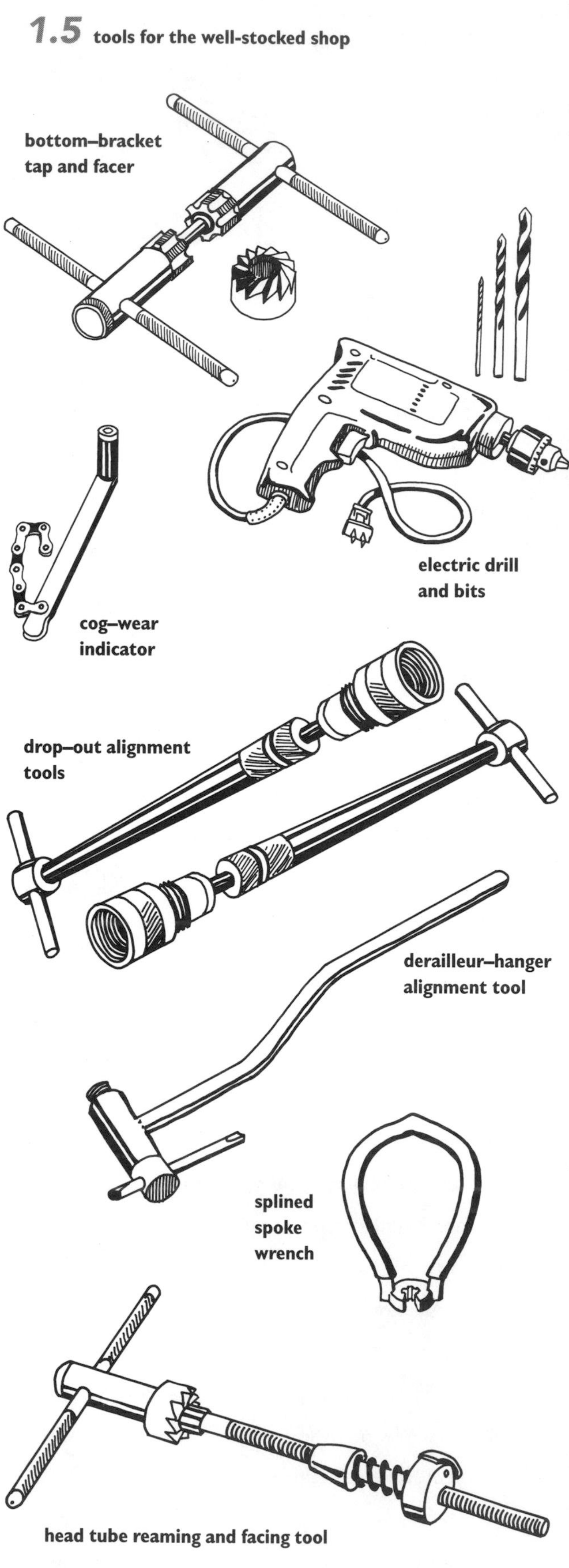

you need will immensely increase the enjoyment of working on a bike. It is hard to do a job with loving care if you are frustrated by not being able to find the cable cutter. Placing small parts in a bench-top organizer, one with several rows of little drawers, is another good way to keep chaos at bay.

1-6: TOOLS TO CARRY WITH YOU WHILE RIDING

A. FOR MOST RIDING:

You can keep everything you need for light repairs (Fig. 1.6) in a small bag under your seat. Some people may prefer a fanny pack. As you stock this bag, look for tools and parts that are light and serviceable. Many of the tools are available in combination, and sold as "multi-tools." Make sure you try all tools at home before depending on them on the road.

- **Spare tube or tubular.** Always carry one. Make sure the valve matches the ones on your bike. If rarely needed, keep it in a plastic bag to prevent deterioration.
- **Tire pump/CO_2 cartridge.** If a pump, the bigger the better, but road pumps need also to be thin to attain high pressures. Mini-pumps are okay, but they're slow. Make sure the pump has the right head for your type of valves. If you prefer air cartridges, get the correct size for the spare tube or tubular (probably 12 grams, unless you are filling a huge touring tire, in which case you may need a 16-gram cartridge).
- At least **two plastic tire levers**, preferably three (clincher tires only)
- **Patch kit**. You'll need something after you've used your spare tube. Check it at least every year to make sure the glue has not dried up. You can also bring glueless patches.
- **Small screwdriver** for adjusting derailleurs and other parts.

1.6 tools to take on all rides

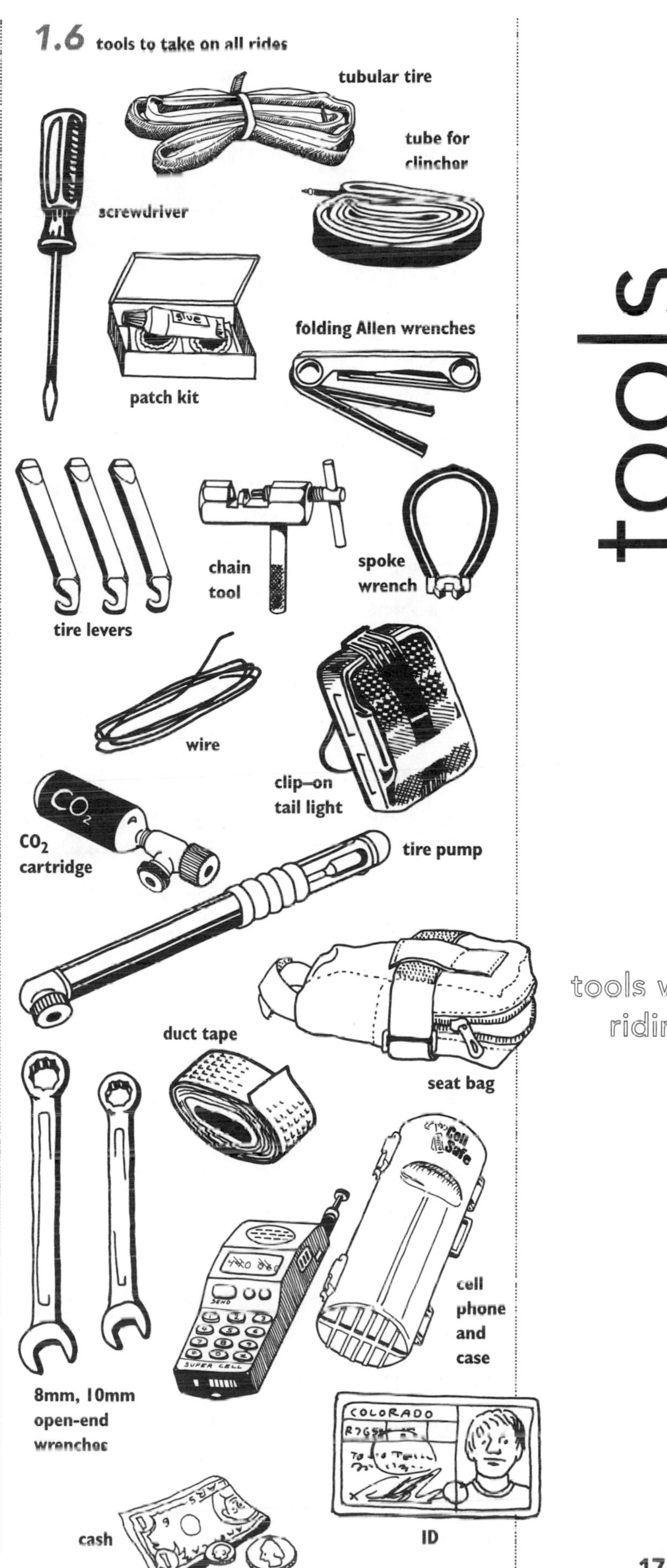

tools

tools while riding

- ✧ Compact set of **Allen wrenches** that includes 2.5mm, 3mm, 4mm, 5mm and 6mm sizes. (You may need to take along an 8mm on a long tour, too, if your crank bolts are that size.)
- ✧ 8mm and 10 mm **open-end wrenches** for pre-1980s bikes.
- ✧ Properly sized **spoke wrench**.
- ✧ Small amount of **duct tape**.
- ✧ Small amount of **wire**.
- ✧ Small clip-on **tail light**.
- ✧ **Identification.**
- ✧ **Cash** for food, phone calls and to boot sidewall cuts in tires.
- ✧ A **cell phone** is not a bad idea. You can get a cell-phone case to fit in a water bottle cage.

B. FOR LONG OR MULTIDAY TRIPS:

These items in Fig. 1.7 are in addition to the items in Fig. 1.6.

- ✧ Spare **folding clincher tire** and a **second spare tube** or **tubular**.
- ✧ **Chain tool.** Get a light one that works.
- ✧ **Spare chain links** from your chain. If you are using a Shimano chain bring at least two “sub-pin” rivets.
- ✧ **Spare spokes.** Innovations in Cycling sells a really cool folding spoke made from Kevlar. It's worth getting one or two for emergency repairs on a long ride.
- ✧ Small plastic bottle of **chain lube**.
- ✧ Small tube of **grease**.
- ✧ Compact 15mm **pedal wrench**. Be sure to get one with a headset wrench on the other end.
- ✧ **Matches.**
- ✧ A lightweight aluminized folding **emergency blanket**.
- ✧ **Rain gear.**

1.7 tools for extended trips on the road

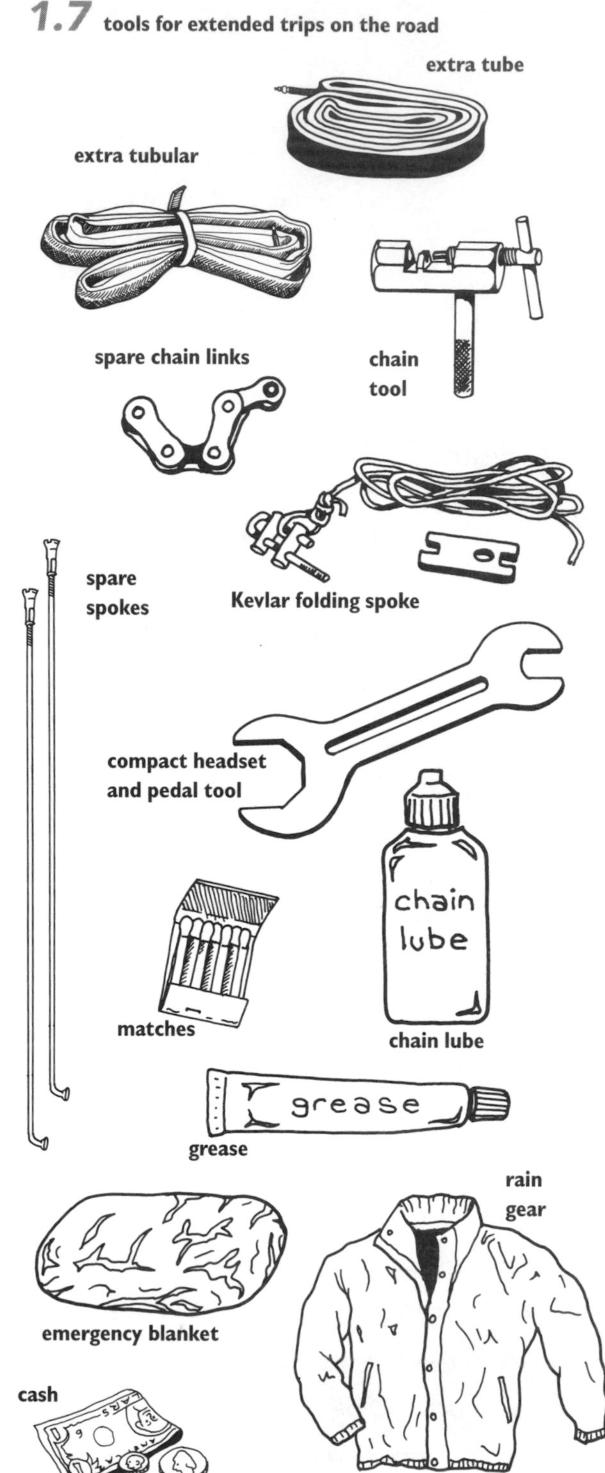

Note: *Read Chapter 3 on emergency repairs before embarking on a lengthy trip.*

If you are planning a bike-centered vacation, be sure to take along a “Level 1” tool kit in your car, some headset wrenches and incidentals like duct tape and sandpaper.

Basic stuff

Pre-ride inspection, wheel removal, general cleaning and mechanical methods guide

tools

Chain lubricant
Rags

OPTIONAL

Solvent (citrus based)
Chain-cleaning tool
Old water bottle

"Basic research is what I am doing when I don't know what I am doing." —Werner von Braun

It is a good idea to get in the habit of checking your bike before heading out on a ride. Performing this inspection regularly can help you avoid getting stranded far from home due to parts failure. You should also know how to properly remove and reinstall a wheel, so that you can deal with minor annoyances like flat tires or jammed chains. And even if you do absolutely nothing else to your bike, keeping its chain clean and properly lubricated, as outlined in this chapter, will make every ride smoother and quieter.

2-1: PRE-RIDE INSPECTION

1. Check to be sure that the quick-release levers or axle nuts (the ones that secure the hub axle to the dropouts) are tight.

2. Check the brake pads for excessive or uneven wear.

3. Grab and twist the brake pads and brake arms to make sure the bolts are tight.

4. Squeeze the brake levers. This should bring the pads flat against the rims (or slightly toed in) without hitting the tires. Make certain that you cannot squeeze the levers all of the way to the handlebars. For details, see Chapter 7 on brake adjustment.

5. Spin the wheels. Check for wobbles while eyeing on the rims, not the tires. Make sure that the rims do not rub on the brake pads.

6. Spin the wheels again, checking for wobbles while eyeing on the tires this time. If a tire wobbles excessively on a straight rim, it may not be fully seated in the rim. There is usually a mold line or an edge of a tape strip on the tire that should be parallel to the rim edge all of the way around. Look for areas where the tire is bulged larger, and/or the

mold line or tape edge is higher above the rim or deeper into the rim than the rest of the way around the tire. To fix an improperly seated tire, you need to completely deflate the tire and carefully seat it uniformly all of the way around before re-inflating.

7. Check the tire pressure. On most road bike tires, the proper pressure is between 80 and 120 pounds per square inch (psi). Look to see that there are no foreign objects sticking in the tire. If there are, you may have to pull the tube out and repair or replace it. If you have an aversion to fixing flats, turn to the section on tire sealants (i.e., goop inside the tube that fills small holes) in Chapter 6.

8. Check the tires for excessive wear, cracking or gashes.

9. Be certain that the handlebar and stem are tight and that the stem is lined up with the front tire.

10. Check that the gears shift smoothly and the chain does not skip or shift by itself. Ensure that each indexed ("click") shift moves the chain one cog, starting with the first click. Make sure that the chain does not overshift the smallest or biggest rear cog or the inner or outer front chainring.

2.1 **releasing the brake**

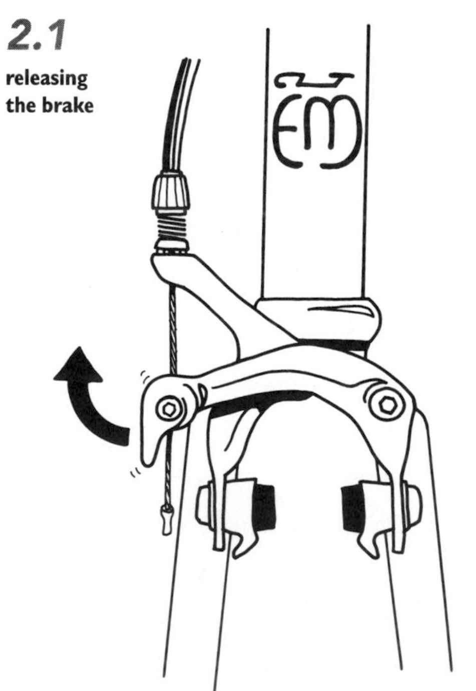

2.2 **releasing a Campagnolo brake**

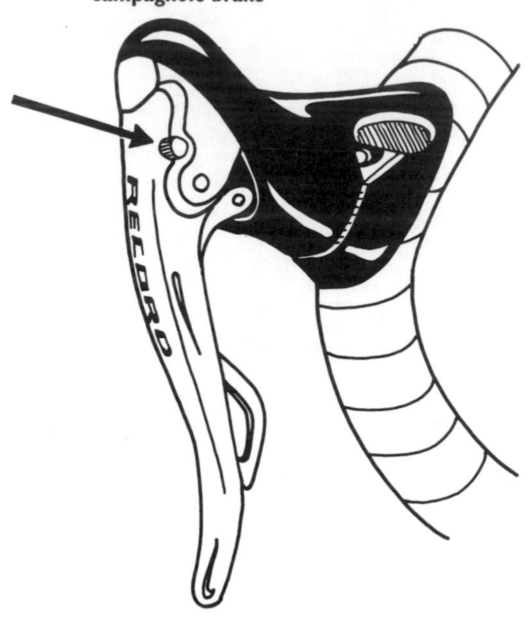

11. Check the chain for rust, dirt, stiff links or noticeable signs of wear. It should be clean and lubricated (being aware that over-lubricated, gooey chains pick up lots of dirt, particularly in dry climates). The chain should be replaced on a road bike about every 1500 to 2500 miles of paved riding—see section 4-6 to accurately evaluate chain wear.

12. Apply the front brake and push the bike forward and back. The headset should be tight and not make "clunking" noises or allow the fork any fore-aft play.

13. If all this checks out, go ride your bike! If not, check the table of contents, go to the appropriate chapter and fix the problems before you go out and ride.

wheel removal

2-2: REMOVING THE FRONT WHEEL

You can't fix a flat if you can't remove the wheel. Front wheel removal is also generally required for roof racks or for putting a bike in a car. As outlined in the following sections, wheel removal involves releasing the brake and opening the hub quick-release or bolt-on skewer, or the axle nuts on inexpensive bicycles.

2-3: RELEASING THE BRAKE

Most brakes have a quick-release mechanism to open the brake arms so that they spring away from the rim, allowing the tire to pass between the pads. Most sidepull road brakes have a lever on the brake caliper that is flipped up to open the brake (Fig. 2.1). Alternatively, Campagnolo Ergo Power systems have a pin near the top of the brake lever that is pushed outward to allow the lever (and consequently the caliper) to open wider (Fig. 2.2).

Center-pull brakes (rare now, but common on older bikes) have a cable-hanger yoke that must be pulled down to release from the straddle cable while the pads are held against the rim.

Cyclo-cross bikes and some touring bikes have cantilever-type brakes, which mount on pivots that are attached to fork legs or seatstays. The newest cantilevers, commonly called "V-brakes" after the Shimano design that popularized them, are released by pulling the end of the curved cable guide tube (a.k.a. "the noodle") out of the horizontal link atop one of the brake arms while squeezing the pads against the rim with the other hand. Most standard cantilever brakes are released by pulling the enlarged head of the straddle cable out of a notch in the top of the brake arm while holding the pads against the rim with the other hand. Really old cantilever brakes are released like the center-pull brakes mentioned in the previous paragraph.

2.3 opening quick-release skewer

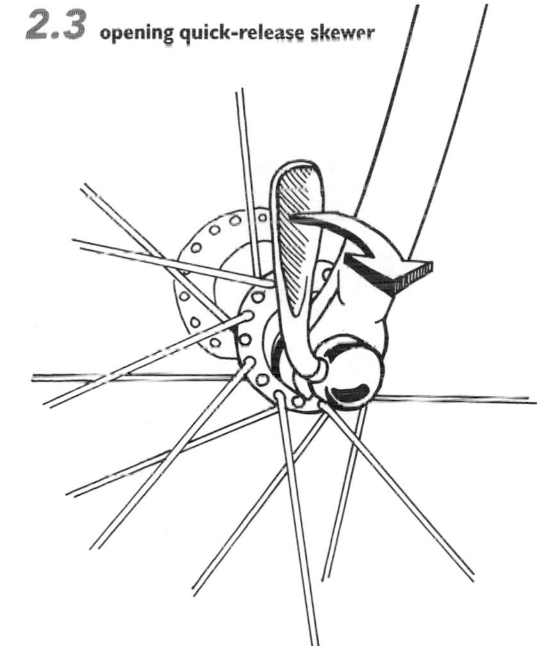

2-4: DETACHING A FRONT WHEEL WITH A QUICK-RELEASE SKEWER

You don't need a tool for this.

Note: *Some bikes have bolt-on skewers (Fig. 2.4), often made of titanium to save weight. The wheel is removed by unscrewing the skewer with a 5mm Allen wrench.*

1. Pull the lever outward to open it (Fig. 2.3).
2. After opening the quick-release lever, the wheel should fall out. If not, you may have wheel-retention tabs on the fork ends, which are designed to keep the wheel in place even if the quick-release inadvertently opens (or, more likely, is left open by mistake). In this case, unscrew the nut on the opposite end of the quick-release skewer's shaft until it clears the fork's wheel-retention tabs.
3. Lift the bike so the wheel falls out.

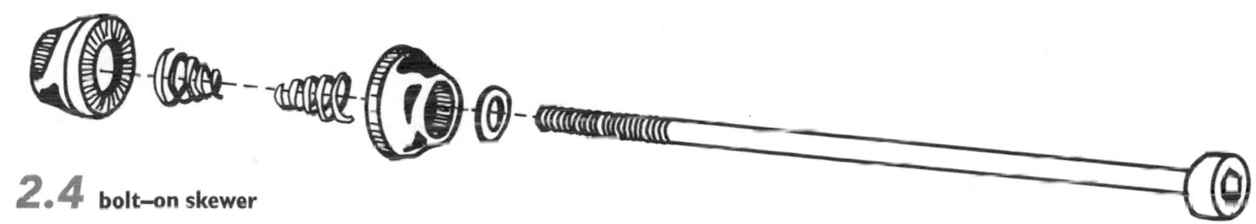

2.4 bolt–on skewer

2-5: DETACHING A WHEEL WITH AXLE NUTS

1. Unscrew the nuts on the axle ends (usually with a 15mm wrench) until they allow the wheel to fall out (Fig. 2.5). Really old road bikes may have wing nuts for finger-tightening instead.

2. Your bike may have some type of wheel-retention system consisting of nubs or bent tabs on the fork ends, or an axle washer with a bent tooth hooked into a hole in the fork end. These systems prevent the wheel from falling out if the axle nuts loosen. Loosen the nuts enough to clear the retention tabs on the fork ends. Note that it's not usually necessary to remove the nuts completely.

3. Pull the wheel out.

2-6: INSTALLING THE FRONT WHEEL

front wheel installation

Leaving the brake open, lower the fork onto the wheel so that the bike's weight pushes the top of the dropout slots down onto the hub axle. This will seat the axle fully into the fork and center the rim between the brake pads. If the fork or wheel is misaligned, you will need to hold the rim centered between the brake pads when securing the hub (and get the untrue wheel or bent fork fixed or replaced soon). Continue with the appropriate hub-securing step.

2-7: TIGHTENING THE QUICK-RELEASE SKEWER

The quick-release skewer is not a glorified wing nut and should not be treated as such.

1. Hold the quick-release lever in the "open" position.

2. Tighten the opposite end nut until it snugs up against the face of the dropout. (If you have no wheel-retention tabs on the fork, and you did not unscrew the skewer nut, this step is unnecessary.)

2.5 **loosening axle nut**

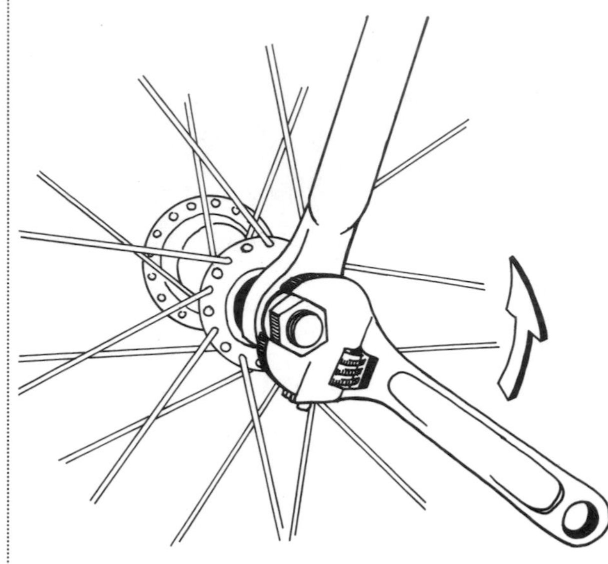

3. Push the lever over (Fig. 2.6) to the "closed" position (it should now be at a 90-degree angle to the axle). It should take a good amount of hand pressure to close the quick-release lever properly; the lever should leave its imprint on your palm for a few seconds.

4. If the quick-release lever does not close tightly, open the lever again, tighten the end nut a quarter turn and close the lever again. Repeat until tight.

5. If, on the other hand, the lever cannot be pushed down flat, then the nut is too tight. Open the quick-release lever, unscrew the end nut a quarter turn or so, and try closing the lever again. Repeat this procedure until the quick-release lever is fully closed and snug. When you are done, it is important to have the lever pointing straight up or toward the back of the bike so that it cannot hook on obstacles and be accidentally opened.

6. Hit the top of the tire with your open palm to check that the wheel is not loose and you cannot bang it out.

2.6 **tightening the quick release**

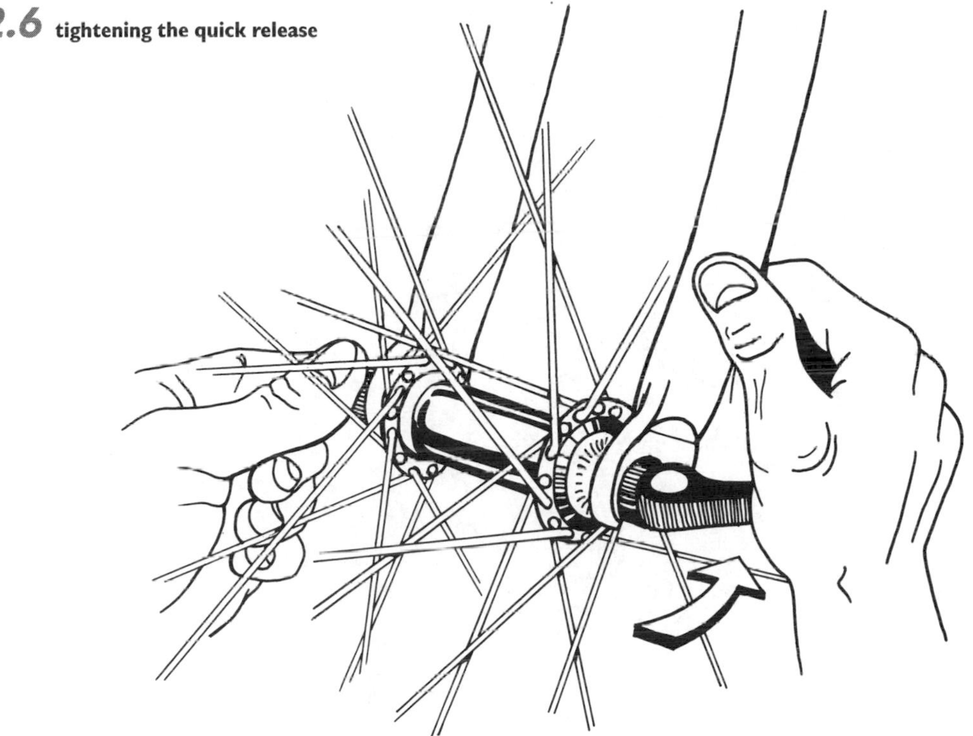

2-8: TIGHTENING BOLT-ON SKEWERS (FIG. 2.4)

Hold the end nut with one hand and tighten the skewer with a 5mm hex key. Control Tech recommends 65 in-pounds of tightening torque for steel bolt-on skewers and 85 in-lbs for titanium ones. You can approximate accurate tightening torque by using a short hex key and tightening as tightly as you can with your fingers. These skewers can be over-tightened; avoid it by being conscious of how much pressure a quick-release skewer applies and do not go higher than that.

2-9: TIGHTENING AXLE NUTS

Snug up the nuts clockwise (opposite direction of fig. 2.5) with a wrench (usually 15mm) a little from each side until they are quite tight. In the case of wing nuts, the procedure is the same; the tools are your fingers.

2-10: CLOSING THE BRAKES

The steps required to close the brakes are always the reverse of what you did to release them.

1. With most road bikes, closing the brake caliper is simply a matter of flipping closed the quick-release lever on the sidepull brake caliper (Fig. 2.1 in reverse). With Campagnolo Ergo Power, you pull the brake lever and push the pin inward into its original position to engage the shallower notch in the lever body (Fig. 2.2).

2. With a cantilever brake (cyclo-cross and some touring bikes), hold the brake pads against the rim with one hand and hook the enlarged end of the straddle cable back into the end of the brake arm with your other hand. On antique bikes with center-pull brakes, hook the straddle cable yoke under the straddle cable.

3. Check that the brake cables are connected securely by squeezing the levers. Lift the front end of the bike and spin the front wheel, gently applying the brakes several times. Check that the pads are not dragging. If they are, re-center the wheel (or adjust the brakes as described in Chapter 7). If everything is reconnected and centered properly, you're done. Go ride your bike.

2.7 removal and installation of rear wheel

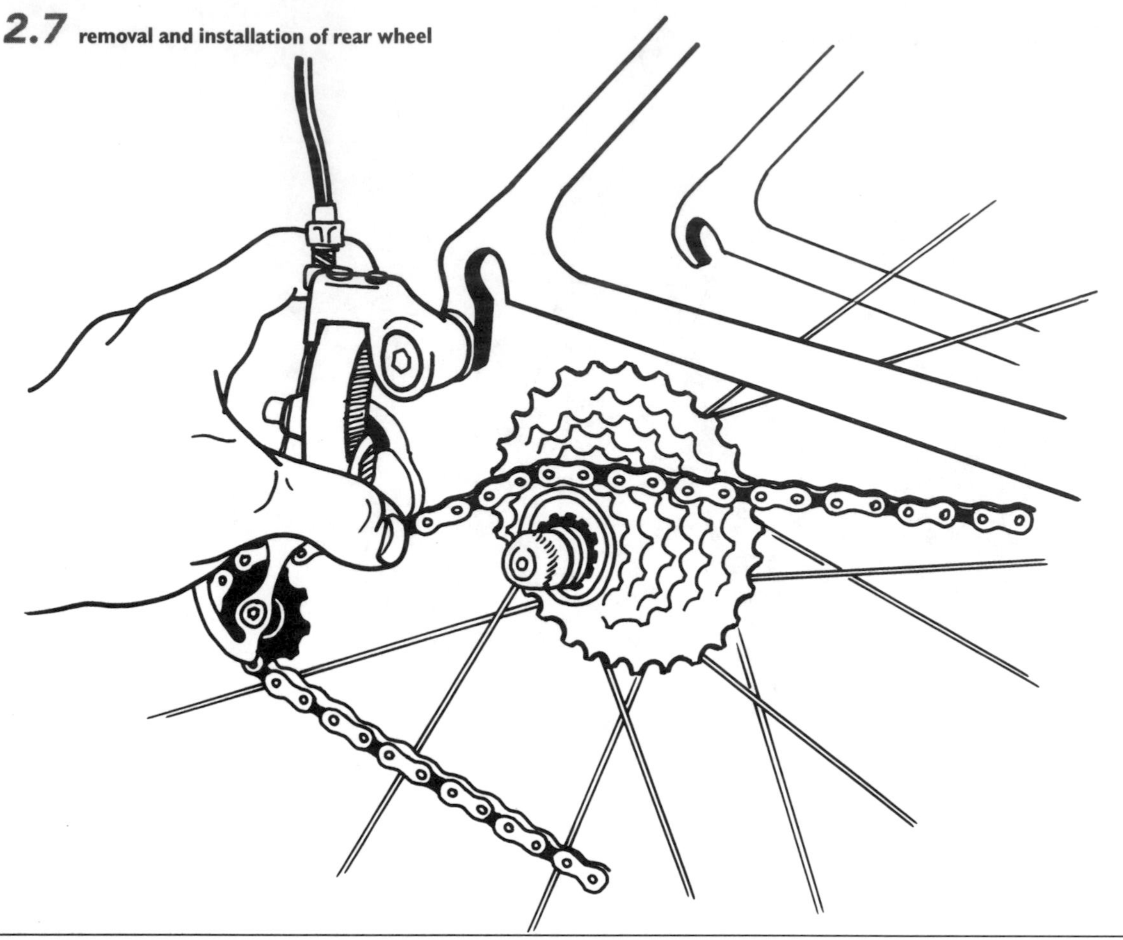

rear wheel removal and installation

2-11: REMOVING THE REAR WHEEL

Removing the rear wheel is just like removing the front, with the added complication of the chain and cogs.

1. Open the brake, as outlined above.

2. Shift the chain onto the smallest cog. Do this by lifting the rear wheel off of the ground, turning the cranks and shifting.

3. To release the wheel from the rear dropouts and the brakes, follow the same procedure as with the front wheel. When you push the wheel out, you will need to move the chain out of the way. This is usually a matter of grabbing the rear derailleur, pulling it back so the jockey wheels (pulley wheels) move out of the way, while pushing forward on the quick release or axle nuts with your thumbs, and letting the wheel fall as you hold the bike up (Fig. 2.7). If the bottom half of the chain catches the wheel as it falls, lift the wheel and jiggle it upward to free it.

2-12: INSTALLING THE REAR WHEEL

1. Check to make sure that the rear derailleur is shifted to its outermost position (over the smallest cog).

2. Slip the wheel between the seatstays and between the brake pads. Maneuver the upper section of chain onto the smallest cog (Fig. 2.7).

3. Set the bike down on the rear wheel.

4. As you let the bike drop down, pull the rear derailleur back with your right hand and pull the axle ends back into the dropouts with your index fingers. Use your thumbs to push forward on the rear dropouts, which should now slide over the axle ends. (If the axle does not slip into the dropouts, you may need to spread the dropouts apart or squeeze them toward each other as you pull the wheel in.)

5. Check that the axle is fully seated in the dropouts, which should result in the wheel being centered between the brake pads. If it is not, hold the

2.8 loop the chain over a dowel rod for cleaning

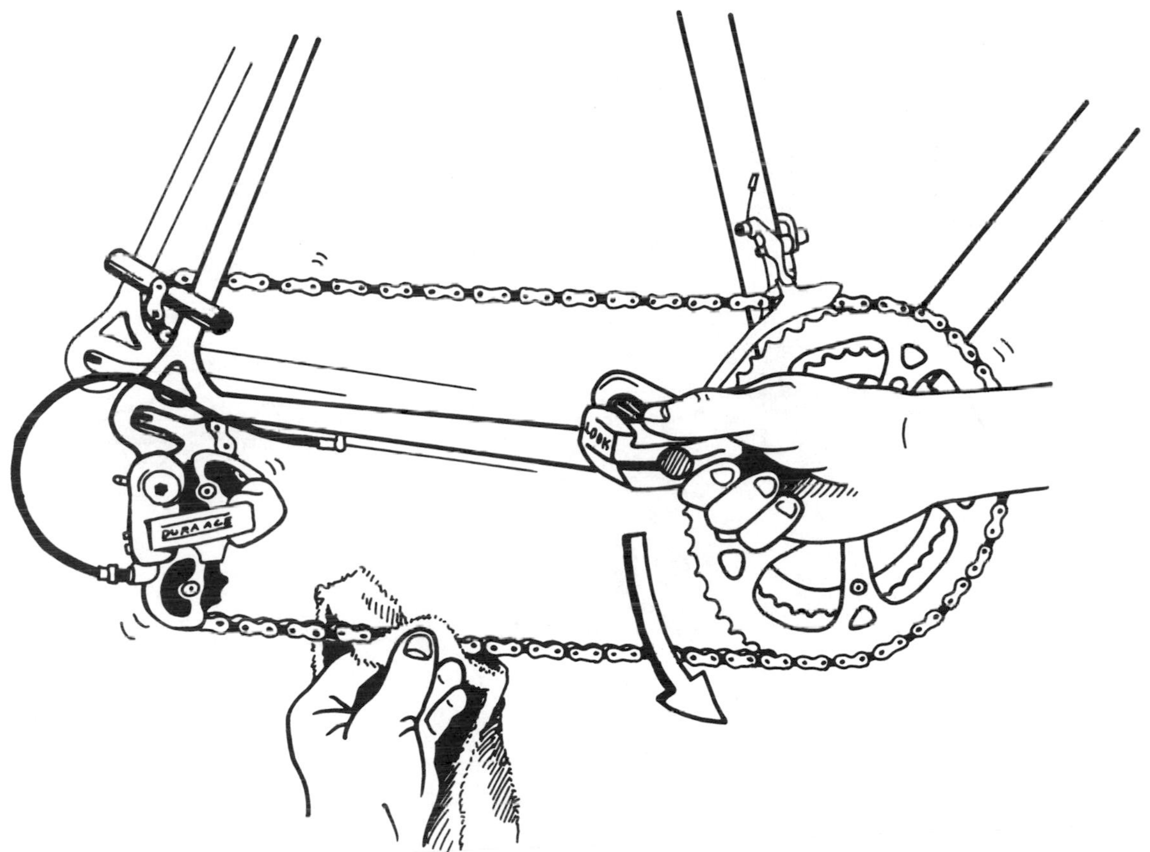

rim in a centered position as you secure the axle. This should not be necessary if your wheel and frame are both aligned and your brakes are centered.

6. Tighten the quick-release skewer, bolt-on skewer, or axle nuts the same way as explained for the front wheel.

7. Reconnect the rear brake the same way as you did on the front wheel. You're done. Go ride your bike.

2-13: CLEANING YOUR BICYCLE

Most cleaning can be done with soap, water and a brush. Soap and water are easier on you and the earth than stronger solvents, which are generally only needed for the drivetrain, if at all.

Avoid using high-pressure car washes to clean your bike. The soaps used are corrosive, and the high pressure forces them into bearings, pivots and frame tubes, causing extensive damage over time.

The best way to set up your bike for cleaning is to put it in a bike stand. In the absence of a stand, you can hang the bike from a garage ceiling with rope. No good? Turn it upside down so it rests on the saddle and handlebars. Alternatively, you can remove the front wheel and stand the bike on the fork and bars, but you'll need to lean it against something, too, to prevent it from pivoting around its headset.

1. The wheels can be cleaned easily while on the bike. Remove the wheels to clean the frame, fork, and components.

2. If the bike has a chain hanger (a little nub attached to the inner side of the right seatstay, a few centimeters above the dropout), hook the chain over it. If not, pull the chain back over a dowel stick (Fig. 2.8) or an old rear hub secured in the dropouts.

2.9 cleaning jockey wheels

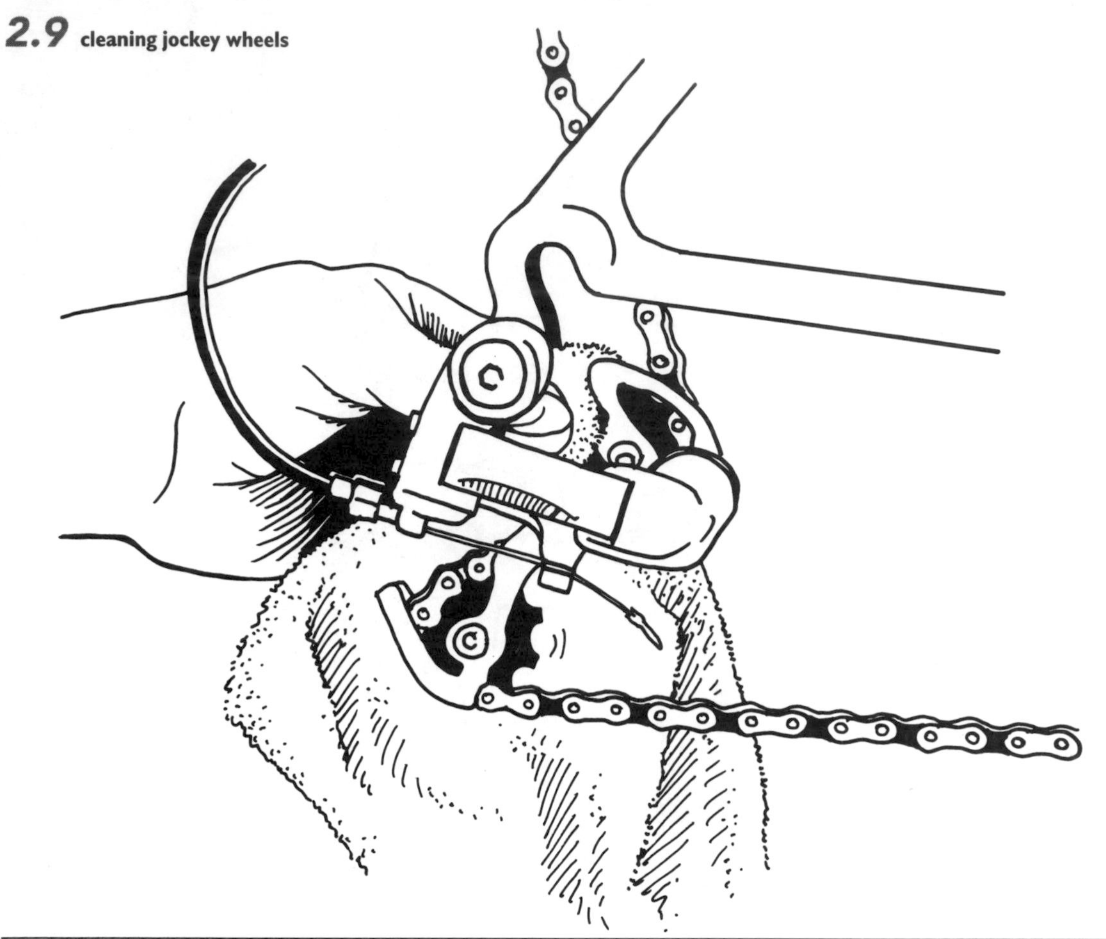

3. Fill a bucket with hot water and dish soap. Using a stiff nylon-bristle scrub brush, scrub the entire bike and wheels. Leave the chain, cogs, chainrings and derailleurs for last.

4. Rinse the bike with water by hosing it off (low pressure!) or wiping it with a wet rag. Avoid getting water in the bearings of the bottom bracket, headset, pedals or hubs. Note, too, that most frames and forks have tiny vent holes in the tubes; these were drilled at the factory to allow gasses to escape during welding. The holes are often open to the outside on the seatstays, fork legs, chainstays, and seatstay and chainstay bridges. Avoid getting water in these holes. Taping over the vent holes is a good idea, and leaving them permanently taped to keep water out is even better.

drivetrain cleaning

2-14: CLEANING THE DRIVETRAIN

The drivetrain consists of an oil-covered chain running over gears and through derailleurs. Sounds messy, doesn't it? Well, it is. In fact, since the whole affair is generally exposed to the elements, it inevitably picks up lots of dirt.

In glorious opposition to this, the drivetrain is also what transfers your energy into the bike's forward motion, which means that it should be kept fastidiously clean so that it can move freely. Frequent cleaning and lubrication are required to keep it rolling well, and to extend the life of your bike.

Fortunately, the drivetrain rarely needs to be completely disassembled for intensive cleaning. If you keep after it, regular maintenance can be confined to wiping down the chain, derailleur pulleys and chainrings with a dry rag.

1. To wipe the chain, turn the cranks while holding a rag in your hand and grabbing the chain (Fig. 2.8).

2. Holding a rag, squeeze the teeth of the jockey

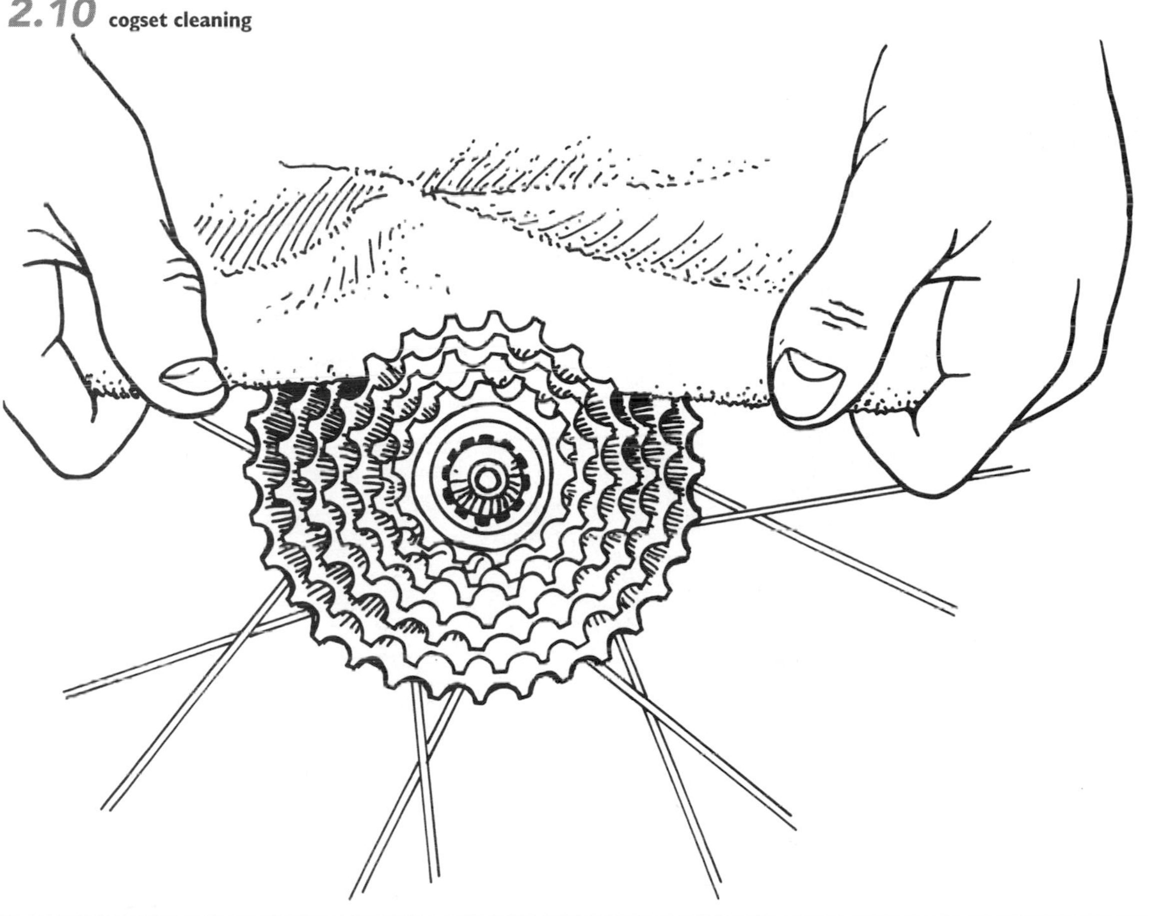
2.10 cogset cleaning

wheels between your index finger and thumb as you turn the cranks (Fig. 2.9). This will remove grease and dirt that has built up on the jockey wheels.

3. Slip a rag in between each pair of rear cogs and work it back and forth until each cog is clean (Fig. 2.10).

4. Wipe down the derailleurs and the front chainrings with the rag.

Your chain will last much longer if you perform this sort of quick cleaning regularly, followed by dripping chain lube on the chain and another light wipe down. You will also be able to skip the kind of heavy-duty solvent cleanings that become necessary when a chain gets really grungy.

You can also remove packed-up road grit from derailleurs and cogs with the soapy water and scrub brush. Note, however, that the soap will not dissolve the dirty lubricant that is all over the drivetrain; rather the brush will smear it all over the bike if you're not careful. Use a different brush than the one you use for cleaning the frame. Follow it with a cloth wipe down.

2-15: CLEANING THE CHAIN WITH SOLVENT

When a chain gets really dirty, the only way to rescue it is with an immersion in solvent—a nasty task worth avoiding by performing the regular maintenance noted above. In fact, if you are sparing with the chain lube—that is, if you only drip it on the chain rollers where it is needed, rather than spraying it all over the chain—you can minimize, if not avoid, the need for solvent cleaning with its associated disposal and toxicity problems.

If you determine that using a solvent is unavoid-

2.11 solvent cleaning of the chain

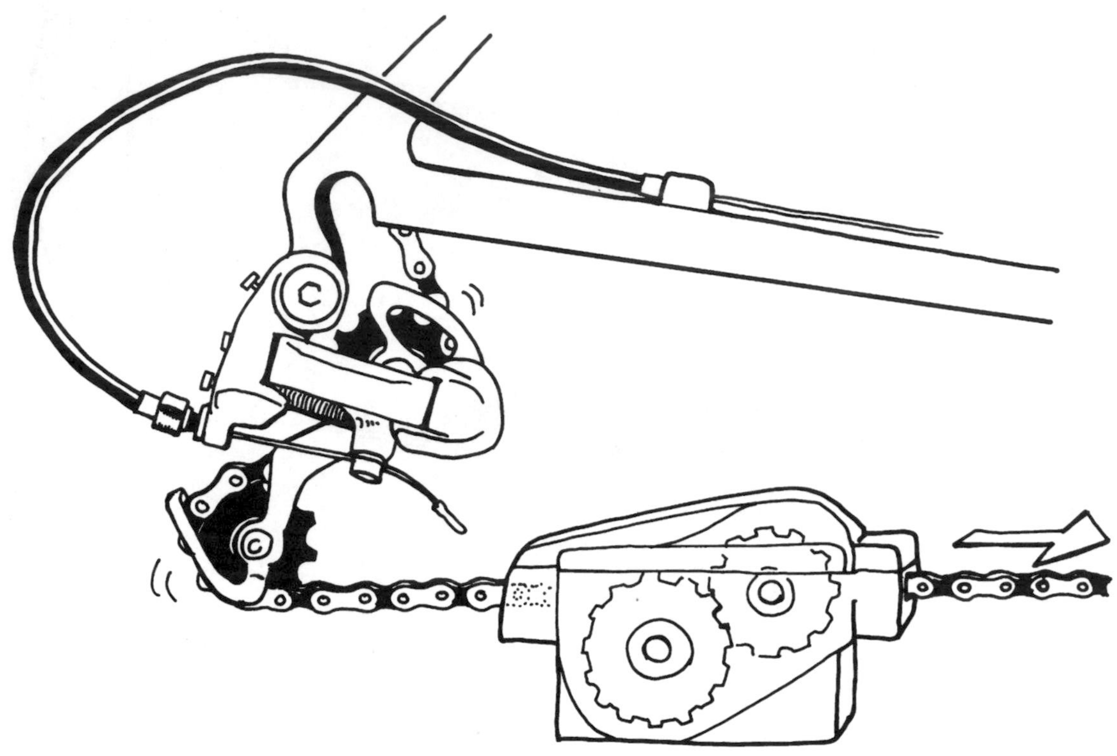

able, work in a well-ventilated area, use as little solvent as necessary, and pick an environmentally friendly mixture. There are many citrus-based solvents on the market that will reduce the danger to your lungs and skin, and be less of a major disposal problem. If you are using a lot of solvents, organic ones such as diesel fuel can be recycled, which may be a preferable solution to using citrus solvents, as long as you protect yourself from the fumes with a respirator. All solvents suck the oils from your skin, so be sure to wear rubber gloves, even with so-

2.12 drip oil only where it is needed

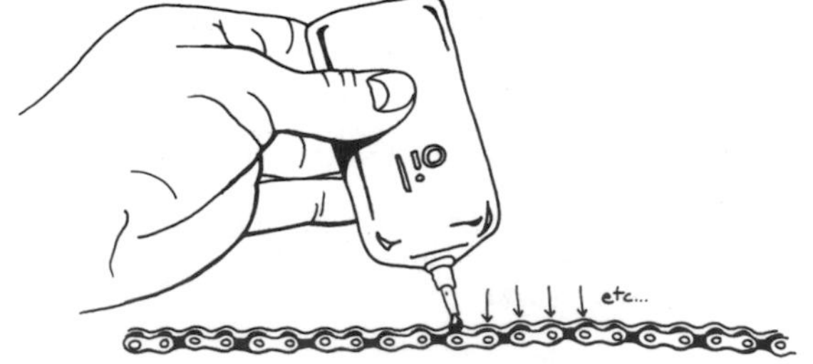

called "green" solvents.

A self-contained chain cleaner with internal brushes and a solvent bath is a quick and convenient way to clean a chain (Fig. 2.11), but it may not clean well deep inside the rollers. A nylon brush or an old toothbrush dipped in solvent is good for cleaning cogs, pulleys and chainrings, and it can be used for a quick clean of the chain as well. The only way to thoroughly clean the chain, however, is to remove it and clean it in a solvent bath.

1. Follow the directions in Chapter 4 for removing the chain.
2. Put the chain in an old water bottle about a quarter-full of solvent.
3. Shake the bottle vigorously to clean the chain. Hold the bottle close to the ground, in case it leaks.
4. Hang the chain to dry completely, especially inside the rollers.
5. Install the chain on the bike, following the

directions in Chapter 4.

6. Drip chain lubricant into each of the chain's links and rollers, one at a time (Fig. 2.12). Put a dot on your starting point with an indelible marker to make sure you hit each link.

7. Lightly wipe down the chain with a clean rag to remove excess lubricant on the outside, where it is not needed.

8. After this sorry episode is concluded, wipe down the chain regularly and lubricate it as necessary using the one drop/one link method outlined above, to avoid another visit to solvent city.

You can re-use much of the solvent by allowing it to settle in a clear container over a period of days or weeks. Decant and save the clear stuff and dispose of the sludge.

2-16: GENERAL GUIDE TO PERFORMING MECHANICAL WORK

I. Threaded Parts

A. All threads must be prepped before tightening. Depending on the bolt in question (see below), prep with lubricant, thread-lock compound, or an anti-seize compound. Clean off excess thread-prepping compound to minimize dirt attraction.

1. Lubricated threads: Most threads should be lubricated with grease or oil. If a bolt is already installed, you can back it out and drip a little chain lube on it, and tighten it back down. Bolts that appreciate lubrication include crank bolts, pedal axles, cleat bolts on shoes, derailleur- and brake-cable-anchor bolts, and control-lever mounting bolts.

2. Locked threads: Some threads need to be locked in order to prevent them from vibrating loose; these are bolts that need to stay in place but are not tightened down fully for some reason or other. Examples include derailleur limit screws, jockey wheel center bolts, brake mounting bolts, and

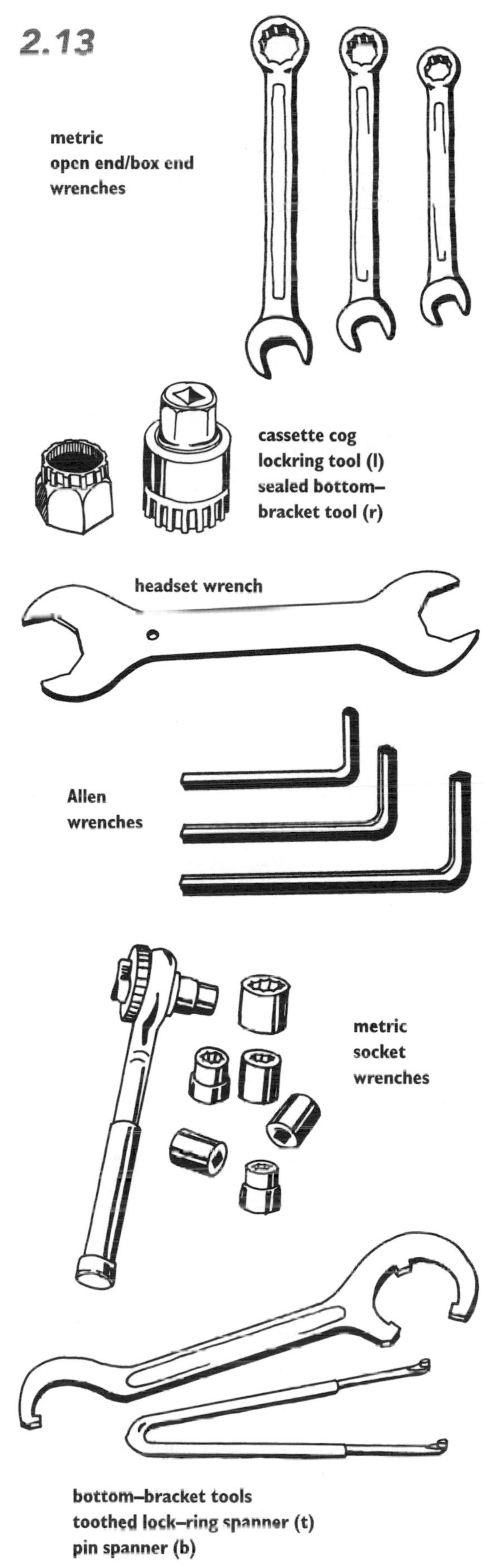

basic stuff

general guide to mechanical work

spoke nipples. Use Loctite, Finish Line Threadlock, or the equivalent on bolts; use Wheelsmith Spoke-Prep or the equivalent on spokes.

3. Anti-Seize threads: Some threads have a tendency to bind up and gall, making full tightening as well as extraction problematic. They need anti-seize compound on them to prevent galling. Any steel or aluminum bolt threaded into a titanium part (this includes any parts mounted to titanium frames, like bottom bracket cups), and any titanium bolt threaded into a steel or aluminum part, must be coated with anti-seize compound. Use Finish Line Ti-Prep or the equivalent.

Cautionary note: *Never thread a titanium bolt into a titanium part; even with anti-seize, these will almost certainly gall and rip apart when you try to remove them. If you must break this rule, use a liberal coating of anti-seize compound on the threads, and every six months or so unscrew the bolt, clean it and reapply the compound.*

B. Wrenches (see Fig. 2.13 for various types) must be fully engaged before tightening or loosening.

1. Hex keys must be fully inserted into the bolt head, or the wrench and/or bolt hex hole will round off. Shallow bolt heads, such as those used on shoe cleat bolts, are especially susceptible, so be careful. And be sure to clean dirt and rocks out of bolt heads to get the hex key in all of the way.

2. Open-end, box-end, and socket wrenches must be properly seated around a hex bolt, or it will round off. Bicycles employ lots of soft aluminum nuts and bolts in the headset, brakes and cranks that are easily damaged by a bad wrench fit.

3. Splined wrenches must be fully engaged or the splines will be damaged or the tool will snap. Be especially careful when removing a cassette lockring; if you strip the splines, you've got a real problem on your hands.

4. Toothed-lockring spanners need to stay lined up on the lockring; if they slide off, they will not only tear up the lockring, they will also damage the frame paint. Such lockrings are found in the bottom-bracket adjustable cup.

5. Pin spanners need to be fully seated in the holes to prevent slipping out and damaging the holes in the part. You'll find pin holes in bottom bracket adjustable cups and crank bolt collars.

C. Tightening torque: a full list of specific tightening torques is in Appendix E. Generally, tightness can be classified in three levels:

1. Snug (10-30 inch-pounds); small set screws (like computer magnet mounting screws), bearing pre-load bolts (like on Aheadset top cap), and screws going into plastic parts need to be snug.

2. Firmly tightened (30-80 inch-pounds); cable anchor bolts, shoe cleat bolts, and brake mounting bolts need to be firmly tightened.

3. Really tight (300-600 inch-pounds); crankarm bolts, cassette lockring bolts and bottom bracket cups need to be really tight.

II. Cleanliness

A. Do not expect parts to work by just squirting or slathering lubricant on them (meanwhile patting yourself on the back for maintaining your bike). The lube will pick up lots of dirt and get very gunky.

B. Do not expect parts to work by washing them and not lubricating them. They will get dry and squeaky.

III. Test Riding

Always ride the bike—slowly at first, and then harder—after adjusting in the bike stand. Parts behave differently under load.

Emergency repairs

"Eat a live toad the first thing in the morning and nothing worse will happen to you the rest of the day." —Anonymous

If you ride your bike a fair distance from home, sooner or later you are likely to encounter a situation that has the potential to turn into an emergency. The best way to avoid an unpleasant surprise is to plan ahead and be prepared before it happens, which is what this chapter is all about. Proper planning involves steps as simple as bringing along a few tools, spare tubes, food and extra clothes. And, of course, a little knowledge.

This chapter will acquaint you with ways to deal with most "emergencies," whether you have all the tools you need or not. Generally, any problem you're likely to encounter will involve only one component on the bike—a flat tire, a broken derailleur cable, or something similar—and in most cases it is pretty easy to find a workaround that will get you home. True, you always have the option of walking, but this chapter is designed to help you avoid that miserable fate.

Incidentally, a cell phone (or at least some change for a pay phone) is worth carrying on long solo rides, just in case something does break in a big way. Bottle-shaped cell-phone cases are available to keep your phone in one of your water bottle cages.

On the other hand, you may find yourself with a perfectly functioning bicycle and a fully charged phone and still be in dire straits because you're either lost, cold, dehydrated or bonking (i.e., your body has run out of fuel) or injured. Carefully read the final portion of this chapter for pointers on how to avoid these things and what to do if the worst does happen.

3-1: RECOMMENDED TOOLS

The take-along tool kit for your seat bag is described in Chapter 1, Section I-6. If you're going to be a

tools

Take-along tool kit shown in Fig. 1.6 —and Fig. 1.7, too, for longer tours.

long way from civilization, take along the extra tools recommended for longer trips.

3-2: FLAT TIRE PREVENTION

The best way to avoid flats is to always have good tires on your bike. Check them regularly for wear, cracking and tread cuts. Steer clear of potholes, broken glass and nails (Ha! As if!), and you'll rarely have a problem.

Flat tires can be minimized with the use of tire sealants; "Slime" is one that works well. Tire sealants usually consist of a viscous liquid full of chopped fibers that plug holes in the tube as they occur (use of Slime is covered in Chapter 6). Sealant can be injected into an existing tube, or you can purchase new tubes with sealant already inside. Note, however, that sealant adds detectable weight to your wheels and is unnecessary if you ride on good roads and keep your tires properly inflated.

If you do have Slime or another tire sealant in your tube and your tire gets low due to a puncture (this is most likely to happen when you put your bike away for a few weeks), put more air in and spin the wheel, or ride the bike for a couple of miles to get the sealant to flow out to the hole. Note that sealant will not fill a puncture if the hole in the tube is on the rim side, since the liquid will be thrown to the outside when the wheel turns.

Sealants cannot fill large punctures and blowouts, although amazingly big holes can be plugged sufficiently to get you home if you locate where the sealant is squirting out through the tire. Rotate the wheel so that spot is at the bottom and wait. The sealant may pool up enough there to plug the hole. Add more air and continue.

Plastic tire liners that fit between the tire and

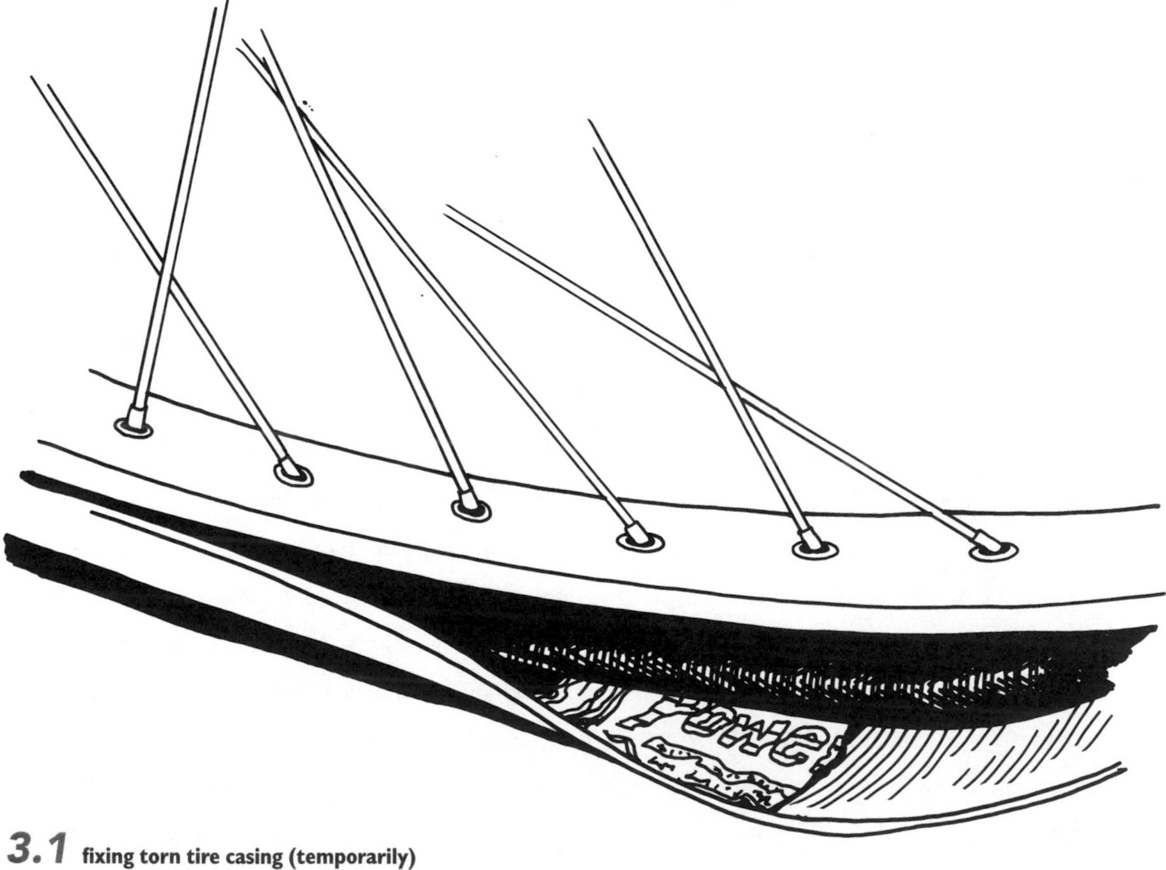

3.1 **fixing torn tire casing (temporarily)**

tube are another strategy often brandished to ward off flats, but I don't recommend them. Most are so stiff that they decrease traction and cornering ability, and they can slip sideways and cut into the tube.

3-3: FIXING FLAT TIRES

A. If you have a spare or a patch kit:

Simple flat tires are easy to deal with. The first flat you get on a ride is most easily fixed by installing your spare tube (Chapter 6). Make sure you remove whatever caused the flat (you'll probably see it sticking up from the tread), and feel around the inside of the tire for any other sharp objects.

If you can't find a thorn, nail, piece of glass or the like in the tire or tube, check the rim to see whether the flat was caused by a protruding spoke or nipple, a metal shard from the rim, or the edge of a spoke hole protruding through a worn rim strip. The rim strip is the piece of plastic or rubber that covers the spoke holes in the well of the rim. Many rim strips are totally inadequate, being either too narrow or prone to cracking or tearing. Also, metal hunks left from the drilling of rims during manufacture can work their way out into the tube.

In fact, these flats are so common that on a new bike I recommend removing the tires and tubes before the first ride and checking the rims. Shake out any metal fragments that may be present. If the rim strips consist of limp, narrow strips of soft rubber or cloth, replace them with high-quality plastic or adhesive cotton rim strips, or apply a couple of layers of reinforced packing tape (the kind that has lengthwise fibers inside) to cover the spoke holes in place of the rim strips.

After you run out of spare tubes, additional flats must be patched (also covered in Chapter 6).

B. Torn sidewall

Rocks and glass can cut tire sidewalls. The likelihood of sidewall problems is reduced if you do not ride with tires so old that the cords are rotten and weak. If your tire's sidewall is torn or cut, the tube will stick out. Just patching or replacing the tube isn't going to solve the problem. Without reinforcement, your tube will blow out again very soon.

First, you have to look for something to reinforce the tire sidewall (Fig. 3.1). Dollar bills work surprisingly well as tire boots. The paper is pretty tough and should hold for the rest of the ride if you are careful. (I told you that cash will get you out of bad situations. Credit cards are not acceptable for this purpose.) Business cards are a bit small but work better than nothing. You might even try an energy bar wrapper or a piece of a plastic soda bottle. A small piece of a tire liner cut in an oval might be a good addition to your patch kit for this purpose. You get the idea.

1. Lay the cash or whatever inside the tire over the gash, or wrap it around the tube at that spot. Place several layers between the tire and tube to support the tube and prevent it from bulging out through the hole in the sidewall.
2. Put a little air in the tube to hold the makeshift reinforcement in place.
3. Mount the tire bead on the rim. You may need to let a little air out of the tube to do so.
4. After making sure that the tire is seated and the boot is still in place, inflate the tube to about 75 psi, if you are good at estimating without a gauge. Pressures lower than this will allow the boot to move around and may also lead to a pinch flat if you cross a train track.

Check the boot periodically on the ride home to make certain that the tube is not bulging out again.

C. No more spare tubes or patches

Now comes the frustrating part: You have run out of spare tubes, and have used up all of your patches (or your CO_2 cartridge is empty and you don't have a pump), and still you have a flat tire. The situation is obvious: You are going to have to ride home without air in your tire.

Riding a flat for a long way will destroy the tire, and it will probably damage the rim, too. You can minimize that damage, though, by filling the space in the tire with grass, leaves or similar materials. Pack it in tightly and then remount the tire on the rim. This should make the ride a little less dangerous, by minimizing the flat tire's tendency to roll out from under the bike during a turn.

3-4: JAMMED CHAIN

When the chain gets jammed between the chainrings and the chainstay, it can be surprisingly difficult to extract. You may find that you tug and tug on the chain, and it won't come out. Well, chainrings are flexible, and if you apply some mechanical advantage, the chain will come free quite easily.

Insert a screwdriver or similar thin lever between the chainring and the chainstay, and pry the space open while pulling the chain out (Fig. 3.2). You will probably be amazed at how easy this is, especially in light of how much hard tugging would not free the chain.

If you still cannot free the chain, disassemble the chain with a chain tool (Chapter 4, Section 4-7), pull it out, and put it back together (Section 4-9 through 4-11).

3-5: BROKEN CHAIN

Chains seldom break on the road, but it does happen. It has happened to me with a bad cogset, causing the chain to skip. It "breaks" by a chain plate popping off the end of a rivet. As the chain rips apart, it can cause collateral damage as well. The

3.2 freeing jammed chain

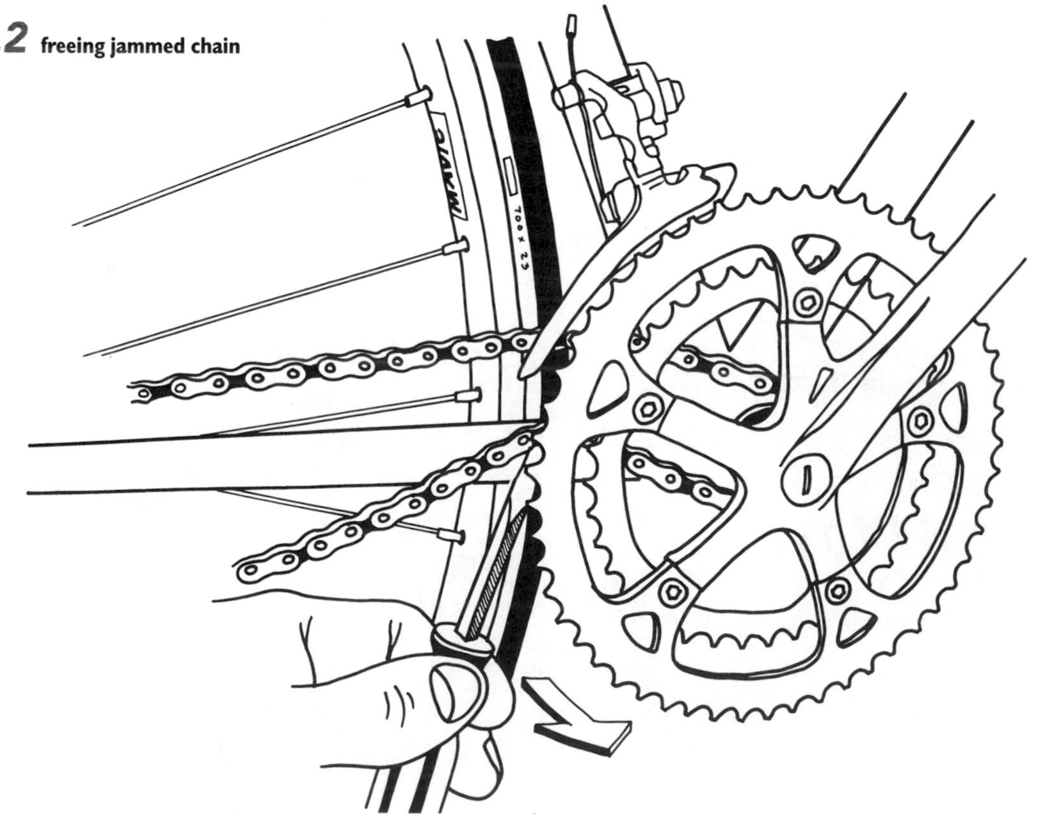

open chain plate can snag the front derailleur cage, bending it or tearing it off, or it can jam into the rear dropout.

When a chain breaks, the end link is certainly shot, and some others in the area may be as well.

1. Remove the damaged links with the chain tool. (You or your riding partner did remember to bring a chain tool, right?) Again, the procedures for removing the damaged links and reinstalling the chain are covered in Chapter 4, Section 4-7 through 4-11.

2. If you have brought along extra chain links, replace the same number you remove. If not, you'll need to use the chain in its shortened state; it will still work, but you probably won't be able to use the largest cogs when on the big chainring.

3. Join the ends and connect the chain (Fig. 3.3); the procedure is in Chapter 4, Sections 4-9 and 10. Some lightweight chain tools and multitools are more difficult to use than a shop chain tool. Some flex so badly that it is hard to keep the push rod lined up with the rivet. Others pinch the plates so tightly that the chain link binds up. It's a good idea to find these things out before you need the tool on the road.

3-6: BENT WHEEL

If the rim is banging against the brake pads, or worse yet the frame or fork, pedaling becomes very difficult. If you haven't hit a pothole or something similar which has bent the rim, the cause is probably a loose or broken spoke. Another culprit could be a broken rim — fairly rare, even with ultra lightweight tubular wheels.

3-7: LOOSE SPOKES

If you have a loose spoke or two, the rim will wobble all over the place.

1. Find the loose spoke (or spokes) by feeling all of them. The really loose ones, which would cause a wobble of large magnitude, will be obvious. If you

3.3 fixing broken chain

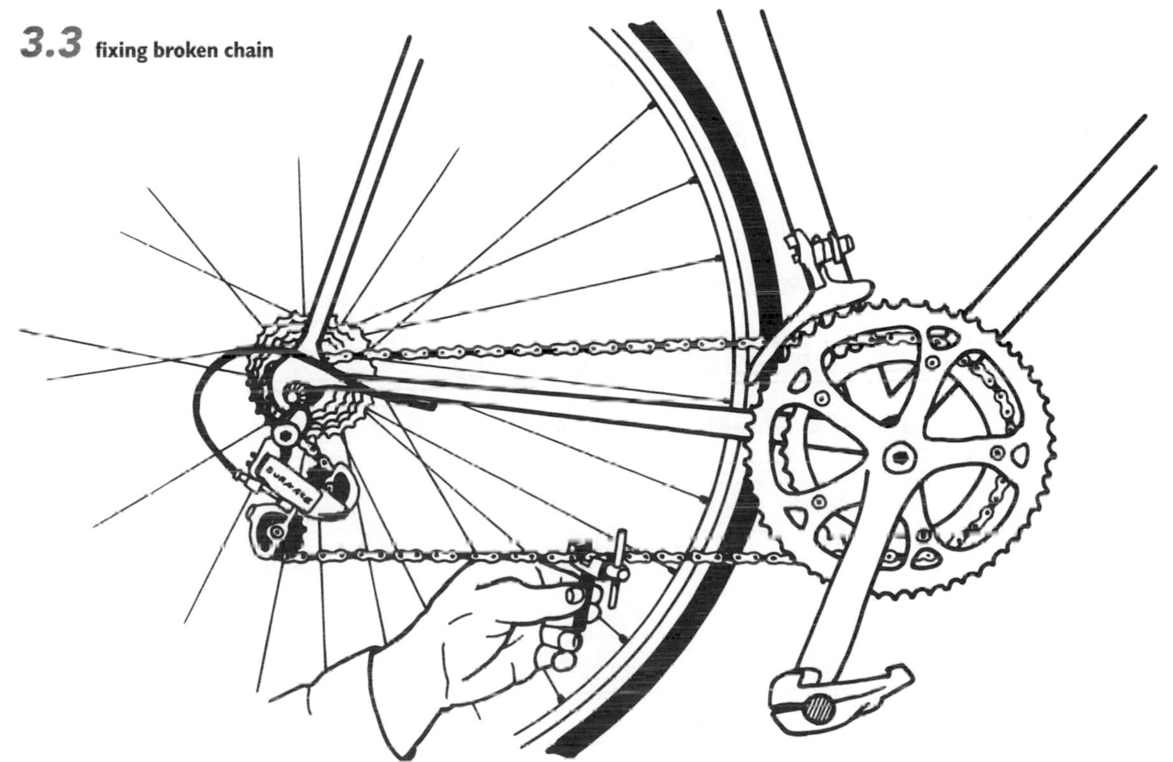

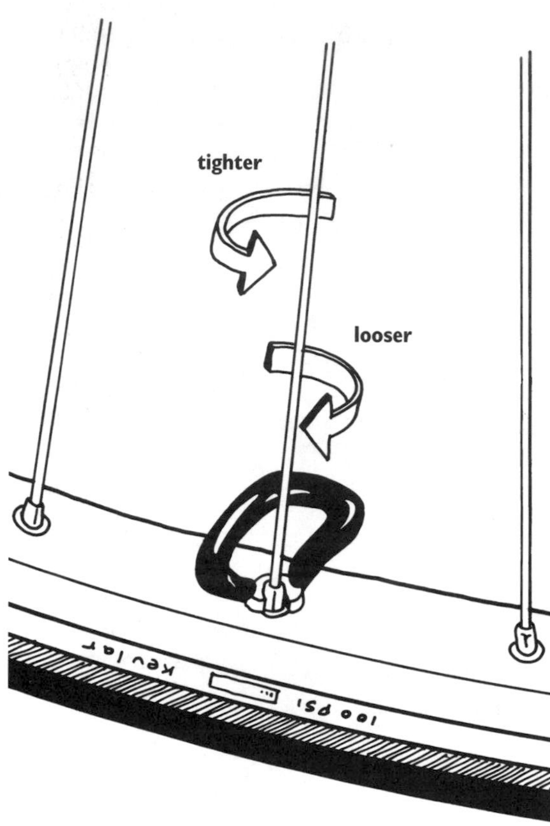

3.4 tightening and loosening

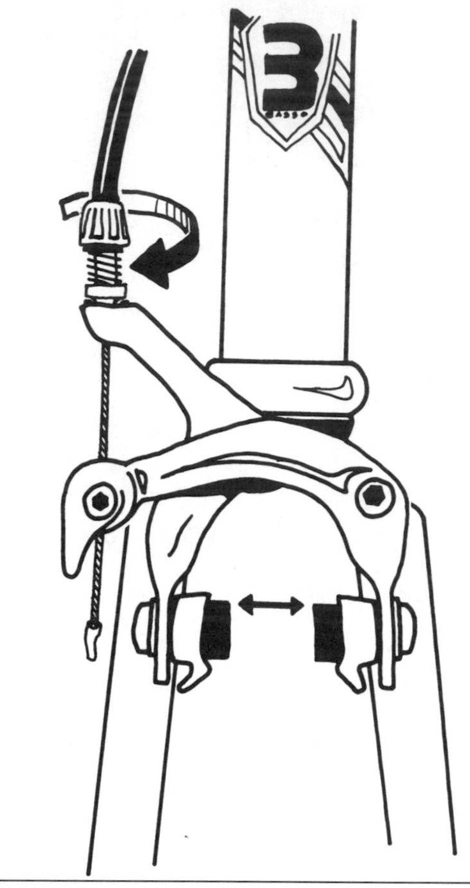

3.5 loosening the brake cable tension

find a broken spoke, skip to the next section (3-8). If you have no loose or broken spokes, skip ahead to section 3-10.

spokes

2. Get out the spoke wrench that you carry for such an eventuality. If you don't have one, skip to section 3-9 below.

3. Mark the loose spokes, if necessary, by tying blades of grass, sandwich bag twist-ties, tape or the like around them.

4. Tighten the loose spokes (Fig. 3.4), and true the wheel, following the procedures in Chapter 6, Section 6-8.

3-8: BROKEN SPOKES

If you broke a spoke, the wheel will wobble wildly.

1. Locate the broken spoke.

2. Remove the remainders of the spoke, both the piece going through the hub, and the piece threaded into the nipple. If the broken spoke is on the freewheel side of the rear wheel, you may not be able to remove it from the hub, since it will be behind the cogs. If so, skip to step 6 after wrapping it around neighboring spokes to prevent it from slapping around (Fig. 3.6).

3. Get out your spoke wrench. If you have no spoke wrench, skip to section 3-9 below.

4. If you brought a spare spoke of the right length or the Kevlar replacement spoke mentioned in Chapter 1, Section 1-6B, you're in business. If not, skip to step 6. Put the new spoke through the hub hole, weave it through the other spokes the same way the old one was, and thread it into the spoke nipple that is still sticking out of the rim. Mark it with a pen or a blade of grass tied around it. With the Kevlar spoke, thread the Kevlar through the hub hole, attach the ends to the enclosed stub

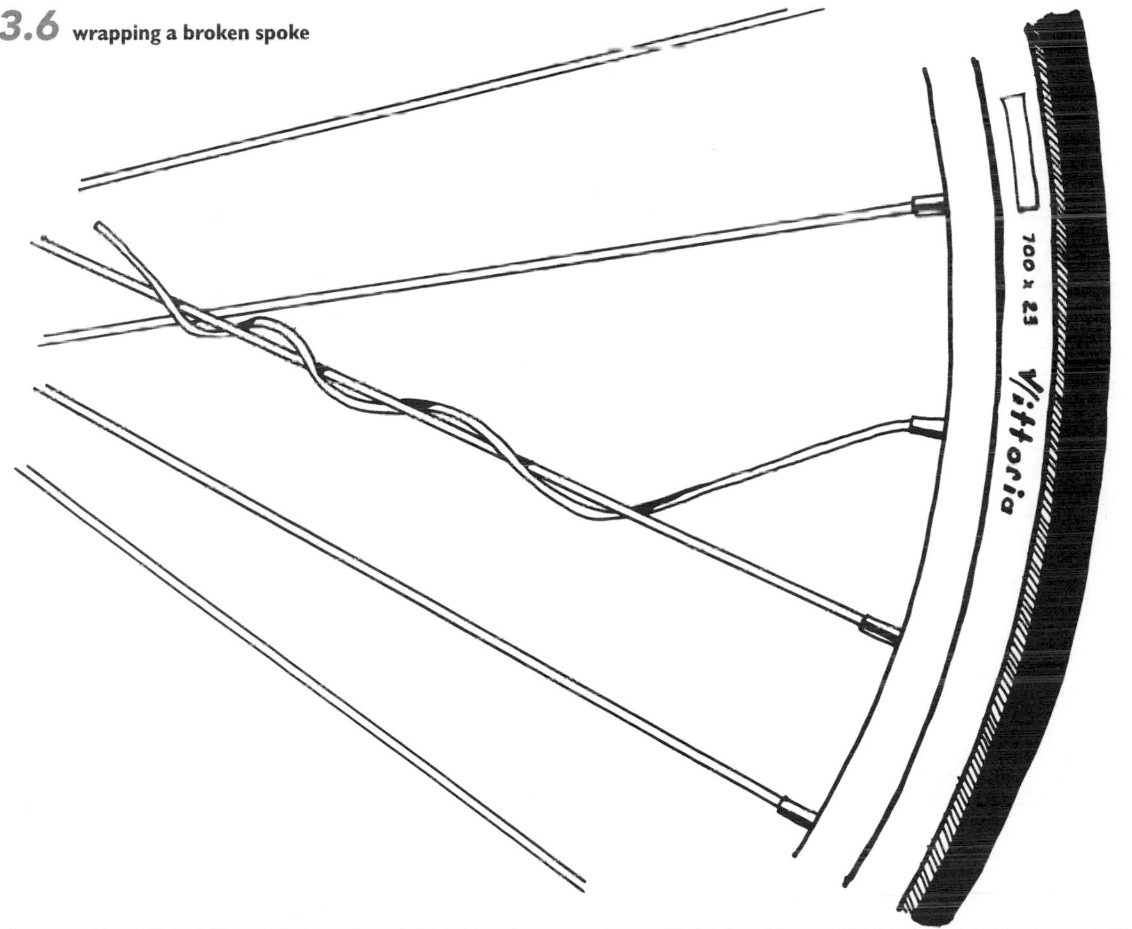

3.6 wrapping a broken spoke

of spoke, adjust the ends to length, tie them off, and tighten the spoke nipple.

5. Tighten the nipple on the new spoke with a spoke wrench (Fig. 3.4), checking the rim clearance with the brake pad as you go. Stop when the rim is reasonably straight, and finish your ride.

6. If you can't replace the spoke and you do have a spoke wrench, bring the wheel into rideable trueness by loosening the spoke on either side of the broken one. These two spokes come from the opposite side of the hub and will let the rim move toward the side with the broken spoke as they are loosened. A spoke nipple loosens clockwise when viewed from its top (Fig. 3.4). Ride home, conservatively, as this wheel will rapidly get worse.

7. Once at home, replace the spoke, following the procedure in Chapter 6, Section 6-9, or take it to a bike shop for repair. If you break a spoke more than once on a wheel, re-lace the wheel with new spokes. The rim may need replacement as well.

3-9: NO SPOKE WRENCH

If the rim is banging the brake pads, but the tire is not hitting the chainstays or fork blades, simply open the brake so that you can get home, as detailed here. If the tire is hitting the frame or fork, you may need more extreme measures to temporarily straighten it; see the next section.

1. Open the brake caliper quick-release lever as far as is necessary for the pads to clear the rim. If the pads still rub, loosen the brake cable tension by screwing in (clockwise) the barrel adjuster on the caliper (Fig. 3.5). Remember that braking effectiveness on that wheel will be greatly reduced or nonexistent, so ride slowly and carefully.

2. If the rim is still banging the brakes, and you

3.7 fixing a bent rim

have a wrench to loosen the brake cable (usually 5mm Allen), do so, and then clamp it back down. You now have no brake on this wheel; ride carefully.

3. If this still does not cut it, you can disconnect the cable and remove the brake caliper from the fork or brake bridge, put it in your pocket, and pedal home slowly. You will usually need a 5mm Allen wrench for this.

straightening a bent rim

3-10: BENT RIM

If the rim is only mildly out of true, and you brought your spoke wrench, you can fix it. The procedure for truing a wheel is explained in Chapter 6, Section 6-8.

If the wheel is really whacked out, spoke truing won't do much. To get it to clear the brakes so that you can pedal home, follow the steps in section 3-9 above.

If the wheel is bent to the point that it won't turn, even when the brake is removed, you can beat it straight as long as the rim is not broken.

1. Find the area that is bent outward the most and mark it.

2. Leaving the tire on and inflated, hold the wheel by its sides with the bent part at the top facing away from you.

3. Smack the bent-outward section of the rim against flat ground (Fig. 3.7).

4. Put the wheel back in the frame or fork, and see if anything has changed.

5. Repeat the process until the wheel is rideable. You may be surprised how straight you can get a wheel this way.

3-11: DAMAGED FRONT DERAILLEUR

If the front derailleur is mildly bent, straighten it

3.8 opening front derailleur cage

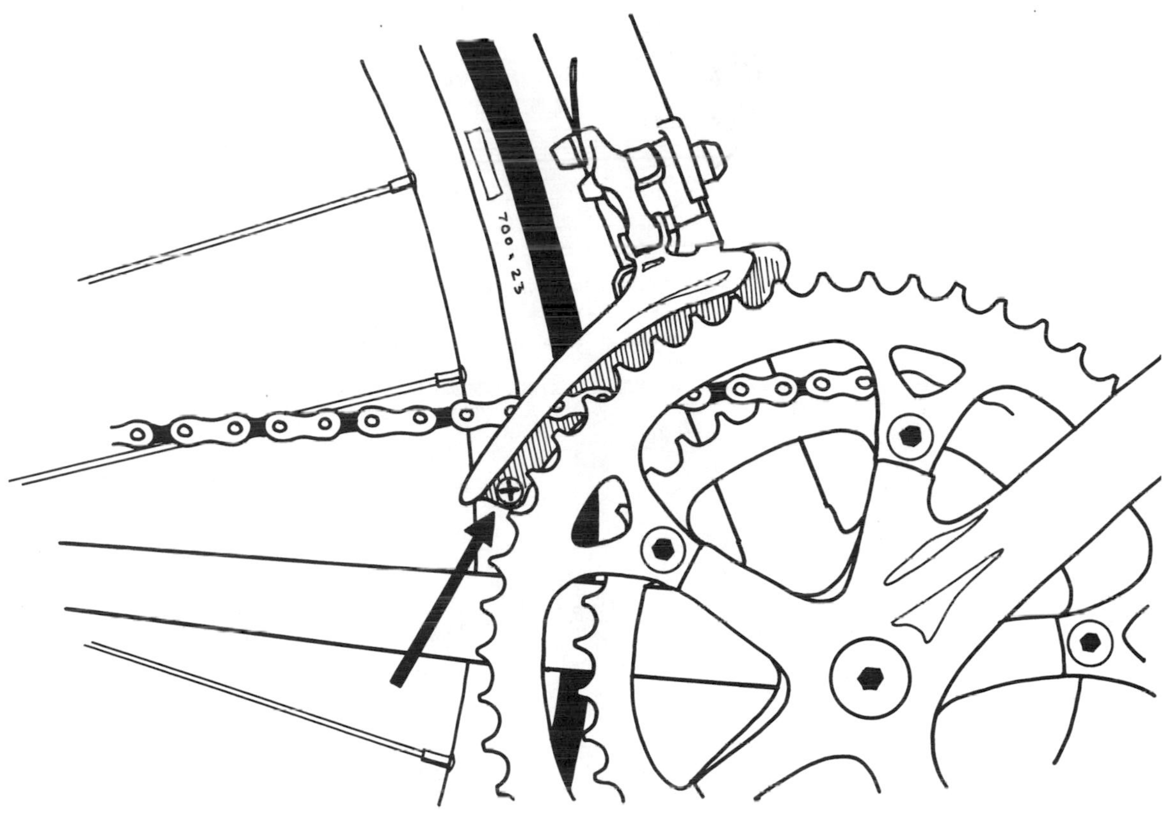

with your hands or leave it until you get home.

If it has simply rotated around the seat tube or twisted in the braze-on (the chain, your foot, or a pants leg can catch it and turn it), reposition it so the cage is just above, and parallel to, the chainrings. Tighten the derailleur in place (usually with a 5mm Allen wrench).

If the derailleur is broken or so bent that you can't ride, or if the braze-on is bent, you will need to remove the derailleur or route the chain around it as described below. (If the braze-on is bent, trying to straighten it will either dent or crack the seat tube or cause a crack to form in the near future. You will need to have a framebuilder remove the braze-on and put a new one on.)

A. With only a screwdriver:

1. Get the chain out of the derailleur cage. To do this, open the derailleur cage by removing the screw at its tail (Fig. 3.8). If, for some reason, the derailleur cage can't be opened this way, you'll have to open the chain with a chain tool (see below).

2. Bypass the derailleur by putting the chain on a chainring that does not interfere with it (either shift the derailleur to the inside and put the chain on the big chainring, or vice versa).

B. With Allen wrenches and a screwdriver (or a chain tool):

1. Remove the derailleur from the seat tube, usually with a 5mm Allen wrench.

2. Remove the screw at the tail of the derailleur cage with a screwdriver, if it has one.

3. Pry open the cage, and separate it from the chain. You can also disassemble the chain, pull it out of the derailleur, and reconnect it (Chapter 4).

4. Manually put the chain on whichever chainring is most appropriate for the ride home. If in

damaged front derailleur

doubt, put it on the inner one (or middle one, if you have a triple).

5. Tie the cable up so it won't catch in your wheel.

6. Stuff the derailleur in your pocket and ride home.

3-12: DAMAGED REAR DERAILLEUR

If the upper jockey wheel gets lost, put the lower one on top and thread a wire or zip-tie through three threaded Presta-valve collar nuts (off your tube valves) as a lower wheel. If one of the jockey-wheel bolts gets lost, and you found the jockey wheel, try replacing the bolt with one of the water-bottle-cage bolts. If the rear derailleur cage return spring breaks, the chain will hang loosely. If you have a bungee cord, hook it to the lower cage, around the skewer (put the lever on the drive side), and up to the seat-tube bottle cage.

If the rear derailleur gets bent just a bit, you can probably straighten it enough to get home. If it gets really bent or broken or one of the jockey wheels falls off, you will need to bypass the derailleur, effectively turning your bike into a single-speed for the remainder of your ride (Fig. 3.9).

1. Open the chain with a chain tool (Chapter 4, Section 4-7) and pull it out of the derailleur.

2. Pick a gear combination in which you think you can make it home most effectively, and set the front derailleur over the chainring you have picked. Be aware that the chain will tend to fall off of the chainrings, or move down to smaller cogs, unless it is really tight.

3. Wrap the chain over the chainring and the rear cog you have chosen, bypassing the rear derailleur entirely.

4. Remove any overlapping chain, making the chain as short as you can while still being able to connect the ends together.

5. Connect the chain with the chain tool as described in Chapter 4, Section 4-9.

6. Ride home.

3.9 bypassing a damaged rear derailleur

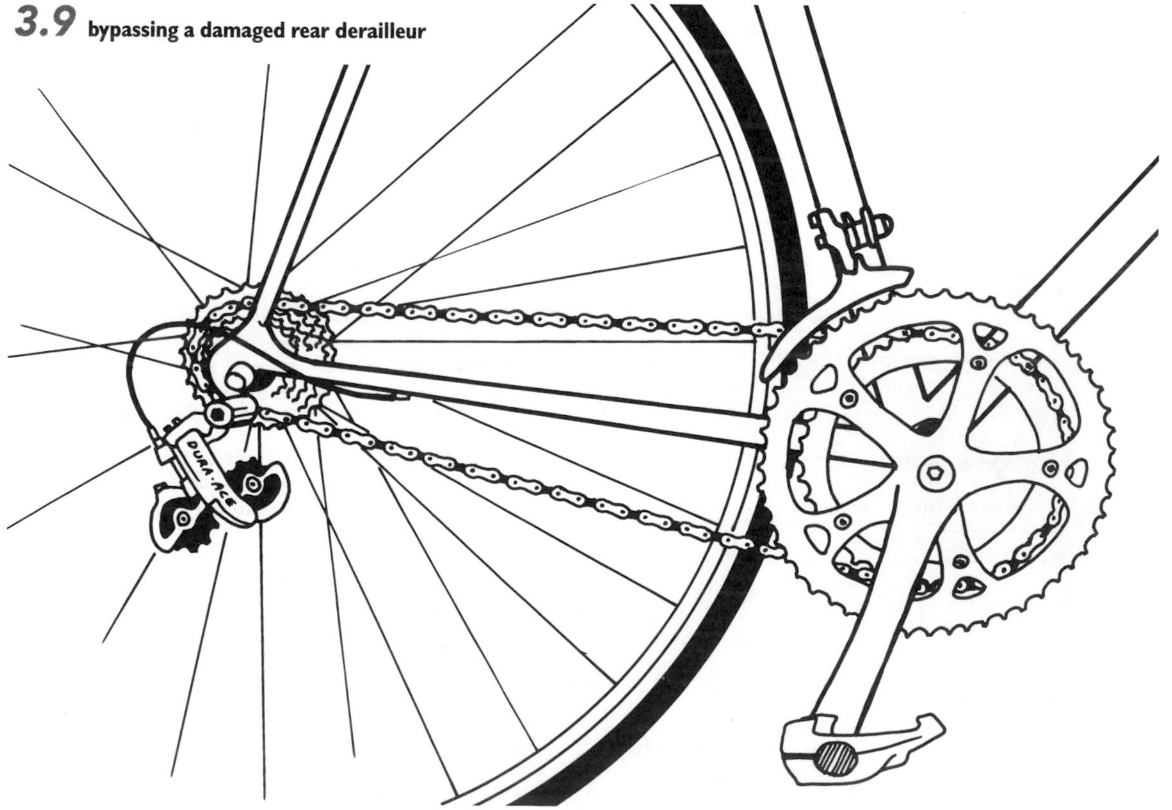

3-13: BROKEN FRONT DERAILLEUR CABLE

The chain will be on the inner chainring, and you will still be able to use all of your rear cogs. Leave it on the inner ring and ride home.

3-14: BROKEN REAR DERAILLEUR CABLE

The chain will be on the smallest rear cog, and you will still be able to use both (or all three) front chainrings. You have three options:

Option 1. Leave it on the small cog and ride home.

Option 2. Move the chain to a larger cog, push inward on the derailleur with your hand, and tighten the high-end limit screw on the rear derailleur (usually the upper one of the two screws) until it lines up with a larger cog (see Fig. 3.10). Move the chain to that cog and ride home. You may have to fine-tune the adjustment of the derailleur stop screw to get it to run quietly without skipping.

Option 3. If you do not have a screwdriver, you can push inward on the rear derailleur while turning the crank with the rear wheel off of the ground to shift to a larger cog. Jam a stick in between the derailleur cage plates to prevent it from moving back down to the small cog (Fig. 3.11).

3-15: BROKEN BRAKE CABLE

Ride home slowly and carefully. Very slowly. Very carefully.

3-16: BROKEN SEAT RAILS OR SEAT POST CLAMP

If you can't tape or tie the saddle back on, try wrapping your gloves or some clothing over the top of the seat post to pad it. Otherwise, remove the seat post and ride home standing up.

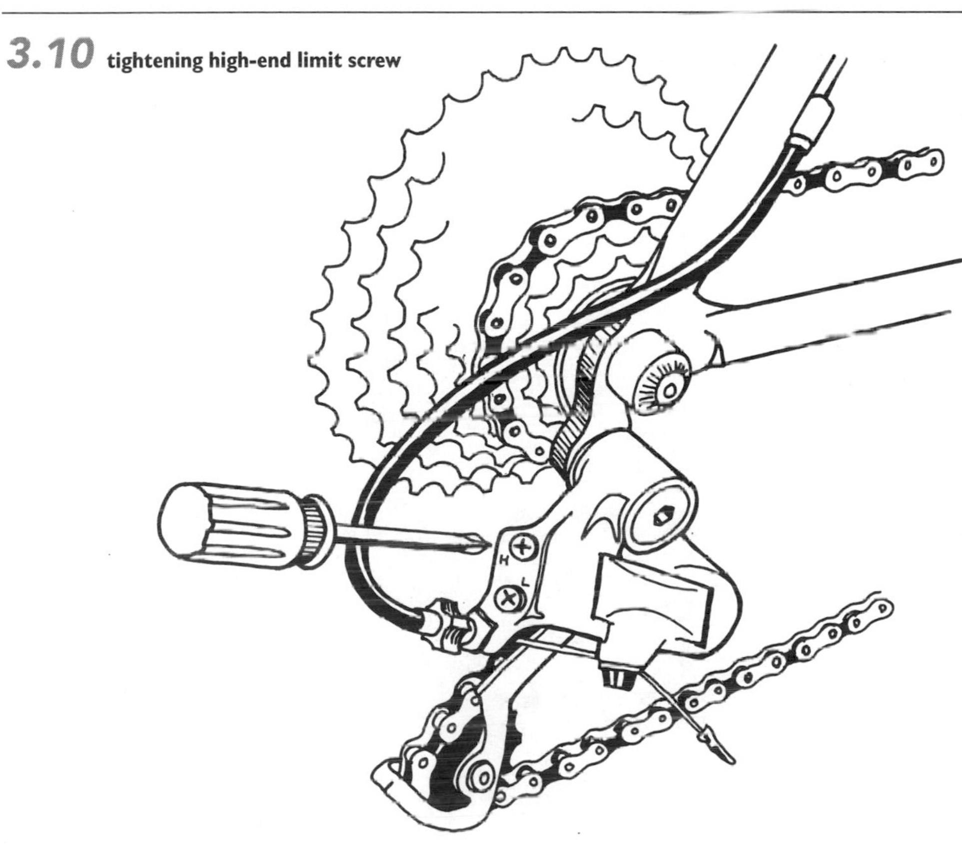

3.10 tightening high-end limit screw

3-17: BROKEN SEAT POST SHAFT

Ride home standing up.

3-18: BROKEN HANDLEBAR

It's probably best to walk home (or phone home for a ride). You could splint it by jamming a stick inside and ride home very carefully, but the stick could easily break, leaving you with no way to control the bike. A sudden impact of your face with the road would follow.

If it is splinted, hold the pieces together with duct tape. If the break is adjacent the stem, slide the stem over the break so it clamps both pieces.

3-19: FROZEN PARTS

Riding in snow or freezing rain can freeze shift cables where they pass under the bottom bracket, or freeze the derailleurs themselves and fill the cogs you are not using with ice. You will just have to stay in that gear. But if the freehub mechanism freezes, you won't be able to coast for even a second. You may be able to free it by peeing on it and hitting it with a stick until it rotates counter clockwise again.

3-20: PREPARE FOR EVERY RIDE

1. Always take plenty of water.
2. Tell someone where you are going and when you expect to return. If you know of someone who is missing, call the police or sheriff, or see to it that someone goes out looking for them in a car.
3. Take extra food for any ride over an hour.
4. Take a road map if you don't know the area. Be willing to ask for directions (not to reinforce any stereotypes, but have you noticed how so many guys are reluctant to do this, but women aren't? Wise up, fellows).
5. Take a cell phone and/or bring change for a pay phone.
6. Take matches, extra clothing and food, and perhaps a flashlight and an aluminized emergency blanket, in case you have to spend some time huddled under a tree.
7. Ride carefully and attentively on wet roads,

3.11

gravel-covered turns, and areas with lots of traffic, especially traffic turning into and out of side roads.

8. Wear a helmet. It's hard to ride home with a cracked skull.

9. Don't ride beyond your limits if you are a long way from home or civilization. Take a break. Get out of the hot sun. Avoid dehydration and bonk by drinking and eating enough.

10. Have your bike in good working order before you leave.

In short, make appropriate decisions when taking long rides. Prepare well. Just because you have a $4000 bike and are riding on paved roads, you are not immune to mechanical problems, getting exhausted, cold, bonked, injured, lost or caught out in the dark.

IV

The chain

"Take care of the luxuries and the necessities will take care of themselves." —Dorothy Parker

tools

Chain lubricant
12-inch ruler
Chain tool
Lots of rags

OPTIONAL

Solvent (citrus-based)
Chain-cleaning tool
Old water bottle
Caliper
Pliers
Solvent tank
Shimano TL-CN24 link-spacing tool
Rohloff or Park chain-elongation indicator
Rohloff cog-wear indicator

The bicycle chain is one of those wondrous technological breakthroughs that we take for granted, but without which a bike would be a clumsy and inefficient contraption. The chain is nothing more than a simple series of links connected by rivets. Rollers surround each rivet between the link plates and engage the teeth of the cogs and chainrings. Nothing to it, and yet it is an extremely efficient method of transmitting mechanical energy from the pedals to the rear wheel. In terms of weight, cost and efficiency, the bicycle chain has no equal—and believe me, people have tried endlessly to improve upon it.

Perhaps because it is so simple and familiar, the chain is often ignored. To keep your bike running smoothly, though, you do have to pay at least some attention to it. It needs to be kept clean and well-lubricated in order to utilize your energy most efficiently, shift smoothly and operate noiselessly. And because its length increases as it wears, thus contacting gear teeth differently than intended, it needs to be replaced regularly to prolong the working life of other, more expensive, drivetrain components.

4-1: LUBRICATION

For best results, use a lubricant intended for bicycle chains. Most lubes sold for this purpose work reasonably well at the basic task of keeping the chain protected and happy.

If you want to get fancy about it, you can assess the type of conditions in which you ride and choose a lubricant intended for those conditions. Some lubricants are "dry," which means that they are formulated to pick up less dirt in dry conditions. Other lubes are "sticky" and therefore less prone to wash off in wet conditions.

Lubricant companies usually advise against

4.1 **Drip oil only where it is needed**

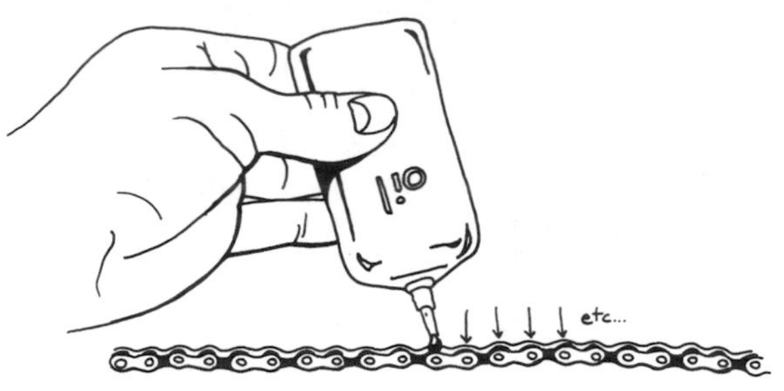

4.2 **wiping chain**

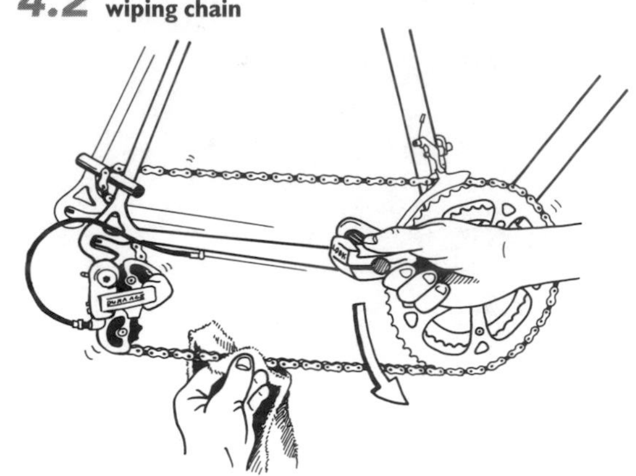

switching among types, and there is probably something to this from the standpoint of maintaining particular properties. That is, once you start using a "dry" lube, for example, it's best to stick with it if most of your riding calls for that type of stuff. But from a lubrication standpoint, there are few, if any, real incompatibilities among brands and types. The main thing is to take care of the chain regularly. If that means using a different brand of oil from time to time, due to travel or changing weather, so be it.

Chain lubes are generally sold in spray cans and in bottles. Sprays should be avoided for regular maintenance chores, because they tend to spew too much oil over everything. The chain only needs a reservoir of oil inside each link; on the outside, the thinnest film is sufficient to keep corrosion at bay. More oil on the outside than that will only attract dirt and gunk; it does nothing to improve the function of the chain.

1. Drip a small amount of lubricant across each roller from the inside out (Fig. 4.1), periodically moving the chain to give easy access to the links you are working on. If you are in a hurry, you can turn the crank slowly while dripping lubricant onto the chain as it goes by. This is better than not lubricating the chain, but it will cause you to apply too much lubricant. That, in turn, will cause the chain to pick up dirt faster, and you'll then wear out your chain sooner.

2. Wipe the chain off lightly with a clean rag to remove excess oil.

3. If you want to do a champion job, perform this task at night, before putting the bike to bed, and then wipe the chain clean again the next morning, or before the next ride. That way, you'll remove additional oil that has seeped onto the outside, where it isn't needed.

If you're riding in wet conditions, you'll need to apply lubricant frequently (after every ride, or even several times during a long rainy ride). The lubricant for wet conditions needs to adhere well to the chain and not be easily washed off; this usually means a thick and sticky lubricant—even a grease. For dry conditions, a smaller amount of a lubricant that does not pick up dirt is preferable.

4-2: CLEANING

Cleaning the chain can be accomplished in a number of ways.

Frequent wiping and lubrication

The simplest way to maintain a chain is to wipe it down frequently and then lubricate it. If this is done prior to every ride, you will never need to clean your chain with a solvent. The lubricant softens the old sludge buildup, which is driven out of the chain when you ride.

4.3 chain cleaning on the bike

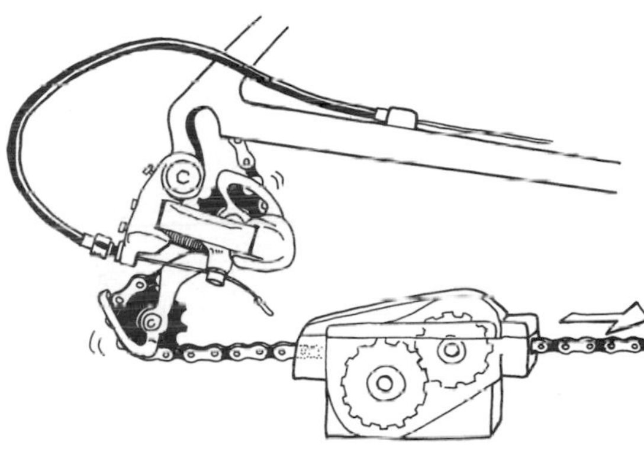

The problem, you're undoubtedly eager to point out, is that the fresh lubricant also picks up new dirt and grime. True, but if this gunk is wiped off before it is driven deep into the chain, and the chain is re-lubricated frequently, it will stay relatively clean and supple. Chain cleaning can be performed with the bike standing on the ground or in a bike stand.

1. With a rag in your hand, grasp the lower length of the chain (between the bottom of the chainring and the rear derailleur lower jockey wheel).

2. Turn the crank backward a number of revolutions, pulling the chain through the rag (Fig. 4.2). Periodically rotate the rag to present a clean section of it to the chain.

3. Lubricate each chain roller as above (Fig. 4.1).

4-3: CHAIN-CLEANING UNITS

Several companies make chain-cleaning gizmos that scrub the chain with solvent without removing the chain from the bike. Removing the chain regularly is admittedly a pain, and it shortens chain life, too, so there is some place for these things. They are generally made of clear plastic and have two or three rotating brushes that scrub the chain as it moves through the solvent bath (Fig. 4.3).

Most chain cleaners are supplied with a non-toxic, citrus-based solvent. For your safety and other environmental reasons, I strongly recommend that you purchase non-toxic citrus solvents for your chain cleaner, even if the unit already comes with a petroleum-based solvent. If you recycle used petroleum solvent, then use that.

Citrus chain solvents often contain some lubricants as well, so they won't dry the chain out. The lubricant inside the solvent is one reason diesel fuel used to have such a following as a chain cleaner. A really strong solvent without lubricant (acetone, for example) will displace the oil from inside the rollers. It will later evaporate, leaving a dry, squeaking chain that is hard to rehabilitate. The same can happen with a citrus-based solvent without a lubricant included, especially if the chain is not allowed to dry sufficiently before it is re-lubricated.

Procedure

1. Remove the top of the chain cleaner case and pour in solvent up to the fill line.

2. Place the unit up against the bottom of the chain, and reinstall the top so that the chain runs through it.

3. Turn the bike's crank backward (Fig. 4.3).

4. Remove the unit, wipe off the chain with a clean cloth, and let it dry.

5. Lubricate as above (section IV-2).

4-4: REMOVAL AND CLEANING

You can also clean the chain by removing it from the bicycle and cleaning it in a solvent. I don't recommend this strategy because, except in the case of a chain with a master link, repeated disassembly weakens the chain. On a road bike, chain breakage is not much of an issue, but it can happen if the chain skips from a worn cog. The skipping can cause a link plate, weakened from opening, to pry apart so that the head of a rivet pops out of it, tearing the chain.

Chain disassembly and reassembly also expands

4.4 checking chain wear... If the curved tooth with the "S" (indicating steel cogs) falls completely into the chain, replace it. (The "A" side is for aluminum cogs.)

the size of the rivet hole where you put it together, allowing the rivet to pop out more easily. Shimano supplies special "subpins" for reassembly of its chains that are meant to prevent this. A hand-opened "master link" can avoid the chain weakening of pushing pins out. Master links are standard on Taya chains and on Sachs and SRAM chains of 1998 and beyond; the aftermarket "Super Link" from Lickton Cycle can also be installed into all but the narrowest of chains (Campagnolo 10-speed, for example).

If you do disassemble the chain (see section 4-7 for instructions), you can clean it well, even without a solvent tank. Just drop the chain into an old jar or water bottle half filled with solvent and agitate. Using an old water bottle or jar allows you to clean the chain without touching or breathing the solvent—something to be avoided even with citrus solvents.

Procedure

1. Remove the chain from the bike (section 4-7 below).
2. Drop it in a water bottle or jar.
3. Pour in enough solvent to cover the chain.
4. Shake the bottle vigorously (low to the ground, in case the top pops off).
5. Hang the chain to air dry.
6. Reassemble it on the bike (see section 4-8, 9, 10, 11 below).
7. Lubricate it as above.

Allow the solvent in the bottle to settle for a few days so you can decant the clear stuff and use it again. I'll say it again: it is important to use a citrus-based solvent. It is not only safer for the environment, it is gentler on your skin and less harmful to breathe. Wear rubber gloves when working with any solvent, and use a respirator meant for volatile organic compounds if you are not using a citrus-based solvent. There is no sense in fixing your bike so it goes faster if you end up becoming a slower, sickly bike rider.

4-5: CHAIN REPLACEMENT

As the rollers, pins and plates wear out, the chain will grow in length. That, in turn, will hasten wear and tear on the other parts of the drivetrain. An elongated chain will concentrate the load on each individual gear tooth, rather than distributing it over all of the teeth that the chain contacts. The abnormal load will cause the gear teeth to become hook-shaped and the tooth valleys to become wider.

If such wear has already occurred, a new chain will not solve the problem. A new chain will not mesh with deformed teeth, and it is likely to skip whenever you pedal hard. The only cure is to replace the chain, the chainrings and the rear cogset. So before all of that extra wear and tear takes place, get in the habit of replacing the chain on a regular basis.

Chain life varies depending on chain type, maintenance, riding conditions, and strength and weight of the rider. As a ballpark number, figure on replacing the chain every 1000–1500 miles, especially if ridden in dirty conditions by a large rider. Lighter riders riding mostly on clean, dry roads can extend replacement time to 2000–3000 miles.

4-6: CHECKING FOR CHAIN ELONGATION

The most reliable way to see whether the chain is worn out is to employ a chain-elongation indicator, such as the model made by Rohloff (Fig. 4.4). The indicator falls completely into the chain if the chain is shot. If the chain is still in good shape, the indicator's tooth will not go all of the way in.

Another way to measure for elongation is with an accurate ruler. Chains are measured on an inch standard, and there should be exactly an integral number of links in 1 foot:

1. Set one end of the ruler on a rivet edge, and measure to the rivet edge at the other end of the ruler.

2. The distance between these rivets should be 12 inches exactly. If it is 12 1/8 inches or greater, replace the chain; if it is 12 1/16 inches or more, it is a good idea to replace it (and a necessity to do so if you have any titanium or aluminum cogs or an 11-tooth small cog).

Chain manufacturer Sachs (SRAM) recommends replacement if elongation is 1 percent, or 1/2-inch in 100 links (50 inches). If the chain is off of the bike, you can hang it next to a new chain; if it is more than a half-link longer for the same number of links, replace it.

4-7: CHAIN REMOVAL

The following procedure applies to all standard derailleur chains except those with a "master link." Master-link equipped chains include all Taya chains, chains with Lickton's "Super Link", and "Power Link"-equipped SRAM or Sachs chains; all of these

4.5 pushing in the pin

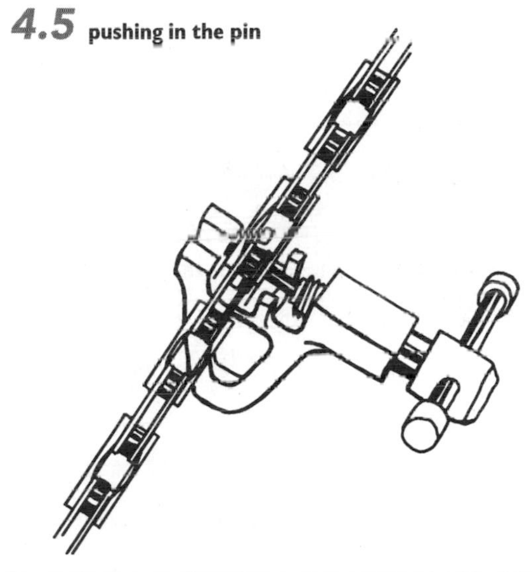

chains snap open by hand at the master link (see section 4-11), although they can also be opened at any other link with a chain tool as described below. Campagnolo 10-speed chains have a master link that cannot be opened, so open it like any other chain.

1. Place any link over the back teeth on a chain tool (Fig. 4.5).

2. Tighten the chain-tool handle clockwise to push the link rivet out. Unless you have a Shimano chain and a new "subpin" for it, don't drive the pin all the way out. Instead, be careful to leave a millimeter or so of rivet protruding inward from the chain plate to hook the chain back together when reassembling.

3. Separate the chain by bending it away from the pushed-out pin.

Incidentally, removing the chain from the bike creates an ideal opportunity to check the rear derailleur limit-screw adjustment. The derailleur limit screws are the marshals that keep the derailleur from moving too far at the travel extremes—keep it, in other words, from shifting into the spokes, or throwing the chain into the dropout. See the next chapter, and figure 5.3, for a look at the limit screws.

To check the limit adjustments with the chain out

of the way, shift the derailleur to high gear and, looking at the derailleur from the rear, see whether the jockey wheel in the cage is aligned with the smallest cog. Then push the derailleur inward until it contacts the inner adjustment screw and look to see whether the jockey wheel is aligned below the largest cog. If either adjustment is off, adjust the limit screw using the procedure in the next chapter, section 5-2.

4-8: CHAIN INSTALLATION

1. Determine the chain length. If you are putting on a new chain, determine how many links you will need in one of the following two ways:

Method 1. Assuming your old chain was the correct length, compare the two and use the same number of links.

Method 2. With a standard double-chainring setup, route the chain through the derailleurs and over the large chainring and smallest cog. The jockey wheels in the rear derailleur should then align vertically (Fig. 4.6).

If you have a triple crankset (three chainwheels up front) and a long-cage rear derailleur on your bike, wrap the chain around the big chainring and the biggest cog without going through either derailleur. Bring the two ends together until the ends overlap; one full link (Fig. 4.7) should be the amount of overlap (Fig. 4.8). Remove the remaining

4.6 **proper chain length with a double**

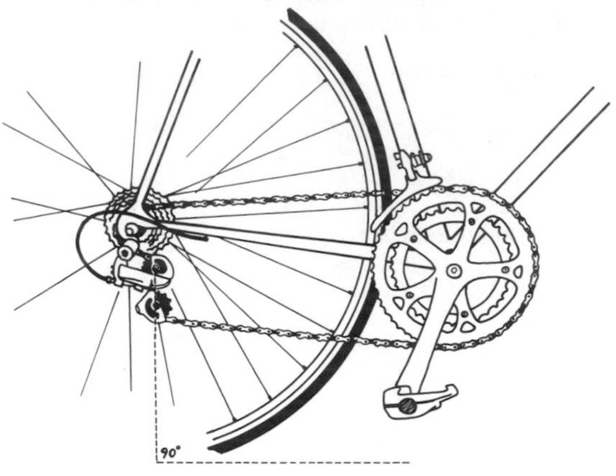

4.7 **one link**

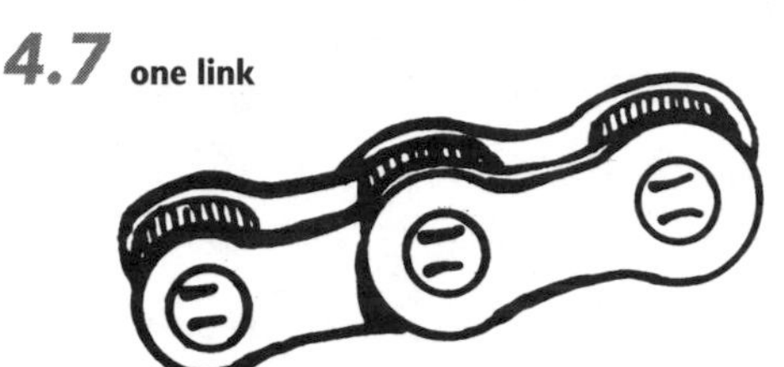

4.8 **determining chain length with a triple**

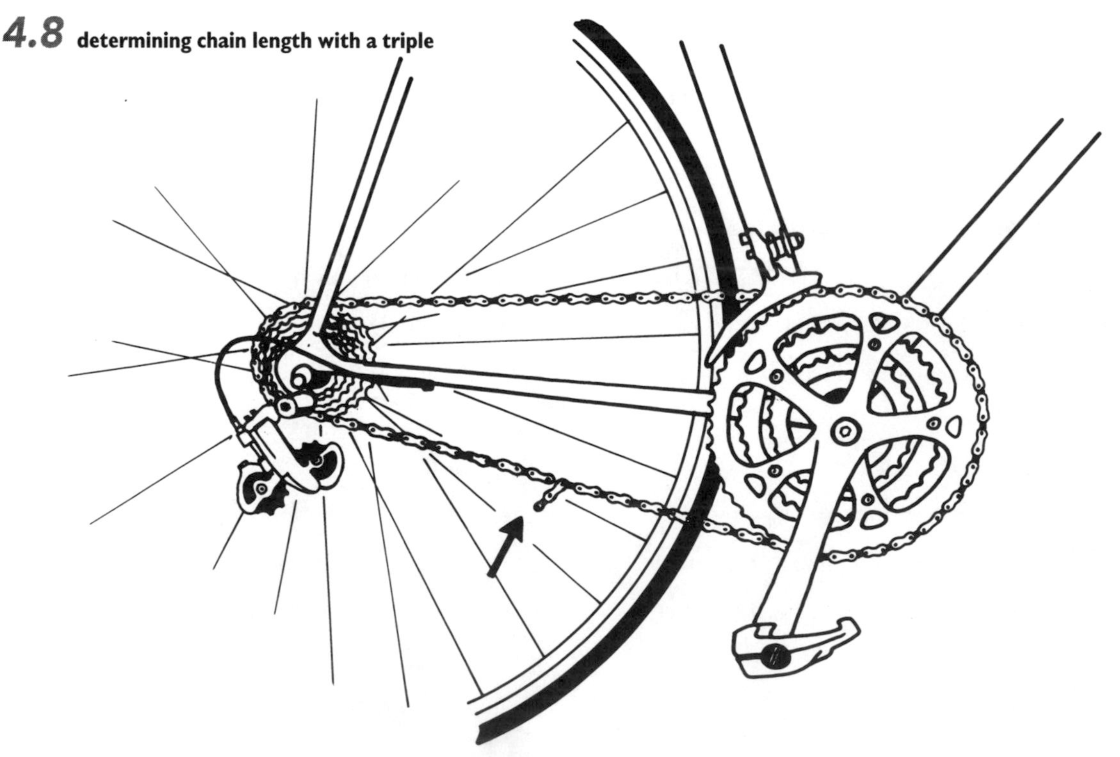

chain installation

links, and save them in your spare tire bag so you have spares in case of chain breakage on the road.

2. Route the chain properly: Shift the derailleurs so that the chain will rest on the smallest cog in the rear and on the smallest chainring up front. Starting with the rear-derailleur pulley that is farthest from the derailleur body (this will be the bottom pulley once the chain is taut), guide the chain up through the rear derailleur, going around the two jockey pulleys. Make sure the chain passes inside of the prongs on the rear derailleur cage. Guide the chain over the smallest rear cog and through the front derailleur cage. Wrap the chain around the smallest front chainring and bring the chain ends together so they meet.

3. Connect the chain: Connecting a chain is much easier if the link rivet that was partially removed when the chain was taken apart is facing outward (toward you). Positioning the link rivet this way allows you to use the chain tool (Fig. 4.9) in a much more comfortable manner (driving the rivet toward the bike, instead of back at you).

4-9: CONNECTING A STANDARD CHAIN

Note: *Campagnolo 10-speed chains require a special "permalink" with two pins and a special tool. Not heeding this could result in injury if the chain breaks.*

1. Push the ends together, snapping the end link over the little stub of pin you left sticking out to the inside between the opposite end plates. You will need to flex the plates open as you push the link in to get the pin to snap into the hole.

2. Push the rivet through with the chain tool (Fig. 4.10) until the same amount protrudes on either end. If you have a nine-speed system and your chain tool seems to have prongs that are getting bent as you push the rivet, see the note in section 4-10, No. 5 below.

4.9 installing the chain pin

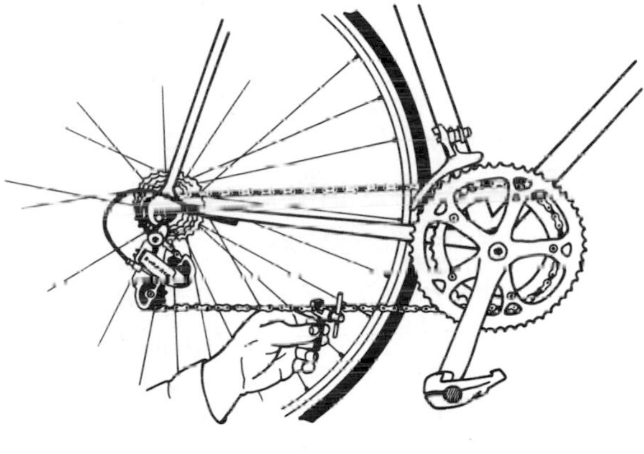

4.10 pushing in the pin

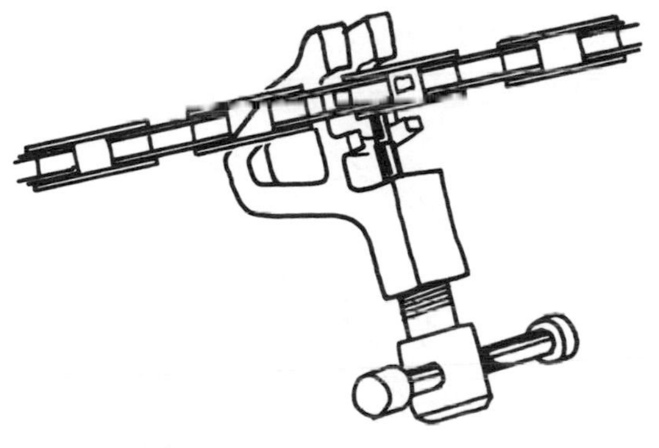

4.16 a stiff link

4.17 freeing a stiff link

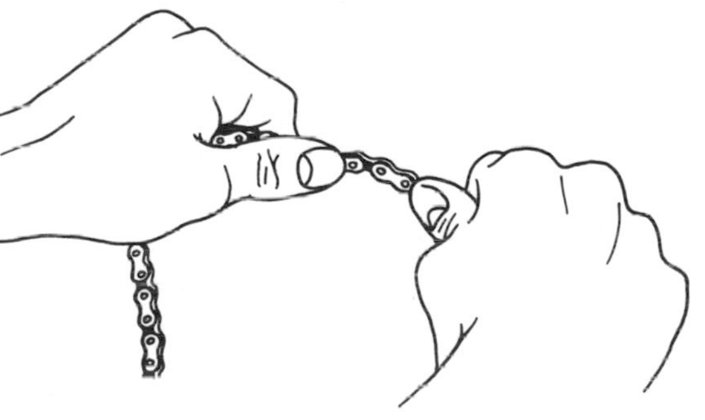

4.11 freeing a stiff link

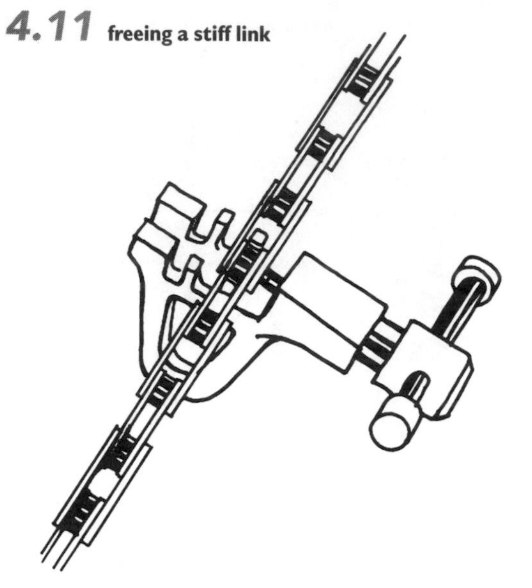

4.12 breaking off Shimano subpin

connecting a chain

3. Free the stiff link (Fig. 4.16), either by flexing it back and forth with your fingers (Fig. 4.17), or, better, by using the chain tool's second set of teeth as illustrated in Fig. 4.11.

4. Put the link over the set of teeth on the tool closest to the screw handle (Fig. 4.11).

5. Push the pin a fraction of a turn to spread the plates apart.

4-10: CONNECTING A SHIMANO CHAIN

1. Make sure you have a Shimano "subpin," which looks like a doubly long rivet with a point on one end. It has a breakage groove at the middle of its length. It comes with a new Shimano chain. If you are re-installing an old Shimano chain, get a new subpin at a bike shop, and make sure it is the right length for the chain (nine-speed chains are narrower than seven/eight-speed chains). If you don't have a subpin and are going to connect it anyway, follow the procedure for above in section 4-9, but be aware that the chain is now more likely to break than if it had been assembled with the proper subpin. And a broken chain is no fun; it can wreck other parts, and you can get injured.

2. Remove any extra links, pushing the appropriate rivet completely out.

3. Line up the chain ends.

4. Push the subpin in with your fingers, pointed end first. It will go in about halfway.

5. With the chain tool, push the subpin through until there is only as much left protruding at the tail end as the other rivets in the chain. If you have a nine-speed chain and an older chain tool, you may find that the prongs in the tool to hold the chain are too far from the backing plate of the tool and will get bent. Shimano tools that work on all Shimano chains are the TL-CN22 and TL-CN31. Many other brands also work.

6. Break off the leading half of the subpin with a pair of pliers (Fig. 4.12).

7. The chain should move freely. If not, flex it back and forth with your thumbs at this rivet. (Fig. 4.17)

4.13 Taya Master Link

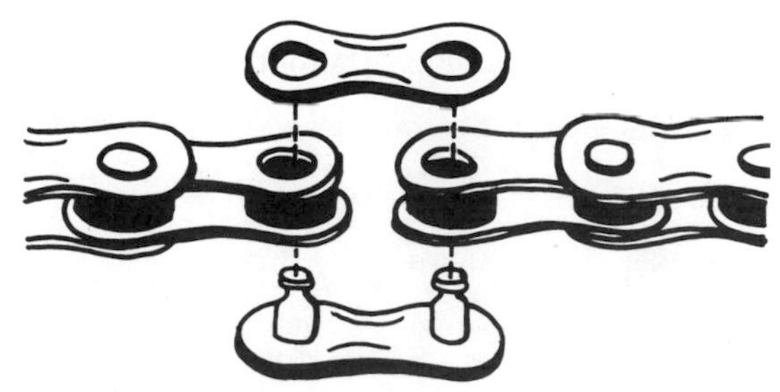

4.14 SRAM Power Link (also Sachs Power Link and Lickton's Super Link)

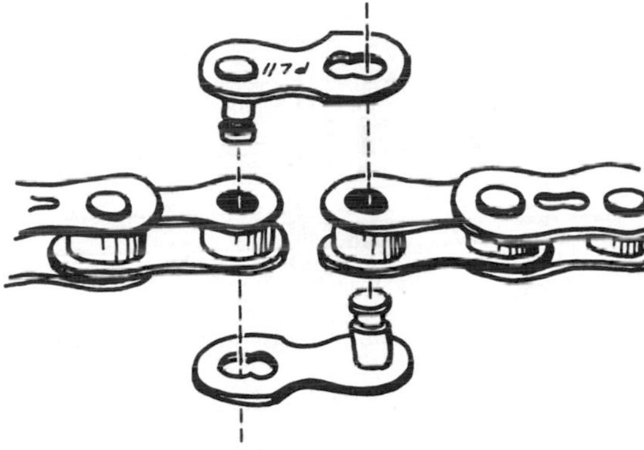

4-11: CONNECTING AND DISCONNECTING A MASTER LINK

A. Taya Chain link

Connecting

1. Connect the two ends of the chain together with the master link that has two rivets sticking out of it (Fig. 4.13).

2. Snap the outer master link plate over the rivets and into their grooves. To facilitate hooking each keyhole-shaped hole over its corresponding rivet, flex the plate with the protruding rivets so that the ends of the rivets are closer together.

Disconnecting

1. Flex the master link so that the pins come closer together.

2. Pull the plate with the oval holes off of the rivets.

B. Lickton's Super Link and SRAM (Sachs) Power Link

These links are the same; SRAM (Sachs) licenses Lickton's design. The link is made up of two symmetrical links, each of which has a single pin sticking out of it (Fig. 4.14). There is a round hole in the center of each plate that tapers into a slot on the end opposite the pin.

Connecting

1. Put the pin of each half of the link through the hole in each end of the chain; one pin will go down and one up.

2. Pull the links close together so that the each pin goes through the keyhole in the opposite plate.

3. Pull the chain ends apart so that the groove at the top of each pin slides to the end of the slot in each plate.

Disconnecting

1. While squeezing the master link plates together, push the chain ends toward each other so that the pins slide down the slot to the keyhole in each plate.

2. Pull the two halves of the master link apart.

Note: *In practice, this is almost impossible to do.*

TROUBLESHOOTING CHAIN PROBLEMS

4-12: CHAIN SUCK

"Chain suck" is the horribly appropriate name for a condition that occurs when the chain does not release from the bottom of the chainring. Instead, it sticks to the ring and gets "sucked" up until it hits the chainstay. Sometimes, the chain becomes wedged between the chainstay and the chainring.

Chain suck is rare on a double chainring setup on a road bike, but it does happen. It is more likely with a triple crank, but fortunately still rare.

A number of things can cause chain suck. To eliminate it, try the simplest methods first.

Reducing chain suck

1. Clean and lube the chain and see if it improves; a dry, rusty chain will hold the curved shape of the chainring too long.

2. Check for tight links by watching the chain move through the derailleur jockey wheels as you slowly turn the crank backward. Loosen tight links by flexing them side to side with your thumbs (Fig. 4.17), or with tool (Fig. 4.11).

3. If chain suck persists, check that there are no

bent or torn teeth on the chainring. Try straightening any broken or torn teeth you find with pliers.

4. If the chain still sucks, try another chain with wider spacing between link plates (if it is too narrow, it can pinch the chainring). You can use a caliper to compare link spacing of various chains. Shimano has a link-spacing tool that checks link-plate separation. The TL-CN24 (Fig. 4.15) tool slips down between links to assure that they are at least 2.38mm apart, which is Shimano's minimum plate-spacing specification for 7/8-speed chains.

5. Another approach is to replace the inner (and perhaps middle) chainring. The new, un-worn rings will release the chain more easily, and some chainrings are thinner than others.

6. If the problem still persists, an "anti-chain suck" device that attaches under the chainstays may help. Ask at your bike shop about what is available.

4-13: SQUEAKING CHAIN

Squeaking is caused by dry or rusted surfaces inside the chain rubbing on each other.

1. Wipe down and lubricate the chain.

2. If the squeak does not go away after a single ride with fresh lubricant, replace the chain. (If the initial remedy does not work, the chain is too dry inside and probably rusted as well. Chains seldom heal from this condition. Life is too short and bike riding is too joyful to put up with the sound of a squeaking chain.)

4-14: SKIPPING CHAIN

There can be a number of causes for a chain to skip and jump as you pedal.

A. Stiff links

1. Turn the crank backward slowly to see if a stiff chain link (Fig. 4.16) exists; a stiff link will be visible because it will be unable to bend properly as it goes through the rear derailleur jockey wheels.

4.15 checking plate spacing with TL-CN24 tool

4.16 a stiff link

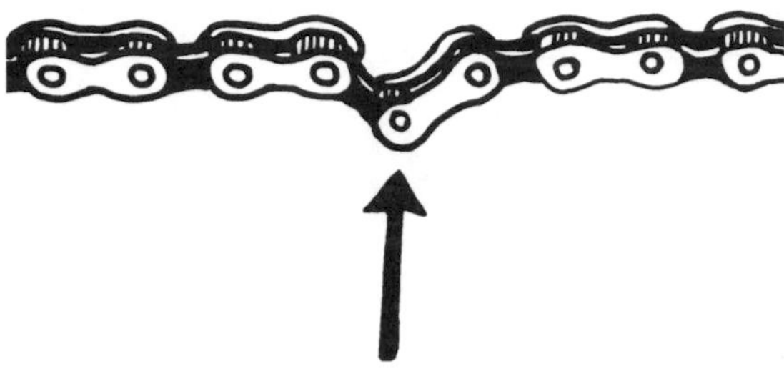

It will jump and move the jockey wheels as it passes through.

2. Loosen stiff links by flexing them side to side between the index finger and thumb of both hands (Fig. 4.17) or by using the second set of teeth on a chain tool (Fig. 4.11). Set the stiff link over the teeth closest the screw handle, and push the pin a fraction of a turn to spread the link.

3. Wipe down and lubricate the chain (Figs. 4.1, 4.2).

B. Rusted chain

A rusted chain will squeak. If you watch it move through the rear derailleur, it will look like many links are tight; the links will not bend easily and will cause the jockey wheels to jump back and forth.

1. Lubricate the chain (Fig. 4.1).

2. If this does not fix the problem after a few miles of riding, replace the chain.

C. Worn-out chain

If the chain is worn out, it will be elongated and will skip because it does not mesh well with the cogs.

4.17 freeing a stiff link

4.11 freeing a stiff link

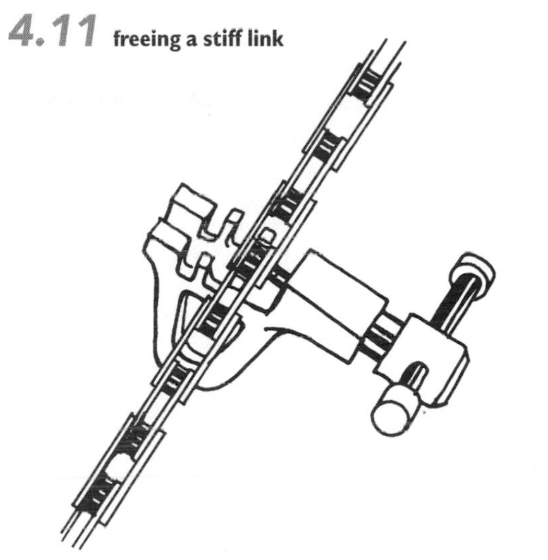

A new chain will fix the problem if the condition has not persisted long enough to ruin some cogs.

1. Check for chain elongation as described above in section 4-6.

2. If the chain is worn out, replace it.

3. If replacing the chain does not help or actually makes matters worse, see the next section.

D. Worn cogs

If you just replaced the chain and it is now skipping, at least one of the cogs is worn out. If this is the case, the chain will probably skip on the cogs you use most frequently and not on others.

1. Check each cog visually for wear. If its teeth are hook-shaped, the cog is shot and should be replaced. Rohloff makes a simple "HG-Check" tool that checks for cog wear by putting tension on a length of chain wrapped around the cog (see Chapter 6). If the last chain link on the tool can be flipped in and out of the tooth pocket while the tool is under tension, the cog is worn out.

2. Replace the offending cogs or the entire cassette or freewheel. See cog installation in Chapter 6, section 6-16.

3. Replace the chain as well, if you have not just done so. An old chain will wear out new cogs rapidly.

E. Maladjusted rear derailleur

If the rear derailleur is poorly adjusted or bent, it can cause the chain to skip by lining up the chain between gears.

1. Check that the rear derailleur shifts equally well in both directions and that the chain can be pedaled backward without catching.

2. Adjust the rear derailleur by following the procedure described under the rear derailleur section in Chapter 5, section 5-2.

F. Sticky shift cable

If the shift cable does not move freely enough to let the derailleur spring over to be lined up under the cog, the chain will jump off under load. Frayed, rough, rusted or worn cables or housings will cause the problem, as will overly thick cables or kinked or sharply bent housings. Replacing the shift cables and housings (Chapter 5) should eliminate the problem.

G. Loose rear-derailleur jockey wheel(s)

A loose jockey wheel on the rear derailleur can cause the chain to skip by letting it move too far laterally.

1. Check that the bolts holding the jockey wheel to the cage are tight, using an appropriately sized wrench (usually 3mm Allen).

2. Tighten the jockey-wheel bolts if necessary, holding the Allen wrench close to the bend so that you don't have enough leverage to over-tighten them. If the jockey-wheel bolts loosen regularly, put Loctite or another thread-lock compound on them.

H. Bent rear derailleur or rear-derailleur hanger

If the derailleur or derailleur hanger is bent, adjustments won't work. You will probably know when it happened, either when you shifted your derailleur into your spokes, when you crashed onto the derailleur, or when you pedaled a plastic bag or a tumbleweed through the derailleur.

1. Unless you have a derailleur-hanger-alignment tool and know how to use it (Chapter 14, Fig. 14.5), take the bike to a shop and have it checked for correct dropout-hanger alignment. Some bikes, especially those made out of aluminum or carbon, have a replaceable (bolt-on) right rear dropout and derailleur hanger, which you can purchase and install yourself.

2. If a straight derailleur hanger does not correct the misalignment, the rear derailleur is bent. This is generally cause for replacement of the entire derailleur (See Chapter 5, section 5-1). With some derailleurs, you can replace the jockey-wheel cage, which is usually what is bent. If you know what you are doing and are careful, you can sometimes bend a bent derailleur cage back with your hands. It seldom works well, but it's worth a try if your only other alternative is to replace the entire rear derailleur. Just make sure you don't bend the derailleur hanger in the process.

I. Worn derailleur pivots

If the derailleur pivots are worn, the derailleur will be loose and will move around under the cogs, causing the chain to skip. Replacing the derailleur is the solution.

J. Bent rear-derailleur mounting bolt

If the mounting bolt is bent, the derailleur will not line up straight. To fix it, get a new bolt and install it following the "upper-pivot overhaul" in Chapter 5, section 5-33. Observe how the spring-loaded assembly goes together during disassembly to ease reassembly.

V

The shifting system

"Never mistake motion for action." —Ernest Hemingway

Riding a bike is much more enjoyable when the derailleurs are working well. It is so sweet to feel the chain respond quickly and positively to shifting commands. On the other hand, it can really ruin a ride to have the chain shift unexpectedly or skip when you pedal hard.

Derailleurs, fortunately, are simple beasts. When they act up, a few turns of some screws or a cable-tension adjustment usually get them working again. Master this chapter and you will be able to fix most shifting problems on your bike in seconds, even when you are on the road.

This chapter is organized with all cable-operated systems at the beginning and electric systems at the end.

5A: THE REAR DERAILLEUR

The rear derailleur (Figs. 5.1, 5.3) moves the chain from one rear cog to another, and it also takes up chain slack (such as when the front derailleur is shifted or the bike bounces over a bump). It bolts to a hanger on the frame's rear dropout about which it can pivot (Fig. 5.2).

Two jockey wheels (pulley wheels) that live in a guide assembly called a chain cage hold the chain tight and help guide the chain as the derailleur shifts. Depending on the model, a rear derailleur has either one or two springs that pull the jockey wheels tight against the chain, creating a desirable amount of chain tension.

Increasing the tension on the shift cable (as when you shift to a lower gear) moves the derailleur inward toward the larger cogs. When cable tension is released (that is, when you shift to a higher gear), a spring between the derailleur's two parallelogram plates pulls the chain back toward the smallest cogs. The two limit screws on the rear derailleur (Fig. 5.3) prevent the derailleur from moving the chain too far to the inside (into the spokes) or to the outside (into the dropout).

tools

2mm, 3mm, 4mm, 5mm and 6mm hex keys
Grease
Small and large screwdrivers
Pliers
Indexed-housing cutters
Cable cutters

OPTIONAL

Crochet hook
Vernier caliper

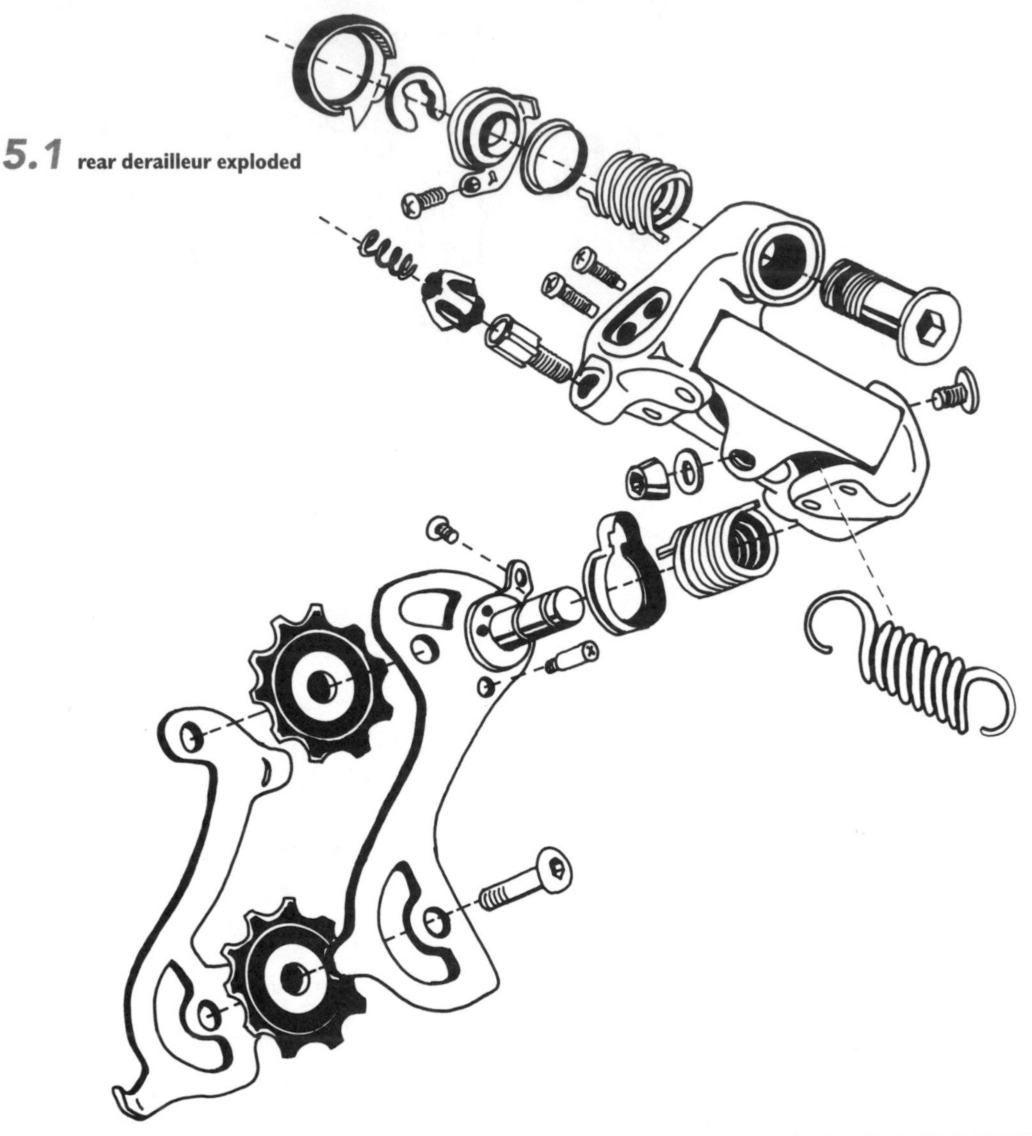

5.1 **rear derailleur exploded**

rear derailleur installation

In addition to limit screws, most rear derailleurs have a barrel adjuster located at the back of the derailleur, where the cable enters it (Fig. 5.3). The barrel adjuster increases cable tension when it is unscrewed (and reduces cable tension when it is screwed in), and is thus used to fine-tune the shifting adjustment to land the chain precisely on each cog with each corresponding click of the shifter.

Rear derailleurs also often have a screw underneath and to the rear (visible in Fig. 5.2). This screw, conventionally called the "B-tension" screw (for no particular reason—sorry), presses against the dropout or a tab attached to the dropout, and is largely responsible for controlling the space between the bottom of the cogs and the upper jockey wheel (Figs. 5.4, 5.5). The other factor affecting the size of this space is chain length.

5-1: REAR DERAILLEUR INSTALLATION

1. Apply a small amount of grease to the derailleur's mounting bolt and then start threading the bolt into the large hole on the right rear dropout.

2. Pull the derailleur back so that the "B" adjusting screw or tab on the derailleur ends up behind the tab on the dropout (Fig. 5.2).

3. Tighten the mounting bolt until the derailleur fits snugly against the hanger.

5.2 right rear dropout

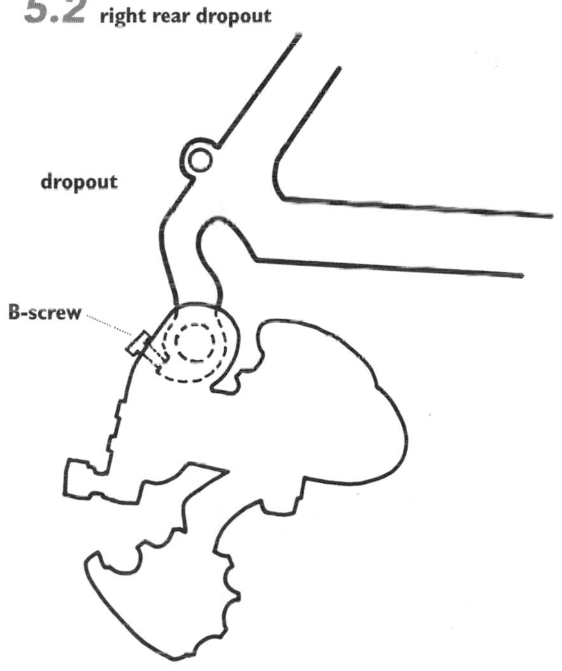

5.3 limit screws and barrel adjuster

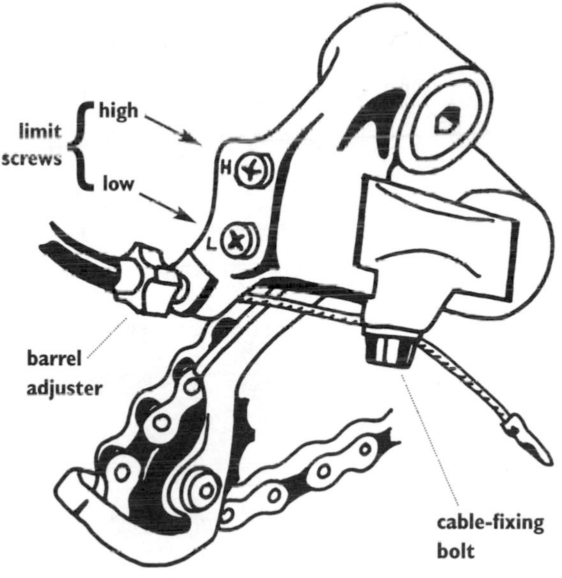

4. Route the chain through the jockey wheels and connect it. (See Chapter 4, Sections 4-8 to 4-11).

5. Install the cables and housings (see Sections 5-6 to 5-13 below).

6. Pull the cable tight with a pair of pliers, and tighten the cable-fixing bolt (Fig. 5.19).

7. Follow the adjustment procedure described below.

5-2: ADJUSTMENT OF REAR DERAILLEUR AND RIGHT-HAND SHIFTER

Perform all of the following derailleur adjustments with the bike in a bike stand or hung from the ceiling. That way, you can turn the crank and shift gears while you put the derailleur through its paces. After adjusting it off of the ground, test the shifting while riding. Derailleurs often perform differently under load than in a bike stand.

Before starting, lubricate or replace the chain (Chapter 4) so that the whole drivetrain runs smoothly.

A. Limit screw adjustments

The first and most important rear derailleur adjustment is of the limit screws. Properly set, these screws (Fig. 5.3) should make certain that you will not ruin your frame, wheel or derailleur by shifting into the spokes or by jamming the chain between the dropout and the smallest cog. It is never pleasant to see your expensive equipment turned into shredded metal. Adjustment requires nothing but a small screwdriver; remember, it's lefty loosy, righty tighty for the limit screws.

B. High-gear limit screw adjustment

This screw limits the outward movement of the rear derailleur. You tighten or loosen this screw until the derailleur shifts the chain to the smallest cog quickly but does not over shift.

How do you determine which limit screw works on the high gear? Often, it will be labeled with an "H," and it is usually the upper of the two screws (Fig. 5.3). If you're not certain, try both screws. Whichever one moves the derailleur when the cable tension is released (and the chain is on the smallest cog) is the one you're looking for. On most derailleurs, you can also see which screw to adjust by looking in between the derailleur's parallelogram side plates. You will see one tab on the back end of each plate. Each is designed to hit a limit screw at one end of the movement. Shift to the smallest cog, and notice which screw is touching one of the tabs; that is the high-gear limit screw.

All of these adjustments require knowing how to work your shift levers. If you want a refresher on shifting Shimano STI or Campagnolo ErgoPower, skip to Section 5-16.

1. Shift the chain to the large front chainring.

2. While slowly turning the crank, shift the rear derailleur to the smallest rear cog (highest gear) (Fig. 5.4).

3. If there is hesitation in the chain's shifting movement, loosen the cable a little to see if it is stopping the derailleur from moving out far enough. Do this by turning the barrel adjuster on the derailleur or down-tube barrel adjuster clockwise, or by loosening the cable-fixing bolt.

4. If the chain still won't drop smoothly and without hesitation to the smallest cog, loosen the high-gear limit screw one quarter turn at a time, continuously repeating the shift, until the chain repeatedly drops quickly and easily.

5. If the derailleur throws the chain into the dropout, or it tries to go past the smallest cog, tighten the cable by turning the barrel adjuster counterclockwise (or tighten the high-gear limit screw one quarter turn) and re-do the shift. Repeat until the derailleur shifts the chain quickly and easily into the highest gear without throwing the chain into the dropout.

C. Low-gear limit screw adjustment

This screw stops the inward movement of the rear derailleur, preventing it from going into the spokes. This screw is often labeled "L," and it is usually the bottom screw (Fig. 5.3). You can check which one it is by shifting to the largest cog, maintaining pressure on the shifter, and turning the screw to see if it changes the position of the derailleur.

1. Shift the chain to the inner chainring on the front. Shift the rear derailleur to the lowest gear (largest cog, Fig. 5.5). Do it gently, in case the limit screw does not stop the derailleur from moving into the spokes.

2. If the derailleur touches the spokes or pushes

5.4 high gear

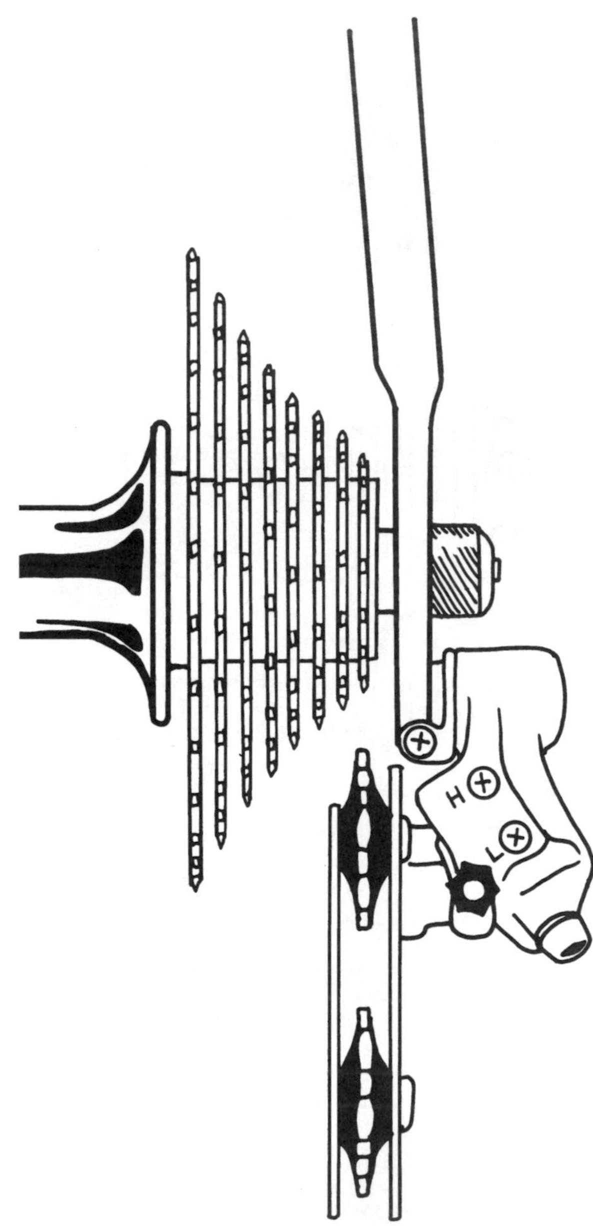

rear derailleur adjustment

5.5 low gear

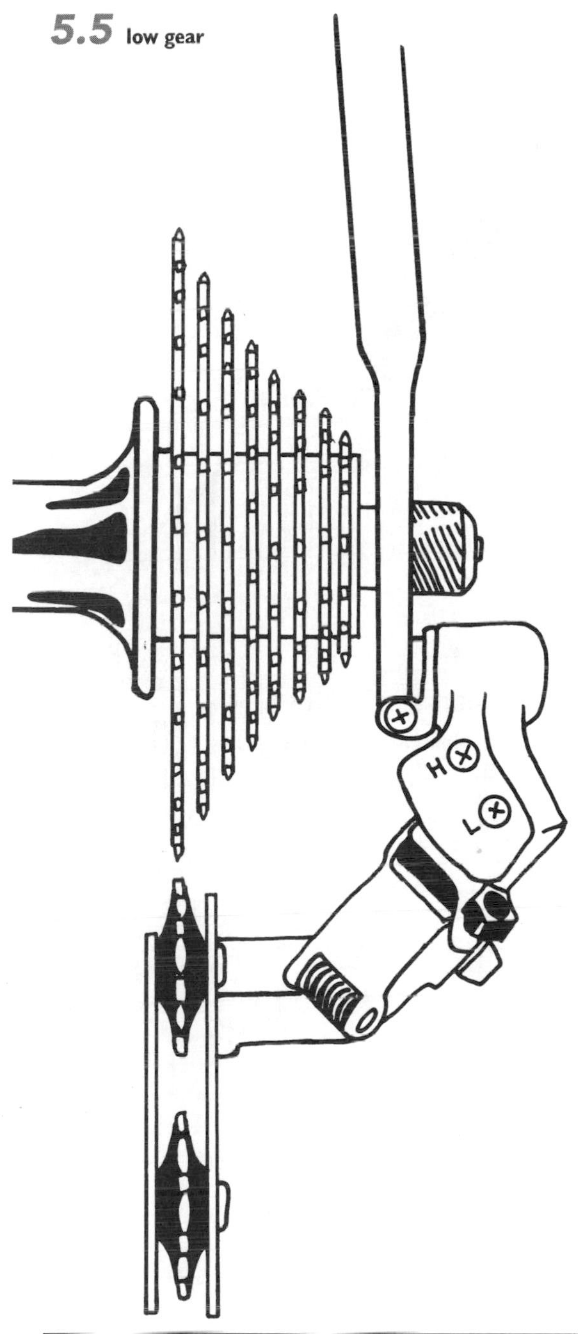

the chain over the largest cog, tighten the low-gear limit screw until it does not.

3. If the derailleur cannot bring the chain onto the largest cog, loosen the screw one quarter turn. Repeat this step until the chain shifts easily up to the largest cog but does not touch the spokes or push the chain over the top of the cog.

D. Cable tension adjustment on indexed rear shifters

With an indexed shifting system (one that "clicks" into each gear), it is the cable tension that determines whether the derailleur moves to the proper gear with each click.

1. With the chain on the large chainring in the front, shift the rear derailleur to the smallest cog. Keep clicking the shifter until you are sure it will not let out any more cable.

2. Shift back one click; this should move the chain smoothly to the second cog.

3. If the chain does not climb to the second cog, or if it does so slowly, increase the tension in the cable by unscrewing (counterclockwise) either the cable barrel adjuster on the derailleur (Fig. 5.3) or the barrel adjuster on the frame cable stop (Fig. 5.6)—or the notched lever adjuster on the frame for Shimano STI. (If you have downtube shifters, the only barrel adjuster is at the rear derailleur.) If you run out of barrel-adjustment range, re-tighten both adjusters, loosen the cable-fixing bolt on the derailleur and pull some of the slack out of the cable. Tighten the cable-fixing bolt and repeat the adjustment.

4. If the chain overshifts the second cog or comes close to overshifting, decrease the cable tension by turning one of the barrel adjusters clockwise (that is, screw it in). If both barrel adjusters are already screwed in, you will need to loosen the cable at the cable-fixing bolt.

5. Keep adjusting the cable tension in small increments while shifting back and forth between the two smallest cogs until the chain moves easily in both directions.

6. Shift the rear derailleur back and forth between the smallest five cogs, again checking for precise and quick movement of the chain from cog to cog. Fine-tune the shifting by making small adjustments to the cable-tensioning barrel adjuster.

7. Shift to the inner ring in the front and to the largest cog in the rear. Shift up and down one click

in the rear, again checking for symmetry and precision of chain movement in either direction between the two largest cogs. Fine-tune the barrel adjusters until you get it just right.

8. Go back through the gears. With the chain on the big chainring, the rear derailleur should shift easily on all but perhaps the largest one or two cogs in the rear. With the chain on the inner chainring, the rear derailleur should shift easily on all but perhaps the two smallest cogs. Fine tune while riding.

E. Cable-tension adjustment on frictional rear shifters

If you do not have indexed shifting, adjustment is complete after you remove the slack in the cable. With proper cable tension, when the chain is on the smallest cog, the derailleur should move as soon as the shift lever does. If there is free play in the lever, tighten the cable by turning the barrel adjuster on the derailleur counterclockwise. If your rear derailleur has no barrel adjuster, loosen the cable-fixing bolt, pull tension on the cable with pliers, and re-tighten the bolt.

F. Final details of rear derailleur adjustment: "B-screw" adjustment

You can get a bit more precision by adjusting the small screw ("B-screw") that changes the derailleur's position against the derailleur hanger tab on the right rear dropout (Fig. 5.2). Viewing from behind with the chain on the inner chainring and largest cog (Fig. 5.5), adjust the screw so that the upper jockey wheel is close to the cog, but not pinching the chain against the cog. Repeat on the smallest cog (Fig. 5.4). You'll know that you've moved it in too closely when it starts making noise when you turn the crank.

Note: *If, despite your best efforts, you cannot get the rear derailleur to shift well, be quiet and do not throw the chain off. Refer to the chain-line discussion under "Troubleshooting" at the end of this chapter.*

5.6 barrel adjuster on downtube cable stop

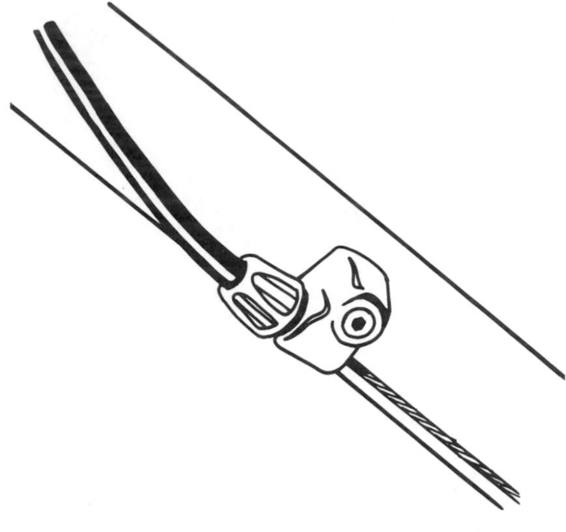

5.7 front-derailleur boss on seat tube with derailleur and mounting bolt

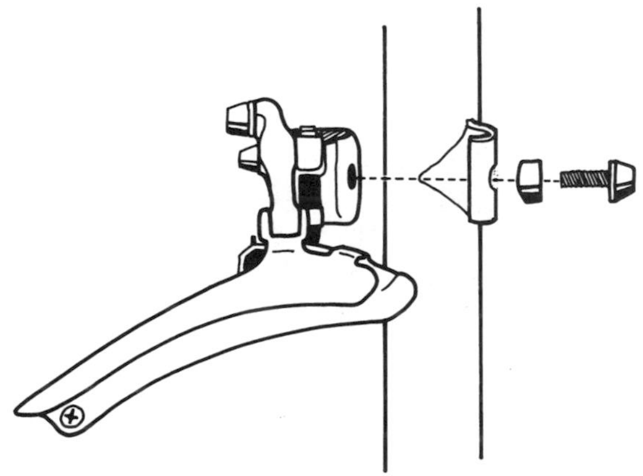

5.8 band-clamp front derailleur

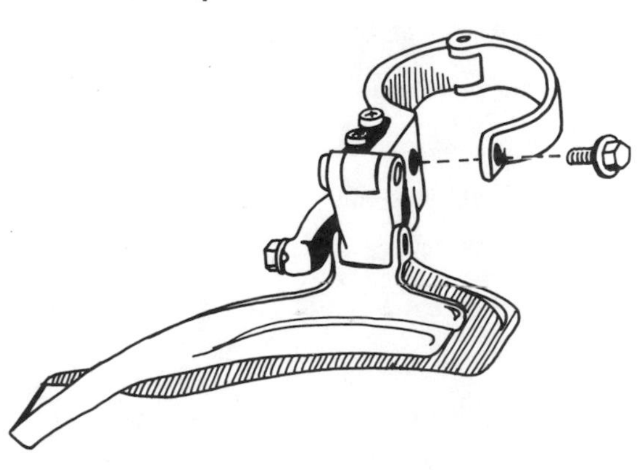

5B: THE FRONT DERAILLEUR

The front derailleur moves the chain between the chainrings. The working parts consist of a steel cage, a linkage mechanism, and an arm attached to the shifter cable. The front derailleur is attached to the frame, usually by a bolt passing through a front-derailleur boss attached to the frame's seat tube (Fig. 5.7). A braze-on-type front derailleur may alternatively bolt into a separate wrap-around clamp that has an ear shaped like a welded-on front-derailleur boss. A derailleur may also have an integral band clamp surrounding the seat tube (Fig. 5.8).

5-3: FRONT DERAILLEUR INSTALLATION

1. Clamp the front derailleur to the frame boss or around the seat tube.
2. Adjust the height and rotation as described in section 5-4A below.
3. Tighten the clamp bolt (Fig. 5.7 or 5.8).

5-4: FRONT DERAILLEUR AND LEFT HAND SHIFTER ADJUSTMENT

A. Position adjustments

A 5mm hex key is all you need to adjust the position of a front derailleur attached to a welded-on front-derailleur boss. With an integrated seat-tube-clamp front derailleur, the position is adjusted with a 5mm Allen (or 8mm box) wrench on the band-clamp bolt.

1. Position the height of the front derailleur so that the outer cage passes about 1-2mm ($^1/_{16}$ to $^1/_8$ inch) above the highest point of the outer chainring (Fig. 5.9).
2. Position the outer plate of the derailleur cage parallel to the chainrings or to the chain in the lowest and highest gears when viewed from above.

5.9 proper front-derailleur vertical clearance

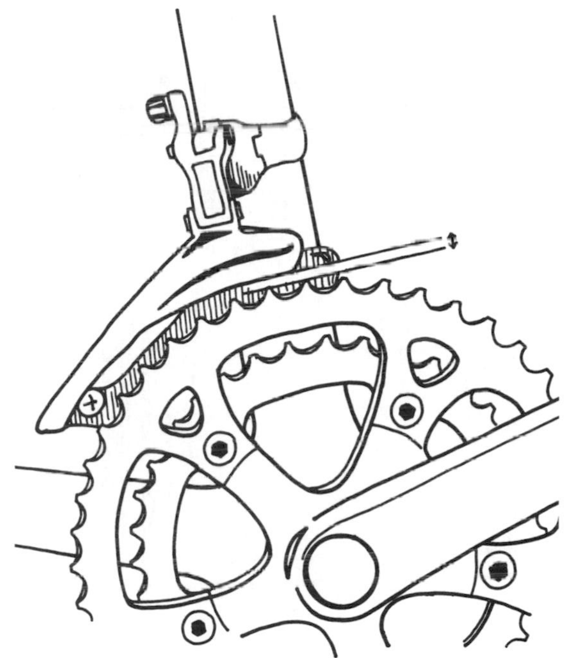

Check this by shifting to the big chainring and smallest cog and sighting from the top (Fig. 5.11). Similarly, when on the inner chainring and largest cog, the inner cage plate should parallel the chainring or the chain (Fig. 5.10).

B. Limit-screw adjustments

The front derailleur has two limit screws that stop the derailleur from throwing the chain to the inside or outside of the chainrings. These are sometimes labeled "L" for low gear (small chainring) and "H" for high gear (large chainring) (Fig. 5.12). On most derailleurs, the low-gear screw is closer to the frame.

If in doubt, you can determine which limit screw controls which function by the same trial-and-error method outlined above for the rear derailleur. Shift the chain to the inner ring, then tighten one of the limit screws. If turning that screw moves the front derailleur outward, then it is the low-gear limit screw. If turning that screw does not move the front derailleur, then the other screw is the low-gear limit screw.

5.10-11 proper front-derailleur rotational alignment

5.12 front-derailleur limit screws

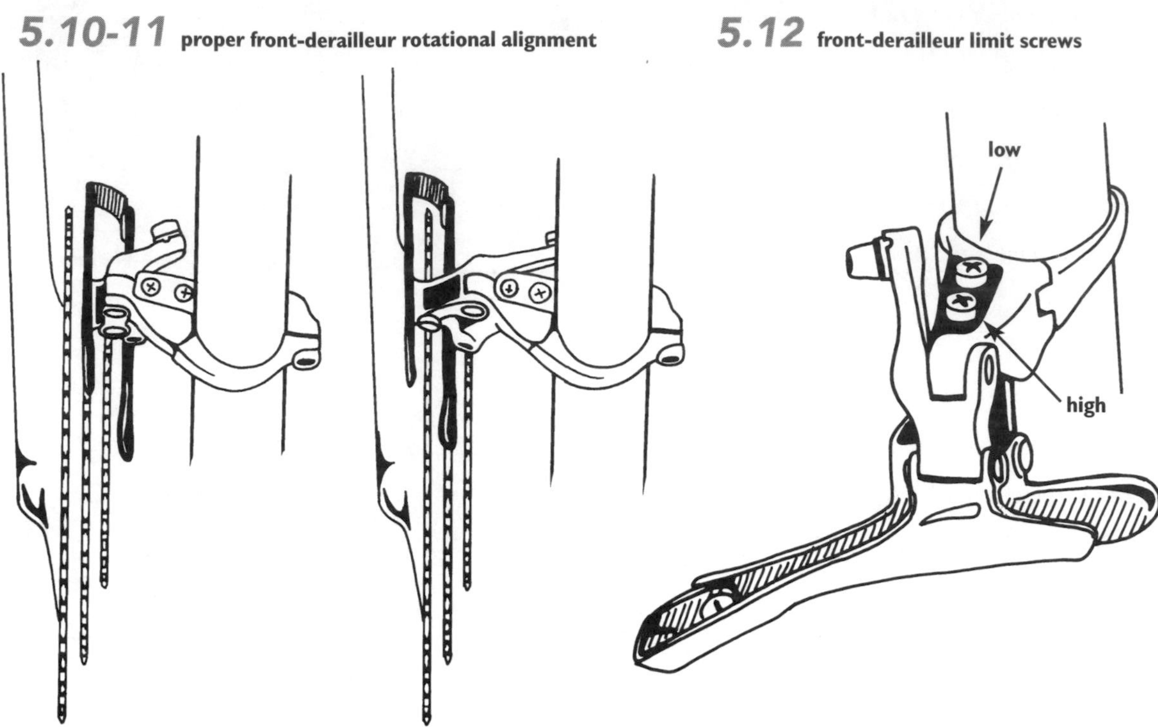

C. Low-gear limit-screw adjustment

1. Shift back and forth between chainrings.

2. If the chain drops off of the inner ring to the inside, tighten the low-gear-limit screw (clockwise) one quarter turn, and try shifting again.

3. If the chain does not shift easily onto the inner chainring, loosen the low-gear-limit screw one quarter turn and repeat the shift.

D. High-gear limit-screw adjustment

1. Shift the chain back and forth between chainrings.

2. If the chain jumps over the big chainring, tighten the high-gear-limit screw one quarter turn and repeat the shift.

3. If the chain is sluggish going up to the big chainring or does not go up at all, loosen the high-gear-limit screw one quarter turn and try the shift again.

E. Cable-tension adjustment

1. With the chain on the inner chainring, remove any excess cable slack by turning the barrel adjuster on the cable stop (Fig. 5.6) counterclockwise (or loosen the cable-fixing bolt, pull the cable tight with pliers, and tighten the bolt).

2. Check that the cable is loose enough to allow the chain to shift smoothly and repeatedly from the outer (or middle on a triple) to the inner chainring.

3. Check that the cable is tight enough so that the derailleur starts to move as soon as you move the shifter. Fine tune while riding.

Note: *This tension adjustment should work for indexed as well as friction shifters. With indexed front shifting, you may want to fine-tune the cable tension to avoid noise from the chain dragging on the derailleur in some cross gears, or to get more precise shifting.*

Another note: *Some front derailleurs have a cam screw at the end of the return spring to adjust the spring tension. For quicker shifting to the smaller rings, increase the spring tension by turning the screw clockwise one-quarter or one-half turn.*

Note on shifting trouble: *If you cannot get the front derailleur to shift well, not rub in cross gears, or not throw the chain off, refer to the chain-line discussion* *under "Troubleshooting" at the end of this chapter.*

And if you just can't stop it from falling off to the inside, install a Third Eye Chain Watcher (Fig. 5.30), a plastic gizmo hose clamped to the seat tube that nudges the chain back up onto the inner ring whenever it tries to climb off.

5-5 FRONT-DERAILLEUR FEATHERING ADJUSTMENT

"Feathering" is adjusting the front derailleur slightly to not rub the chain in cross gears.

1. Shimano STI shifters

To stop the chain from rubbing while on the inner ring and a small rear cog, you push the brake lever inward about half as far as you would to shift to the big chainring and let go. You will feel a soft click, and the front derailleur will stay a few millimeters out from its farthest-in position.

If the chain is rubbing in a cross-gear while on the big chainring, move the derailleur inward a couple of millimeters by pushing the chain-dump lever (the small lever behind the brake lever) inward lightly a few degrees. When you feel a soft click, let go.

With most road bikes, if the derailleurs are adjusted properly, the frame is in alignment, and the chain and chainline are to Shimano specification, these feathering positions will eliminate chain rub in all of the cross gears except perhaps a small-small or big-big combination.

Note: *You lose the feathering adjustment of an STI lever if you are using it with a triple crank.*

2. Campagnolo ErgoPower shifters

With Campagnolo ErgoPower, the front shift lever has a number of closely spaced click stops; it does not have two definitive "indexed" positions. This means that you can move the derailleur in small increments by a single click in either direction. Feathering is simple and obvious, and you can generally avoid chain rub in any gear. The front shifter's incremental movements are small enough to find a rub-free position as long as the outer chainring is not bent and the frame is aligned properly. You may want to play with the left barrel adjuster a bit as you ride to get the chain tension just right for noise-free operation in cross-gears.

5C: SHIFT CABLES AND HOUSINGS

To function properly, derailleurs need to have clean, smooth-running cables (also called "inner wires"). As with replacing a chain, replacing cables is a maintenance operation, not a repair operation. Do not wait until cables break to replace them. Replace any cables that have broken strands, kinks, or fraying between the shifter and the derailleur. You should also replace housings (also called "outer wires") if they are bent, mashed, just plain gritty or the color clashes with your bike (this is really important!).

CABLE INSTALLATION/REPLACEMENT

5-6: BUYING CABLES

1. Buy new cables and housing with at least as much length as the ones you are replacing.

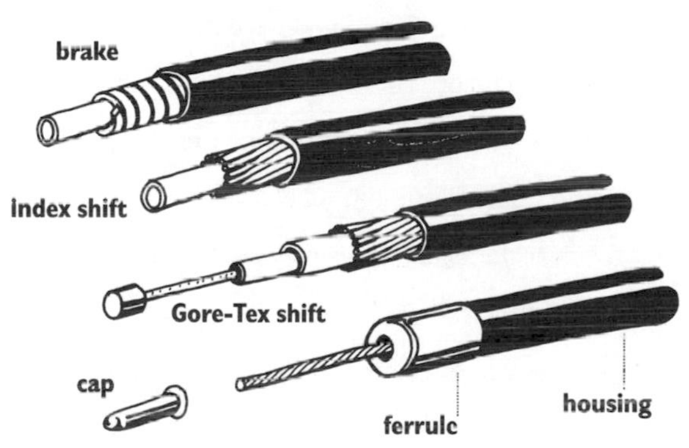

5.13 cable-housing types and end caps

2. Make sure that the cables and housing are for indexed systems. These cables will stretch minimally, and the housings will not compress in length. Under its external plastic sheath, indexed housing is not made of steel coil like brake housings; it is made of parallel (coaxial) steel strands of thin wire. If you look at the end (Fig. 5.13), you will see numerous wire ends sticking out surrounding a central Teflon tube (make sure the housing you buy has this liner!).

3. Buy two cable-end crimp caps (Fig. 5.13) to prevent fraying, and a tubular cable-housing end (ferrule) for each end of every housing section. These ferrules will prevent kinking at the cable entry points, cable stops, shifters and derailleurs.

4. It is a good idea to buy extra cables, cable caps and ferrules (Fig. 5.13) to keep on hand in your work area. They're inexpensive, and if you have a small supply you will be able to change cables when you need to without making a special trip to the bike shop to get a little cable-end cap.

5-7: CUTTING HOUSING TO LENGTH

1. Use a special cutter made for the purpose; Park, Shimano, and Wrench Force sell them (see Chapter 1 tools). Standard wire cutters (i.e., "side cutters") will not cleanly cut index-shift housing.

2. Cut the housing to the same lengths as the pieces you are replacing. If you have no old housings for comparison, cut the new pieces so that they curve smoothly. When you turn the bars, the housing should not pull or kink. Allow enough length so that the rear derailleur can swing backward (Fig. 5.14) and forward (Fig. 5.15) freely.

3. With a nail or toothpick, open each Teflon sleeve-end that has been smashed shut by the cutter.

4. Place a ferrule over each housing end (Fig. 5.13).

5.14 rear derailleur swinging back to check housing length

5.15 rear derailleur swinging forward to check housing length

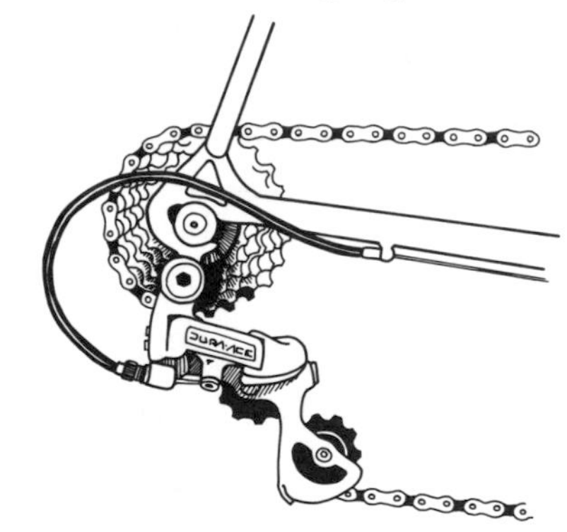

5-8: REPLACING SHIFT CABLE IN SHIMANO STI SHIFT/BRAKE LEVER

1. Disconnect the cable at the derailleur and snip off the cable-end cap (if installed).

2. Shift the inner chain-dump lever to the gear setting that lets the most cable out. This will be the highest-gear position for the rear shift lever (small cog), and the lowest for the front (small chainring).

3. Pull the brake lever to reveal the shift cable access hole on the outboard side of the lever. Push the cable until the cable head emerges from the hole far enough to grab it. Pull out the old cable and recycle it.

4. The recessed hole into which the cable head seats should be visible through the access hole. Thread the new cable through the hole and out through the inboard side of the lever (Fig. 5.16).

5. Guide the cable through each housing seg-

cable installation and replacement

ment (making sure each segment has a ferrule on the end; see Fig. 5.13) and cable stop and re-connect it at the derailleur cable-fixing bolt.

6. Clip the cable 1–2cm past the bolt and crimp on a cap to prevent fraying (Fig. 5.21).

5-9: REPLACING SHIFT CABLE IN CAMPAGNOLO ERGOPOWER LEVER

1. Disconnect the cable at the derailleur and snip off the cable end cap (if installed).

2. Push the cable until the cable head emerges from the cable hole in the slot near on the bottom of the lever (it's toward the outboard side, just outboard of the little gear teeth; Fig. 5.17). Push the cable head out far enough to grab it. Pull out the old cable and recycle it.

3. Click the thumb lever until it will click no more.

4. Push the new cable in through the hole and up through the lever body until it emerges from the housing-entry hole at the upper base of the lever body on the outboard side.

5. Guide the cable through each housing segment (making sure each segment has a ferrule on the end; see Fig. 5.13) and cable stop and re-connect it at the derailleur cable-fixing bolt.

6. Clip the cable 1–2cm past the bolt and crimp on a cap to prevent fraying (Fig. 5.21).

Note: *The ErgoPower cable hook is too small to fit a Shimano cable head—just another of those maddening parts incompatibilities. You can file the Shimano head down enough to fit in, but expect to need to push hard with pliers to get the cable back out next time.*

5-10: REPLACING CABLE IN A DOWN-TUBE SHIFT LEVER, BAR-END LEVER, OR SHIFT LEVER ON AN AERO' HANDLEBAR

1. Disconnect the cable at the derailleur and snip off the cable end cap.

2. Flip the lever forward to the gear setting that lets the most cable out. This will be the highest gear position for the rear shift lever (small cog), and the lowest for the front (small chainring).

3. Push the cable until the cable head pops out of the hole in the shift lever. Pull out the old cable and recycle it.

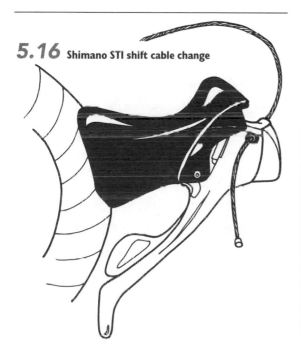

5.16 **Shimano STI shift cable change**

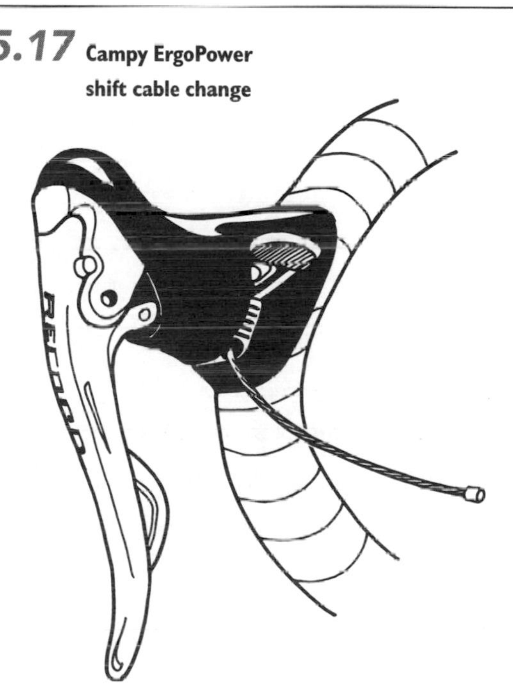

5.17 **Campy ErgoPower shift cable change**

4. Thread the new cable through the hole and out through the other side of the lever (Fig. 5.18).

5. Guide the cable through each cable stop and housing segment (making sure each segment has a ferrule on the end; see Fig. 5.13) and re-connect it at the derailleur cable-fixing bolt.

6. Clip the cable 1–2cm past the bolt and crimp on a cap to prevent fraying (Fig. 5.21).

5-11: ATTACH CABLE TO REAR DERAILLEUR

1. Put the chain on the smallest cog so the rear derailleur moves to the outside.

2. Run the cable through the barrel adjuster, and route it through each of the housing segments until you reach the cable-fixing bolt on the derailleur. Make sure that the rear shifter is on the highest-gear setting; this ensures that the maximum amount of cable is available to the derailleur.

3. Pull the cable taut and into its groove under the cable-fixing bolt (Fig. 5.19).

4. Tighten the bolt. On most derailleurs this takes a 5mm Allen wrench.

5. Clip the cable 1–2cm past the bolt and crimp on a cap to prevent fraying (Fig. 5.21).

5-12: ATTACH CABLE TO FRONT DERAILLEUR

1. Shift the chain to the inner ring so that the derailleur moves farthest to the inside. This ensures that the maximum amount of cable is available to the derailleur.

2. With a 5mm hex key, tighten the cable to the cable anchor on the derailleur while pulling the cable taut with pliers, using the groove into which the cable is supposed to fit (Fig. 5.20).

3. Clip the cable 1–2cm past the bolt and crimp on a cap to prevent fraying (Fig. 5.21).

5.18 **down-tube shifter cable change**

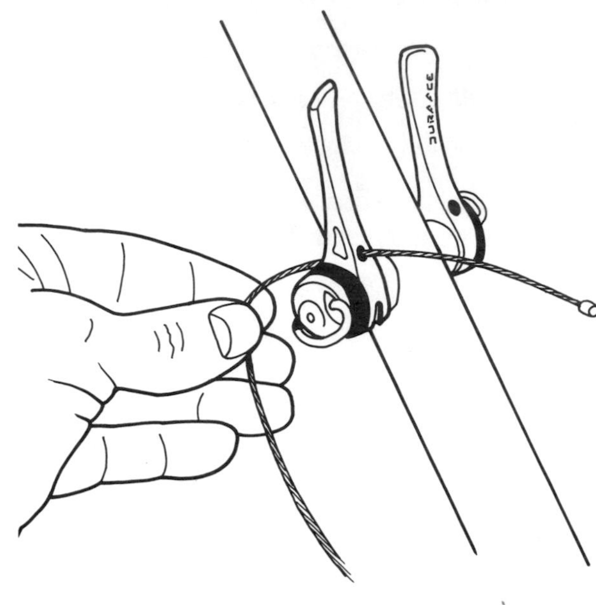

5-13: FINAL CABLE TOUCHES

A high-quality cable assembly includes the cable-housing-end ferrules (Fig. 5.13) throughout, and crimped cable caps (Fig. 5.21); cables are clipped about 1–2cm past the cable-clamp bolts.

5-14: CABLE LUBRICATION

New cables and housings with Teflon liners do not need to be lubricated. Old cables can be lubricated with chain lubricant. Grease sometimes slows their movement, but some manufacturers recommend (and supply) their own molybdenum disulfide grease for cables.

1. Disconnect the cable at the derailleur, and clip off the cable-crimp end. Be aware that if the cable frays at all when clipped, you may not be able to slide this old cable back in through the housings and may have to replace the entire cable.

2. Coat with lubricant the areas of the cable that will be inside of the cable housing segments. Squirt lubricant into each housing section.

Note: *If you have any trouble re-installing the cable* *due to fraying, or the housings are dirty and rusty, you might as well replace the cables perhaps the housings as well.*

Another note: *On bikes with a slotted chainstay cable stop, pull the housing out of the stop, slide it up the cable, and lubricate that section of cable without disconnecting it from the derailleur.*

5-15: STEPS TO REDUCE CABLE FRICTION

In addition to replacing your cables and housings with good quality cables and lined housings, there are other specific steps you can take to improve shifting efficiency.

1. The most important friction-reducing steps are to route the cable so that it makes smooth bends, and make sure it is just long enough that turning the handlebars does not increase the tension on the shift cables.

2. Choose cables that offer especially low friction. "Die-drawn" cables, which have been mechanically pulled through a die (a small hole in a piece of hard steel), move with lower friction than standard cables. Die-drawing flattens the outer strands, smoothing the cable surface. Thinner cables and lined housings with a large inside diameter also reduce friction.

3. An electric (Mavic Mektronic) shifting system eliminates cable friction from the rear shifter and maybe just the ticket for a tandem, where the long cable run always creates friction problems.

5D: THE SHIFTERS

Shimano STI, Campagnolo ErgoPower, Mavic Mektronic, down-tube, and bar-end levers (Figs. 5.16, 5.17, 5.18, 5.27 and 5.28) all move the derailleurs, but they do so in very different ways.

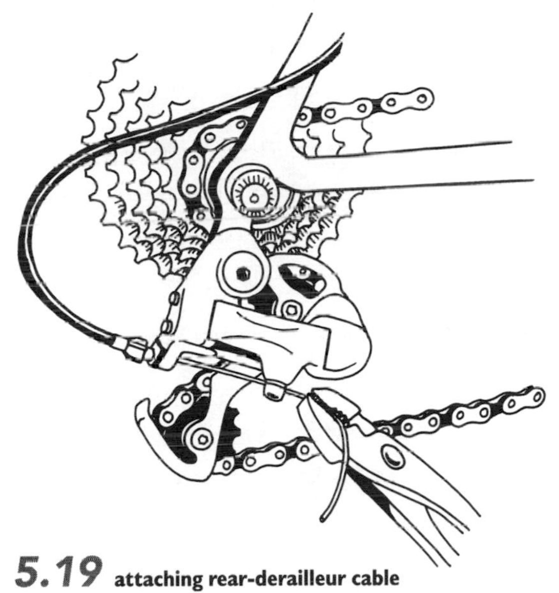

5.19 attaching rear-derailleur cable

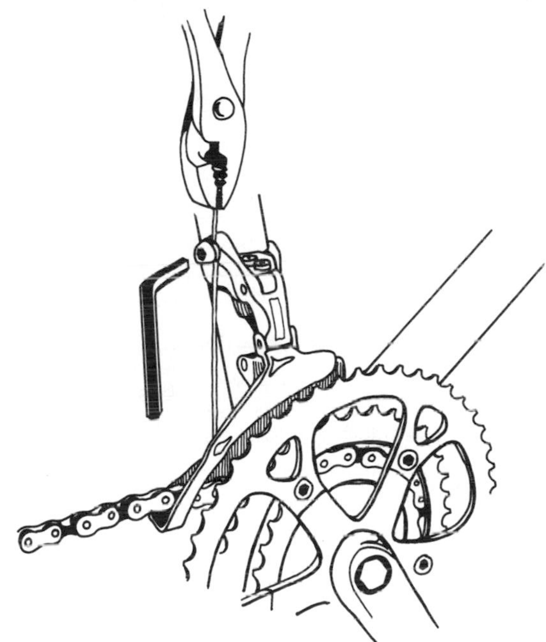

5.20 attaching front-derailleur cable

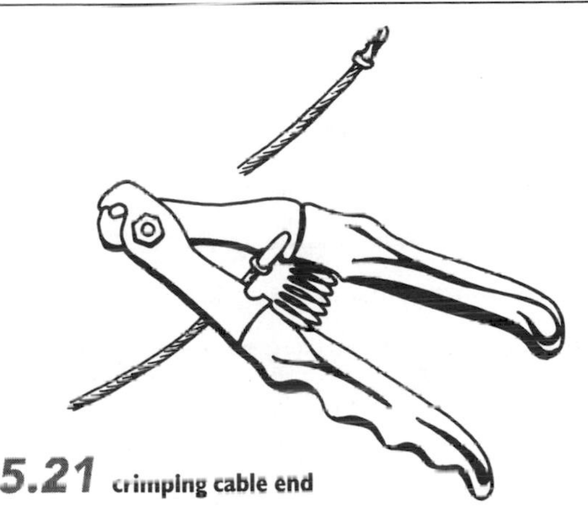

5.21 crimping cable end

5-16: OPERATING INTEGRATED SHIFT-BRAKE LEVERS

Rear Shimano STI—right-hand lever (Fig. 5.16):

To shift to a larger cog (lower gear), push the brake lever to the left (inward) with your fingers. The most you can move the chain is three cogs with a single push.

To shift to a smaller cog (higher gear), push the smaller lever to the left (inward) with your second finger. It will click only one gear at a time.

Front Shimano STI—left-hand lever:

To shift to a larger chainring (higher gear), push the brake lever to the right (inward) with your fingers. It takes a firm push. If it moves a small click but the chain does not climb up the outer ring, give it another push, and it will. If you have a triple, you can shift only one chainring at a time.

To shift to a smaller chainring (lower gear), push the smaller lever to the right (inward) with your second finger. If you have a triple, you can shift only one chainring at a time.

To feather the front derailleur so that it does not rub on the chain in a cross-gear (see Section 5-5 for more on this):

When on the inner chainring, give the brake lever a gentle inward push until you hear a soft click.

When on the outer chainring, give the inner lever a gentle push until you feel the soft click. This may take some practice, as you can easily overdo it, dropping the chain onto the inner ring.

Rear Campagnolo ErgoPower—right-hand lever (Fig. 5.17):

To shift to a larger cog (lower gear), push the finger lever behind the brake lever to the left (inward) with your fingers. Depending on model and year, you can move the chain up to three cogs with a single push.

To shift to a smaller cog (higher gear), push the thumb lever down (yes, with your thumb). Depending on model and year, you can move the chain across three to ten cogs with a single push.

Front Campagnolo ErgoPower—left-hand lever:

To shift to a larger chainring (higher gear), push the finger lever behind the brake lever to the left (inward) with your fingers. If the chain does not climb up the outer ring, give it another push and it will. If you have a triple, you can shift only one chainring at a time.

To shift to a smaller chainring (lower gear), push the thumb lever down.

To feather the front derailleur so that it does not rub on the chain in a cross-gear (see Section 5-5 for more on this):

When on the inner chainring, give the finger lever a gentle inward push to move one click at a time.

When on the outer chainring, give the thumb lever a single-click push at a time.

Rear Mavic Mektronic—right-hand lever (Figs. 5.27, 5.28):

To shift to a larger cog (lower gear), push the upper yellow button on the button set that is below the computer (standard) or the left button clamped on the bar (triathlon type). Or flip the little yellow lever on the back of the brake lever back toward you. Or flip the yellow button on the top of the brake hood upward. The most you can move the chain by holding a button is three cogs with a single push.

To shift to a smaller cog (higher gear), push the lower yellow button on the button set that is below the computer (standard) or the right button clamped on the bar (triathlon type). Or push the little yellow lever on the back of the brake lever away from you. Or push the yellow button on the top of the brake hood downward. The most you can move the chain by holding a button is three cogs with a single push.

Front Mavic Mektronic—left-hand lever:

To shift to the larger chainring (higher gear), push forward on the lever on the side of the brake hood.

To shift to the smaller chainring (lower gear), pull back on the lever on the side of the brake hood.

5-17: REPLACING/INSTALLING INTEGRAL BRAKE/SHIFT LEVERS

Shifters can be replaced as an entire unit and sometimes as separate parts. Brake/shift levers are generally labeled right and left, but if you're in doubt, you can tell which is which because the levers should flip to the inside. If you are replacing the entire brake lever/shift lever unit:

1. Remove the handlebar tape and bar plugs.
2. Remove the old brake lever by loosening the brake lever's mounting bolt with a 5mm Allen wrench and sliding the lever assembly off. The position of the bolt varies. On current dual-control levers it is on the outboard side of the lever under the lever hood. Slip the hex key down from the top between the lever body and the hood rather than trying to roll back the hood far enough to get at it from outside of the hood (Chapter 7, Fig. 7.10). On Campagnolo ErgoPower, the bolt is on the outboard side toward the top; on Shimano STI it is on the middle of the outboard side, and on Mavic Mektronic, it is on the outboard side toward the bottom.
3. Slide the new lever on the bar to where you like it (be careful with the wires on Mektronic). A good rule of thumb is to put a straightedge against the bottom of the bar and slide the lever down until its end touches the straightedge. The lever can sit a little higher than this, but generally not any lower. Put a long straightedge across the top of both levers to make sure they are level with each other.
4. Tighten the mounting bolt.
5. Install the barrel-adjuster cable stops on the shifter bosses, if not already in place.
6. Install the cables (see Chapter 5 Sections 5-6 to 5-15 and Chapter 7 Sections 7-6 and 7-C1.)
7. Wrap the handlebar tape (see Chapter 11, section 9-9).

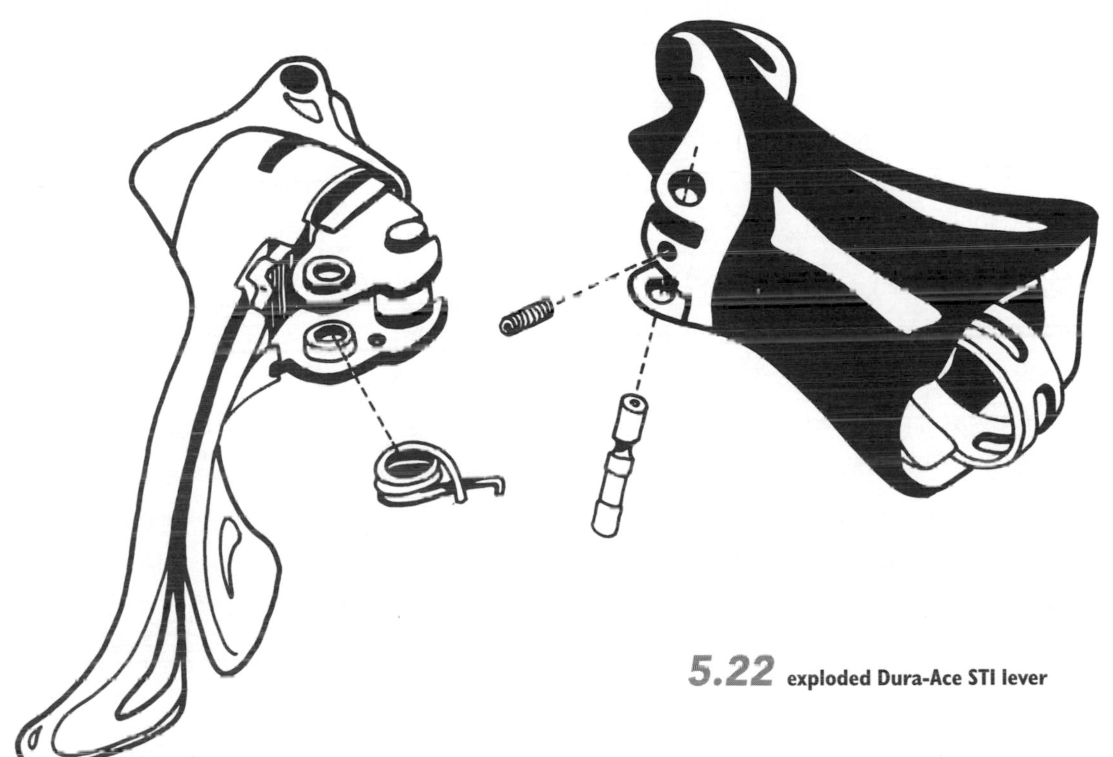

5.22 exploded Dura-Ace STI lever

overhauling STI and Ergo Power levers

5-18: REPLACING SHIFTER UNIT ON STI INTEGRAL BRAKE/SHIFT LEVER

If you have a jammed Shimano STI shifter, you cannot really go into the mechanism like a watchmaker and replace parts. Shimano doesn't sell the internal parts separately, and opening the mechanism voids the warranty. But you can replace the entire shifter unit of two blades with the internal ratchet. Note that this may be false economy; you save the lever base, rubber hood and band clamp but pay over half of the cost of a pair of levers for a single blade assembly. For Dura-Ace 9-speed, you pay about $15 more for an entire lever than for the blade assembly, and for Dura-Ace 8-speed, you pay around $80 less for an entire lever than for the blade assembly! But if you find a bargain somewhere, here's the procedure:

1. Remove the shift and brake cables.

2. With a 2mm hex key, remove the set screw holding the pivot axle in place under the lever. Expect it to make noise unscrewing and be hard to remove. There is a lot of threadlock compound on it to keep it from vibrating loose.

3. Push out the axle and catch the spring.

4. Pull off the old blade assembly (Fig. 5.22) and insert the new blade assembly.

Note: *If you have a lever that is FlightDeck-computer compatible, you will need to unscrew the cover on the inboard side of the lever under the gum hood and push the end of the wiring harness up through the lever as you pull off the blade. With the new one, fish the wires back in the same way and replace the cover to hold the little rubber part and the four terminals in place.*

5. Replace the return spring and axle.

6. Replace the set screw, putting some threadlock compound on it first.

5-19: OVERHAULING CAMPAGNOLO ERGOPOWER LEVERS (LEVEL 3)

LEVEL 3

This is an extremely satisfying maintenance task. As with any mechanism that has lots of precision internal parts, it can be great fun, if you are in the right state of mind, to take an ErgoPower lever all apart, clean it up, put it back together, and feel it work more smoothly afterward.

Ride enough hours with your levers, especially in rain and muck, and they will get dirty inside and will work so much better if you clean 'em up and re-grease 'em. Also, every ErgoPower lever has two little G-shaped springs that click into teeth in a ratchet, giving you the indexing steps. These springs can get worn, flattened, or broken, and shifting performance will drop off or cease to exist. These G-springs are the same for every model and year, so get a couple, if you think you need them, and follow along. Your levers will be good as new again!

As is typical with Campagnolo parts, every little ErgoPower gubbin is replaceable. Refer to the exploded diagrams, Fig. 5.23A (8-speed right-hand lever) and Fig. 5.23B (9- or 10-speed right-hand lever). You can also magnify all those parts and find their part numbers for your particular year and model of lever on Campagnolo's Web site, www.campagnolo.com.

The following instructions cover overhaul and lubrication, as well as replacing broken or damaged index springs. When I mention 8-speed levers, I am referring to 1992-1997 ErgoPower levers, both right and left. The lever body and the rubber hood comes to a point on top of these (and the lever body allows a brake cable to be installed "old-style" straight into the top of the lever, as well as "aero'-style" under the handlebar tape). The reference to 9- and 10-speed levers applies to 1998 and later levers (both

5.23A exploded Campagnolo ErgoPower lever—eight speed

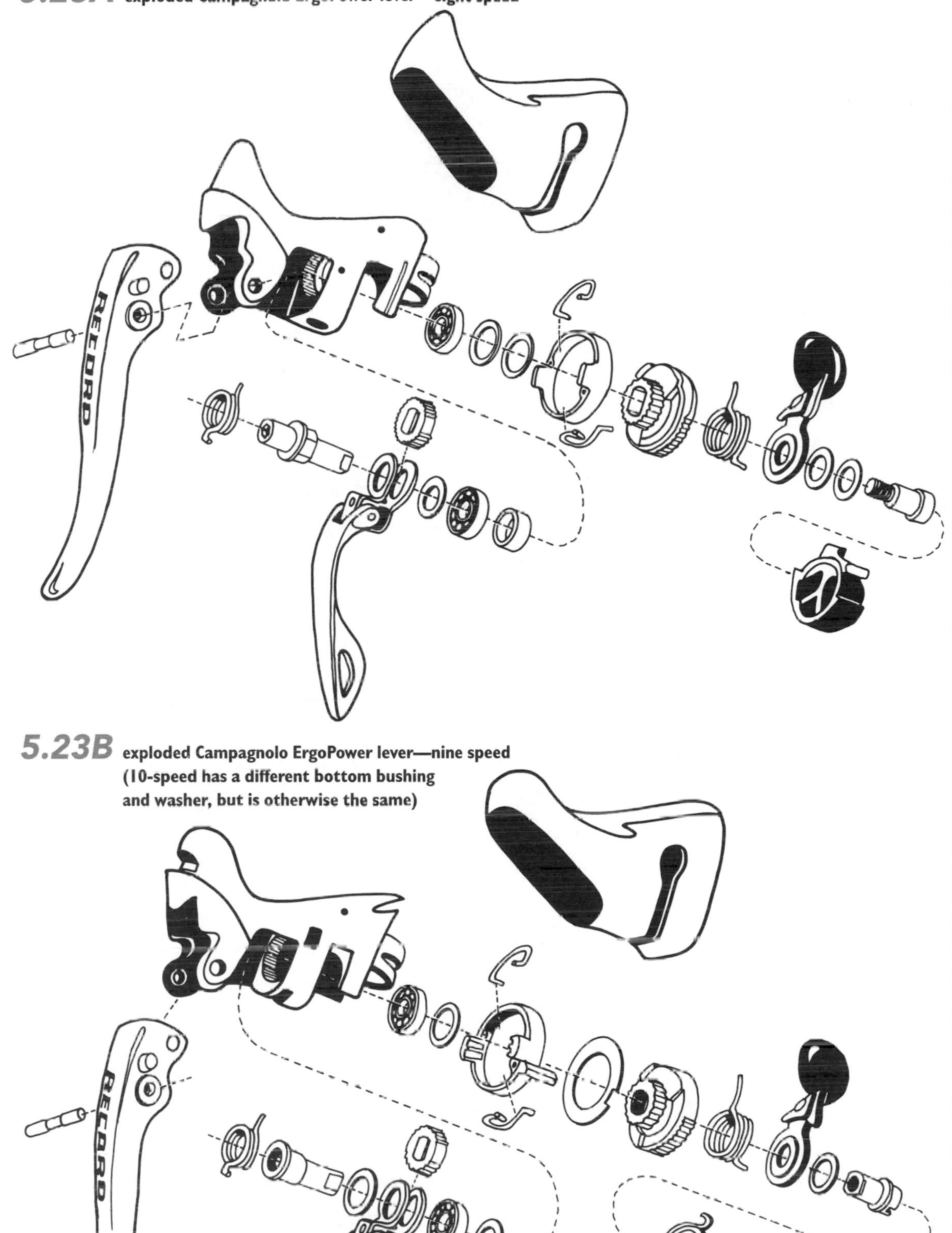

5.23B exploded Campagnolo ErgoPower lever—nine speed (10-speed has a different bottom bushing and washer, but is otherwise the same)

sides) whose lever body (and rubber hood) are rounded on top and only allow the brake cable to be routed under the tape to the base of the lever.

1. Remove the rubber hood—it's easier to pull it off of the base of the lever, but it will come off over the top as well. On composite lever bodies, pull off the plastic piece that covers the bottom of the shift mechanism, with pliers, if necessary. Push out the lever-pivot pin by tapping it out with a blunt nail and a hammer. Support the lever body near the pin so that the edge of the lever does not flex outward as you tap. Pull off the brake lever.

2. Clamp the lever body onto the end of a handlebar held in a vise so that the bar-clamp strap is right at the edge of the bar and the lower part of the lever body is hanging off the end of the bar; you want to be able to get at the lever's mechanism from the bottom. Hold the bar in the vise so that the lever is upside down.

With a 9- or 10-speed lever, shift to the lowest-gear position with the finger lever to release tension on the flat coil spring at the bottom of the lever; you can see it stick out around the large flat washer when you get to the low-gear position.

With an 8-speed lever, you do the opposite; shift the thumb lever to the highest-gear position.

3. Hold the top nut with one hex key while you unscrew and remove the bottom bolt with another hex key. On a 9- or 10-speed lever, the top nut takes a 5mm hex key, and the lower bolt takes a 3mm. On an 8-speed lever, the nut and bolt both accept 4mm hex keys, and the bolt may have a brass washer or two on it, so watch for them.

Important note: *The bolt on a right-hand 8-speed lever is left-hand threaded, so it unscrews in a clockwise direction!*

4. With an 8-speed lever, skip to Step 6.

With a 9- or 10-speed lever, remove the bottom washer, pop the compensation spring (a flat coil) out with a thin screwdriver, and take out the thin play-removing washer, if installed.

5. Hold the (9- or 10-speed) assembly together with your thumb while shifting to the high-gear position with the thumb lever. Hold the thumb lever in place and, with needle-nose pliers, pull out the next part: the bushing in the center of the coil spring.

6. Pop out the thumb lever, the ratchet spring, the ratchet, and, on a 9- and 10-speed right-hand lever, the notched washer. The two G-shaped index springs, which are the most common replacement item in ErgoPower levers, are now visible. One or two washers that sit on top of the cartridge bearing underneath may come out with the ratchet. If not, you can pop the washer(s) out after Step 7 and clean, grease and replace it/them at that time.

7. Pop the G-spring carrier and G-springs out. Clean and grease all parts.

If you need to replace the finger-lever assembly, it will come out as is now, with the pins and bearings intact.

8. Put the new (or clean and re-greased) G-springs on the underside of the G-spring carrier, and coat them with grease to hold them in place. Push the G-spring carrier back into place in the lever body.

9. On a right-hand 9- and 10-speed lever, replace the notched washer on top of the G-spring carrier with the washer's tab facing down. The notch fits around the vertical post on the G-spring carrier. This washer (and the vertical carrier post) do not exist in left-hand 9- and 10-speed levers or in 8-speed ones, so skip to step 10.

10. Drop the (greased) indexing ratchet down onto the pivot post so that the flats in both parts interlock. Make sure that the cable hook on the ratchet butts against the outboard side of the lever body. Slip the long end of the return spring down

into the ratchet, out the ratchet's slot, and into the hole in the lever body, dropping the (greased) spring down into the ratchet with the short end of the spring sticking up.

11. Push the small hole in the thumb-lever ring onto the up-pointing end of the ratchet spring, with the convex side of the ring facing the spring. Push back on the thumb-lever ring to align it over the ratchet.

On 9- and 10-speed levers, while holding the thumb-lever ring down, push the central bushing down through the ring. Push down and turn the bushing (on 9-speed, use a 5mm hex key; on 10-speed, use a large screwdriver in the larger set of slots) until the flats on the end of the bushing engage the flats on the end of the top bolt protruding into the ratchet. If there were washers on the bushing, make sure you have installed them.

On 10-speed levers, the bushing is larger in diameter and has flats that engage over the flats on the top bolt, rather than inserting into them. An unfortunate consequence of this larger diameter of the bushing is that it is harder to push the bushing into place without disengaging the return spring from the thumb lever. Keep at it until you get it.

On 8-speed levers, insert the bolt, with any washers it had on it, down through the thumb-lever ring until it engages the nut. While holding the nut with a 4mm hex key inserted into the top of the lever, tighten the bolt with another 4mm hex key. Remember that the bolt is reverse-threaded on a right-hand 8-speed lever! Skip to step 16 now.

12. Steps 12-15 only apply to 9- and 10-speed levers. While holding the bushing in place, shift the finger lever all the way to the lowest-gear position.

13. Lay the flat compensation spring on top of the thumb-lever ring. The inner end of the spring hooks into a notch in the end of the bushing, and the outer spring end hooks around either the post on the spring carrier (right-hand lever) or the outboard edge of the lever body (left-hand lever).

14. Holding the flat spring down, tip the bushing back and forth until you feel the flats in the end of the bushing disengage from the flats on the top bolt (do this with the 5mm hex key on 9-speed, and with the large screwdriver on 10-speed). Still holding the spring down, turn the bushing about a quarter to a half turn to wind the spring (counterclockwise on the right lever; clockwise on the left lever), and jiggle the bushing back and forth with the 5mm hex key or large screwdriver until its flats re-engage the top bolt.

(Campagnolo suggests an alternative method for steps 13 and 14, which I find to be more of a hassle, but you may prefer: When laying the flat spring in place, hook the inner spring end into a more advanced bushing slot; the outer end of the spring will be squished up against the back wall of the lever body. While holding the bushing with the 5mm hex key or large screwdriver, pull the outer spring end with a hooked awl or small crochet hook, and pull it to the post [right-hand lever] or to the notch in the lever-body's outboard wall [left-hand lever].)

15. Holding the flat spring down with your finger, slide the large washer under your finger and on top of the flat spring so it snaps over the end of the bushing. The 10-speed washer has two notches to fit the larger slots in the bushing. Start the 3mm Allen bolt while holding the other end of the pivot shaft with a 5mm hex key. Snug the bolt down.

16. Check the mechanism. If it works smoothly, re-install the brake lever, the bottom cap, and the rubber hood (engaging all of the hood's nubs into holes, slots and protrusions in the lever body). It's easier to pull the hood on over the levers from the front than from the base of the lever body.

Congratulations! You are done!

5.24 exploded Campagnolo Super Record frictional lever

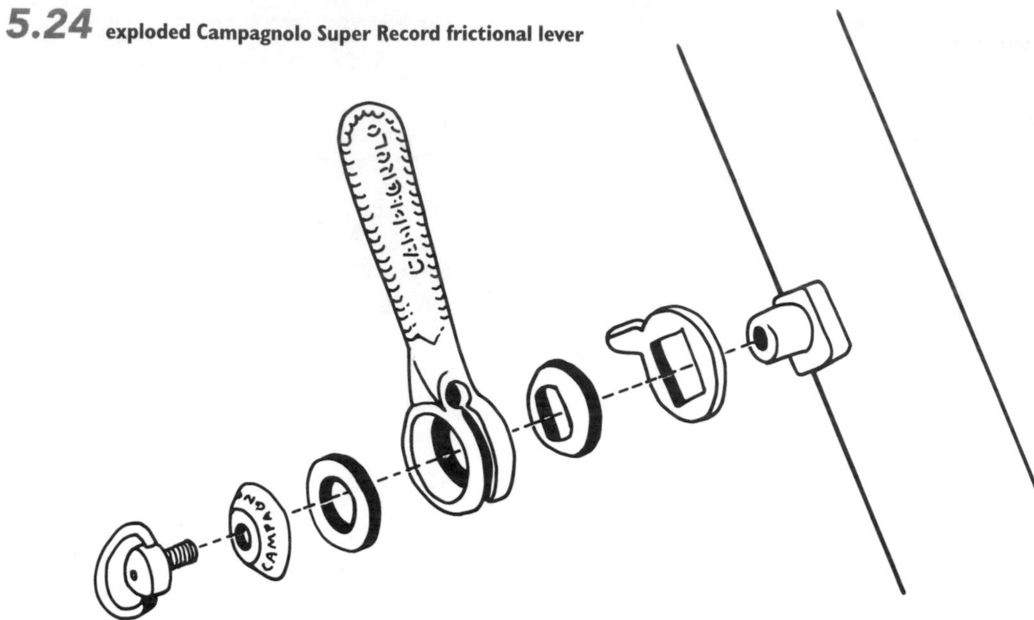

5-20: OVERHAUL OR REPLACE DOWN-TUBE SHIFTERS

Much of this instruction will also apply to shifters attached to bosses on the end of aero' bars as well as bar-end shifters.

1. Remove the screw holding the shifter to the frame's shifter boss, and pull the shifter off.

2. If you have a frictional shifter (Fig. 5.24), all of its pieces come apart. To get the shifter working smoothly, simply clean the parts, grease them, and put them back together. If you have an indexed Shimano shifter, the mechanism cannot be serviced. Buy a new lever if the mechanism has failed.

3. Replace the stop piece that fits over the square base of the shifter boss. With old frictional shifters, this is simply a washer with a square hole and a bent tab. With more recent shifters, this is a cast piece that has a square stop on it that is to be lined up along the down tube projecting forward.

4. Put on the brass or plastic washer, slip the shifter on, install the top washer(s) and the screw. Some Shimano left-hand shifters have a return spring in them and must be installed with the lever flipped down in order to fit properly over the stop on the base. It is not until the screw is tightened down that one of these spring-loaded levers will stay in place when rotated counter clockwise to its starting position, pointed forward, parallel with the downtube.

5. Install the cable and tighten it at the derailleur.

overhauling down-tube shifters
—
derailleur maintenance

5E: DERAILLEUR MAINTENANCE

5-21: JOCKEY-WHEEL MAINTENANCE

With proper attention, the jockey wheels on the rear derailleur will last a long time. They should be wiped off every time you wipe down and lubricate the chain (daily is a good idea). The only other maintenance involved is a light overhaul every 1000–2000 miles.

The mounting bolts on jockey wheels also should be checked regularly. If a loose jockey-wheel bolt falls off while you are riding, you'll need to follow the procedure for a "broken rear derailleur on

5.25 exploded jockey wheels

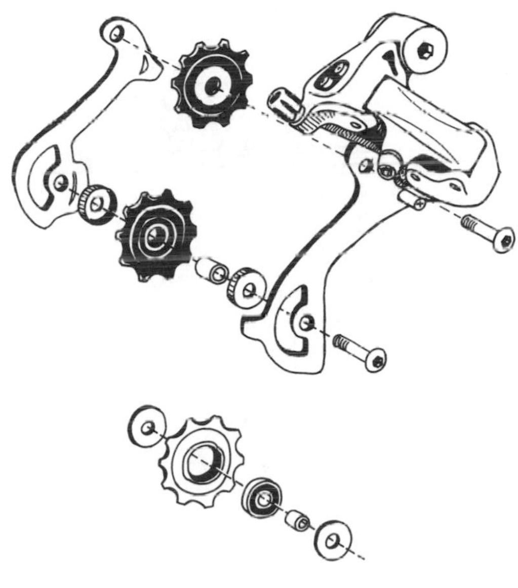

the road" in Chapter 3, Section 3-12.

Standard jockey wheels turn on a bushing made of steel or ceramic. Some high-end models have cartridge bearings. A washer with a inwardly bent rim is usually installed on both sides of a standard jockey wheel. Some jockey wheels also have rubber seals around the edges of these washers.

5-22: OVERHAULING STANDARD JOCKEY WHEELS

1. Remove the jockey wheels by undoing the bolts that hold them to the derailleur (Fig. 5.25). This usually takes a 3mm Allen wrench.

2. Wipe all parts clean with a rag. Solvent is usually not necessary but can be used.

3. If the teeth on the jockey wheels are broken or badly worn, replace the wheels.

4. Smear grease over each bolt and bushing and inside each jockey wheel.

5. Reassemble the jockey wheels onto the derailleur. Be sure to orient the cage plate properly (the larger part of the cage plate should be at the bottom jockey wheel).

5-23: OVERHAULING CARTRIDGE-BEARING JOCKEY WHEELS

If the cartridge bearings (lower jockey wheel in Fig. 5.25) in high-end jockey wheels do not turn freely, they can usually be overhauled.

1. With a single-edge razor blade, pry the plastic cover off of one side or, preferably, both sides of the bearing (Fig. 6.29). (Steel covers on bearings cannot be removed. If such a bearing is not turning freely, the entire bearing needs to be replaced.)

2. With a toothbrush and solvent, clean the bearings. Use citrus-based solvent, and wear gloves and glasses to protect skin and eyes.

3. Blow the solvent out with compressed air or your tire pump and allow the parts to dry.

4. Squeeze new grease into the bearings and replace the covers.

5-24: REAR DERAILLEUR OVERHAUL

Except for the jockey wheels and pivots, most rear derailleurs are not designed to be disassembled. If the pivot springs seem to be operating effectively, all you need to do is overhaul the jockey wheels (see above), and clean and lubricate the parallelogram and spring as follows.

5-25: MINOR REAR DERAILLEUR WIPE AND LUBE

1. Clean the derailleur as well as you can with a rag, including between the parallelogram plates.

2. Drip chain lube on both ends of every pivot pin.

3. If you have the clothespin-type spring in the parallelogram (as opposed to the full coil spring running diagonally from one corner of the parallelogram to the other), put a dab of grease where the spring end slides along the underside of the outer parallelogram plate.

5-26: REAR-DERAILLEUR UPPER-PIVOT OVERHAUL

LEVEL 3

This applies to Shimano and similar derailleurs.

1. Remove the rear derailleur; it usually takes a 5mm Allen wrench to unscrew it from the frame and to disconnect the cable.

2. With a screwdriver, pry the circlip (Fig. 5.26) off of the threaded end of the mounting bolt. Don't lose it; it will tend to fly when it comes off.

3. Pull the bolt and spring out of the derailleur (Fig. 5.1).

4. Clean and dry the parts with or without the use of solvent.

5. Grease liberally, and replace the parts.

6. Each end of the spring has a hole that it needs to go into. If there are several holes, and you don't know which one it was in before, use the middle one. (If the derailleur does not keep tension on the chain well enough, you can later try another hole that increases the spring tension.)

7. Push it all together, and replace the circlip with pliers.

5-27: REAR DERAILLEUR LOWER-PIVOT OVERHAUL

LEVEL 3

This applies to Shimano and similar derailleurs.

1. Locate and unscrew the tall cage-stop screw on the derailleur cage (Fig. 5.1); it is located near the upper jockey wheel. It is designed to maintain tension on the lower pivot spring and is what prevents the cage from springing all of the way around. Once the screw is removed, slowly guide the cage around until the spring tension is relieved.

2. Unscrew the lower pivot bolt using a 4mm,

5.26 rear-derailleur pivots

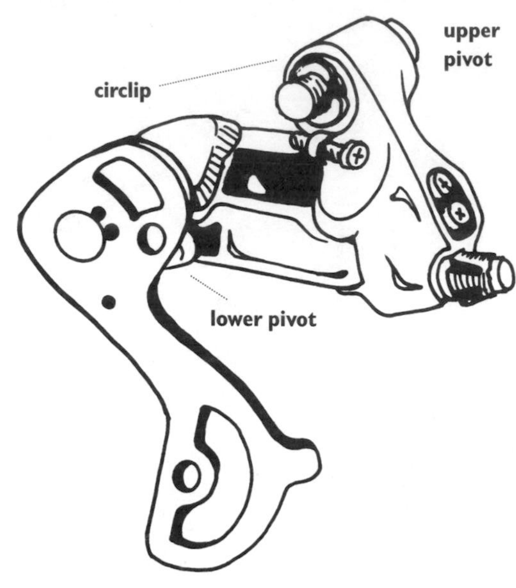

5mm, or 6mm Allen wrench. Be sure to hold the jockey-wheel cage to keep it from twisting.

3. Determine in which hole the spring end has been placed, then remove the spring.

4. Clean and dry the bolt and the spring with a rag. Solvent may be used if necessary.

5. Grease all parts liberally.

6. Replace the spring ends in their holes in either piece. Use the middle hole if you have a choice and aren't certain which it came out of.

7. Screw the bolt back into the jockey-wheel cage plate.

8. Twist the jockey-wheel cage plate counter-clockwise to tension the spring, and replace the cage-stop screw.

5-28: REAR DERAILLEUR PARALLELOGRAM OVERHAUL

LEVEL 3

Very few derailleurs can be completely disassembled. Those that can (Mavic cable-actuated derailleurs) have removable pins holding them together. The pins have circlips on the ends which can be popped off with a screwdriver to remove the pins. If you have such a derailleur, disassemble it in a box so the circlips do not fly away, and make note of where each part belongs so that you can get it back together again. Clean all parts, grease them, and reassemble.

5-29: REPLACING STOCK REAR DERAILLEUR BOLTS WITH LIGHTWEIGHT VERSIONS

LEVEL 3

Lightweight aluminum and titanium derailleur bolts are available as replacement items for many derailleurs. Removing and replacing jockey-wheel bolts is simple, as long as you keep all of the jockey-wheel parts together (Fig. 5.25) and put the inner cage plate back on the way it was. Upper and lower pivot bolts (Fig. 5.1) are replaced following the instructions outlined earlier in this chapter for overhauling the pivots (Sections 5-26 and 5-27).

5F: TROUBLESHOOTING REAR DERAILLEUR AND RIGHT-HAND SHIFTER PROBLEMS

Once you have made the adjustments outlined above, the drivetrain should be quiet in operation and shift smoothly. The drivetrain should stay in gear, even if you turn the crank backward. If you cannot fine-tune the adjustment so that each click with the right shifter results in a clean, quick shift, you need to check some of the following possibilities. For skipping- and jumping-chain problems, see also the Troubleshooting section at the end of Chapter 4.

5-30: SHIFTER COMPATIBILITY

Make certain that the shifter and derailleur are made by the same company. If the brands are different, make sure that they are designed to work together. For instance, Modolo makes an integral brake/shift lever that can be set up to work either Campagnolo or Shimano derailleurs.

If the shifter and derailleur are incompatible, you will need to change one of them (probably whichever item is less costly). For more on compatibility, see Section 5-38 below.

5-31: STICKY CABLES

Check to see whether the derailleur cables run smoothly through the housing. Sticky cable movement will cause sluggish shifting. Lubricate the cable by smearing it with chain lube or a specific lubricant that came with your shifters (Section 5-14). If lubricating the cable does not help, replace the cable and housing (see Sections 5-6 to 5-13).

5-32: BENT REAR DERAILLEUR HANGER

A bent hanger will hold the derailleur crooked and bedevil shifting. Instructions for straightening the hanger are in Chapter 15, Section 15-4.

5-33: BENT REAR DERAILLEUR CAGE

A bent derailleur cage will align the jockey wheels at angle. Mild bending can be straightened by hand; eyeball the crankset for a vertical reference.

5-34 LOOSE OR WORN-OUT REAR DERAILLEUR

Grab the derailleur and twist it with your fingers to feel for excessive play. Loose pivots, a symptom of a worn-out rear derailleur, will cause the rear derailleur to be loose and floppy. Replace it if it has this problem.

A loose mounting bolt will also mess up shifting by allowing the derailleur to flop around. Tighten the bolt.

TROUBLE-SHOOTING

—

Mavic Mektronic installation

5G: ELECTRIC SHIFTING; INSTALLING AND ADJUSTING MAVIC MEKTRONIC

Mavic Mektronic (Figs. 5.27, 5.28) is the wireless offspring of Mavic Zap, the original widely available electric shifting system. Shifts are initiated by pushing buttons on the brake lever, or at other remote locations. All shift buttons are hard-wired to the computer, which registers normal computer functions as well as displaying which rear cog the chain is on.

The system is powered by three batteries, which are located in the computer, the derailleur, and the wheel sensor (which is mounted to the fork). The batteries last a long time because the power to perform the shifts comes from your feet; the upper jockey wheel drives a ladder-shaped ratchet back and forth continuously. When the shift instruction comes from the computer, a solenoid on one side or the other of the ladder ratchet drives a pin into the ratchet, which forces the derailleur in or out one cog space.

5-35: MEKTRONIC INSTALLATION AND ADJUSTMENT

LEVEL 2

Installation:

Install the levers as in section 5-17. Install the computer bracket at a 10-degree incline on the handlebar adjacent the stem (road version) or on top of the stem (triathlon version) with Zip-ties. The triathlon version also has an additional shift-button set to be installed on the aero' bar (also with Zip-ties). Tape all wires down, and install the front derailleur cable as in section 5.C.

Mount the magnet on a spoke near the spoke nipple, and Zip-tie the sensor high on the fork so its mark lines up with the magnet and clears it by 2-3mm. Mount the rear derailleur to the dropout with a 4mm hex key.

Adjustment:

Computer and computer/derailleur interface:

First, it is imperative that the computer face be angled up at least 10 degrees up from horizontal (Fig. 5.28) or it may not function properly. And when mounting the system, make sure that the derailleur, fork sensor and computer mounting bracket are all installed before you stick the computer on the bracket.

Initially, the computer must be set up to recognize the derailleur. Do this in a quiet area away from PC or TV screens, running motors, power lines or other potential sources of interference. Depress both black buttons on the computer simultaneously while pushing one of the yellow shift buttons anywhere in the system. The screen will turn on for four seconds. Release the three buttons and order a shift by pushing any yellow shift button. Wait for four to five seconds before pedaling and ordering a shift to ascertain that initialization has succeeded and that the displayed cog is the correct one (see Section 5-37 if it is not).

It is not necessary to repeat the process when changing batteries, but it is if you ever change the computer or derailleur. The initialization ensures that your derailleur will not be shifted by someone else's Mektronic computer.

Rear derailleur:

The rear derailleur (Fig. 5.27) moves one Shimano 9-speed cog space with each shift. It works acceptably with Campagnolo 9-speed as well, but use a Shimano chain for best operation. Since there is no cable to hold it in its initial position, you must set its position with a knurled knob on the derailleur.

5.27 Mavic Mektronic rear derailleur

5.28 Mavic Mektronic brake/shift lever, shift buttons and computer tipped up at greater than 10 degrees from horizontal

With the bike in a bike stand, push the derailleur over so that the chain is riding on a medium-sized cog. Check to see that the upper jockey wheel is lined up directly under the cog. Turn the knob clockwise to move the derailleur inward, counter-clockwise to move it outward. Try it on the smallest cog as well. (To free the knob for ease of rotation, push inward on the derailleur.)

Shift the derailleur from cog to cog while turning the crank; it should shift up as easily as down. If it is sluggish in one direction, move the derailleur a bit in that direction with the knurled knob.

Ride the bike and notice the shifting. If necessary, stop and fine-tune the derailleur position with the knob.

5-36: MEKTRONIC COMPUTER MAINTENANCE

Reset the daily mileage, elapsed time, and max and average speeds by pushing both black buttons for two seconds.

Do not store the bike with the LCD screen in the sun for prolonged periods when not in use. And do not spray pressurized water at the computer or sensor.

All three batteries in the three components of the system are the same, making it easy to carry a spare. Mavic claims a life expectancy for the derailleur battery of 1–3 years, 2–4 years for the computer battery, and 3–5 years for the sensor battery. But if used on a tandem (where the length of broadcast of communication signals is longer), battery life drops to a year on the derailleur and the computer. See Section 5-37 below for diagnosing battery problems.

After replacing a battery, reset the computer by pushing a shift button while simultaneously holding down both black buttons on the computer (do this in the event of any irregular display as well). All of your wheel size, cog-size, miles/kilometer, odometer and clock settings will be cleared and will have to be reset.

To set any computer function, go to the display showing that function by pushing either black button repeatedly until you get there. To get into reset mode, hold the right black button down for more than two seconds until the display blinks. Release the button. The left button now changes the setting, while the right button moves to the next digit and ultimately exits from reset mode.

Derailleur:

Wipe off the derailleur jockey wheels frequently. Periodically lubricate and check bolt tightness of jockey wheels.

5-37: TROUBLESHOOTING MAVIC MEKTRONIC

The "BAT" icon is highlighted in black on the screen:

One of the batteries is nearly dead. If the indicator just came on, you should have enough juice in it to get you home (if not, you have a single-speed, but you can at least manually set the derailleur on the gear you want to ride home in, and it will stay there).

Now you know is that one of the batteries is low, but which one is it? To find out, hold the left black button down for two or more seconds. The status of each battery will scroll past; in each case, one icon will be highlighted, while the arrow in the upper right-hand corner of the screen will point either up (battery is good) or down (battery is low). When the "ATM" icon is highlighted, you are seeing the status of the computer battery; "ODO" is for the sensor battery, and the little cog-shaped icon is the indicator for the derailleur battery.

After replacing a battery, reset the computer by pushing a shift button while simultaneously holding down both black buttons on the computer (do this in the event of any irregular display as well). All of your wheel-size, cog-size, miles/kilometer, odometer and clock settings will be cleared and will have to be reset (see Section 5-36 for setting procedure).

When replacing the derailleur battery, wait 10 minutes after removing the old battery before installing the new one.

"BAT" comes on at beginning of ride but is off by the end:

It may have been so cold at the start of your ride that the battery voltage indicated too low. Confirm by using above battery diagnosis procedure.

No display:

Push any button to wake the computer from its energy-saving mode. If there is still no display, replace the computer battery.

Cog size displayed is larger than actual cog:

While pedaling, shift all of the way in to the largest cog and keep pushing that button until the correct largest cog appears on the screen.

Cog size displayed is smaller than actual cog:

While pedaling, shift all of the way out to the smallest cog and keep pushing that button until the correct smallest cog appears on the screen.

Display is dark:

Put the bike in the shade.

Slow display response:

The computer may be too cold. Check it again when it is warmer.

Speed is not shown:

Adjust the relative positions of the sensor and the wheel magnet.

Screen does not display cog size after a shift is ordered, whether or not the shift is accomplished.

Check that the computer is set into the bracket properly (it should click into place). Check that the screen is angled up at least 10 degrees from horizontal. If that doesn't fix it, replace the computer battery and reset the computer (see above). Still problems? Replace the derailleur battery and reset the computer (remember to wait 10 minutes after removing the old battery before installing the new one).

No shift occurs, but the computer display flashes:

Re-initialize the computer (section 5-35). If this does not work, replace the computer batter.

No shift occurs, and the computer display is unchanged when pushing any yellow shift button (the display should flash and show the new

cog size), but the batter diagnostic does not indicate battery problems:

Possibility 1:

The contact between the mounting bracket and the computer may not be good. Snap the computer in and out of the mount to clear the contacts and ensure that it is in place. Try flexing the bracket while commanding a shift (early triathlon mounts had contacts that did not protrude enough, and this can bring them into contact). Cleaning the contacts with sandpaper may also be called for.

Possibility 2:

If you store your bike in your office near computer equipment, the derailleur battery can be dead, but not show up that way in the battery diagnostic. This is because the derailleur awakens regularly from its sleeping mode to check for incoming shift messages. If the derailleur is near a personal computer or power supply for prolonged periods, it may be awake all of the time, which would rapidly drain the battery. The battery diagnostic on the Mektronic computer requires communication between the derailleur and the computer, which would be impossible with a dead battery. The Mektronic computer would consult its memory of the last ride and indicate that the battery is fine.

Derailleur is on the smallest or largest cog and won't shift back:

After a crash, one of the solenoids in the rear derailleur may be engaged mechanically into the ladder-shaped ratchet. The derailleur will shift all of the way in one direction, but it won't shift back because both solenoids will be engaging. Free a stuck solenoid electrically by commanding a shift in the direction in which it has already moved as far as it can (for example, if it is on the smallest cog, push the yellow switch on the back side of the brake lever to tell it to shift again to the smallest cog).

5.F: TROUBLESHOOTING FRONT DERAILLEUR AND REAR SHIFTER PROBLEMS

5-38: COMPATIBILITY ISSUES BETWEEN BRANDS, MODELS AND 5-, 6-, 7-, 8-, 9- AND 10-SPEEDS

The number of rear cogs on a road bike keeps going up every few years. But does any of the old stuff work with any of the new stuff? And can you mix Shimano and Campagnolo parts?

Well, if you have resolutely stuck with your old frictional down-tube shifters, you can let Campagnolo and Shimano throw however many cogs they want at you, and you will still be able to shift. That old Campagnolo Nuovo Record shifter and derailleur worked on five cogs, six cogs, seven cogs, eight cogs, nine cogs, and it will probably work on 10 cogs! Modern indexed systems shift more precisely, but they don't offer that kind of flexibility.

Compatibility problems occur because the chain required gets narrower as the number of cogs goes up. The spacing also narrows between chainrings, between rear derailleur jockey-wheel plates, between front-derailleur cage plates, and between the right rear hub flange and the largest cog. Also, the rear hub axles have gotten longer. The spacing between rear dropouts (and hence the rear axle "overlock" dimension) was at 120mm during 5-speed days, 126mm during the 6- and 7-speed era and it is now 130mm for 8, 9, and 10 speeds.

Threaded freewheels:

The 5-, 6- and 7-speed era marked the beginning of the transition from freewheels that threaded onto the rear hub to cassette freehubs built into the hub onto which separate cogs could be installed. With some minor exceptions, freewheels were completely compatible with every hub, since nearly all shared the same threading. Spacers sometimes had to be moved around from one end of the axle to the other to prevent the chain from dragging on the frame in the smallest cog. And, of course, you had to get a longer axle and re-dish the wheel when frames went from 120mm to 126mm rear spacing. But that was about it.

Freewheels did appear with eight speeds, so you could still space your old hub one more time with a new axle to 130mm. But freewheel makers threw in the towel when we hit 9 speeds.

Five-speed freewheel cogs were spaced farther apart than current cogs, and there was no consistency of cog spacing between brands or even between different pairs of cogs on the same freewheel. There did not have to be, since the rider was manually lining up the derailleur with each cog. You were also lucky to have a 13-tooth first cog, rather than the 14-tooth that the previous generation saw as a high gear.

The first Suntour 6-speed freewheels were called "Ultra-6" and had narrower spacing between cogs (and a narrower chain) so they would fit on a 120mm rear hub. Not everyone embraced narrowness, but many riders wanted 12-tooth cogs. Splitting the difference, many frames of the era (especially Italian ones) were built with 126mm rear spacing, and equipped with 6-speed freewheels with cogs set at the old wide spacing.

compatability of brands and models

Suntour answered with "Ultra-7" narrow-spaced freewheels and chains. Sedis started making narrow chains as well, and narrow spacing became the standard, carrying on into 8-speed.

Cassette freehubs:

Shimano's spacing between cogs has gone from 3.65mm for 5- and 6-speeds, to 3.10mm for 7-speed, 3.00mm for 8-speed, and 2.65mm for 9-speed.

The original Shimano freehubs appeared around 1980 and accepted six speeds widely spaced on a 126mm hub. The first five cogs were splined to fit on the splined freehub body, and the last cog threaded on. Shimano chains, called "Uniglide," were wide and had the bent-plate configuration of present-day Shimano chains. Shimano began making its first indexed shifting systems in the mid-80s as well.

When Suntour came out with narrow Ultra-7 freewheels in the early 1980s, Shimano countered with wider freehub bodies that fit seven widely spaced cogs and the wide Shimano chain. These hubs had unique flanges with all of the spokes emerging on the outside to reduce wheel-dish problems brought on by the wide cassette on a 126mm hub. The wheels still fell apart under the loads of big riders, though. The smallest cog still threaded on, and all of the spline grooves were the same width, but the width caused the first freehub incompatibility with previous models.

In the second half of the 1980s, Shimano succumbed to the rising popularity of narrow chains, and it made narrow bent-plate (Uniglide) chains. Its new freehub body was the old 6-speed length, and it fit seven narrowly spaced cogs. But the new cogs would not fit on the old freehub bodies for two reasons. The new freehubs were splined end-to-end and had internal threads at the outboard end to fit a lockring holding the cogs on instead of a threaded small cog. And one spline groove was wider than the others, since the new cogs had shifting ramps that had to be oriented a particular way relative to the adjacent cog in order to shift properly. You could have weathered the short-lived wide-7 freehubs, but now you really had to throw out all of your old wheels and cogs.

The 1990s began with the introduction of 8 speeds. Shimano had dictated that frames now had to have 130mm rear ends to accommodate new hubs with wider freehub bodies. The one-wide-spline arrangement and threaded lockrings continued, but you could not fit eight cogs on a 7-speed body.

This set the stage for 9 speeds, which had narrower spacing, a narrower chain, and fit on 8-speed freehubs at first. But the desire for an 11-tooth cog forced the reduction of the freehub diameter by removing the outboard 2-3mm of spline ridges, so you had to get new hubs again (unless you were handy enough with a file or a grinder to knock off the last couple of millimeters of the spline ridges to be flush with the freehub outer diameter). This Shimano freehub configuration carries on into the new millennium.

But what about Suntour, Mavic and Campagnolo? Well, all of them began making freehub bodies and cogs with their own spline configurations, and only Campagnolo's systems survived the shakeout. Suntour disappeared completely from the road market, while Mavic went with the flow, making Shimano-compatible hubs. Mavic today makes cogs and spacers to adapt to 8- or 9-speed Shimano or Campagnolo systems; you can use Mavic cogs with spacers for any of these standards, or you can use Mavic spacers within a Shimano 9-speed cogset to make it compatible with a 9-speed Campagnolo derailleur and shifters.

Campagnolo, the great, reliable and unchanging bastion of compatibility and small-parts availability in the 1970s and early 1980s disappointed its faithful when it came out with 9 speeds. During the 8-speed era, it had been selling complete wheels with 8-speed freehub bodies of its own standard. Its 9-speed freehub body, however, has much deeper splines that do not fit Campy 8-speed cogs, so those beautiful and expensive 8-speed wheels are now junk. (But for one minor exception, you cannot get a new 9-speed Campy freehub body and install it on an 8-speed Campy hub.) However, Campagnolo's 10-speed cogsets, introduced in 1999, do fit on Campy 9-speed freehub bodies, since the 6.1mm-wide 10-speed chain is narrower yet. The tooth-to-tooth distance on Campagnolo 9-speed is 4.55mm, it is 4.15mm on 10-speed.

Chainrings:

The spacing between chainrings keeps getting narrower with more speeds, as does the width and index-spacing of the front derailleur. If you have upgraded piecemeal, you may find your 9-speed chain falling between the two chainrings held over from an earlier 7- or 8-speed system. The narrow chain will generally slip uselessly as you pedal, but it can jam between the rings as well, causing all sorts of expensive havoc. This potential raises its head again with a 10-speed chain on 9-speed chainrings.

Chainring teeth are made to fit closer together either by reducing the thickness of the chainring-mounting flats on the crank spider arms, or by offsetting the teeth to one side of the chainring. Shimano 7-, 8-, and 9-speed spider arms are all the same thickness, but the teeth on Shimano 9-speed chainrings are offset toward each other.

Campagnolo's spider arms got thinner when going from 7- and 8-speed to 9-speed, but the chainring teeth got offset going to 10-speed, and the spider arms stayed the same as 9-speed. You can upgrade a Campagnolo 9-speed crank to 10-speed by changing the rings.

Shifting compatibility of models within brands:

All Campagnolo shifting system components can be interchanged within models. In other words, you can use Athena 9-speed ErgoPower shifters with a Veloce rear derailleur, Mirage front derailleur, Record cogs, Chorus crank and Neutron wheel. The same holds true if all components are 8-speed.

Shimano components have more interchangeability exceptions. Until 9-speed came out, the stroke length for Dura-Ace derailleurs was different from all other Shimano derailleurs, mountain or road. Put another way, you could use any Shimano shifter you wanted with any Shimano derailleur except for Dura-Ace.

With the advent of 9 speeds, all Shimano rear derailleurs and shifters work together. But the same is not true with front derailleurs. If you try to use a road STI shift/brake lever with a top-swing (low-mount) top-pull mountain-bike front derailleur (you might do this for a triple on a hybrid bike, for instance), it won't work. You can use any Shimano top-mount, top-pull front derailleur with road STI, though. And all current Shimano cassettes fit on any Shimano freehub model designed for the same number of speeds.

Shifting compatibility between brands:

Until the advent of 9 speeds, a Campagnolo cogset did not shift acceptably on a Shimano indexed drivetrain, and vice versa. But the limited amount of space available for 9 speeds brought Shimano's and Campagnolo's cog spacing close enough that rear wheels could be switched back and forth between the two with decent shifting performance—not as good as you would pay the big bucks for, perhaps, but acceptable for normal riding, and certainly good enough for wheel changes during races. Neutral-support vehicles only had to stock one variety of 9-speed wheels to cover every rider in the peloton.

Of course, 10-speeds have changed all of that again.

Mavic Zap was designed for Shimano 8-speed systems, and Mavic Mektronic is built for Shimano 9-speed systems, but it works decently on Campagnolo 9-speed cassettes as well.

As for front derailleurs and cranksets, mixing parts seems to cause few problems as long as you use parts designed for the same number of speeds. Campagnolo and Shimano road front derailleurs and cranksets work fine with each other's road shifters. Mavic Mektronic left levers work with either Campagnolo or Shimano front derailleurs.

All 9-speed chains work with all 9-speed systems. And any 8-speed chain works on any 7-speed or 8-speed system. It is worth experimenting, though, because you may find that a Shimano chain, for instance, will improve the shifting on a Campagnolo system. The 7- and 8-speed chains are 7-7.2mm wide; 9-speed chains are 6.5-6.7mm wide; and Campagnolo's 10-speed chain is 6.1mm wide.

5-39: CHAIN SUCK

Though relatively rare on road bikes, chain suck (where the chain sticks to the chainring and is dragged around until it jams between the chainring and the chainstay) can still occur. See Troubleshooting at the end of Chapter 4, Section 4-12.

5-40: CHAINLINE

improving chainline

Chainline is the relative alignment of the front chainrings with the rear cogs; it is the imaginary line connecting the center of the middle chainring with the middle of the cogset (Fig. 5.29). This line should in theory be straight and parallel with the vertical plane of the bicycle. Even owners of new bikes may discover poor chainlines on their bikes, due to mismatched cranks and bottom brackets.

Assuming that the frame is aligned properly (see Chapter 15, Section 15-5), chainline is adjusted by moving or replacing the bottom bracket to move the cranks left or right. You can roughly check the chainline by placing a long straightedge between the two chainrings (or, in the case of a triple, against the middle chainring) and back to the rear cogs; it should come out in the center of the rear cogs. (If that's not good enough for your purposes, a more precise method is outlined below.)

If your chain falls off to the inside no matter how much you adjust the derailleur's low-gear limit screw, cable tension, and derailleur position, or you have chain rub, noise, or auto-shift problems in mild cross-gears that are not corrected with derailleur adjustments, a likely culprit is poor chainline.

5-41: PRECISE CHAINLINE MEASUREMENT

You will need a caliper with a Vernier (or digital) scale. If you have a triple, you may want to consult the chainline discussion in Chapter 5 of *Zinn and the Art of Mountain Bike Maintenance.*

The position of the plane centered between the two chainrings, as measured from the center of the seat tube to the center between the chainrings, is often called the chainline, although this is only the front point of the line.

1. Find the position of the plane centered between the chainrings, or front point of the chainline (**CL_F** in Fig. 5.29).

a. Measure from the left side of the down tube to the outside of the large chainring (**d_1** in Fig. 5.29). (Do not measure from the seat tube, this tube is often ovalized at the bottom).

b. Measure the distance from the right side of the down tube to the inside of the inner chainring (**d_2** in Fig. 5.29).

c. To find CLF (the front chainline), add these two measurements, and divide the sum by two.

$$CL_F = (d_1 + d_2)/2$$

2. Find the rear end point of the chainline (**CL_R** in Fig. 5.29), which is the distance from the center of the plane of the bicycle to the center of the cogset.

a. Measure the thickness of the cog stack, end to end (**t** in Fig. 5.29).

5.29 measuring chain line

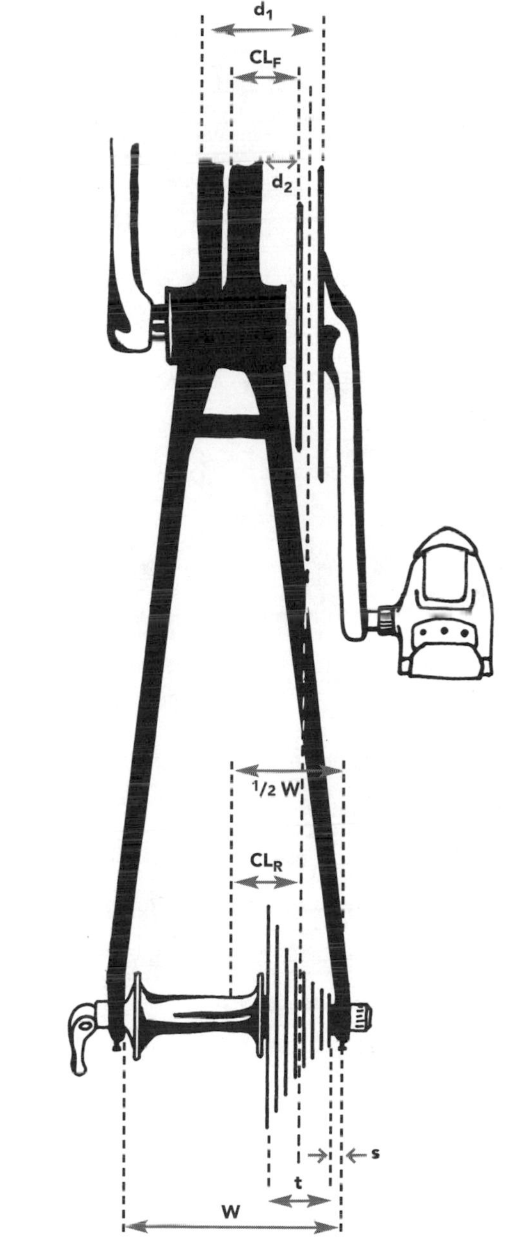

b. Measure the space between the face of the smallest cog and the inside face of the dropout (**s** in Fig. 5.29).

c. Measure the length of the axle from dropout to dropout (**w** in Fig. 5.29); this length is also called the "axle overlock dimension," referring to the distance from locknut face to locknut face on either end. Generally, on any road bike built since the late 1980s, this will be 130mm.

d. To find **CL_R**, subtract one-half of the thickness

of the cog stack and the distance from the inside face of the right rear dropout from one half of the rear axle length.

$$\mathbf{CL_R = w/2 - t/2 - s}$$

3. If $\mathbf{CL_F = CL_R}$ (the rear chainline), the chainline is perfect. This may not be possible to attain, however, due to considerations of chainstay clearance, and prevention of chain rub on large chainrings in cross gears. Shimano specifies a "chainline" (meaning $\mathbf{CL_F}$, the front point of the chainline) of 43.5mm for a double and 45.0mm for a triple on road bikes. $\mathbf{CL_F}$, the rear end point of the chain line, on the other hand, usually comes out around 42.6mm for Shimano 9-speed, 41.8mm for Campagnolo 9-speed, and 41.7mm for Campagnolo 8-speed.

Your bike will shift best and run quietest if you get the chainline ($\mathbf{CL_F}$) at around 42mm. However, this ideal may cause problems on your particular bike because (a) the inner chainring might rub the chainstay, (b) the front derailleur may bottom out on the seat tube before moving inward enough to shift to the inner chainring (this is particularly a problem with bikes with triples and oversized seat tubes), or (c) when crossing to the smallest cog from the inner chainring, the chain may rub on the next larger ring (this is not a problem if you simply avoid those cross gears).

precise chainline measurement

My general recommendation is to have the chainrings in toward the frame as far as possible without rubbing the frame or bottoming out the front derailleur before it shifts cleanly to the inner chainring.

4. To improve the chainline, move the chainrings, since there is little or nothing you can do with the rear cog position. The chainrings are moved by using a different bottom bracket, by exchanging bottom bracket spindles with a longer one, or by moving the bottom bracket right or left (bottom bracket installation is covered in Chapter 8).

5.30 **Third Eye Chain Watcher**

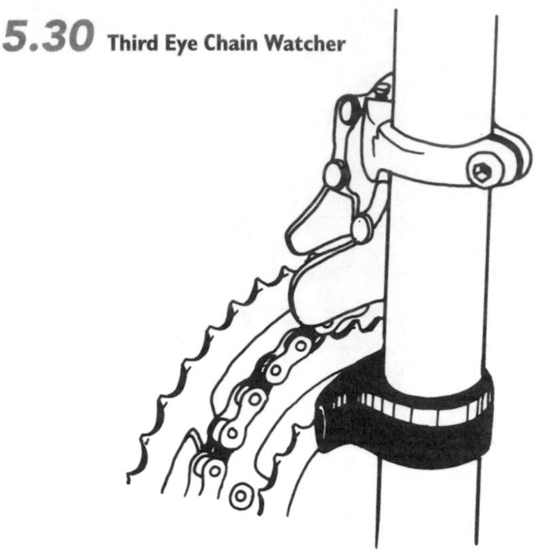

Note: *Some brand-new bikes have terrible chainlines that can only be corrected by buying a new bottom bracket. This usually has to do with a conceptually impaired bean-counting product manager selecting the parts for a given bike model. Product managers know that customers often pay attention to the quality and brand of the cranks on the bike but pay little heed to the quality of the bottom bracket—an unseen part. A cheap bottom bracket that does not match the cranks is often specified to save the manufacturer some money. The cranks will sit too far out, and the chainline will stink. You will end up having to replace the long bottom bracket with a shorter one if you want the bike to shift decently. Good shops will replace the bottom bracket before selling it to you.*

Another note: *The chainline can also be off if the frame is out of alignment (Chapter 15, Section 15-5). If that's the case, it is probably something you cannot fix yourself.*

5. If improving the chainline does not fix your problem, or if you don't want to mess with the chainline, buy and install a Third Eye Chain Watcher (Fig. 5.30). This is an inexpensive plastic gizmo that clamps around the seat tube next to the inner chainring. Adjust its position so that it nudges the chain back on when the chain tries to fall off to the inside.

VI

Wheels and tires

"All you need in this life is ignorance and confidence, and then success is sure." —Mark Twain

Most road bike wheels are strung together with spokes connecting the hub to the rim. The rim, which serves as both support for the tire and as a braking surface, is supported and aligned by the tension on the spokes. Bearings in the hub, when clean and properly adjusted, allow the wheel to turn freely around the axle.

Composite wheels, be they disc wheels or three-, four- or five-spoke wheels, generally use rigid members to hold the wheel up. An exception is the Spinergy Rev-X, which relies on tension on eight flat carbon spokes to support the wheel. Composite wheels generally cannot be trued, although the rim is replaceable on some models.

Wheels intended for aerodynamic efficiency either have solid sides (disc wheels) or have aerodynamically shaped rims and few spokes, which are often themselves aerodynamic in shape. The spokes can be steel, titanium, or composite (often carbon fiber).

A cassette freehub or a freewheel allows the rear wheel to spin while coasting, and it engages when force is applied to the pedals (Fig. 6.1).

The tires provide suspension as well as grip and traction for propulsion and steering. The air pressure in the tire is the primary suspension system on a road bike.

Two types of road tires are available. "Clinchers" (Fig. 6.2) are held into a C-shaped rim by a steel or Kevlar bead on each edge of the tire. A separate inner tube inside of the clincher holds the air in. "Tubulars" (Fig. 6.3) have a casing that is wrapped around an inner tube and stitched or glued together. The tire is glued onto a box-section rim that has no vertical rim walls like a clincher rim.

This chapter addresses how to fix a flat or replace a tire or tube, true a wheel, fix a broken spoke or bent rim, overhaul hubs, change rear cogs, and lubricate cassettes and freewheels. Have at it.

tools

Tire levers
Pump
Patch kit
Spoke wrench
Grease
5mm hex keys
13mm, 14mm, 15mm cone wrenches
Metric open-end wrenches or adjustable wrenches

OPTIONAL

Tubular rim cement
Teflon tape
Pliers
Miter clamp
Leather sewing needle
Braided high-test fishing line
Thimble
Barge cement (or other strong contact cement)
Truing stand
Tire sealant
Freehub cassette lockring remover
Freewheel remover
Citrus solvent
Soft hammer
Rohloff cog-wear indicator
Freehub Buddy
Fine-tip grease gun

6.1 the whole thing

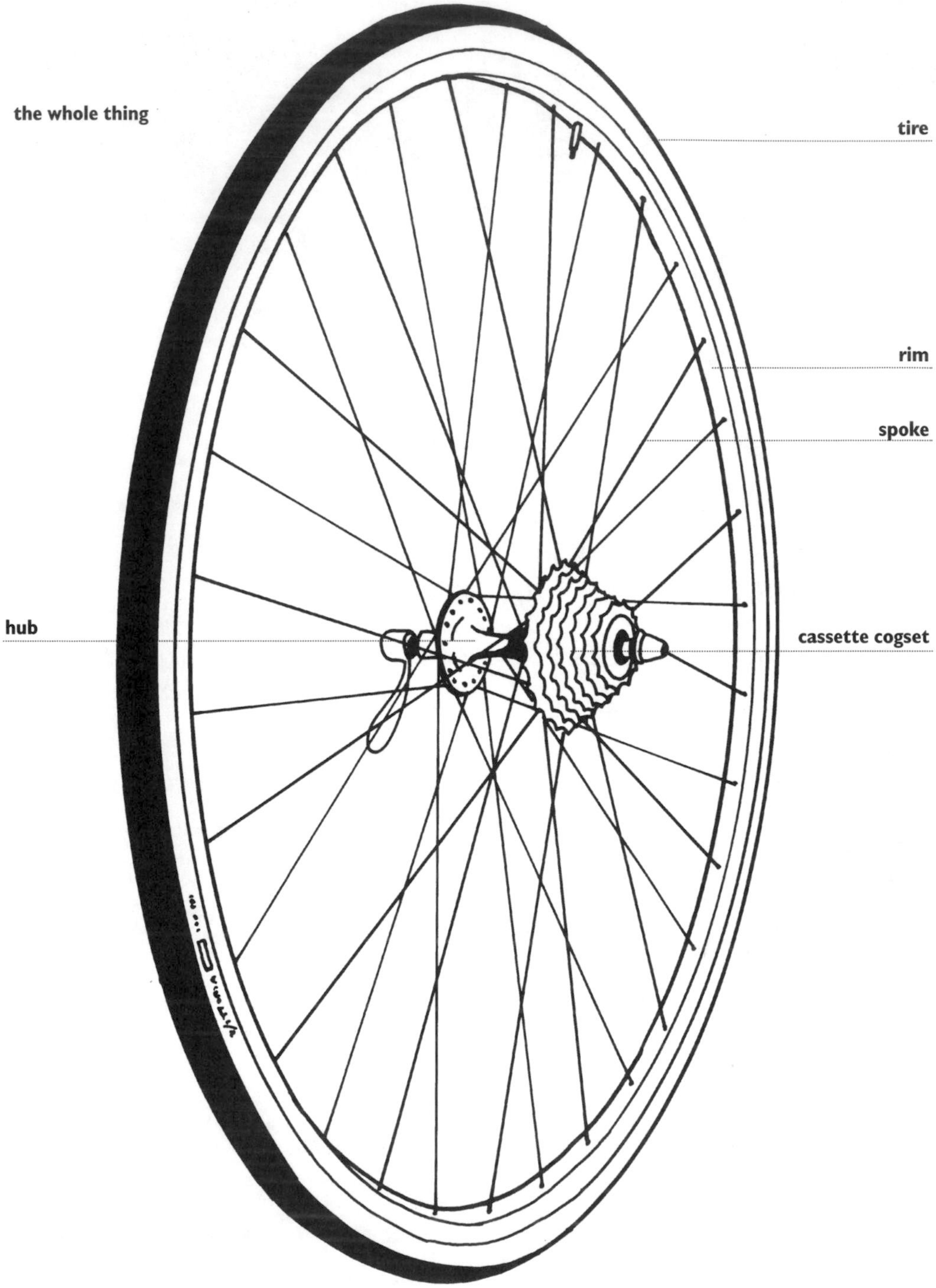

tire
rim
spoke
hub
cassette cogset

6.2 clincher tire

PRO Kevlar 700x23

6.3 tubular tire

Vittoria 700x23

tires

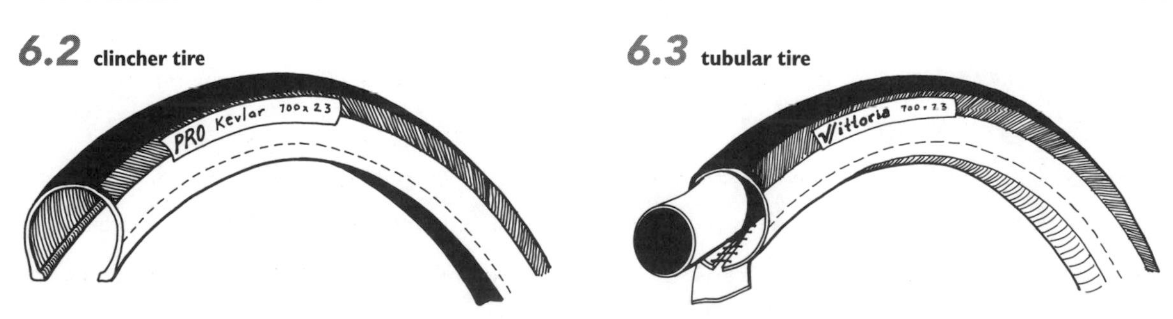

6.4 Presta valve

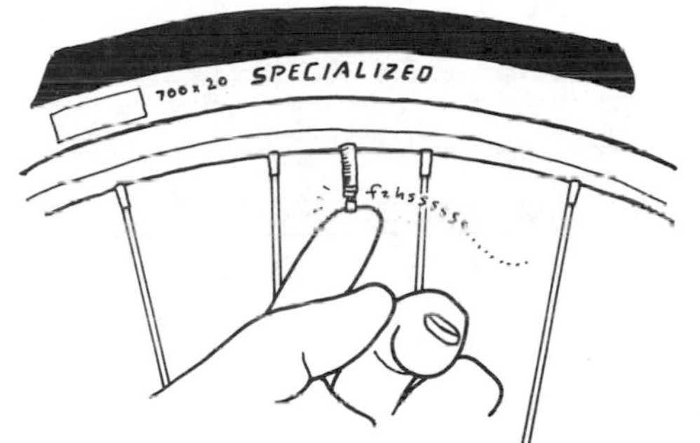

6.5 Schrader valve

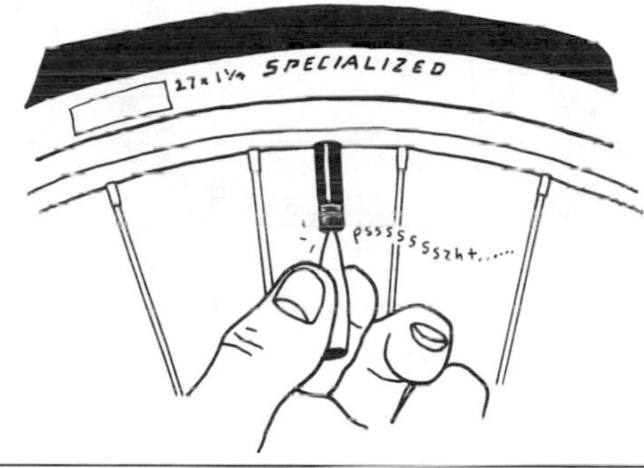

6.6-7 removing clincher tire with levers

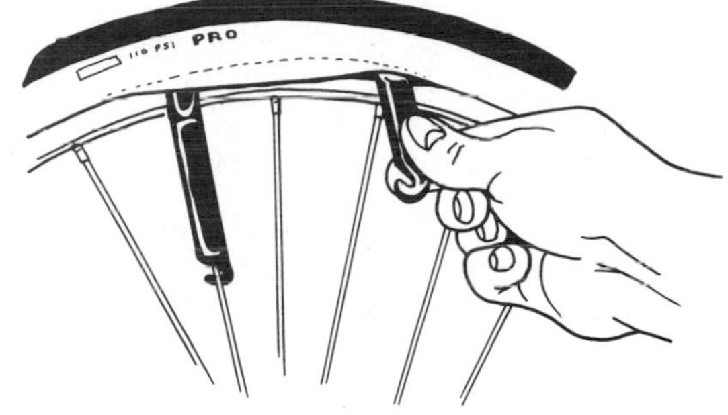

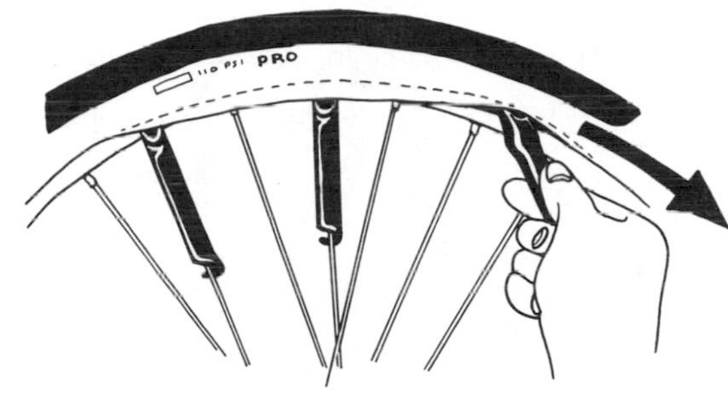

6A: CLINCHER TIRES

Replacing or repairing tires and inner tubes

6-1: REMOVING THE TIRE

1. Remove the wheel (See Chapter 2, Section 2-2 and 2-11).

2. If your tire is not already flat, deflate it.

First remove the valve cap (if installed) to get to the valve.

Most road tires have "Presta," or "French" valves. These valves are thinner than "Schrader" valves (the kind found on cars) and have a small threaded rod with a tiny nut on the end. To let air out, unscrew the little nut a few turns, and push down on the thin rod (Fig. 6.4). To seal, tighten the little nut down again (with your fingers only!); leave it tightened down for riding.

To deflate a Schrader valve, push down on the valve pin with something thin enough to fit in that won't break off, like a pen cap or a paper clip (Fig. 6.5).

Note: *If you have deep-section rims (i.e., Mavic Cosmic, Campagnolo Shamal, Vento, or Bora; Hed, Rolf, Spinergy, Zipp or any of a myriad of others), the wheels will likely have "valve extenders"—thin threaded tubes that screw onto the Presta valve stems. To deflate the tire, you need to insert a thin rod (a spoke is perfect) into the valve extender to release the air.*

Some inner tubes now come with extra-long Presta valves for deep-section wheels. These are operated just like standard Presta valves.

3. If you can push the tire bead off the rim with your thumbs without using tire levers, by all means do so, since there is less chance of damaging either the tube or the tire if you avoid the use of levers or other tools. It's easiest if you start just to one side or the other of the valve.

4. If you can't get the tire off with your hands alone, insert a tire lever, scoop side up, between the rim sidewall and the tire until you catch the edge of the tire bead. Make sure you do not pinch the tube between the lever and the tire. Again, start

6.8 removing the inner tube

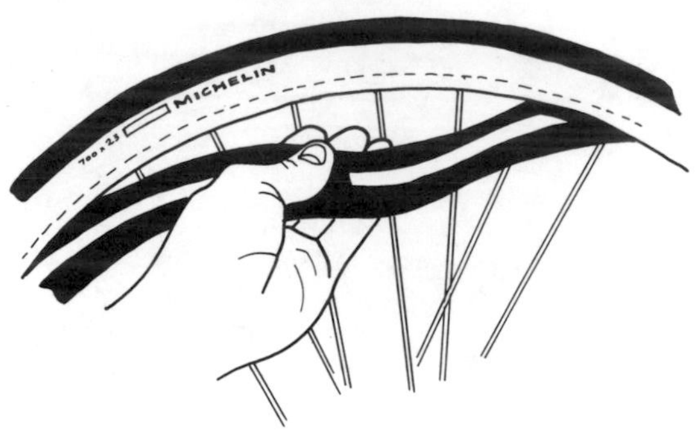

near the valve. This allows the beads on the side opposite the valve to drop into the center of the rim, effectively reducing the diameter about which the tire is stretched.

5. Pry down on the lever until the tire bead is pulled out over the rim (Fig. 6.6).

If the lever has a hook on the other end, hook it onto the nearest spoke. Otherwise, keep holding it down.

6. Place the next lever a few inches away, and do the same thing with it (Fig. 6.6).

7. If needed, place a third lever a few inches farther on, pry it out, and continue sliding this lever around the tire, pulling the bead out as you go (Fig. 6.7). Some people slide their fingers around under the bead, but beware of cutting your fingers on sharp tire beads.

Note: *There are a few different quick tire levers on the market that work differently and more quickly than the separate standard tire levers. If the tire bead is very tight on the rim, though, using separate tire levers may be the only method that works effectively.*

8. Once the bead is off on one side, pull the tube out (Fig. 6.8).

If you are patching or replacing the tube, you do not need to remove the other side of the tire from the rim. If you are replacing the tire, the other bead should come off easily with your fingers. If it does not, use the tire levers as outlined above.

6-2: PATCHING AN INNER TUBE

1. If the leak location is not obvious, put some air in the tube to inflate it until it is two to three times larger than its deflated size. Be careful. You can explode it if you put too much air in, especially with lightweight latex or urethane tubes.

2. Listen/feel for air coming out, and mark the leak(s).

3. If you cannot find the leak by listening, submerge the tube in water. Look for air bubbling out (Fig. 6.9) and mark the spot(s).

Keep in mind that you can only patch small holes. If the hole is bigger than the eraser end of a pencil, a round patch is not likely to work. A slit up to an inch long or so can be repaired with an oval patch.

6-3: STANDARD PATCHES

Use a patch designed for bicycle tires; it will generally have a thin, usually orange, gummy edge surrounding a slightly thicker patch of black rubber. Rema and Delta are common brands.

1. Dry the tube thoroughly near the puncture.

2. To provide a suitable surface for the patch, rough up and clean the tube surface within about a 1-inch radius around the hole with a small piece of sandpaper (usually supplied with the patch kit). Do not touch the sanded area. If the patch kit you are using came with a little metal "cheese grater" for the purpose, discard it and replace it with sandpaper. The grater-style rougheners tend to do to your

6.9 checking for puncture

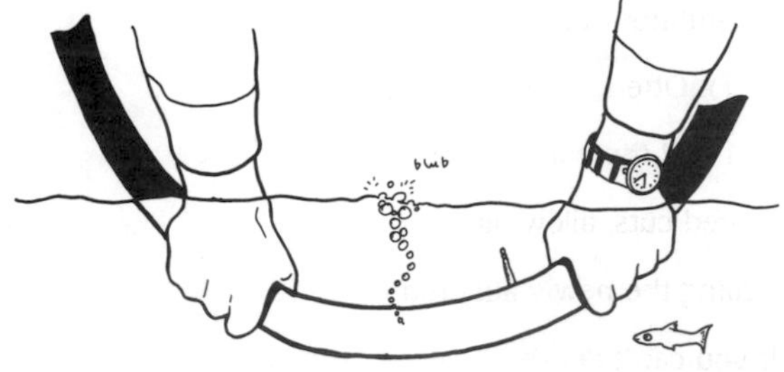

6.11 removing cellophane

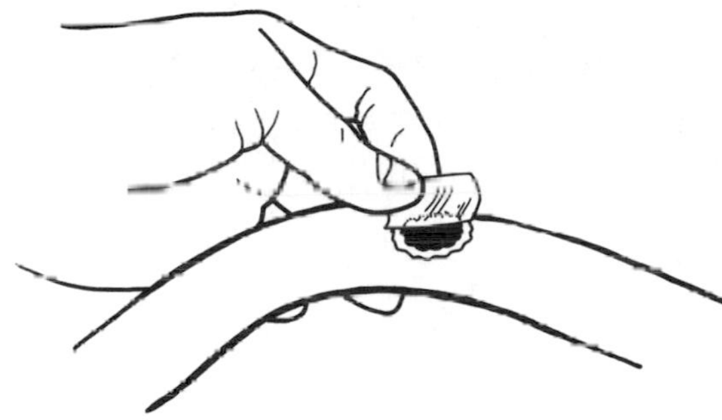

tube what they do to cheese.

3. Apply patch cement in a thin, smooth layer all over an area centered on the hole (Fig. 6.10). Use the end of the glue container or a brush, rather than your finger, to spread the glue around. Cover an area that is bigger than the size of the patch. By the way, the glue is similar to rubber cement, so if the tube in your patch kit has dried out you can use any rubber cement sold in stationery and hardware stores for the purpose. If you do this, and use the brush attached to the top of the bottle cap, wipe the brush almost dry before spreading the cement on the tube. You only need a thin layer for the patch.

4. Let the glue dry 10 minutes or so until there are no more shiny, wet spots.

5. Peel the patch from its foil backing (but do not remove the cellophane top cover yet).

6. Stick the patch over the hole, and push it down in place, making sure that all of the gummy edges are stuck down. With the tube sitting on a hard surface, burnish the patch with the plastic handle of a screwdriver to stick the edges down securely.

7. Remove the cellophane top covering, being careful not to peel off the edges of the patch (Fig. 6.11). Often, the cellophane top patch is scored. If you fold the patch, the cellophane will split at the scored cuts, allowing you to peel outward and avoid pulling the newly adhered patch up off of the tube. If you can't get the cellophane off without peeling up the patch, just leave it alone. It won't do any harm in the tire.

6-4: GLUELESS PATCHES

There are a number of adhesive-backed patches on the market that do not require cement to stick them on. Most often, you simply need to clean the area around the hole with the little alcohol pad supplied with the patch. Let the alcohol dry, peel the backing, and stick on the patch.

The advantages of glueless patches is that they are very fast to use, take little room in a seat bag, and you never open your patch kit to discover that your glue tube is dried up. On the downside, I have not found any glueless patches that stick nearly as well as the standard type. With a standard patch installed, you can inflate the tube without having it in the tire to look for more leaks. If you do that with a glueless patch, the patch usually lifts enough to start leaking. You must install the tube in the tire and on the rim before putting air in it after glueless patching. And it is probably not a permanent fix, like a Rema-type patch would be.

6-5: INSTALLING PATCHED OR NEW TUBE

If you've just fixed a flat, feel around the inside of the tire to see if there is still anything sticking through that can puncture the tube again. Sliding a

6.12-13 **installing tire by hand**

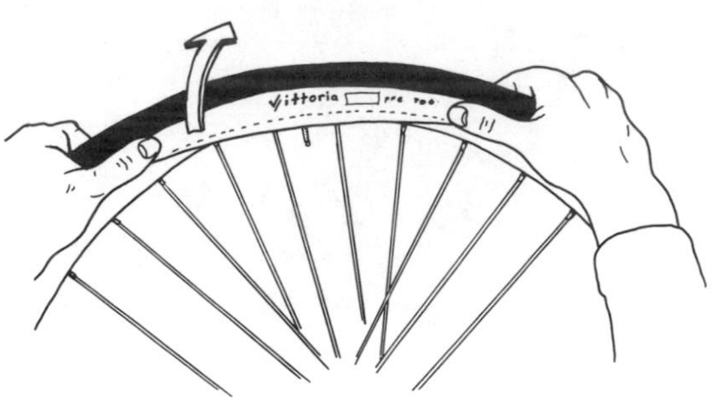

installing a patched or new tube

rag all the way around the inside of the tire works well for this. The rag will catch on anything sharp, and will save your fingers from being cut by whatever is stuck in the tire.

1. Replace any tire that has damaged areas (inside or out) where the casing fibers appear to be cut or frayed.

2. Examine the rim to be certain that the rim tape is in place and that there are no spokes or anything else sticking up that can puncture the tube. Replace the rim tape if necessary. Two layers of fiberglass strapping tape works great.

3. By hand, push one bead of the tire onto the rim.

4. (Optional) Smear baby powder around the inside of the tire and on the outside of the tube, so the two do not adhere to each other. Don't inhale this stuff, by the way.

5. Put just enough air in the tube to give it shape. Close the valve, if Presta.

Note: *If you have deep-section rim and a standard-length Presta valve, you will need to install a valve extender so you can get air into the tire once it is on the rim. To install valve extenders so they seal properly and allow easy inflation, unscrew the little nut on the Presta valve against the mashed threads at the top of the valve shaft (they are mashed to keep the nut from unscrewing completely). Back the nut firmly into these mashed threads with a pair of pliers so the nut stays unscrewed and does not tighten back down against the valve stem and prevent air from going in when you pump it. You also should wrap a turn or two of Teflon pipe thread tape around the top threads on the valve stem before screwing on the valve extender to seal it. If you do not, air will leak out when pumping, and the pressure gauge on your pump will not give an accurate reading of the pressure in the tire. Tighten the valve extender onto the valve stem with pliers.*

6. Push the valve through the valve hole in the rim.

7. Push the tube up inside the tire all of the way around.

8. Starting at the side opposite the valve stem, push the tire bead onto the rim with your thumbs. Be sure that the tube doesn't get pinched between the tire bead and the rim.

9. Work around the rim in both directions with your thumbs, pushing the tire onto the rim (Fig. 6.12). Finish from both sides at the valve (Fig. 6.13), deflating the tube when it gets hard to push more of the tire onto the rim. You can often install a tire without tools. If you cannot, use tire levers, but make sure you don't catch any of the tube under the edge of the bead. Finish the same way, at the valve.

10. Re-seat the valve stem by pushing up on the valve after you have pushed the last bit of bead onto the rim (Fig. 6.14). You may have to manipulate the tire so that all the tube is tucked under the tire bead.

11. Go around the rim and inspect for any part of the tube that might be protruding from under the edge of the tire bead. If you have a fold of the tube under the edge of the bead, it can blow the tire off the rim when you inflate it or while you are riding. It will sound like a gun went off next to you and will leave you with an unpatchable tube.

12. Pump the tire up. Generally, 85–100 psi is correct for a good-quality road tire. Much more, and you are pushing the limits of some tires. Much less, and you run the risk of a pinch flat or "snake bite."

6-6: PATCHING TIRE CASING (SIDEWALL)

Unless it is an emergency, don't do it! If the tire casing is cut, get a new tire. Patching the tire casing is dangerous. No matter what you use as a patch, the tube will find a way to bulge out of the patched hole, and when it does your tire will go flat immediately. Imagine coming down a steep hill and suddenly your front tire goes completely flat ... you get the picture.

In an emergency, you can put layers of non-stretchable material between the tube and tire (see Chapter 3, Section 3-3B, Fig. 3.1). Candidates for this duty include a dollar bill, an empty energy bar wrapper (or two), or even a short section of the exploded tube (double thickness is better).

6.14 seating the tube

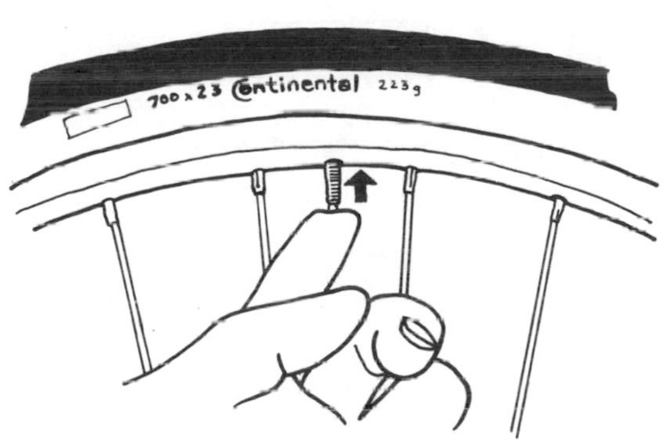

6B: TUBULAR TIRES

Tubular tires, or sew-ups, are expensive, hard to install (they must be glued to the rim), hard to repair, and these days can even be hard to find. So why bother with them?

For one thing, tubular wheelsets are generally lighter than clincher wheelsets, because tubular rims do not require flanges for the tire bead. Tubular tires by themselves are usually lighter than clinchers, too, although the difference these days is often quite small.

Another reason for the continuing popularity of these quirky throwbacks is that a lot of people say that they ride and corner better than clinchers. And being sewn together, they can be made to hold extremely high pressures.

But perhaps the main reason to consider tubulars is their inherent safety. In the event of a blowout, they stay on the rim. Clincher tires, when flat, fall into the rim well, and you may find yourself trying to ride on the slippery metal rim, rather than on a piece of rubber.

Tubulars usually deflate more slowly when punctured than clinchers, too, since the air can only escape through the puncture hole. Clinchers can let air escape all the way around the rim.

If these advantages appeal to you—and the disadvantages mentioned above don't put you off—tubulars are a worthwhile alternative to the standard clincher set-up.

6-7: REMOVING A TUBULAR

1. Remove the wheel (See Chapter 2, Section 2-2 and 2-11).

2. If the tire is not already flat, deflate it: Tubular tires have "Presta," or "French" valves. To let air out, unscrew the little nut atop the valve stem a few turns, and push down on the thin rod (Fig. 6.4). To

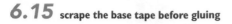

6.15 scrape the base tape before gluing

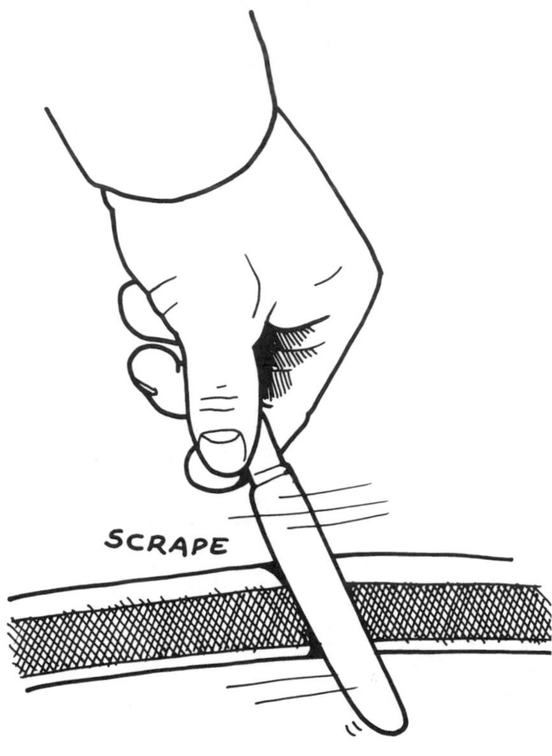

seal, tighten the little nut down again (with your fingers only!); leave it tightened for riding.

Note: *If you have deep-section rims (i.e., Mavic Cosmic, Campagnolo Shamal, Vento or Bora; Hed, Rolf, Spinergy, Zipp or any of a myriad of others), the wheels will likely have "valve extenders"—thin threaded tubes that screw onto the valve stems. To deflate the tire, you may need to insert a thin rod (a spoke is perfect) into the valve extender to release the air.*

Some tubulars now come with extra-long Presta valves for deep-section wheels. These are operated just like standard Presta valves.

3. Push the tire off of the rim in one section with your thumbs pushing up against one side. Avoid using tools. If you use a tool to pry the tire away from the glue, you will tear the base tape at the least and more likely tear casing cords as well. The tire will always be lumpy in that area after such damage.

4. Peel the tire off the rim by hand.

6-8: GLUING TUBULAR TIRES

LEVEL 2

Gluing tubular tires to the rims properly is critical to continuing the attachment you have with your epidermis. I can say from experience and from watching many riders roll improperly glued tires off of rims that you do not want it to happen to you. Follow these steps and your tire will really be secure! Pay particular attention to the second step, since all the rim cement in the world will not keep your tire on if it is not adhered to the tire.

1. Before gluing a new tubular, stretch it first over the rim (Fig. 6.16). To do this, install the tire without any glue on it using the method described in step 6.

2. Scrape the base tape of the tubular to produce a good gluing surface. The base tape on most tires is cotton and has a coating of latex over it, to which the rim cement will not bond well. The tire can roll off of even a thick layer of cement on the rim if the base tape has not been properly prepared. This step does not apply to most Continental tubulars, which usually have no latex over the base tape.

Start by pumping the tire (not on the rim) until it turns inside out and the base tape faces outward. Using the serrations of a table knife or the rough side of a metal file, scrape the base tape back and forth (Fig. 6.15) until the latex coating on the tape balls up into little sticky hunks. I have also heard of people brushing rubbing alcohol on the base tape to make the surface tacky. I generally discourage the use of solvents on the base tape for fear of solvent penetrating the tape and dissolving the glue holding the tape onto the tire. I have seen many a tire roll right off of the base tape, even though the tape is well-adhered to the rim.

3. Prepare the rim for glue. With a new rim, clean off any oil with alcohol and rough up the glu-

ing surface with sandpaper. A power die grinder with a sandpaper roll on it works great for roughing up a hard anodization layer on the rim, if you have access to one.

With a rim that has been glued before, you can just apply a uniform layer of glue, unless there is a really thick, lumpy layer of old glue on the rim. In this case, scrape the big lumps off and get the surface as uniform as you can.

4. Put a thin layer of glue on the rim, edge-to-edge, and edge-to-edge on the base tape of the tire, as well. I recommend squeezing a bead out of the tube and then putting a plastic bag over your finger and spreading the glue on the tire and rim thinly and uniformly. Let it dry a couple of hours. Repeat.

Pro track riders do this procedure at least six times, as the more thin layers you have, the better the bond. Tandem track sprinters need lots more layers yet. More than two layers is not necessary for most road use.

Let the second layer dry overnight, or at least several hours in the warm sun. The glue on the rim and the tire should feel dry to the touch and will not get all over your hands and legs when you stretch the tire.

I recommend using red rim glue made specifically for tubulars, of which there are several brands, rather than clear glues, some of which stay tacky and do not harden up. This may be attributable to solvent in the glue, which can break down the glue holding the base tape onto the tire. The only disadvantage to the red glues is that they harden up; if you leave them on for years, they get so dried out that the tire is not held well and needs to be re-glued.

If you are in a hurry and need to use the wheel within a few hours, you can use 3M Fast Tack automotive trim adhesive as a rim cement. Many riders swear by it. In my experience, it dries faster but

6.16 stretch the tubular over the rim

does not seem to bond as strongly as red rim glue and can cause the solvent softening of the base tape glue.

5. After the glue on the rim and tire has dried overnight (or a couple of hours with Fast Tack), smear another thin layer of glue on the rim. Let this set for 15 minutes.

6. Deflate and mount the tire as follows. Stand the wheel up with the valve hole facing up. Put the valve stem through the hole, and, leaning over the wheel, grab the tire and stretch outward as you push the base tape into the top of the rim. Keep stretching down on the tire with both hands, using your body weight, as you push the tire down around the rim (Fig. 6.16). I like to lean hard enough on the tire that my feet lift repeatedly off of the ground. The further you can stretch the tire at this point, the easier it will be to get the last bit of tire onto the rim.

Lifting the rim up to horizontal with the valve

side against your belly, roll the last bit of the tire onto the opposite side of the rim. If you can't get the tire to pop over the rim, peel the tire back and start over, pushing down again from the valve stem. You want to avoid the temptation of prying a stubborn tire onto the rim with screwdrivers or other tools, as you will likely tear cords in the base tape and tire casing, leading to a bulge in the tire in this area.

7. By pulling the tire this way and that, get the edge of the base tape aligned with the rim. You want to see the same amount sticking out from the rim all the way around on both sides around the wheel.

8. Pump the tire to 100 psi and spin the wheel, looking for wobbles in the tire. If you find that the tread snakes back and forth as you spin the wheel, deflate the tire and push it over where required. Reinflate and check again, repeating the process until the tire is as straight as you are willing to get it. The final process will depend somewhat on how accurately the tubular was made; you'll find that some brands and models glue on straighter than others.

9. Pump the tire up to 120–130 psi and leave it overnight to bond firmly.

You can get an even better bond by using a woodworker's band (miter) clamp around the entire inflated tire. The miter clamp (see Chapter 1, Fig. 1.3) is a piece of nylon webbing with a cam-lock buckle on it. Depress the tab on the buckle to let out enough strap to surround the inflated tire and wheel. Pull the end of the strap to tighten the loop around the tire. Use a wrench to tighten the clamp and put extra pressure down on the tire to conform its bottom surface to the rim and bond it tightly. Tomorrow you can release the miter clamp (using the thumb release tab) and go ride or race on this wheel.

6-9: CHANGING A TUBULAR TIRE ON THE ROAD

If you get a puncture out on the road with a tubular tire, you will find that it is easier to deal with than a flat clincher. You want to make sure that you are carrying a spare tubular that already has glue on the base tape. For your spare, bring along an old tubular that has been glued to a rim in the past, or, with a new tire as a spare, follow steps 1-4 in section 6-8 above.

Remove the wheel and pull the flat tire off of the rim. If you did a good gluing job, this may take some doing. (On the other hand, if the tubular is easy to peel off, you need to improve your gluing technique.) Stretch the spare tire onto the rim as in steps 6 and 7 in section 6-8 above. Pump it up hard (over 100 psi) to get it to stay on the rim for the rest of the ride. Corner carefully going home, as the glue bond is marginal. When you get home, glue a tire securely on the rim before riding that wheel again.

6-10: PATCHING TUBULAR TIRES

LEVEL 2

In the early 1980s, my racing buddies and I spent countless hours patching tubular tires, often while sitting in the car on the way to distant races. Now that everyone trains on clinchers, nobody seems to patch tubulars any more. Tubulars are arguably still the best tires for racing, being lighter, requiring lighter rims, and being able to hold tremendous pressures due to being sewn together (the high air pressure reduces the rolling resistance of the tire on the road). However, even though tubulars are expensive, it makes no sense to patch a racing tire, since you invest too much time, energy and money competing in races to run the risk of puncturing a bad tire.

If for some reason you still wish to patch a tubular, here are the steps involved:

changing a tubular on the road — patching a tubular

1. Remove the tire from the rim.

2. Pump up the tire to 70 psi, or as high as you can, and find the leak by submerging the inflated tire in a bucket of water. If you're lucky, air will come out through a hole in the tread. In the case of a pinched tube, though, the air may seep out through the casing randomly at the stitches, and be hard to localize. See the next step for help.

3. In the region 2 inches on either side of the puncture, peel away the base tape covering the stitching. If you were unable to precisely locate the hole, try submerging the inflated tire now to watch the bubbles coming out through the stitching. Peel more base tape back if necessary until you are sure that you have exposed the stitching at the hole.

4. Deflate the tire and carefully cut the outer layer of stitching threads for an inch or so on either side of the hole. Pull the casing open in that spot, and pull enough of the tube out through the hole to find and access the hole(s) in it.

5. Patch the tube in the same manner as outlined in section 6-2 above, using the same type of recommended patches.

6. Push the tube back in place, and sew the opening in the stitching closed by hand. I recommend using a leather needle with a triangular-cross-section tip and braided high-test fishing line. Stitch one way across the opening, turn the tire around and double back over the stitches again. For obvious reasons, be careful not to poke the tube. You may need a thimble to push the needle in and a pair of pliers to pull it out on each stitch.

Inflate the tire to 70 psi or so to make sure all of the leaks have been patched.

7. Deflate the tire and coat the peeled-back section of base tape and the exposed stitching area with contact cement. Barge glue for shoes works great. Wait 15 minutes or so for the glue to set, and carefully stick the base tape back down over the stitching. (If the tape stretched when you pulled it loose, it's permissible to cut it and overlap the ends.)

8. Coat the rim and the tire base tape with a thin layer of rim cement. Let it sit 15 minutes to an hour. Since this is an old tire, there should already be a good layer of rim cement on the tire and the rim.

9. Glue the tire onto the rim (see section 6-8).

6-11: TIRE SEALANTS

Tire sealants can virtually eliminate flat tires caused by tread punctures; they do not fix sidewall cuts. The most popular tire sealant, Slime, is a primordial green goo full of chopped fibers; when poured into an inner tube, it flows to punctures and seals them. There are other brands and colors of tire sealants as well; these instructions generally apply to them all.

Only use Slime in a clincher tube without cuts in it. The tube must also have a Schrader valve in good condition (Fig. 1.1, 6.5). By the way, you can put sealant in a tube that already has a slow leak; simply inject it as below, pump it up, and spin the wheel for about five minutes.

Note: *If you have Presta valves (Fig. 6.4), and you want to use tire sealant, you can purchase tubes with sealant already inside.*

A. Slime installation into a tube that's already installed in a tire

1. Shake the Slime bottle.

2. Remove the Schrader valve core using the valve cap/core-remover packaged with the Slime.

3. Rotate the wheel so the valve stem is at the 4 o'clock position.

4. Cut off the bottle spout, and connect the bottle spout and valve stem with the supplied tubing.

5. Squeeze the bottle slowly to inject the Slime.

6. Stop squeezing after injecting 4 ounces.; wait several minutes to clear the stem.

7. Remove the tube.

8. Screw the valve core firmly back into the valve stem in a clockwise direction.

9. Inflate the tube.

If the tube has a leak, spin the wheel for five minutes to spread the Slime around in the tube.

B. Maintaining tire-sealant-filled tubes

Inflating: Always have the stem at 4 o'clock and wait a minute for the sealant to drain away; if you don't, sealant will leak out, eventually clogging the valve.

Sealing punctures:

1. If you find the tire has gone flat, pump it up and ride it a bit to see if it seals.

2. If you get numerous punctures, you may need to pump repeatedly and ride before the tube seals up.

3. Pinch flats, caused by pinching the tube between the tire and rim, are hard to seal because the two "snake-bite" holes are on the side. Try laying the bike on the same side as the holes.

4. Imbedded nails and other foreign objects can be removed; spin the wheel to seal the hole.

5. Punctures on the rim side of the tube will not seal, because the sealant is thrown to the outside by centrifugal force.

6. Sidewall gashes need to be patched, and the tire needs to be replaced.

truing a wheel

6C: RIMS & SPOKES

6-12: TRUING A WHEEL

For more information on truing wheels, see Chapter 12 on wheel building, section 12-4.

If the wheel has a mild wobble in it, you can fix it by adjusting the tension on the spokes. An extreme bend in the rim cannot be fixed by spoke truing alone, since the spoke tension on the two sides of the wheel will be so uneven that the wheel will rapidly fall apart.

1. Check that there are no broken spokes in the wheel, or any spokes that are so loose that they flop around. If there is a broken spoke, follow the replacement procedure in the following section, 6-13. If there is a single loose spoke, check to see that the rim is not dented or cracked in that area. I recommend replacing the rim if it is. If the rim looks okay, mark the loose spoke with a piece of tape, and tighten it up with the spoke wrench until it feels the same tension as adjacent spokes on the same side of the wheel (pluck the spoke and listen to the tone). Then follow the truing procedure below.

2. Grab the rim while the wheel is on the bike, and flex it side to side to check the hub bearing adjustment. If the bearings are loose, the wheel will clunk side to side. The play in the bearings will have to be eliminated before you true the wheel or the rim will wobble erratically due to the loose hub. Follow the hub adjustment procedure, Section 6-16D, steps 28-31, in this chapter.

3. Put the wheel in a truing stand, if you have one. Otherwise, leave it on the bike and suspend the bike in a bike stand or from the ceiling, or turn it upside down on the handlebars and saddle.

4. Adjust the truing stand feeler, or hold one of your brake pads so that it scrapes the rim at the biggest wobble.

5. Where the rim scrapes, tighten the spoke (or spokes) that come(s) to the rim from the opposite side of the hub, and loosen the spoke(s) that come(s) from the same side of the hub (Figs. 6.18 and 6.19). This will pull the rim away from the feeler or brake pad.

When correcting a wheel that is laterally out of

6.17 tightening and loosening spokes

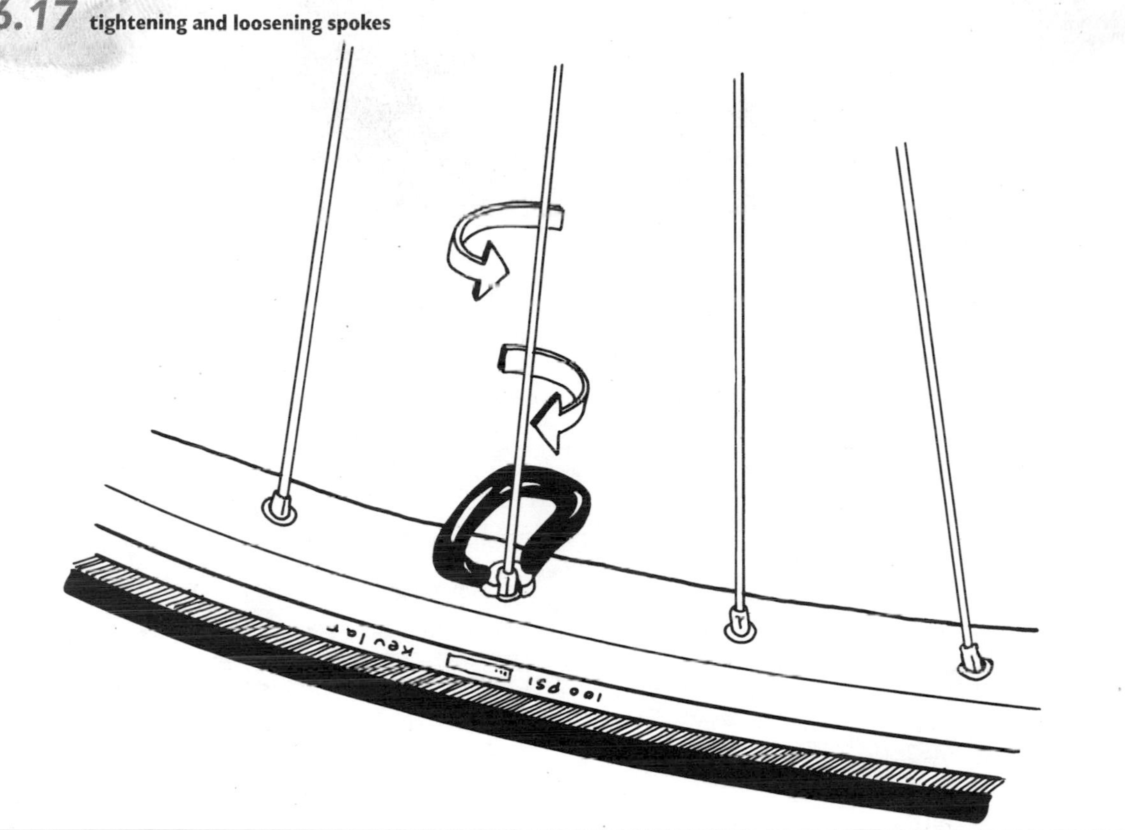

true (wobbles side-to-side), always adjust spokes in pairs: one spoke coming from one side of the wheel, the other from the opposite side. Tightening spokes is like opening a jar upside down. With the jar right-side up, turning the lid to the left (counter clockwise) opens the jar, but this reverses when you turn the jar upside down (try it and see). Spoke nipples are just like the lid on that upside-down jar: When the nipples are at the bottom of the rim, counter-clockwise tightens, and clockwise loosens (Fig. 6.17). The opposite is true when the nipples to be turned are at the top. It may take you a few attempts before you catch on, but you will eventually get it. If you temporarily make the wheel worse, simply undo what you have done and start over.

It is best to tighten and loosen by small amounts (about a quarter-turn at a time), decreasing the amount you turn the spoke nipples as you move

6.18-19 lateral truing

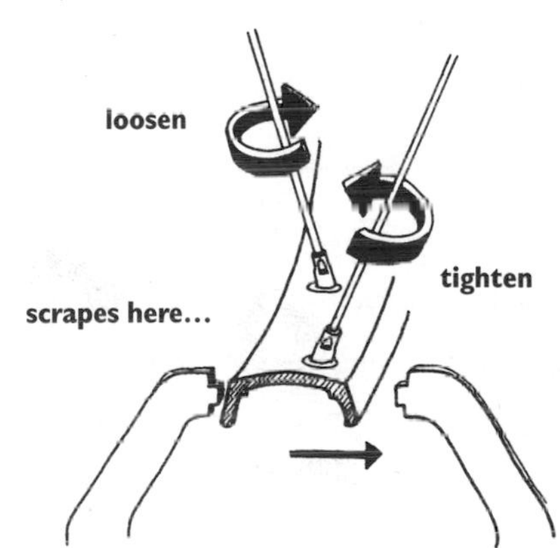

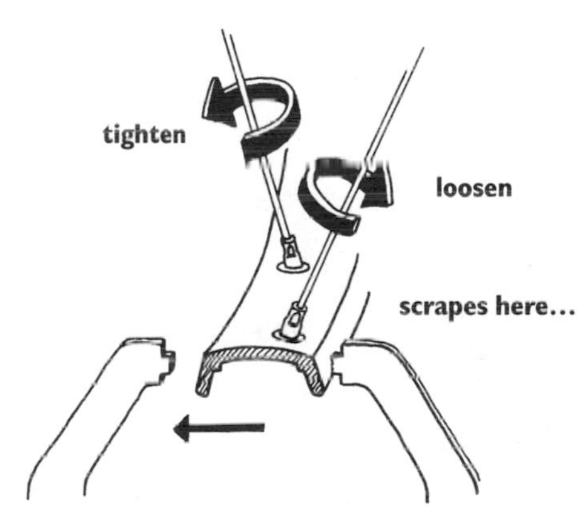

6.20 weaving a new spoke

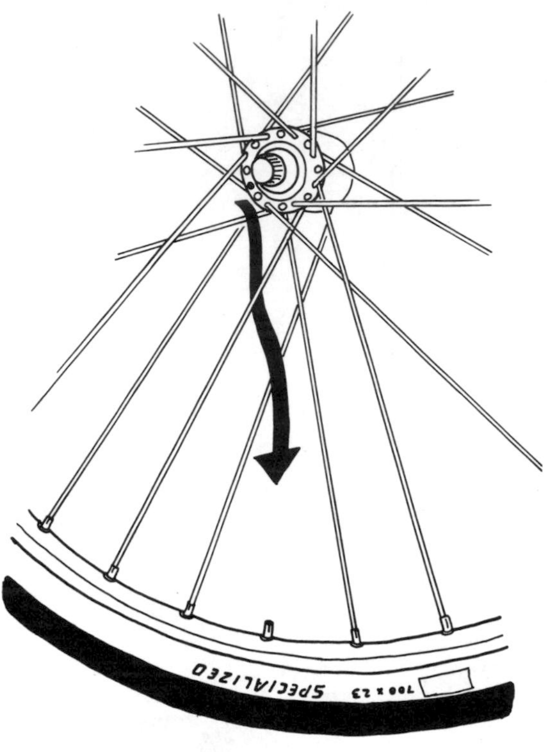

away from the spot where the rim scrapes the hardest. If the wobble gets worse, then you are turning the spokes the wrong direction.

6. As the rim moves into proper alignment, readjust the truing-stand feeler or the brake pad so that it again finds the most out-of-true spot on the wheel.

7. Check the wobble first on one side of the wheel and then the other, adjusting spokes accordingly, so that you don't end up pulling the whole wheel off center by chasing wobbles only on one side. As the wheel gets closer to true, you will need to decrease the amount you turn the spokes; otherwise, you will over-correct.

8. Accept a certain amount of wobble, especially if you are truing the wheel in a bike; the method is not very accurate and is not at all suited for making a wheel absolutely true. If you have access to a wheel dishing tool, check to make sure that the wheel is centered (Chapter 12, section 12-5).

6-13: REPLACING A BROKEN SPOKE

LEVEL 2

Go to the bike store and get a new spoke of the same length. Remember: the spokes on the front wheel are usually not the same length as the spokes on the rear wheel. Also, the spokes on the drive (right) side of the rear wheel are almost always shorter than those on the non-drive (left) side.

1. Make sure you are using a replacement spoke of the proper thickness and length.

2. Thread the spoke through the spoke hole in the hub flange. If the broken spoke is on the drive side of the rear wheel, you will need to remove the cassette cogs or the freewheel to get at the hub flange (Sections 6-20 and 6-21).

3. Weave the new spoke in with the other spokes just as it was before (Fig. 6.20). It may take some bending to get it in place.

4. Thread it into the same nipple, if the nipple is in good shape. Otherwise, use a new nipple; you'll need to remove the tire, tube, and rim strip (or the tubular tire) to install the nipple.

5. Mark the new spoke with a piece of tape, and tighten it up about as snugly as the neighboring spokes on that side of the wheel.

6. Follow the steps for truing a wheel as outlined above, section 6-12.

6D: HUBS

6-14: OVERHAULING HUBS

LEVEL 2

Hubs should turn smoothly and noiselessly. If you maintain them regularly, you can expect them to still be running smoothly when you are ready to give up on the rest of your bike.

All hubs have a "hub shell" that contains the axle

6.21 front hub with cartridge bearing

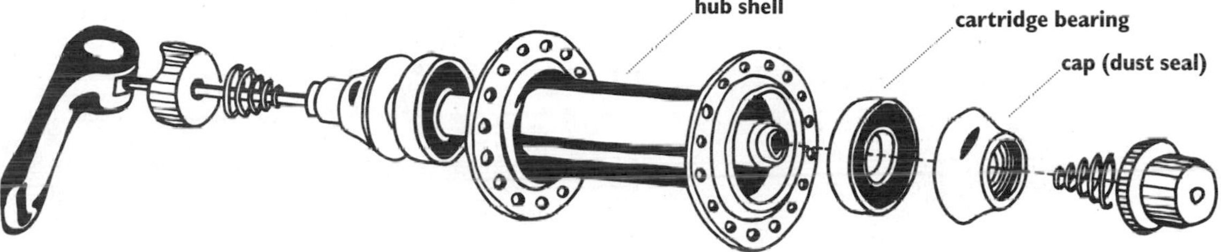

6.22 front hub with standard ball bearings

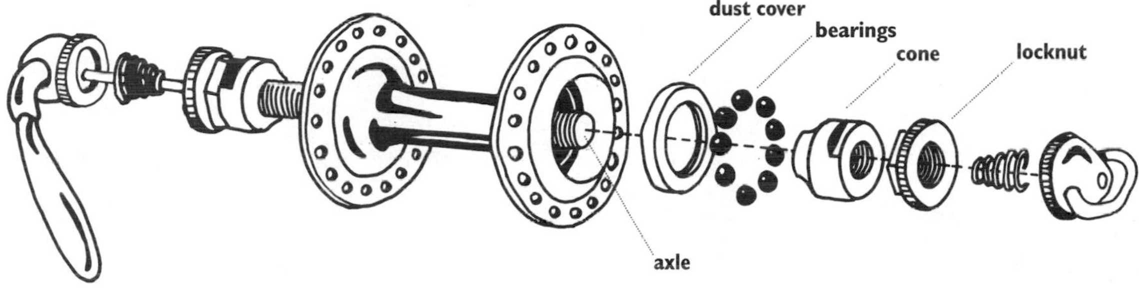

and bearings and is connected to the rim with spokes, or in the case of disc wheels, by sheets of composite material. Beyond that, they diverge into two types: the standard "cup and cone" type (Fig. 6.22), and the "sealed bearing" (or "cartridge bearing") type (Fig. 6.21).

Standard cup-and-cone hubs have loose ball bearings that roll along very smooth bearing surfaces called "races" or "cups;" an axle runs through the center of the hub. Conical nuts, called "cones" (Fig. 6.22), thread onto the axle. The cones create an inner race for the bearings. In high-quality hubs, the cup and cone surfaces that contact the bearings are precisely machined to minimize friction. The operation of the hub depends on the smoothness and lubrication of the cones, ball bearings, and bearing races. The cones are held in place on the axle by one or more spacers (washers) followed by threaded locknuts that tighten down against the cones and spacers to keep the hub in proper adjustment. The rear hub will have more spacers on both sides, especially on the drive side (Fig. 6.31).

The term "sealed-bearing" hub is a bit of a misnomer, since many cup-and-cone hubs offer better protection against dirt and water than some sealed-bearing hubs. The phrase "cartridge-bearing hub" is more accurate, since the distinguishing feature of these hubs is that the bearings, races and cones are assembled as a complete unit at the bearing factory, and then plugged into a hub shell machined to accept the cartridge. Cartridge-bearing front hubs have two bearings, one on each end of the hub shell (Fig. 6.21). Rear hubs (Fig. 6.30) may have a cartridge bearing on the left side only, and may employ a stock Shimano freehub with loose hub bearings as well as loose freehub bearings on the drive side. Some manufacturers make their own freehubs and have cartridge bearings on both sides of the hub as well as internal to the freehub.

Cartridge-bearing hubs can have any number of axle assembly types. Some have a threaded axle with locknuts quite similar to a cup-and-cone hub. More common in the high end are aluminum axles, often very fat with correspondingly large bearings.

6.23 loosening and tightening locknut

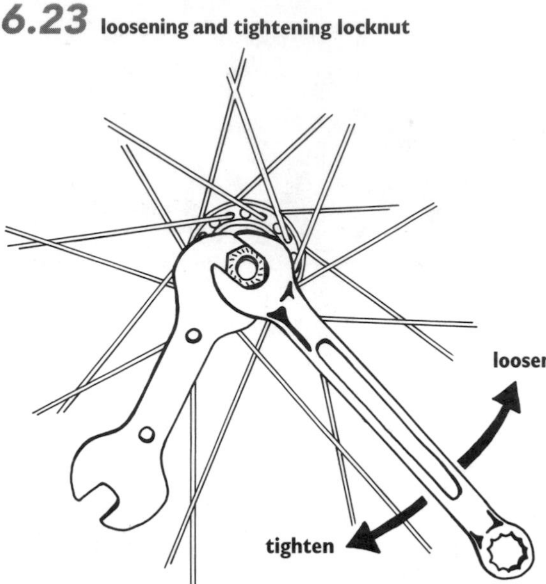

Their end caps usually snap on or are held on with set screws or circlips. The end caps may also thread into the axle and accept a 5mm hex key in the end of each cap.

6-15: ALL HUBS, PRELIMINARY

1. Remove the wheel from the bike (Chapter 2, Sections 2-2 and 2-11).

2. Remove the quick-release skewer or the nuts and washers holding the wheel onto the bike.

overhaul standard "cup-and-cone" hubs

6-16: OVERHAUL STANDARD "CUP-AND-CONE" HUB, FRONT OR REAR

To isolate problems, take some time to evaluate the hub's condition before disassembling it. Spin the hub while holding the axle, and turn the axle while holding the hub. Does it turn roughly? Is the axle bent or broken? Wobble the axle side to side. Is the bearing adjustment loose?

a. Disassembly:

1. Set the wheel flat on a table or workbench. Slip a cone wrench of the appropriate size (usually 13mm, 14mm or 15mm) onto the wrench flats on one of the cones. On a rear wheel, work on the left (non-cog) side.

2. Put an appropriately sized wrench or adjustable wrench on the locknut on the same side.

3. While holding the cone with the cone wrench, loosen the locknut (Fig. 6.23). This may take considerable force, since the parts are usually tightened against each other very securely to maintain the hub's adjustment. Make sure that you are unscrewing the locknut counterclockwise ("lefty loosey, righty tighty").

4. As soon as the locknut loosens, move the cone wrench from the cone on top to the cone on the opposite end of the axle, in order to hold the axle in place as you unscrew the locknut. On a rear hub, put another open-end wrench on the opposite locknut. Unscrew the loose locknut with your fingers; use a wrench if necessary.

5. Slide any spacers off, keeping track of where they came from. If they will not slide off, the cone will push them off when you unscrew it. Note that some spacers have a small tooth or "key" that corresponds to a notch on the axle. Keep these lined up to facilitate removal.

6. Unscrew the cone from the axle. Again, you may need to hold the opposite cone with a wrench. An easy way to keep track of the various nuts, spacers and cones is to lay them on your work bench in the order they were removed. If that seems too casual, you can slide a twist-tie through all the parts in the correct order of orientation. Either method serves as an easy guide when reassembling the hub.

7. To catch any bearings that might fall out, put your hand over the end of the hub from which you removed the nuts and spacers and flip the wheel over. Have a rag underneath the wheel to catch stray bearings.

8. Pull the axle up and out, being careful not to lose any bearings that might fall out of the hub or might stick briefly to the axle. Leave the cone, spac-

ers, and locknut all tightened together on the opposite end of the axle from the one you disassembled. If you are replacing a bent or broken axle, measure the amount of axle sticking out beyond the locknut. Put the cone, spacers and locknut on the new axle identically.

9. Remove all of the ball bearings from both sides of the hub. They may stick to a screwdriver with a coating of grease on the tip, or you can push them down through the center of the hub and out the other side with the screwdriver. Tweezers or a magnetic screwdriver might also be useful for removing bearings. Put the bearings in a cup, a jar lid, or the like. Count the bearings, and make sure you have the same number from each side.

10. With a screwdriver, gently pop off the seals that are pressed into either end of the hub shell (Fig. 6.24). Be careful not to deform them; leave them in if you can't pop them out without damage. If they are not removed, it is tedious, but not impossible, to clean the dirty grease out of their concave interior with a rag and a thin screwdriver.

b. Cleaning:

11. Wipe out the hub shell with a rag. Remove all dirt and grease from the bearing surfaces. Using a screwdriver, push a rag through the hub shell and spin it to clean out the hub shell axle hole. Wipe off the outer faces of the shell. Finish with a very clean rag on the bearing surfaces, which should be shiny and completely free of dirt or grease. If the hub has been neglected, the grease may have solidified and glazed over so completely that you will need a solvent to remove it. Use gloves with the solvent. If you have a rear cassette hub, take this opportunity to lubricate the cassette. (See section 6-22 on lubricating cassettes and freewheels.)

12. Wipe down the axle, nuts and cones with a rag. Clean the cones well with a clean rag; strive for spotless. Again, solvent may be required if the grease has solidified. Get any dirt out of the threads on the disassembled axle end to prevent the cone from pushing the dirt into the hub upon reassembly.

6.24 removing dustcap

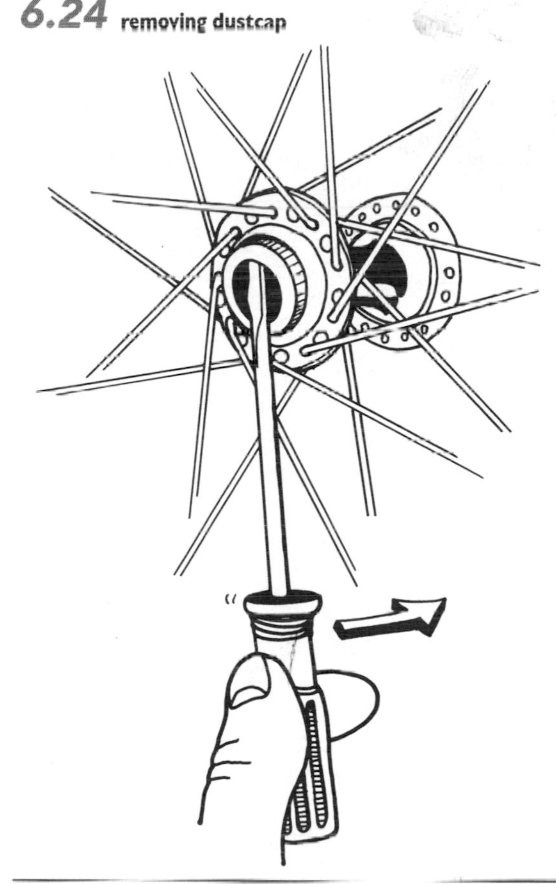

13. Wipe the grease and dirt off the seals. A rag over the end of a screwdriver is sometimes useful to get inside. Again, glaze-hard grease may have to be removed with a solvent. Keep solvent out of the freehub body.

Note: *Using new ball bearings when overhauling standard "cup and cone" hubs assures round, smooth bearings; however, do not avoid performing an overhaul just because you don't have any new ball bearings. Inspect the bearings carefully. If there is even the slightest hint of uneven wear or pitting on the balls, cups or cones, throw the bearings out and complete the overhaul with new bearings. Err on the side of caution.*

14. Wipe off the bearings by rubbing all of them

6.25 **push inward on the axle and flip the wheel over**

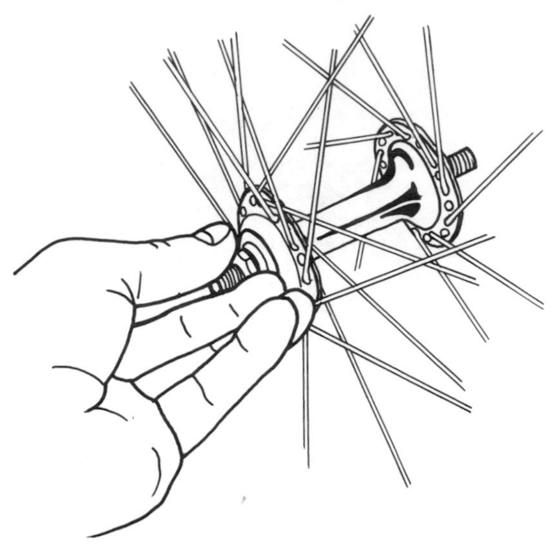

6.26 **seat the bottom cone in the bearings**

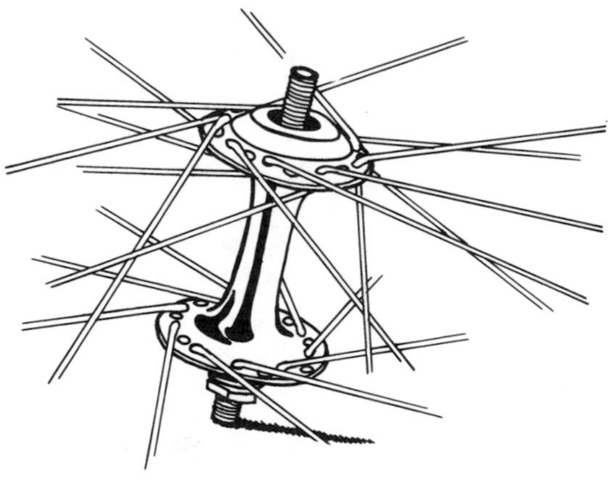

together between two rags. This may be sufficient to clean them completely, but small specks of dirt can still adhere to them, so I advise the next step as well.

15. If you are overhauling low-quality hubs, skip to step 16.

Otherwise, polish the bearings. I prefer to wash them in a plugged sink with an abrasive soap like Lava, rubbing them between my hands as if I were washing my palms. This really gets them shining, unless they are caked with glaze-hard grease. Make sure you have plugged the sink drain! This method has the added advantage of getting my hands clean for the assembly step. It is silly to contaminate your super-clean parts with dirty hands. If there is hardened glaze on the bearings, soak them in solvent. If that does not remove it, buy new bearings at the bike shop. Take a few of the old bearings along so you get the right size.

16. Dry all bearings and any other wet parts. Inspect the bearings and bearing surfaces carefully. If any of the bearings have pits or gouges in them, replace all of them. Same goes for the cones. A patina or lack of sheen on balls and cones indicates wear and is cause for replacement. Most bike shops stock replacement cones. If the bearing races (or cups) in the hub shell are pitted, the only thing you can do is buy new hubs. Regular maintenance can prevent pitted bearing races.

c. Assembly and lubrication:

17. Press the seals or dust covers in on both ends of the hub shell.

18. Smear grease with your clean finger into the bearing race on one end of the hub shell. I like using light-colored or clear grease so that I can see if it gets dirty, but any bike grease will do. Grease not only lubricates the bearings, it also forms a barrier to dirt and water, so use enough grease to cover the balls halfway. Too much grease will slow the hub by packing around the axle.

19. Stick half of the ball bearings into the grease, making sure you put in the same number of bearings that came out. Distribute them uniformly around in the bearing race.

20. Smear grease on the cone that is still attached to the axle, and slide the axle into the hub shell. Lift the wheel up a bit (30-degree angle), so you can push the axle in until the cone slides into position, keeping all the bearings in place. On rear hubs, it is important to replace the axle and cone assembly into the same side of the hub from which it was removed to preserve drive-side cog spacing.

21. Holding the axle pushed inward with one

hand to secure the bearings, turn the wheel over (Fig. 6.25).

22. Smear grease into the bearing race that is now facing up. Lift the wheel and allow the axle to slide down just enough so that it is not sticking up past the bearing race. Make sure no bearings fall out of the bottom. If the race and bearings are properly greased and the axle remains in the hub shell, they are not likely to fall out.

23. While the top end of the axle is still below the bearing race, place the remaining bearings uniformly around in the grease. Make sure you have inserted the correct number of bearings.

24. Slide the axle into place by setting the wheel down on the table, so that the wheel rests on the lower axle end, seating the cone into the bearings (Fig. 6.26).

25. Cover the top cone with a film of grease and then, using your fingers, screw it into place, seating it snugly onto the bearings.

26. In correct order, slide on the washer and any spacers. Watch for those washers with the little tooth or "key" that fits into the lengthwise groove in the axle.

27. Use your finger to screw on the locknut. Note that the two sides of the locknut are not the same. If you are unsure about which way the locknut goes back on, check the orientation of the locknut that is on the opposite end of the axle (this locknut was not removed during this overhaul and is assumed to be in the correct orientation). As a general rule, the rough surface of the locknut faces out so that it can get a better purchase on the dropout.

d. Hub adjustment:

28. Thread the cone onto the axle until it lightly contacts the bearings. The axle should turn smoothly without any roughness or grinding, and there should be a small amount of lateral play. Thread the locknut down until it is snug against the cone.

29. Place the cone wrench into the flats of the hub cone. While holding the cone steady, tighten the locknut with another wrench (Fig. 6.27). Tighten it about as snugly as you can against the cone and spacers, in order to hold the adjustment. Be sure that you are tightening the locknut and not the cone; you can ruin the hub if you tighten the cone hard against the bearings.

30. If there is too much play in the axle when you are done, or if the bearings are tight, loosen the locknut while holding the cone with the cone wrench. If the hub is too tight, unscrew the cone a bit. If the hub is too loose, screw the cone in a bit. You may need to put a wrench on the opposite-side cone to effectively tighten or loosen the cone you are adjusting.

31. Repeat Steps 28-30 until the hub adjustment feels right. There should be a slight amount of axle end play so that the pressure of the quick release skewer will compress it to perfect adjustment. (A nutted hub—no quick release—should be adjusted with no bearing play.) Tighten the locknut firmly against the cone to hold the adjustment.

6.27 loosening and tightening locknut

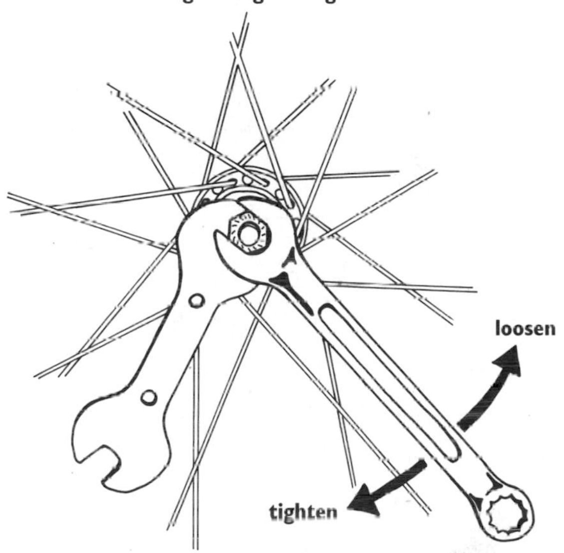

Note: *You may find that tightening the locknut against the cone suddenly turns your "Mona Lisa" perfect hub adjustment into something slightly less beautiful. If it is too tight, back off both cones (with a cone wrench on either side of the hub, each on one cone) a fraction of a turn. If too loose, tighten both locknuts a bit. If still off, you might have to loosen one side and go back to step 29. It's rare that I get a hub adjustment perfectly dialed-in on the first try, so don't be dismayed if you have to tinker with the adjustment a bit before it's right.*

32. Put the skewer back into the hub. Make sure that the conical springs have their narrow ends toward the inside (Fig. 6.22).

33. Install the wheel in the bike and tighten the skewer. Check that the wheel spins well without any side play at the rim. If it needs readjustment, go back to Step 31.

34. Congratulate yourself on a job well done! Hub overhaul is a delicate job, and it makes a difference in the longevity and performance of your bike.

6-17: OVERHAUL CARTRIDGE-BEARING HUB

cartridge hub overhaul

LEVEL 2

Cartridge-bearing hubs generally do not need much maintenance. If you ride through water above the hubs, however, you can expect water and dirt to get through any kind of seal. If the ball bearings inside the cartridges get wet, they should be overhauled or replaced.

There are many types of cartridge-bearing hubs, and it is outside the scope of this book to explain how to disassemble every one of them. Generally, though, there will be end caps that can be removed by: (1) pulling or prying them off, (2) sliding them off after loosening a set screw on each cap, (3) unscrewing the caps with a 5mm Allen wrench inserted into the 5mm hex flats in the through-hole in either axle end, or (4) yanking the cassette straight off of the hub by hand.

Once the end cap is removed, you can often smack the end of the axle with a soft hammer or on a table to dislodge the opposite bearing (Fig. 6.28). Pop the other bearing out the same way. The axle usually has a shoulder on each side, internal to the bearings, which can force the bearings out when tapping on the end of the axle. Cartridge bearings are vulnerable to lateral stress; if you have to use a lot of force to pound them out, they will need to be replaced. Be careful when tapping them back in; hold one of the old bearings against each new bearing, and tap the old bearing with the hammer to drive the new one into place.

Once the cartridge bearings are out, you can sometimes overhaul them (otherwise you'll need to buy new ones):

1. Gently pop the bearing covers off with a single-edge razor blade (Fig. 6.29).

2. Squirt citrus-based solvent into the bearing under pressure (wear rubber gloves and protective glasses) to wash out the grease, water and dirt. Scrub with a clean toothbrush.

3. Dry the bearing with compressed air.

4. Pack the bearing with grease and snap the bearing covers back on.

5. Reassemble the hub the opposite way it came apart. Sometimes the bearings will be out of alignment slightly after installation, making the hub noticeably hard to turn. A light tap on either end of the axle with a soft hammer will often free them.

Note: *Reinstalling the bearings in most of today's cartridge-bearing hubs is relatively easy: simply press the bearings with your hand, or use the shoulder on the axle as a punch to press the bearings into place. In most cases, even a soft hammer is not necessary.*

6.28 **tapping out cartridge bearing**

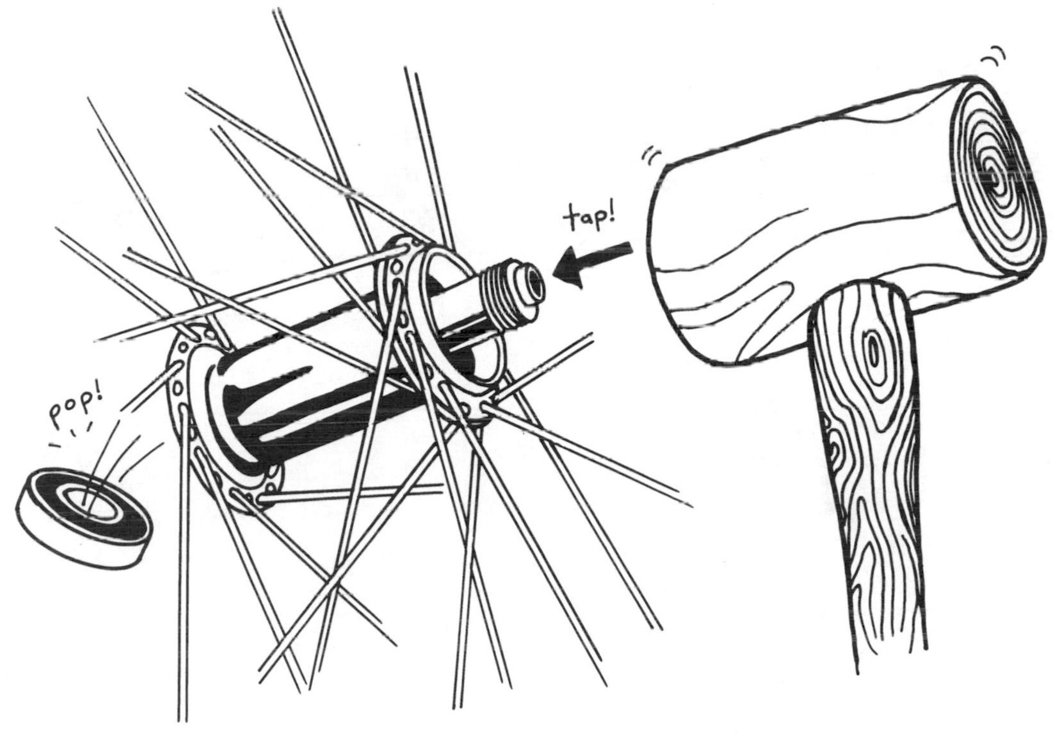

However, with older cartridge-bearing hubs (Suntour, Sanshin, Specialized, and others), it isn't so easy. The tolerance between the hub cups and the outer surface of the bearing is so tight that these bearings must be pressed in or pounded in with a hammer. A direct blow from a hammer would ruin the bearing, so with these types of hubs, it is best to use either an old cartridge bearing or a similarly sized disc of metal that acts on the outer bearing edge to tap the bearings into the hub.

6-18: GREASE GUARD HUBS

Wilderness Trail Bikes, Suntour, Campagnolo and others make high-end hubs, some labeled Grease Guard, equipped with grease ports that accept a small-tipped grease gun. Injecting grease into the ports forces lubricant through the bearings from the inside and flushes the old grease out of the outside. Also, look for these grease ports on the freehub body under the cogs. Grease injection systems do not eliminate the need for overhauling your hubs, but they extend the amount of time between overhauls. While convenient, these systems are only as good as you are about using them.

6.29 **removing bearing seal**

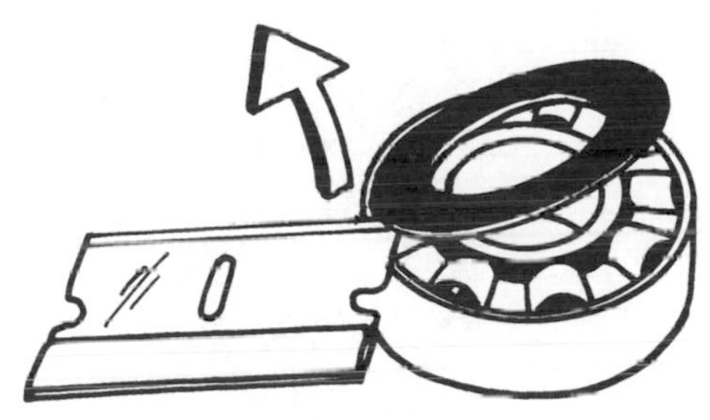

6E: FREEHUBS, FREEWHEELS AND COGS

Freehubs and freewheels allow the rear wheel to turn freely independent of the chain. Most rely on a series of pawls that engage when pressure is applied to the pedals and disengage when the rider is coasting.

A freehub is an integral part of the rear hub. The

6.30 rear freehub with cartridge bearings and cassette cogs

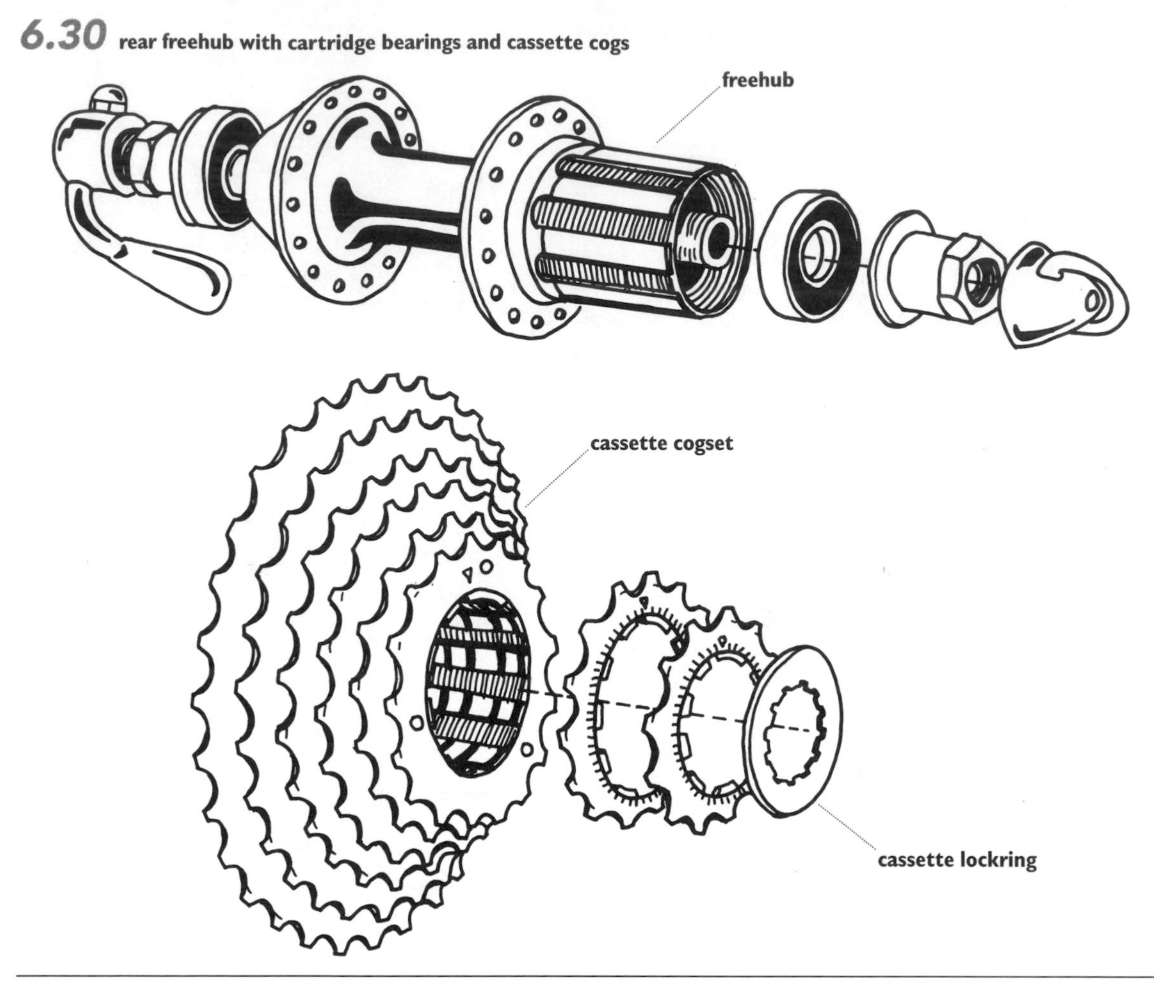

6.31 threaded rear hub with standard ball bearings and freewheel

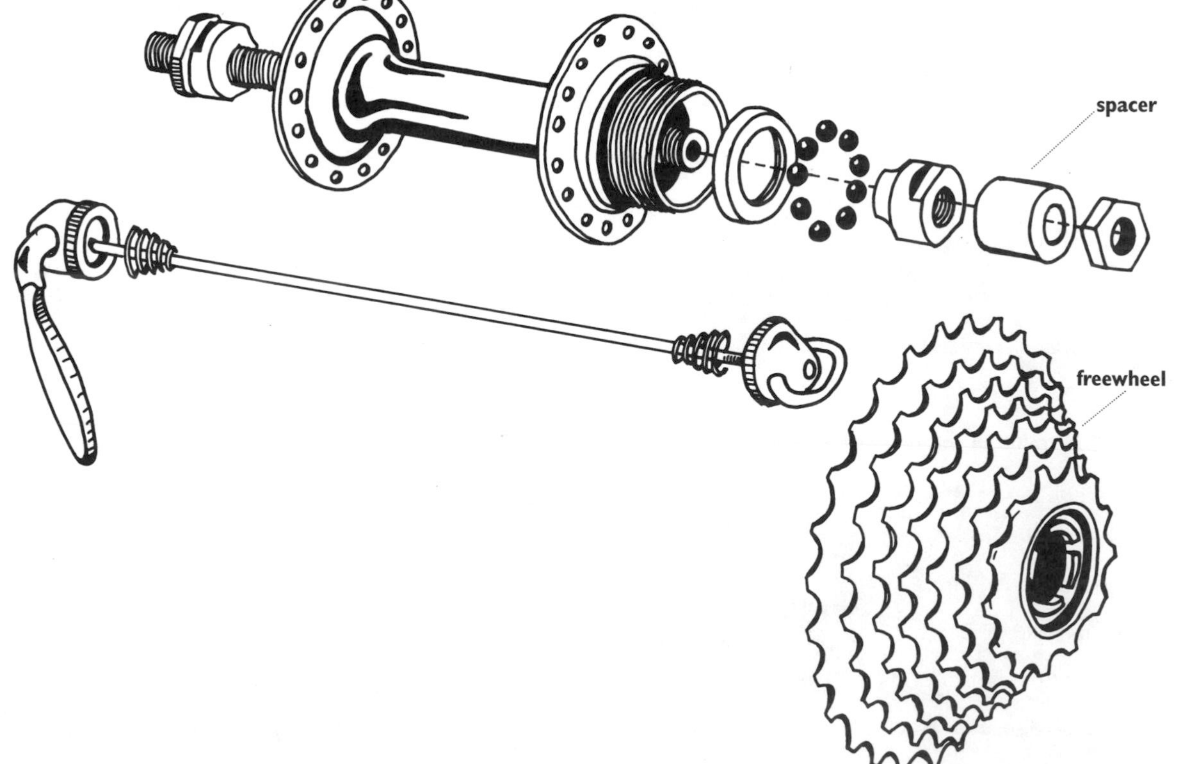

cogs slide onto the longitudinal splines of the freehub body (Fig. 6.30). Changing gear combinations is accomplished by removing the cogs from the freehub body and putting on different ones. A freehub can usually be lubricated without removing it from the hub.

A freewheel is a separate unit with the cogs attached to it. The entire freewheel threads onto the drive side of the rear hub (Fig. 6.31). Thread-on freewheels have fallen out of fashion relative to freehubs; changing cogs on freewheels is difficult, and freewheels do not support the drive side of the hub axle. Freewheels can only be removed with a freewheel tool that matches the pattern of the freewheel. Entire freewheels with different gear combinations can be interchanged in this way.

Fixed-gear cogs, as used on track bikes or some winter-training setups on the road do not freewheel; the cog drives the chain forward. There are two kinds of fixed gears: a standard 3/32-inch width for a standard road chain, and a 1/8-inch width for a track chain. Neither can be used with a derailleur, and the frame needs to have long horizontal dropouts in order to pull the wheel back enough to tension the chain.

When put on a standard threaded road wheel, a fixed-gear cog can unscrew when pedaled backward, but the cog is meant to be removed with a chain whip. On a track wheel, there is a second set of threads outboard of the standard hub threads. These threads are smaller in diameter and are left-hand threaded. A left-hand-threaded lockring holds the cog on and is tightened whenever the rider pushes backward on the pedals. The cog is removed by unscrewing the lockring in a clockwise direction with a lockring spanner of the appropriate size, and then unscrewing the lockring in a counterclockwise direction with a chain whip.

6.32 cleaning cogs

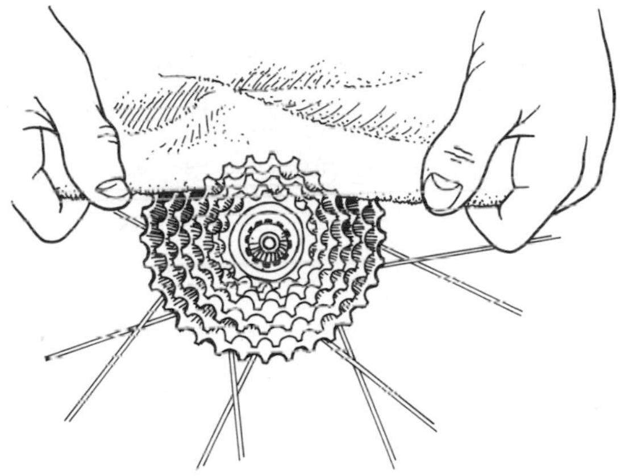

6-19: CLEANING REAR COGS

The quickest, albeit perfunctory, way to clean the rear cogs is to slide a rag back and forth between each pair of cogs while they are on the hub (Fig. 6.32). The other way—usually unnecessary unless the bike has been neglected—is to remove them (see section 6-20 below) and wipe them off with a rag or immerse them in solvent.

6-20: CHANGING CASSETTE COGS

1. Get out a chain whip, a cassette lockring remover, a wrench (adjustable or open) to fit the remover, and the cog(s) you want to install. (Some very old freehubs have a threaded smallest cog instead of a lockring. These require two chain whips and no lockring remover.)

2. Remove the skewer.

3. Wrap the chain whip around a cog at least two up from the smallest cog, wrapped in the drive direction to hold the cassette in place.

4. Insert the splined lockring remover into the lockring; it's the internally splined ring that holds the smallest cog in place. Unscrew it in a counterclockwise direction while using the chain whip to keep the cassette from turning (Fig. 6.33). If the lockring is so tight that the tool pops out without loosening it, install and tighten the skewer, sans

springs, through the hub and lockring tool. Loosen the lockring a fraction of a turn, remove the skewer, and unscrew the lockring the rest of the way.

5. Pull the cogs straight off. Some cassette cogsets are comprised of single cogs separated by loose spacers, some cogsets are bolted together, and some cogsets are a combination of both.

6. Clean the cogs with a rag or a toothbrush; use solvent if necessary, observing the usual precautions.

7. Inspect the cogs for wear. If the teeth are hooked, they may be ripe for replacement. Rohloff makes a cog-wear indicator tool; if you have access to one, use it according to its supplied instructions.

8. a. If you are replacing the entire cogset, just slide the new set on. Usually, you'll find that one spline is wider than the others (Fig. 6.34).

b. If you are installing a nine-speed cassette, see the note under step 9.

c. If you are replacing some individual cogs within your cogset, be certain that they are of the same type and model. For example, not all 16-tooth Shimano cogs are alike. Most cogs have shifting ramps, differentially shaped teeth, and other asymmetries. They differ with model as well as with sizes of the adjacent cogs, so you need to buy one for the exact location and model. Install cogs in decreasing numerical sequence with the numbers facing out.

Some bolt-together cogsets can be disassembled for cleaning and then reinstalled onto the freehub as separate cogs to facilitate future cog changes and cleaning (the bolts are there for the manufacturer's convenience, not yours). Note that there are two kinds of bolt-together cogsets: those with three long thin bolts holding the stack of cogs and spacers together (Fig. 6.30), and those with cogs bolted or riveted to an aluminum spider that has internal splines to fit on the cassette body. For the type with the three bolts, just unscrew the bolts, take it apart, and put in the replacement cogs. The other type is not to be disassembled from the aluminum spider, and the individual cogs are not to be replaced; you

6.33 removing a cassette lockring

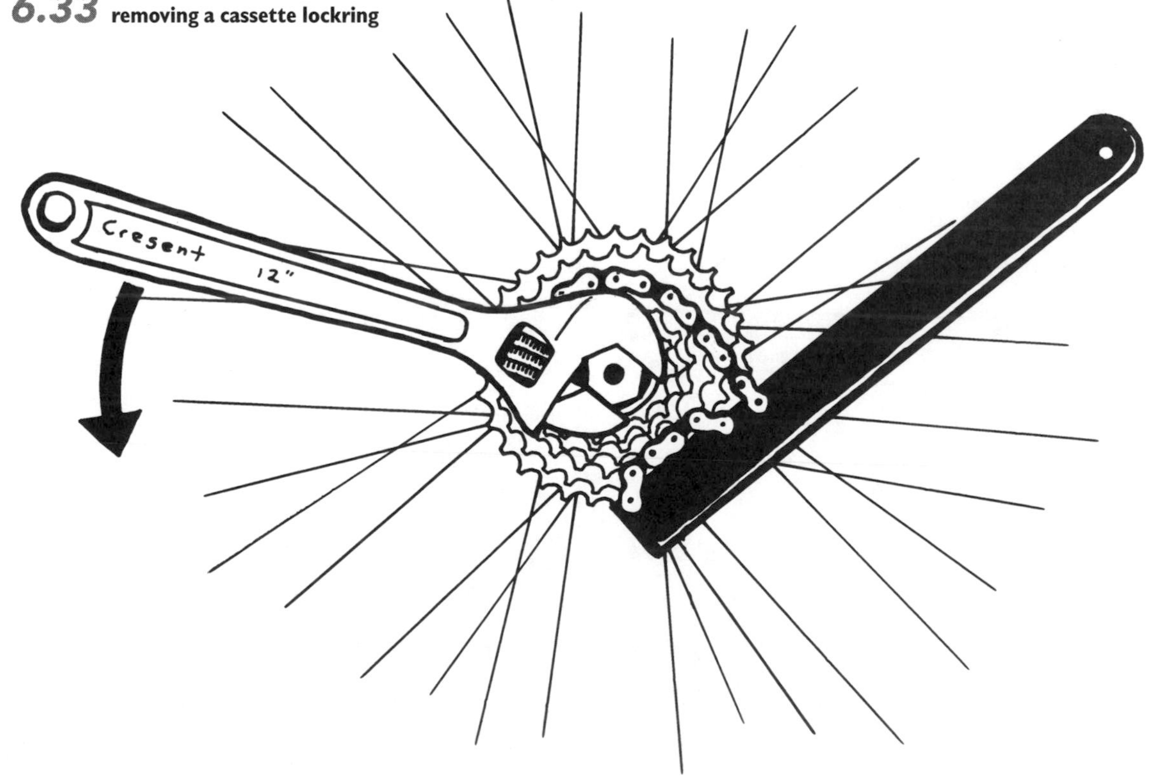

replace each carrier with attached cogs as a complete assembly.

9. With everything back in place, tighten the lockring with the lockring remover and wrench. (If you have the old type with the thread-on first cog, tighten that with a chain whip instead.) Make sure that all of the cogs are seated and can't wobble side to side, which would indicate that the first or second cog is sitting against the ends of the splines. If the cogs are loose after tightening the lockring, loosen the lockring, line up the first and second cogs to make sure they are in place, and tighten the lockring again.

Note on compatibility: *The above instructions for removing and replacing cogs apply for 9-, 8-, 7-, and 6-speed cogsets. But the freehub body is usually different for each, so make sure you only use a 7-speed cogset on a 7-speed freehub body, etc.*

Note on 11-tooth cogs: *While all Shimano 8-speed freehubs are wide enough for a 9-speed cogset, some 8/9-speed freehub bodies will not accept 11-tooth cogs (for instance, 1992–94 Shimano 8-speed freehub bodies will not accept 11-tooth cogs). To accept the small 11-tooth cog, the splines of current freehub bodies stop about 2mm before the outer end of the freehub body. You can file the last 2mm of splines off of an old-style 8-speed freehub so it will accept an 11-tooth cog. The steel is very hard on high-end freehubs, so a grinder may be needed for this job.*

6-21: CHANGING FREEWHEELS

If you have a freewheel (Fig. 6.31) and want to switch it with another one, follow this procedure. Replacing individual cogs on an existing freewheel is beyond the scope of this book, and is rarely done these days due to unavailability of spare parts.

1. Obtain the appropriate freewheel remover for your freewheel, and round up a big adjustable wrench to fit it.

2. Remove the quick-release skewer, and take the springs off of it.

3. Slide the skewer back in from the left side, place the freewheel remover into the end of the freewheel so that the notches or splines engage, and thread the skewer nut back on, tightening it against the freewheel remover to keep it from popping out of its notches.

4. Put the big adjustable wrench onto the flats of the freewheel remover, and loosen it (counterclockwise). It may take considerable force to free it, and you may even need to put a large pipe on the end of the wrench for more leverage. Set the tire on the ground for traction as you do it. As soon as the free-

6.34 spline vs. spleen

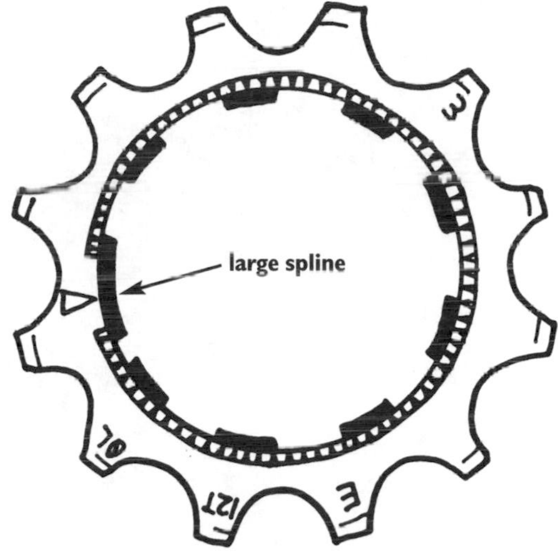

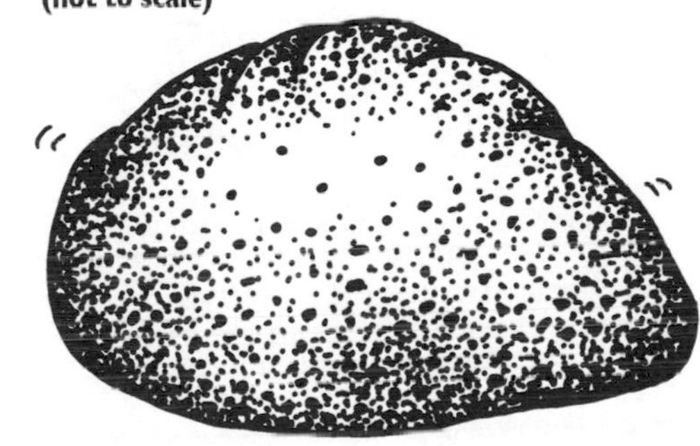

6.35 prying out freehub dust cover with a J-tool

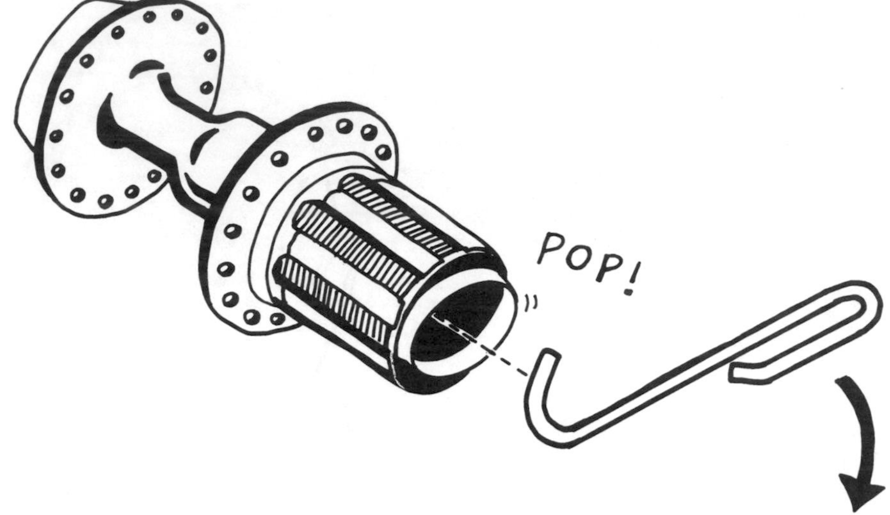

wheel pops loose, loosen the skewer nut before continuing; otherwise, you may snap the skewer in two.

5. Loosen the skewer nut a bit, unscrew the freewheel a bit more, etc., until it spins off freely and there is no longer any danger of having the freewheel remover pop out of the notches.

6. Remove the skewer and spin off the freewheel.

7. Grease the threads on the hub and the inside of the new freewheel.

8. Thread on the new freewheel by hand. You can snug it down with the freewheel remover and a wrench if you like, but it will tighten itself into place with the first few pedal strokes anyway.

9. Replace the skewer with the narrow ends of its conical springs facing inward (Fig. 6.31).

lubricating freehubs

6-22: LUBRICATING FREEHUBS

LEVEL 2

Freehubs and freewheels can usually be lubricated simply by dripping chain lube into them. Some high-end freehubs have grease-injection holes on the freehub body; remove the cogs to get at the hole, and grease often to avoid grease thickening up inside.

If the freehub has teeth on the faces of the hub shell and freehub (DT-Hügi or old Mavic freehubs have these radial teeth), just drip oil into the crease between the freehub and the hub shell as you turn the freehub counterclockwise.

1. Disassemble the hub axle assembly (see Section 6-14).

2. Wipe clean the inside of the drive-side bearing surface.

3. With the wheel laying flat and the freehub pointed up toward you, flow chain lube between the bearing surface and the freehub body as you spin the freehub counterclockwise. You will hear the clicking noise of the freehub pawls smooth out as lubricant reaches them. Keep it flowing until old black oil flows out of the other end of the freehub.

LEVEL 3

a. Thorough Shimano freehub lubrication: By far the best way to lubricate a Shimano freehub is to inject lubricant under pressure into it with a Morningstar "Freehub Buddy" tool (Chapter 1, Fig.1.4). To use this tool, you must pry out the freehub dust cover (Fig.6.35) to expose the hub bearing race. Push the Freehub Buddy into the

6.36 lubricating a Shimano freehub through a Freehub Buddy

bearing race, and inject the lubricant of your choice into the threaded hole in the center of the Freehub Buddy: The lubricant squirts out through the lube galley hole in the side of the tool between the two O-rings. The smaller O-ring on the Freehub Buddy seals off the hub through-hole to prevent lubricant from going in there, and the larger O-ring prevents lube from squirting back out the front of the freehub.

The Freehub Buddy accepts many different lubricants. I recommend force-threading the tip of a tube of outboard motor gear oil into the threaded hole in the Freehub Buddy and squeezing the gear oil in (Fig.6.36). Outboard gear oil is a great lubricant that is the perfect weight for a freehub. You can also force-thread the tip of a turkey baster or a tube of grease into the Freehub Buddy's threaded hole. Fill the turkey baster with oil or your own custom mixture of oil and grease. Aerosol chain lube can also be squirted into the Freehub Buddy via an adapter that accepts the long, thin tube that comes with the spray lube.

Whatever lubricant you use, squeeze it into the Freehub Buddy until all the old dirty lubricant squeezes through the freehub and out the back end of it. Keep going until clean lube oozes out.

The Freehub Buddy is the only way you can get a lubricant thicker than thin chain lube into your freehub, and a thicker lubricant protects better. Be careful not to use too thick of a lubricant, however. Filling a freehub with thick grease may cause the pawls to stick in cold weather. They won't snap into the freehub teeth to lock it up when you want to pedal forward. You could end up freewheeling in both directions!

Note, too, that many freehub dust caps will be ruined upon removal; they are usually made of stamped sheet metal. Shimano does not sell them separately. Morningstar sells machined removable dustcaps with an O-ring seal. Contact Morningstar Tooling at 9925 Kirkelie Rd., Frazier Park, CA 93225.

LEVEL 3

b. Campagnolo freehub lubrication: Remove the hub axle, and pull the freehub straight off. Older models require wrapping a twist-tie around the three pawls as they expose themselves from the hub shell as you pull; if you don't do this, the three pawls and the three springs will fly away. Wipe off the pawls, spring, and slide the freehub back in. Again, older models require using a twist-tie to hold the pawls in place as you push it in. Pull the twist-tie off after the pawls are inside the hub shell and before the freehub is pushed all the way in.

LEVEL 2

c. Lubrication of recent high-end DT-Hügi freehubs: Lay the wheel on its side, cogs up, and grasp the cogset and pull straight up; it will pull the hub end cap off and the freehub will come off. Clean and grease the spring, both star-shaped ratchets, and the teeth they engage. Push the freehub and dustcap back on.

4. Wipe off the excess lube, and continue with the hub overhaul (Sections 6-16, 6-17).

6-23 LUBRICATING FREEWHEELS

1. Wipe dirt off of the face of the fixed part of the freewheel surrounding the axle.

2. With the wheel lying flat and the cogs facing up, drip lubricant into the crease between the fixed and moving parts of the freewheel or cassette as you spin the cogs in a counterclockwise direction. You will hear the clicking noise inside get smoother as the lubricant seeps in. Keep the flow of lubricant going until old, dirty oil flows out the back side around the hub flange.

3. Wipe off the excess oil.

VII

Brakes

"What do I say to complaints that my brakes are no good?
I'll tell you this: Anyone can stop.
But it takes a genius to go fast."—Enzo Ferrari

By far the most common brake for road bikes is the dual-pivot sidepull brake (Fig. 7.1). The predecessor of the dual-pivot road brake is the center-pivot sidepull brake (Fig. 7.2), which is also a very powerful and lightweight brake. And going way back to the 1970s, dual-pivot centerpull brakes (Fig. 7.3) were the standard, although a couple of other dual-pivot centerpull brakes that did not require a cable hanger or a straddle cable (notably Shimano AX, Campagnolo Record and Croce d'Aune) had brief popularity in the 1980s.

Center-pull cantilever brakes (Fig. 7.4) and sidepull cantilever brakes (i.e., V-brakes, Fig. 7.5) are found on cyclo-cross bikes and many touring bikes and tandems. Both types are light, simple and offer good clearance for mud and big tires. V-brakes and cantilevers pivot on bosses attached to the frame and fork, with V-brakes offering the advantage of not requiring a cable hanger fixed to the frame or fork, since the cable routes directly to the brake arm. But a road brake lever does not pull enough cable to operate a V-brake without some sort of adapter installed to increase cable pull. Hence the continuing popularity of center-pull cantilevers.

And there has long been a tiny contingent using hydraulic brakes that drive the pads straight toward the rim by hydraulic pressure. Road models mount in the same bolt hole as standard road brakes, but mountain-bike versions that mount on the cantilever bosses can be used on cyclo-cross bikes and touring bikes with cantilever studs. Hydraulic brakes are beyond the scope of this book; please consult Chapter 7 of *Zinn and the Art of Mountain Bike Maintenance* for details on these brakes.

tools

2mm, 3mm, 4mm, 5mm and 6mm hex keys
Cable cutter
Wet chain lube
Grease
Pliers

OPTIONAL

8mm socket wrench
8mm, 10mm open-end wrenches
13mm, 14mm cone wrenches
Adjustable wrench

7-1: RELEASING BRAKES TO REMOVE A WHEEL

Road tires are often narrow enough to slip past the brake pads without opening the brakes further. With a wide tire or with a brake adjusted for very little clearance between the rim and the pads, the brake will need to be opened a bit. The following instructions describe how to open the vast majority of road brakes out there, both old and new. When you put your wheel back in, remember to follow these instructions in reverse so that your brakes will work when you need them.

Shimano (Fig. 7.1) and other dual-pivot sidepull brakes besides Campagnolo and Mavic:

Flip open the quick-release lever on the brake arm.

Campagnolo and Mavic dual-pivot sidepull brakes and Campagnolo dual-pivot centerpull brakes:

These brakes do not have a quick-release mechanism on the brake caliper. Instead, there is a cable-release button on the brake lever. On Campagnolo (Fig. 7.6), push the button inward so that it clears the edge of the lever housing and allows the lever to flip open wider. On a Mavic Mektronic lever (Fig. 5.28), slide the chrome button on the front downward to release the lever.

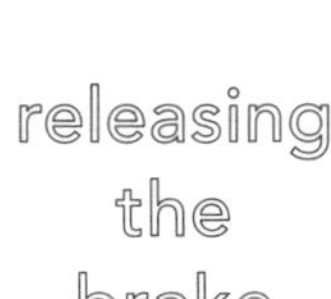

Center-pivot sidepull brakes (Fig. 7.2):

Flip open the lever on the brake arm, same as on a Shimano dual-pivot sidepull brake. While older Campagnolo brakes open this way (post-mid-1980s), Campagnolo center-pivot sidepulls have the quick-release on the brake lever (as in Fig. 7.6) and not on the caliper.

V-brakes (Fig. 7.5):

Hold the pads against the rim and pull the cable noodle back and up to release it from the brake arm link.

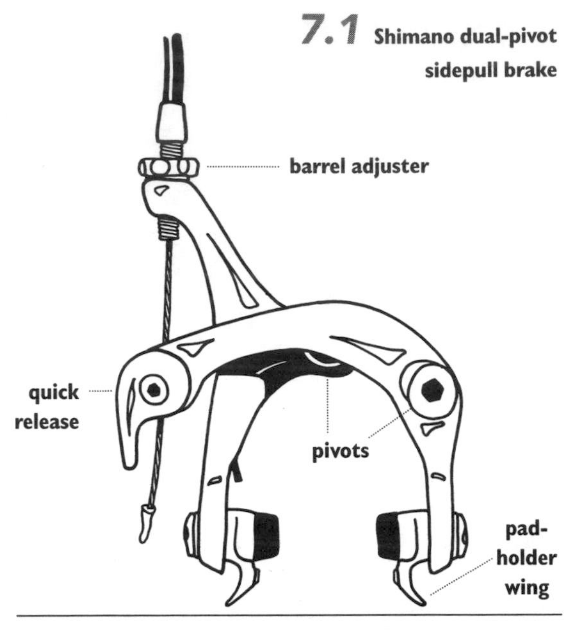

7.1 Shimano dual-pivot sidepull brake

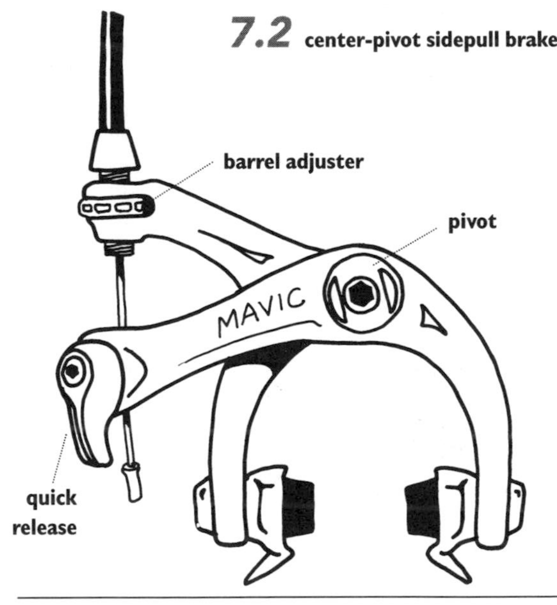

7.2 center-pivot sidepull brake

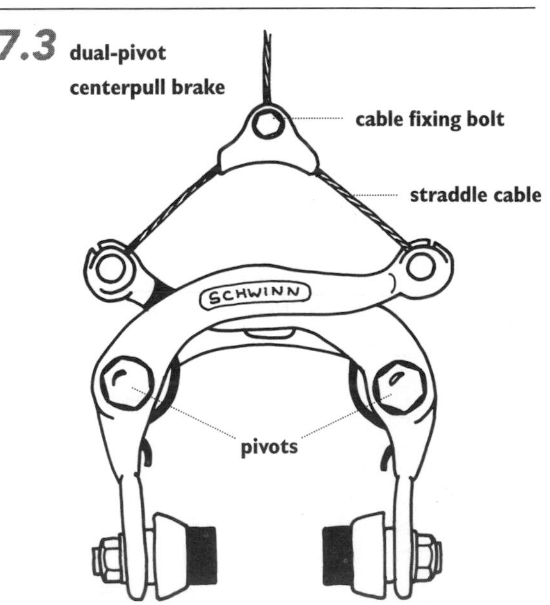

7.3 dual-pivot centerpull brake

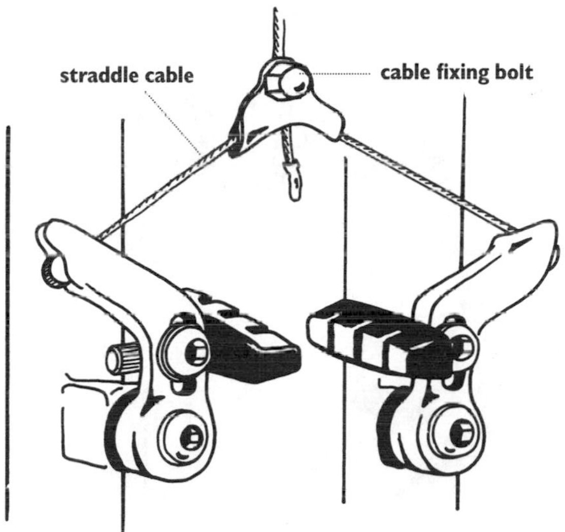

7.4 center pull cantilever brake

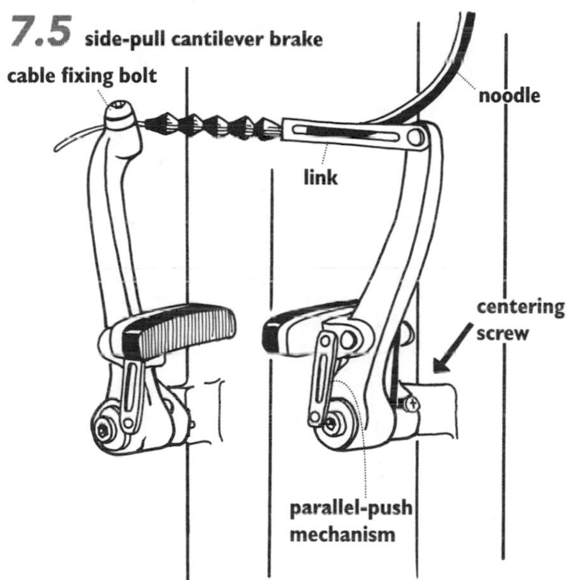

7.5 side-pull cantilever brake

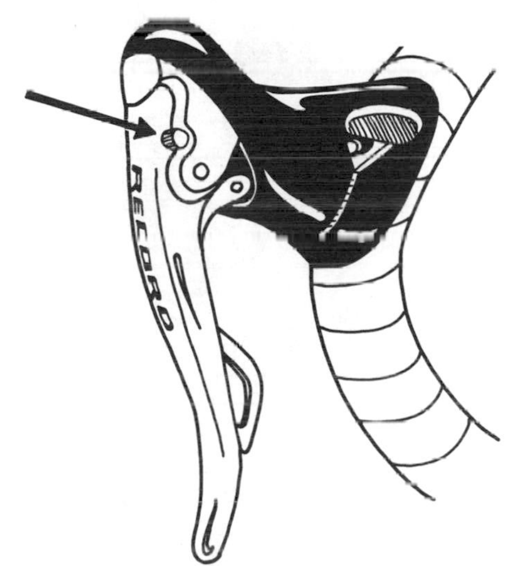

7.6 cable-release button on a Campagnolo Ergo-Power lever

Cantilevers (Fig. 7.4) and ancient dual-pivot centerpull brakes (Fig. 7.3):

Hold the pads against the rim and pull the head of the straddle cable out of the hook at the end of one brake arm.

Shimano AX dual-pivot centerpulls:

Pull the cable barrel adjuster up and out.

7A: CABLES & HOUSINGS

Given that cables transfer braking force from the levers to the brakes, their proper installation and maintenance are critical to good brake performance. If there is excess friction in the cable system, the brakes will not work properly, no matter how well the brakes, calipers and levers are adjusted. Cables with broken strands should be replaced immediately.

7-2: CABLE TENSIONING

As brake pads wear and cables stretch, the cable needs to be tightened. The barrel adjuster on the brake arm of any sidepull road brake (Fig. 7.7), and on top of Shimano AX and Campagnolo centerpulls serves exactly this purpose.

Cantilevers, V-brakes and old centerpulls (Figs. 7.3, 7.4 and 7.5): Since there is no barrel adjuster on a road brake lever, cable-tensioning requires a barrel adjuster on a cable stop on the frame, or it requires loosening the cable-fixing bolt, pulling the cable taut, and tightening the bolt again.

The cable should be tight enough that the lever cannot be pulled to the bar, yet loose enough that the brakes—assuming they are centered and the wheels are true—are not dragging on the rims.

7-3: INCREASING CABLE TENSION

1. Back out the barrel adjuster on the caliper by turning its collar nut clockwise (on most brakes) when

viewed from above (Figs. 7.1, 7.2 and 7.7). The underside of the adjuster nut usually has bumps that drop in and out of notches in the top of the brake arm, so you may wish to hold the pads against the rim with your thumb and fingers to make turning the nut easier.

2. Increase the tension sufficiently that the brake lever does not hit the handlebar when the brake is applied fully, yet not so tight that the brake rubs or comes on with very little movement of the lever. Lock in the adjustment with the notches in the top of the arm engaging the adjuster.

3. You may find that the barrel adjuster cannot take up enough cable slack alone to get the brakes as tight as you want. If so, you need to tighten the cable at the brake. First, screw the barrel adjuster back in most of the way. This leaves some adjustment in the system for brake setup and cable stretch over time. Loosen the bolt clamping the cable at the brake (Figs. 7.3, 7.4, 7.5, 7.9). Check the cable for wear. If it's badly frayed, replace it. (See Cable Installation, section 7-6 below.) Otherwise, pull the cable tight, and re-tighten the clamping bolt. Tension the cable as needed with the barrel adjuster.

cable tensioning and maintenance

7-4: REDUCING CABLE TENSION

1. Turn the barrel adjuster (Figs. 7.1, 7.2, 7.7 counter-clockwise when viewed from the top until your brake pads are properly spaced from the rim.

2. Let the notches and bumps in the barrel adjuster and brake arm engage to lock in the adjustment.

3. Double-check that the cable is tight enough that the lever cannot be squeezed all the way to the handlebar.

7-5: CABLE MAINTENANCE

1. If the cable is frayed or kinked or has any broken strands, replace it. (See Cable installation, section 7-6 below.)

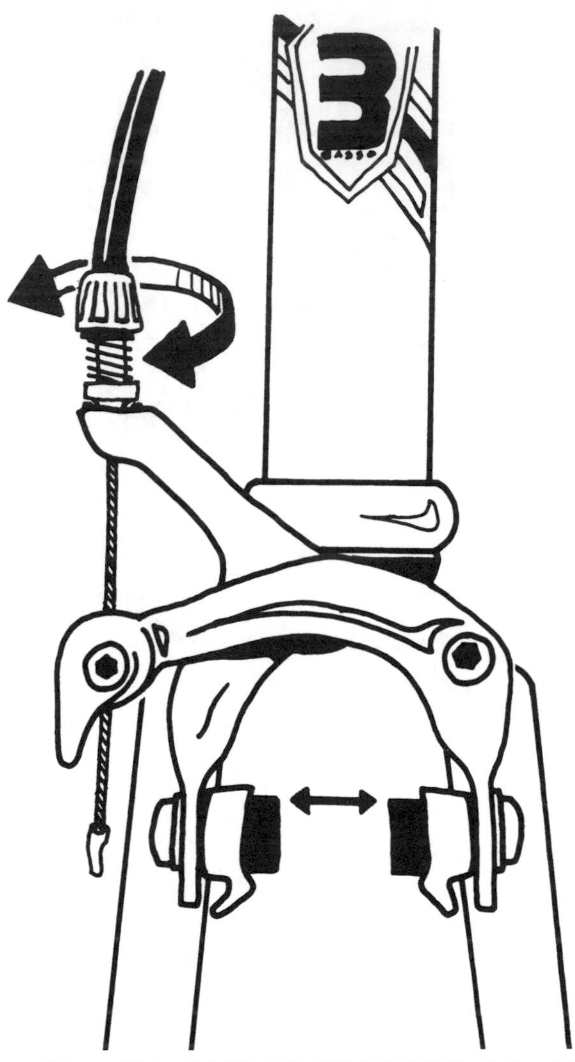

7.7 turning the barrel adjuster on the brake arm of sidepull road bike

7.8 insert the cable into the lever, through the cable hook, and out the exit hole

2. If the cable is not sliding well, lubricate it. Use an oil-based chain lubricant (not a chain wax or other dry lube) or molybdenum disulfide grease, if possible. Lithium-based greases and chain waxes can eventually gum up cables and restrict movement.

3. To lubricate, open the brake (via the cable quick release as when you remove a wheel; see section 7-1).

4. If you have slotted cable stops, pull the ends of the rear brake cable housing segments out of each stop. On the front brake, and on the rear brake if your bike does not have slotted cable stops, you will have to disconnect the cable at the brake, clip off the cable end, and pull out the entire cable.

5. Slide the housing up the cable, wipe the cable clean with a rag, rub chain lubricant on the cable section that was inside the housing, and slide the housing back into place. If you have pulled the housing completely off of the cable, squirt chain lube through the housing as well.

6. If the cable still sticks, replace the cable and housing.

7-6: CABLE REPLACEMENT AND INSTALLATION

1. Disconnect the cable at the brake caliper, clip off the cable end cap, and pull out the old cable from the lever. You will need to pull the lever and then let it back a bit to free the head of the cable from the cable hook in the lever.

Note: *When installing a new cable, it is a good idea to replace the housings as well, even if they seem okay. Daily riding in particularly dirty conditions may require cables and housings to be replaced every few months. As with chains and derailleur cables, brake-cable replacement is a maintenance operation, not a repair operation. don't wait until a cable breaks or seizes up to replace it.*

2. Purchase good-quality cables and lined housings. For cables, try using "die-drawn" cables; the exterior strands have been flattened by being pulled through a constricting die. They will move with less friction. For housing, you'll find that most brake-cable housing is spiral-wrapped to prevent splitting under braking pressure (see Chapter 5, Fig. 5.13). Plastic-lined housing reduces friction and is a must.

3. Cut the housing sections long enough to reach the brakes, and route them so that they do not make any sharp bends. If you are replacing existing housing, look at the bends before removing the old housings (after unwrapping the handlebar tape to get at them). If the housing bends are smooth and do not bind when the front wheel is swung through its arc, cut the new housings to the same lengths. Otherwise, cut each new segment longer than you think necessary and keep trimming it back until it gives the smoothest path possible for the cable, without the cable tension being affected by steering. Use a cutter specifically designed for cutting housings, or a sharp side-cutter.

4. After cutting, make sure the end faces are flat. If not, square them off with a file or a clipper.

5. If the end of the Teflon liner is mashed shut after cutting, open it up with a sharp object like a nail or a toothpick.

6. Slip a ferrule over each housing end for support (see Chapter 5, Fig. 5.13). Some brake arm barrel adjusters function as a ferrule and will not fit one.

7. Decide which hand you want to control which brake (the standard is the right hand controlling the rear brake, but if you're the only one riding the bike, you can switch it around to match the set-up on your motorcycle, for example). Install the housings into each housing stop, brake lever, and brake caliper.

8. Tighten the adjusting barrel on the brake caliper to within one turn of being screwed all of

the way in (Fig. 7.7).

9. Insert the cable into the lever, through the cable hook, and out the cable exit hole (Fig. 7.8). On current brakes, the cable exits the inboard side of the lever under the edge of the lever hood so that it can be wrapped under the handlebar tape. Many brake levers prior to 1988 or so, and almost all of them prior to 1980 had the cable coming out of the top of the lever.

10. Slide the cable through the housings and to the brake, making sure there is a ferrule (cylindrical cap) on the end of the housing, if one will fit into the barrel adjuster.

Note: *With new cables and lined housing, it is usually best not to use a lubricant on the cable. It is not necessary, so why run the risk of it gumming up inside the housing and attracting dirt? (Down the road, when the cable starts to stick, you may need to lubricate it; see section 7-5.)*

11. Attach the cable to the brake. (See section on your type of brake.) Pull it taut and tighten the cable-clamping bolt (Fig. 7.9). Pull the lever as hard as you can and hold it for 60 seconds to stretch the new cable.

7.9 **pull the cable taut and tighten the brake cable-clamping bolt**

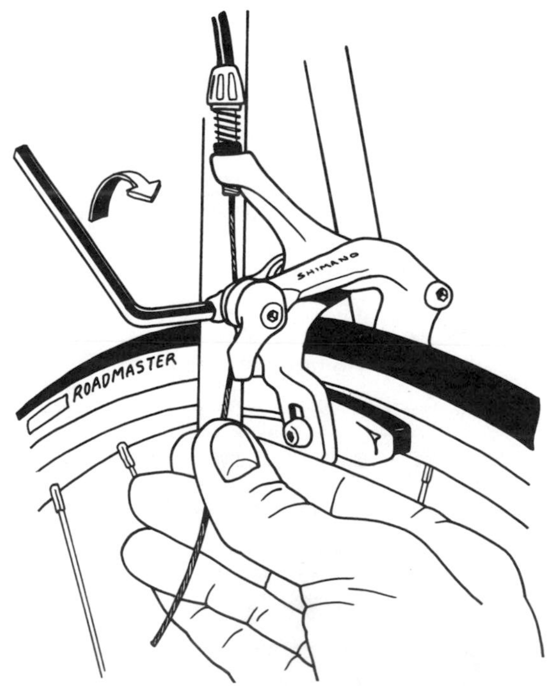

12. Adjust cable tension with the caliper barrel adjuster (as in sections 7-2, 3, and 4).

13. Cut off the cable about an inch past the cable-fixing bolt. Crimp an end cap on the exposed cable end to prevent fraying (Fig. 5.21 in Chapter 5). Wrap the handlebar tape (see Chapter 11, section 11-9).

Note: *Once the cable has been properly installed, the lever should snap back quickly when released. If it does not, re-check the cable and housing for free movement and sharp bends. Release the cable quick-release and hold the pads to the rim with your hand while checking the lever for free movement. With the cable still loose, check that the brake pads do not drag on the tire as they return to the neutral position; make sure the brake arms rotate freely on their pivots, and check that the brake arm return springs snap the pads away from the rims. If the lever and caliper move freely and spring back strongly, and if there are no obvious binds in the system, check for frayed strands within the housing sections, and then try lubricating the cable (section 7-5).*

7B: BRAKE LEVERS

The levers must operate smoothly and be set up so that you can reach them easily while riding.

7-7: LEVER LUBRICATION/SERVICE

1. Lubricate all pivot points in the lever with grease or oil.

2. Check return-spring function on lever (note, though, that not all levers have springs in them).

3. Make sure that the lever or lever body is not bent in a way that hinders movement.

4. Check for stress cracks. If you find any, replace the lever.

5. Replace torn or cracked lever hoods.

7-8: LEVER REMOVAL, INSTALLATION, AND POSITIONING

Most current brake levers integrate the brake lever and the shifter in a single unit (Figs. 7.6, 7.10).

1. Remove the handlebar tape.

2. Loosen the brake lever's mounting bolt with a 5mm Allen wrench and slide the lever off. The position of the bolt varies. On current dual-control levers it is on the outboard side of the lever under the lever hood. Slip the hex key down from the top between the lever body and the hood rather than trying to roll back the hood far enough to get at it from outside (Fig. 7.10). On Campagnolo ErgoPower (Fig. 7.6), the bolt is on the outside toward the top; on Shimano STI (Fig. 7.10) it is on the middle of the outer side, and on Mavic Mektronic (Fig. 5.28), it is on the outside toward the bottom.

Old-style brake levers have the mounting bolt in the center of the lever body, and it is reached by pulling the lever and sticking the hex key straight in. Campagnolo and other European levers from the early 1980s and before used a hex nut (accessed with an 8mm socket wrench) rather than an Allen bolt.

3. Slide the new lever on the bar to where you like it. A good rule of thumb is to put a straightedge against the bottom of the bar and slide the lever down until its end touches the straightedge. The lever can sit a little higher than this if you like, but generally not any lower. Put a straightedge across the top of both levers to make sure they are level.

4. Tighten the mounting bolts.

5. Install the cables (see Chapter 5, Sections 5-6 to 5-15, and Section 7-6 above).

6. Wrap the handlebar tape (see Chapter 11, section 11-9).

7.10 **tightening an STI brake/shift lever to the bar with a 5mm hex key**

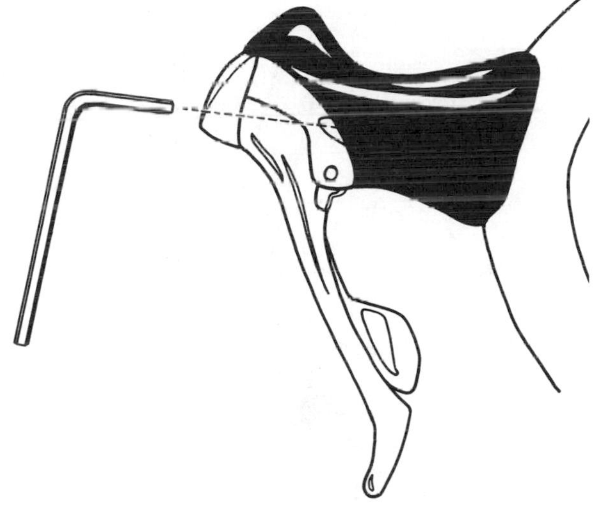

7-9: LEVER REACH

There is no reach-adjustment screw on a road brake lever. If you have small hands and have difficulty reaching the levers, there are a few things you can try.

First, you can try different positions on the bar for the lever. This may bring the lever closer to the bar.

Another option is to buy a bar with a different bend that puts the palm of the hand closer to the lever. There are some bars specifically made to accomplish this.

Finally, you can try to buy a smaller lever. This used to be relatively simple when brake levers were just brake levers. But now that levers incorporate the shifters, you cannot swap a shorter lever from another manufacturer, and the levers made by derailleur manufacturers do not come in different reaches. You can buy a whole new brake/derailleur system to get one with a reach you prefer, if necessary, but I recommend investigating a different handlebar first.

7.11 tightening a caliper to the brake bridge with a 5mm hex key

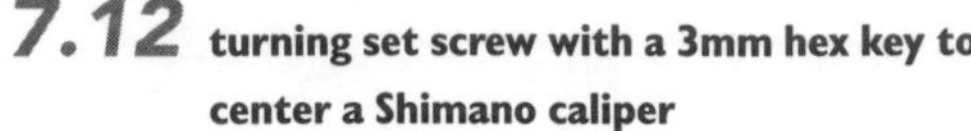

7.12 turning set screw with a 3mm hex key to center a Shimano caliper

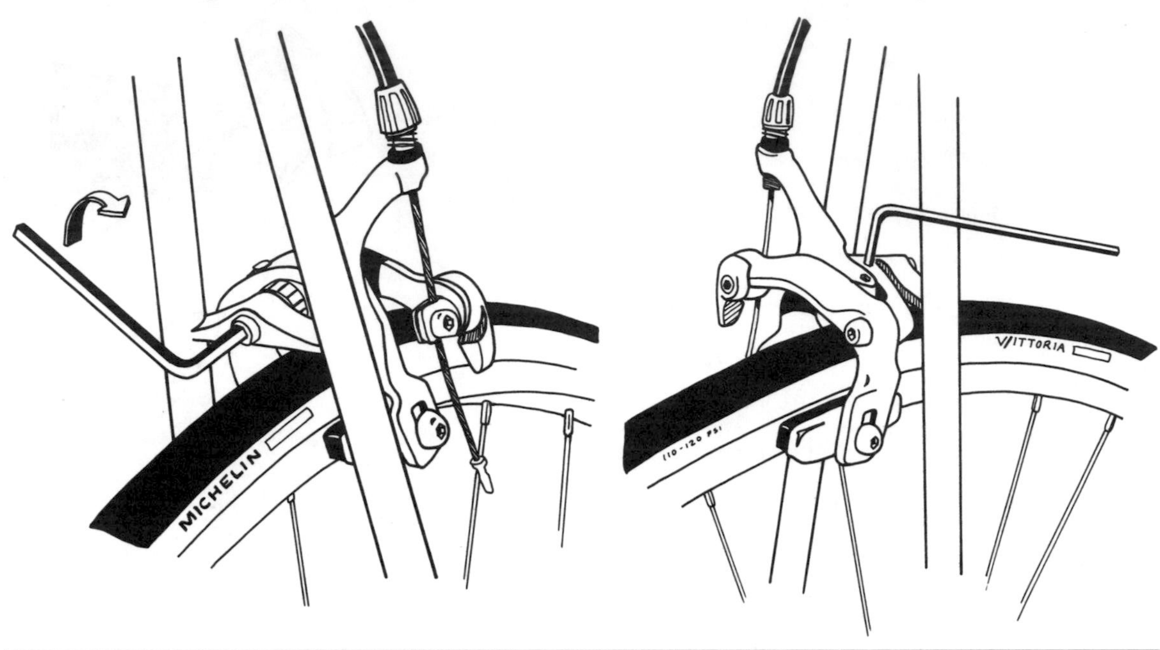

7C: BRAKE CALIPERS

The caliper of a brake is the part that grabs the wheel rim. In most cases, a road caliper is a sidepull device that bolts through a hole in the brake bridge or fork crown (Figs. 7.1, 7.2, 7.11, 7.12). But "caliper" can also refer to the pair of arms of a cantilever or V-brake that attach to pivot posts welded onto the frame and fork (Figs. 7.4, 7.5). And then there are those old centerpull calipers (Fig. 7.3) from 1970s Raleighs and Peugeots.

dual-pivot sidepull brake calipers

7C.1: DUAL-PIVOT SIDEPULL BRAKE CALIPERS

Dual-pivot sidepull brakes (Figs. 7.1, 7.11) have become the industry standard. They are powerful and easy to keep in adjustment.

Campagnolo and Mavic dual-pivot brakes have some features distinct from Shimano. And Shimano brakes generally share similar features with Asian copies.

1. Installation

Stick the center bolt through the hole in the brake bridge or fork crown and tighten it in place with a 5mm hex key inserted into the recessed nut (Fig. 7.11). Hold it roughly centered over the wheel as you tighten the nut.

2. Cable hook-up

Route the cable housing into the barrel adjuster on the upper brake arm. If one will fit into the barrel adjuster, install a ferrule on the end of the housing; see Section 7-6. Push the cable through the housing and the barrel adjuster and under the cable-fixing-bolt washer on the lower brake arm. Pull the cable taut, and tighten the bolt with a 5mm hex key (Fig. 7.9). Have the quick-release on the caliper (or on the lever on Campagnolo or Mavic Mektronic) open as you do this. Close it after the cable is connected.

3. Centering

You are trying to achieve an equal amount of space between the pad and the rim on each side. The simplest and quickest way to center these brakes requires no tools. Just grab the brake and twist the entire thing into position (don't mess with the mounting bolt; leave it tight). Or just pull outward on the pad that is closer to the rim. But do make sure before riding that the recessed nut on the back of the brake bridge or fork is tight (Fig. 7.11).

The centering method built in by Campagnolo and Shimano consists of a set screw, while Mavic brakes involve the mounting bolt.

Campagnolo has a 2mm hex set screw on the side opposite the cable, just above the pad on the arm. As you tighten the screw, the pad on that side moves away from the rim. Loosen the screw, and the other pad (the one on the cable side) moves away from the rim.

Shimano's set screw is on the upper end of the opposite brake arm. It takes a 3mm hex key (Fig. 7.12), and tightening it moves the pad on that side away from the rim. Loosen it, and the other pad (the one on the cable side) moves away from the rim.

Mavic dual-pivot sidepulls require working a 5mm hex key in the recessed mounting nut along with a 14mm cone wrench on the nut behind the brake caliper (similar to center-pivot centering—Fig. 7.14).

4. Pad adjustment

Loosen the pad-mounting bolt with a hex key (generally 4mm or 5mm). Slide the pad up and down along the groove in the arm to get the pad even with the height of the rim's braking surface. Twist the pad in the vertical plane to have the top edge of the pad follow the curve of the top edge of the rim (Fig. 7.13). While squeezing the brake lever to hold the pad against the rim, tighten the bolt. Make sure the pad does not twist as you tighten (if it does, you will have to hold it with your fingers as you cinch the bolt).

Current Campagnolo brakes also have an orbital adjustment of the pads to align the face of the pad flat against the rim and to allow a toe-in adjustment of the pad. A concave washer nests against the convex face of the pad holder to allow this. If you have brake squeal or want to reduce grabbiness, toe the pads in a bit so the forward end of the pad is a little bit closer to the rim than the rearward end. A 1mm toe-in is sufficient to eliminate squeal and grabbiness.

Note: *Users of Shimano pre-built wheels with Dura-Ace or Ultegra brakes will want to remove the little plastic screw in the pad-holder wing (below the pad—see Fig. 7.1). Otherwise, as soon as the pad gets a bit worn, that screw will thump-thump-thump against the bend in the spoke where it exits the side of the rim.*

5. Spring tension adjustment

Campagnolo dual-pivot brakes have a set screw that pushes on the end of the return spring. It is located on the side of the arm above the cable-side pad. If you tighten this screw (with a 2mm hex key), you tighten the spring, thus making the brake both harder to pull and quicker to snap back. There is no tension adjustment on Shimano brake springs or on the leaf spring in new Mavic brakes. Some springs can be bent with pliers to increase tension.

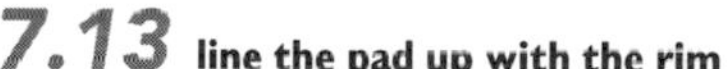

7.13 line the pad up with the rim

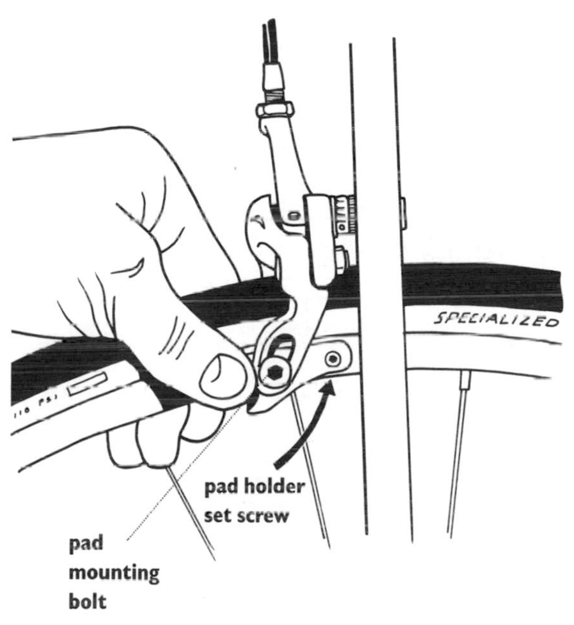

6. Cable tension adjustment

Follow the instructions in sections 7-2 through 7-4.

7. Pad replacement

When the pads get so worn that the grooves cut into the pads are almost gone, you ought to replace them.

Most pads these days are molded in one piece with the mounting nut insert or stud, so you just unscrew the pad and bolt the new one in place.

High-end Shimano, Campagnolo and Mavic dual-pivot brakes surround the pad with an aluminum holder which is bolted to the brake arm. The pad can be replaced separately by sliding it from the holder. Shimano and Mavic pad holders have a set screw (Fig. 7.13) that must first be backed out to free the pad.

It is not easy to slide any pad in or out of the holder. You may have to yank out the old pad with pliers and slide in the new pad with the aid of a vise. When you re-install the pad to the brake arm, make sure that the closed end of the pad holder faces forward. Otherwise, the first time you brake hard, you may see two pieces of rubber fly ahead of you and feel two more hit the backs of your legs. You may not remember anything after that.

center-pivot sidepull brake calipers

7C.2: CENTER-PIVOT SIDEPULL BRAKE CALIPERS

Center-pivot sidepull brakes (Fig. 7.2) are still on lots of bikes, since they were the standard from the late 1970s to the early 1990s. They, too, work great and are easy to set up and adjust. Many adjustments are the same as those on dual-pivot brakes.

1. Installation

Stick the center bolt through the hole in the brake bridge or fork crown and tighten it in place with a 5mm hex key inserted into the recessed nut (Fig. 7.11). Hold it roughly centered over the wheel as you tighten the nut.

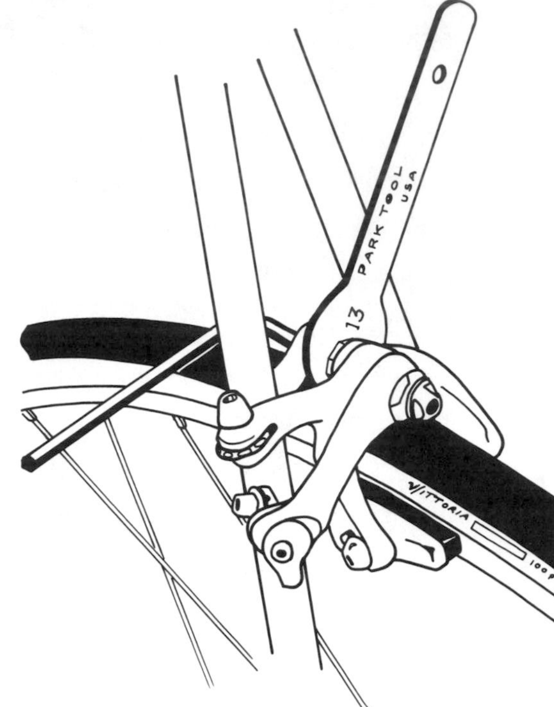

7.14 centering a center-pivot sidepull brake with a cone wrench

Some older bikes do not have a countersunk hole in the back of the brake bridge and fork crown. With these, you need a brake with a longer center bolt and a standard nut, which you tighten with a 10mm box wrench.

2. Cable hook-up

Route the cable housing into the barrel adjuster on the upper brake arm. If one will fit into the barrel adjuster, install a ferrule on the end of the housing; see Section 7-6. Push the cable through the housing and the barrel adjuster and under the cable-fixing bolt washer on the lower brake arm. Pull the cable tight and tighten the bolt with a 5mm hex key (same as with a dual-pivot brake, Fig. 7.9) or an 8mm box wrench. Have the quick-release on the caliper (or on the lever on some later Campagnolo levers) open as you do this.

3. Centering

You want an equal amount of space between the pad and the rim on each side. Turn the brake the direction you need with a cone wrench (usually 13mm or 14mm) slipped onto the flats of the center bolt between the brake and the frame (Fig. 7.14). Hold the brake-mounting nut at the same time, making sure that it is tight when you are finished.

4. Pad adjustment

Loosen the pad-mounting bolt with a hex key or box wrench. Slide the pad up and down along the groove in the arm to get the pad even with the height of the rim's braking surface. Twist the pad in the vertical plane to have the top edge of the pad follow the curve of the top edge of the rim (same as with a dual-pivot brake, Fig. 7.13). While squeezing the brake lever to hold the pad against the rim, tighten the bolt. Make sure the pad does not twist as you tighten (if it does, you will have to hold it with your fingers as you cinch down on the bolt).

5. Spring tension adjustment

Some center-pivot sidepulls have a spring-tension adjusting screw. And on some Shimano center-pivot brakes, the piece of plastic at each end of the spring can be reversed to tighten or loosen the spring. The hole through which the end of the spring slides is offset in the wafer-shaped plastic piece. Push inward on the end of the spring to free the plastic wafer from the brake-arm tab, flip it over, and push it back in place under the tab. If the hole is to the outside, the spring is looser; if the wafer is flipped so the hole is toward the inside, the spring is as tight as it is going to get.

6. Cable tension adjustment

Follow the instructions in sections 7-2 through 7-4.

7. Pad replacement

When the pads are worn down to the point that the grooves cut into the pads are almost gone, you ought to replace them.

Many pads are molded in one piece with the mounting nut insert or mounting stud, so you just unscrew the pad and bolt the new one in place.

Some brake pads are held inside a holder which is bolted to the brake arm. You slide the rubber pad alone out of the holder, but often it is not easy. You may have to yank out the old pad with pliers and slide in the new pad with the aid of a vise. When you re install the pad to the brake arm, make sure that the closed end of the pad holder faces forward. Otherwise, the first time you brake hard, you may see two pieces of rubber fly ahead of you and feel two more hit the backs of your legs. You may not remember anything after that.

7C.3: CANTILEVER AND SIDEPULL-CANTILEVER (V-) BRAKE CALIPERS

Some cyclo-cross, touring and tandem bikes have cantilevers or V-brakes. Both types mount on pivot studs attached to the frame and fork.

Standard cantilever brakes have two separate arms that are pulled toward each other when the brake cable pulls up on a link wire connecting the two arms (Fig. 7.4). Short-arm cantilever brakes work acceptably with road levers. A cable stop is required on the frame's seatstays and another one below the stem.

V-brakes (Figs. 7.5, 7.15) have tall, cantilever-like arms, a horizontal cable hook link on top of one arm, and a cable clamp on the top of the other. A curved aluminum guide pipe, or "noodle," hooks into the horizontal link and takes the cable from the end of the housing and out through the link and directs it toward the cable clamp on the opposite arm. V-brakes usually have long, thin brake pads with threaded posts. Some V-brakes have "parallel-push" linkages (Fig. 7.5) that move the brake pads horizontally rather than in an arc around the brake boss like a cantilever. Simple V-brake designs (Fig. 7.15) mount the pad directly to the arm so that it moves in a cantilever-like arc.

V-brakes are extremely powerful, but they require more cable pull than road brakes and don't work with road levers unless you install a cam unit that increases the cable pull. This cam unit usually replaces the noodle and bolts onto the cable-fixing bolt. A cable stop is bolted onto the end of the cable and hooks into the brake link.

The adjustment and pad positioning of cantilevers and V-brakes would monopolize an unacceptable number of pages in this book, so please consult Chapter 7 of *Zinn and the Art of Mountain Bike Maintenance* for details on the adjusting of these brakes (as well as for hydraulic rim brakes and disc brakes).

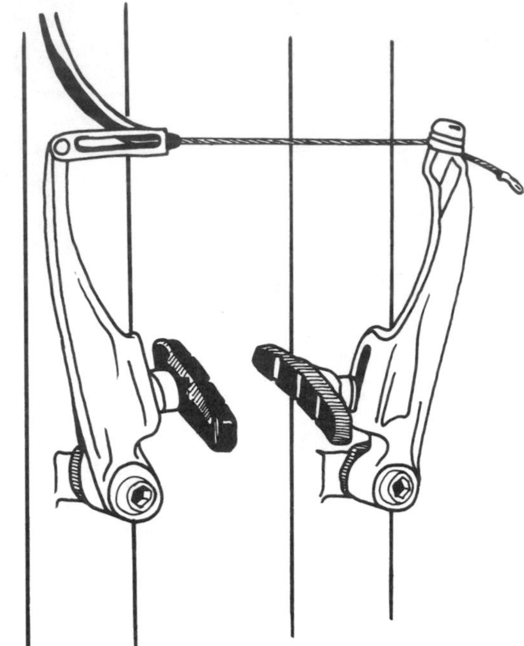

7.15 **simple V-brake**

7C.4: SHIMANO AX AND CAMPAGNOLO RECORD AND CROCE D'AUNE CENTERPULL CALIPERS

Not many of these little items were produced, but they were coveted as high-end brakes, so there are still some around. They attach in the same manner as sidepull calipers, and the pad adjustment and cable-tension adjustment procedure is pretty much the same as well. The major differences have to do with cable connection and centering.

The cable housing stops at a barrel adjuster above the center of the brake. The cable goes straight down through a crosswise hole in the cable-fixing bolt. The Shimano fixing anchor is in a separate triangular piece that tends to turn as you tighten the bolt.

Centering either of these brakes could not be simpler. Just grab the part sticking straight up (with the cable entry on top) and twist it as needed. Make sure the mounting nut is tight behind the fork or brake bridge.

Shimano and Campagnolo road centerpull calipers

—

TROUBLE-SHOOTING

7-10: TROUBLESHOOTING

1. Squealing brakes:

Possible causes for noise are grease or oil on the rim and/or pad; toe-out of the pads under hard braking so that the heel of the pad does the work; brake arms that are too flimsy for the rider (and chatter or toe-out when the brakes are applied); and ceramic-coated rims paired with pads not intended for ceramic braking surfaces.

In the case of dirty or oily rims, clean them with solvent (rubbing alcohol may be sufficient), and wipe them clean. In the case of dirty pads, reveal a clean layer of the pad with sandpaper.

If your pads toe-out while braking, you should toe them in. Some pads (recent Campagnolo) have an orbital adjustment on the pads that allows toe-in. Otherwise, the only way to toe road pads is to remove the pad, put an adjustable wrench on the end of the brake arm, and twist it. This will help eliminate squeal on a brake with flimsy arms, too. If the arms flex too much for you, get new brakes.

High-end rims with ceramic braking surfaces can squeal if the pads are not specifically made for ceramic rims. Easy enough; get new pads.

2. Insufficient braking power:

Possible causes include flexing of brake arms or lever; stretching of cable; compression of brake housing; squishing of pads; or insufficient coefficient of friction between the pads and rim.

If the brake arms or levers are too flexible, you need new brakes, but you can try eliminating the other factors first and see if braking power comes up enough for you.

If the cables and housings are old, frayed, thin, or cheap, chances are the cable is stretching more than a new one would, and the cable housing is compressing more than new housing would. Replace both.

If the pads are too soft, they will squish rather than applying full pressure against the rim. Replace them with higher-quality ones.

Insufficient friction is common with chromed steel rims (found only on cheap bikes). The only cure is to fit especially aggressive pads (or replace the rims—not a bad idea, since chromed steel rims do not provide much braking power when wet).

Another cause of weak braking power can be oil and grime on the rims and pads (or water, but that will dry off soon). Sand the pads and clean the rim with solvent. The pads might also be overly worn and need replacement. And finally, the pads may not work with your particular rim. Try different pads.

3. The levers come back to the bar before the bike slows down enough:

Check that the brake quick-release is closed. If so, the cable needs to be tightened. See Section 7-3. The causes in the last item above (Insufficient braking power) may also apply.

4. Brake rubs on wheel:

Possible causes include off-center caliper, brakes too tight, or untrue wheel. If one pad rubs all of the way around the rim, see Section 7C for centering the brake caliper. If both pads rub all of the way around, loosen the cable as in Section 7-4. If the wheel wobbles back and forth against the pad(s), true the wheel; see Chapter 6, Section 6-12 or Chapter 13 Section 13-4).

5. Pads do not meet flat to the rim:

Other than on late-model Campagnolo brakes, if the pad will not mount so it meets the rim flat or slightly toed-in, the only way to adjust it is to remove the pad and twist the end of the arm with an adjustable wrench. (Late-model Campy brakes have an orbital pad mount that allows freedom of adjustment in all planes, once the pad bolt is loosened.)

If one pad toes in and one toes out, it is possible that either the brake center-bolt is bent or the brake hole in the frame or fork is drilled crooked.

6. Brake caliper returns slowly or not at all:

Possible causes: the caliper's center bolt or secondary pivot bolt is bent or the nuts on it are too tight where it passes through the brake arm; the end of the spring is not riding in its plastic friction piece or it needs lubrication; or the cable is sticking.

You can adjust the tightness of the pivot-bolt nuts and replace bent bolts.

Replacing the end of the spring in its plastic friction reducing piece is easy enough, and you can put a dab of grease between the spring and the spring tab on the arm for those springs without the friction-reducing piece.

If the cable is sticking, replace or lubricate it (see Sections 7-5 and 7-6).

7. Brake arms are loose or the front nut is missing from a center-pivot sidepull brake:

The nut(s) holding the caliper together have loosened up or are missing. Tighten the nuts until there is no play in the caliper, yet it still moves freely. If the brake has two nuts, make sure they are both there (the end of the bolt should be observed by the front cap-nut), and hold the back one with one wrench while you tighten the front one against it with another wrench.

8. You just got new brakes for your old (pre-1980) racing bike or for a touring bike and, (a) the pads will not slide down far enough to hit the rim, and/or (b) the hole on the back of the fork crown and/or brake bridge is too small for the recessed brake nut:

You need to get a long-reach brake for the pads to hit the rim, and to fit the small, unrecessed brake hole, you need to get a brake with a long center bolt and a standard nut and washer. This either means you need to buy a new brake with these features, which will be a low-end brake, or you need to find a good, old brake. In the 1980s, Campagnolo and others made top-quality brakes with your choice of brake reach and center-bolt style.

You can evern get drop-style center bolts for old Campagnolo single-pivot sidepull brakes to lower a short-reach brake so the pads can reach the rim on a long-reach frame.

Cranks and bottom brackets

"When someone tells you something defies description, you can be pretty sure he's going to have a go at it anyway."—Clyde B. Aster

tools

5mm, 6mm, 7mm and 8mm hex keys
14mm socket wrench
Crank puller
Chainring nut tool
Pin spanner (or adjustable pin tool)
Splined bottom bracket wrench
Adjustable wrench
Toothed lockring spanner
Grease

OPTIONAL

15mm and 16mm socket wrenches
Dustcap pin tool
3/8-inch drive socket handle

The crankset consists of the crankarms, bottom bracket, chainrings, chainring bolts, and crank bolt (Figs. 8.1A and B). The forces applied through this system are large, so all parts need to be quite tight to prevent ruining expensive components by using them when loose. In addition, bottom bracket bearings need to run smoothly under high loads in order not to sap your energy.

8A: CRANKARMS AND CHAINRINGS

8-1: CRANK REMOVAL AND INSTALLATION

To take off the crankarms, you will need, depending on the crankset, either a large hex key alone, or a crank puller along with a socket wrench or large hex key (Figs. 8.2 and 8.3).

Most Shimano cranks and their clones are secured with a crank bolt accepting either an 8mm hex key or a 14mm socket wrench. Current Campagnolo cranks accept an 8mm hex key; older Campagnolo cranks take a 7mm hex key or a 15mm socket. Early-1980s Shimano Dura-Ace and 600 Dyna-Drive cranks are removed with a 6mm hex key, and you may still find pre-1980 French (TA, Stronglight) cranks with 16mm bolts.

A. Removal:

1. Older cranksets (and some current inexpensive ones) have a dust cap covering the crank bolt. If it's there, remove it. Depending on type, it may take a 5mm Allen wrench, a two-pin dust cap tool, or a screwdriver.

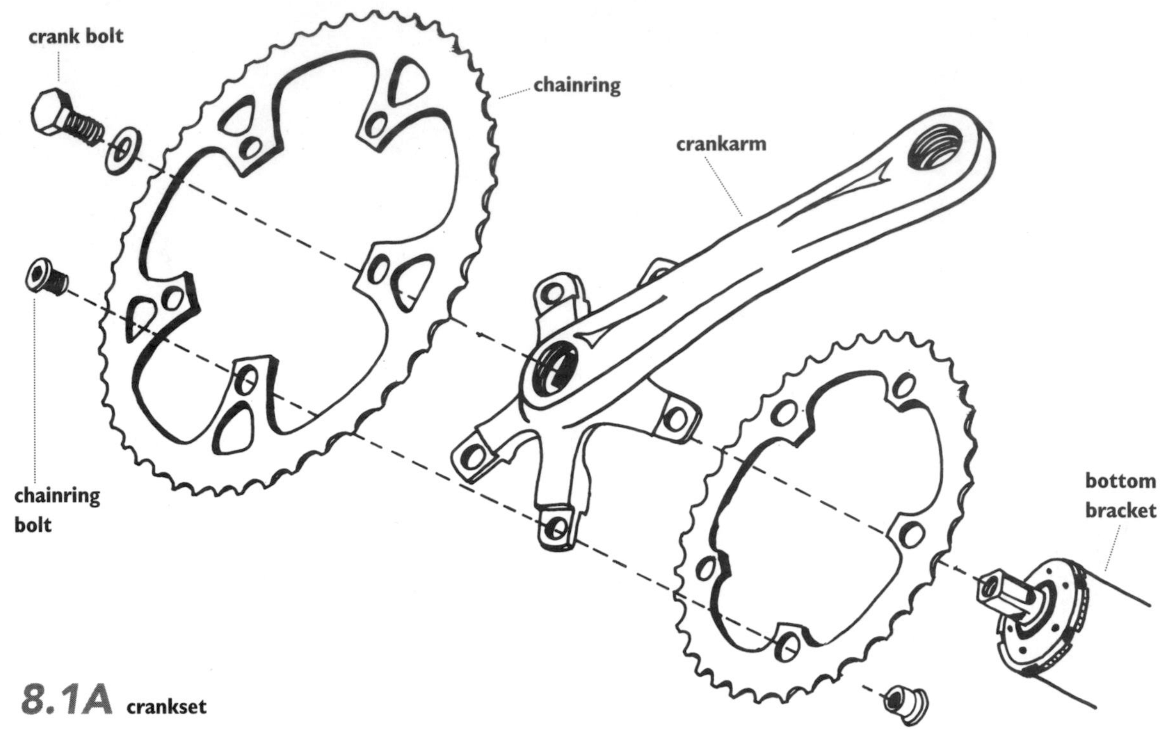

8.1A crankset

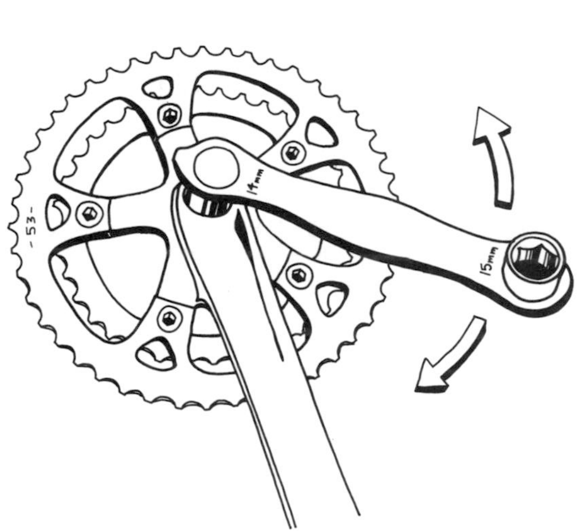

8.2 removing and installing crank bolt

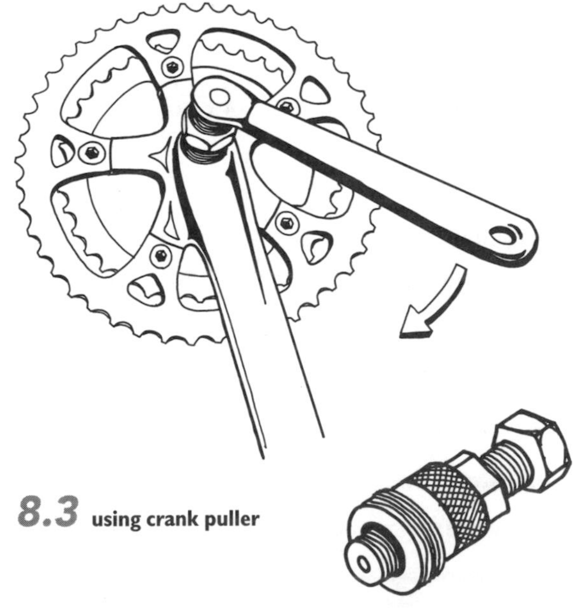

8.3 using crank puller

2. Unscrew the crank bolt, using the appropriate wrench (Fig. 8.2). If the crank does not pull off as the bolt unscrews (see "Note" below), make sure you remove the washer under the bolt after you remove the bolt (Fig. 8.1A). A washer left in will prevent the crank puller from pushing on the end of the axle. If the crank comes right off, skip the following steps.

Note: *Most current high-end Shimano and recent Campagnolo road cranks, as well as old Shimano Dyna-Drive, are self-extracting; that is, they require no crank puller. A ring threaded into the crank holds down the crank bolt; as the bolt is unscrewed, its outer lip pushes on the ring and pushes the crank off. Sometimes the ring is not properly secured, and it unscrews. In this case, you need to hold the ring by its* *two holes with a pin tool while you unscrew the bolt with a hex key. If this fails (and you do not have a Shimano splined-pipe-axle bottom bracket, Fig. 8.13), you can unscrew and remove the ring, remove the crank bolt and use a crank puller (see below).*

3. Holding the crank puller (Fig. 8.3) in your hand, unscrew its center push bolt so that the inner and outer threaded ends of the tool are flush.

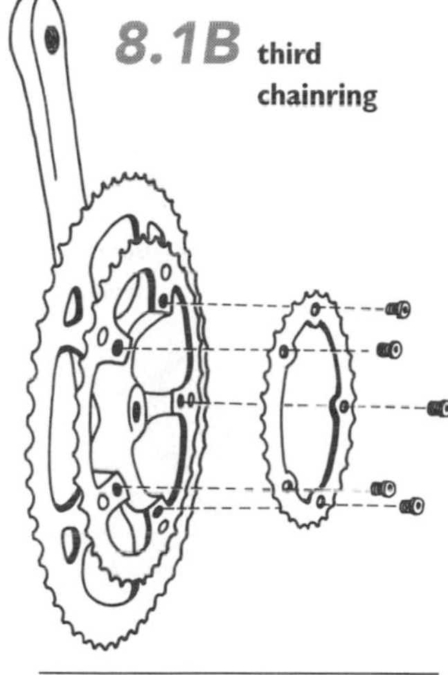

8.1B third chainring

4. Thread the outer part of the crank puller into the hole in the crankarm. Thread it in as far as it can go (preferably by hand; clean the threads if it won't thread in easily); otherwise, you will not engage sufficient crank threads when you tighten the push bolt, and the threads will be damaged. Future crank removal depends on those threads being in good condition.

5. Tighten the push bolt clockwise (Fig. 8.3), either with a wrench, or a socket wrench handle or a built-in handle, until the crankarm pulls off of the axle. Unscrew the puller from the crankarm.

B. Installation:

1. Slide the crankarm onto the bottom bracket axle. Clean off all grease from both parts. Greasing the axle would allow the soft aluminum crank to slide too far onto the hard steel or titanium axle and could deform the square hole in the crank. With a splined spindle and crank, grease is irrelevant either way.

2. Install the crank bolt. Apply grease to the threads, and tighten (Fig. 8.2). If you have a torque wrench, here is an excellent place to break it out and tighten the bolt to about 300 to 435 inch-pounds (see Appendix E). If you're not using a torque wrench, make sure the bolt is quite snug, but don't muscle it into submission.

3. Replace the dust cover, if the crank has one.

4. Removing and reinstalling the right crankarm could position the crank further inboard than it was previously, which will affect shifting, so check the front derailleur adjustment. (See Chapter 5, Section 5-5.)

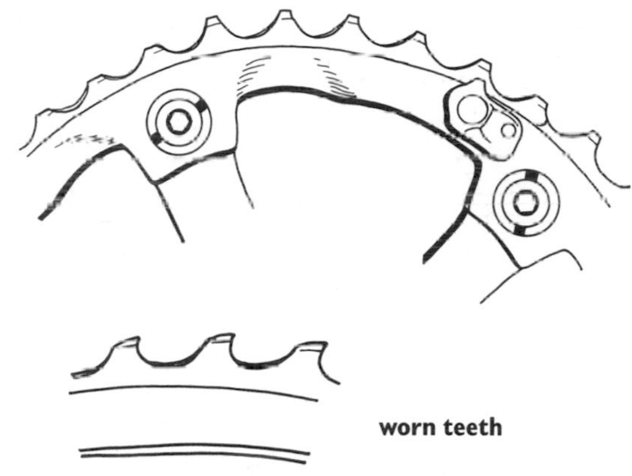

8.4 chainring shifting ramps and asymmetrical teeth

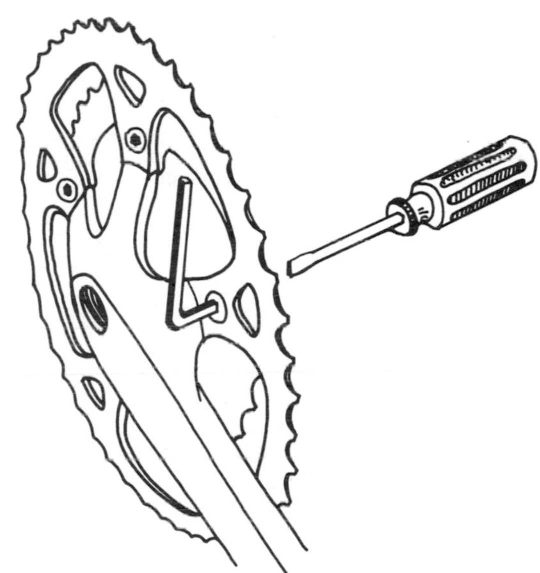

8.5 removing and installing chainring bolts

8-2: CHAINRINGS

You should get into the habit of checking the chainrings regularly. They do wear out and need to be replaced. It's hard to say how often, so include

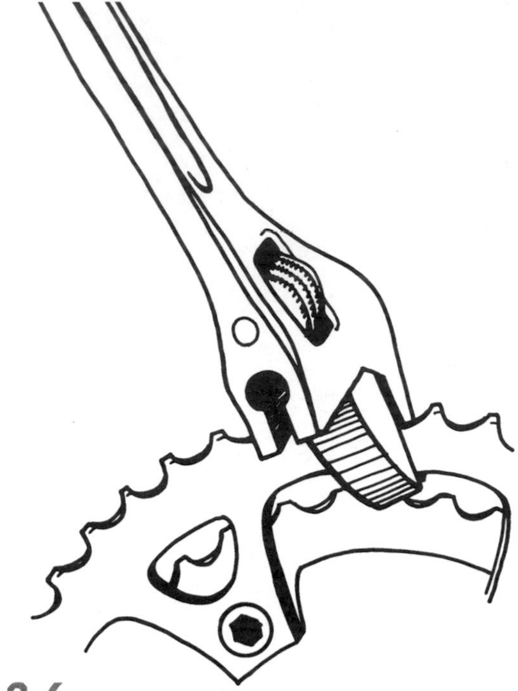

8.6 straightening warped chainrings

chainrings as part of your regular maintenance checklist. Always check them for wear when you replace the chain.

The chainring teeth should be checked periodically for wear; the chainring bolts should be checked periodically for tightness; the chainrings themselves should be checked for trueness by watching them as they spin past the front derailleur.

1. Wipe the chainring down and inspect each tooth. The teeth should be straight and uniform in size and shape. Caution: Don't be deceived by the erratic tooth shapes on modern chainrings designed to facilitate shifting (Fig. 8.4); check if the odd shapes repeat regularly. Shifting ramps on the inboard side, meant to speed chain movement between the rings often look like cracks.

If the teeth are worn hook-shaped, the chainring needs to be replaced. The chain should be replaced as well (see Chapter 4, Section 4-5), since this tooth shape effectively changes the spacing between teeth and accelerates wear on the chain.

Another wear evaluation method is to lift the chain from the top of the chainring; the greater the wear of either part, the further the chain separates. If it lifts more than one tooth, the chain, and perhaps the chainring as well, needs to be replaced.

2. Remove minor gouges in the chainrings with a file.

3. If an individual tooth is bent, try bending it back carefully with a pair of pliers or a Crescent wrench (Fig. 8.6). If it breaks off, take the message and buy a new chainring.

4. While turning the crank slowly, watch where the chain exits the bottom of the chainring. See if any of the teeth are reluctant to let go of the chain. If the chain gets pulled up a bit as it leaves the bottom of the chainring, it can get sucked up between the chainring and the chainstay. Locate any offending teeth and see if you can correct the problem. If the teeth are really chewed up or cannot be improved with pliers and a file, the chainring should be replaced.

chainring bolts

8-3: CHAINRING BOLTS

Check that the bolts are tight by turning them clockwise with a 5mm Allen wrench (Fig. 8.5). If, as you try to tighten the bolt, its nut turns, hold the nut with a two-pronged chainring-nut tool designed especially for this purpose, or with a screwdriver (Fig. 8.5).

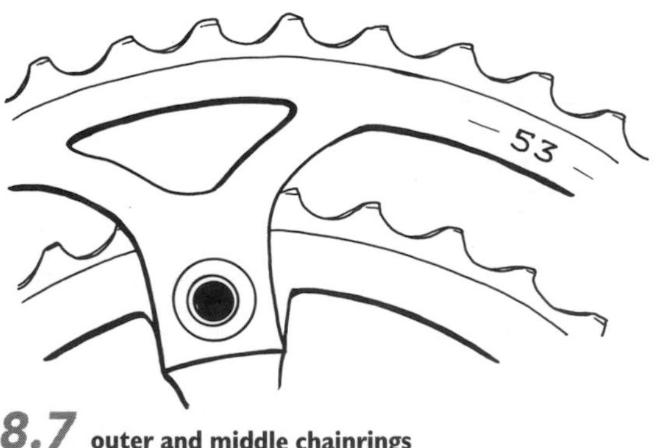

8.7 outer and middle chainrings

8.8 **Shimano LX, XT and XTR cranks use a cassette system for the rings**

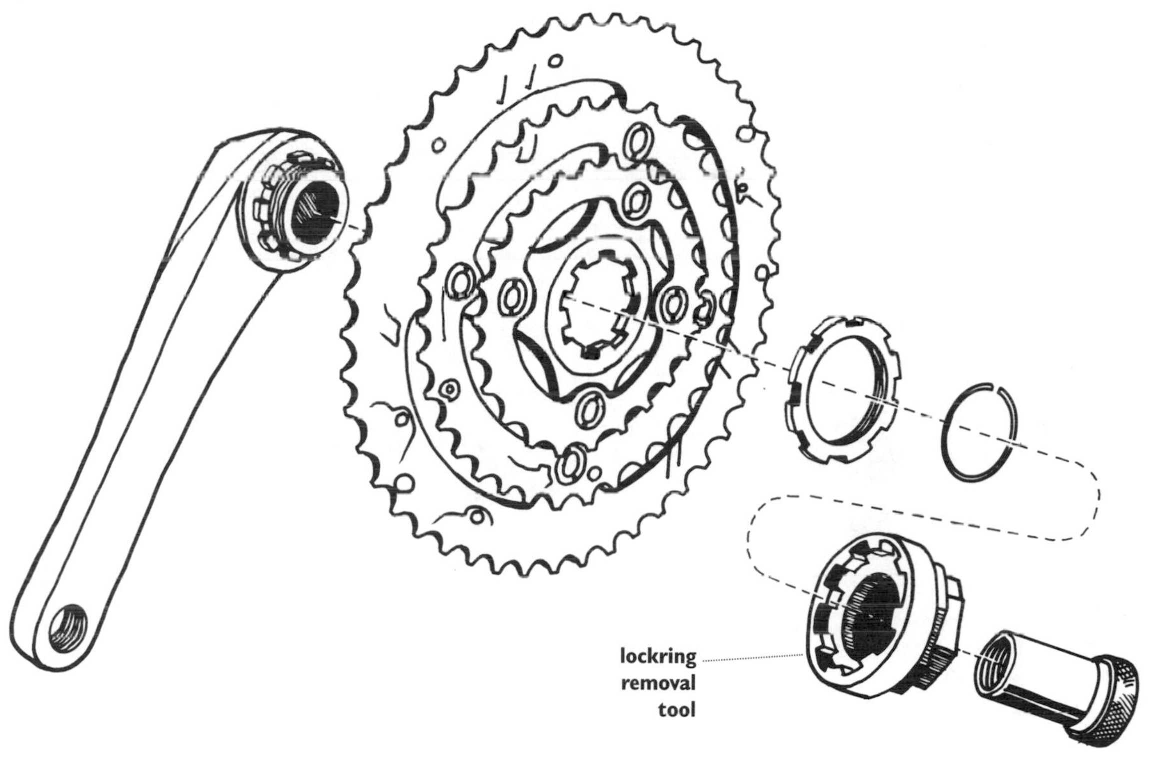

8-4: WARPED CHAINRINGS

Looking down from above, turn the crank slowly and see whether the chainrings wobble back and forth relative to the plane of the front derailleur.

If they do, make sure there is no play in the bottom bracket by grabbing the crankarms and attempting to rock the bottom bracket axle back and forth. If there is play, adjust the bottom bracket (step 15, Section 8-8). It is normal to have a small amount of chainring wobble and flex when you pedal hard, but excessive wobbling will compromise shifting. Small, localized bends can be straightened with a Crescent wrench (Fig. 8.6). If a ring is really bent, replace it.

8-5: BENT CRANKARM SPIDERS

If you installed a new chainring and are still seeing serious back-and-forth wobble, chances are good that the spider arms on the crank are bent. If the crank is new, this is a warranty item, so take it to your bike shop.

8-6: CHAINRING REPLACEMENT

A. Double chainrings

Replacing either of the chainrings on a double (or the two largest chainrings on a triple) is easy (Fig. 8.7).

1. Unscrew the chainring bolts with a 5mm Allen key (Fig. 8.5). You may need to hold the nut on the backside with either a chainring-nut tool or a thin screwdriver.

2. Install the new chainrings, lubricate the bolts, and tighten them (Fig. 8.5).

Note: *Whenever you change the size of the outer chainring, you must reposition the front derailleur for proper chainring clearance, as described in Chapter 5, Section 5-5.*

B. To replace the inner chainring on a triple:

1. Pull off the crankarm (Section 8-1, Figs. 8.2 and 8.3).

2. Remove the 5mm Allen bolts holding the chainring. They are threaded directly into the crankarm (Fig. 8.1B).

8.9 **bottom bracket assembly**

3. Install the new ring, and lube and tighten the bolts.

Note: *Some triple cranks have chainrings that come off as a set; these are generally mountain cranks, but they can be used on a road bike. Current Shimano XT and XTR cranks rely on a thread-on cassette system that allows you to spin off all three chainrings from the crankarm as a unit (Fig. 8.8). After removing a circlip (by prying it off with a screwdriver), a special lockring tool loosens the chainring-cassette lockring; a female-threaded tool that goes on the crank bolt holds the lockring tool in place (Fig. 8.8). Once the cassette is off, you can interchange chainrings within the set or simply pop on a whole new set.*

Inexpensive cranks often have chainrings riveted to the crank or riveted to each other and bolted to the crank as a unit. If the chainrings are damaged, you may have to replace the entire crankset.

4. Replace the crankarm (Section 8-1, Fig. 8.2).

8B: BOTTOM BRACKETS

Most bottom brackets simply thread into the frame's bottom bracket shell (Fig. 8.9). Simple enough, but it's important to remember that not all of these threads are the same.

Almost all current road bikes use English standard threads. That translates into a 1.370-inch diameter and a thread pitch of 24 threads per inch. These numbers are usually engraved on the bottom bracket cups. If you are replacing a bottom bracket, make sure that the new cups have the same threads. It is important to remember that the drive side (right side) of an English standard bottom bracket has left-hand threads. In other words, turning counterclockwise tightens the drive-side cup (Fig. 8.16). Meanwhile, the left cup has right-hand threads that are, therefore, tightened clockwise.

Other threads you may run across are Italian (with a 36mm diameter, and note that both cups have right-hand threads), French and Swiss (both of these come in 35mm diameter, but use different thread directions). The latter two thread patterns are very rare, although French threading was common until the early 1980s.

The most common type of bottom bracket in the 1990s is the Shimano-style cartridge bottom bracket with splined cups (Fig. 8.10). The most common bottom bracket in the 1980s and before was the "cup and cone" style with loose ball bearings (Fig.

8.10-14 types of bottom brackets

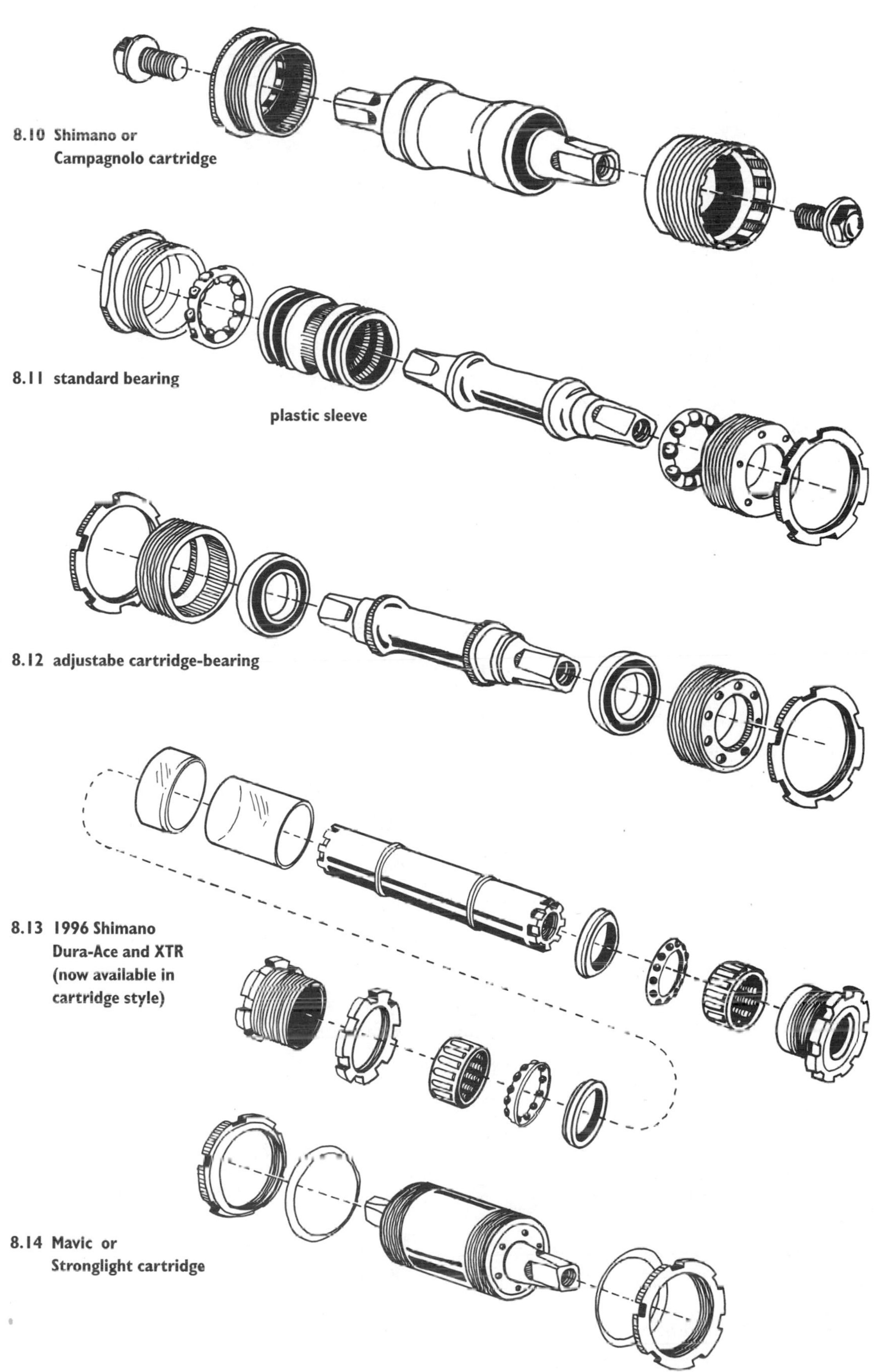

8.15 tightening and loosening left bottom bracket cup

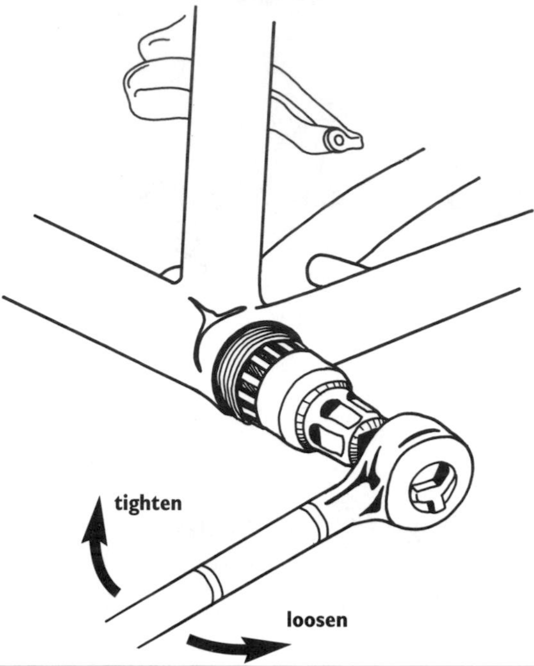

8.11). Another bottom bracket type has a sealed cartridge bearing on either end secured by an adjustable cup and lockring at either end (Fig. 8.12). Shimano's latest bottom brackets both cartridge adn cup-in-cone, have a large tubular axle with splined, not square, ends (Fig. 8.13).

Some bottom brackets do not thread into the bottom bracket shell. One rare type utilizes cartridge bearings held into an unthreaded bottom bracket shell by snap rings in machined grooves. Another type includes a cartridge threaded on each end (Fig. 8.14); it slips into the bottom bracket shell and is held in place by lockrings threaded onto the cartridge.

bottom bracket installation

8C: BOTTOM-BRACKET INSTALLATION

LEVEL 2

The most important item in bottom bracket installation is to make sure that the axle length in the bottom bracket is correct. If it's incorrect, the chainrings will not line up well with the rear cogs (i.e., the chainline will be off; see Chapter 5, Section 5-40). Some bikes come from the factory with the wrong length bottom bracket. No amount of fiddling with the derailleurs will get such a bike to shift properly. Get a bottom bracket specifically recommended for your crankset and double-check that it has the proper threading for your frame. Before installing a new bottom bracket of a different brand and model than your crank, see Fig. 5.34, and read the chainline section (5-40) at the end of Chapter 5.

Always grease the threads when installing bottom brackets (or use an anti-seize compound on them).

8-7: INSTALLATION OF SHIMANO OR CAMPAGNOLO CARTRIDGE-SEALED BOTTOM BRACKETS (AND CLONES)

As of this writing, most road bottom brackets are Shimano-style sealed cartridge units (Fig. 8.10) that are installed with a splined tool (Fig. 1.3).

1. Slide the cartridge into the bottom-bracket shell, paying particular attention to the "right" and "left" markings on the cartridge. The cup with the raised lip is the drive-side cup (the cup on the left in Fig. 8.10). The drive-side cup is left-hand threaded on an English-thread bottom bracket and right-hand threaded on an Italian-threaded one.

2. Using the splined cup tool (for Shimano or Campagnolo) with either an open-end wrench or a 3/8-inch drive socket wrench on it, tighten the drive-side cup into the drive side of the bottom bracket shell until the lip seats against the face of the shell. The recommended torque is in Appendix E.

Note: *Again, on most bikes, this cup will tighten counterclockwise.*

3. Insert the non-drive-side cup, and, with the

same tool, turn it clockwise until it fits tightly against the cartridge (Fig. 8.15). (See Appendix E for recommended torque.) There is no adjustment of the bearings to be done; you can put on the crank now.

8-8: INSTALLATION OF CUP-AND-CONE BOTTOM BRACKETS

LEVEL 2

Cup-and-cone (or "loose-ball") bottom brackets (Figs. 8.11 and 8.13) use ball bearings that ride between cone-shaped bearing surfaces on the axle and cup-shaped races in the threaded cups. One cup, called the fixed cup (the cup on the left in Fig. 8.11), has a lip on it and fits on the drive side (right side) of the bike. The other, called the adjustable cup (the right cup in Fig. 8.11), has a lockring that threads onto the cup and against the face of the bottom bracket shell. The individual ball bearings are usually held together

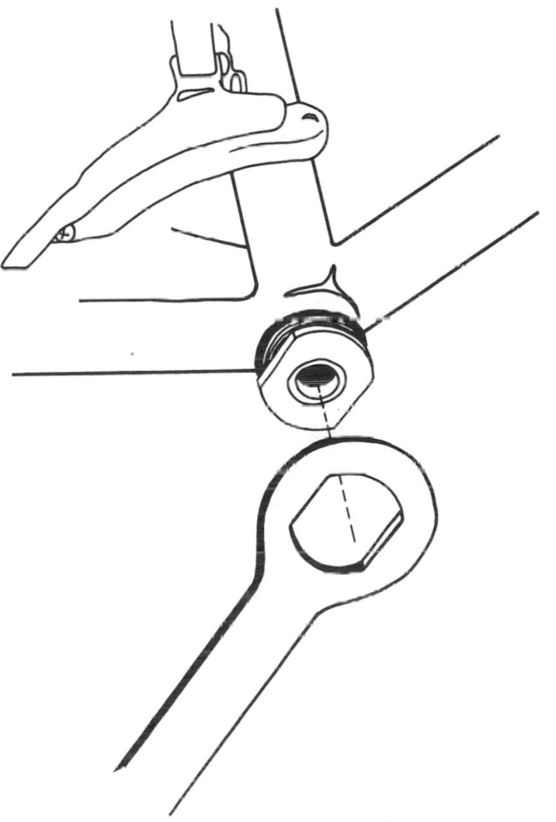

8.16 driveside fixed cup

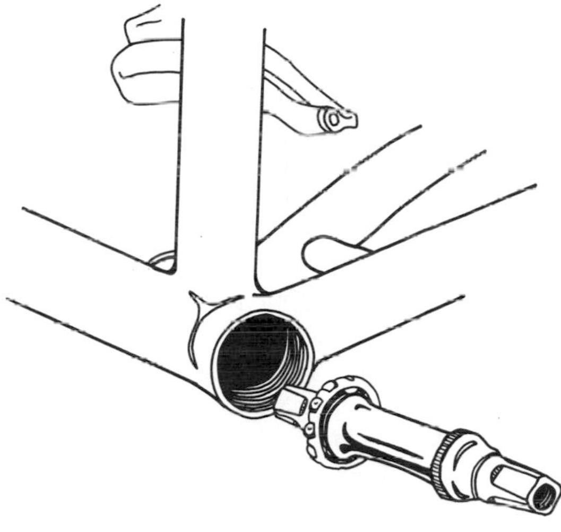

8.17 placing axle in shell

by a retaining cage, which varies in shape depending on bottom bracket. Some folks prefer to do without the retainer; it works fine either way.

In order for cup-and-cone bottom brackets to turn smoothly, it is important that the bearing surfaces of the cups are parallel. Since the cups thread into the bottom bracket shell, the threads on both sides of the shell must be lined up with each other, and the end faces of the shell must be parallel. If you have any doubts about your frame, it is a good idea to have the bottom bracket shell tapped (threaded) and faced (ends cut parallel) by a qualified shop possessing the proper tools.

1. Unless you have a fixed-cup tool, have a shop install the fixed cup for you. The shop tool assures that the cup goes in straight and very tightly. The tool pictured in Fig. 8.16 can be used in a pinch, but it can let the cup go in crooked and will slip off before you get it really tight. The fixed cup must be very tight (see Appendix E for torque) so it does not vibrate loose. Remember that English-threaded fixed cups are tightened counterclockwise.

2. Wipe the inside surface of both cups with a clean rag, and put a thin layer of clean grease on the bearing surfaces. Apply enough so that the balls

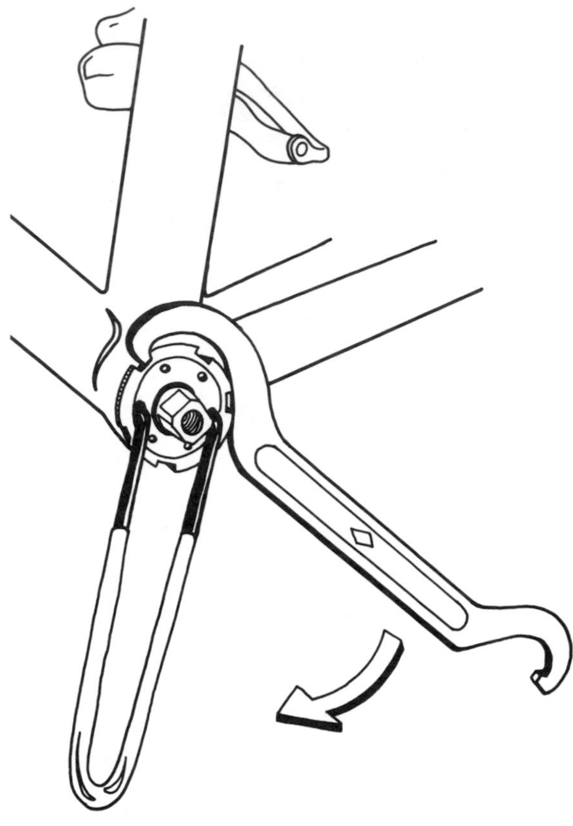

8.18 tightening lockring

will be half-covered; more than that will be wasted and will attract dirt.

3. Wipe the axle (also called a spindle) with a clean rag.

4. Figure out which end of the bottom-bracket axle is the drive side. The drive side may be marked with an "R;" if not, you can tell by choosing the side with the longer end (when measured from the bearing surface). If there is writing on the axle, it will usually read right-side-up for a rider sitting on the bike. If there is no marking and no length difference, the axle orientation is irrelevant.

5. Slide one set of bearings onto the drive-side end of the axle (Fig. 8.17). If you're using a retainer cage, make sure you put it on right. The balls, rather than the retainer cage, should rest against the axle bearing surfaces. Since there are two types of retainers with opposite designs, you need to be careful to avoid binding, as well as smashing of the retainers. If you're still confused, there is one easy test: If it's in right, it'll turn smoothly; if it's in wrong, it won't.

If you have loose ball bearings with no retainer cage, stick them into the greased cup. Most set-ups rely on nine balls; you can confirm that you are using the correct number by inserting and removing the axle and checking to make sure that they are evenly distributed in the grease with no extra gap for more balls.

6. Slide the axle into the bottom bracket so that it pushes the bearings into the fixed cup (Fig. 8.17). You can use your pinkie stuck through from the other side to stabilize the end of the axle as you slide it in.

7. Insert the protective plastic sleeve (shown in Figs. 8.11 and 8.13) into the shell against the inside edge of the fixed cup. The sleeve keeps dirt and rust from falling from the frame tubes into the bearings, so if you don't have one, get one.

8. Now turn your attention to the other cup. Place the bearing set into the greased adjustable cup. If you are using a bearing retainer, make sure it is properly oriented. If you are using loose balls, press them lightly into the grease so they stay in place.

9. Without the lockring, slide the adjustable cup over the axle and tighten it clockwise by hand into the shell, being certain that it is going in straight. Screw the cup in as far as you can by hand—ideally, all the way until the bearings seat between the axle and cup.

10. Locate the appropriate tool for tightening the adjustable cup. Most cups have two holes that accept the ends, or pins, of an adjustable cup wrench called a "pin spanner" (Fig. 1.3). The other common type of adjustable cup has two flats for a

wrench; on this type, you may use an adjustable wrench.

11. Carefully tighten the adjustable cup against the bearings, taking great care not to overtighten. Turn the axle periodically with your fingers to ensure that it moves freely. If it binds up, you have gone too far, back it off a bit. The danger of overtightening is that the bearings can force dents into the bearing surfaces of the cups, and the bearings will never turn smoothly again.

12. Screw the lockring onto the adjustable cup, and select the proper tool for it. Lockrings come in different shapes, and so do lockring spanners; make sure yours mate properly with each other.

13. Tighten the lockring against the face of the bottom-bracket shell with the lockring spanner while holding the adjustable cup in place with a pin spanner (Fig. 8.18). If you turn the bicycle upside down, you can pull down harder on the wrenches.

14. As you snug the lockring against the bottom-bracket shell, check the axle periodically. The lockring can pull the cup out of the shell minutely and loosen the adjustment. The axle should turn smoothly without free play in the bearings. I recommend installing and tightening the drive-side crankarm onto the drive end of the axle (Fig. 8.2) at this time so you can check for free play by wiggling the end of the crank; it will give you a better feel for any looseness in the system.

15. Adjust the cup so that the axle play is just barely eliminated. While holding the cup in place, tighten the lockring as much as you can (Fig. 8.18) so the bottom bracket does not come out of adjustment while riding (recommended torque is in Appendix E; tightening it as much as you can is about right). You may have to repeat this step a time or two until you get the ideal adjustment.

8-9: INSTALLATION OF OTHER TYPES OF BOTTOM BRACKETS

The two bottom-bracket types mentioned above probably represent about 95 percent of the road bikes in circulation. There are, however, a few variations worth mentioning.

A. Cartridge-bearing bottom brackets with adjustable cups (Fig. 8.12) are reasonably easy to install. These come with an adjustable cup at each end. With this type, you simply install the drive-side cup and lockring, slide the cartridge bearing in (if it is not already pressed into the cup), slip the axle in, and then install the other bearing, cup and lockring. Tighten each lockring while holding the adjustable cup in place with a pin spanner (Fig. 8.18). Adjust for free play as in Section 8-8, steps 11-15.

The advantage of having two adjustable cups is that you can center the cartridge by moving it side to side in the bottom-bracket shell. If the chainrings end up too close or too far away from the frame (see chainline discussion and Fig. 5.34 in the Troubleshooting section at the end of Chapter 5, Section 5-40), you can move one cup in and one out to shift the position of the spindle.

Sometimes cartridge-bearing bottom brackets bind up a bit during adjustment and installation. A light tap on each end of the axle usually seats them.

B. Stronglight (or Mavic) cartridge bottom brackets (Fig. 8.14) require each end of the bottom-bracket shell to be chamfered at an angle to seat the angled lockrings. You need to go to a shop equipped with the correct cutting tool for this. Once the bottom-bracket-shell chamfer has been cut, you simply slip the cartridge into the shell, slide on one of the angled plastic rings from either end (pictured in Fig. 8.14), and screw on a lockring, angled side inward, from either side. Holding the cartridge with a pin spanner, tighten the lockrings on each side (Fig. 8.18). The beauty of these bottom brackets is that they work independently of the shell threads, so they can be installed in shells with ruined threads or non-standard threads. Mavic stopped producing them in 1995, but Stronglight now makes them.

C. An unthreaded bottom-bracket shell with snap-ring grooves accepts only a type of bottom bracket without cups (not pictured); snaprings retain the bearings. This type was popular at the beginning of the 1980s but has virtually disappeared on new bikes. With a cupless bottom bracket, seat the cartridge bearings against the stops on either end of the axle. Install one snap-ring with snap-ring pliers into the groove in one end of the shell. Push the entire assembly of axle and two bearings in from the other side of the bottom-bracket shell. Install the other snap-ring, and you're done.

8D: OVERHAULING THE BOTTOM BRACKET

LEVEL 2

A bottom-bracket overhaul consists of cleaning or replacing the bearings, cleaning the axle and bearing surfaces, and re-greasing them. With any type, both crankarms must be removed (Section 8-1).

overhauling bottom brackets

8-10: OVERHAULING CARTRIDGE BOTTOM BRACKETS

LEVEL 2

Standard cartridge bottom brackets (Fig. 8.10) are sealed units and cannot be overhauled. They must be replaced when they stop performing properly. Remove the cranks as in Section 8-1. Remove the bottom bracket by unscrewing the cups with the splined cup tool (Fig. 8.15), and install a new bottom bracket as directed in Section 8-7, above.

8-11: OVERHAULING CUP-AND-CONE BOTTOM BRACKETS

LEVEL 2

Cup-and-cone bottom brackets (Fig. 8.11) can be overhauled entirely from the non-drive side, after you have removed the crankarms as described in Section 8-1.

1. Remove the lockring with the lockring spanner (as in Fig. 8.18, except the lockring spanner and the rotation direction will be reversed).

2. Remove the adjustable cup with the tool that fits yours (usually a pin spanner (Fig. 1.3), installed into the cup as in Fig. 8.18).

3. Leave the fixed cup in place, and check that it is tight in the frame by putting a fixed cup wrench on it and trying to tighten it (counterclockwise for English thread, clockwise for Italian), (Fig. 8.16).

4. Clean the cups and axle with a rag. There should be no need for a solvent unless the parts are glazed.

5. Clean the bearings with a citrus-based solvent, without removing them from their retainer cages. A simple way to do this is to drop the bearings in a plastic bottle, fill it with solvent, cap it and shake it. A toothbrush may be required afterward, and a solvent tank is certainly handy if you have access to one. If your bearings are not shiny and in perfect shape, replace them. Balls with dull luster and/or rough spots or rust on them should be replaced.

6. Wash the bearings in soap and water to remove the solvent and any remaining grit. Towel them off thoroughly, and then let them dry completely. An air compressor is handy here.

7. Follow the installation procedure described in Section 8-8.

8. Install the crankarms as in Section 8-1, Fig. 8.2.

8-12: OVERHAULING OTHER TYPES OF BOTTOM BRACKETS

LEVEL 2

If any cartridge-bearing bottom bracket becomes difficult to turn, the bearings must be replaced. If they are pressed into cups, then you may also have to buy new cups. Be doubly sure to get the correct size.

1. Reverse the installation procedure outlined above in Section 8-9 to remove the bottom bracket.

2. Replace the bearings.

3. Re-install the bottom bracket (Section 8-9) and crankarms (Section 8-1).

8E TROUBLESHOOTING CRANK- AND BOTTOM-BRACKET NOISE

8-13: CREAKING NOISES

Mysterious creaking noises can drive you nuts. Just as you think you have your bike tuned to perfection, a little noise comes along to ruin your ride. What's worse is that these annoying little creaks, pops and groans can be a bear to locate.

Pedaling-induced noises can originate from almost anything connected to your crankset, including movement of the cleats on your shoes, loose crankarms on the bottom-bracket axle, loose chainrings, or poorly adjusted pedal- or bottom bracket-bearings. Of course, noise could also originate from seemingly unrelated components like the seat, seatpost, frame, wheels, or handlebars.

Before spending hours overhauling the drivetrain, spend some time trying to isolate the source of the noise. Try different pedals and shoes and wheels. Pedal out of the saddle, and pedal without flexing the handlebars. If the source of the creak turns out to be the saddle, seatpost, pedals, wheels, or handlebars, turn to the appropriate chapter for directions on how to correct the problem.

If the creaking is definitely in the crank area:

1. Check to make sure that the chainring bolts are tight, and tighten them if they are not (Fig. 8.5).

2. If that does not solve the problem, make certain that the crankarm bolts are tight (Fig. 8.2). If they are not, the resulting movement between the crankarm and the bottom-bracket axle is a likely source of noise. If the crank is of a different brand than the bottom bracket, check with the manufacturers or your local shop to make sure that they are recommended for use together. Incompatible cranks and axles will never properly join and are a potential problem area.

3. Rusting can break the glue bond between a Shimano cartridge bottom bracket and one or both of its cups, allowing movement between cartridge and cup. This movement can make creaking noises when pedaling. To quiet it down, remove the cartridge, grease the inside of the cup(s) as well as the threads, and re-install the bottom bracket.

4. The bottom bracket itself can creak due to improper adjustment, lack of grease, cracked bearings, worn parts, or loose cups. All of these things require adjustment or overhaul procedures, outlined in Section 8C of this chapter.

5. If you have an unpainted titanium or aluminum frame, check to make sure that the front derailleur clamp is tight. The noise from a loose clamp while pedaling, especially under heavy load, can seem to emanate from the crankset.

6. Now for the bad news. If creaking persists, the problem could be rooted in the frame. Creaks can originate from cracks in and around the bottom-bracket shell. Or the threads in the bottom bracket shell could be so worn that they allow the cups to move slightly. Neither of these is a good sign—unless, of course, you were hoping for an excuse to buy a new frame.

8-14: CLUNKING NOISES

1. Crankarm play: Grab the crankarm and push on it side to side.

a. If there is play, tighten the crankarm bolt (Fig. 8.2; torque spec is in Appendix E).

b. If there is still crankarm play, and you have a cup-and-cone bottom bracket (Figs. 8.11, 8.13) or a cartridge-bearing bottom bracket with a lockring on each side (Fig. 8.12), adjust the bottom bracket axle end play (steps 11-15, Section 8-8).

c. If bottom-bracket adjustment does not eliminate crankarm play, or you have a non-adjustable cartridge bottom bracket (Fig. 8.10), the bottom bracket is loose in the frame threads. With a cup-and-cone bottom bracket, you can go back to Section 8-8 and start over, making sure that the fixed cup is very tight. A cheater bar (extension tube) may need to be used on the fixed-cup wrench to tighten it to high enough torque. Adjustable-cup lockrings need to be equally tight (Fig. 8.18), once the axle end play is adjusted properly.

d. The lockrings and fixed-cup flanges must be flush against the bottom bracket shell all of the way around; if they are not, the bottom bracket must be removed, and the bottom bracket shell must be tapped (threaded) and faced (cut parallel) by a shop equipped with the tools.

e. If the crankarm play persists or the bottom-bracket fixed cup or lockring will not tighten up completely, then either the bottom-bracket cups are stripped or undersized, or the frame's bottom-bracket-shell threads are stripped or oversized. Either way, it's an expensive fix, especially the frame replacement option! Get a second opinion if you reach this point. If you can find a Mavic or Stronglight cartridge bottom bracket (Section 8-9B, Fig. 8.14), you can still use a frame with stripped threads.

2. Pedal end play: Grab each pedal and wobble it to check for play. See Overhauling Pedals, Section 9B in Chapter 9 if you find axle end play.

8-15: HARD-TO-TURN CRANKS

If the cranks are hard to turn, you need to overhaul the bottom bracket (see Section 8C, above), unless you want to continue intensifying your workout or boost the egos of your cycling companions. The bottom bracket may be shot and need to be replaced.

8-16: INNER CHAINRING DRAGS ON CHAINSTAY

The bottom bracket axle is too short, or the square hole in the crankarm is so deformed that the crank slides on too far, or you have switched to a larger inner chainring. A misaligned frame, with either bent chainstays or a twisted bottom bracket shell, can cause chainring rub as well.

With an adjustable cartridge-bearing bottom bracket with a lockring on each end, it is possible to fix the problem by offsetting the entire bottom bracket to the left (Fig. 8.18).

If the bottom bracket axle is too short, replace it with one of the correct length.

If the square hole in the crank is badly deformed, replace the crankarm. There's no other cure; it will continue to loosen up and cause problems otherwise.

If the chainring is too large, get a smaller one.

A badly misaligned frame needs to be replaced.

Note: *See Section 5-40 at the end of Chapter 5 (Fig. 5.34) on chainline to establish proper crank-to-frame spacing.*

Pedals

"Experience is that marvelous thing that enables you to recognize a mistake when you make it again." —F. P. Jones

tools

15mm pedal wrench
2.5mm, 3mm, 4mm, 5mm and 6mm hex keys
Phillips-head screwdriver
Small flat-blade screwdriver
Snap ring pliers
8mm, 9mm, 10mm, 12mm, 20mm and 22mm box wrenches
13mm cone wrench
Shimano, Look splined pedal axle tools
Grease
Fine-tipped grease gun
Chain lubricant

OPTIONAL

Splined Campagnolo pedal cap tool
Torx drivers
8mm socket wrench
Speedplay grease fitting
Threadlock compound

To best serve its purpose, a bicycle pedal needs only to be firmly attached to the crankarm, and provide a stable platform for the shoe. A simple enough task, but you'd be amazed at the different approaches that have been taken to achieve this goal.

Still, for the purpose of our discussion, there are two basic types of road pedals. One, the standard cage-type pedal with a toeclip and strap (Fig. 9.2), is the simplest and cheapest. The second, or "clip-in" type (Fig. 9.1), retains the foot with spring-loaded clips (like a ski binding) and is almost universal on mid- to high-end road bikes. Clip-in pedals are sometimes called "clipless," since they have no toeclip.

Cage-type pedals are fairly common on lower-end bikes. They are relatively unintimidating for the novice rider, and the frame (or "cage") that surrounds the pedal provides a large, stable platform (Fig. 9.2). A symmetrical BMX-style pedal has an identical top and bottom, and it can be used with just about any type of shoe. If you mount toeclips on these without straps, your feet won't slide forward and will release easily in almost any direction.

One-sided road cage pedals (Fig. 9.2) are designed to be used exclusively with toeclips, since they cannot be pedaled upside-down very well. A toe strap keeps your foot on the pedal and also allows you to pull on the upward part of the pedal stroke, giving you more power, a fluid pedal stroke

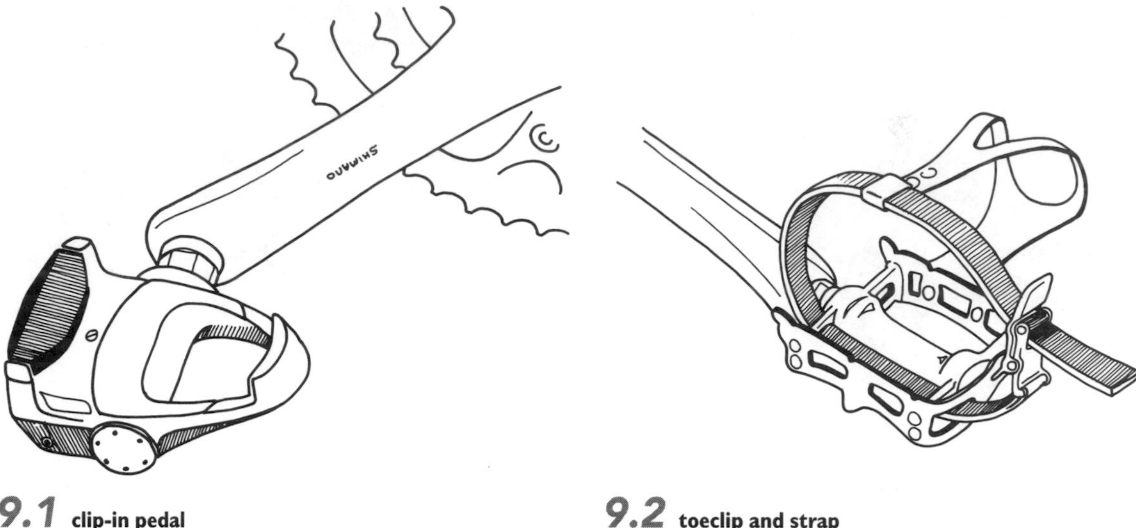

9.1 clip-in pedal

9.2 toeclip and strap

and balanced muscle development. Of course, as you add clips and straps, the pedal becomes harder to enter and to exit, and running shoes with aggressive tread become increasingly difficult to use.

Clip-in models (Fig. 9.1, 9.3, 9.4) offer all of the advantages of toeclips and straps coupled with a slotted cleat mounted on a stiff shoe, yet they allow easier entry and exit from the pedal. Clip-in pedals are more expensive and require special shoes and accurate mounting of the cleats. Your choice of shoes is limited to stiff-sole models that accept cleats for your particular pedal. Once you have them properly mounted and adjusted, you will find that clip-in pedals waste less energy through flex and slippage and allow you to transfer more power directly to the pedals.

This chapter explains how to remove and replace pedals, how to mount the cleats and adjust the release tension with clip-in pedals, how to troubleshoot pedal problems, and how to overhaul and replace spindles on almost all road pedals. Incidentally, I use the terms "axle" and "spindle" interchangeably.

9-1: PEDAL REMOVAL AND INSTALLATION

Note that the right pedal axle is right-hand threaded and the left is left-hand (reverse) threaded. Both unscrew from the crank in the pedaling direction. There's an interesting bit of history behind the threading of pedal axles this way. In the early days of cycling, fixed-gear bikes were the norm, and it was decided that if the pedal bearings were to seize up, the pedal should unscrew from the crank rather than tear up the rider's strapped-in feet. This isn't a concern on a modern bike, since the freewheel elimates the bodily danger of a seized pedal, and the bearing quality makes seizing highly unlikely.

A. Removal:

1. Slide a 15mm pedal wrench onto the wrench flats of the pedal axle (Fig. 9.3). Or, if the pedal axle is designed to accept it, you can use a 6mm Allen wrench from the back side of the crankarm (Fig. 9.4). The latter is particularly handy on the road, since you probably won't be carrying a 15mm wrench. But if you are at home and the pedal is really tight it will be easier to use the standard pedal wrench.

2. Unscrew the pedal in the appropriate direction. The right, or drive-side, pedal unscrews counterclockwise when viewed from that side. The left-side pedal is reverse threaded, so it unscrews in a

clockwise direction when viewed from the left side of the bike. Once loosened, either pedal can be unscrewed quickly by turning the crank forward with the wrench engaged on the pedal spindle and the rear wheel off the ground.

B. Installation:

1. Use a rag to wipe the threads clean on the pedal axle and inside the crankarm.

2. Apply a light coat of grease to the pedal threads.

3. Start screwing the pedal in with your fingers, clockwise for the right pedal, counterclockwise for the left.

4. Tighten the pedal with the 15mm pedal wrench (Fig. 9.3) or a 6mm Allen wrench (Fig. 9.4). This can be done quickly by turning the cranks backward with the wrench engaged on the pedal spindle.

9A SETTING UP CLIP-IN PEDALS

Setting up clip-in pedals involves installation and adjustment of the cleats on the shoes, and adjusting the pedal release tension.

There are a number of different "mounting platforms" for road pedals, and your shoe sole must be

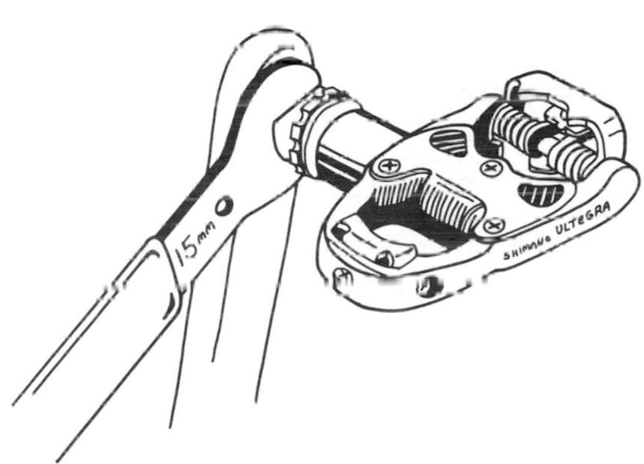

9.3 removing pedal with 15mm wrench

9.4 removing pedal with a 6mm Allen wrench

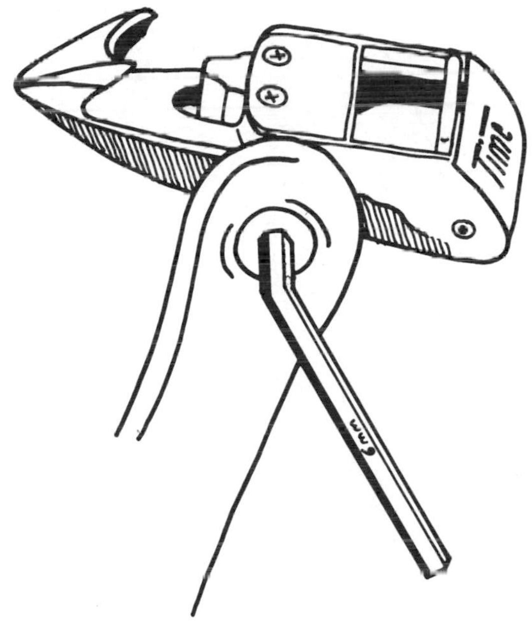

compatible with your pedal cleats. The original clip-in road pedal system was the Look, which has three 5mm x 0.8mm threaded holes arranged in a triangular pattern (Fig. 9.5). The Time pedal system requires a flat surface with four smaller threaded holes (Fig. 9.6). Shimano Pedaling Dynamics, or SPD, cleats mount with two side-by-side 5mm x 0.8mm-thread screws, spaced 14mm apart. They screw into a movable threaded cleat-mounting plate behind two longitudinal grooves in the sole (Fig. 9.7). Lastly, Shimano's SPD-R pedal requires a shoe with a single lengthwise slot in the sole with a 5mm x 0.8mm threaded hole at either end moving on a threaded backing plate behind the slot (Fig. 9.8). (Diadora pedals have yet another mounting pattern, but they are no longer on the market and so will not be covered here.) Pedal manufacturers not listed in this paragraph mount on one or several of these shoe-hole patterns.

Incidentally, many shoe and pedal manufacturers make adapter plates to fit various shoes and pedals

9.5 **Look cleat drill pattern**

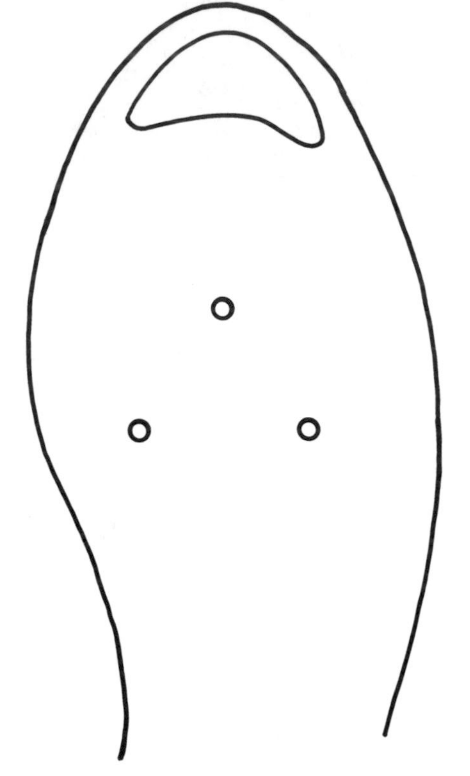

9.6 **Time cleat drill pattern**

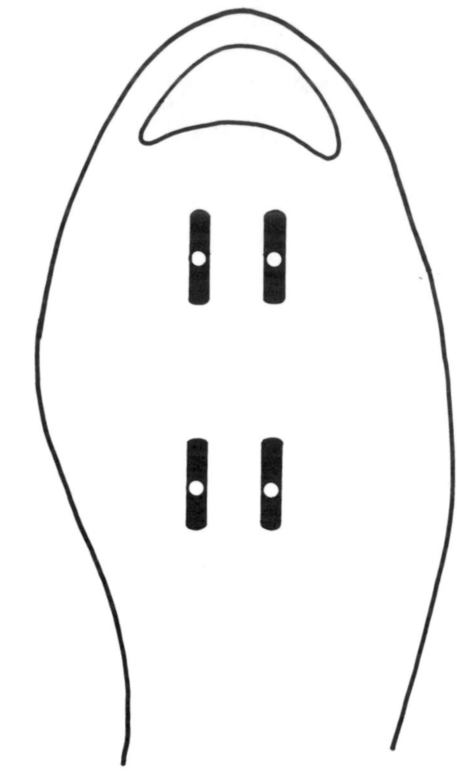

to each other, so that if you have a favorite pair of shoes it may be possible to make them work with an unrelated set of pedals.

9-2: INSTALLING AND ADJUSTING PEDAL CLEATS ON THE SHOES

installing and adjusting cleats

The cleat is important because its position determines the fore-aft, lateral (side-to-side), and rotational position of your foot. If the cleats aren't properly oriented, the misalignment could eventually cause hip, knee or ankle problems.

1. Put the shoe on, and mark the position of the ball of your foot (the big bump behind your big toe) on the outside of the shoe. This will help you position the cleat so the ball of your foot will be above or just ahead of the pedal spindle. Take the shoe off, and continue drawing the line straight across the bottom of the shoe.

2. Grease the cleat screw threads, and screw the cleat that came with the pedals onto the shoe; this usually requires a 4mm Allen wrench or a Phillips-head or standard screwdriver. Make sure you orient the cleat in the appropriate direction. Some cleats have an arrow indicating forward (Fig. 9.9); if yours do not, the instructions accompanying the pedals will specify which direction the cleat should point, and in some cases, on which shoe an asymmetrical cleat should be mounted.

SPD and SPD-R cleats require rubber "pontoons" on a plate mounted under the cleat (Fig. 9.9). The pontoons guide the small cleat into the pedal. The pontoons are not necessary on a mountain-bike shoe with tread to guide the cleat.

3. Position the cleat. Temporarily place it in the middle of its lateral- and rotational-adjustment range. Setting the fore-aft position requires knowing where the pedal spindle is positioned relative to the cleat. Many cleats have a mark on the side indicat-

9.7 SPD cleat drill pattern

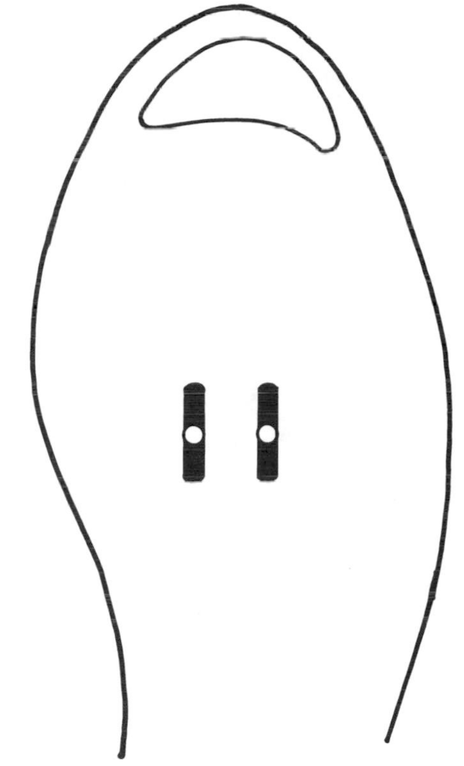

9.8 SPD-R cleat drill pattern

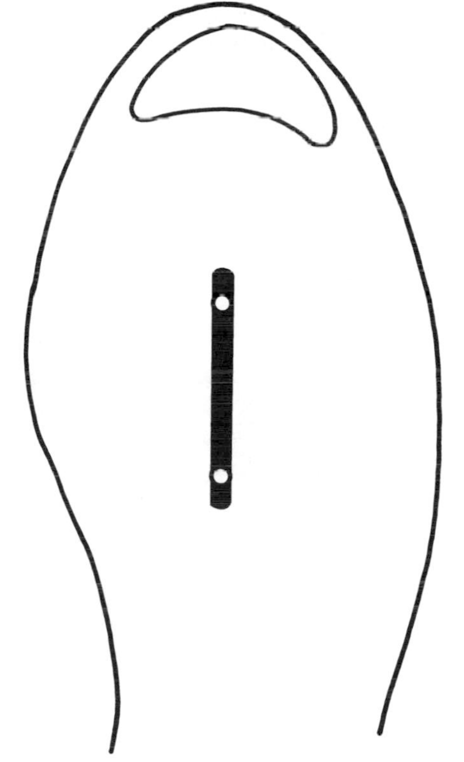

ing the spindle position (Fig. 9.10). If your cleat has this, line up the cleat mark 1 centimeter behind the line you drew in Step 1 across the shoe sole. With an SPD pedal, line up the mounting screws 1 centimeter behind the mark you made in Step 1 (Fig. 9.9). With a Speedplay cleat, place the center of the hole in the middle of the cleat 1 centimeter behind the mark you made in Step 1.

If the cleat has neither centering marks nor is it SPD, you will have to tighten the screws and set the shoe in the pedal. When the shoe is level, you want the ball of the foot between 0 and 1 centimeter forward of the pedal spindle. Putting the ball further forward is usually helpful to develop power, while high-cadence spinning is usually enhanced with the ball of the foot further back. If you know which type of rider you are, you can set the shoe as appropriate. Otherwise, split the difference and shoot for the middle of the range.

Make sure you don't put an old-style Time rear cam on the wrong shoe, or you will not be able to release by twisting outward.

Note: *There are many SPD- and Look-style "private label" pedals under various brand names on the market. The cleat-mounting and tension-adjustment instructions for SPD or Look pedals generally apply to these models as well.*

4. Snug the screws down enough to prevent the cleat from moving when clipped in or out of the pedals, but don't tighten them fully. Follow the same steps with the other shoe.

5. To set the lateral cleat position, put the shoes on, sit on the bike, and clip into the pedals. Ride around a bit. Notice the position of your feet. Generally, the closer your feet are to the plane of the bike, the more efficient your pedaling will be, but you don't want them in so far that your ankles bump the cranks. Take the shoes off and adjust the

9.9 cleat centered 1cm behind ball-of-foot-line

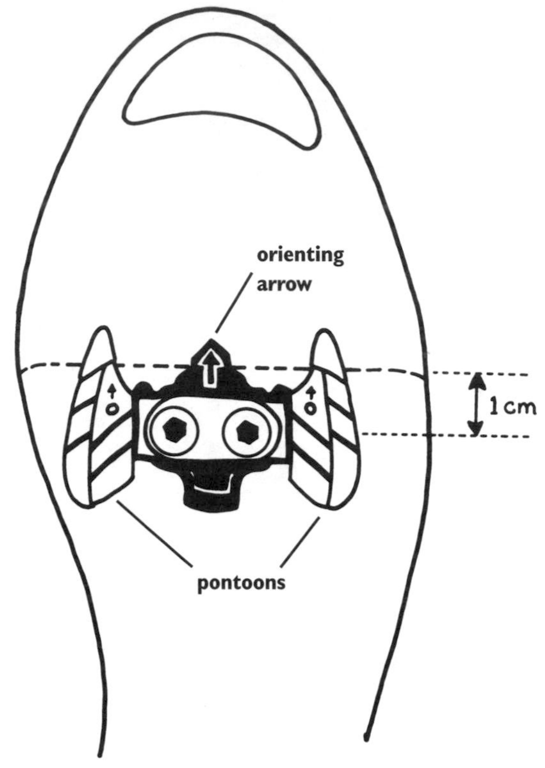

9.10 Look cleat with mark for pedal center

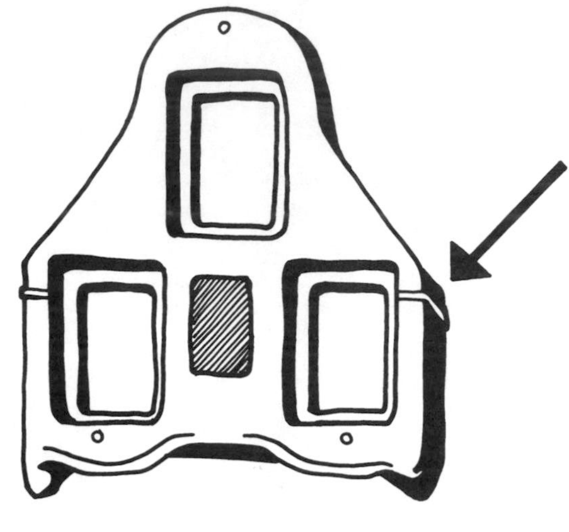

cleats laterally, if necessary, to move the feet side to side. Get back on the bike and clip in again. Note that Time and Power pedals have no lateral cleat adjustment.

6. To set rotational position, ride around some more. Notice if your feet feel twisted and uncomfortable. You may feel pressure on either side of your heel from the shoe. If necessary, remove your shoes and rotate the cleat slightly. Most pedals now offer free-float, allowing the foot to rotate freely for a few degrees before releasing. Precise rotational cleat adjustment is less important if the pedal is free-floating. Some Look pedals have a dial on the back of the clip to set the amount of free-float rotation. I recommend starting with the greatest amount of free-float angle. You can reduce the float later if you desire.

SPD-R cleats come in three styles: one with a wide tip for "fixed" operation, and two narrower-tip models for different amounts of free-float. Vertical cleat play can be eliminated by raising rubber bumpers on the pedal body. Dura-Ace SPD-R pedals have a 3mm nut on the bottom of the pedal to push the bumper up, while Ultegra SPD-R pedals require removing three screws on the face of the pedal to interchange the two pads with thicker ones.

7. Once your cleat position feels right, trace the cleats with a pen so that you can tell if the cleat stays put. While holding the cleat in place, tighten the bolts down firmly. Hold the Allen wrench close to the bend so that you do not exert too much leverage and strip the bolts. There is little danger of over-tightening with a screwdriver, but do take care that the blade (or Phillips tip) fits well in the screw slot (or Phillips cross). Push down firmly while tightening to avoid stripping the head of the screw.
Note: *If you have a small torque wrench, the recommended tightening torque for most cleat screws is 43-52 inch-pounds (see Appendix B).*

9. When riding with new shoes or pedals, bring cleat-tightening tools along, since you may want to fine-tune the cleat adjustment over the course of a few rides.

9-3: ADJUSTING RELEASE TENSION OF CLIP-IN PEDALS

If you find the factory release-adjustment setting to be too loose or too restrictive, you can adjust it on many clip-in pedals; exceptions are Bebop, Diadora, Power, Speedplay and Time. The adjusting screws are usually located on top, on the side, or at the rear of the pedal (Figs. 9.11, 9.12). The screws affect the tension of the nearest set of clips. The adjuster screws are usually operated with a small (usually 3mm) Allen wrench or a small screwdriver.

1. Locate the tension-adjustment screws. Most Looks have a screw (either slotted or 2.5mm or 3mm hex head) on top of the platform (Fig. 9.11); Look Anatomics and Campagnolo ProFits have a 3mm hex screw on the side. Ritchey, Shimano SPD and SPD-R (Fig. 9.12) have a 3mm hex screw on the back of the clip.

Note: *There are many SPD- and Look-style "private label" pedals under various brand names on the market. The cleat-mounting and tension-adjustment instructions for SPD or Look pedals generally apply to these pedals as well.*

2. To loosen the tension adjustment, turn the screw counterclockwise; to tighten it, turn it clockwise (Figs. 9.11, 9.12). It's the classic "lefty loosey, righty tighty" approach. There usually are click stops in the rotation of the screw. Tighten or loosen one click at a time (1/4-1/2 turn), then ride the bike to test the adjustment. Many types include an indicator that moves with the screw to show relative adjustment. Make certain that you do not back the screw out so far that it comes out of the spring plate or can vibrate loose; feel for at least the first "click" to hold it in place.

Note: *With Ritchey pedals, you will decrease the amount of free-float in the pedal as you increase the release tension.*

9B OVERHAULING PEDALS

LEVEL 2

Like a hub or bottom bracket, pedal bearings and bushings need to be cleaned and re-greased regularly.

There is a wide variation in road pedal designs. This book is not big enough to go into great detail about the inner workings of every single model. Speaking in general terms, pedal guts fall into two broad categories: ones that have loose ball bearings (Figs. 9.15, 9.16 and 9.23), and those

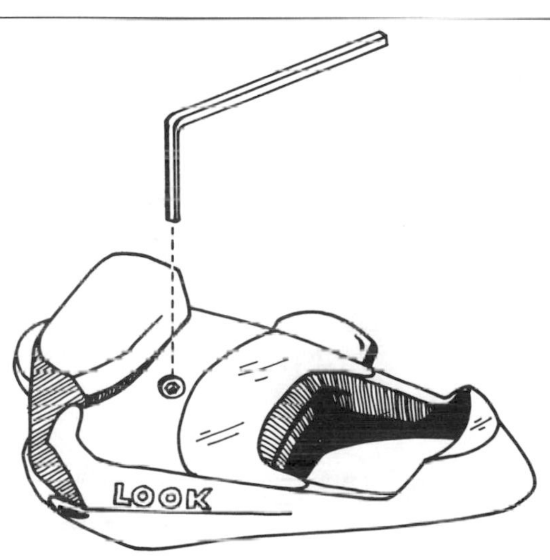

9.11 tension screw on Look pedal

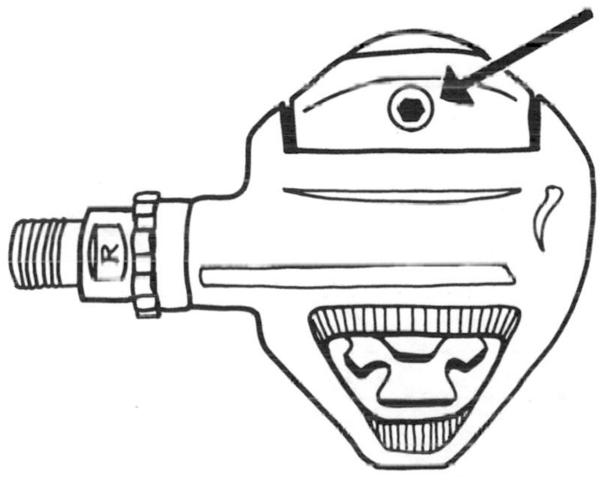

9.12 tension screw on Ritchey, Shimano pedals

9.13 tool for removing Shimano pedal axle assembly

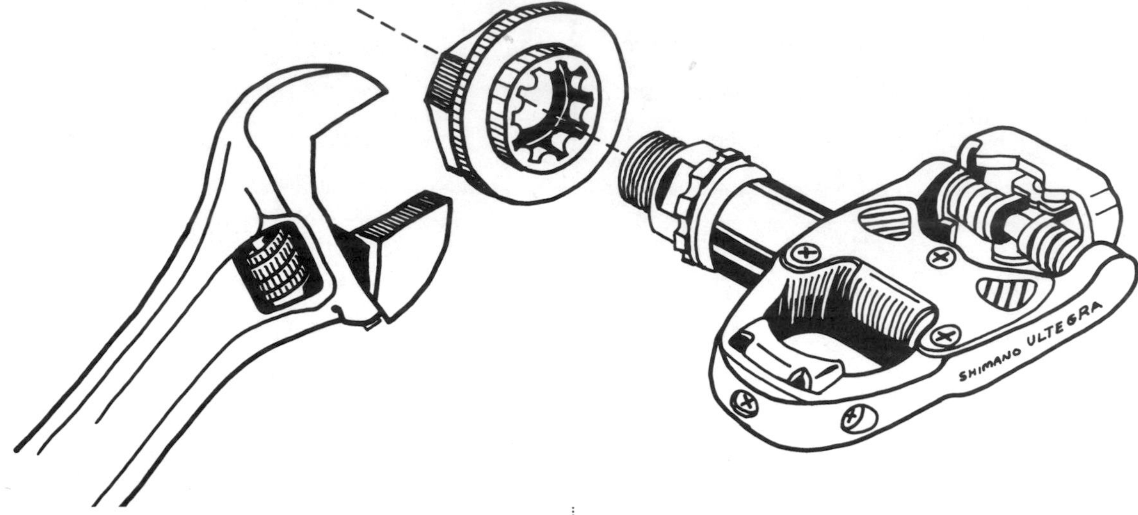

that have cartridge bearings (Figs. 9.17-21).

Many pedals are closed on the outboard end and have a nut surrounding the axle on the inboard end (Figs. 9.13-9.17). The axle assembly installs into the pedal as a unit and is accessed by this inboard nut. Some axles are held in by a snap ring (Figs. 9.18 and 9.20). The axle assemblies on older pedal designs (Fig. 9.23) and some new ones as well (Figs. 9.19 and 9.21) are accessed from the outboard end by removing a dust cap.

1. Remove the pedal from the bike (Figs. 9.3 and 9.4).

2. Before you start, figure out how the pedal is put together so you will know how to take it apart; the following paragraphs and the illustrations on subsequent pages should help. In a few cases, the workings of the pedal guts may not be clear until you have completed Step 1 in the overhaul process, which begins on page 152.

Most Shimano pedals have two sets of loose bearings and a bushing which come out as a complete axle assembly (Fig. 9.16). You will see the tiny ball bearings at the small end of the axle (Fig. 9.22). Dura-Ace SPD-R pedals have a set of ball bearings

9.14 a 22mm wrench gets at the axle assembly in a Campagnolo ProFit pedal

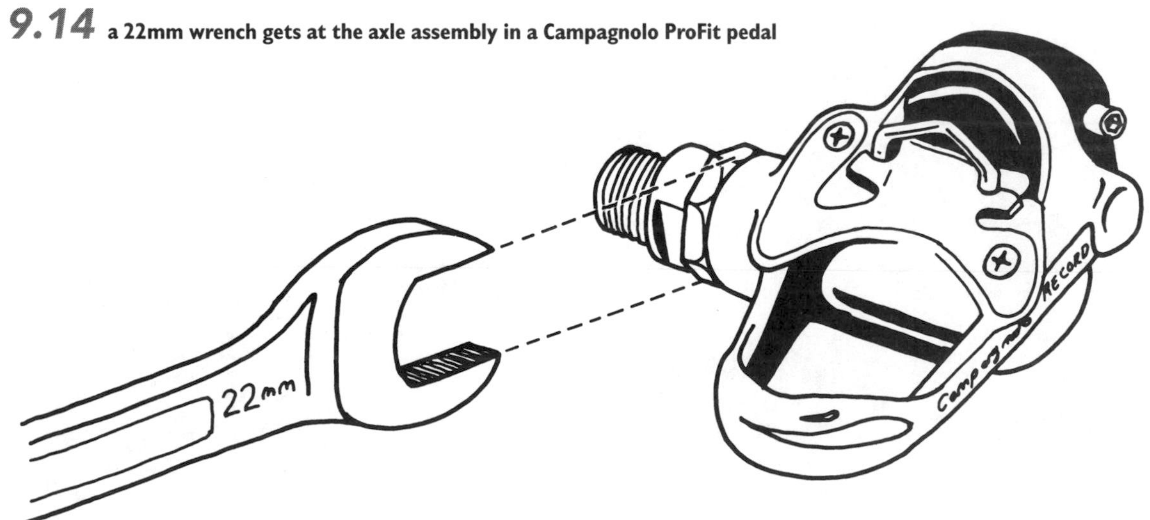

9.15-21 types of clip-in pedals

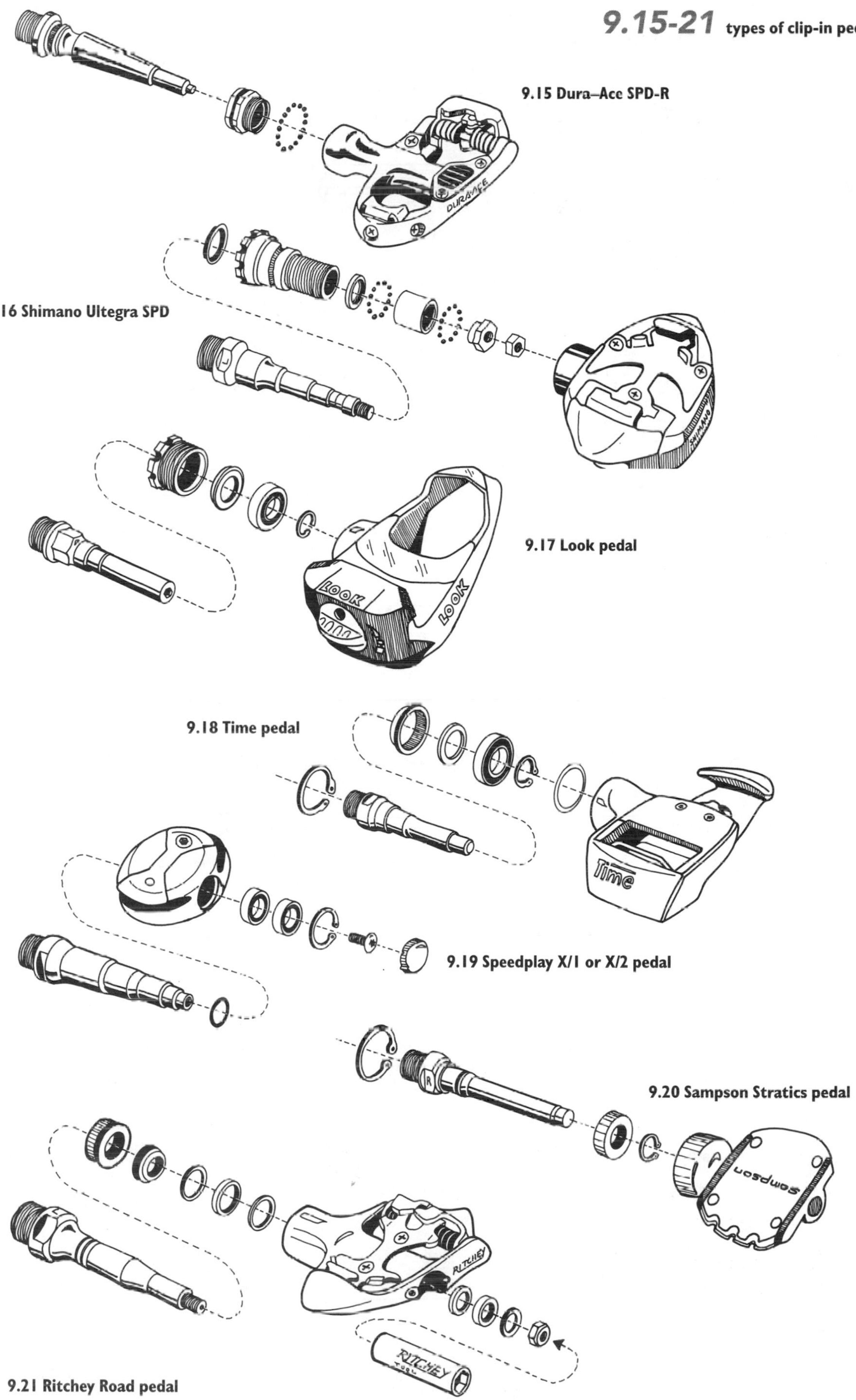

9.15 Dura–Ace SPD-R

9.16 Shimano Ultegra SPD

9.17 Look pedal

9.18 Time pedal

9.19 Speedplay X/1 or X/2 pedal

9.20 Sampson Stratics pedal

9.21 Ritchey Road pedal

9.22 **most Shimano axles have two nuts, used to adjust bearing play**

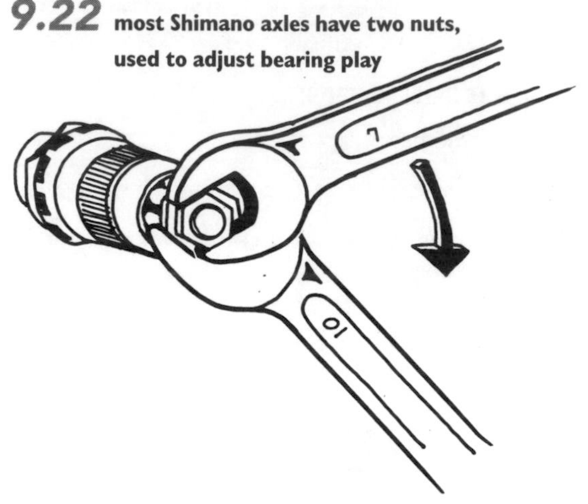

on each end of the spindle and a 6mm inside diameter (I.D.) set of needle bearings just inboard of the outboard bearings (Fig. 9.15).

Speedplay X/3 pedals have an inboard 10mm I.D. brass bushing and an outboard 6mm I.D. cartridge bearing.

The Campagnolo Record ProFit (Fig. 9.14) pedal has one inboard and two outboard 17mm O.D. cartridge bearings.

Look, Diadora and Time pedals have an inboard cartridge bearing (19mm, 24mm and 24mm O.D., respectively) and one or two pressed-in outboard needle bearing sets (Figs. 9.17 and 9.18).

Speedplay X/1 and X/2 pedals have an inboard pressed-in needle bearing and an outboard pair of cartridge bearings (Fig. 9.19).

Sampson Stratics (Fig. 9.20) pedals have a 24mm outside diameter (O.D.) plastic "bearing" on the inboard side and a plastic bushing inside the pedal body.

Ritchey road pedals (Fig. 9.21) have two sets of pressed-in needle bearings, one with an I.D. of 10mm and the other 7mm.

Power Pedal axles are not removable. The bearings are lubricated through the small grease fitting on the bottom of the pedal until clean grease squeezes out of the inboard side.

9-4: OVERHAULING PEDALS CLOSED ON THE OUTBOARD END

LEVEL 3

1. Make sure your pedal does not have a dust cap or screw cover on the outboard end. If it does, skip to Section 9-5.

Unless you have a Time, Diadora or Sampson pedal, remove the axle assembly by unscrewing the nut surrounding the axle where it enters the inboard side of the pedal (Figs. 9.13 and 9.14). See note below regarding thread direction.

Most Shimano pedals are disassembled with a plastic splined tool (Figs. 1.2, 1.3), as are some Looks. Use a large adjustable wrench or a vise to hold the tool (Fig. 9.13). Most other pedals take a 20mm or 22mm open-end wrench (Fig. 9.14). You may find that you will want to hold the pedal body in a padded vise while unscrewing the nut with a wrench.

Note: *The threads inside the pedal body are reversed from the crankarm threads on the axle; the internal threads on the drive-side pedal are left-hand threaded, and vice versa. That means the right axle assembly unscrews clockwise, and the left axle assembly unscrews counterclockwise. It's confusing, but like the bottom bracket threads, pedal bodies are threaded so that pedaling forward tightens the assembly.*

The nut is often made of plastic and can crack if you turn it the wrong way, so be careful. Hold the pedal body with your hand or a vise while you unscrew the assembly. The fine threads take many turns to unscrew.

Campagnolo ProFit (Fig. 9.14) and many Look pedal axle assemblies are unscrewed with a 22mm open-end wrench; Dura-Ace SPD-R (Fig. 9.15) axle assembly removal requires a 20mm wrench. More recent Look axles are accessed with a special Look splined tool similar to the one that unscrews most

Shimano pedals (Fig. 9.13). Note that original Shimano clip-in road pedals are actually Looks with Shimano axle assemblies, and Campagnolo clip-in pedals prior to 1997 (other than an unfortunate attempt by Campagnolo itself in the late 1980s) are also Looks with Campagnolo axle assemblies.

Time, Diadora and Sampson pedal axles are retained by a snap ring on the crank side (Figs. 9.18 and 9.20). Popping the snap ring out requires inward-squeezing snap ring pliers. There is also a snap ring on a Power Pedal, but there is no point in removing it, since the clutch bearing and axle assembly is pressed in, and you will not be able to pull it out.

With Time, Look, Sampson or Diadora, skip to step 3.

2. Once you have removed the pedal body, take a look at the axle/bearing/bushing assembly. You will notice either one or two nuts on the thin end of the axle that serve to hold the bearings and/or bushings in place. Remove the nut or nuts as follows.

If the axle has a single nut on the end, simply hold the axle's large end with the 15mm pedal wrench and unscrew the little nut with a 9mm or 12mm wrench (or whatever fits it). The nut will be tight, since it has no locknut.

If the axle has two nuts on the end (Fig. 9.16), they are tightened against each other. To remove them, hold the inner nut with one wrench while you unscrew the outer nut with another (Fig. 9.22). On Shimano pedals, the inner nut does double duty as the bearing cone; be careful not to lose the tiny ball bearings as you unscrew the cone!

3. Clean all of the parts.

If it is a loose-bearing pedal, use a rag to clean the ball bearings, the cone, the inner ring that the bearings ride on at the end of the plastic sleeve (it looks like a washer), the bearing surfaces on either end of the little steel cylinder (or cylinders, in the case of Campagnolo Looks), the axle, and the inside of the plastic or aluminum axle sleeve (Fig. 9.16). To get the bearings really clean, wash them in the sink in soap and water with the sink drain plugged; the motion is the same as washing your hands, and results in both the bearings and your hands being clean for a sterile reassembly. Blot dry.

9.23 loose bearing pedal exploded

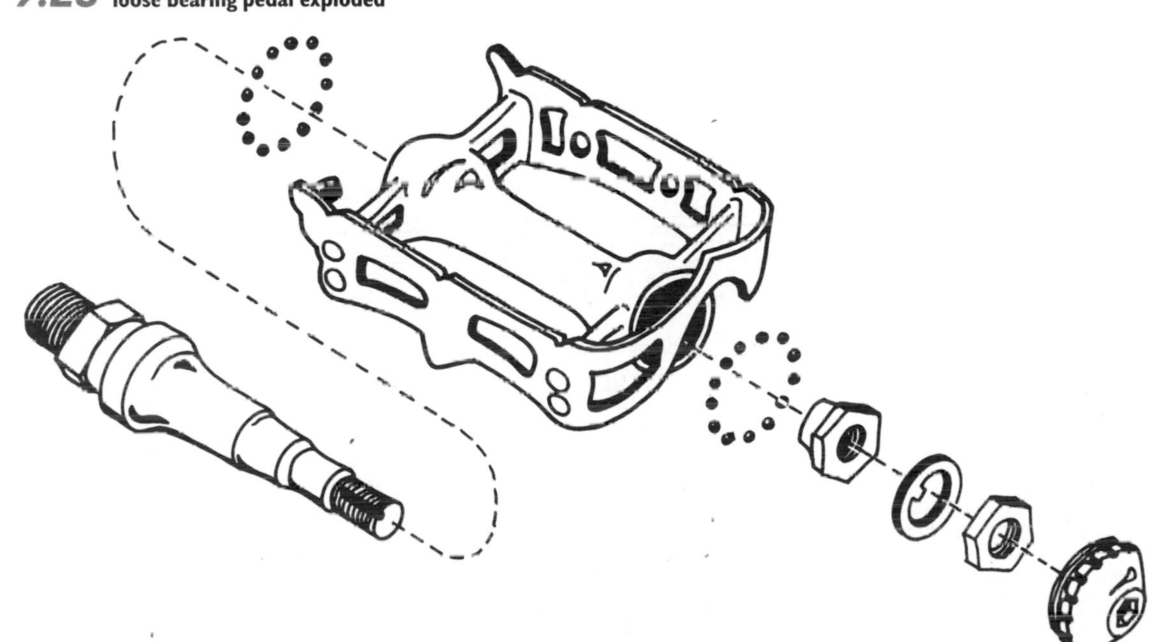

If, on a pedal with a cartridge bearing (Figs. 9.17-9.21), the bearing is dirty or worn out, it is best to replace it. These units usually have steel bearing covers that cannot be pried off without damaging them, nor can the covers be replaced. Plastic covers can be pried off and the bearing re-greased.

Needle bearings (Dura-Ace SPD-R/PD-7700, Look, Time, Diadora, Figs. 9.15, 9.17, 9.18) can be cleaned with solvent and a thin toothbrush slipped inside the pedal body bore. The needle bearings usually just need grease, though, since they are well isolated from dirt.

On a Sampson (Fig. 9.20), just wipe down the axle, the plastic "bearing" and the pedal body bore. Do the same for an inexpensive bushing-only pedal.

4. Lightly grease everything and reassemble the parts as they were, a simple process with bushings, cartridge bearings, and needle bearings, not so simple with loose bearings!

With a loose-bearing pedal, you have some exacting work to place the bearings on their races and screw the cone on while they stay in place. With most Shimano guts (Fig. 9.16), grease the bushing inside the axle sleeve, and slide the axle into the sleeve. Slide the steel ring, on which the inner set of bearings rides, down onto the axle and against the end of the sleeve. Make sure that the concave bearing surface faces away from the sleeve. Coat the ring with grease, and stick half of the bearings (usually 12) onto the outer surface of the ring. Slip the steel cylinder onto the axle so that one end rides on the bearings. Make sure that all of the bearings are seated properly and none are stuck inside of the sleeve.

overhauling pedals closed on the outboard end

To prevent the bearings from piling up on each other and ending up inside the sleeve instead of on the races, grease the cone and start it on the axle a few threads. Place the remaining half of the bearings on the flanks of the cone. Being careful not to dislodge the bearings, screw the cone in until the bearings come close to the end of the cylinder without touching it. While holding the axle sleeve, push the axle inward until the bearings seat against the end of the cylinder. Make sure that the first set of bearings is still in place. Screw the cone in without dislodging the inboard bearings by avoiding turning the axle or the cylinder. Tighten the cone with your fingers only, and loosely screw on the locknut.

Pre-1997 Look-style Campagnolo pedal guts are similar to Shimano, except that the bearing race is machined into the axle (rather than being a separate ring), and there are two cylinders, not one. Orient the cylinders so that their bearing races face outward and otherwise follow the above steps.

With Dura-Ace SPD-R/PD-7700 pedals (Fig. 9.15), you needed to push back on the bearing cup (on the end of the 20mm nut that holds the axle into the pedal body) to remove the ball bearings in the first place. Grease the cup and push back on it again to allow enough space between the cup and the cylinder to set each of the 17 balls onto the edge of the cup with a small screwdriver.

5. Adjust the axle assembly. (Time, Look, Diadora and Sampson skip this step.)

Pedals with a small cartridge bearing and a single nut on the end of the axle, like Campagnolo Record ProFit, require that you tighten the nut against the cartridge bearing while holding the other end of the axle with the 15mm pedal wrench. Tighten it enough to remove play but not enough to bind the axle.

On pedals with two nuts on the end of the axle, hold the cone or inner nut with a wrench and tighten the outer locknut down against it (Fig. 9.22). Check the adjustment for freedom of rotation, and be sure there is no lateral play. Readjust as necessary by tightening or loosening the cone or inner nut and re-tightening the locknut.

6. Replace the axle assembly in the pedal body. Smear grease on the inside of the pedal hole; this will ease insertion and act as a barrier to dirt and water. Screw the sleeve in with the same wrench you used to remove it (Figs. 9.13 and 9.14). ***Remember:*** *Pay attention to proper thread direction (see note in Step 1)! Tighten carefully; it is easy to overtighten, which can crack a plastic nut.*

7. Put the pedals back on your bike, and go ride.

9-5: OVERHAULING PEDALS WITH A DUST CAP ON THE OUTBOARD END

LEVEL 2

Note: *Assess the value of your pedals and your time before continuing. Well-made older racing pedals like Campagnolo deserve careful attention, but many non-clip-in pedals are not worth the effort of overhaul.*

1. Remove the dust cover from the outboard end of the pedal with the appropriate tool. This could be a pair of pliers, a flat or Phillips screwdriver, a coin, an Allen wrench or a splined tool made especially for your pedals; it's pretty easy to figure out which one is needed to remove the cap. Dig the dustcap out from Ritcheys (Fig. 9.21) and Speedplay X/1 and X/2 (Fig. 9.19) with a sharp pick or a sharpened nail (Ritcheys first require removal of a 2.5mm hex screw holding down the corner of the dustcap). ***Note:*** *Speedplay bearings can be re-greased without removing the axle. On an X/1 or X/2, insert Speedplay's "Speedy Luber" grease-injection fitting, and squirt grease in with a fine-tip bicycle grease gun until it squirts out the other end. On an X/3, after removing the screw from the outboard end, pump grease in with a fine-tip grease gun while slowly turning the spindle until you see grease at the opposite end.*

2. Hold the wrench flats on the inboard end of the axle with a pedal wrench, and unscrew the locknut with the appropriate-size socket wrench (or box wrench, if there is room for it).

Ritchey road pedals require a deep, thin-wall 8mm socket; Ritchey makes a double-ended thin 8mm socket for the purpose that you can turn with an 8mm hex key in the other end.

On a Speedplay X/1 or X/2 pedal, remove the Torx T15 or T20 screw on the outboard end under the dust cap (Fig. 9.19) with the appropriate Torx driver. You may have to heat the bolt with a soldering iron to soften the thread-lock compound.

On a Speedplay X/3, carefully pry the two halves of the pedal apart with a knife or razor blade after removing the 2.5mm pedal body screws from either side. Lift the axle assembly out and remove the 8mm locknut from the end of the spindle. Pull the bearings, bushing and O-ring off of the spindle. Clean and grease the parts, and replace the cartridge bearing and bushing if necessary. Reassemble the parts onto the axle, and tighten the locknut snugly against the bearing (35-40 inch-pounds). When you reassemble the pedal, seal it from water by caulking the inside edges of the pedal body halves and putting on a new O-ring.

3. Remove the axle.

If it is a loose-bearing pedal (Fig. 9.23), hold the pedal over a rag to catch the bearings and then unscrew the cone. Keep the bearings from the two ends separate in case they differ in size or in number. Count them so you can put the right numbers back in when you reassemble the pedal. The guts should look like Fig. 9.23.

If the pedal does not have loose bearings (Fig 9.19, 9.21), the procedure is different.

With a Ritchey (Fig. 9.21), once you have

9.24 dropping in bearings

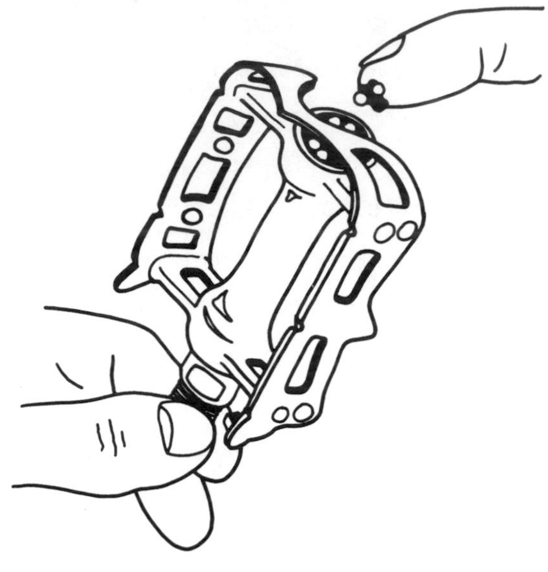

removed the 8mm locknut, you can pull the axle out. The pedal has two pressed-in needle bearings inside. Scrub them with solvent and a rag or thin brush, if they are dirty. Removal of bad needle bearings requires a special tool to pull them out.

With a Speedplay X/1 or X/2 pedal (Fig. 9.19), you pull the axle out and re-install the Torx screw in the end of the axle. Remove the little snap ring from the outboard end of the pedal bore with inward-squeezing snap ring pliers. Push the axle back in and carefully push the cartridge bearings out. The cartridge bearings are easily replaceable, but if the needle bearings are in bad shape, you will have to buy a new pedal body from Speedplay with the needle bearings already pressed in. You can clean them as above with Ritcheys.

With Ritchey or Speedplay, dry and grease the needle bearings and put the pedals back together the reverse of disassembly. Do not overtighten the Ritchey locknut; remove bearing play, but don't bind the axle. Put thread-lock compound on the Speedplay Torx end bolt, and tighten it snugly (35-40 inch-pounds).

Skip to step 11 with Ritchey and Speedplay.

4. With a rag, clean the bearings, cones and bearing races. Clean the inside of the pedal body by pushing the rag through with a screwdriver. If there is a dust cover on the inboard end of the pedal body, you can clean it in place, or pop it out with a screwdriver and clean it separately.

5. If you want to get the bearings really clean, wash them in a plugged sink with soap and water. The motion is the same as washing your hands, and it results in both the bearings and your hands being clean for a sterile reassembly. Blot dry.

6. If you removed it, press the inboard dust cover back into the pedal body. Smear a thin layer of grease in the inboard bearing cup and replace the bearings. Once all of the bearings are in place, there will be a gap equal to about half the diameter of one bearing.

7. Drop the axle in and turn the pedal over so that the outboard end is up. Smear grease in that end, and replace the bearings (Fig. 9.24).

8. Screw the cone in until it almost contacts the bearings, then push the axle straight in to bring the cone and bearings together; this prevents the bearings from piling up and getting spit out as the cone turns down against them. Without turning the axle (which would knock the inboard bearings about), screw the cone in until it is finger-tight.

9. Slide on the washer and screw on the lock nut. While holding the cone with a cone wrench, tighten the lock nut (similar to Fig. 9.22, but you will be holding the cone with a 13mm or similar cone wrench, not the pictured 10mm standard open-end wrench).

10. Check that the pedal spins smoothly without play. Readjust as necessary by tightening or loosening the cone and re-tightening the locknut.

11. Replace the dust cap.

12. Install the pedals and go for a ride.

TROUBLESHOOTING PEDAL PROBLEMS

9-6: CREAKING NOISE WHILE PEDALING

a. The shoe cleats need grease on the tip or they are loose and need to be tightened, or they are worn and need to be replaced (see Section 9-2).

b. Pedal bearings and pedal-body threads need cleaning and lubrication (see Section 9.B and 9-4 to 9-6).

c. The noise is originating from somewhere other than the pedals (see Chapter 8 Troubleshooting section or Appendix A).

9-7: RELEASE OR ENTRY WITH CLIP-IN PEDALS IS TOO EASY OR TOO HARD

a. Release tension needs to be adjusted (see "Adjusting pedal release tension," section 9-3).

b. Pedal-release mechanism needs to be cleaned and lubricated. Clean off mud and dirt, and drip chain lubricant on the springs and a dry lubricant (like White Lightning) on the cleat-contact surfaces of the clips (Fig. 9.25).

c. The cleats themselves need to be cleaned and lubricated. Clean off dirt and mud, oil the springs and put a dry chain lubricant or dry grease like pure Teflon on the contact ends of the cleats.

d. The cleats are worn out. Replace them (Section 9-2).

e. The clips on the pedal are bent or the guide plates on top of the pedal are worn, bent, broken or missing. Straighten bent clips if you can, or replace them. If you can't repair or replace the clips, you may have to replace the entire pedal. On Speedplays, the top and bottom metal plates may need replacing.

g. If it is hard to clip into your pedals, check the metal cleat guide plate at the center of an SPD-type pedal. It is held on with Phillips screws, and they may be loose or have fallen out, or the guide plate can be bent or broken. Tighten loose mounting screws and replace missing or damaged guide plates.

h. If you have small feet, and it is hard to get in and out of a pedal that has a large cleat (Look and copies, Campagnolo) or a large adapter plate, the curvature of your shoe sole may be so extreme that the center of the cleat hits the center of the pedal before the ends have clipped in. The fix may be as simple as removing the little rubber plug from under your Look cleat. You may also need to shim the front and rear of the cleat away from the shoe, or file down the center of the cleat.

9-8: YOU EXPERIENCE KNEE AND JOINT PAIN WHILE PEDALING

a. Cleat misalignment often causes pain on the sides of the knees (see Section 9-2).

b. You need more rotational float. Consider a pedal that offers more float (or replace fixed cleats with floating ones, or adjust your Look pedals for more float).

9.25 **lubricate the springs and cleat contact areas**

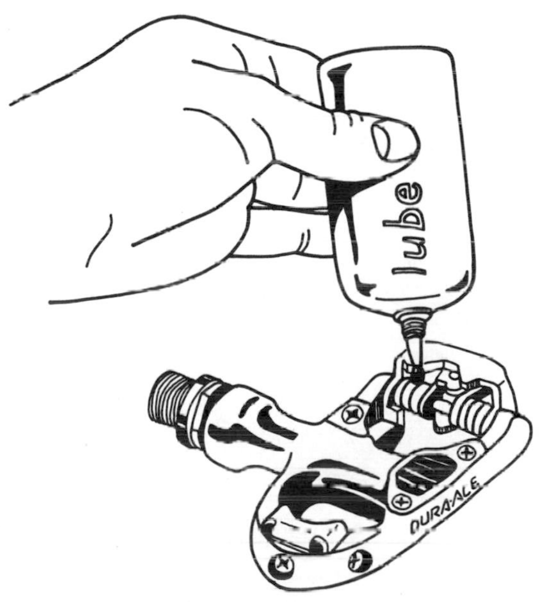

c. If your foot naturally rolls outward (supinates), and your shoe and cleat tip your feet further out (since most people pronate, this correction is built into some shoes), then there is likely to be an increase in the tension on the iliotibial (I-T) band, the tendon connecting the hip and calf. This will eventually cause pain on the outside of the knee. You need to see a specialist, because you may need custom orthotics for your shoes to correct the problem.

d. Fatigue and improper seat height can also contribute to joint pain. Pain in the front of the knee right behind the kneecap can indicate that your saddle is too low. Pain in the back of the leg behind the knee suggests that your saddle is too high.

Caution: *If any of these problems result in chronic pain, consult a specialist.*

Saddles & seatposts

"I do most of my work sitting down.
That's where I shine."—Robert Benchley

tools

4mm, 5mm and 6mm hex keys
Screwdriver
Grease

OPTIONAL

Soft hammer
Securely mounted vise
Penetrating oil
Hacksaw
Flex hone
Electric drill
Cutting oil

After a few hours on the bike, I can pretty much guarantee that you will be most aware of one component on your bike: the saddle. It is the part of your bike with which you are most ... uh ... intimately connected. Nothing can ruin a good ride faster than a poorly positioned or uncomfortable saddle.

The seatpost connects the saddle to the frame. A few bicycles, such as the Softride, employ a flexible beam attached to the front of the frame instead of a seatpost. These are covered separately at the end of this chapter.

10-1: SADDLES

Most bike saddles are made up of a flexible plastic shell, some padding, a cover and a pair of rails (Fig. 10.1). Not much to it, which perhaps explains why there are countless variations on this theme: Some have extra thick padding or high-tech gel cushions; some have depressions, holes or splits in the shell to reduce pressure on sensitive areas; some reduce weight with rails made of titanium, hollow steel or even braided carbon fiber; others have synthetic covers, covers made from Kevlar or covers made from the finest full-grain leather money can buy.

You can expect to spend anywhere from $20 to $200 for a decent saddle, yet price may not be the

10.1 Modern lightweight saddle

10.3 Brooks leather saddle

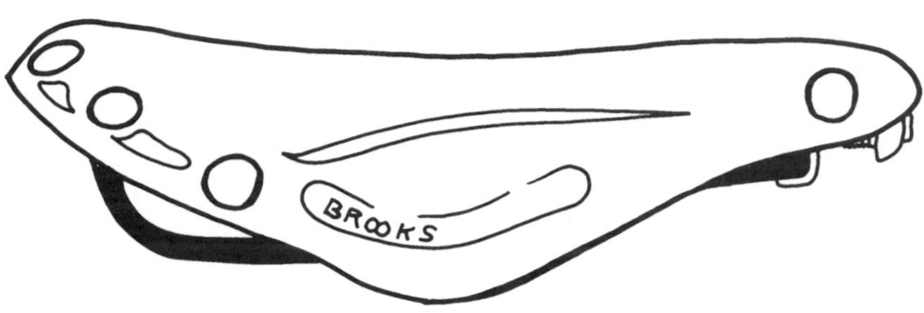

saddle designs

best indicator of what makes a saddle really good—namely comfort. My best advice is to ignore weight, fashion and looks, and choose a saddle that is comfortable. I could go on for pages about hi-zoot gel padding, scientifically designed shells that support some parts and don't contact others and flex just right, as well as all sorts of factors that engineers consider when designing a saddle. None of it would count for squat if, after reading it, you ran out and bought a saddle that turned out to be a giant pain in the rear. People are different and saddles are different. Try as many as you can before buying one.

The current marketing war raging over saddles that are designed to prevent male impotency (Fig. 10.3) can blind a consumer's ability to select appropriately. If you buy a saddle out of fear, and it is uncomfortable, you have done yourself a disservice. Don't take it on faith or scientific studies that such a saddle must be protecting you, even if you don't particularly like it; if it hurts or you get numb, it isn't working for you. What works for one person won't necessarily work for another.

Determine which saddle shape and design is the most comfortable for your body. Then—and only then—start looking at things like titanium rails, fancy covers and all of the other things that improve a saddle. Some people can only find comfort on 400-gram saddles with tons of thick padding. Others can ride for hours on a skinny little 200-gram Selle Italia Flite. It's a matter of preference. Any decent bike shop worth its weight in titanium should let you try a saddle for a while before locking you into a sale. And keep in mind that the position of the saddle can be as important as the shape.

Brooks and Ideale saddles have no plastic shell, foam padding or cover. They are constructed from a single piece of thick leather attached to a steel frame with large brass rivets (Fig. 10.2). This was the main type of saddle up until the 1980s. Brooks still makes them this way, updated with titanium rails in some models. This sort of saddle requires a long break-in period and frequent applications of a

10.2 saddle designed to not contact the perineum

leather-softening compound that comes with the saddle or from a shoe store. As is the case with a lot of old bike parts, you either love 'em or you hate 'em. If you're not familiar with them by now, you'll probably hate 'em, so go out and buy a nice comfortable modern saddle (Fig. 10.1 or 10.3).

A saddle with a plastic shell and foam padding requires little maintenance, except to keep it clean. Check periodically that the rails are not bent or cracked (a clear sign that you need to replace your saddle).

10-2: SADDLE POSITION

Even if you have found the perfect saddle, it can still feel like a medieval torture device if it isn't properly positioned. Saddle placement is the most important part of finding a comfortable riding position. Not only does saddle position affect how you feel on the bike, but it affects your control and efficiency as well. With the saddle in the right place you suddenly become a much better rider. See Appendix C, Section C-3 for a detailed explanation of setting saddle and handlebar position. Following are some short guidelines.

There are three basic elements to saddle position: tilt, fore-and-aft position, and saddle height (Fig. 10.4). Proper saddle height (Fig. 10.4) is key to effectively transferring power to the pedals. The ideal height on a road bike places your leg in a 90- to 95-percent extension when you're riding. If your frame is the correct size, you should have no trouble achieving this without pulling the post out beyond its height-limit line. Appendix C has more detail on this.

A common cause of numb crotch and butt fatigue (and even sore arms and shoulders) is an improperly tilted saddle (Fig. 10.4). The general rule of thumb is that you should keep the saddle level when you first install it. After a while, some people find that they prefer a slight upward or downward tilt to their saddles. I strongly recommend against making that tilt much more than 1/4 inch. Too much

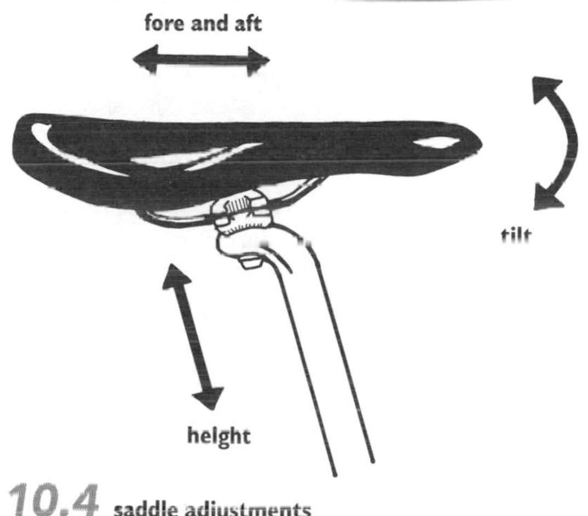

10.4 saddle adjustments

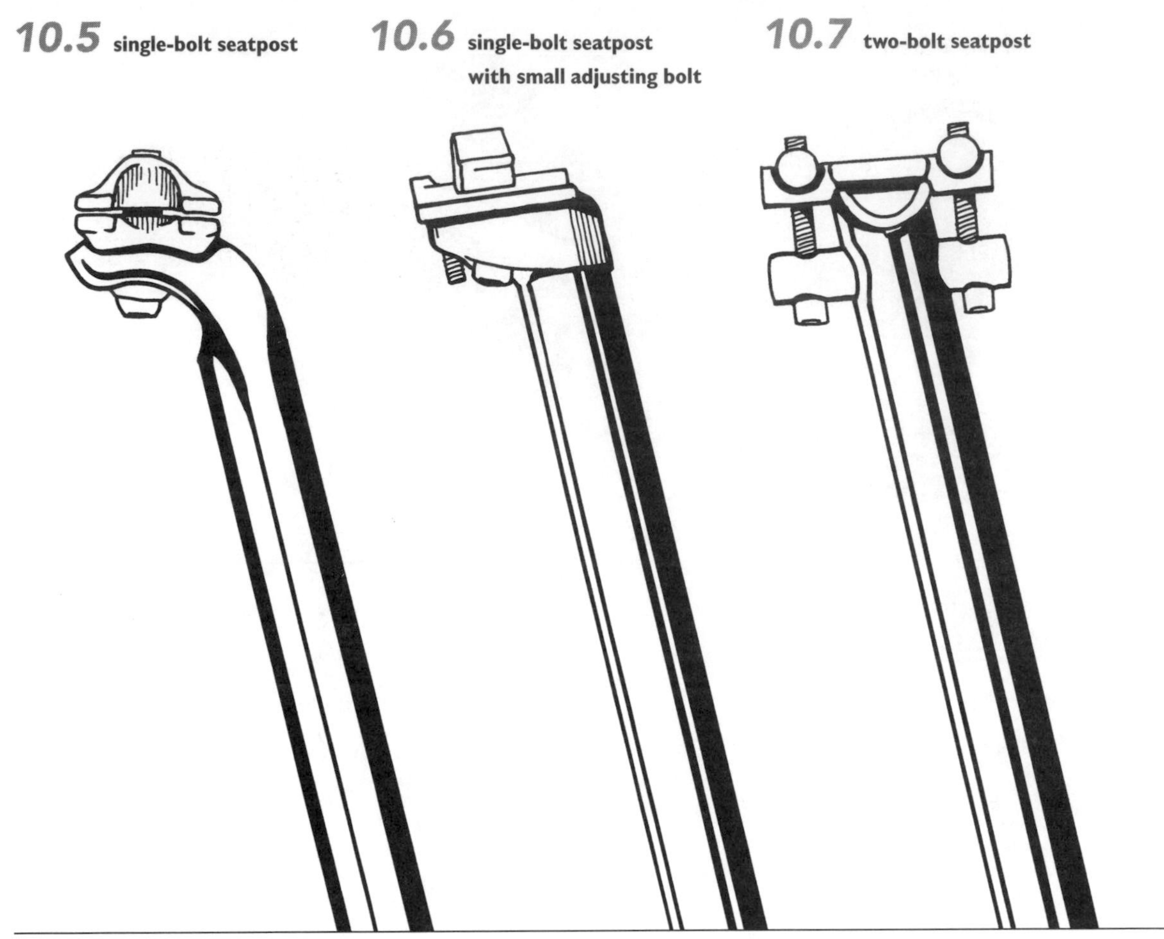

10.5 single-bolt seatpost

10.6 single-bolt seatpost with small adjusting bolt

10.7 two-bolt seatpost

upward tilt places too much of your body weight on the nose of the saddle. Too much downward tilt will cause you to slide down the saddle as you ride. That puts unnecessary pressure on your arms, back and shoulders as they fight to oppose the forward slide.

Fore-and aft-position (Fig. 10.4) determines where your butt sits on the saddle (or get a new one, if it is too wide for you), the position of your knees relative to the pedals, and how much of your weight is transferred to your hands. Regardless of manufacturer, all saddles are designed to have your butt centered over the widest part. If this is not where you sit, reposition the saddle. You want to have a comfortable bend in your arms, without feeling too cramped or stretched out. If you find that your neck and shoulders feel tighter than usual and your hands are going numb, then redistribute your weight by moving the saddle back.

Fore-and-aft saddle position also affects how your legs are positioned relative to the pedals. Ideally, your position should be such that your knee pushes straight down on the forward pedal when the crankarms are in a perfectly horizontal position. Appendix C explains how to determine this precisely.

Butt pain is intimately connected to handlebar position, as are other aches and pains. The shorter the upper-body reach and higher the handlebars, the more weight will go on the butt. On the other hand, the longer the reach and lower the bars, the more the pelvis rotates forward, and the pressure point moves from the sit bones to the soft tissue of the perineum and genital area. As a general rule, a novice rider will want a shorter reach and higher bars, and perhaps a correspondingly wider saddle, than an experienced rider. Once again, consult Appendix C.

10.8 saddle installation on single-bolt seatpost

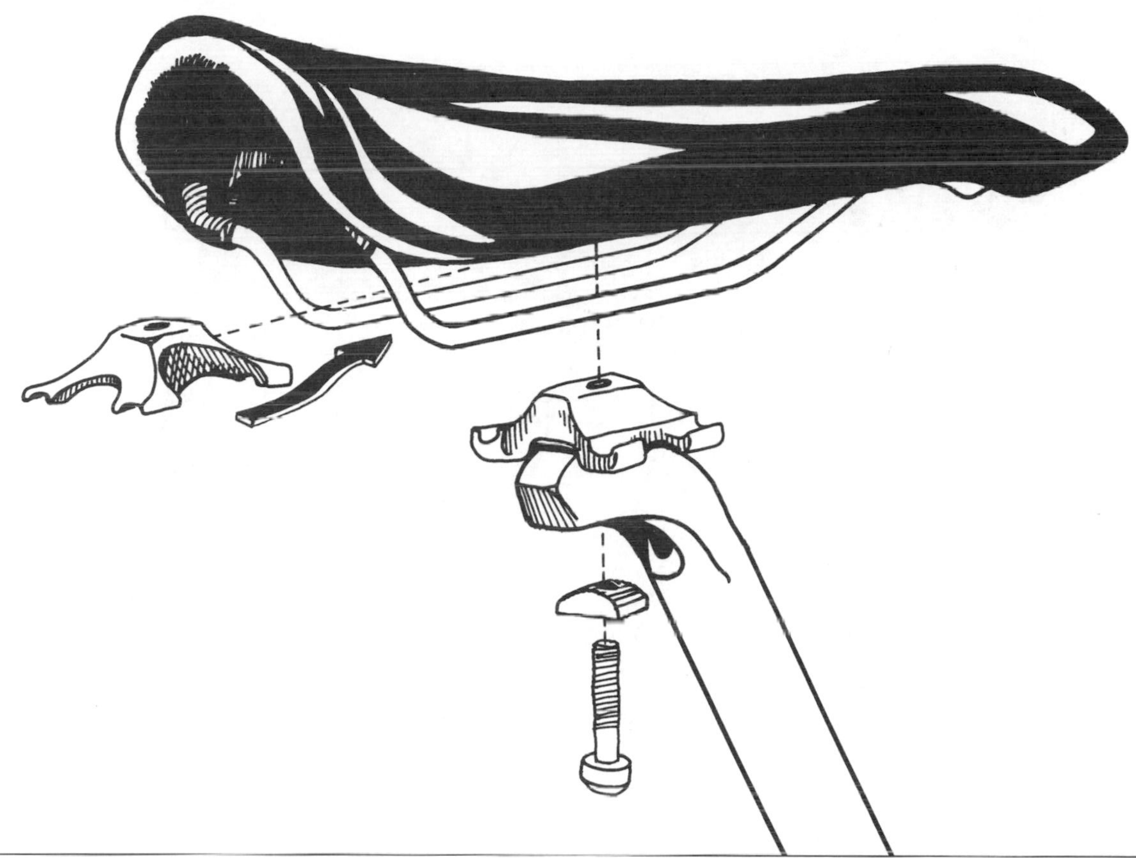

10-3: SEATPOST MAINTENANCE

A standard seatpost requires little maintenance other than removing it from the frame every few months. Wipe it down, regrease it and the inside of the frame's seat tube, and then reinstall it. This keeps it clean and moving freely for the purposes of adjustability; it also should prevent the seatpost from getting stuck in the frame (a very nasty and potentially serious problem). The procedures for installing a new seatpost and for removing a stuck seatpost are outlined later in this chapter.

Regularly check any seatpost for cracks or bends so that you can replace it before it breaks with you on it.

Since suspension seatposts are rare on road bikes, maintenance of them is not covered here, but it is covered in *Zinn and the Art of Mountain Bike Maintenance*.

10-4: INSTALLING A SADDLE

Remember the heavy steel posts you had on bikes as a kid (or on a cheap adult bike)? Those seatposts had a single horizontal bolt that pulled together a number of knurled washers with ears to hold the saddle rails. They are cheap to make, being simply a steel tube with some washers and a bolt, but they cannot hold up to adult use.

Fortunately, most seatposts don't have these clamps anymore. Much more secure (and generally lighter) is a post with one or two vertical bolts holding an aluminum clamshell together.

Most posts have either one (Fig. 10.5) or two bolts (Figs. 10.6 and 10.7) for clamping the saddle.

Two-bolt posts usually rely on one of two systems. In one, the two bolts work together by pulling the saddle into the clamp (Fig. 10.7). On others, a smaller second bolt holds the tilt angle

10.9 saddle installation on two-bolt seatpost

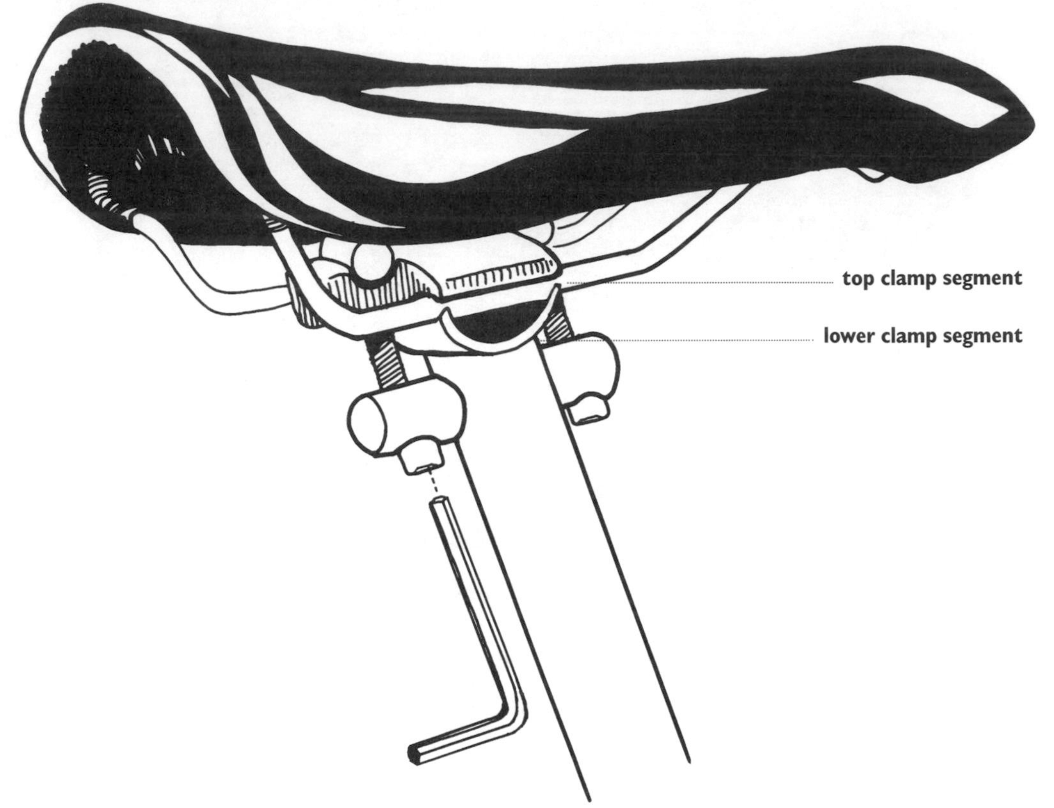

(Fig. 10.6). It is reasonably easy to figure out how to remove, install and adjust the saddle, no matter what kind of post you have.

saddle installation

10-5: SADDLE INSTALLATION ON SEATPOST WITH A SINGLE VERTICAL BOLT

Posts with a single vertical bolt (Fig. 10.5) usually have a two-piece clamp that fastens onto the saddle rails. On most models, saddle tilt is controlled by moving the clamp and saddle along a curved platform. Before you tighten the clamp bolt, make sure there is not a second, much smaller bolt (or "set screw") that adjusts seat tilt. If one is present, skip to the next section (10-6).

1. Loosen the bolt until there are only a couple of threads still holding onto the upper clamp.

2. Turn the top half of the clamp 90 degrees and slide in the saddle rails. Do it from the back where the space between the rails is wider. You might need to remove the top clamp piece completely from the bolt if it is too large to fit between the rails. If you do disassemble the clamp, pay attention to the orientation of the parts so you can put it back together the same way.

3. Set the seat rails into the grooves in the lower part of the clamp, and set the top clamp piece on top of the rails (Fig. 10.8). Slide the saddle to the desired fore-aft position.

4. Tighten the bolt and check the seat tilt. Readjust if necessary.

10-6: SADDLE INSTALLATION ON SEATPOST WITH LARGE CLAMP BOLT AND SMALL SET SCREW

This post type is illustrated in Fig. 10.6.

1. Loosen the large bolt until the top part of the clamp can be moved out of the way or removed so that you can slide the saddle rails into place.

2. Set the saddle rails between the top and bottom sets of grooves in the seat clamp. Slide the saddle to the desired fore-aft position. Tighten the large bolt.

3. To change saddle tilt, loosen the large clamp bolt, adjust the saddle angle as needed by turning the set screw, and re-tighten the clamp bolt. Repeat until the desired adjustment is reached. Caution: Do not use the set screw to make the clamp tight! Do not adjust the set screw unless the clamp bolt is loose!

Note: *On these types of seatposts, the set screw may be vertical or horizontal. On posts with a vertical set screw (Fig. 10.6), the screw is usually adjacent the clamp bolt. A horizontal set screw can be placed at the top front of the seatpost, pushing back on the clamp. With such a set screw, push down on the back of the saddle with the clamp bolt loose to make sure the clamp and set screw are in contact. Another type of post has a horizontal tilt-adjusting bolt that passes crosswise through a slot in the seatpost clamp. On this type, the saddle can be fully tightened down, yet the tilt-adjust screw can be loosened and the saddle tipped differently and re-tightened without adjusting the clamp bolt.*

10-7: INSTALLING SADDLE ON SEATPOST WITH TWO EQUAL-SIZED CLAMP BOLTS

This post type is illustrated in Fig. 10.7.

1. Loosen one or both of the bolts and open the clamp enough to slide the saddle rails into the grooves of the clamp.

2. Slide the saddle to the desired fore-aft position. Tighten down one or both of the clamp bolts completely.

3. Loosen one clamp bolt and tighten the other to change the tilt of the saddle (Fig. 10.9). Repeat as necessary.

4. Complete by tightening both bolts.

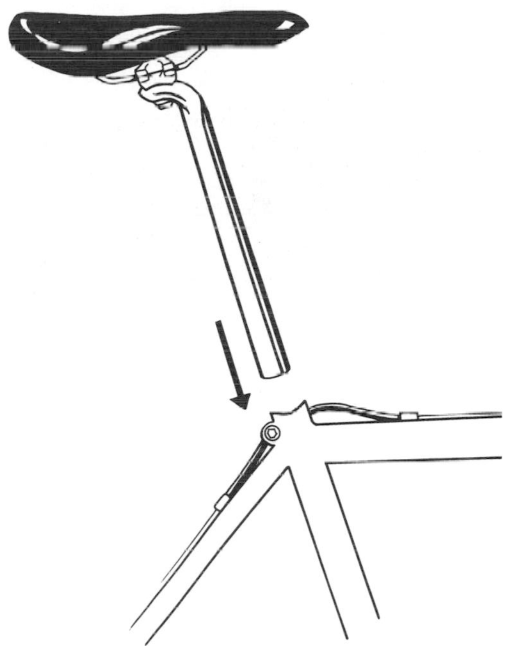

10.10 seatpost installation into the frame

10-8: SEATPOST INSTALLATION INTO THE FRAME

1. Check for irregularities, burrs, and other problems inside the seat tube visually and with your finger; if there are some you may need to sand or otherwise clean up inside the seat tube. It may be necessary for a bike shop to ream the seat tube if a post of the correct size will not fit.

2. Grease the seatpost and the inside of the seat tube. Grease the seat-lug-binder bolt. If you are using a sleeve or shim to adapt an undersized seatpost to fit the frame, grease it inside and out, and insert it.

3. Insert the seatpost (Fig. 10.10), and tighten the binder bolt. Some binder bolts are tightened with a wrench (usually a 5mm hex key), and some require two wrenches (usually two 5mm hex keys or two open-end wrenches).

4. After the saddle is attached, adjust the seat height to your desired position. It is a good idea to mark this height on the post with an indelible marker or a piece of tape. This way, if you remove it, you can just slide it right back into the proper place.

10.11 saddle on Softride beam

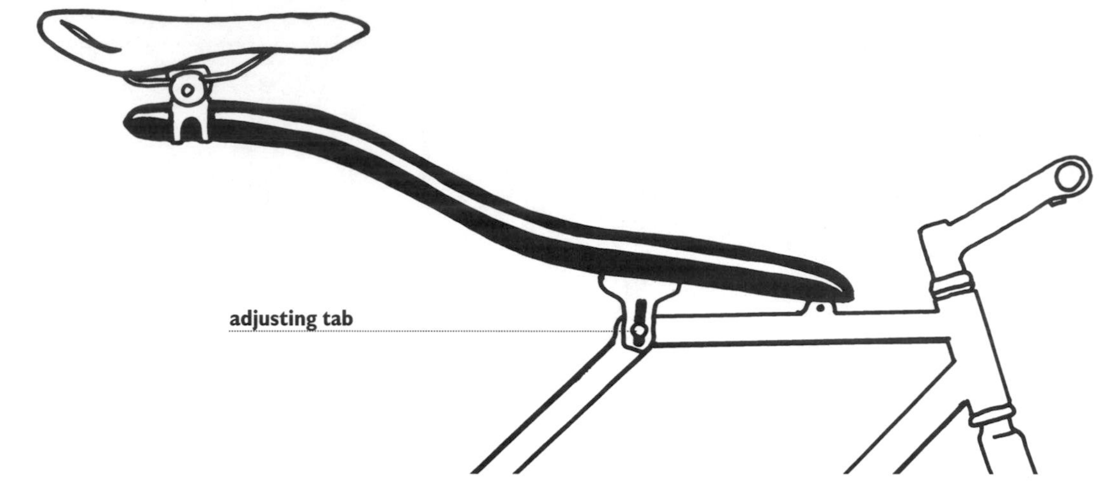

10-9: INSTALLING A SOFTRIDE SUSPENSION BEAM ONTO FRAME

LEVEL 2 The frame must be built to accept the beam, or you must purchase a retrofit kit from Softride to install it on a standard frame.

1. Attach the beam to the front frame-mounting bracket with a steel pin. The underside of the beam's nose has a small steel eyelet that fits between two tabs on the bracket, which is located on the top of the frame's top tube (Fig. 10.11). With a soft hammer, tap the included pin through the bracket, through the eye on the bottom of the beam, and out through the hole in the other side of the bracket.

2. Attach the beam to the rear frame-mounting bracket, located a few inches behind the front eyelet. The rear mount on the beam consists of two curved tabs separated by the width of the frame's mounting bracket that extend down. Long, curved slots in each tab (Fig. 10.11) are used to adjust the saddle height. Pass the bolt through one of the rectangular washers (with its knurled side pointing inward) and into the slot of one tab. Then pass it through the round end cap of the cylindrical frame mount, the frame mount itself and out through the second end cap, the other oval tab hole and the other rectangular washer. Screw on the nut after lining up the offset end cap holes so they fit into the mounting bracket with the bolt in place.

3. Swing the beam up to the desired height, with the fixing bolt loose. For starters, set it about an inch higher than what your normal seat height would be, to offset the beam's flex. If you reach the end of the adjustment in the bracket tab slots and the seat is still not as high as you need it to be, rotate the rear frame-mount end caps. The caps' offset holes offer two height positions for this very reason.

4. Tighten the fixing bolt. Readjust saddle height as needed.

installing a Softride suspension beam

—

removing a stuck seatpost

10-10: REMOVING A STUCK SEATPOST

LEVEL 3 This is a Level 3 job because of the risk involved. It may be best to entrust this to a shop, because if you make a mistake you run the risk of destroying your frame. If you're not 100-percent confident in your abilities, go to someone who is—or at least to someone who will be responsible if they screw it up.

1. Remove the seat-lug-binder bolt. Sounds easy enough.

2. Squirt penetrating oil around the seatpost, and

let it sit overnight. To get the most penetration, remove the bottom bracket (Chapter 8), turn the bike upside down, squirt the penetrating oil in from the bottom of the seat tube, and let it sit overnight.

3. The next day, stand over the bike and twist the saddle.

4. If Step 3 does not free the seatpost, you will need to move into the difficult and risky part of this procedure.

You will now sacrifice the seatpost. Remove the saddle and all of the clamps from the top of the seatpost. With the bike upside down, clamp the top of the seatpost into a large bench vise that is bolted to a very secure workbench. Congratulations, you have just ruined your seatpost. Don't ever ride it again.

Grab the frame at both ends, and begin to carefully apply a twisting pressure. Be aware that you can easily apply enough force to bend or crack the frame, so be careful. If the seatpost finally releases, it often makes such a large "pop" that you will think that you have broken many things!

5. If step 4 does not work, you need to go to a machine shop and get the post reamed out of the seat tube.

If you still insist on getting it out yourself, you should really sit down and think about it for a while. Will the guy at the machine shop really charge you so much money that it is worth the risk of completely destroying your frame yourself?

Do you still insist on doing this yourself? Okay, but don't say I didn't warn you.

Take a hacksaw and cut off the post a little more than an inch above the frame. (Now you really have destroyed your seatpost, so I don't have to warn against riding it again.) Remove the blade from the saw and wrap a piece of tape around one end. Hold on to the taped end and slip the other end into the center of the post. Carefully—very carefully—make two outward cuts about 60 degrees apart. Your goal is to remove a pie-shaped wedge from the hunk of seatpost stuck in your frame. Be careful; this is where many people cut too far and go right through the seatpost into the frame. Of course, you wouldn't do that, would you?

Once you've made the cut, pry or pull this piece out with a large screwdriver or a pair of pliers. Be careful here, too. A lot of over-enthusiastic home mechanics have damaged their frames by prying too hard.

Once the wedge is out, work the remaining piece out by curling in the edges with the pliers to free more and more of it from the seatpost walls. It should eventually work its way out.

With the post out of the frame, clean the inside of the seat tube thoroughly. A flex hone, sold in auto parts stores (or rented at rental stores) for reconditioning brake cylinders, is an excellent tool for the purpose. Turn the frame upside down, put the hone in your electric drill, and be sure to use plenty of honing fluid or cutting oil as you work. If you do not know how to use a hone, it may be best to take the frame to a bike shop to have the job done or try sandpaper wrapped around your fingers.

Inasmuch as removing a stuck post is so miserable that no one wants to do it twice, I'm certain that I do not need to remind you to grease the new post thoroughly before inserting it in the frame, and check it regularly thereafter as outlined above.

10-11: TROUBLESHOOTING PROBLEMS IN THE SEAT AND SEATPOST

1. Loose saddle.

Check the bolts. They are probably loose. Tighten the bolts and set the desired saddle tilt, after setting fore-aft saddle position (Section 10-2). Check for any damage to the clamping mechanism, and replace the post if necessary. If you need help, look up the instructions that apply to your seatpost.

2. Stuck seatpost.

This can be a serious problem. Follow the instructions in Section 10-10 carefully, or you might damage your frame.

3. Saddle squeaks with each pedal stroke.

Some saddle rail materials—titanium especially—squeak against the aluminum clamp. Take the saddle off and generously grease the rails where they contact the clamp. No luck? The rails may be loose in the saddle base. Put up with it or get a new saddle.

4. Creaking noises from the seatpost.

A seatpost can creak from moving back and forth against the sides of the seat tube while you ride. Pull the post from the frame and regrease the post and seat tube.

Some frames use a collar to adapt the seat tube to a certain seatpost diameter. Remember that the internal diameter of the seat tube is larger below the collar. I have seen bikes that creaked because the bottom of the seatpost rubbed against the sides of the seat tube below the extension of the collar. You can solve that problem by shortening the seatpost a bit with a hacksaw. If you do saw off the post, make sure that you still have at least 3 inches of seatpost inserted in the frame for security.

If the creaking originates from the post head where the saddle is clamped, check the clamp bolts. Lubricate the bolt threads and you will be able to tighten them a bit more.

Shock-absorbing seatposts can squeak as they move up and down. Try greasing the sides of the inner shaft. Grease the elastomers inside, too.

5. Seatpost slips down.

Tighten the seat-lug-binder bolt. If the seat lug is pinched closed, and the post still slips down, you may be using a seatpost with an incorrect diameter, or the seat tube on your bike may be oversized or has stretched. Double-check the seat-tube diameter with calipers, or ask your local shop to do so.

Try putting a larger seatpost in the frame, and replace yours if you find one that fits better. If the next size up is too big, you may need to shim your existing post. Cut a 1-inch x 3-inch piece of aluminum from a pop can. Pull the seatpost out, grease it and the pop-can shim, and insert both back into the frame. Bend the top lip of the shim over to prevent it from disappearing inside the frame. You may need to experiment with various shim dimensions until you find a piece that will go in with the seatpost and will also prevent slippage. Fortunately, they're cheap.

On a titanium frame with an integral seat binder (one that is welded to the seat tube, as opposed to an external clamp), the seat tube will stretch if the binder is chronically overtightened. If the post is slipping because the binder slot has closed up, contact the frame manufacturer for assistance. You might be able to rescue the situation by filing the slot and binder wide enough to keep it from pinching closed (a tedious job, but titanium will yield to a normal metal file). Plug the seat tube with a greasy rag to keep metal filings from falling into the bottom bracket, and suspend the frame upside down to encourage the filings to go elsewhere.

By the way, don't try this until you get the go-ahead from the framebuilder; attacking the frame in this manner will undoubtedly void the warranty in the absence of explicit authorization. If filing isn't recommended, you will probably have to return the frame to the manufacturer for more comprehensive repair.

XI

Stems, handlebars and headsets

"I may not have gone where I intended to go, but I think I have ended up where I intended to be." —Douglas Adams

On a bike, you maintain or change your direction by applying force to your handlebars. If everything works properly, variations in that pressure will result in your front wheel changing direction. Pretty basic, right? Right, but there is a series of parts between the handlebars and the wheel that makes that simple process possible. The parts of the steering system are illustrated in Fig. 11.1. In this chapter, we'll cover most of that system by going over handlebars, stems and headsets.

11A STEMS

The stem connects to the fork's steering tube and clamps around the handlebar. Stems come in one of two basic types, for threaded or unthreaded steering tubes. The threads referred to have nothing to do with the stem; they're for the headset.

As of this writing, the vast majority of forks on road bikes are threaded, which means that the steering tube on the fork has external threads at the top onto which the headset screws for attachment and adjustment. Stems for threaded steering tubes (Fig. 11.2) have a vertical "quill," which extends down into the steering tube of the fork, and a horizontal shaft, or extension, that connects to the handlebars. The stem binds to the inside of the steering tube by means of a conical or wedge-shaped plug pulled up by a long bolt that runs through the quill (Fig. 11.3).

Unthreaded steering tubes, which are the standard on mountain bikes, are becoming more popular on road bikes as well. Stems for unthreaded steering tubes (Fig. 11.4) have a clamping collar in place of the quill. Since the steering tube has no

tools

4mm, 5mm and 6mm hex keys
2-32mm headset wrenches
Hammer
Screwdriver
Hacksaw
Flat file
Round file
Glue stick
Electrical tape
Grease
Citrus solvent

OPTIONAL

Star-nut installation tool
Threadless saw guide
Channel-lock pliers
Securely mounted vise
Headset cup remover
Crown race remover
Headtube reamer
Crown race facer
Headset press
Crown race slide punch

11.1 parts of the steering system

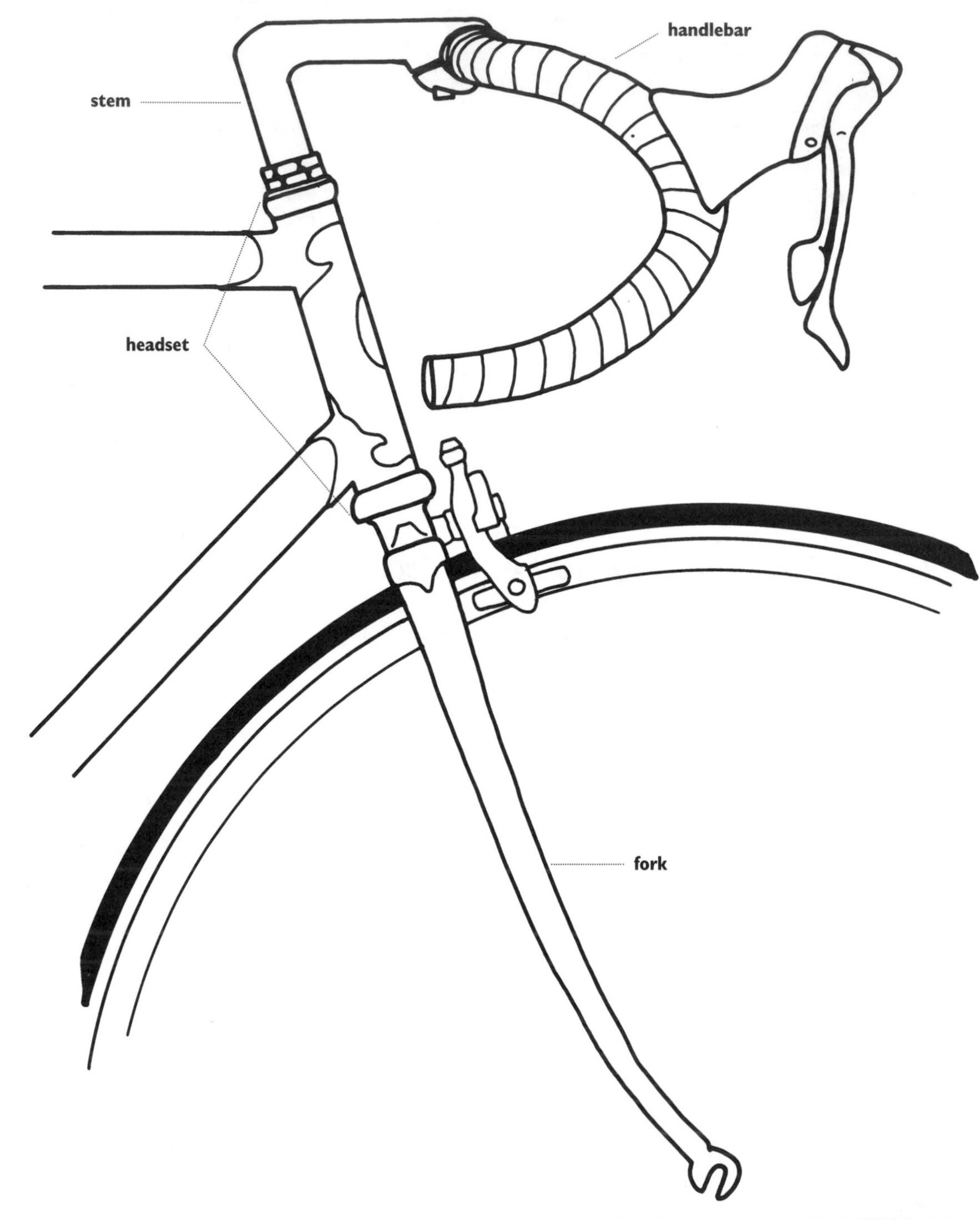

the steering system

threads, the top headset cup slides on and off. In this case, the stem plays a dual role. It clamps around the steering tube to connect the handlebars to the fork, and it also keeps the headset in proper adjustment by preventing the top headset cup from sliding up the steering tube (Figs. 11.5 and 11.6).

Traditionally, road stems are bent at an angle of about 73 degrees so that, when installed on the bike, the extension is horizontal. Stems on track bikes historically tended to be angled downward when mounted on the bike. Stems with 90-degree angles and greater, resulting in an upward angle on the assembled bicycle, are becoming commonplace on road bikes and even on track bikes.

11-1: REMOVE STANDARD QUILL-TYPE STEM FROM THREADED FORK

1. Unscrew the stem-fixing bolt on the top of the stem about three turns or so. Most stem bolts take a 6mm Allen wrench. Some stems have a rubber plug on top of the stem that must be removed to get at the stem bolt.

2. Tap the top of the bolt down with a mallet or hammer (Fig. 11.7) to disengage the plug or wedge from the bottom of the quill. If the head of the bolt is recessed down in the stem so that a hammer cannot get at it, leave the Allen wrench in the bolt and tap the top of the Allen wrench until the wedge is free.

3. Pull the stem out of the steering tube. If the stem will not budge, see Section 11-6A in this chapter.

11-2: INSTALL AND ADJUST HEIGHT OF STANDARD STEM IN THREADED FORK

LEVEL 2

1. Generously grease the stem quill, the bolt threads, the outside of the wedge or conical plug, and the inside of the steering tube. If this is the first time you've done this, I know what you're thinking: "Why put grease on something that I want to wedge together?" Don't worry; the grease won't prevent the wedge from keeping the stem tight. What the grease will do is prevent the parts from seizing or rusting together so that you can't get them apart again.

2. Thread the bolt through the stem and into the wedge or plug until it pulls it into place, but not so far as to prevent the stem from inserting into the steering tube.

3. Slip the stem quill into the steering tube (Fig. 11.3) to the depth you want. Make sure the stem is inserted beyond its height-limit line. Tighten the bolt until the stem is snug but can still be turned.

4. Set the stem to the desired height, line it up with the front wheel, and tighten the bolt. It needs to be tight, but don't overdo it. You can overtighten the stem bolt to the point that it puts a bulge in the steering tube, so be careful.

11-3: REMOVE CLAMP-TYPE STEM FROM THREADLESS STEERING TUBE

1. Loosen the horizontal bolt(s) clamping the stem around the steering tube.

2. With a 5mm (usually) Allen wrench, unscrew and remove the adjusting bolt in the top cap covering the top of the stem clamp and steering tube

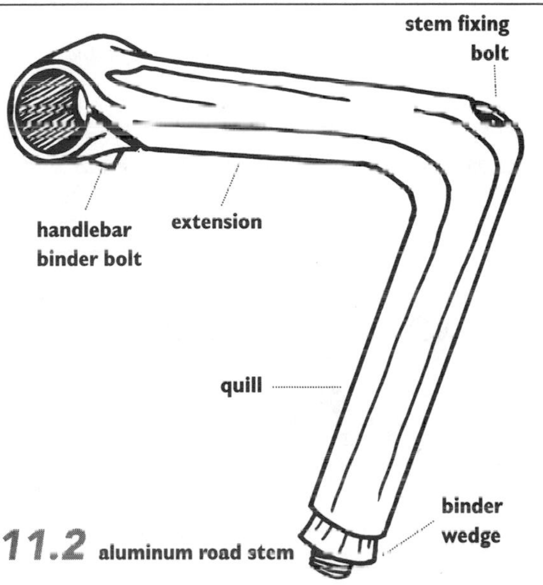

11.2 aluminum road stem

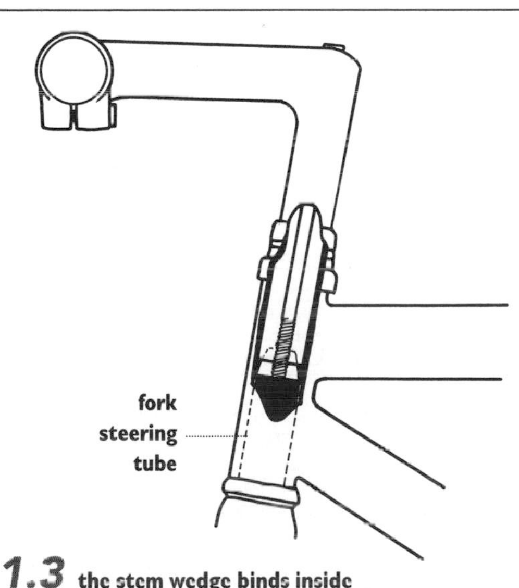

11.3 the stem wedge binds inside the fork steering tube

11.4 threadless stem

11.5 threadless headset and stem cutaway

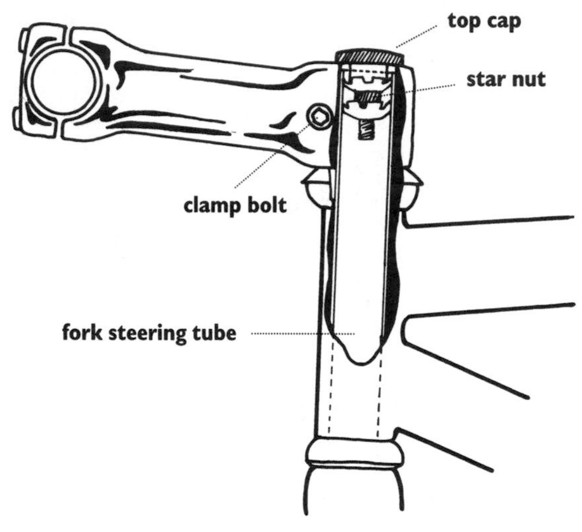

(Fig. 11.8). The fork can now fall out, so hold the fork as you unscrew the bolt.

Note: *Some threadless headsets do not use a top cap. For instance, DiaTech threadless headsets have a collar beveled internally on the top and bottom to adjust headset compression. Without a top cap, as soon as you loosen the stem, the fork can slip out.*

3. With the bike standing on the floor, or while holding the fork to keep it from falling out, pull the cap and the stem off of the steering tube. Leave the bike standing until you replace the stem, or slide the fork out of the frame, keeping track of all headset parts.

4. If the stem will not budge, see Section 11-6B in this chapter.

11-4: INSTALL AND ADJUST HEIGHT OF STEM ON THREADLESS STEERING TUBE

LEVEL 2

Installing and adjusting the height of a stem on a threadless fork is much more complicated than installing and adjusting the height of a standard stem in a threaded fork. That's why this step is listed with a Level 2 designation. Because the stem is integral to operation of the headset (Fig. 11.6), any change to the stem position alters the headset adjustment.

1. Stand the bike on its wheels, so the fork does not fall out. Grease the top end of the steering tube. Loosen the stem clamp bolts, and grease their threads. Slide the stem onto the steering tube.

2. Set the stem height to the desired level. If you want to place the stem in a position higher than directly on top of the headset, you must put some spacers between the bottom of the stem clamp and the top piece of the headset. No matter what, there must be contact (either directly or through spacers) between the headset and the stem. Otherwise, the headset will be loose.

Note: *Some manufacturers produce a pinch-binding headset-adjustment-holding ring with which you can raise or lower the stem without affecting the adjustment of your headset. You slide the ring onto the steer-*

11.6 threadless headset cup held in place by stem

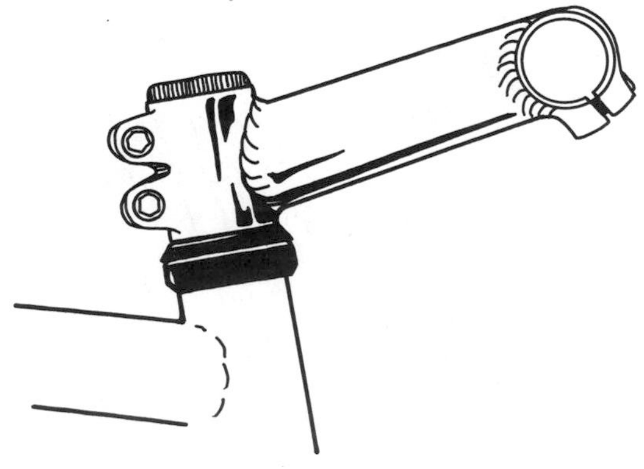

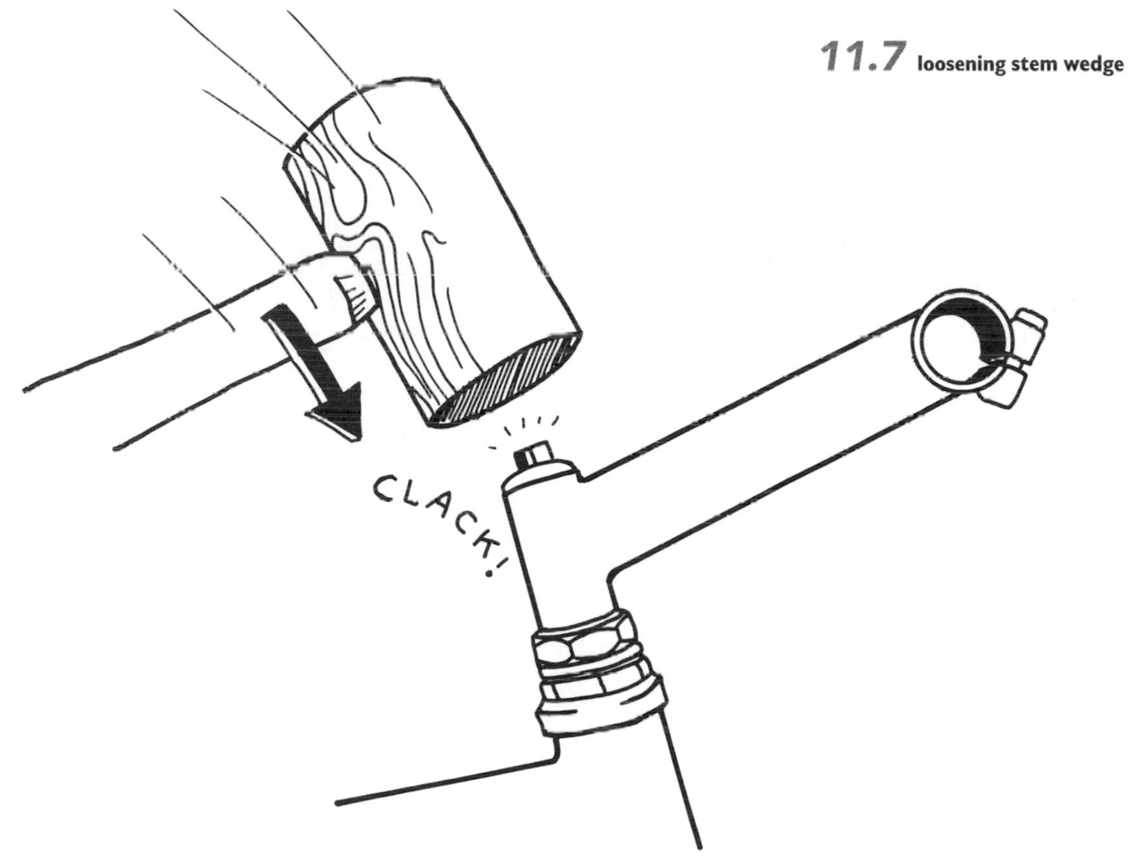

11.7 loosening stem wedge

ing tube on top of the headset and below the stem. Once the headset position is set, you tighten the pinch bolt on the ring. After that is in place, you can raise the stem without throwing the headset out of adjustment.

Many new stems are 1 1/8" with a simple split shim to fit 1" steering tubes. 3T also makes an enclosed headset cap/shim allowing adjustment of a 1 1/8-inch stem on a 1-inch steering tube. With 3T's long, slotted shim, you can slide the stem up and down on the shim while the headset adjustment is held in place by the bolt through the shim's enclosed top. (It surrounds the steerer and its lower flange pushes down on the headset.)

3. Check the steering tube length: In order to adjust the threadless headset, the top of the stem clamp (or spacers placed above it) should overlap the top of the steering tube by 3–6mm (1/8–1/4 inch) (Fig. 11.9). If it does, skip ahead to step 4.

11.8 loosening and tightening bolt on threadless–style headset

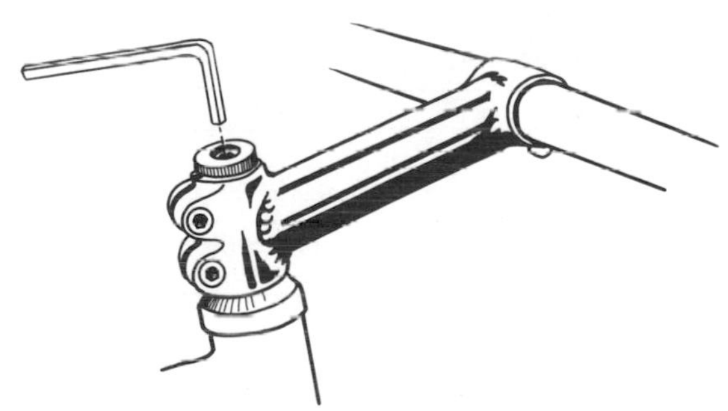

11.9 measuring distance between stem clamp and top of steering tube

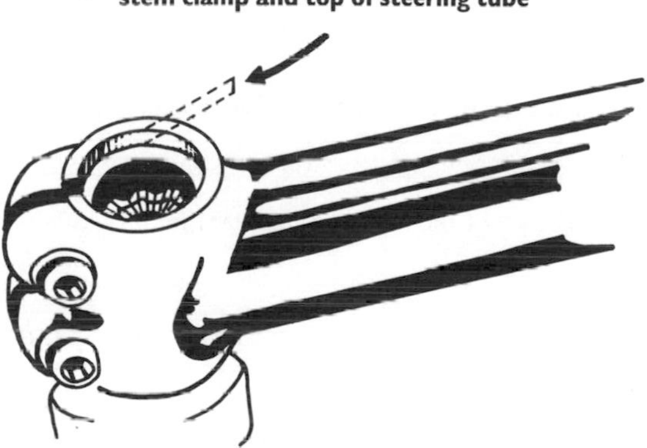

a. Steering tube too short: If the top of the stem clamp overlaps the top of the steering tube by more than 6mm (1/4 inch), the steering tube is too short to set the stem height where you have it. If you have spacers below the stem, remove some until the top edge of the stem clamp overlaps the top of the steering tube by 3–6mm. If you cannot or do not wish to lower the stem any further, you will need a fork with a longer steering tube, or a stem with a shorter clamp, or a stem that is angled upward more to achieve the desired handlebar height. Stems for threadless steering tubes with clamps of differing lengths are available as are stems of varying angles. Replacing the stem is a lot cheaper and easier than replacing the fork.

b. Steering tube too long: If the top of the steering tube is less than 3mm (1/8 inch) below the top edge of the stem clamp (or if sticks up above the top of the stem clamp), you have a choice. If you want the option to raise the stem for a higher handlebar position, stack some headset spacers on top of the stem clamp until the spacers overlap the top edge of the steering tube by at least 3mm.

If, on the other hand, you are sure you will never want the stem any higher, you can cut off the excess tube. First, mark the steering tube along the top edge of the stem clamp and remove the fork from the bike. Make another mark on the steering tube 3mm below the first mark. Place the steering tube in a padded vise or bike stand clamp. Using the lower mark as a guide, cut the excess steering tube off with a hacksaw or tube cutter. Measure twice; cut once!

Make your cut straight. Mark it straight by wrapping a piece of tape around the steering tube and cutting along it. If you are not sure your cut will be straight, start it a little higher and file it down flat to the tape line. If you really want to be safe, use a tool specifically designed to help you make a straight cut; Park Tool's "threadless saw guide" will do the trick. Remember that you can always shorten the steering tube a little more, but you cannot make it longer!

There is a star-shaped nut (Figs. 11.5 and 11.17) that is inserted inside the steering tube (Fig. 11.9). The bolt through the top cap screws into it to adjust the headset bearings (but not to retain the headset; the stem bolts do that). If the star nut is already inside of the steering tube, and it looks like the saw is going to hit it, you must move the star nut down. See Step 4 below for instructions on how to push the star nut in deeper.

Use a round file on the inside of the tube and a flat file on the outside to remove any metal burrs left by the hacksaw or cutter.

When you have completed cutting and de-burring, put the fork back in, replacing all headset parts the way they were originally installed (Fig. 11.17). Return to Step 1 above.

4. Check that the edges of the star-shaped nut are at least 12mm below the top edge of the steering tube. The nut must be far enough down that the bottom of the headset top cap does not hit it once the adjusting bolt is tightened. If the nut is not in deeply enough, you need to drive it deeper into the steering tube after removing the stem. This is best done with the star nut installation tool (Chapter 1, Fig. 1.4). The tool threads into the nut, and you hit it with a hammer until it stops; the star nut will now be set 15mm deep in the steering tube. If you do not have this tool, go to a bike shop and have the nut set for you. If you insist on doing it yourself, read "pushing the star nut in deeper" below. Just remember that it is easy to mangle the star nut if you do not tap it in straight.

Pushing the star nut in deeper without a star nut installation tool:

a. Put the adjusting bolt through the top cap, and thread it six turns into the star nut.

b. Set the star nut over the end of the steering tube, and tap the top of the bolt with a mallet. Use the top cap as a guide to keep it going in straight.

c. Tap the bolt in until the star nut is 15mm below the top of the steering tube.

Note: *If the wall thickness of the steering tube is greater than standard, the stock headset star nut will not fit in, and it will bend when you try to install it. Even pros sometimes ruin star nuts. It's not a big problem, since replacements can be purchased separately. If yours goes in crooked, take a long punch or rod, set it on the star nut, and drive it all of the way out of the bottom of the steering tube. Dispose of the star nut, and get another.*

If the internal diameter (I.D.) of the steering tube is undersized (standard I.D. is 22.2mm [7/8 inch] on a 1-inch steering tube, 25.4mm [1 inch] on a 1 1/8 inch steering tube, and 28.6mm [1 1/8 inch] on a 1 1/4 inch steering tube) you cannot use the stock star nut from the headset for that size. Get a correctly sized star nut at a bike shop or from the fork manufacturer. In a pinch, you can make a big stock star nut fit by bending each pair of opposite leaves of the star nut toward each other with a pair of channel-lock pliers to reduce the nut's width. Now you can insert the nut; be aware that it may not grip as well as a properly sized one.

5. Install the headset top cap on the top of the stem clamp (or spacers you set above it). Grease the threads of the top-cap adjusting bolt, and thread it into the star nut inside the steering tube (Fig. 11.8).

6. Adjust the headset. The steps are outlined in Section 11-15.

11-5: STEM MAINTENANCE AND REPLACEMENT SCHEDULE

A bike cannot be controlled if the stem breaks, so make sure yours doesn't break. Aluminum has no fatigue endurance limit, which means that any aluminum part regularly stretched or flexed will eventually fail. Steel and titanium parts repeatedly stressed more than about one-half of their tensile strength will eventually fail as well. Aluminum may fail suddenly; steel and titanium tend to crack first and then tear over time.

What this means is that stems and handlebars are not permanent accessories on your bike. Replace them before they fail on you.

Clean the stem regularly. Whenever you clean it, look for corrosion, cracks and bent or stressed areas. If you find any, replace the stem immediately. If you crash hard on your bike, especially hard enough to bend the bars, replace the stem—and the bar, of course. Err on the side of caution.

Italian stem maker 3T recommends replacing stems and handlebars every four years. If you rarely ride the bike, this is overkill. If you ride hard and ride often, every four years may not be frequent enough. Do what is appropriate for you, and be aware of the risks.

11-6: REMOVING A STUCK STEM

LEVEL 3

A stem can get stuck into (or onto) the steering tube due to poor maintenance. Regular maintenance involves periodically re-greasing the stem and steering tube to enable the parts to slide freely when disassembled. The grease also forms a barrier to sweat and water.

If the stem is really stuck, be careful as you try to remove it; you can—quite easily, in fact—ruin the fork as well as the stem and the headset trying to get it out. In fact, you're better off having a shop work on it, unless you really know what you are doing and are willing to accept the risk of destroying a lot of expensive parts.

A. Removing a stuck stem from a threaded fork

1. Unscrew the stem bolt on top of the stem three turns or more. Smack the bolt (or the Allen wrench in the bolt) with a mallet or hammer (Fig. 11.7) to completely disengage the wedge.

2. Grasping the front wheel between your knees, make one last attempt to free the stem by twisting back and forth on the bars. Don't use all of your strength, because you can ruin a fork and front wheel this way.

3. If the stem didn't budge, squirt penetrating oil around the stem where it enters the headset. Let the bike sit for several hours and add more penetrating oil every hour or so.

4. Turn the bike over, and squirt penetrating oil into the bottom of the fork steering tube so that it runs down around the stem quill. Let the bike sit for several hours and add more penetrating oil every hour or so.

5. Now that it is totally soaked in penetrating oil, try Step 2 again. If the stem does not come free this time, you have to go to your workbench and use that heavy-duty vise. It's solidly mounted, isn't it? Good, because it will need to be.

6. Remove the front wheel (Chapter 2) and the front brake (Chapter 7. Put pieces of wood on each side of the vise. Clamp the fork crown into the vise (Fig. 11.10).

8. Grab both ends of the handlebar and twist back and forth. The stem will generally come free with a very loud pop. If this doesn't work, you may have to saw off the stem just above the headset and have the bottom of the stem reamed out of the steering tube by a machine shop. In this case, unscrew the headset and remove the fork; don't take the bike to a machine shop as an assembly.

11.10 clamping fork crown in vise

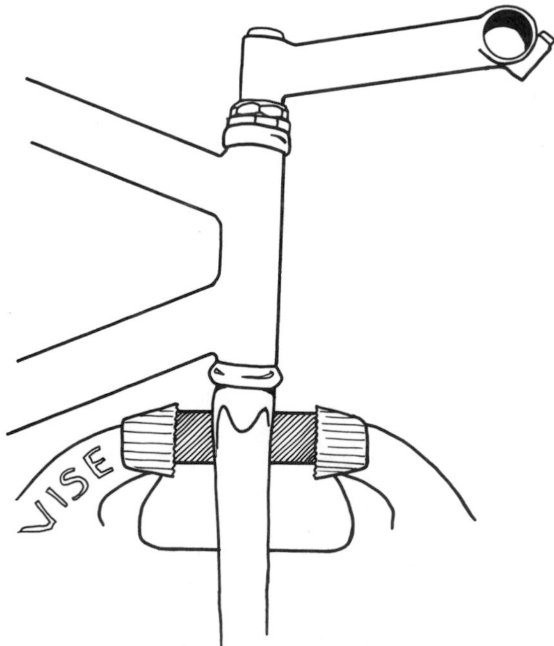

B. Removing a stuck stem from a threadless fork

1. Remove the top cap (Fig. 11.8) and the bolts clamping the stem to the steering tube.

2. Thread the clamp bolts in from the other side. Spread the stem clamp by inserting a coin into the slot between each bolt end and the opposing unthreaded half of the binder lug (Fig. 11.11). Tighten each bolt against each coin so that it spreads the clamp slot open wider. The stem should come right off of the steering tube now.

Note: *If the stem is the type that comes with a single bolt in the side of the stem shaft ahead of the steering tube (Fig. 11.5), loosen the bolt a few turns and tap it in with a hammer to free the wedge. It might require some penetrating oil to free this type of stem from around the steering tube.*

3. If it still will not come free, you may have to use a vise, following instructions 6 and 7 in the last section on freeing a quill-type stem. Failing that, your last resort is to saw through the steering tube at the base of the stem clamp and replace the stem, fork and headset.

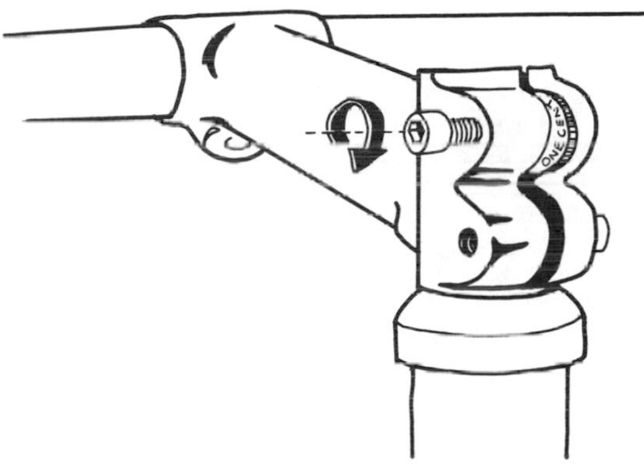

11.11 spread the stem clamp

11B HANDLEBARS

I am generally referring here to standard road drop bars, but most of these comments also apply to the "cow horn" style of handlebar common on triathlon and time-trial bikes.

11-7: HANDLEBAR REMOVAL

1. Remove the handlebar tape (Fig. 11.12), at least from one side.

2. Remove the brake levers (Chapter 7).

3. Loosen the bolt on the stem clamp surrounding the bar. This usually takes a 5mm Allen wrench. Or with a front-opening stem, remove the bolts (or bolt, on a hinged type), and the bar will fall out.

4. Pull the bar out, working the bend around through the stem. If the bar won't budge, or if it will budge but it appears that you will tear up the bar's finish working it out through the stem, or if the bend in the bar will not pass through the stem clamp, you need to open the stem clamp a bit more. On many stems, you can do this by removing the clamp bolt, threading it back in from the opposite side with a coin inserted into the clamp slot, and tightening the bolt against the coin to spread the clamp. (Opening a stem clamp in this way—but from a steering tube—is illustrated in Fig. 11.11.)

11-8: HANDLEBAR INSTALLATION

1. Remove the stem-clamp bolt (or bolts), grease the threads, and replace it (them). Grease the inside of the stem clamp, and grease the clamping area in the center of the bar. Grease keeps the parts from seizing over time, and also will prevent squeaks from developing later.

2. Install the bar and rotate it to the position you find most comfortable. I prefer setting a drop bar so that the bottom flat section (the "drop") is horizontal or aimed down and back toward the rear hub, but the setting you choose is entirely a matter of personal preference.

11-9: HANDLEBAR MAINTENANCE AND REPLACEMENT SCHEDULE

A bike cannot be controlled without handlebars, so you never want one to break on you. Do not look at the bars as a permanent accessory on your bike. All handlebars will eventually fail. The trick is not to be riding them when they do.

Keep the bars clean. Regularly inspect them (under the tape) for cracks, crash-induced bends, corrosion, and stressed areas. If you find any sign of wear or cracking, replace the bars. Never straighten

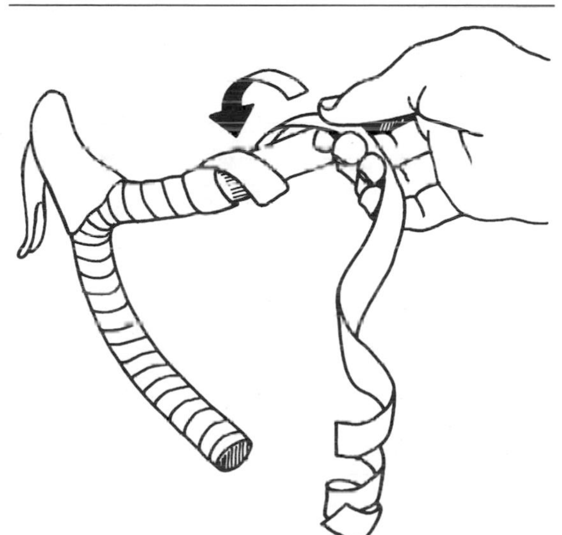

11.12 removing handlebar tape

a bent handlebar! Replace it! If you crash hard on your bike, consider replacing the bars even if they look fine. If the bars have taken an extremely hard hit, it's a good idea to replace them rather than gamble on their integrity.

The Italian stem and bar manufacturer 3T recommends replacing stems and bars every four years. As with a stem, if you rarely ride the bike, this is overkill. If you ride hard and ride often, every four years may not be frequent enough. Do what is appropriate for you, and be aware of the risks.

11-10: WRAPPING HANDLEBAR TAPE

You need both hands free and the bars rigidly held. Clamping the bike in a bike stand or holding it in a stationary trainer should do the trick, but you may need to stabilize the front wheel between your knees or with a strap around the down tube and rim, or a bar-holder from the seatpost to the handlebar. Again, before wrapping, clean the bar and inspect it for cracks, crash-induced bends, corrosion, and stressed areas. If you find any sign of wear or cracking, replace the bar.

Tape down concealed brake and shift cables in a few places with electrical tape or strapping tape (Fig. 11.13). (Pre-1984 or so brake levers have no concealed cables; the brake cable comes out of the top of the lever.) Shimano STI levers have concealed brake cables and exposed shift cables. Both the shift cables and brake cables are concealed on Campagnolo ErgoPower or Mavic Mektronic levers. Tape the cables down where they will be the most comfortable on your hands. Some handlebars have creases in them for the cables; tape the cables down so they stay in the creases. Shimano STI brake cables go along the front of the handlebar. Campagnolo ErgoPower shift cables go along the front of the bar and the brake cables go around the back of the bar.

Smear some Glue Stick on the bar around the outside of all of its bends. These areas are where the handlebar tape tends to creep and separate; the glue will help keep that from happening.

Insert the plugs into the ends of the bar. Lightweight bars tend to have thin walls and consequently larger inside diameter, and many end plugs will not fit tightly in them. In this case, wrap some electrical tape around the insertion prongs of the plug until it fits tightly and won't rattle out.

Handlebar tape sets usually come with two little short pieces. These are to cover the brake-lever-clamp bands. Peel back the edge of the rubber hood on the brake lever, wrap the little tape piece around the clamp band and insert each end under the hood. You

wrapping a handlebar

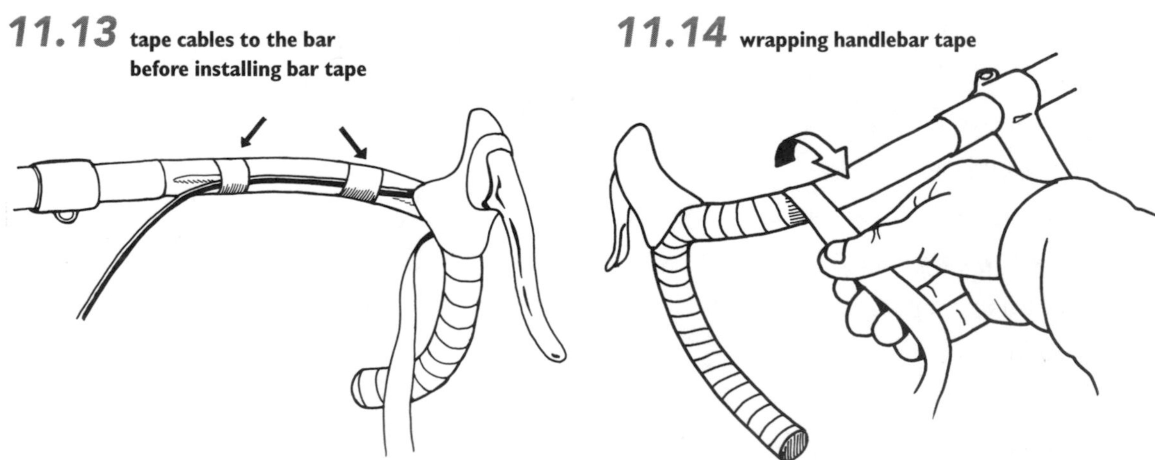

11.13 tape cables to the bar before installing bar tape

11.14 wrapping handlebar tape

may want to tape the ends down with some Scotch tape. Leave the hoods peeled back so that you can wrap the bar tape up onto the edge of the lever body and then cover it with the skirt of the rubber hood.

Peel back the paper backing on the tape and start wrapping at the end of the bar from the inside out. You always want to wrap from the end of the bar so that each wrap holds down the upper edge of the prior one. Wrapping from the top of the bar and finishing at the end plug is a mistake, because your hands will constantly peel back the upper edge of each tape wrap as you ride. The tape will look bad and get torn quickly.

Pull the tape tightly as you wrap, but not enough to break it. Overlap each wrap about one-quarter to one-half of its width (Fig. 11.14). Use as much overlap as you can to increase padding and decrease the chance of the tape slipping enough to reveal the handlebar. The amount of overlap will depend on the length of the tape, the width and drop depth of the bars, and the amount you stretch the tape as you wrap.

When you get to the bulged section of the bar that clamps into the stem, you should have just run out of tape. If you have more, you can re-wrap part of the bar with more overlap, or you can cut off the excess. If the tape doesn't make it to the bulge, you can re-wrap part of the bar with less overlap. If you want to end with only a narrow piece of sticky tape holding it down, you can trim the end of the bar tape to a point, and hold it down with a single width of electrical tape wrapped around a couple of times. You can follow with the decorative tape piece that came with the bar tape. Otherwise, just wrap around the bars a number of times with electrical tape, going wide enough with it to completely cover the square-cut end of the bar tape. Cut or break the electrical tape so that it ends under the bar.

11.15 installing aero' bars

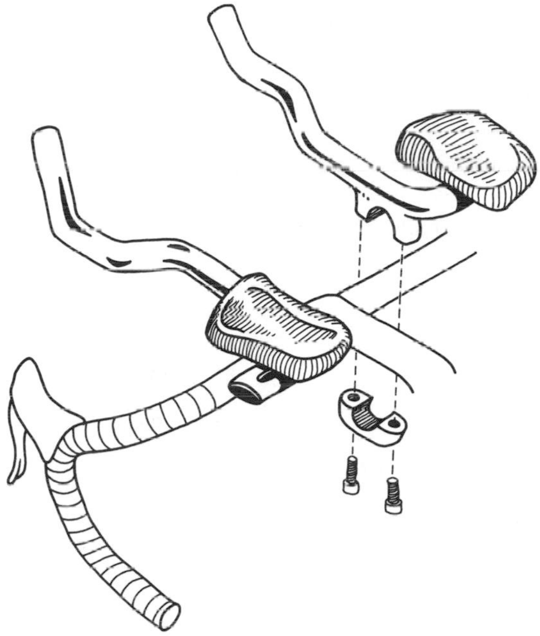

11-11: INSTALLING A CLIP-ON AERO' BAR

Open the clamps that attach around the handlebar by removing the bolts with a hex key. Note: I will refer to the bike's handlebar, when a clip-on is attached to it, as the "base bar." Clip-ons generally mount on the bulge of the base bar, right next to the stem. If the clip-on you have chosen mounts on the thinner-diameter section of the base bar, you will have to peel back some handlebar tape from the section adjacent the bulge.

For starters, set the clip-on bar level or angled upward slightly. Bolt the clip-on clamps around the base bar (Fig. 11.15). You want the bolts tight enough that the clip-on bar won't slip when you hit a bump or pull on it, but you also don't want to crush the base bar. See the Torque Table in Appendix B.

Set the elbow pads in a medium-width position. The pad is often held onto the elbow support with a hook-and-loop fastener such as Velcro; pulling off the pad will reveal the adjusting bolt. Ideally, you want the elbow pad positioned under your elbow or slightly forward of it, and you want the clip-on to be of such a length that your hands grasp the ends comfortably with the elbows on the pads.

11-12: SETTING STEM AND BAR POSITIONS

Setting handlebar height and reach is very personal. Much depends on your physique, your flexibility, your frame, your riding style, and a few other preferences. This subject is covered in depth in Appendix C. Here are some brief suggestions.

- I recommend setting drop handlebars so that the flat section below the bend (the "drop") is horizontal or aimed slightly downward toward the rear hub.
- If you stand a lot when you climb, you will want the bars low enough that you can use your arms efficiently when gripping the brake levers and pulling.
- A low, stretched-out position is better aerodynamically. A low position puts the top of the handlebar about 6–12cm lower than the top of the saddle. With your hands on the drops, a stretched-out position places your elbow at least 2 inches in front of your knee at the top of the pedal stroke.
- If you are using an aero' (clip-on) bar, you want to find a position that maximizes both comfort and aerodynamic efficiency. The lower and more aerodynamic you are trying to be, the more forward you will want to position your saddle to open up the angle between your torso and your thigh. When setting the reach to the bars, a good rule of thumb is to position your elbow pads so that your ear is over the bend in your elbow. As for width, the narrower the elbow pads, the more aerodynamic you will be. Work on getting lower only after you have gotten comfortable and efficient with a narrow position.

11C HEADSETS

There are two basic types of headsets: threaded (Fig. 11.16) and unthreaded (Fig. 11.17). Road headsets generally come in the 1-inch-diameter size, but some road bikes are now appearing with 1 1/8-inch headsets.

The top bearing cup on a threaded headset has wrench flats, a keyed washer stacked on top of it, and a locknut that covers the top of the steering tube. That locknut tightens against the washer and top cup (see Fig. 11.16). Extra spacers may be included under the locknut.

Prior to the 1990s, practically all headsets and steering tubes were threaded. Dia-Compe's AheadSet pioneered the threadless headset, which is a lighter system because it eliminates the stem quill, bolt, and wedge. The AheadSet connection between the handlebars and the stem is more rigid, too. Of course, fork manufacturers prefer threadless headsets, because they do not have to thread their forks and/or offer various lengths of fork steerers; steerer diameter becomes the only variable.

On an unthreaded headset, the top cup and a conical compression ring slide onto the steering tube (Fig. 11.17). The stem clamps around the top of the steering tube and above the compression ring. A nut with two layers of spring-steel teeth sticking out from it (called a "Star Fangled Nut" by Dia-Compe) fits into the steering tube and grabs the inner walls (Fig. 11.5). A top cap sits atop the stem clamp and pushes it down by means of a long bolt threaded into the star nut to adjust the headset (Fig. 11.17). The stem clamped around the steering tube holds the headset in adjustment (Fig. 11.6). Some headsets (DiaTech) omit the star nut and top cap, instead employing a clamp surrounding the steerer between the stem and the headset. The clamp is

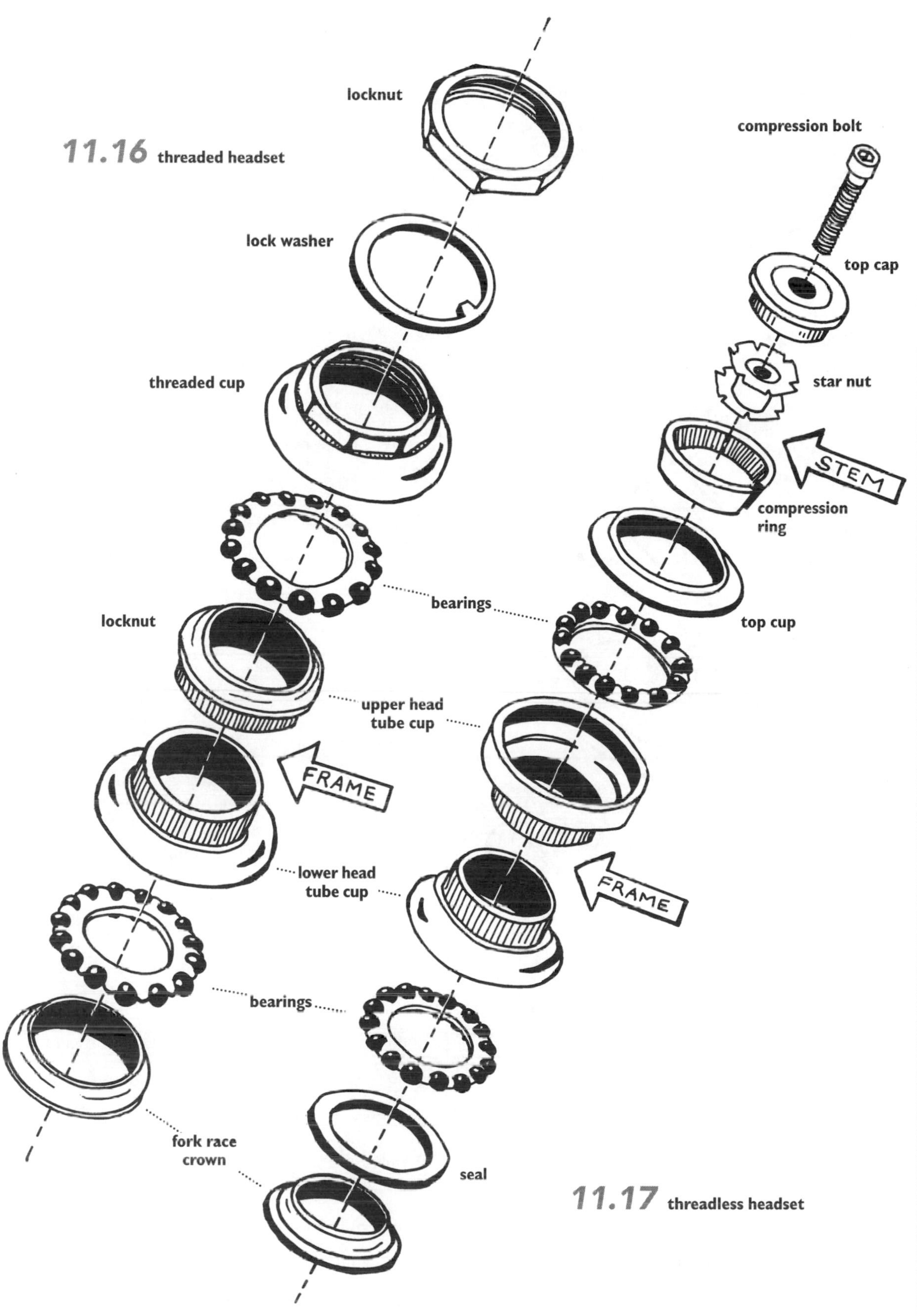

11.16 threaded headset

11.17 threadless headset

11.18 **needle bearings**

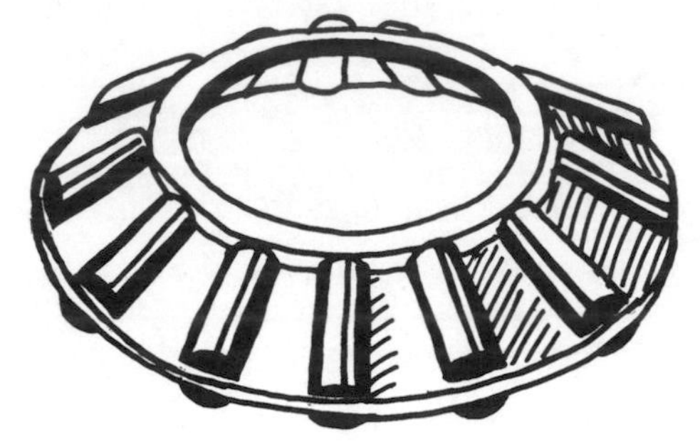

11.19 **cartridge bearing headset**

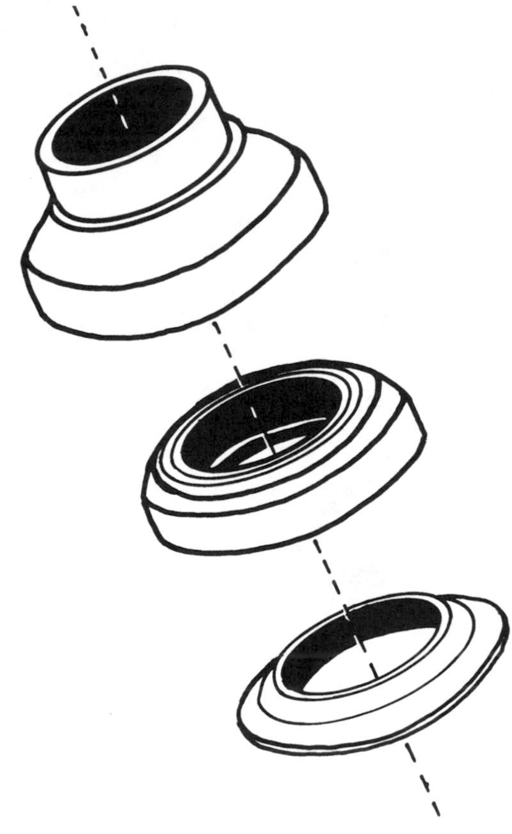

internally tapered to fit over a dual-taper washer and push it—and the headset top cap—down.

Most headsets, threaded or threadless, use ball bearings held in some type of steel or plastic retainer or "cage" (Figs. 11.16 and 11.17) so that you are not chasing dozens of separate balls around when you work on the bike. A variation on this (Stronglight) has needle bearings held in conical plastic retainers (Fig. 11.18) riding on conical steel bearing surfaces.

Cartridge-bearing headsets usually employ "angular contact" bearings (Fig. 11.19), since normal cartridge bearings cannot take the side forces encountered by a headset. Each bearing is a separate, sealed, internally greased unit.

11-13: CHECK HEADSET ADJUSTMENT

If the headset is too loose, it will rattle or clunk while you ride. You might even notice some "play" in the fork as you apply the front brake. If the headset is too tight, the fork will be difficult to turn or feel rough to rotate.

1. Check for headset looseness by holding the front brake and rocking the bike forward and back. Try it with the front wheel pointed straight ahead and then with the wheel turned at 90 degrees to the bike. Feel for back-and-forth movement (or "play") at the lower head cup with your other hand. If there is play, you need to adjust the headset because it is too loose.

If the headset is loose, skip to the appropriate adjustment section, 11-14 or 11-15.

2. Check for headset tightness by turning the handlebars back and forth with the front wheel off the ground. Feel for any binding or stiffness of movement. Also, check for the chunk-chunk-chunk movement to fixed positions characterizing a pitted headset (if you feel this, you need a new headset; skip to Section 11-18). Lean the bike to one side and then the other; the front wheel should turn as the bike is leaned (be aware that cable housings can resist the turning of the front wheel). Lift the bike by the saddle so it is tipped down at an angle with both wheels off of the ground. Turn the handlebar one way and let go of it. See if it returns to center quickly and smoothly on its own. If the headset does not turn easily on any of the above steps, it is too tight, and you should skip to the appropriate adjustment section, 11-14 or 11-15.

3. If the headset is a threaded model, try to turn the top nut and the threaded cup by hand. They should be so tight against each other that they can only be loosened with wrenches. If you can tighten or loosen either part by hand, even if it passed tests one and two above, you still need to adjust the headset; go to section 11-14.

11-14: ADJUSTING A THREADED HEADSET

The secret to good adjustment is simultaneously controlling the steering tube, the adjustable cup, and the locknut as you tighten the latter two together.

Note: *Perform the adjustment with the stem installed. Not only does it give you something to hold onto that keeps the fork from turning during the installation, but there are slight differences in adjustment when the stem is in place as opposed when it is not. Tightening the stem bolt can sometimes bulge the walls of the steering tube slightly (Fig. 11.3), just enough for it to shorten the steering tube and tighten a previously perfect headset adjustment.*

1. Following the steps outlined in Section 11-13, determine whether the headset is too loose or too tight.

2. Put a pair of headset wrenches that fit the headset on the headset's top nut (which I will also call the "locknut") and top bearing cup (or "threaded cup" or "adjustable cup"). Headset nuts come in a wide variety of sizes, so make sure you have purchased the proper size. The standard wrench size for a road bike is 32mm.

Place the wrenches so that the top one is slightly offset to the left of the bottom wrench. That way you can squeeze them together to free the nut (Fig. 11.20).

Note: *People with small hands or weak grip will need to grab each wrench out at the end to get enough leverage.*

3. Hold the lower wrench in place and turn the top wrench counterclockwise about 1/4 turn to loosen the locknut. It may take considerable force to break it loose, since it is generally tight to keep the headset from loosening up.

4. If the headset was too loose, turn the lower (or threaded) cup clockwise about 1/16 of a turn while holding the stem with your other hand. Be careful when tightening the cup; over-tightening it can ruin the headset by pressing the bearings into the bearing surfaces and make little indentations. The headset then stops at the indentations rather than turns smoothly, a condition known as a "pitted" or "brinelled" headset.

If the headset was too tight, loosen the threaded cup counterclockwise 1/16 turn while holding the stem with your other hand. Loosen it until the bearings turn freely, but not to the point where any play develops.

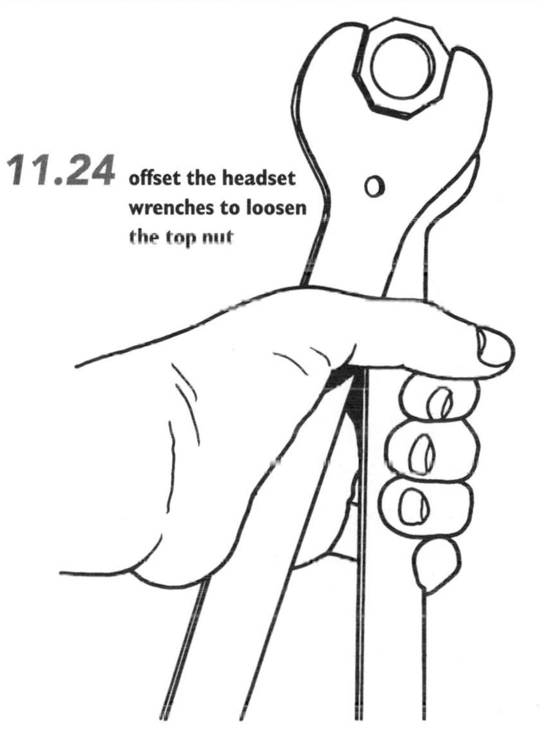

11.24 offset the headset wrenches to loosen the top nut

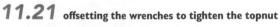

11.21 **offsetting the wrenches to tighten the topnut**

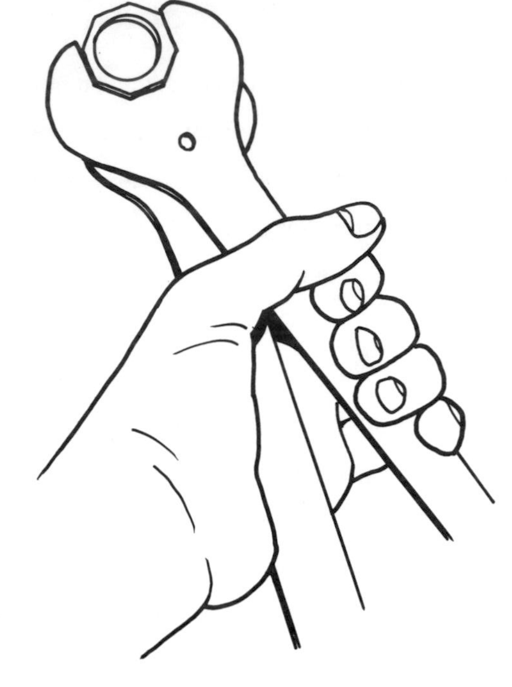

5. Holding the stem, tighten the locknut clockwise with a single wrench. Make sure that the threaded cup does not turn while you tighten the locknut. If it does turn, you either are missing the keyed lock washer separating the cup and locknut (Fig. 11.16), or the washer you have is missing its key. In this case, remove the locknut (the stem has to come out first) and replace the keyed washer. Put the locknut on the steering tube so that the key engages the longitudinal groove in the steering tube. Thread on the locknut, install the stem and re-do the adjustment procedure.

Note: *You can adjust a headset without a keyed washer by working both wrenches simultaneously, but it is trickier, and the headset often comes loose while riding.*

6. Check the headset adjustment again. Repeat Steps 4 and 5 until properly adjusted.

7. Once properly adjusted, place one wrench on the locknut and the other on the threaded cup. Tighten the locknut (clockwise) firmly against the washer(s) and threaded cup to hold the headset adjustment in place (Fig. 11.21).

8. Check the headset adjustment again. If it is off, follow Steps 2-7 again. Once it is adjusted properly, make sure the stem is aligned with the front wheel before riding.

Notes: *If you constantly get what you believe to be the proper adjustment, and then find it to be too loose after you tighten the locknut and threaded cup against each other, the steering tube may be too long, causing the locknut to bottom out. Remove the stem and examine the inside of the steering tube. If the top end of the steering tube butts up against the top lip of the locknut, the steering tube is too long. Remove the locknut and add another spacer.*

If you don't want to add another spacer, file one or 2 millimeters from the steering tube. Be sure to deburr it inside and out, and avoid leaving filings in the bearings or steering tube threads. Replace the locknut and return to Step 5.

Wheels Manufacturing makes a headset locknut called the "Growler." It replaces the locknut and will not come loose, even on bumpy terrain. It threads on like a normal locknut and is adjusted the same way. The only difference between a Growler and a standard locknut is that the Growler is split on one side and has a pinch bolt bridging the split. Once the headset is adjusted, you tighten the pinch bolt to keep the locknut from unscrewing.

11-15: ADJUSTING A THREADLESS HEADSET

threadless headset adjustment

Adjusting a threadless headset is much easier than adjusting a threaded one. It's a Level 1 procedure and usually only takes a 5mm Allen wrench.

1. Check the headset adjustment (section 11-13, above). Determine whether the headset is too tight or too loose.

2. Loosen the bolt(s) that clamp the stem to the steering tube.

3. If the headset is too tight, loosen the 5mm Allen bolt on the top cap about 1/16 of a turn (Fig. 11.22).

If the headset is too loose, tighten the 5mm Allen bolt on the top cap about 1/16 turn (Fig. 11.22). Be careful not to over-tighten it, which will put too much pressure on the bearings and eventually pit the headset. If you're using a torque wrench, Dia-Compe recommends a tightening torque on this bolt of 22 inch-pounds. This is a good place to start, but your headset may require a different torque for proper adjustment.

Note: *Not all threadless stems are adjusted with the top-cap system. DiaTech threadless headsets have no top cap. Instead, a clamping collar below the stem adjusts headset tension. The stem is first clamped in place. The collar is beveled on the inside from both ends, and it slides down an externally beveled ring above it as you tighten the clamp screw. This puts pressure on the headset. As soon as you loosen the stem, the headset comes out of adjustment.*

Adjustment problems:

a. If the cap does not move down and push the stem down, re-do step 2, making sure the stem is not stuck to the steering tube. If the stem won't budge, go to Section 11-6B earlier in this chapter.

b. Another hindrance occurs if the conical compression ring (Fig. 11.17) is stuck to the steering tube, preventing adjustment via the top cap bolt. With the stem off, tap the steering tube down with a mallet, and then push the fork back up to free the compression ring. Grease the ring and the steerer, and reassemble.

c. If the neither the stem nor the compression ring is stuck, yet the cap still does not push the stem down, the steering tube may be so long that it is hitting the lip of the top cap and preventing the cap from pushing the stem down. The steering tube's top should be 3-6mm below the top edge of the stem (Fig. 11.9). If the steering tube is too long, add a spacer above or below the stem, or use a flat file to make the steering tube shorter.

d. Another thing that can thwart adjustment is if the star nut is not installed deeply enough, so the cap bottoms out on the star nut. The highest point of the star nut should be 12–15mm below the top of the steering tube. Tap it deeper with a star-nut-installation tool, or put the bolt through the top cap, thread it five turns into the star nut, and gently tap it in with a soft hammer, using the top cap to keep it going in straight.

Once you have fixed the cause of the adjustment problem, return to step 1 above.

4. Tighten the steering tube clamp bolt, or bolts, on the stem. If using a torque wrench, Dia-Compe recommends a tightening torque of 130 inch-pounds.

5. Re-check the headset adjustment. Repeat Steps 2–4 if necessary. If it is adjusted properly, make sure the stem is aligned straight with the front wheel.

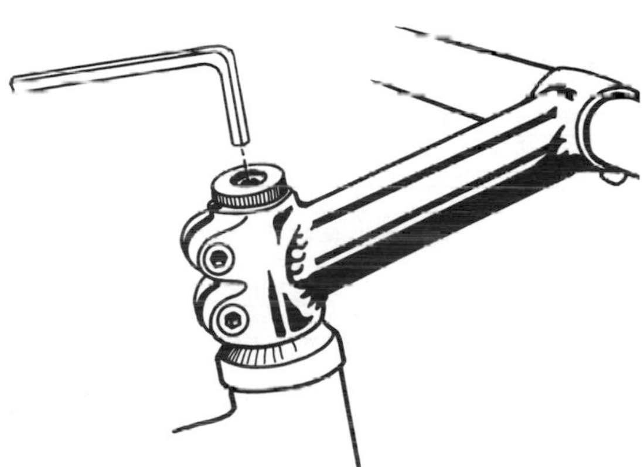

11.22 **loosening and tightening bolt on threadless-style headset**

11-16: OVERHAUL THREADED HEADSET

LEVEL 2

Like any other bike part with bearings, headsets need periodic overhauls. If you use your bike regularly, you should probably overhaul a loose-bearing headset once a year. Headsets with sealed cartridge bearings usually never need to be overhauled; if a bearing fails, you either replace the bearing (Shimano, Fig. 11.19) or, if it has press-in bearings (like Chris King and Dia-Compe's "S" series, Fig. 11.23), you replace the entire cup. If you have a Shimano cartridge-bearing headset, continue with these instructions. If you are replacing a Chris King or Dia-Compe "S" headset cup, move on to the instructions for headset removal.

A bike stand is highly recommended when overhauling a headset.

1. Disconnect the front brake cable (Chapter 7), and remove the stem by loosening the stem bolt three turns, tapping the bolt down with a hammer to free the wedge (Fig. 11.7), and pulling it out.

2. Either turn your bike upside down or be prepared to catch the fork as you remove the upper portion of the headset. To remove the top headset cup, unscrew the locknut and threaded cup with headset wrenches: Place one wrench on the locknut and one on the threaded cup. Loosen the locknut by turning it counterclockwise (Fig. 11.24). It's easiest if the top wrench is angled just to the left of the lower wrench, and you squeeze them together. Unscrew the locknut and the cup from the steering tube. The headset washer or washers will slide off of the steering tube as you unscrew the threaded cup.

overhauling threaded headset

3. Pull the fork out of the frame.

4. Remove any seals that surround the edges of the cups. Make a point of remembering the position and orientation of each.

11.23 Chris King-style pressed sealed bearings

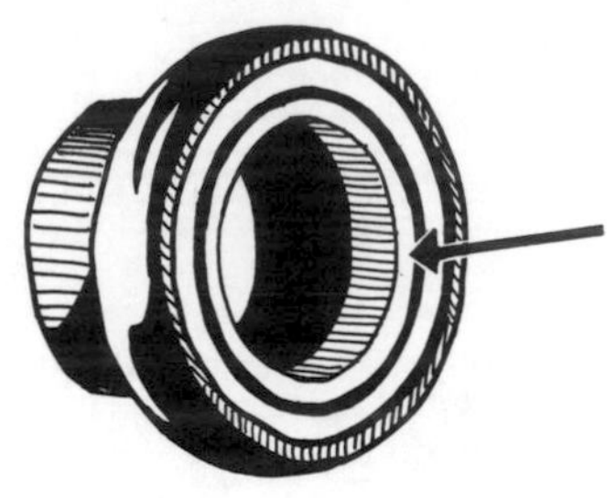

11.24 loosening the locknut

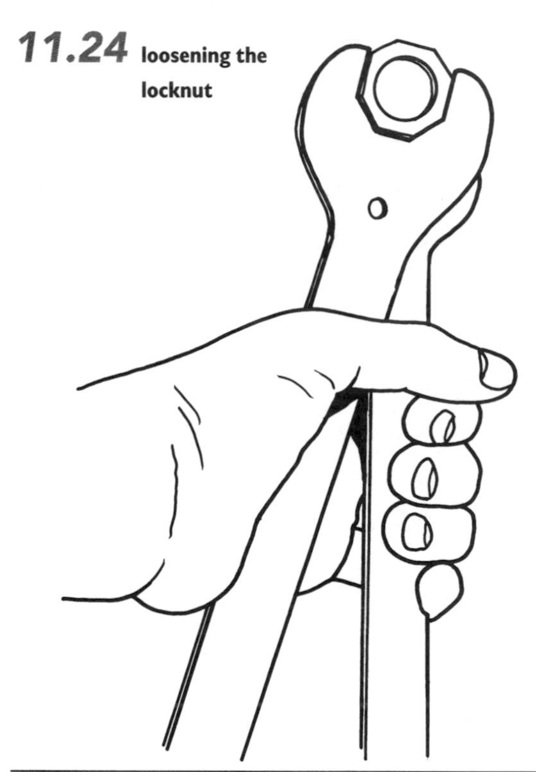

5. Remove the bearings from the cups. If the balls are loose, be especially careful not to lose any. Separate top and bottom sets if they are of different sizes.

6. Clean or replace the bearings.

a. With standard ball-bearing or needle-bearing headsets, put the bearings in a jar or old water bottle along with some citrus-based solvent. Shake. If the bearings from the top and bottom are of different sizes, keep them in separate containers to avoid confusion.

b. With sealed cartridge bearings, check to see if they turn smoothly. If they do not, buy new ones. Either way, skip to Step 8.

7. Blot the bearings dry with a clean rag. Plug the sink, and wash the bearings in soap and water in your hands, just as if you were washing your palms by rubbing them together. This helps keep your hands clean for the assembly steps as well. Rinse bearings thoroughly and blot them dry. Let them air dry completely.

8. Wipe all of the bearing surfaces with clean rags. Wipe the steering tube clean, especially the threads, and wipe the inside of the head tube clean with a rag stuck to the end of a screwdriver.

9. Inspect all bearing surfaces for wear and pitting. If you see pits (separate indentations made by bearings in the bearing surfaces), you need to replace the headset. If that's the case, skip to Section 11-18.

10. Apply grease to all bearing surfaces. A thin film will do, especially if you are using sealed cartridge bearings.

11. Turn the bike upside down in the bike stand. Place a set of bearings in the top cup and a set in the cup on the lower end of the head tube. Make sure you have the bearing retainer right side up so that only the bearings contact the bearing surfaces. If you have installed the retainer upside down it will come in contact with one of the bearing surfaces, and the headset will not turn well. This is a bad thing, since assembling and riding it that way will turn the retainer into jagged chunks of broken metal. To be safe, double and triple check the retainer placement by turning each cup pair in your hand before proceeding.

Most headsets have the bearings set up symmetrically top and bottom (Fig. 11.16). This way, the top piece of each pair is a cup, and the bottom piece is a cone and the bearing retainer rides the same way in both sets. Some headsets, however, place both cups facing outward from the head tube (Fig. 11.17), so the bearing retainers are asymmetrical on either end of the head tube. Also, watch for asymmetry in ball size; Ritchey and recent Campagnolo headsets have smaller balls on top than in the bottom.

Notes: *Stronglight and similar needle-bearing headsets come with two pairs of separate conical steel rings. These are the bearing surfaces that sit on either side of each needle bearing (Fig. 11.18). You will find that one conical ring of each set is smaller than the other ring. Place the smaller one on the lower surface supporting the bearing: for the bottom bearing, place the smaller ring on the fork crown race and, for the top bearing, place the smaller ring on the cup on top of the head tube.*

If you have loose ball bearings with no bearing retainer, stick the balls into the grease in the cups one at a time, making sure that you replace the same number you started with in each cup.

12. Re-install any seals that you removed from the headset parts.

13. Drop the fork into the head tube so that the lower headset bearing set seats properly (Fig. 11.25).

14. Screw on the top cup, with the bearings in it, onto the steering tube. Keeping the bike upside down at this point not only keeps the fork in place, it also prevents grit from falling into the bearings as you thread the cup on.

15. Turn the bike upright. Slide on the keyed washer (Fig. 11.16). Align the key in the groove of the steering tube threads. Screw on the locknut with your hand.

16. Grease the stem quill and insert it into the steering tube (Fig. 11.3). Make certain that it is in deeper than the imprinted limit line. Align the stem with the front wheel and tighten the stem bolt.

17. Adjust the headset as outlined in Section 11-14.

11-17: OVERHAUL THREADLESS HEADSET

Either place the bike upside down in the work stand or be ready to catch the fork when you remove the stem.

1. Disconnect the front brake (Chapter 7), and unscrew the top cap bolt (Fig. 11.22) and the stem clamp bolt, or bolts. Remove the top cap and the stem.

2. Remove the top headset cup by sliding the top cup, conical compression ring (Fig. 11.17) and any spacers off of the steering tube. It may take a tap with a mallet on the end of the steering tube, followed by pushing the fork back up, to free the compression ring.

3. Pull the fork from the frame.

4. Remove any seals that surround the edges of the cups. Remember the position and orientation of each.

5. Remove the bearings from the cups. Be careful not to lose any. Separate top and bottom sets if they are of different sizes.

6. Clean or replace the bearings:

a. With standard ball-bearing or needle-bearing headsets, put the bearings in a jar or old water bottle along with some citrus-based solvent. Shake. If the bearings from the top and bottom are of different sizes, keep them in separate containers to avoid confusion.

b. With sealed cartridge bearings, check to see if they turn smoothly. If they do not, buy new ones. Skip to Step 8.

7. Blot the bearings dry with a clean rag. Plug the sink, and wash the bearings in soap and water in your hands, just as if you were washing your palms by rubbing them together. Your hands will get clean for the assembly steps as well. Rinse bearings thoroughly and blot them dry. Let them air dry completely.

8. Wipe all of the bearing surfaces with clean rags. Wipe the steering tube clean.

9. Inspect all bearing surfaces for wear and pitting. If you see pits (separate indentations made by bearings in the bearing surfaces), you need to replace the headset. If so, skip to section 11-18.

10. Apply grease to all bearing surfaces. If you are using sealed-cartridge bearings, apply grease conservatively.

11. Turn the bike upside down in the bike stand. Place a set of bearings into the top cup and a set into the cup on the lower end of the head tube. Make sure you have the bearing retainer right side up so that only the bearings contact the bearing surfaces. If you have installed the retainer upside down, it will come in contact with one of the bearing surfaces, and the headset will not turn well. This is a bad thing, since assembling and riding it that way will turn the retainer into jagged chunks of broken metal. To be safe, double and triple check the retainer placement by turning each cup pair in your hand before proceeding.

Most headsets have the bearings set up symmetrically top and bottom (Fig. 11.16). This way, the top piece of each pair is a cup and the bottom piece is a cone, and the bearing retainer rides the same way in both sets. Some headsets, however, place both cups (and hence the bearing retainers) facing outward from the head tube (Fig. 11.17).

Note: *If you have loose ball bearings with no bearing retainer, stick the balls into the grease in the cups one at a time, making sure that you replace the same number you started with in each cup.*

12. Re-install any seals that you removed from the headset parts.

13. Drop the fork into the head tube so that the lower headset bearing set seats properly (Fig. 11.25).

overhauling threadless headset

11.25 setting fork in head tube to seat bearings

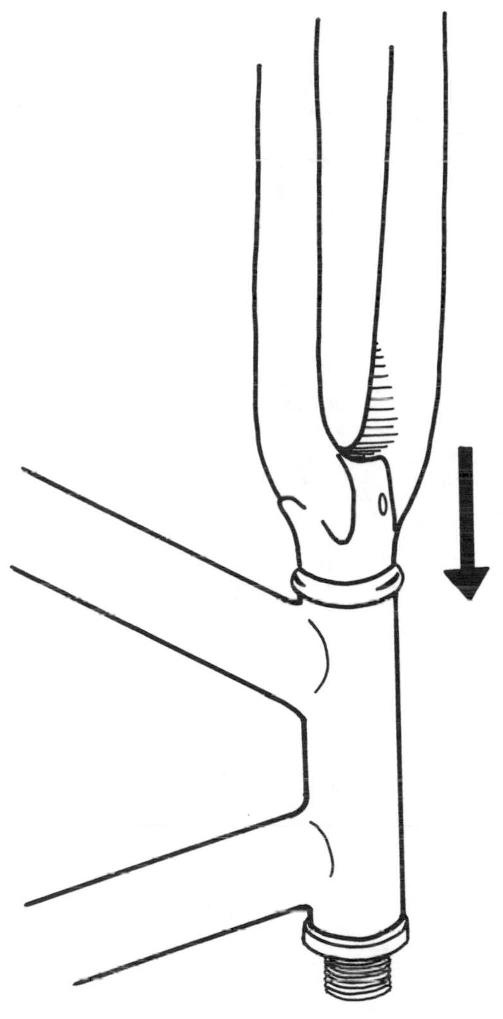

14. Slide the top cup, with the bearings in it, onto the steering tube. Keep the bike upside down at this point; it not only keeps the fork in place, it also prevents grit from falling into the bearings as you put the cup on.

15. Grease the compression ring and slide it onto the (greased) steering tube, so the narrower end slides into the conical space in the top of the top cup (Fig. 11.17). Slide on any spacers you had under the stem. Slide the stem on, and tighten one stem clamp bolt to hold it in place.

16. Turn the bike over. Check that the stem clamp extends 3–6mm above the top of the steering tube (Fig. 11.9) and that the star nut is 12-15mm down in the steering tube. If they are, install the top cap on the top of the stem clamp and steering tube, and screw the bolt into the star nut (Fig. 11.22).

If the steering tube is too long, remove the stem. Add a spacer or file the steering shorter until the stem clamp overlaps it by 3–6mm. If the steering tube is too short, remove spacers from below the stem, if there are any. If there are no spacers to remove, try a new stem with a shorter clamp.

17. Adjust the headset (Section 11-15).

11-18: REMOVE HEADSET

LEVEL 3

1. Remove the front brake. Open the headset and remove the fork and bearings by following Steps 1–5 either section 11-16 or 11-17, depending on headset type.

2. Slide the solid end of the headset-cup remover (sometimes called a headset "rocket," a wonderfully evocative name, as you'll see) through one end of the head tube (Fig. 11.26). As you pull the headset-cup remover through the head tube, the splayed-out tangs on the opposite end of the tool will pull through the cup and spread out.

3. Strike the solid end of the cup remover with a hammer, and drive the cup out (Fig. 11.27). Be careful as you do this, as the remover, or rocket, is liable to launch the cup across the room if hit with sufficient force.

4. Remove the other cup by placing the cup remover into the opposite end of the head tube and repeating Steps 2 and 3 on the opposite end of the end tube.

5. Most road fork crowns are narrower than the diameter of the headset fork crown race, so you can elegantly remove the crown race with a crown race remover or an appropriately sized bench vise. Stand

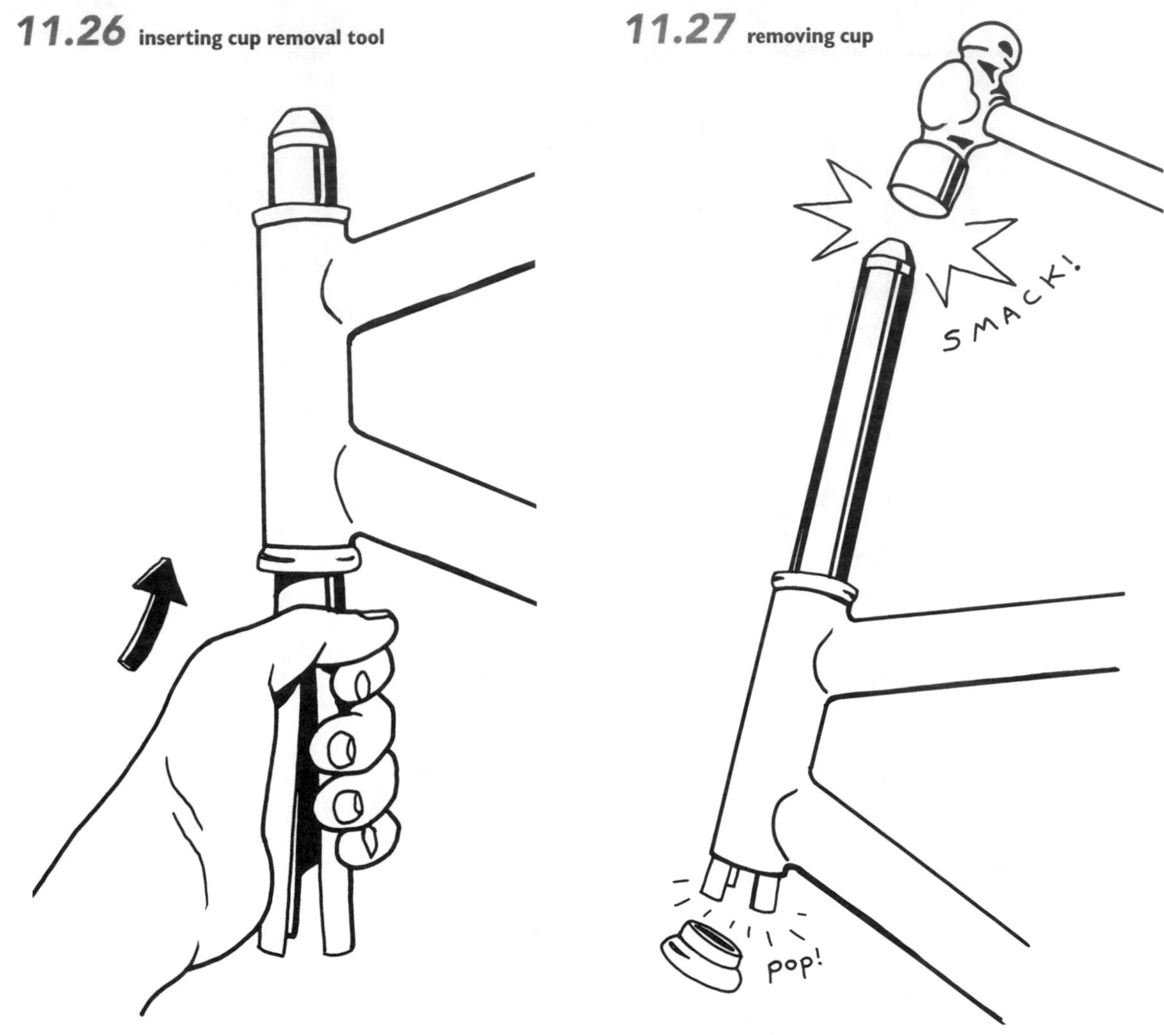

11.26 inserting cup removal tool

11.27 removing cup

removing a headset

the fork upside down on the steering tube. Place the U-shaped crown race remover so it straddles the underside of the fork crown and its ledges engage the front and back edges of the crown race. Smack the top of the crown race remover with a hammer to knock the race off (Fig. 11.29).

To use a bench vise, slide the fork into the vise, straddling its center shaft. Tighten the vise so its faces ever-so-lightly contact the front and back of the fork crown with the lower side of the crown race sitting on top of them. Put a block of wood on the top of the steering tube to pad it. Strike the block with a hammer to drive the fork down and knock the crown race off (Fig. 11.29).

a. If the fork crown is larger in diameter than the fork crown race, you will need to knock the race off with a screwdriver—preferably an old, cheap screwdriver that you no longer use to drive screws. Turn the fork upside down so that the top of the steering tube is sitting on the workbench, or clamp the steering tube horizontally in a vise between a pair of V-blocks. If there are notches at the front and back of the fork crown under the bearing race, place the blade of a large screwdriver into the notch on one side of the crown so it butts against the bottom of the headset fork crown race. If there is no notch, work the screwdriver blade under the race however you can; you may need to first drive a thin blade between the race and fork crown to open a gap. Tap the handle of the screwdriver with a hammer to drive the crown race up the steering tube a bit (Fig. 11.30). Move the screwdriver to the other

11.28 **removing fork-crown race with a crown-race remover**

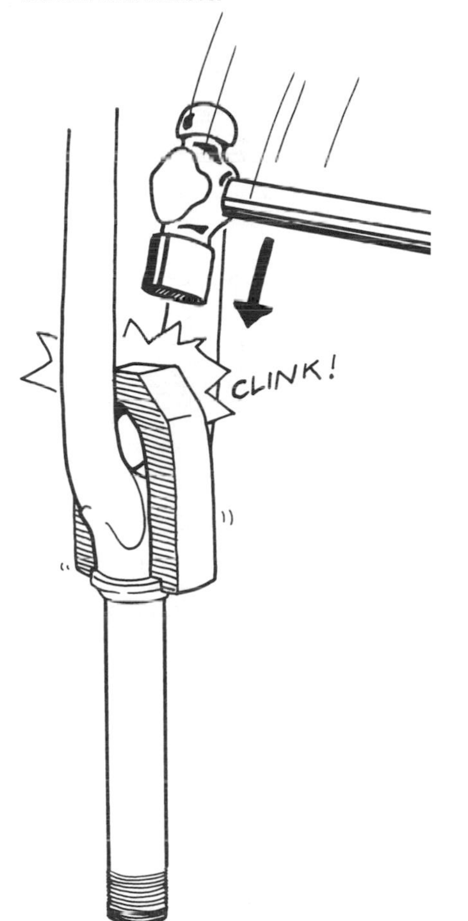

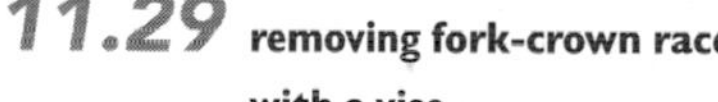

11.29 **removing fork-crown race with a vise**

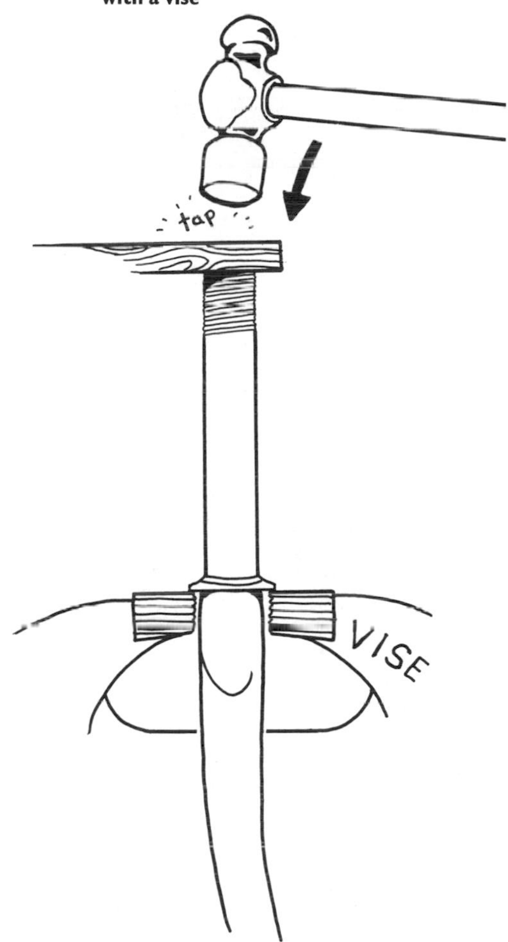

side, and tap it again to move that side of the crown race up a bit. Continue in this way, alternately tapping either side of the crown race up the steering tube, bit by bit, until it gets past the enlarged section of the steering tube and slides off.

11-19: INSTALL HEADSET

LEVEL 3 There is really no good way to install a headset without the necessary tools. If you do not have them, it is better to take the parts to a qualified shop for installation.

1. Frame and fork preparation: If this is a new frame (or one that has "eaten" headsets in the past), ream and face the head tube. If you do not have the tools for this, have a bike shop equipped with the proper tools do it for you. Reaming makes the head tube ends perfectly round inside and of the correct diameter for the headset cups to press in. Facing makes the ends of the head tube parallel so the bearings can turn smoothly and uniformly.

The base of the steering tube also needs to be turned down to the correct diameter for the crown race. The crown race seat on the fork crown must be faced in a way that places the crown race parallel to the head tube cups.

The steering tube (threaded or threadless) must also be cut to the proper length. You can wait until the headset (and stem, in the case of a threadless headset) are installed, or you can figure out the length you need and cut it now. **Remember, you can't go back and add any length afterward, so**

11.31 measuring amount of steerer tube to cut

11.30 removing fork-crown race with a screwdriver

be careful! After a threaded headset is assembled, you can measure the amount as in Fig. 11-31, remove the top nut, and trim that much length off of the top of the steering tube, de-burring it inside and out afterward.

If you are using a threaded headset, and you know its stack height (the stack height is often listed in the headset owner's manual, or a bike shop can look it up in *Barnett's Manual* or *Sutherland's Manual*), measure the length of the head tube and add the headset stack-height to this length. If you are adding extra spacers between the headset nuts, add their thickness in as well. This figure represents the length that the steering tube must be. If the steering tube is already more than 3–5mm shorter than this, you need to find another headset with a shorter stack height (or, if you have included spacers, remove a few).

If the steering tube is longer than this sum, you can cut it down to size. First, thread the headset adjustable cup onto the steerer well away from the cut point, and then cut the steerer to the correct length. Use a flat file to square off the cut, and a round file to remove the burrs the hacksaw left on the inside and outside edges of the steering tube end. Then unscrew the adjustable cup, which, as it comes off the steerer, will dress the threads.

You can follow much the same steps if you are using a threadless headset. Add the headset stack-height to the length of the steering tube and the stem clamp, and subtract 3mm from the total. This is the length the steering tube should be from fork crown to top. I recommend not cutting until the headset is assembled and the stem is installed so you can see if you want some spacers under the stem to raise your bars higher.

If you do not know the headset stack height, or if you're afraid you'll cut the steering tube too short, or if you want to see how it goes together before

11.32 setting fork-crown race

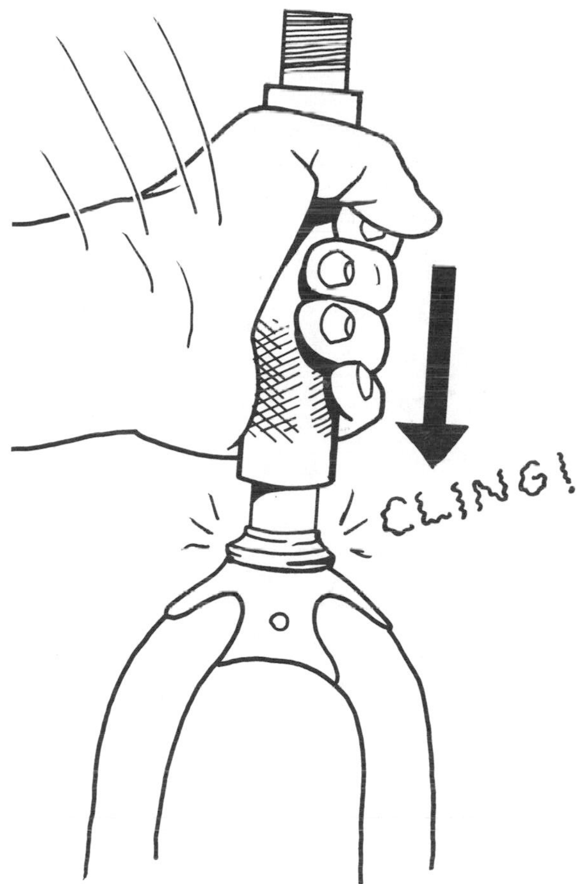

11.33 pressing in headset cups with a headset press

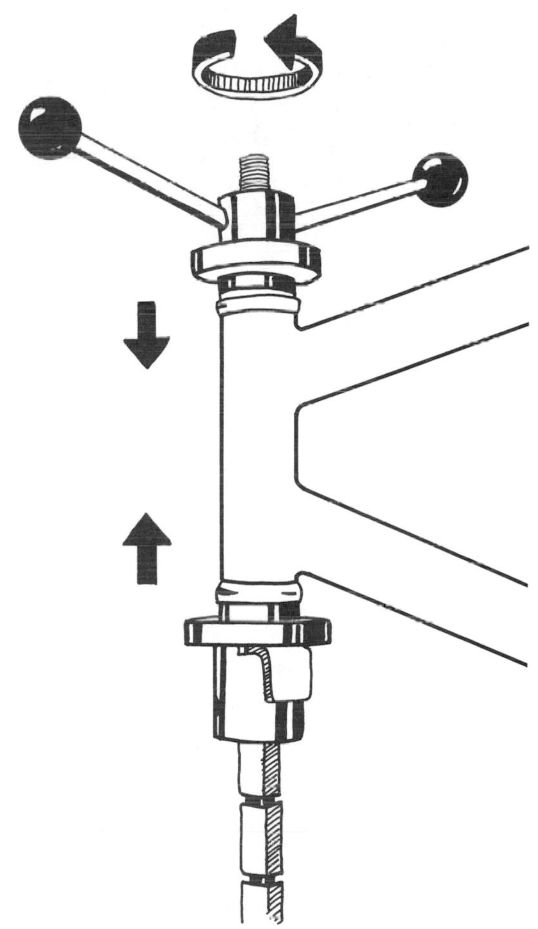

you cut it down, continue with the installation and assembly. When you are ready, cut it to 3–6mm below the top edge of the stem.

2. Put a thin layer of grease on the ends of the headset cups that will be pressed into the head tube, inside the hole in the fork crown race, inside the ends of the head tube itself, and on the base of the steering tube.

3. Slide the fork crown race down on the fork steering tube until it hits the enlarged section at the bottom. Slide the crown race slide punch up and down the steering tube, pounding the crown race down until it sits flat on top of its seat on the fork crown (Fig. 11.32). Some crown race punches are longer and closed on the top and are meant to be hit with a hammer rather than be slid up and down by hand.

Hold the fork up against the light to see if there are any gaps between the crown race and the crown. ***Note:*** *Thin crown races can be bent or broken by the crown race punch. Chris King, Park and Shimano make support tools that sit over the race and distribute the impact from the punch.*

4. Place the headset cups into the ends of the head tube. Slide the headset-press shaft through the head tube. Press the button on the detachable end of the tool and slide it onto the shaft until it bumps into one of the cups (Fig. 11.33). Find the nearest notch on the shaft and release the button. Some headset presses use a system of spacers and cones on both ends of the cups. Follow the instructions to set yours up properly. Whatever you do, be certain that the parts that contact the cups are not touching the bearing races.

Note: *Dia-Compe "S" and Chris King headsets have bearings that are pressed into the cups and cannot be removed (Fig. 11.23). If you use a headset press that pushes on the center of the cups, you will ruin the bearings. You need a press that pushes the outer portion of the cup and does not touch the bearings. Chris King makes tool inserts for this that fits most headset presses, and Park has a headset press with large flat ends for the purpose. On the other hand, some thin aluminum headset cups can be mashed by a flat press surface pushing on the outside of the cup; these need press inserts pushing on the inside of the cups.*

5. Hold the lower end of the cup press shaft with a wrench. That will keep the tool from turning as you press in the cups. Tighten the press by turning the top handle clockwise (Fig. 11.33). Keep tightening the tool until the cups are fully pressed into the ends of the head tube. Examine them carefully to make sure there are no gaps between the cups and the ends of the head tube.

6. Liberally apply grease to all bearing surfaces. If you are using sealed cartridge bearings, a thin film will do.

7. Assemble and adjust the headset, following Sections 11-16 and 11-14 for a threaded headset, and Sections 11-17 and 11-15 for a threadless one.

TROUBLE-SHOOTING

11-20: TROUBLESHOOTING STEM, HANDLEBAR, AND HEADSET PROBLEMS

1. Bar slips.

Tighten the pinch bolt on the stem that holds the bar. If the clamp closes on itself without holding the bar securely, check that the bar is not deformed or smaller diameter than the stem was made to fit and the stem clamp is not cracked or stretched. Replace any questionable parts. You can slide a shim made out of a beer can between the stem and bar to hold it better, but replacing parts is a safer option; there is always a reason why parts that are meant to fit together no longer do!

2. Bar makes creaking noise while riding.

Loosen stem clamp, grease the area of the bar that is clamped in stem, slide the bar back in place, and tighten the stem bolt. If the bar has a sleeved center section, rather than a bulged section, the bar could be creaking inside the sleeve. There's no cure for this; replace the bar.

3. Clip-on bar slips. Tighten clip-on clamp bolts.

4. Stem is not pointed straight ahead.

Loosen bolt (or bolts) securing stem to fork steering tube, align stem with front wheel, and tighten stem bolt (or bolts) again. With a threaded headset, the bolt you are interested in is a single vertical bolt on top of the stem; loosen it about two turns, and tap the top of the bolt with a hammer to disengage the wedge on the other end from the bottom of the stem (Fig. 11.7). With a threadless headset, there are one, two, or three horizontal bolts pinching the stem around the steering tube which need to be loosened to turn the stem on the steerer. Do not loosen the bolt on the top of the stem cap (Fig. 11.22); you'll have to readjust the headset if you do.

5. Fork and headset rattle or clunk when riding.

The headset is too loose. Adjust headset (Section 11-14 or 11-15).

6. Stem/bar/fork assembly does not turn smoothly but instead stops in certain fixed positions.

Headset is pitted and needs to be replaced. See Sections 11-18 and 11-19.

7. Stem/bar/fork assembly does not turn freely.

Headset is too tight. The front wheel should swing easily from side to side when leaning the bike or lifting the front end. Adjust the headset (Section 11-14 or 11-15, depending on type).

8. Stem is stuck in or on fork steering tube.

See Section 11-5.

Cycling computers

"For a list of all the ways technology has failed to improve the quality of life, please press three." —Alice Kahn

tools

Phillips and flat-blade screwdrivers
Electrical tape

A cycling computer can be a useful tool if it is set up correctly, and if you want the information. On the other hand, it can give you incorrect information if not set up properly, and it can also give you information you might be better off not having.

11-1: WHY HAVE A CYCLING COMPUTER?

Most likely, you ride a bike because you love riding. Or at least that is why you started. If having a computer on your handlebar adds to your pleasure, then by all means use one.

You may love watching yourself eat up the miles on a long ride. Or you may get a thrill from seeing how fast you can go downhill. Timing yourself periodically on a favorite loop may bring satisfaction as your times drop with improving fitness. You may like watching your cadence or working on keeping your pedaling rate in a certain range. An altimeter feature may be fun to watch in the mountains.

You may have a specific, periodized workout schedule with which a heart monitor and/or a power meter can assist you in realizing your goals more rapidly. Effectiveness of interval training can be enhanced, since duration, speed, and intensity of the intervals (and, at least as important, the intensity of the rest periods between intervals and the intensity of recovery rides between interval days) can be monitored and even stored for later playback with a power meter and/or a computer with a heart monitor.

On the other hand, if you start using your computer to tell you whether you have ridden "far enough" or "hard enough" or "correctly" today, or this week, or this year, then you may want to recon-

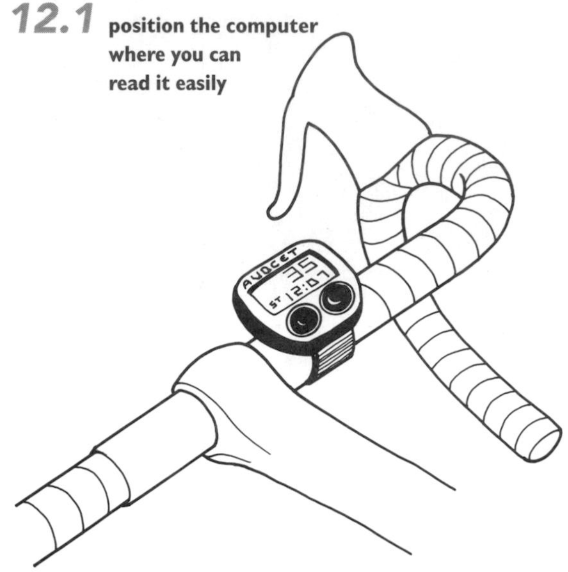

12.1 position the computer where you can read it easily

sider. We all are probably compulsive enough in our work that we don't need to be compulsive in our play as well. My intention in writing this book is to add to your enjoyment of cycling, and I am not interested in you judging yourself harshly about what you have or have not done on a bike. It can be an insidious feature of a cycling computer—that what started as a fun way to monitor yourself becomes a way in which you beat yourself up. And it can creep up on you. Bike riding devolves slowly from fun to drudgery without your noticing, until riding a certain way becomes another thing you "have to" do. Yank the computer off your bike if you see this happen.

12-2: SETTING UP A CYCLING COMPUTER

Computers vary from brand to brand, and, without having this book become an unmanageably large, dry tome, I can't go into the exact details of which buttons to push when for which computer. But I can give you some general guidelines that work for setting up any computer, and you can get the specifics about which buttons to push from the owner's manual or from a friendly guy or gal at the bike shop.

Note that details about setting up a Mavic Mektronic computer are in Chapter 5, sections 5-35 to 5-37.

A. Measure the circumference of the wheel and tire.

1. Inflate the tire mounted on the wheel that will carry the magnet (usually the front), and wrap a piece of tape across the rim and around the tire in one spot.

2. Put a piece of tape crosswise on a hard floor or driveway, and set the wheel on it so that the tape around the tire is lined up over it (Fig. 12.2).

3. Holding the ends of the axle, roll the wheel forward one revolution until the piece of tape is at the bottom again.

4. Put another piece of tape on the floor lined up with the tape on the tire (Fig. 12.2).

5. With a tape measure, find the distance from

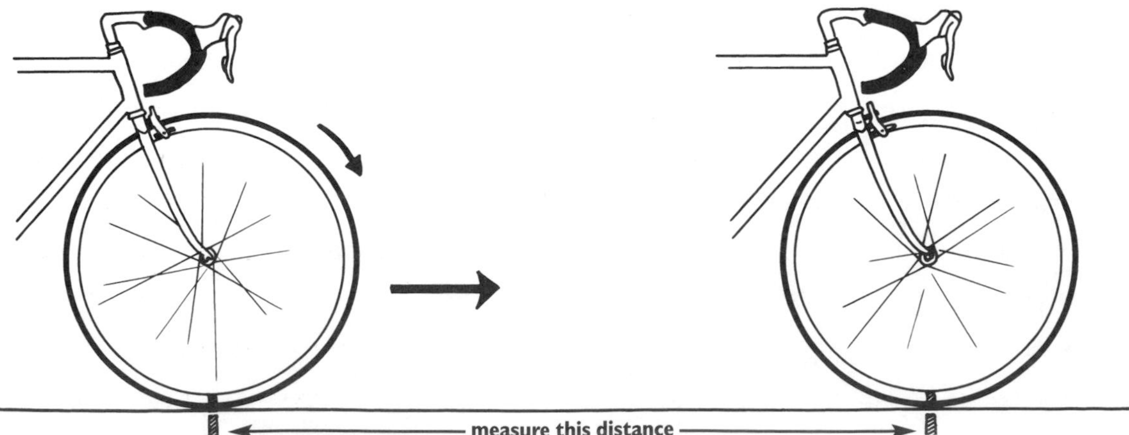

12.2 rolling out the wheel to measure its circumference

leading edge of one piece of tape on the floor to the other. This is the circumference of the inflated tire. Your computer needs this information to properly measure speed and distance, since it is counting revolutions of the wheel and must know distance covered with each revolution.

In the computer owner's manual, you will find either a way to enter the circumference, or you will find a table of code numbers corresponding to ranges of circumference and instructions on how to enter the proper code number.

B. Install the computer and sensor

1. Snap the computer bracket around the handlebar next to the stem (Fig. 12.1). If it fits too loosely onto the bar, wrap the bar at that spot with one of the rubber pieces that come with the computer or with layers of electrical tape. If you have aero' bars, the real estate on the top of your base handlebar will be too cluttered for a computer, and you wouldn't be able to see a computer mounted on the base bar when you are on the aero' bars. Mount the computer on the stem or on a cross-member of the aero' bar, or buy and install a computer mounting stub projecting inward from one tube of the aero' bar.

2. Tighten the screw to secure the mount, and snap the computer onto the mount.

3. If the computer has a wire to the sensor, wrap the wire around the front brake cable to take up slack, and strap the sensor around the fork blade.

To give yourself more flexibility later, don't wrap the sensor around and around the brake wire. Instead, first attach the bracket to the bar and the sensor to the fork. Start twisting the computer wire around the brake cable, from the middle of its slack length and secure it in the center with tape or a zip-tie. Raising the handlebar then does not require disconnecting the sensor and unwinding it; you merely cut the tape or zip-tie to release the wire.

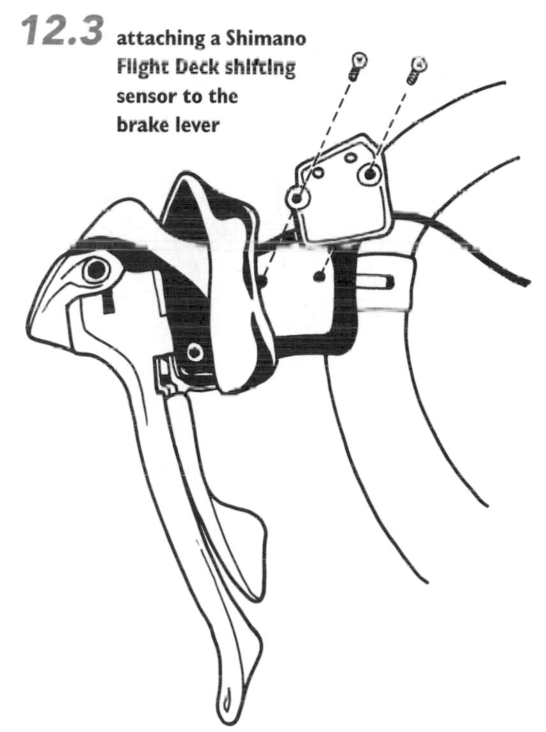

12.3 attaching a Shimano Flight Deck shifting sensor to the brake lever

With a wireless computer, you need only strap the sensor to the fork blade.

The sensor usually mounts to the inside of the fork leg about midway down, but the position may need to be changed later for optimal clearance with the wheel magnet. There is usually a built-in zip-tie on the sensor, or separate zip-ties are used to hold the sensor. Older Avocet computer sensors mount around the dropout, not on the fork leg.

Secure the wire to the fork with tape or zip-ties.

Shimano and Campagnolo cycling computers also have wires that must be connected to the brake levers, since they sense when you shift (Fig. 12.3).

4. Attach the wheel magnet to the spokes. Some magnets have a slotted holder with a collar and a screw to tighten against the spoke (Fig. 12.4). Other magnets sit in a plastic housing that wraps around the spoke and is retained by a screw (Fig. 12.5), or they come in a plastic housing that snaps onto the spoke (Fig. 12.6).

To fit the magnet on aero spokes, file the slot in a slotted magnet holder wider, or use a plastic fold-

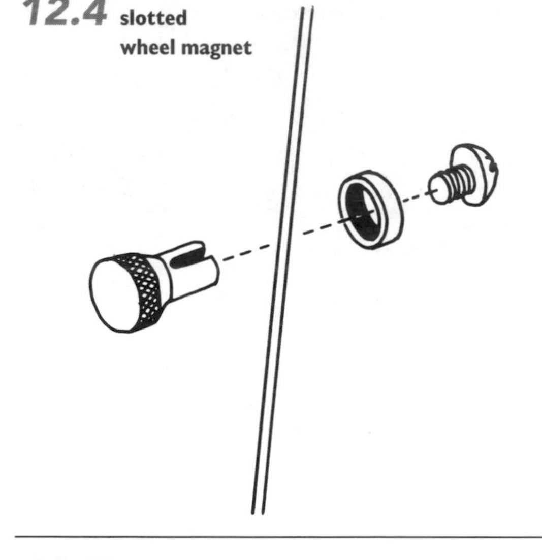

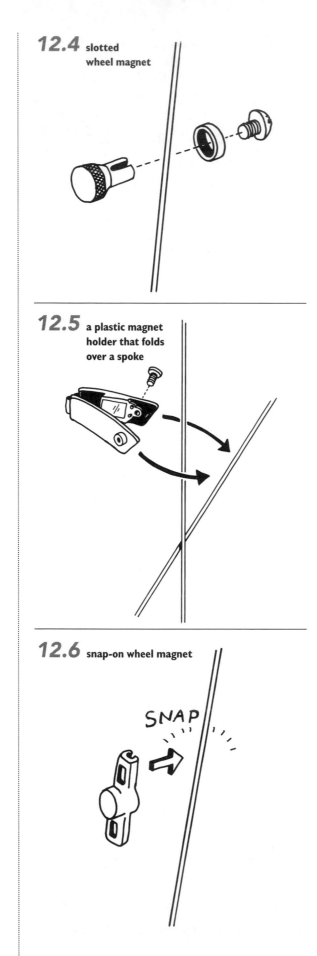

12.4 slotted wheel magnet

12.5 a plastic magnet holder that folds over a spoke

12.6 snap-on wheel magnet

ing type. For a wheel without wire spokes, you can tape a refrigerator magnet onto a disc wheel or onto the side of a composite spoke.

Make sure the wheel magnet passes close to the sensor. If the computer does not indicate a speed when you spin the wheel, the positions of the sensor and/or the magnet need to be changed. Many sensors have a scribed line indicating where the magnet should pass (some sensors have lines at either end, giving you a couple of options). Make sure the magnet passes by the line and that it is close to the sensor (1 to 5mm away), but it doesn't touch (Fig. 12.7). You may need to slide the sensor and the magnet up or down.

Older Avocet computer magnet rings live in a plastic housing that snaps onto the hub. If the hub flange is too far inboard, the sensor will not respond to the magnet, and you will need to clip a second magnet over the first one. If the clips are not in the right spots to fit hub, you can snip the clip tabs off and lace the magnet to the spokes with wire or twist-ties.

5. If the computer has a separate cadence sensor and magnet, the magnet usually goes on the crankarm, and the sensor mounts to the chainstay. The new Campagnolo computers have the cadence sensing mechanism built inside the pedal, while Shimano computers calculate cadence from wheel speed and gear size.

12-3: POWER METERS AND HEART MONITORS

The two primary power meters on the market are the SRM and the Tune Power Tap.

The SRM has strain gauges built into the spider arms on the right crank. The torque on the crank is picked up wirelessly by sensors near the bottom bracket.

12.7 position the magnet close to the sensor and align with one of he scribed lines

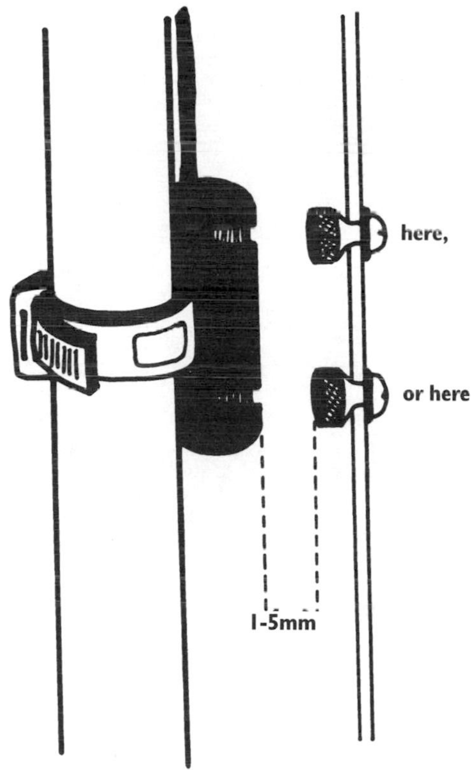

12.8 replacing the computer battery

The Tune Power Tap has strain gauges built into an oversized rear hub. Torque on the hub is communicated wirelessly to a sensor on the seatstay.

Stand-alone heart monitors or Tune or SRM heart monitors require no additional hookups on the bike, just a strap around your chest.

12-4: DIAGNOSING COMPUTER PROBLEMS

A. No display or battery indicator appears on computer screen

The battery probably needs to be replaced. Some computers have a battery not only in the computer (Fig. 12.8) but also in the sensor, so check both places. Some computers have two batteries in the computer itself. A bike shop (or a camera store) should have a battery to match.

If the battery is not the problem, check for broken wires.

B. Computer is on, but speed does not register

The wheel magnet may be missing, or it may be too far from the sensor as it passes by. Adjust the positions of the sensor and the magnet so that the magnet passes close by the scribed line on the sensor but does not touch it (Fig. 12.7).

C. Cadence reading does not display

Check that your computer does have a cadence feature. If so, check that the sensor and magnet on the crank and frame pass closely by each other.

D. Computer reads wrong speed and distance

The wrong wheel size may have been entered. Follow the owner's manual for the button-pushing sequence to find the number programmed into the computer for wheel size. See section 12-2A for measuring wheel circumference.

E. Can't find computer owner's manual

Here are a number of options:

1. Check with a bike shop for a new manual.
2. Get the contact information for the manufacturer or distributor from the bike shop, and contact the company directly.
3. Check the computer maker's Web site for an on-line owner's manual or to order a new one.
4. Learn from a friend or shop employee who knows how to work your computer. Take notes.

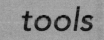

Wheelbuilding

"If you think you can or think you can't, you're right." —*Henry Ford*

tools

Screwdriver
Spoke wrench
Truing stand
Wheel-dishing tool
Spoke prep or grease

Optional

Linseed oil

Congratulations. You have arrived at the task most often used to gauge the talents of a bike mechanic. Next to building a frame or fork, building a good set of wheels is the most critical and most creative of a bike mechanic's tasks.

Despite the air of mystery surrounding the art of wheelbuilding, the construction of a good set of bicycle wheels is actually a straightforward task. Moreover, it is quite rewarding to turn a pile of small parts into a set of strong and light wheels upon which you can corner and descend with confidence. You will be amazed at what they can withstand, and you will no longer go through life thinking that building wheels is something just the "experts" do. With practice and patience, you can build wheels at your house that are as good as any custom-made set, and far superior to those built by machine.

This is not meant to be an exhaustive description of how to build all types of wheel spoking patterns; there are entire books written on the subject—justifiably so, by the way, since the bicycle wheel is an artful engineering miracle that deserves thoughtful exegesis. (If you are interested in a more comprehensive treatment of the subject of wheelbuilding, I recommend *The Barnett's Manual* by John Barnett, *The Art of Wheelbuilding* by Gerd Schraner, or *The Bicycle Wheel* by Jobst Brandt.)

You can, however, build great wheels following the methods presented here. The main text describes how to build a wheel laced in the classic "three-cross" spoking pattern, in which each spoke crosses three other spokes (Fig. 13.1). Section 13-7 details how to build a radially spoked wheel. So let's get started.

13-1: PARTS

1. Gather the parts you need: a rim, a hub (make sure that the hub has the same number of holes as the rim), properly sized spokes and nipples to match. I suggest getting the spokes from your local

wheel parts

13.1 the complete wheel

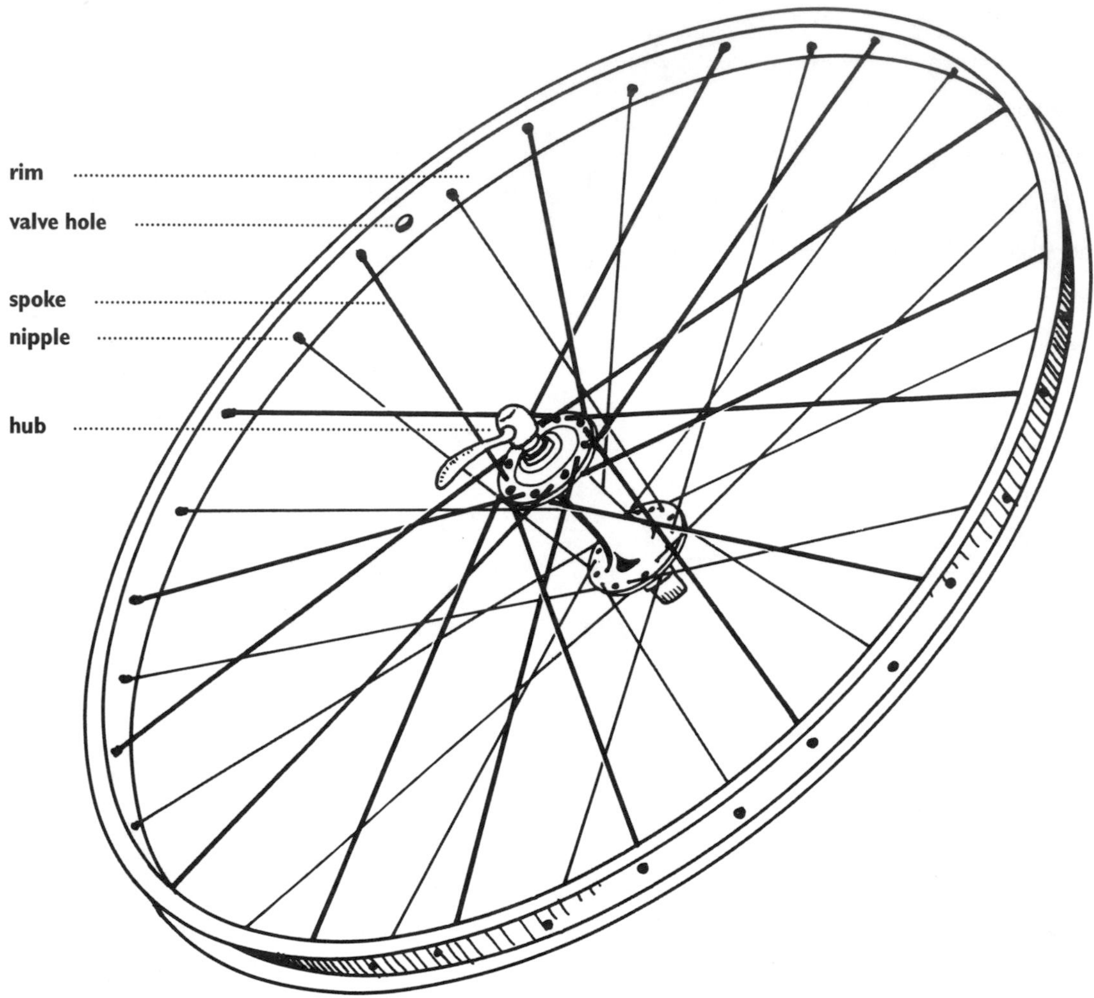

13.2 spoke and nipple

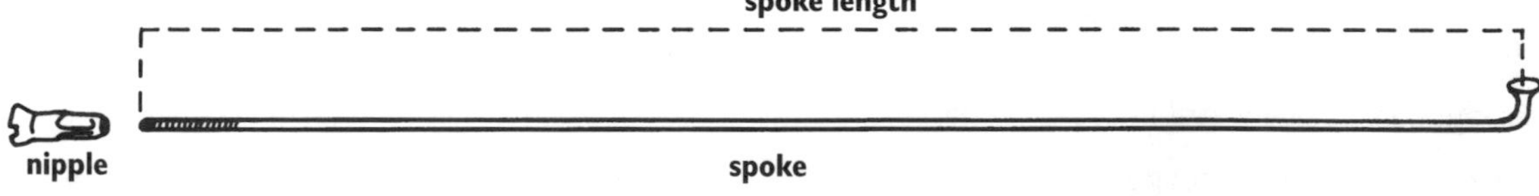

bike shop. This way, a mechanic can help make sure you are get the right spoke lengths (Fig. 13.2) and can counsel you on which gauge (thickness) of spoke to select, as well as which rim makes sense for your weight, budget and kind of riding you plan on doing. Remember when you calculate spoke length to specify that you will be using a "three cross" spoking pattern (unless you are building a radial wheel—see section 13-7).

Note: *If you are replacing a rim on an old wheel, do not use the old spokes. You won't save much money re-using the old spokes, and the rounded-out nipples and weakened spokes will soon make you wish you had bought a new set.*

13-2: LACING THE WHEEL

For the sake of brevity and clarity, I do not mention using spoke prep compound with every instruction to thread a nipple onto a spoke. While the use of thread compound is not mandatory, I think that the wheel is improved with it. It encourages the nipples to thread on more smoothly, it takes up some of the slop between the spoke and nipple threads, and its thread-locking ability discourages the nipples from vibrating loose.

The spoke prep is applied to the spoke threads before the nipples are put on. You do not want too much, as it will be hard to adjust the nipples months and years down the road; you just want the spoke prep in the valleys of the threads. You can get the right amount if you dip the threads of a pair of spokes into the prep compound, and then take two more dry spokes and roll the threads of all four spokes together with your fingers.

If you don't use spoke prep, at least dip each spoke's threads in grease before installing.

1. Divide your spokes into two separate groups, one set for each side of the hub flange. If you are building a rear wheel, you should be working with two different spoke lengths, since spokes on the right-hand side, or drive side, are almost always shorter.

2. Hold the rim on your lap with the valve hole away from you. Notice that the holes alternate being offset upward or downward from the rim centerline.

Note: *If you are building a rear wheel with an OCR (Off Center Rear) rim drilled off center (Ritchey and Bontrager both have OCR models), make sure that you orient the rim so that the spoke holes are offset to the left (non-drive) side (see Fig. 13.3). The rim is meant to reduce wheel dish, so offsetting the nipples to the left reduces the otherwise very steep angle at which drive-side spokes normally hit the rim. The balanced left-to-right spoke tension should increase the lifetime of the wheel, and the lower spoke angle moves the drive-side spokes away from the rear derailleur. So*

13.3 **"OCR" (off-center rear) rim laced correctly**

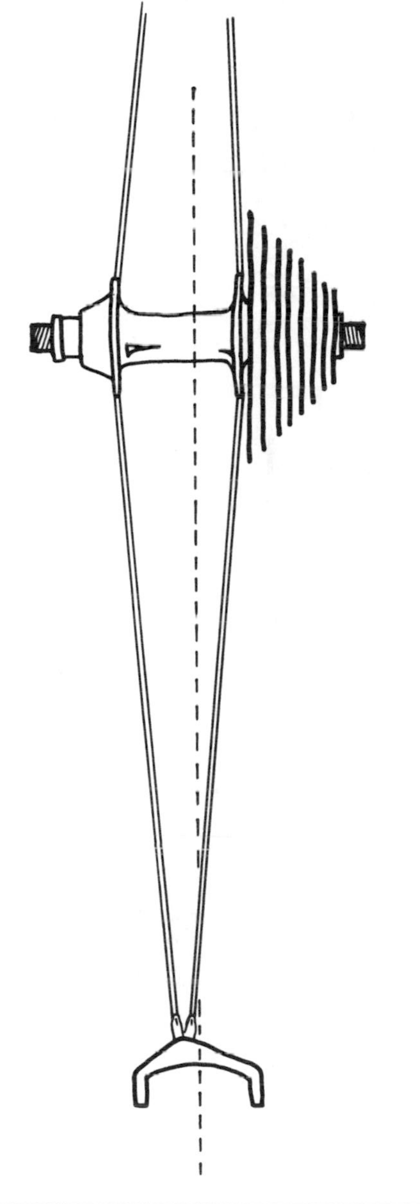

with an OCR rim (Fig. 13.3), have the spoke holes offset downward, toward your lap.

3. Hold the hub in the center of the rim, with the right side of the hub pointing up. On a rear hub, the right side is the drive side. Front hubs are symmetrical; pick a side to be the right side. In the illustrations, the right side has the nut end of the quick release.

A. First set of spokes

4. Drop a spoke down into every other hole in the top (right side) hub flange, so that the spoke

13.4 first half of right-side spokes placed in hub

13.5 first spoke — right side up

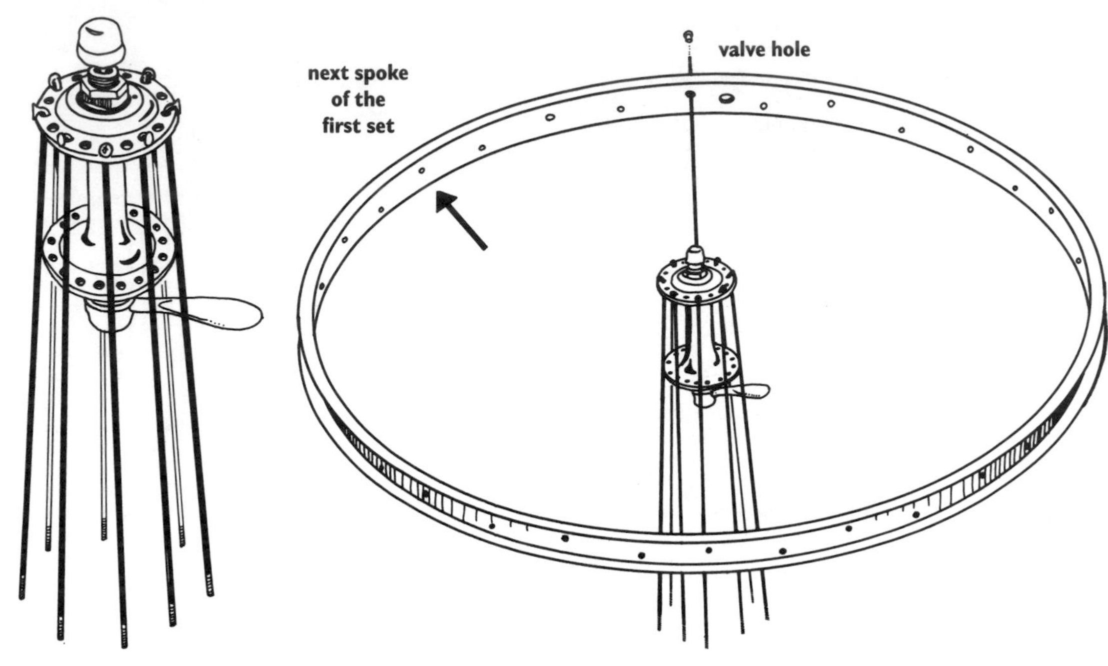

13.6 first set of spokes laced

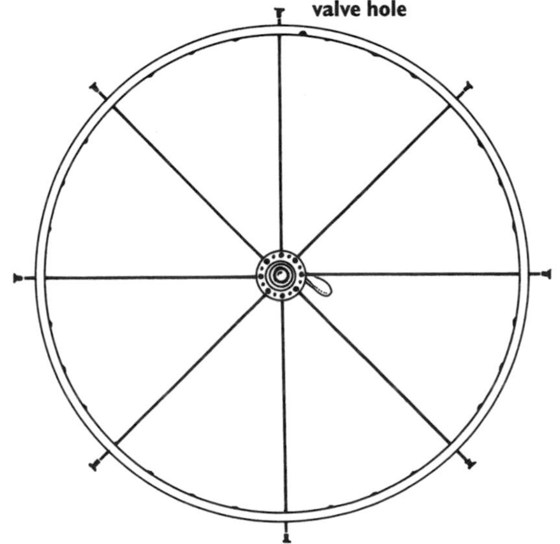

lacing the wheel — second set of spokes

heads are facing up (Fig. 13.4). Make sure if it's a rear wheel that you put the shorter spokes on the right (drive) side. Half of the holes you are looking at are normally countersunk deeper into the hub flange to seat the spoke head, so use those holes.

5. Put a spoke into the first hole counterclockwise from the valve hole and screw the nipple on three turns (Fig. 13.5). Notice that this hole is offset upward (on an OCR rim, this means that the hole is offset upward from the centerline of the spoke holes, not the centerline of the rim). If the first hole counterclockwise from the valve hole isn't offset upward, you have a mis-drilled rim, and you must offset all instructions one hole.

6. Working counterclockwise, put the next spoke on the hub into the hole in the rim four holes away from the first spoke, and screw a nipple on three turns. There should be three open rim holes between these spokes, and the hole you put the second spoke into should also be offset upward.

7. Continue counterclockwise around the wheel in the same manner. You should now have used half of the rim holes that are offset upward, and there should be three open holes between each spoke (Fig. 13.6).

8. Flip the wheel over.

13.8 lacing second set

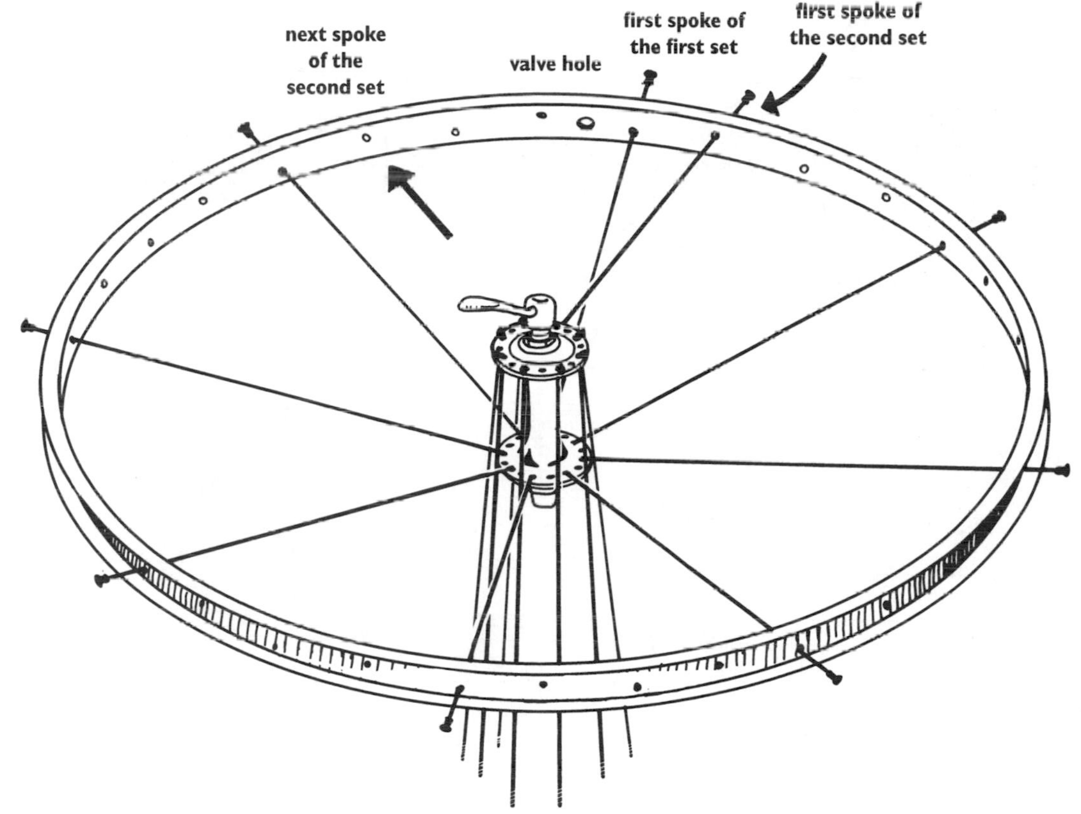

13.7 spoke hole off-set

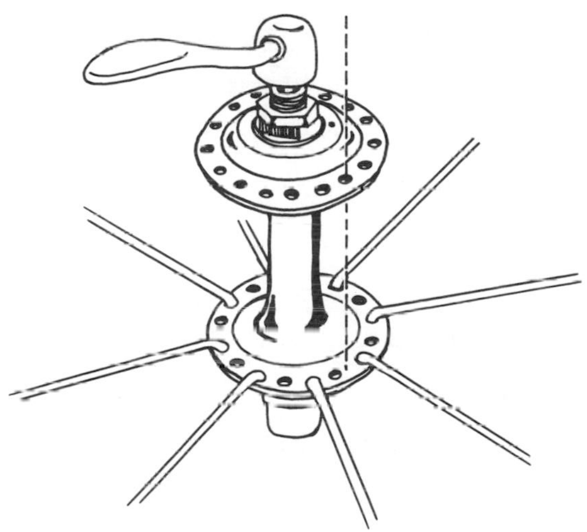

13.9 diverging parallel spokes

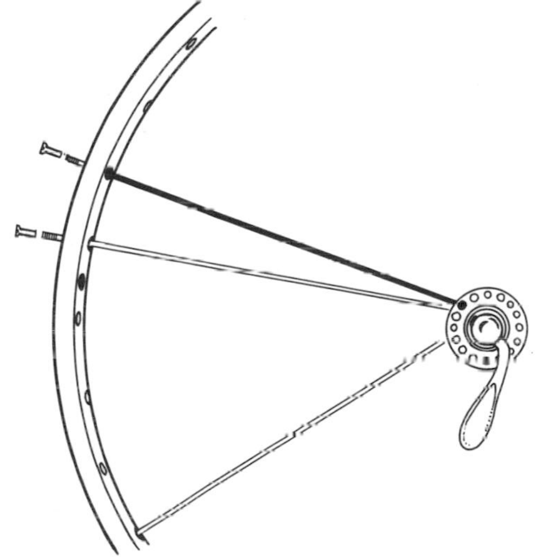

B. Second set of spokes

9. Sight across the hub from one flange to the other. Notice that the holes in one flange do not line up with the holes in the other; each hole lines up in between two holes on the opposite flange (Fig. 13.7).

10. Drop a spoke down through the hole in the top flange that is immediately clockwise from the first spoke you installed (the spoke that is just clockwise from the valve hole).

11. Put this new spoke into the second hole clockwise from the valve hole, next to the first

13.10 second set of spokes laced

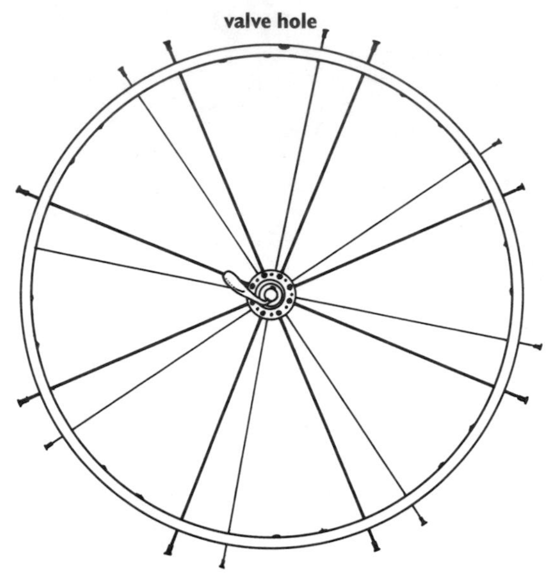

13.11 placing third set of spokes in hub

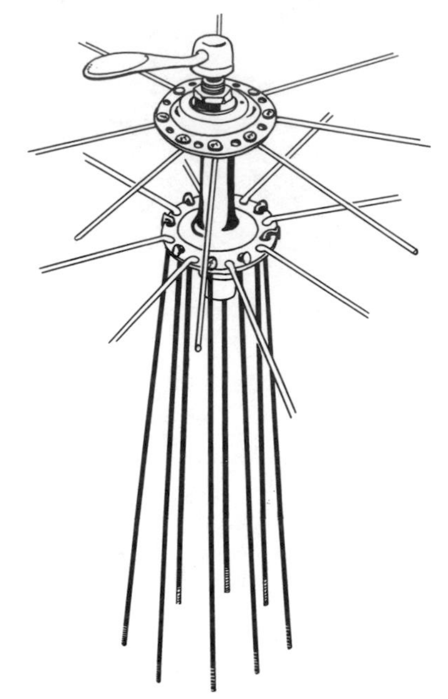

spoke you installed (Figs. 13.8 and 13.9). This hole will be offset upward from the rim centerline.

12. Thread the nipple on three turns.

13. Double check to make sure that the spoke you just installed starts at a hole in the hub's top (left side) flange that is one-half-a-hole space clockwise from the hole in the lower flange where the first spoke you installed started. These two spokes should be diverging but still nearly parallel (Fig. 13.9).

14. Drop a spoke down through the hole in the top (left side) hub flange two holes away in either direction, and continue around until every other hole has a spoke hanging down through it (Fig. 13.8).

15. Working counterclockwise, take the next spoke from the hub and put it in the rim hole that is three holes counterclockwise from the valve hole. This hole should be offset upward and four holes to the left of the spoke you just installed. Thread the nipple on three turns.

16. Follow this pattern counter-clockwise around the wheel (Fig. 13.10). You should have now used half of the rim holes that are offset upward, as well as half of the total rim holes. The second set of spokes should all be in upwardly offset holes, one hole clockwise from each spoke of the first set.

C. Third set of spokes

17. Drop spokes through the remaining holes on the right side of the hub, from the inside out (Fig. 13.11). Remember: if it's a rear wheel, these spokes should be shorter than the spokes used on the left side.

18. Flip the wheel over, grabbing the spokes you've just dropped through to keep them from falling out.

19. Fan the spokes out, so they cannot fall back down through the hub holes.

20. Grab the hub shell and rotate it counterclockwise as far as you can (Fig. 13.12).

21. Pick any spoke on the top (right hand) hub flange that is already laced to the rim. Now find the spoke five hub holes away in a clockwise direction.

22. Take this new spoke, cross it under the spoke you counted from (the one five holes away),

13.13 lacing third set of spokes

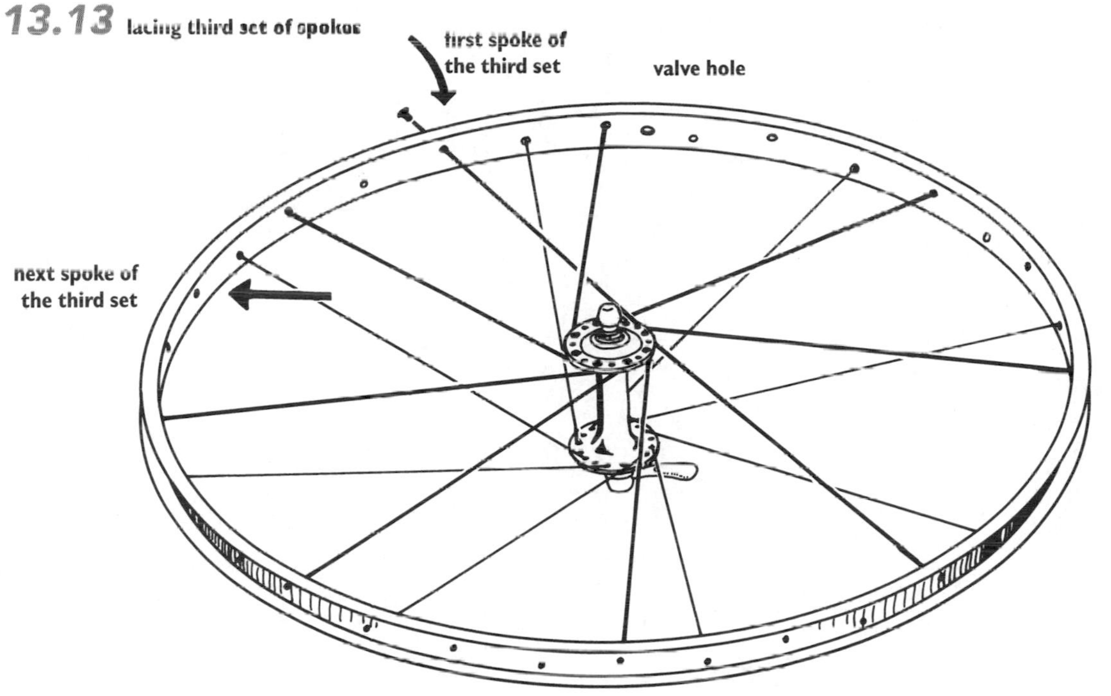

and stick it into the rim hole two holes counterclockwise from that spoke (Fig. 13.13). Thread a nipple on three turns.

23. Continue around the wheel, doing the same thing (Fig. 13.14). You may find a spoke or two that doesn't reach quite far enough. If that's the case, push down about an inch from the spoke elbow to help it reach.

24. Make sure that every spoke coming out of the upper side of the top flange (the spokes that come out toward you with their spoke heads hidden from view) crosses over two spokes and under a third. All three of these "crossing" spokes come from the underside of the same flange, and have their spoke heads facing toward you. These "crossing" spokes begin 1, 3 and 5 hub holes counter-

13.12 rotating hub counterclockwise

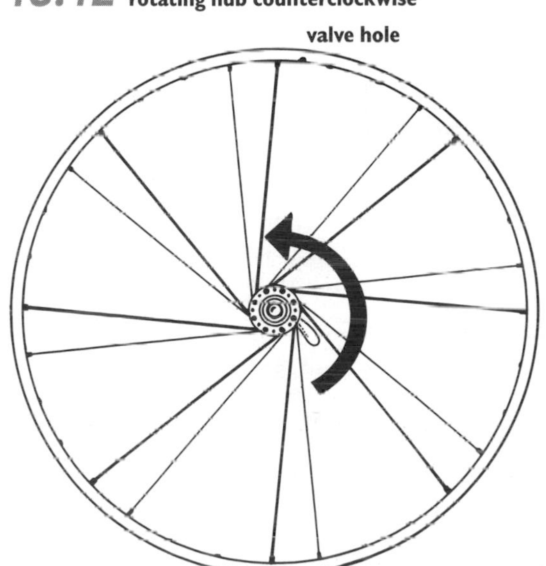

13.14 third set laced

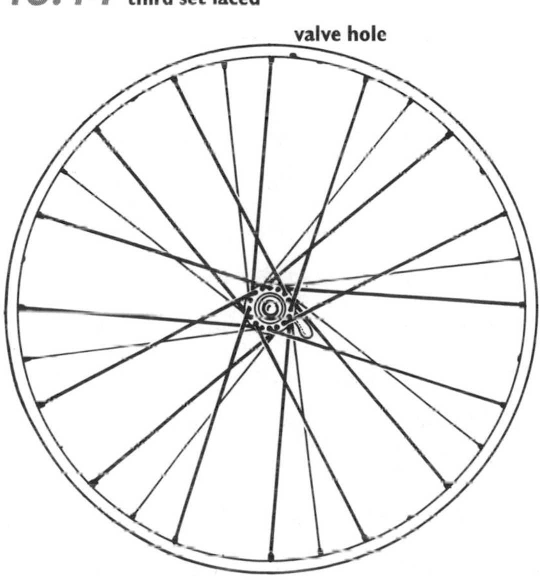

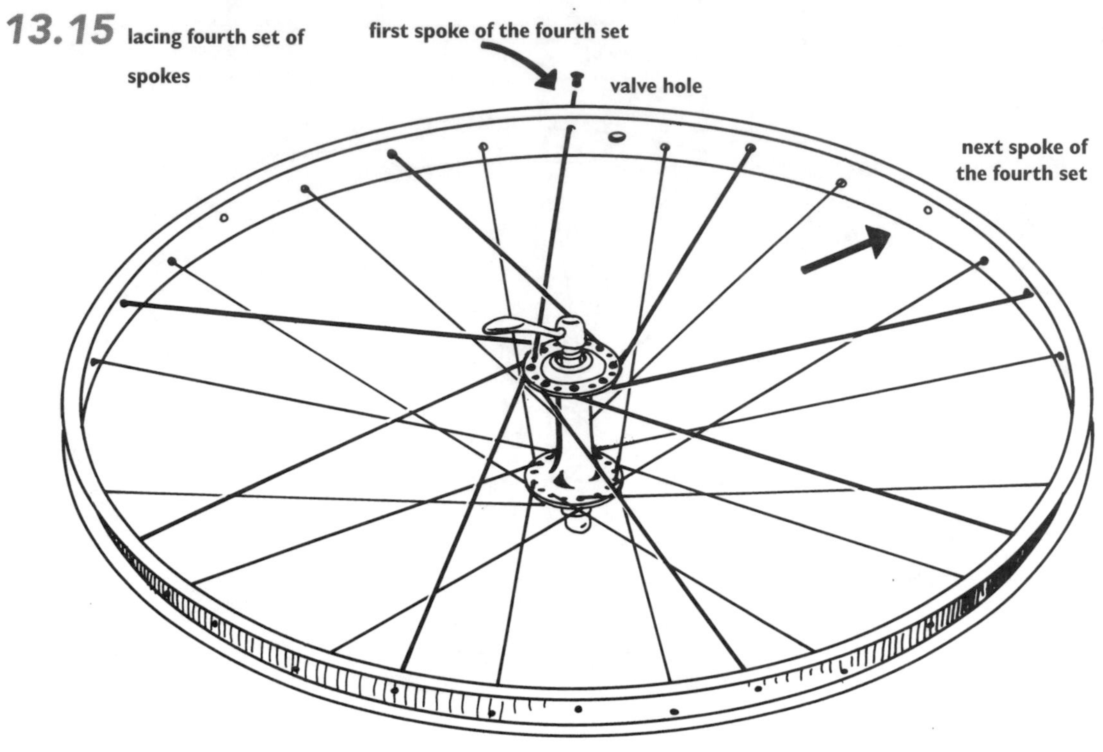

13.15 lacing fourth set of spokes

clockwise from the spoke that you just inserted into the rim (Fig. 13.14). This is called a "three cross" pattern because every spoke crosses three others on its way to the rim (over, over, under). Every upwardly offset hole should now be occupied on the rim.

D. Fourth set of spokes

lacing the wheel — fourth set of spokes

25. Drop spokes down through the remaining hub holes in the bottom flange from the inside out (like Fig. 13.11, but with the other side of the hub up).

26. Flip the wheel over, grabbing the spokes to keep them from falling back down through the holes.

27. Fan the spokes out.

28. Pick any spoke on the top (left-hand) hub flange that is already laced to the rim. Now find the spoke five hub holes away in a counterclockwise direction.

29. Take that spoke, cross it over two spokes and under the spoke you counted from. Stick the spoke into the rim hole two holes clockwise from the spoke it crosses under (Fig. 13.15). Thread a nipple on three turns.

30. Continue around the wheel, doing the same thing until the wheel is laced like Fig. 13.1. You may find that some spokes don't reach far enough. If that's the case, push down on each one about an inch from the spoke elbow to help them reach.

31. Make sure that every spoke coming out from the upper side of the top flange (the spokes that come out toward you with their spoke heads hidden from view) crosses over two spokes and under a third (Fig. 13.1). All three of these "crossing" spokes come from the underside of the same flange, and have their spoke heads facing you. The "crossing" spokes begin 1, 3 and 5 hub holes clockwise from each spoke emerging from the top of upper (left) hub flange (Fig. 13.1). Every hole should now be occupied on the rim. The valve hole should be between "converging parallel" spokes (Fig. 13.16) to make room for the pump head when inflating the tire.

13.16 converging parallel spokes

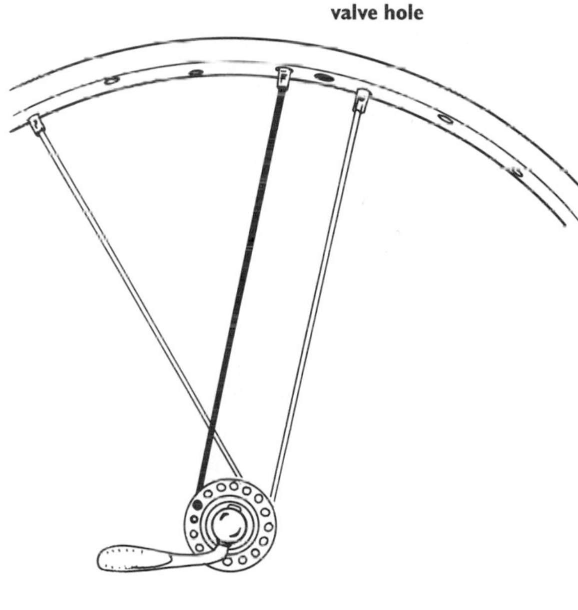

If this is a rear wheel, note that the spokes coming out of the outside of the hub flange on both sides oppose the clockwise twist the chain applies on the cogs. See section 13-6 for more on this.

13-3: TENSIONING THE WHEEL

1. Put the wheel in the truing stand.

2. Tighten each nipple with a spoke wrench until only three threads are visible beyond the bottom of the nipple (see Figs. 13.17-13.20 for rotation direction). From now on, every time you tighten or loosen a spoke nipple, turn it back the opposite direction 1/8 turn afterward. This unwinds the twist in the spoke that your tightening or loosening had just caused.

3. Using your thumb, press the spokes coming outward from the outer side of the hub flanges down at the elbow to straighten their line to the rim. Spokes coming out of the inner side of the flange do not need this.

4. Go around the wheel, tightening each nipple a half-turn. Do this uniformly, and only a half-turn, so that the wheel is not thrown out of true.

5. Check to see if the spokes are tight enough to give a tone when plucked. Squeeze pairs of spokes together and compare with a good wheel with spokes of the same gauge; your wheel should have considerably less tension at this point.

6. Repeat Steps 4 and 5 until the spokes all make a tone but are under less tension than an existing, good wheel. Final tensioning will come with the remainder of the truing process.

13-4: TRUING THE WHEEL

A. Lateral true

Side-to-side trueness is the most obvious wheel parameter when you spin it.

1. Make sure the hub axle has no end play. If it does, adjust the hub (see Hub adjustment in Chapter 6).

2. (Optional) Put a drop of linseed oil around each nipple on the tire side where it seats in the rim to lubricate the contact area between it and the inside of the rim hole.

3. Set the truing stand feelers so that one of them scrapes the side of the rim at the worst lateral wobble (Figs. 13.17 and 13.18).

4. Ending a few spokes on either side of where the rim scrapes, tighten the spokes coming from the opposite side of the hub and loosen the spokes coming from the same side of the hub (Figs. 13.17 and 13.18). Start with a quarter turn on nipples at the center of the scraping area and decrease the amount you turn each nipple as you move away in either direction. This pulls the rim away from the feeler. If it does the opposite, you are turning the nipples the wrong direction. Remember: you normally turn something to the right to tighten and to the left to loosen, but tightening and loosening

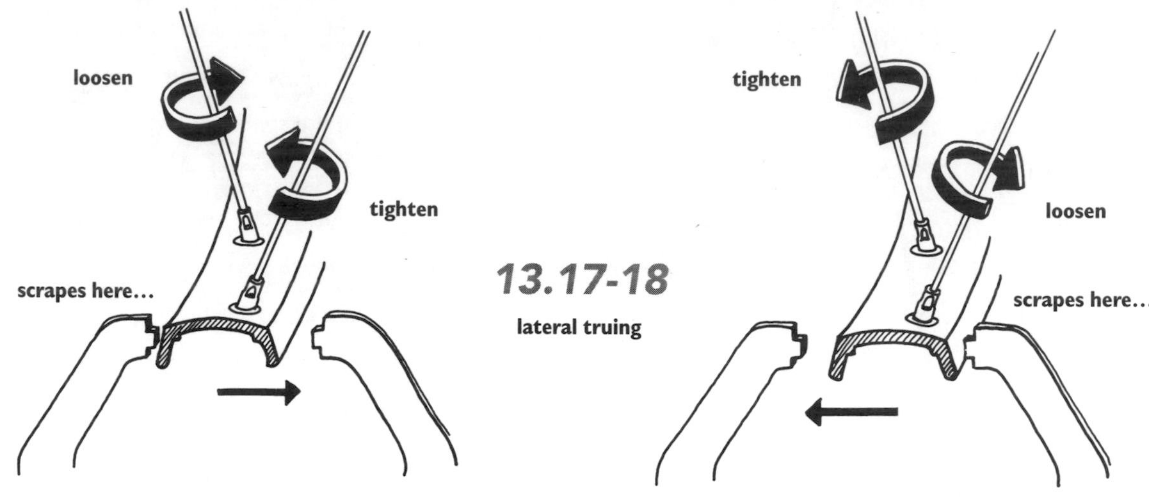

13.17-18
lateral truing

spoke nipples at the bottom of the wheel is the opposite of what you would normally do (Figs. 13.17–13.20). This is because the nipple head is underneath your spoke wrench. Try opening a jar that is upside down and you will immediately understand the principle involved.

5. Work around the wheel in this way, bringing in the feelers as the wheel gets truer.

B. Radial true

While not as obvious as side-to-side trueness, out-of-roundness is more important to the longevity of the wheel, since, as Portia Masterson of the Self Propulsion bike shop in Golden, Colorado, so eloquently puts it, "uniformity of tension is the key to durability." Radial truing can also be somewhat slow and frustrating work. If you find yourself running out of patience for this job, step away for awhile and then start again when you feel fresh and ready.

6. Set the truing-stand feelers so that they now contact the circumference of the rim, rather than the sides.

7. Bring the feelers in until they scrape against the highest spot on the rim (Fig. 13.19).

8. Tighten the spokes a quarter-turn where the rim scrapes. This will pull the rim inward. Decrease the amount of each turn (to an eighth-turn and less) as you move away from the center of the scraping area.

9. Work around the wheel this way, bringing the feelers in as the wheel becomes rounder.

10. Wherever there is a dip in the rim, loosen the spokes (Fig. 13.20).

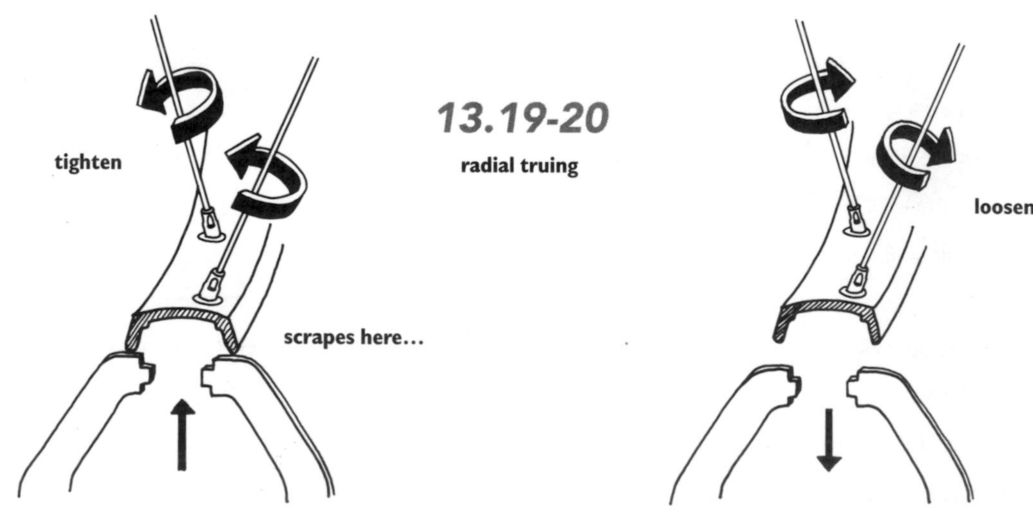

13.19-20
radial truing

If the spokes are too tight at this point, they will be hard to turn and creak and groan as you turn them. When the spokes become hard to turn (i.e., the nipples feel on the verge of rounding off), loosen all of the spokes in the wheel a quarter-turn before continuing. Compare tension with a good wheel with the same gauge spokes; tension at this point should still be lower in the wheel you are building.

13-5: DISHING THE WHEEL

1. Place the dishing tool across the right side of the wheel, bisecting the center (Fig. 13.21).

2. Tighten or loosen the dishing gauge screw until the gauge contacts the outer face of the axle end nut (Fig. 13.21).

3. Flip the wheel over.

4. Place the dishing tool across the other side of the wheel.

5. Check the gap of the dishing gauge with this axle end-nut face (Fig. 13.22). Any gap between the dishing gauge and the axle end-nut face indicates the amount the rim is offset from the centerline of the wheel. If there is no gap, but an overlap instead, reset the dishing gauge on this side (the previously overlapped side). Then flip it over and check the other side (i.e., repeat Steps 3, 4, and 5 on the opposite side).

6. Put the wheel back in the truing stand.

7. Pull the rim toward the center (reducing the gap between the dishing tool and the axle end face) by tightening the spokes on the opposite side of the wheel from the axle end that had the gap between it and the dishing gauge. Tighten a half-turn each — no more. If the spokes start getting really tight (they will creak a lot when tightening, the nipples will start rounding off, and the spokes will feel much tighter than the spokes in a comparable wheel),

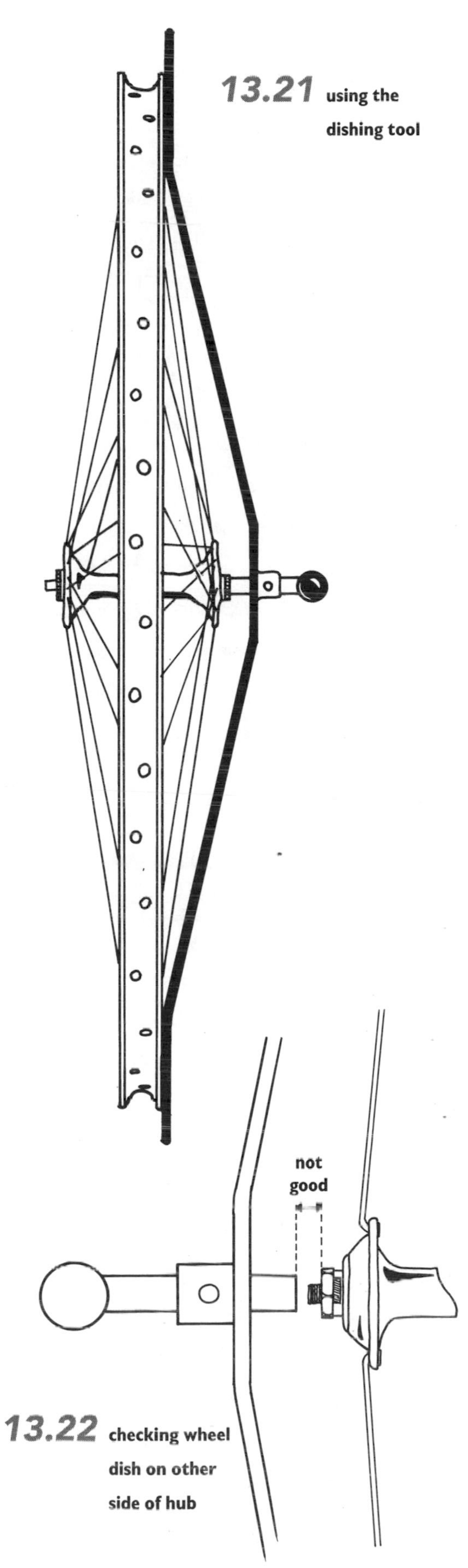

13.21 using the dishing tool

13.22 checking wheel dish on other side of hub

then loosen the spokes uniformly on the opposite side of the wheel.

8. Recheck the wheel with the dishing gauge by repeating Steps 1-5.

9. If the dish is still off (there is still a gap between the dishing gauge and the end nut when you flip it over), repeat Steps 6-8 until the dish is correct (the gap is zero).

10. Stress the spokes by squeezing each pair together with your hands (Fig. 13.23). They will make a "ping" noise as they unwind.

Leaning on the wheel is a quicker way to pre-stress it, but this method has the potential to wreck the wheel if you are not careful. To proceed, set the axle end on the workbench and carefully press down on the rim with your hands at the 9 o'clock and 3 o'clock positions. This will affect an area of about three spokes on each side, so rotate the wheel three spokes, press down again, rotate three more spokes in the same direction, press down again, and so on. After you finish one side, flip the wheel over and do the other side. Do not press down with all your might; while a well-built wheel's lateral strength is impressive, it is still easy to destroy your work with too much pressure.

If pre-stressing throws the wheel way out of true, the spokes are probably too tight. Loosen them all an eighth-turn. Note, though, that some loss of wheel "trueness" is normal. If the loss is minor, you can overlook it and continue with step 11.

11. Repeat "Truing the wheel" steps, followed by the "Dishing the wheel" steps, pre-stressing the spokes frequently as you go. Keep improving the accuracy of the build this way.

12. Bring up the tension to that of a comparable wheel by making small tightening adjustments to every nipple, adjusting dish and true after each time around, until the wheel is as you want it.

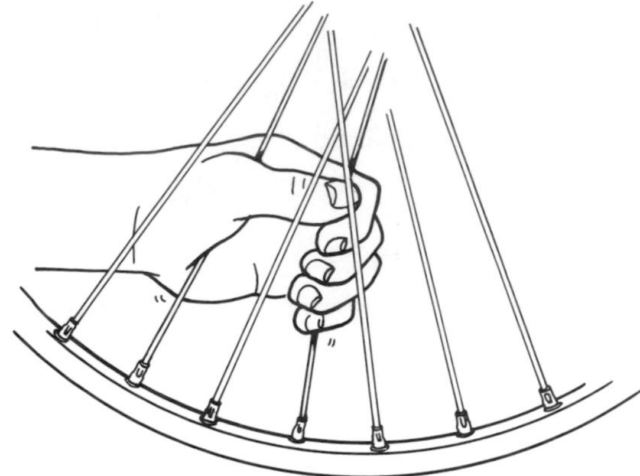

13.23 **relieving tension**

13. If the rim is oily, wipe it down with a citrus-based biodegradable solvent.

14. Congratulate yourself on building your wheel, and show it off to your friends.

13-6: COMMENTS

final comments

Your wheel has some features that you won't find on machine-built wheels. Most significantly, on your rear wheel, the "pulling spokes" are to the outside. In plain speak, this means that you have a spoking pattern that best resists the twisting force on the hub produced by pedaling forces on the chain.

In the wheel you've built, half of the spokes are called "pulling" or "dynamic" spokes, and the other half are called "static" spokes (this is true of any spoking pattern except radial). The pulling spokes are the ones directed in such a way that a clockwise twist on the hub increases the tension in them. If you look at the wheel from the drive side, you will see what I am talking about.

You will also see that the static spokes do not oppose a clockwise twist on the hub. In fact, their tension decreases when you stomp on the pedals.

By placing all of the pulling spokes so that they come from the inside of the hub flanges out (i.e., the spoke heads are on the inward side of the flanges), we have attached the spokes doing the most work the farthest outward on the hub, increasing their angle to the rim, and hence their ability to oppose forces acting on the rim.

If you choose the appropriate parts for your weight and riding style, and have the proper spoke tension, then you should have a strong wheel that will last a long time. Congratulations!

13-7: RADIALLY SPOKED WHEELS

With the advent of stronger rim materials and stiffer rim cross-sections, radially spoked wheels (Fig. 13.24) have become popular. They are simple to build, and radial spoking offers a number of advantages.

A radially spoked wheel is vertically stiffer than a crossed one, since radial spokes allow little opportunity for spokes to absorb energy in the spoking pattern. The radial wheel can be stiffer laterally, too, since all of the spokes can come to the outside of the hub flange and increase the pulling angle to the rim.

A radial wheel is lighter, because the spokes are shorter. Further weight can be removed with fewer spokes, and radial spoking allows any even spoke count to be used (with non-radial patterns, the spoke count must be a multiple of four). And radial spoking allows the use of direct-pull hubs and nail-head spokes (straight spokes without elbows), eliminating a potential weak spot in the spokes.

Radially laced spokes line up behind each other and thus improve the aerodynamics of the wheel. Aero-shaped spokes can improve the aerodynamics further yet, but using aero-shaped spokes in a standard hub often requires slotting the hub holes with a jeweler's file to get the spoke through. If you do this yourself, make sure you only file downward from the hole, toward the meat of the flange. Slotting upward toward the edge greatly weakens the hub and invites the spoke to rip through.

Speaking of torn hub flanges, the warranty of some hubs is voided when spoked radially; Shimano, for one, has this stipulation. The stress is greater on hub holes with radial spoking because the spoke tension in a radial wheel is often higher and because there is less material resisting the hub tearing out when the spoke is pulling straight outward than if it is pulling at an angle along the hub flange.

A completely radial wheel can only be used on the front. On the rear, the drive side (or the non-

13.24 radially spoked front wheel

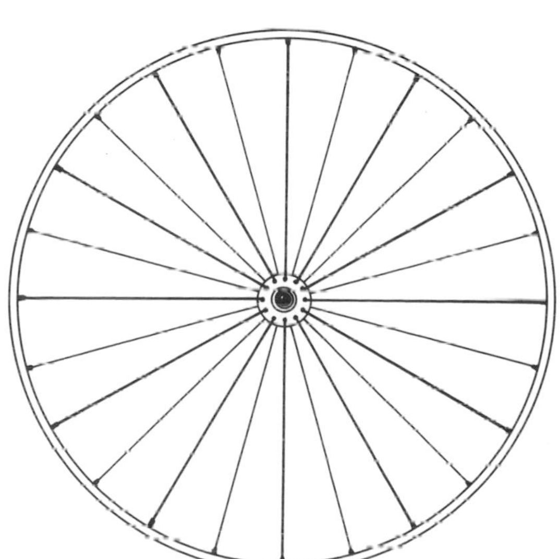

13.25 radial/three-cross rear wheel

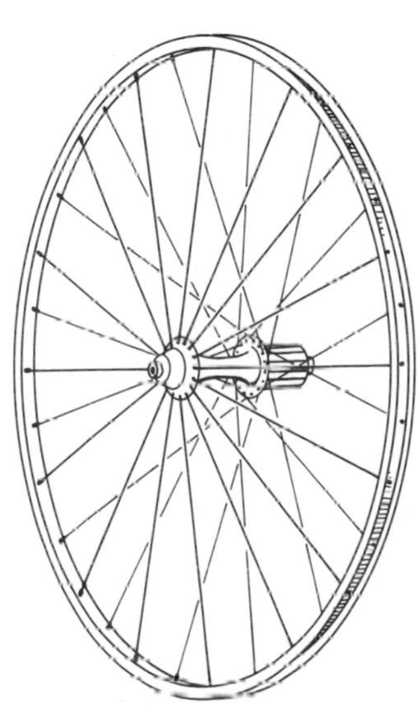

drive side, if the hubshell is oversized and stiff) must still have a crossing pattern to oppose the twist on the hub caused by the chain (Fig. 13.25).

A. How to lace a radial front wheel:

Drop all of the spokes from the inside of each flange outward and lace them straight to the rim.

B. How to lace a rear wheel with a radial left side and a three-cross drive side:

First lace the drive side following the instructions in sections 13-2A, steps 4 through 7, and 13-2C, steps 17 through 24. Now lace the left side spokes outward through the hub flange and straight to the rim.

The tensioning and truing steps are the same as for standard three-cross wheels, but radial spoke tension should be higher to help prevent the spokes from vibrating loose.

13-8: WHEELS FOR BIG RIDERS

wheels for big riders

Building wheels for heavy and tall riders requires greater lateral and vertical stiffness. The weight of the rider can more readily bend and laterally flex the rim, but it creates another problem as well. The heavier rider de-tensions the spokes at the bottom of the wheel more by making the rim more D-shaped at the bottom as it rolls. If the spokes are under less tension, or if the nipple flanges periodically lose contact with the bases of the rim holes, the nipples can unscrew, and the wheel will fall apart. To achieve the higher strength required, you can add the following characteristics.

First, the spoke count needs to be high; 36 or more spokes is highly preferable for riders over 190 pounds. The spokes need to be heavier, since thicker spokes have less stretch as well as less breakage. While 14/15-gauge (2.0mm/1.8mm) double-butted spokes will probably have no more breakage than straight 14-gauge (2.0mm) spokes (since most breakage occurs at the nipple or the elbow, where butted spokes are thick), butted spokes will stretch more, allowing spoke loosening.

The deeper the rim, the higher its hoop strength (vertical stiffness and strength). Unfortunately, most deep aero rims are also thinner to reduce weight and hence lose some strength. Very-deep-section rims work with low spoke counts because of this high hoop strength. The strongest wheel is a deep-section rim drilled for more spokes.

With 8-, 9- and 10-speed rear wheels, dish is high (one side is flatter than the other), meaning that there is a great tension difference between spokes on the two sides. The loose spokes on the left can unscrew, especially under high pedaling forces, and the tight spokes on the right can break. As the chain twists the cogs clockwise, the spokes opposing the twist (the "pulling spokes") get tighter, while the "static spokes" are reduced in tension and can unscrew.

Using radial spokes on the left side (see section 13-7 above) can counteract the problem of grossly uneven tension. With a radial left side, the chain winding up the hub always tightens all of the left side spokes, rather than loosening half of them as happens with a crossing pattern.

An off-center rim, such as a Ritchey OCR, can also help by reducing the wheel dish. The rim holes are offset to the left side (Fig. 13.3), so the drive-side spokes come to the rim at a lower angle and can work with lower tension. The left-side spokes come to the rim at a higher angle and can be under higher tension without forcing the use of dangerously high tensions on the drive side. Before lacing an off-center rim, make sure you read the note in step 2 of section 13-2 above.

XIV

Forks

"Someday we'll look back on this moment and plow into a parked car." —Evan Davis

The fork serves a number of purposes. Most obviously, it connects the front wheel to the handlebars. Of course, the fork allows the bike to be steered, and supports the front brake.

The fork also offsets the front hub some distance forward of the steering axis. This offset distance (called "fork rake"), combined with the steering axis (the "head angle") and the wheel size, determine how your bike is going to handle and steer.

All forks—rigid (Fig. 14.1) or suspended (Figs. 14.2, 14.4, 14.5)—provide at least a minimum amount of suspension by allowing the front wheel to move up and down. The steering axis angles the fork forward from vertical, while the front hub is offset further forward yet, and these things make it possible for any fork to flex along its length and absorb vertical shocks. Suspension forks add a much greater range of vertical wheel travel.

Virtually every road fork is made up of a simple combination of components: the steering tube, the fork crown, the fork legs (sometimes called "blades"), and the fork ends (also called "dropouts" or "fork tips"). Figs. 14.1 & 14.2 illustrate these parts on a rigid fork and a suspension fork. Forks for cyclo-cross bikes and some touring bikes also have cantilever/V-brake bosses (Fig. 14.3). Road forks are manufactured from steel, aluminum, carbon fiber, titanium and countless mixes of these materials.

ROAD SUSPENSION FORK TYPES:

A very small percentage of road bikes come equipped with suspension forks (Figs. 14.2, 14.4, 14.5), which have some sort of springs inside

tools

2mm, 2.5mm, 5mm and 8mm hex keys
8mm open-end wrench
Small screwdriver

OPTIONAL

Ruler
True front wheel
Dropout alignment tools
V-blocks
Vise
4-inch long, 3/8-inch drive, 6mm hex key socket
6-inch socket extension
3/8-inch drive socket handle
Snap ring pliers
Threadlock compound
Automatic transmission fluid
Suspension fork grease
RockShox pump

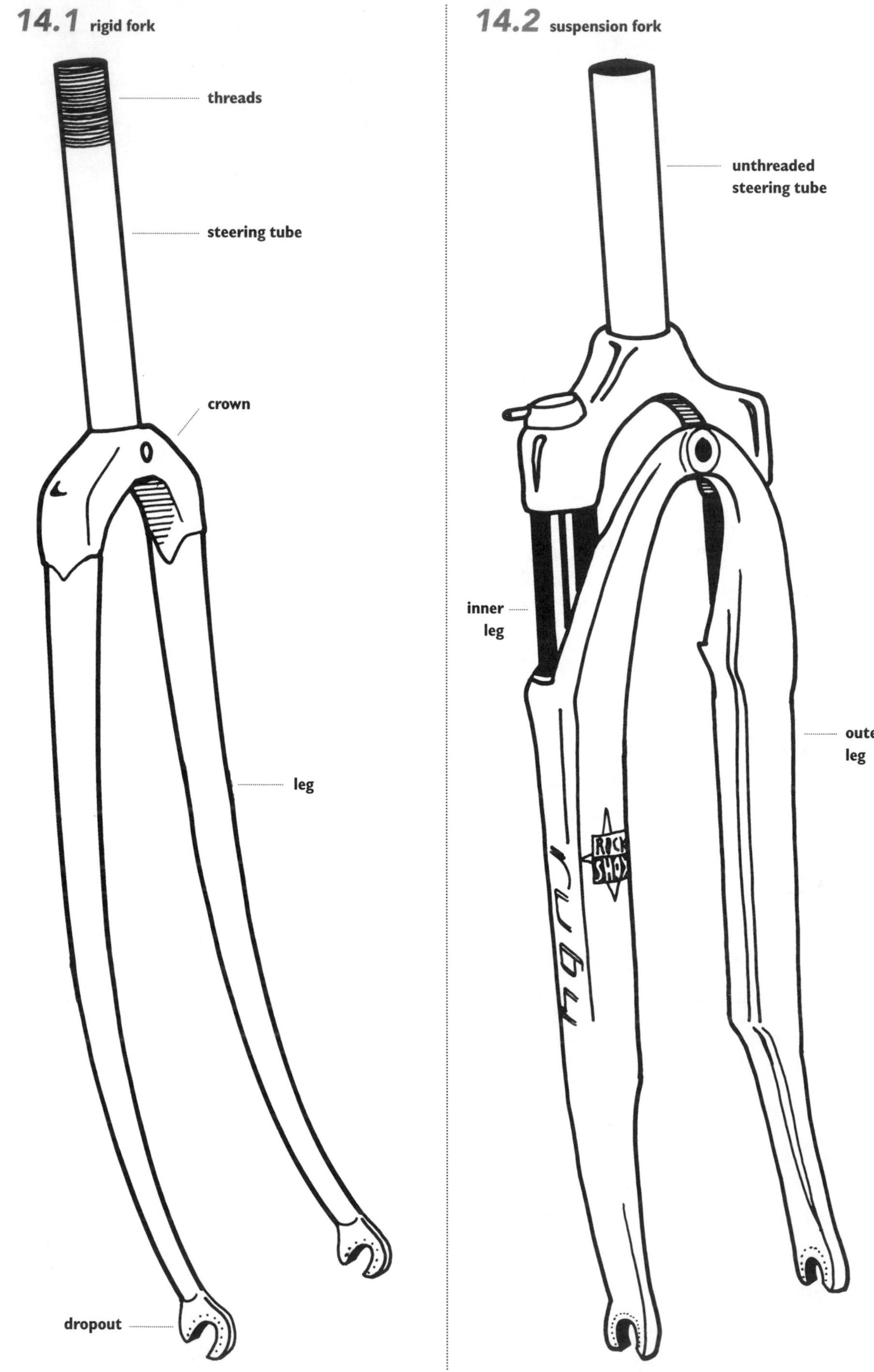
14.1 rigid fork
threads
steering tube
crown
leg
dropout
14.2 suspension fork
unthreaded steering tube
inner leg
outer leg
ROCK SHOX
ruby

that yield to bumps. The springs can be steel or titanium coils, elastic polymer bumpers (elastomers), compressed air, or a combination.

Often included is a damping system to control how fast the spring compresses and rebounds. The damper acts much like a shock absorber on a car or a screen door (you know, the thing that keeps the door from slamming). Hydraulic damping systems are the most common, relying on the controlled movement of oil from one chamber to another. That movement is usually regulated by a system of holes that act to control the rate of flow.

The most common suspension fork design uses "telescoping" fork legs that consist of two sections: inner legs attached to the fork crown and steering tube, and outer legs attached to the front hub that slide up and down over the inner legs (Fig. 14.2). Road versions often have curved outer legs.

Cannondale uses its "Headshok" design on some road bike models (Fig. 14.4). The Headshok incorporates rigid fork legs attached to a single shock unit inside the fork steering tube.

The SUS21 Aeroswing fork (Fig. 14.5) has an elastomer on each side built into the pivot of a bolt-on dropout. The wheel swings back on impact, but not so far that the brake pad hits the tire, if it is adjusted properly. Different dropouts with stiffer or softer elastomers inside can be bolted on to change the ride quality.

14-1: FORK INSPECTION

For the most part, forks are pretty durable, but they do break occasionally. A fork failure can ruin your day, since the means of control of the bike is eliminated. Such loss of control usually precedes the rapid acceleration of your body downward onto the road, resulting in substantial pain.

Ever since I first opened my framebuilding shop,

14.3 cyclo-cross fork

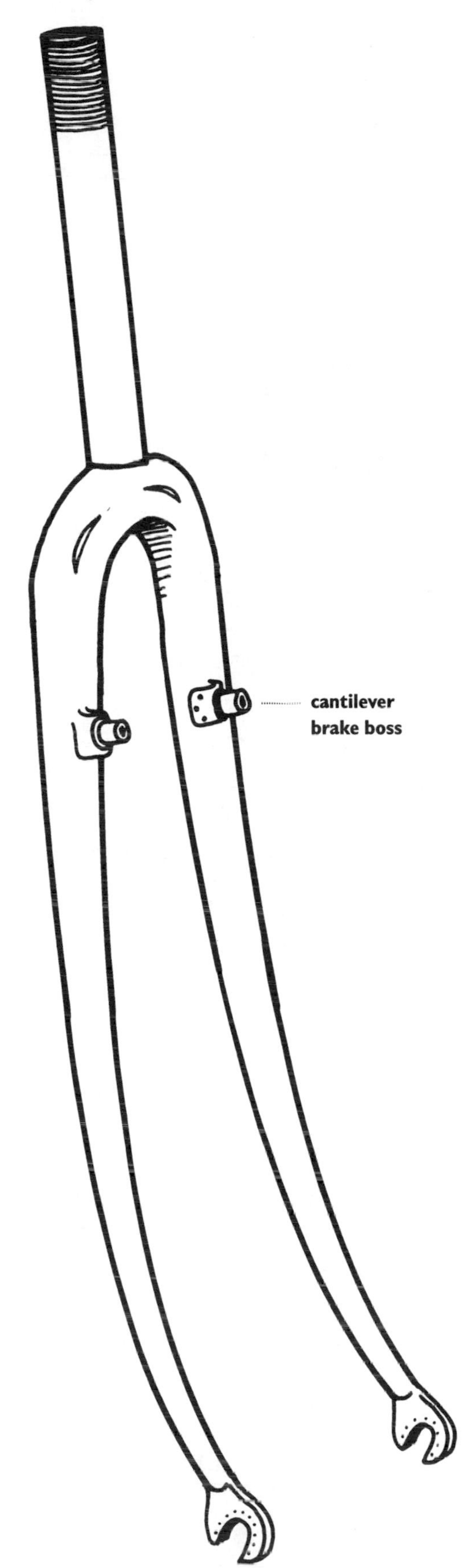

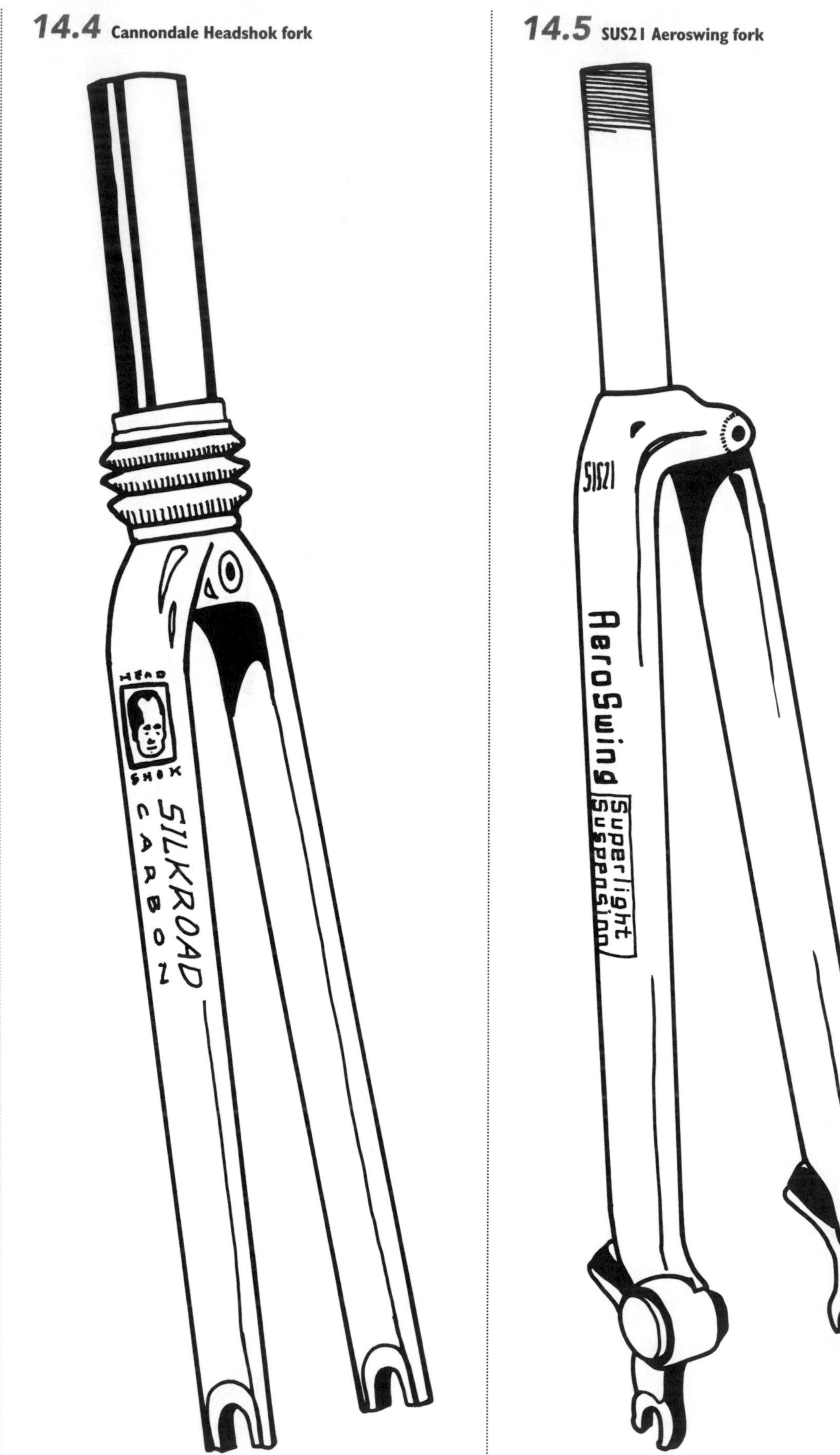

14.4 Cannondale Headshok fork

14.5 SUS21 Aeroswing fork

fork inspection

people have regularly brought in what has grown to be an amazing collection of forks that broke, sometimes with catastrophic consequences. Some had steering tubes broken either at the fork crown or in the threads. Others had fork crowns that broke or separated (releasing a fork leg or two), fork legs that folded, cantilever posts that snapped, and front dropouts that bent over or broke off. You can go a long way toward preventing problems like these by regularly inspecting your fork.

With that in mind, get into the habit of checking your fork regularly for any warning signs of impending failure. Obvious things to look for include bends, cracks and stressed paint. If you have crashed your bike, give the fork an especially thorough inspection. If you find any indication that the fork has been damaged, replace it. A new fork is cheaper than emergency room charges, brain surgery, or an electric wheelchair.

When you inspect a fork, remove the front wheel, wipe any dirt off, and look under the crown and between the fork legs. Carefully examine all of the outside areas. Look for any areas where the paint or finish looks cracked or stretched. Look for bent parts, from little ripples in fork legs to bent dropouts (Fig. 14.6). Skewed or broken cantilever posts are something to look for on cyclo-cross and touring forks (Fig. 14.3).

Put the wheel back in and watch to see if the fork legs twist when you tighten the hub into the dropouts. Check to make sure that a true wheel centers under the fork crown. If it doesn't, turn the wheel around and put it back in the fork to determine whether the misalignment is in the fork or the wheel. If the wheel lines up off to one side when it is in one way and off the same amount to the other side when it is in the other way, the wheel is off, and the fork is straight. If the wheel is skewed off to the same side in the fork no matter which direction you place the wheel, the fork is misaligned.

I recommend overhauling your headset annually (Chapter 11, Sections 11-16 and 11-17); when you do, carefully examine the steering tube for any signs of stress or damage. Check for bent, cracked or stretched areas, stripped threads (Fig. 14.6), a bulging threaded steerer where the stem expands inside or a crimped threadless steerer where the stem clamps around its top.

With a threaded fork, hold the stem up next to the steering tube to make sure that, when your stem is inserted to the depth you have been using it, the bottom of the stem is always over an inch below the bottom of the steering tube threads. If you expand your stem in the threaded region, you are asking for trouble; the threads cut the steering tube wall thickness down by about 50 percent, and each thread offers a sharp breakage plane along which the tube can cleave.

ON SUSPENSION FORKS:

Check for oil leaks or torn, cracked or missing seals around the top of the outer leg.

On SUS21 forks, make sure the bolts anchoring the dropouts are tight.

If you have any doubts about anything on your fork, take it to the expert at your bike shop. When it comes to forks, err on the side of caution.

14-2: FORK DAMAGE

If your inspection has uncovered some damage that does not automatically require fork replacement, here are some guidelines to go by and means of repair.

A. Dents

Not all fork dents threaten the integrity of the fork. A small dent usually poses little risk; a large

14.6 types of fork damage

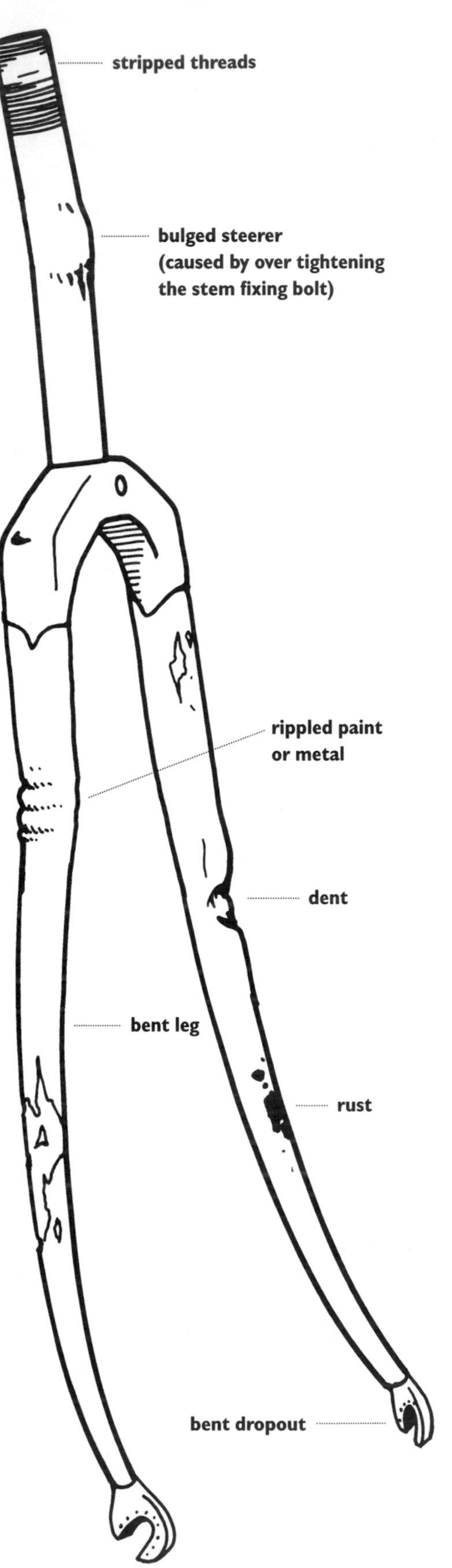

fork damage

dent (Fig. 14.6) demands attention (replace the fork). On a suspension fork, almost any dent can ruin the fork's operation, even if it does not pose a breakage threat, but most suspension fork parts are replaceable.

B. Fork misalignment

Within limits, a rigid steel fork can be realigned if it is slightly off-center (see Section 14-5 in this chapter.) Aluminum, carbon-fiber, titanium and suspension forks cannot be re-aligned. Don't try it!

C. Stripped steering tube threads

If the threads on the steering tube are damaged (Fig. 14.6) so that the headset slips when you try to tighten it, you need to replace the fork. If the steering tube is bulged, it also needs to be replaced, since it can split.

On a steel fork, you can have a framebuilder replace the steering tube, but it is hardly worth it. On telescoping suspension forks, the steering tube/fork crown/inner leg assembly can usually be replaced.

D. Obvious bend, ripple or crease in fork legs

Replace the fork if ripples and bends are obvious (Fig. 14.6). The poor handling and potential breakage pose too great a threat to your safety to be worth saving a few bucks.

E. Bent or stripped cantilever bosses

Some cantilever studs can be unscrewed with an 8mm open end wrench and replaced. It is a good idea to use a thread-locking compound on the threads of the new mount.

On many touring and cyclo-cross forks, the entire cantilever boss is welded on (Fig. 14.3). This usually means that you have to buy a new fork. If you have a framebuilder in your area, he or she may be able to weld or braze a new one on a steel fork. You will also need to repaint the fork; all that work may cost more than a new fork, by the way.

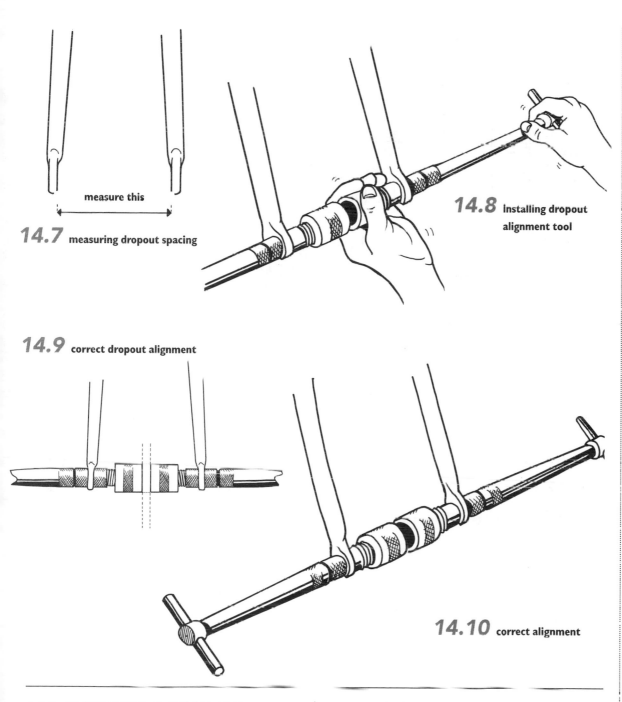

measure this

14.7 measuring dropout spacing

14.8 Installing dropout alignment tool

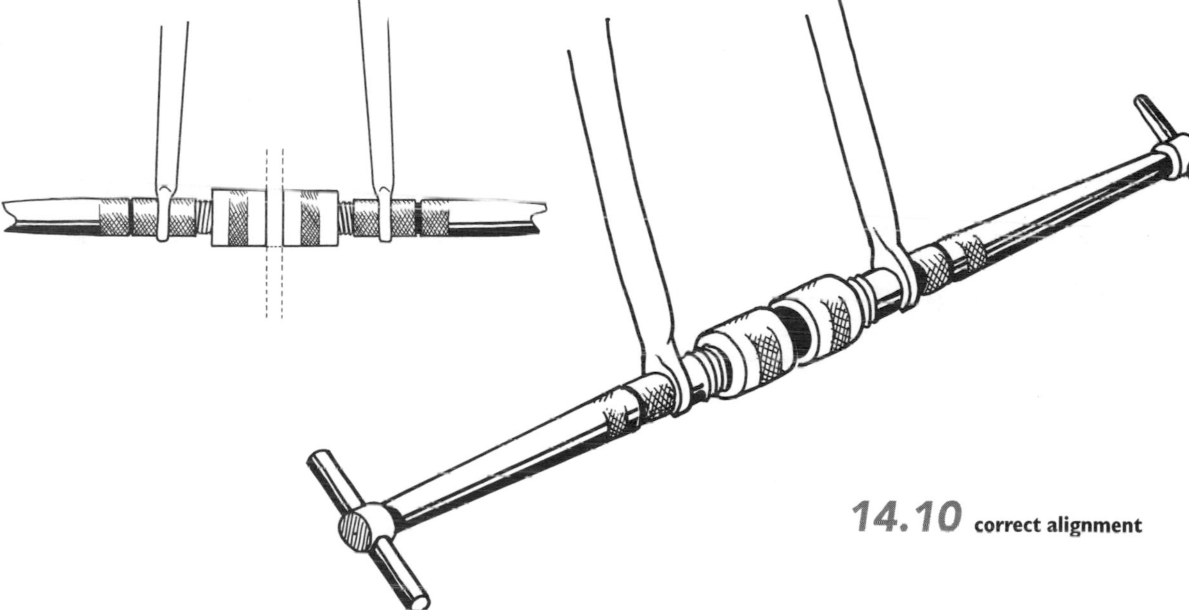

14.9 correct dropout alignment

14.10 correct alignment

14-3: MAINTAINING STANDARD ROAD FORKS

Beyond touching up the paint on steel forks and performing regular inspections, the only maintenance procedure with a rigid fork is to check the alignment (Section 14-4) if your bike is handling badly. You can perform minor realignment on a steel fork if you find that it is off center, but note that it is risky enough to qualify as a Level 3 job. Do not try to realign titanium, carbon-fiber or aluminum forks.

14-4: CHECK FORK ALIGNMENT

LEVEL 3

You will need a ruler, a true front wheel, and dropout alignment tools (Fig. 1.5). If you have an aluminum, titanium, carbon-fiber, or suspension fork, this procedure is diagnostic only, because you should not try to realign any of these forks. Checking the alignment may help explain bike-handling problems.

If you find the alignment to be off more than a

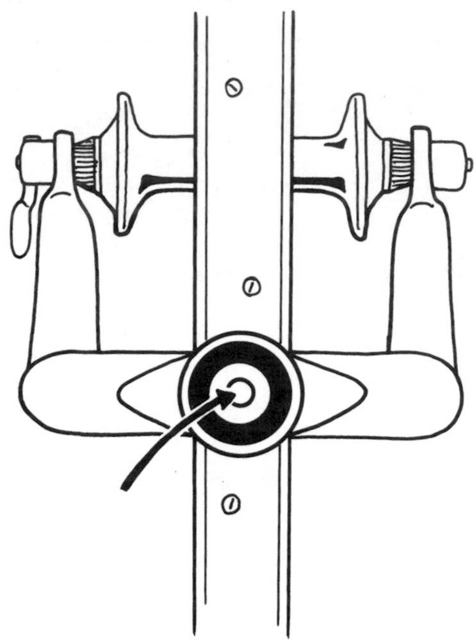
14.11 correct alignment of valve hole in a straight fork

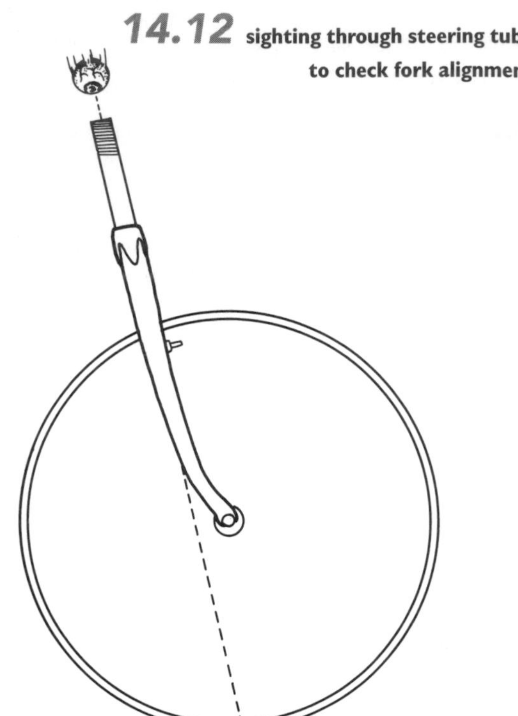
14.12 sighting through steering tube to check fork alignment

fork alignment

couple of millimeters in any direction with any fork other than a steel unsuspended one, you will need a new fork. If the fork is new, misalignment should be covered by the warranty.

If a steel fork is more than 8mm off in any direction, you ought to get a new fork. If the dropouts of a steel fork are slightly bent, you can realign them. You can also take a moderately bent (less than 8mm off) steel fork to a framebuilder or a bike shop for realignment. Make sure that whomever you take it to is properly equipped with a fork jig or alignment table and is well versed in the art of "cold setting" (a fancy term for bending) steel forks.

1. Remove the fork from the bike. (Chapter 11, Sections 11-16 and 11-17)

2. With the front wheel out, measure the spacing between the faces of the dropouts (Fig. 14.7). Adult bikes should have a spacing of 100mm between the inner surfaces of the dropouts. (Some low-end kids' bikes have narrower spacing—about 90mm or so. If that's the type of bike you are working with, don't bother checking alignment; it isn't worth the trouble.) Remember that you are measuring the distance between the flat surfaces that meet the hub axle faces (and not between wheel-retaining nubs that protrude inward from the dropouts). Dropout spacing up to 102mm and down to 99mm is acceptable. Beyond that in either direction means a trip to the bike shop for a new fork. If you have a steel fork, you can take it to a bike shop or framebuilder for alignment.

3. Clamp the steering tube of the fork in a bike stand or between V-blocks in a vise. Install the dropout-alignment tools (Fig. 14.8). The tools are made so that they can be used on either the fork or the rear triangle of the bike, so they have two axle diameters and spacers for use in the wider rear dropouts. Move all of the spacers to the outside of the dropouts so that only the cups of the tools are placed inside of the dropouts. Install the tools so that the shafts are seated up against the tops of the dropout slots. Tighten the handles down.

4. Ideally, the ends of the cups on the dropout aligning tools should be parallel and lined up with

each other (Fig. 14.9). The cups of Campagnolo dropout alignment tools are non-adjustable and are nominally 50mm in length; the ideal space between their ends is 0.1-0.5mm. The cups on Park dropout aligning tools (illustrated in Figs. 14.8, 14.9, and 14.10) are adjustable in length, so that you can bring the faces up close to each other no matter what the dropout spacing. If they are lined up with each other, and the dropouts are spaced between 99mm and 102mm apart, continue on to step 5. If a steel rigid fork's dropouts are not lined up straight across with each other (Fig. 14.10), and the dropouts are within the 99-102mm spacing range, skip to Section 14-5 to align them.

Note: *It is very important that the dropout faces are parallel before continuing with step 5, or the rest of the alignment procedures will be a waste of time. Clamping the hub into misaligned dropouts will force the fork legs to twist. If the dropouts are misaligned, any measurement of the side-to-side and fore-aft alignment of the fork legs will not be accurate.*

5. Remove the tire from a front wheel. Make sure the wheel is true and properly dished (Chapter 13, Sections 13-4 and 13-5).

6. Install the wheel in the fork. Make sure the axle is seated against the top of the dropout slot on either side, and make sure the quick-release skewer is tight. Lightly push the rim from side to side to make certain that there is no play in the front hub. If there is play, you first must adjust the hub (Chapter 6).

7. Look down the steering tube and through the valve hole to the bottom side of the rim (Fig. 14.11). The steering tube should be lined up with this line of sight through the wheel (Fig. 14.12). When you are sighting through the steering tube and the valve hole, you should see the same amount of space between either side of the rim and the sides of the steering tube. You should also see the center of the bottom side of the rim through the valve hole. Turn the wheel around and install it again so that what was the right end of the axle is now the left, and vice versa. Sight through the steering tube and the wheel valve hole again.

Placing the wheel in the fork both ways corrects for deformation in the axle or any wobble in the wheel. If the wheel is true and dished properly, and the axle is in good shape, the wheel should line up exactly as it did before. If it does not line up, but the wheel is off by the same amount to one side as it is to the opposite side when the wheel is turned around, the wheel is off and the fork is fine side-to-side.

If this test indicates the fork is up to 2-3mm off to the side, that is close enough; continue on. If it is off by more than 3mm, get a new fork or have it aligned by a framebuilder (if it is steel, that is; do not try to realign suspension, titanium, carbon-fiber or aluminum forks).

Note: *If you are sighting through the wheel in this way and you cannot see the bottom side of the rim through the valve hole because the hub is in the way, the fork has big problems. In order for the bike to handle properly, the fork must have some forward offset of the front hub from the steering axis. This offset, or "rake," is usually around 4cm. If you sight through the*

14.13 checking fore-aft fork leg alignment

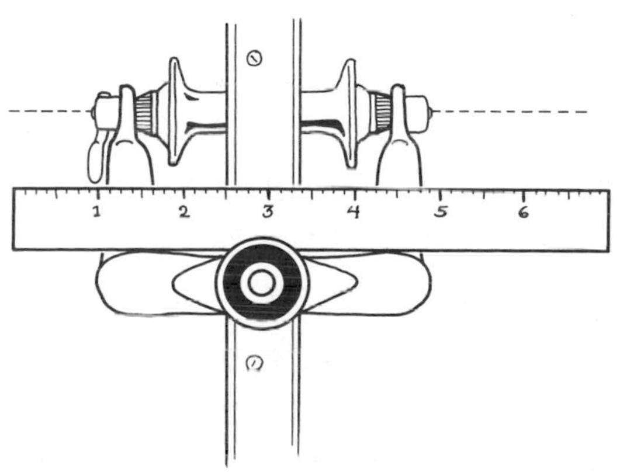

steering tube and see the front hub, the fork is bent backward so much that it has little or no offset! If this is the case, you need a new fork.

8. With the wheel in the fork, place a ruler on edge across the fork blades just below the fork crown (Fig. 14.13). Make sure the ruler is perpendicular to the steering tube.

9. Holding the ruler in place, lift the fork toward a light source so that you are sighting across the ruler and the front hub toward the light. The ruler's edge should line up parallel with the fronts of the dropouts (or with the axle ends sticking out of either end of the hub) (Fig. 14.13). This test will tell you whether one fork leg is bent back relative to the other one. If the two line up parallel or very close to that, the fork alignment has checked out completely, and you can put it back in the bike. If one fork leg is considerably behind the other, you need to get a new fork or have this one aligned.

14-5: ALIGN DROPOUTS ON RIGID STEEL FORK

align dropouts on rigid steel fork

LEVEL 3

You can only do this with a steel, non-suspension fork!

Dropouts are easy to tweak out of alignment; simply pulling the bike off of a roof rack and failing to lift it high enough to clear the rack skewer will do it. Forks can also come with misaligned dropouts to start with.

If the dropout is bent more than 7 degrees or so, or if the paint is cracked at the dropout where it is bent, it may be dangerous to bend it back. Replace the fork.

1. Install dropout-alignment tools and check alignment as described in Step 3 and 4 under "Check fork alignment."

2. If the dropouts are not aligned, and the fork spacing is between 99mm and 102mm, you can align the dropouts. If the fork spacing is wider than 102mm or less than 99mm, there is no point in aligning the dropout faces, because you must bend the fork legs as well to correct the spacing. Without an alignment table or fork jig, you cannot do this accurately. You should get a new fork, or have a qualified mechanic or framebuilder align your steel fork.

If your fork spacing is between 99mm and 102mm apart, clamp the crown or unicrown of the fork very tightly between two wood blocks in a well-anchored vise.

3. Grab the end of the dropout-alignment tool handle with one hand and the cup of the tool with the other (Fig. 14.8). Bend each dropout until the open faces of the dropout-alignment tools are parallel, and the edges line straight up with each other (Fig. 14.9).

4. Remove the tools, and continue with "Check fork alignment," Section 14-4, Step 5.

14-6: MEASURING SUSPENSION FORK TRAVEL

Suspension forks (Figs. 14.2, 14.4, 14.5) are still rare on road bikes, but their usage is growing. This and the following sections cover telescoping forks with elastomer, coil, and air-oil springs.

A. Measure sag

"Sag" is the amount of fork compression that occurs when the rider sits on the bike without moving. Since most road suspension forks do not have protective fork boots, you can simply put a zip tie around the upper tube ("inner leg") and push it down against the top of the seal on the lower tube ("outer leg"). Now sit on the bike and get off again. Measure the distance the zip tie slid up the upper tube from the seal (Fig. 14.14). It should be 3 to 5mm. If it is more, the spring setting is too soft; if it is less, the spring setting is too hard.

If fork boots are present on the fork, you'll need

a friend to help you. Have your friend measure the distance from the top of the outer leg to the bottom of the fork crown when you are on the bike and again when you are off of the bike. The difference between the two measurements is the sag.

B. Measure maximum possible travel

The fork's full travel can be measured by releasing the spring from the fork, or you can believe the manufacturer's advertised travel for your fork.

1. Remove the springs from both fork legs.

The RockShox Ruby Road (Figs. 14.2 and 14.15) has a rubber top plug on one side that must be pried up with a small screwdriver, revealing the top cap. Unscrew the top cap with an 8mm hex key and remove the spring stack. The other leg has a lockout lever which must be moved to the "off" position. Remove the lockout knob screw with a 2mm hex key, lift off the lockout knob, and, with a 17mm socket wrench, remove the spring stack.

With an air-oil fork, release the air from both legs. On RockShox Paris-Roubaix air-oil forks with ball-needle valves (Fig. 14.16), remove either the Phillips screw or the plastic snap-on cap covering the air hole, turn the compression damping adjuster to the highest setting, moisten the ball-pumping needle, and stick it down into the hole to release the air. On forks with Schrader valves, simply remove the valve cap and push down on the valve pin to let the air out.

2. Measure the distance from the bottom of the crown to the top of the outer leg when the fork is fully extended and again when it is fully compressed. The difference between these numbers is the total available travel.

C. Measure travel used while riding

Put a zip tie around the upper tube and slide it down against the top of the upper seal on the lower tube. Ride the bike normally; when you return, measure the distance the zip tie has slid up from the seal. Compare this with the total travel found in part B above. If you have a lock-out on your fork, you can get the softest possible ride by setting the springs so that you use up the full travel when you hit the biggest bump you would foresee encountering, and use the lockout when you want your fork to be stiff.

14-7: MINOR MAINTENANCE OF TELESCOPING SUSPENSION FORKS

Road suspension forks, since they operate in a clean environment relative to mountain-bike forks, nor-

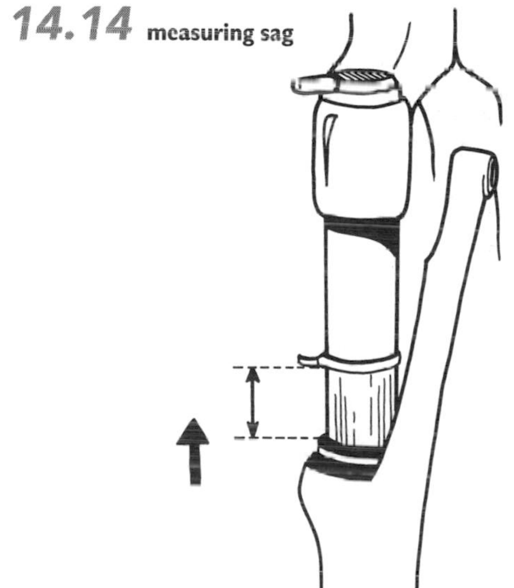

14.14 measuring sag

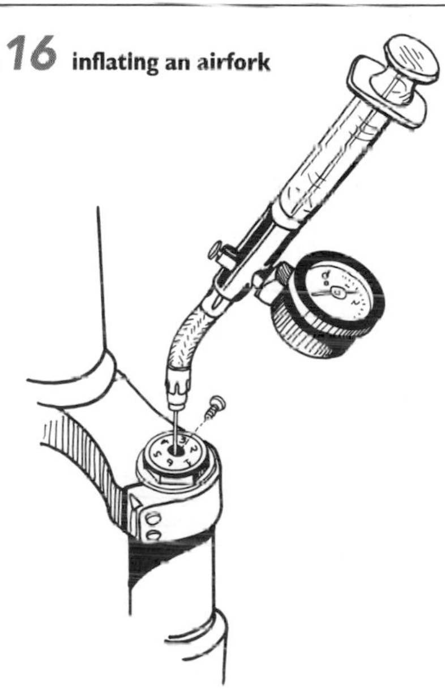

14.16 inflating an airfork

14.15 RockShox Ruby suspension fork

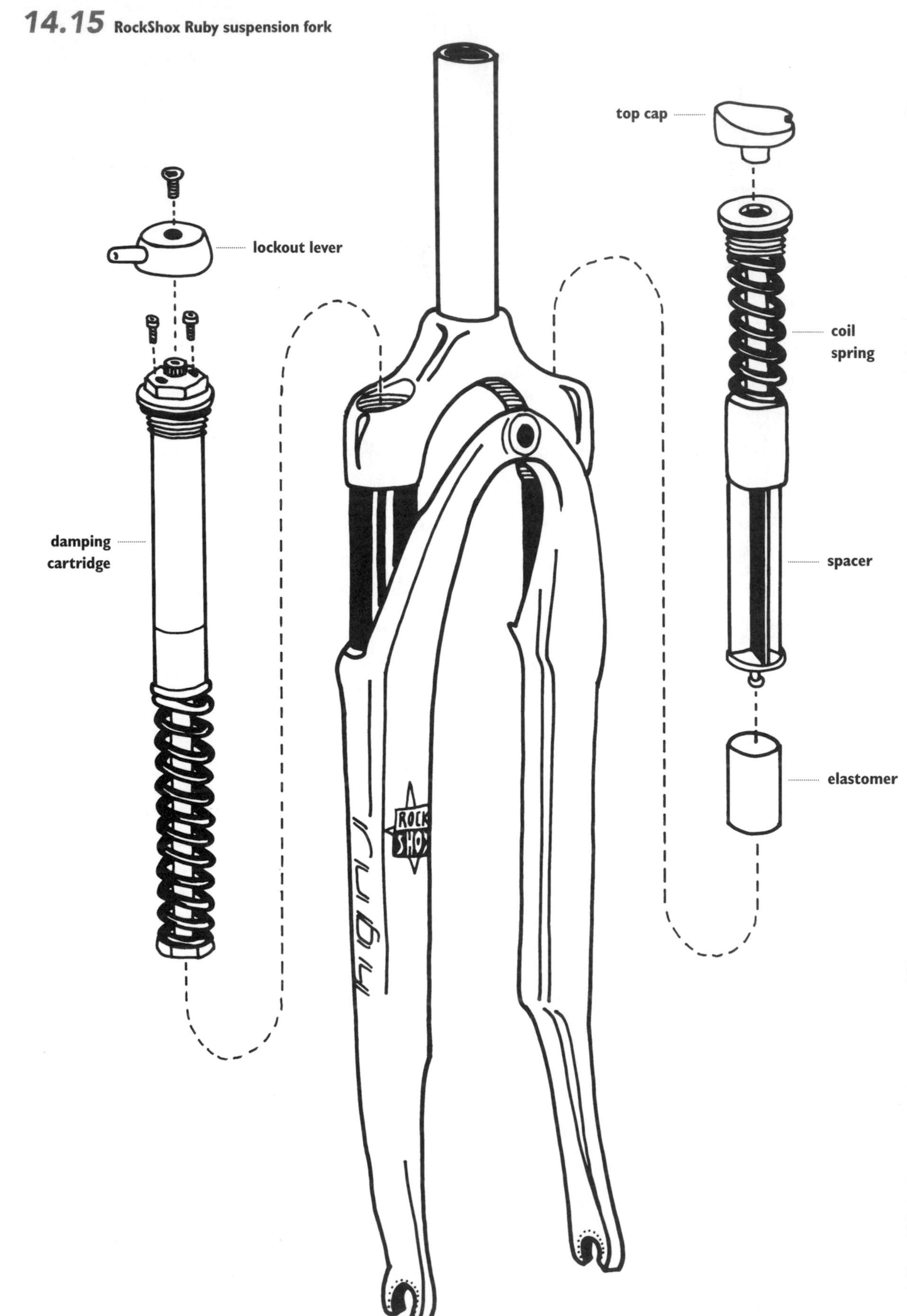

mally need little maintenance. And many current suspension forks incorporate oil baths to minimize maintenance. The oil splashes around and keeps the seals and sliders lubricated.

If the fork does not have an oil bath, you can greatly increase the life of the seals as well as the time between fork overhauls by performing the following procedure frequently. Stickiness in suspension forks is usually caused by a dry or dirty dust seal rubbing on a dry or dirty inner leg.

1. With the fork boots off or slid up, wipe off the outside of the seal on top of each outer leg and the length of the inner leg between the outer leg and crown.

2. Put a thin coat of a non-lithium grease (like Englund EDL or "Judy Butter") on the outside of the seals and inner legs.

14-8: TUNING COIL SPRING/ELASTOMER FORKS

A. Lock-out system

Some road suspension forks have a lock-out device that can be used when no suspension is desired. This is a nice feature for sprinting or climbing out of the saddle—even for long climbs in the saddle or racing any smooth stretch, when the bobbing of the fork would rob energy from propulsion.

Generally, the lock-out works by closing off an orifice in the oil-filled damping chamber. On a Ruby, the system is engaged by a lever on top of the crown (Fig. 14.14). Cannondale Headshok forks (Fig. 14.4) have a knob on top of the steering tube above the stem that can be rotated to lock out the fork.

B. Setting spring preload

Spring preload is the amount the spring resists compression when the fork is at rest, and it can be adjusted on many coil spring/elastomer forks. Preload determines the way a spring responds to the forces applied to it. On road coil spring/elastomer forks, the spring stack must be removed to adjust preload (unlike mountain-bike forks, where you can adjust the preload simply by turning the adjuster knobs on the top of the fork crown).

The RockShox Ruby Road (Figs. 14.2 and 14.15) has a spring stack in each leg, one under a lock-out lever on the right and one under a rubber plug on the left. Reveal the left top cap by prying off the rubber top plug with a small screwdriver. Unscrew the top cap with an 8mm hex key and remove the spring stack. The right leg's lock-out lever must first be moved to the "off" position and the lock-out knob screw removed with a 2mm hex key. Lift off the lock-out knob, and with a 17mm socket wrench, remove the spring stack.

The preload of the left stack is increased by moving the slotted preloader further down on the solid spacer, and reduced by moving it up. Slide the preloader off of the spacer and back on into a different set of grooves (Fig. 14.15).

The preload of the right spring is changed by removing or adding spacers on the spring after removing the spring cap screw with a 2.5mm hex key (Fig. 14.15). Make the same adjustment to both sides. Replace the spring stacks and top caps (RockShox recommends 60 inch-pounds of torque), and put the lockout knob and rubber cover back on.

Preloading the springs does not limit the full travel for large bumps; it alters the force required to initially move the springs when you encounter smaller bumps. Varying the preload also changes the fork's sag.

C. Replacing elastomers and coil springs

To make major changes in the fork's spring rate, you must change the springs inside of the fork (Fig. 14.15). Manufacturers usually color-code the elastomers and coil springs for stiffness. You can also tell the difference between stiff and soft elastomer bumpers by squeezing them between your fingers (some manufacturers refer to the elastomers as "MCUs" for "Micro-Cellular Units," referring to small air voids trapped inside the elastomers). Extra springs usually come with the fork, or you can buy them from a dealer.

The fork needs stiffer springs (or more spring pre-load) if it sags excessively when you sit on it. The fork needs softer springs if hard impacts with large bumps do not use the fork's full travel.

1. Remove the springs the same way as in section 14-8B above.

2. Clean any old grease off of the spacers you found in the fork.

3. Pull off the old springs and replace them with the coil springs and/or elastomers that you intend to use.

4. Apply a new coating of grease to the new parts and everything you just cleaned. Make sure you grease the outside of the coil springs to reduce the noise of the springs rubbing inside the legs.

5. Put the spring stacks in the fork legs (Fig. 14.15), and screw the caps down. (RockShox recommends 60 inch-pounds). Replace the rubber cover and the lockout knob.

overhauling Ruby fork legs

14-9: OVERHAULING RUBY FORK LEGS

LEVEL 3

This section only applies to RockShox Ruby Road forks.

1. Remove the front brake from the fork arch (with a 5mm hex key), and remove the front wheel.

2. Pull out the spring stacks as described in Section 14-8B above (Fig. 14.15).

3. Compress the fork completely.

4. You will need a 6mm, 3/8 inch drive hex-key socket that is at least 4 inches long, and you will need to put it on the end of a 6-inch socket extension. Stick it down inside the inner leg and push it through the cap on top of the plunger until it engages the 6mm hex plunger bolt. Tap on the top of the extension with a hammer until it fully engages the bolt. Since the bolt is tight and threadlocked, if you do not have the hex key fully engaged, the bolt and/or the hex key will strip. Gripping the lower-leg assembly between your knees, hold the fork while you unscrew the bolt. Do the same on the other leg.

5. Slide off the lower-leg assembly (Fig. 14.15), being aware that it has an oil bath in it that could spill. Pour out the oil into an oil-recycling container.

6. With inwardly squeezing snap ring pliers, remove the snap ring inside the end of each inner leg, and pull out and clean the plunger assembly and top-out bumper. Clean the inner legs (upper tubes) with a lint-free rag, and inspect for nicks and scratches.

7. With a rag on the end of your finger, clean the seals on the top of the outer legs and the top bushing on each side. With a rag wrapped around a rod, clean the bottom bushing down deep in each outer leg.

8. On each side, grease the plunger assembly and top-out bumper, and push it back into place in the end of the inner leg with the clear washer and snap ring to hold it in place. Make sure the sharp edge of the snap ring is toward the open end of the inner leg (that way, the spring cannot force the snap ring out of the bottom of the inner leg, as it conceivably could if the rounded edge were facing outward).

9. Clean the plunger bolts and put threadlock compound on them.

10. Pour 10ccs of 8-weight hydraulic oil (automatic transmission fluid is okay) into the outer legs

and slosh it around to coat all of the seals and bushings. Smear the same oil or some Judy Butter or Englund grease on the inner legs. Carefully slip the inner legs through the seals on the outer legs, and slide the fork together, gently rocking the two pieces to allow the inner legs to slip through the bushings and bottom out. Install and tighten the plunger bolts with the 6mm hex key and extension. RockShox recommends 120 inch-pounds of torque.

11. Re-install the spring stacks and caps as in Section 14-8B above.

14-10: ADJUSTING PARIS-ROUBAIX AIR/OIL FORKS

It would be hard to come up with a spring lighter and more easily adjustable than one made of air! This section only applies to RockShox Paris-Roubaix Road forks.

1. Adjust air pressure

Compressed air acts as the spring in this type of fork. Greater air pressure means a stiffer fork, and vice versa. It is a good idea to check and correct air pressure every couple of weeks, as it may lose air over time.

Do not use a tire pump on the fork; the large stroke volume puts too much air into the fork too quickly. The RockShox pump looks like a large syringe with a gauge on it (Figs. 1.2, 14.16). The ball valve on each leg is located beneath either a Phillips screw or a plastic pry-off cap on top of the compression-damping adjusting knob (Fig. 14.16).

Tighten down the compression-damping adjustment knob before inserting the pump needle. This will help you avoid pinching the rubber valve on the top of the adjuster rod inside, causing it to leak. Moisten the needle, and insert it into the valve hole (Fig. 14.16). Pump both legs up to the pressure recommended for your weight in your owner's manual.

You might want to experiment with different pressures to find what you like best or to get 3–5mm of sag and the boing you want over those train tracks by your house.

2. Adjust compression damping

The compression damping determines how large an impact is required to initiate movement of the fork.

Compression damping can be adjusted by turning the knobs on top of the fork crown. Doing so varies the size of orifices separating the oil-filled chambers. Turning the knob clockwise increases the compression damping, meaning that a larger bump (or pedaling force) is required to start the fork moving. When riding on a paved road, tighten it all of the way down to minimize the fork movement due to pedaling.

3. Other adjustments

You can make several other adjustments to Paris-Roubaix forks, including oil height, oil viscosity, valve-spring preload, rebound bleed hole size and compression bleed hole size. Check your owner's manual if you want to mess with these.

14-11: OVERHAULING PARIS-ROUBAIX FORKS

LEVEL 3

I won't go into much detail, since there are so few of these forks out there. I just want to assure you that it is not very scary. You can pull the upper and lower halves of the fork apart once you deflate it and remove the snap ring on the top of each outer leg (under the wiper) with inwardly-squeezing snap ring pliers.

Changing the oil requires unscrewing the top caps and pouring the oil into an oil-recycling container. You can continue to remove snap rings and take the inner-leg assembly apart down to the last washer and micro-clean every little part if you like, or you can simply wipe the intact inner legs down at this stage.

Clean the inside of the outer legs with a clean rag on a rod. Grease the inner legs and the insides of the outer legs with Judy Butter or Englund fork grease. Rock the inner legs back into place, and secure them with the snap rings, making sure that the sharp edge of the snap rings faces up. Pour ATF (automatic transmission fluid) or 5-wt. or so shock oil into the fork up to the height indicated in your owner's manual for your weight.

14-11: FORK UPGRADES

You may be able to improve the ride of your bike by replacing the fork. There are a number of reasons to do this. To lighten the bike and add gee-whiz value, you could get a carbon-fiber fork. To soften the ride, you could get a suspension fork or an aluminum fork. To stiffen the ride, you could get a steel fork. To lighten the bike and get a more rigid fork-to-bar connection, you could switch to a threadless system (see Chapter 11 on headsets to see the difference between threaded and threadless systems). And to reduce aerodynamic drag, you could get an aero' fork.

Make sure you get a fork with the same length steering tube as your old fork (unless you are also switching to a threadless system, in which case you will just get a long, unthreaded steerer). Chapter 11 covers the installation of the headset.

With most telescoping road suspension forks (except Cannondale Headshok), the front brake is attached to the fork brace, which is thinner than a fork crown (Fig. 14.2). As a result, a short brake bolt is needed, rather than a long front-brake bolt. You will either need to mount a rear brake on the front or get a rear center bolt and install it into your front brake.

Frames

"Duct tape is like The Force.
It has a light side, a dark side,
and it holds the universe together...." —Carl Zwanzig

tools

2.5mm, 3mm, 4mm and 5mm hex keys
A true rear wheel
Oil
Grease

OPTIONAL

Derailleur hanger alignment tool
String
Ruler
Dropout alignment tools
Metric taps
Bottom bracket tap set
Electric drill
Drill-bit set
16mm wrench
8mm open-end wrench

Pay close attention to the frame, because it is the most important part of your bike. It is the one item that is nearly impossible to fix on the road, and if it fails, the consequences can be serious.

15-1: FRAME DESIGN

The traditional rigid "double-diamond" design of a road bike frame relies on a "front triangle" and a "rear triangle" (Fig. 15.1); never mind that the front triangle is not actually a triangle—or much of a diamond, for that matter.

Referring to Fig. 15.2, the angle of the seat tube relative to the horizontal (the "seat angle") determines the fore-aft position of the rider relative to the pedals. It also plays a role in determining the weight distribution on the wheels. And seat angle partially dictates the length of the chainstays, since the more tipped-back the seat tube is, the further back the rear wheel will have to be to avoid hitting it.

For a given top-tube length and front-end geometry, the seat angle also dictates whether your feet hit the front wheel or not when pedaling around a tight, low-speed turn (the interference is called, quaintly these days, "toe-clip overlap"). And unless the frame tubing is altered to compensate, the vertical and lateral compliance of the rear of the bike will increase with shallower seat angles and correspondingly longer chainstays.

The angle of the head tube relative to the horizontal (the "head angle"), in combination with the fork rake (explained at the beginning of Chapter 14) and wheel diameter, determines much of the steering and handling characteristics of the bike. These two items also dictate in large part how much shock

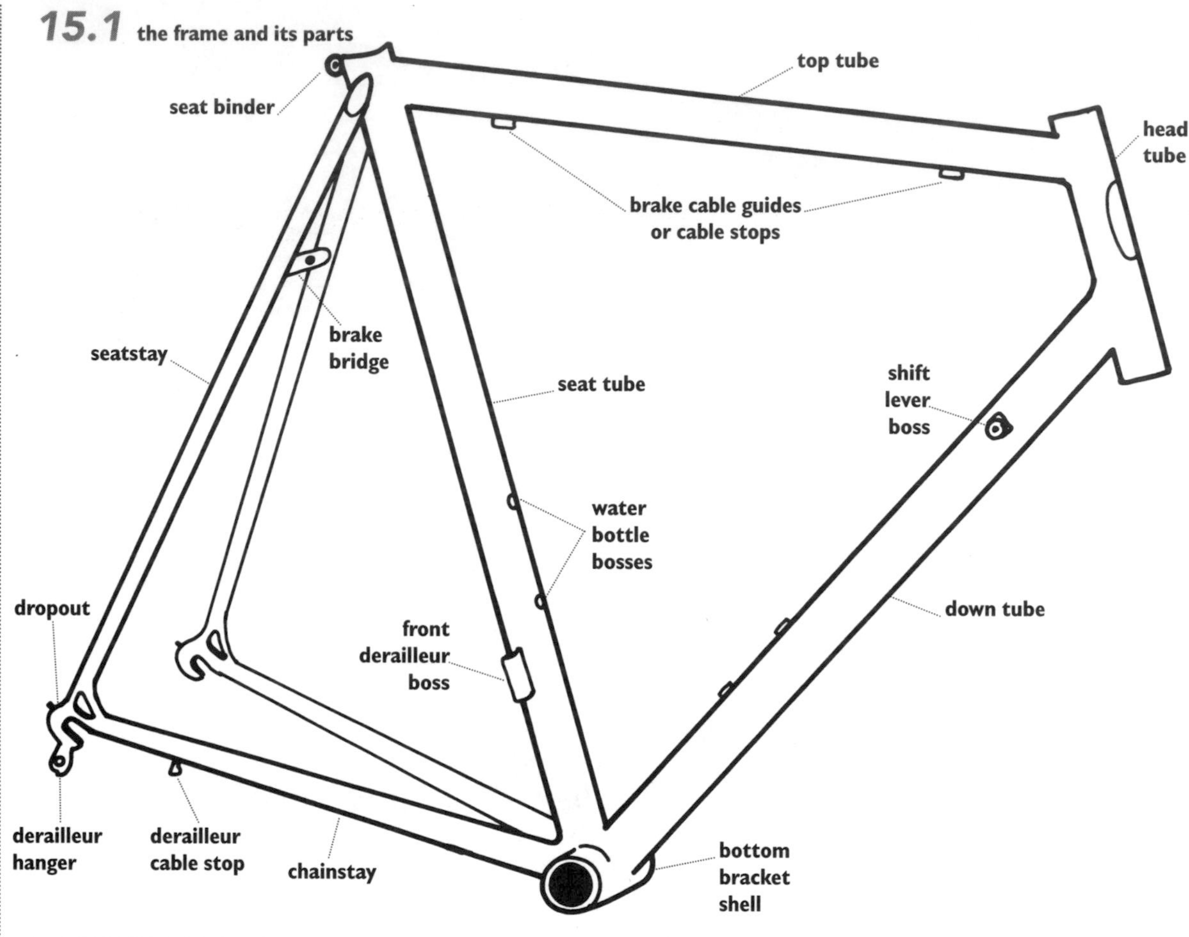

is absorbed by the fork.

The height of the bottom bracket above the ground determines how much clearance you will have for your pedals when rounding a turn. (Low bottom brackets impart a feeling of stability. Compromises between cornering clearance and stability are often made by framebuilders, especially in pro-level bikes where it is assumed the rider will have sufficient experience to always corner with the inner crank up.) Along with the seat-tube length and angle, the bottom-bracket height also helps determine the stand-over clearance your crotch has over the top tube.

The top-tube length, along with the stem length, seat angle, and seat fore-aft position on the seatpost, determines your reach to the handlebars.

The seat-tube length (or "frame size") determines the amount of seatpost extension you will get for a given seat height, as well as the minimum seat height possible on the bike. It also is one of the variables determining stand-over height.

The wheelbase is the distance between the wheel axles. It determines the minimum possible turning radius.

Some frames are designed for improved aerodynamic performance and have wing-shaped tubes and a low-profile design to reduce air drag.

15-2: FRAME MATERIALS

A materials evolution has accompanied the development of the bicycle ever since its birth. Wood was the material of choice for the first bikes, but was soon replaced by steel, aluminum, and even bamboo. Steel and aluminum are the materials most commonly used to build frames today, but titanium, carbon composites and metal matrix composites

15.2 frame dimensions

top tube length

seat angle

seat tube length

frame materials

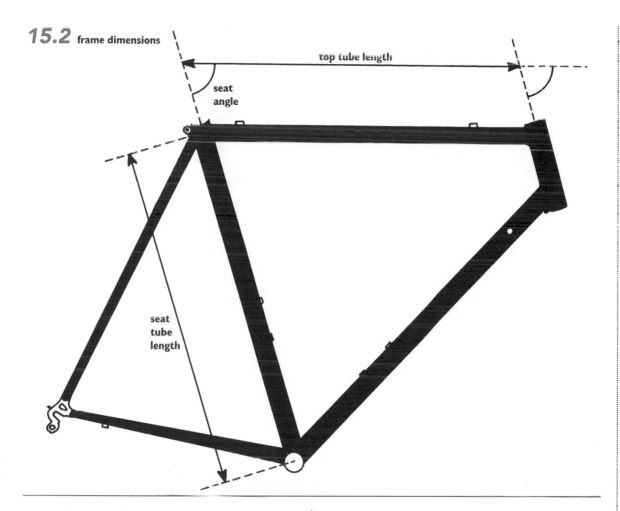

account for a significant share at the high end. Bicyclists are reaping benefits from the end of the Cold War by riding on parts made of materials produced by former defense contractors looking for new markets after their gravy train dried up.

Since the materials used in road frames come in a variety of grades with varying costs and physical properties, let's assume for the following discussion that I am talking about the highest grades used in bicycles. For example, the aluminum used in pop cans and window frames is a lot different than the 7000-series aluminum used in high-end bicycle frames.

Steel has the highest modulus of elasticity (a principal determinant of stiffness) as well as the highest density and tensile strength of any of the metals commonly used in frames. Aluminum has a much lower modulus, density and tensile strength than steel; titanium has a modulus, density and tensile strength between the two. With good frame design and construction combined with intelligent selection of tube properties, diameters, shapes and wall thicknesses, long-lasting frames with comparable stiffness-to-weight and/or strength-to-weight ratios can be built from any of these metals.

Butting of metal tubing reduces weight by putting thicker material at the tube ends and thinning the center sections. "Double-butted" means that both ends are thicker than the center sction, while "triple-butting" and "quad-butting" refer to gradation steps in the thickness at the ends.

Alloying and heat-treating of most metals makes a huge difference in their tensile strengths. Low-carbon steel (like gas pipe) is soft and easy to bend and break. High-carbon steels alloyed with chromium, molybdenum and other materials are far stronger;

heat-treating makes them stronger yet. The same goes for aluminum. The latest rage in aluminum for bicycles sees the metal alloyed with an element called scandium, which raises its strength considerably. Most aluminum frames require a post-weld heat-treatment step or they will be soft and breakable.

Titanium alloyed with 3 percent aluminum and 2.5 percent vanadium (3Al/2.5V) is far stronger than commercially pure (CP) titanium, which is 98 percent titanium. Titanium alloyed with 6 percent aluminum and 4 percent vanadium (6Al/4V) is stronger yet, but as of this writing is still not drawn into tubing, so all 6/4 bike tubes are made from rolled and welded sheet, which reduces aesthetics and ultimate strength somewhat. Titanium, like steel, requires no post-weld heat-treatment, but it must be welded in an inert-gas atmosphere or it will oxidize and become extremely brittle.

Advertising claims touting one frame-tubing material over another can be misleading, since you may not know whether a manufacturer is comparing its material with the high-strength alloyed forms of competitors' materials. If scandium-alloyed aluminum is compared with commercially pure titanium, for example, it comes off looking much better than if it were compared with hardened 6/4 or 3/2.5 titanium, but the consumer just sees "titanium" listed in the advertisement.

Carbon-fiber and similar composite frame materials consist of fibers embedded in a resin (plastic) matrix. These materials can be very light, very strong and very stiff. Bikes can be built by gluing carbon-fiber tubes into lugs (usually made of carbon fiber or aluminum), or they can be molded in a single piece ("monocoque" construction).

The big advantage of composites is that extra composite fabric can be added into sections of the mold to add thickness precisely where extra strength is needed. The tricky part is holding the composite parts together in a frame that does not come apart.

Metal-matrix composite frame materials contain additions of ingredients that improve mechanical properties (usually tensile strength). These additions are not alloying materials (i.e., they are not melted together with the metal), since that would generally contaminate the metal. Rather, particles of sand-like materials (aluminum oxide, silicon oxide, etc.) are worked into the metal (usually aluminum) without melting the particles. The trick with metal-matrix composites is making them weldable without weakening the frame at the joints.

Framebuilders endlessly experiment with all sorts of exotic materials that offer mechanical advantages. Beryllium, for example, was commonly used in the defense industry. Its light weight and low density coupled with high strength and stiffness made it an ideal material to use on the nose cones of nuclear missiles. Well, they're not making too many of those any more, so a few folks have tried building bikes out of the stuff. It works great but has the drawback of being poisonous if ingested or inhaled; I advise against trying to taste or snort a Beryllium frame.

15-3: FRAME INSPECTION

You can avoid potentially dangerous frame failures by inspecting your frame frequently. If you find damage, and you are not sure how dangerous the bike may be to ride, take it to a bike shop for advice.

1. Clean the frame every few rides, so that you can spot problems early.

2. Inspect all tubes for cracks, bends, buckles, dents, and paint stretching or cracking, especially near the joints where stress is highest. If in doubt,

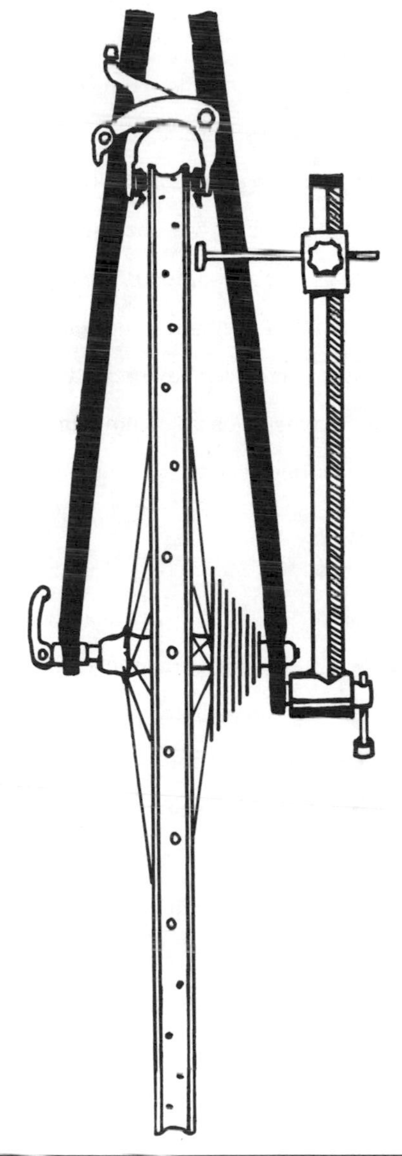

15.3 **checking derailleur-hanger alignment**

take it to an expert for advice.

3. Inspect the rear dropouts and the welds or glue joints around the brake bridge and chainstay bridge for cracks (see Fig. 15.1 for names and locations of frame parts). Check to be sure the dropouts (and brake bosses and cable hangers on cyclo-cross and touring frames) are not bent. Some dropouts and brake bosses bolt on and are replaceable, and some cable hangers are glued in and replaceable. Otherwise, badly bent or broken dropouts, brake bosses, and cable hangers need to be replaced; a framebuilder in your area may be able to do the job.

4. Remove the seatpost every few months and invert the bike to remove any water that might have collected in the seat tube. On steel frames, look for deeply rusted areas. Look and feel for rust inside, or for rust falling out. I recommend squirting oil or a rust-preventing spray for bicycle frames inside the tubes periodically. Remember to grease both the seatpost and the inside of the seat tube when you reinsert the seatpost. After sanding off the rust, touch up any external areas where the paint has come off with touch-up paint or nail polish (hey, it's available in lots of cool colors).

5. Check that a true and properly dished rear wheel sits straight in the frame, centered between the chainstays and seatstays and lined up in the same plane as the front triangle. Check that tightening the hub skewer does not result in bowing or twisting of either the chainstays or the seatstays.

15-4: CHECK AND STRAIGHTEN REAR DERAILLEUR HANGER

LEVEL 3

1. If you have a hanger-alignment tool (Fig. 1.5), thread it into the derailleur hanger on the right dropout (Fig. 15.3).

2. Install a true rear wheel in the frame.

3. Swing the tool around, measuring the spacing between its arm and the rim all of the way around. The arm of the tool should be the same distance from the rim at all points. Some tools, like the one shown in Fig. 15.3, have a set-screw extending from the arm that you can adjust to check the spacing; others require you to measure the gap with a ruler or caliper

4. If the tool has play in it, keep it pushed inward lightly as you perform all of the measurements, or you will get inconsistent data.

5. If the spacing between the tool arm and the rim is not consistent (within a millimeter or two all

15.4 checking frame alignment with a string

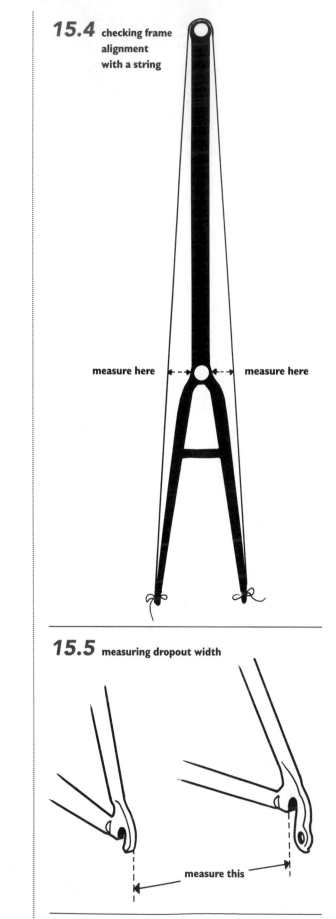

measure here

measure here

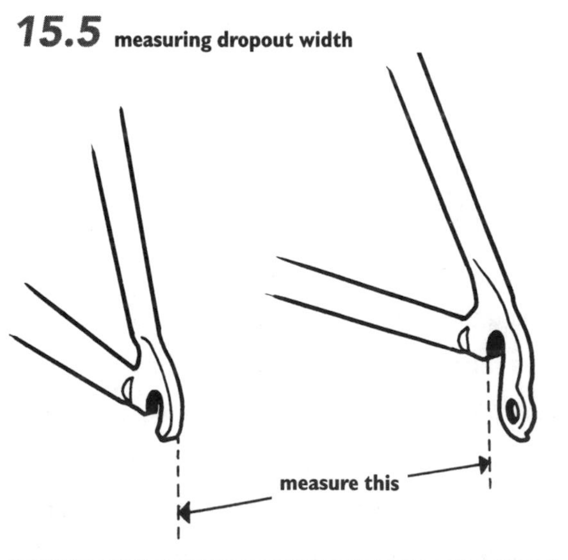

15.5 measuring dropout width

of the way around), carefully bend the hanger by pulling outward lightly on the arm of the tool where it is closest to the rim.

6. If the derailleur hanger is severely bent, you may not be able to align it without breaking it (you may even have trouble threading the tool in, because the threaded hole will be ovalized). If you have a replaceable bolt-on dropout, replace it.

7. If the threads or the hanger itself are really screwed up, and you do not have a replaceable dropout, see Section 15-7B below for other derailleur hanger options.

15-5: CHECK FRAME ALIGNMENT AND ADJUST DROPOUT ALIGNMENT

LEVEL 3

Exacting alignment checks require a precision surface plate, an uncommon tool in the home workshop. Thus, the following methods for determining frame alignment are inexact, but sufficient for determining gross alignment woes.

If you find problems more severe than moderately bent dropouts or a misaligned derailleur hanger, do not attempt to correct them. Adjusting frame alignment, if it can be done at all, should only be performed with an accurate frame alignment table by someone who is practiced in its use.

1. With the frame clamped in a bike stand, tie the end of a string to one rear dropout. Stretch it tightly around the head tube, and tie it symmetrically to the other dropout (Fig. 15.4).

2. Measure from the string to the seat tube on each side (Fig. 15.4). The measurement should be the same within a millimeter.

3. Put a true and properly dished rear wheel in the frame and check that it lines up in the same plane as the front triangle. Make certain that the wheel is centered between the seatstays and chain-

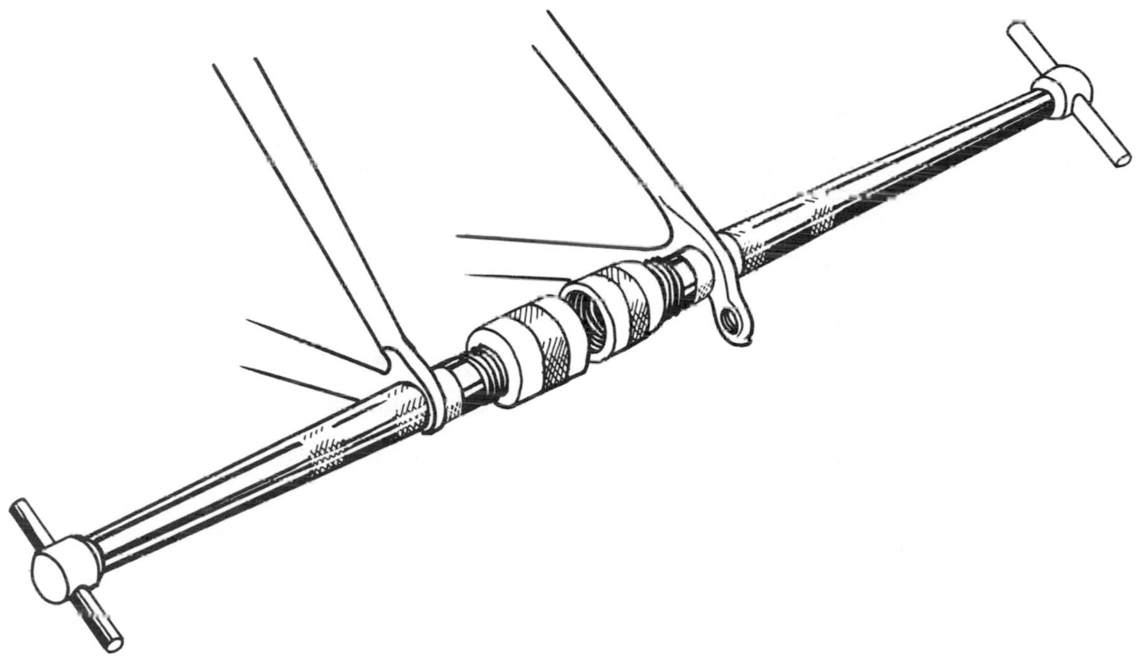

15.6 using dropout alignment tools on rear dropouts

stays. The hub should slide easily into the dropouts without requiring you to pull outward or push inward on the dropouts. Tightening the hub quick release should not result in bowing or twisting of frame members.

4. Remove the wheel and measure the spacing between the dropouts (Fig. 15.5). For 8-, 9- or 10-speed rear hubs, this spacing should be 130mm. Measure the width of the rear hub with a caliper to see what the rear-end spacing of the frame should be. If the spacing on the frame is 1mm less or 1.5mm more than nominal, it is acceptable. For instance, if you have a frame whose rear spacing should be 130mm, acceptable spacing is 129mm to 131.5mm.

5. If you have dropout alignment tools, put them in the dropouts so their shafts are fully seated into the dropouts (Fig. 15.6). Arrange the tool spacers (and the cups, if they are adjustable) so that the faces of the cups are within a millimeter of each other. Tighten the handles on the tools. The tool cups should line up straight across from each other, with their faces exactly parallel.

If the tools do not align, one or both dropouts are bent. If you have replaceable dropouts, go ahead and replace one or both of them. If you have a composite or bonded rear triangle of any kind, there is nothing you can do about the problem if the bike is not equipped with replaceable dropouts.

If the bike has a steel rear triangle, you can align the dropouts by bending them carefully with the dropout alignment tools. Hold the cup of the tool with one hand and push or pull on the handle with the other.

Aluminum or titanium rear dropouts can sometimes be aligned, but it is something you should have a shop do. Titanium is hard to bend since it keeps springing back, and you run a great risk of breaking aluminum by bending.

Caution: *Never heat the dropouts (or any part of the frame) for alignment purposes. Doing so could irreparably change the strength, temper, or hardness of the part, and lead to further damage.*

15-6: CORRECTING FRAME DAMAGE

Other than alignment items covered above, the only frame problems you can correct are damaged threads, chipped paint, and small dents. Broken braze-ons and bent, broken or deeply dented tubes call for a new frame or require a framebuilder to perform the repair.

15-7: FIXING DAMAGED THREADS

A road frame has threads in the bottom bracket shell, the brake bosses, the waterbottle bosses, and the rear derailleur hanger. Some bikes have a threaded seat binder, some have cantilever brake bosses, and some also have a small threaded hole in the bottom of the bottom-bracket shell to which a plastic derailleur cable guide is bolted.

1. If any threads on the frame are stripped or cross-threaded, try chasing through the threads with the appropriate thread tap. Then replace the bolt or bottom bracket cup with a new one.

The following tap sizes are commonly found on most road bikes:

Waterbottle bosses and the hole for a plastic shift cable guide:	**5mm X 0.8**
Seat binders and brake bosses:	**6mm X 1**
Derailleur hanger:	**10mm X 1**
Bottom-bracket shells:	**1.37 inches X 24**

(Remember, the drive side (right side) bottom-bracket threads are left-hand threaded; the other side is right-hand threaded.)

Whenever you re-tap any threads, use oil on the tap (use canola vegetable oil on titanium threads). Specific thread-cutting oil is not necessary on old threads since they are already cut.

2. Turn the tap forward (clockwise) a bit, then turn it back, then forward (two steps forward and one back), etc. to prevent the tap from binding and possibly breaking. Be aware that taps are made of very hard and brittle steel. If you put any side or twisting forces on small taps, they can easily break. If the tap breaks, you'll have a real mess; the broken tap in the hole is harder than the frame and it's impossible to drill the broken tap out. If you break off a tap in the frame, do not try to get it out yourself. Take it to a bike shop, a machine shop, or a framebuilder before you break off what little is left sticking out. Unless you put the tap in crooked, breaking one should not be a problem when re-tapping damaged frame threads since these threads will be so worn; getting them to find any metal to bite into will probably be your biggest problem.

IMPORTANT NOTE: *Tapping a bottom-bracket shell requires expertise. If you have never done it before and want to do it yourself, get some expert supervision. In addition to making sure that you place the correct tap in the correct end of the shell, you must also be certain that the taps go in straight. Most bottom-bracket taps have a shaft between the two taps to keep them parallel to each other (see Fig. 1.5). They must both be started at the same time from both ends. If you mess up the threads, you can ruin your frame. So if in doubt, ask an expert.*

If tapping the threads and using a new bolt does not solve your problem, here are some specific remedies:

A. Damaged waterbottle bosses

Some bike shops have a tool that rivets bottle bosses into the frame. Check for this first, since you can avoid a new paint job that way. But note that these riveted bosses tend to loosen up over time, especially if the bottle cage bolts are overtightened. Otherwise, take the bike to a framebuilder to get a new boss welded or brazed in.

B. Damaged rear derailleur-hanger threads

Some bikes have replaceable rear dropouts that bolt onto the frame. Another option is to use a

15.7 **inserting dropout saver**

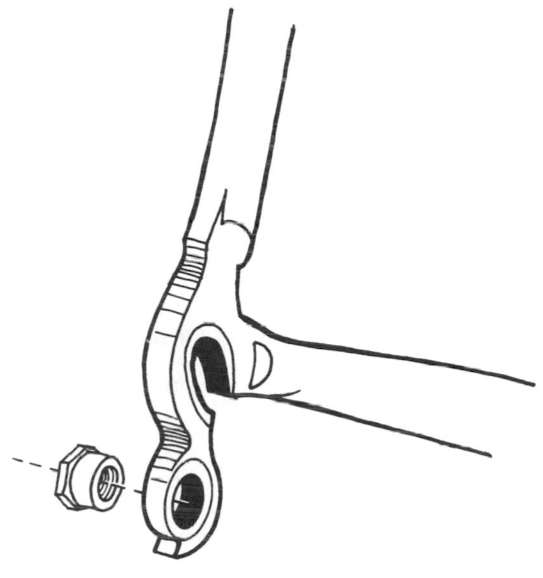

"Dropout Saver" derailleur-hanger backing nut (Fig. 15.7) made by Wheels Manufacturing and available at bike shops. The Dropout Saver is simply a sleeve threaded the same as the dropout, with 16mm wrench flats. You drill out the hole in the damaged derailleur hanger with a 15/32-inch drill bit, push the dropout saver in from the back side, and screw in the derailleur. Dropout Savers come in two lengths, depending on the thickness of the dropout.

Another option is to saw off the derailleur hanger with a hacksaw and use a separate derailleur hanger from a cheap bike that fits flat against the outside of the dropout and is held in by the hub axle bolts or quick release. The final options are to have the dropout replaced by a framebuilder. Or you could always get a new frame.

C. Damaged seat binders

Drill out the threads and install a quick-release or a bolt and nut. Seat-binder threads rarely get stripped, however; it is usually the bolt that is the problem.

D. Damaged bottom-bracket-shell threads

You can use an old-style Mavic (now Stronglight) bottom bracket (Chapter 8, Section 8-9B, Fig. 8.14), if you can still find one, since it does not depend on the threads in the shell to anchor it. Mavic stopped producing these bottom brackets in 1995, but Stronglight now makes them. You must have a shop bevel the ends of the bottom-bracket shell with a special Mavic cutting tool. If the shop has the cutting tool, it likely will have the tools to install the bottom bracket as well.

E. Damaged bottom bracket cable-guide threads

A new hole in the bottom of the bottom bracket can be drilled and tapped, or the stripped hole can be tapped out with larger threads for a larger screw. Make sure the screw you use is short enough that it does not protrude into the inside of the bottom-bracket shell.

F. Damaged brake posts and bosses

Some brake posts are replaceable; they have wrench flats (usually 8mm) at the base, and they thread into a boss welded to the frame. If the posts are not of this type, you will have to ask a framebuilder to install a new boss.

15-8: REPAIR CHIPPED PAINT AND SMALL DENTS

Fixing paint chips is simply a matter of cleaning the area and applying a bit of touch-up paint. Sand any chipped paint or rust completely away before repainting. Use a touch-up paint made for your bike, model paint of a similar color, or use fingernail polish.

Small dents can be filled with automotive body putty, but there is little point to filling them if you are only doing a paint touch-up, since the repaired area probably won't look that great anyway.

There are plenty of frame painters around the country who can fill dents, repaint frames, and can even match original decals. Many of them advertise in bike magazines or can be found on the Internet.

15-9: PIVOTLESS SUSPENSION FRAME MAINTENANCE

Suspension frames are rare on road bikes, but the majority of those that do exist have no pivots on which suspension members rotate. Instead, they rely on the flexibility of various frame members. Suspension frames without moving pivots fall into two broad categories: beam bikes, where the saddle is mounted not on a seatpost but rather out on the end of a long cantilevered beam (Fig. 10.11), and bikes with a shock that depend on the flexure of the chainstays, rather than the pivoting of a rear swingarm.

The beam suspension with the longest heritage is the Softride "visco-elastic" flexible composite beam (Fig. 10.11), and many framebuilders have offered frames for it. Zipp and Softride beams also exist that do not flex along their length, but rather at the mount on the frame. Softride and Zipp beams themselves are generally maintenance-free; the mounting points on the frame feel high forces and are candidates for failure, though. Inspect the beam-mounting points on the frame periodically for fatigue indications (stretched, bulged, or cracking metal or paint). Installation and replacement of the Softride flexible beam is covered in Chapter 10, section 10-9.

Another simple and lightweight rear-suspension design relies on the flexure of the chainstays coupled with a small shock behind the seat tube or radically curved seatstays. It is a good idea to check the chainstays frequently for indications of fatigue (stretched, bulged, or cracking metal or paint) as well as the seatstays and shock-mounting points. If a shock is used, it should be kept lubricated and tuned to your weight and riding style.

appendices

"It is better to know some of the questions than all of the answers." —James Thurber

APPENDIX A

troubleshooting index

This index is intended to assist you in finding and fixing problems. If you already know wherein the problem lies, consult the Table of Contents for the chapter covering that part of the bike. If you are not sure which part of the bike is affected, this index can be of assistance. It is organized alphabetically, but, since people's descriptions of the same problem vary, you may need to look through the entire list to find your symptom.

This index can assist you with a diagnosis and can recommend a course of action. Following each recommended action are listed chapter numbers to which you can refer for the repair procedure.

SYMPTOM	LIKELY CAUSES	ACTION	CHAPTER
bent wheel	1. maladjusted spokes	true wheel	6
	2. broken spoke	replace spoke	6
	3. bent rim	replace rim	13
bike pulls to one side	1. wheels not true	true wheels	6
	2. tight headset	adjust headset	11
	3. pitted headset	replace headset	11
	4. bent frame	replace or straighten	15
	5. bent fork	replace or straighten	14
	6. loose hub bearings	adjust hubs	6
	7. low tire pressure	inflate tires	2, 6
bike shimmies at high speed	1. frame cracked	replace frame	15
	2. frame bent	replace or straighten	15
	3. wheels way out of true	true wheels	6
	4. loose hub bearings	adjust hubs	6
	5. headset too loose	tighten headset	11
	6. soft frame/heavy rider	replace frame	15
	7. poor frame design	replace frame	15
bike vibrates when braking	see *chattering and vibration when braking* in "strange noises", three pages on		
brake doesn't stop bike	1. maladjusted brake	adjust brake	7
	2. worn brake pads	replace pads	7
	3. wet rims	keep braking	7
	4. greasy rims	clean rims	7
	5. sticky brake cable	lube or replace cable	7
	6. steel rims in wet	use aluminum rims	13
	7. brake damaged	replace brake	7
	8. sticky or bent brake lever	lube or replace lever	7
brake rubs on rim	1. brake misaligned	adjust brake	7
	2. untrue wheel	true wheel	6, 13

SYMPTOM	LIKELY CAUSES	ACTION	CHAPTER
chain falls off in front	1. maladjusted front derailleur	adjust front derailleur	5
	2. chain line off	adjust chain line	8
	3. chainring bent or loose	replace or tighten	8
chain jams in front between chainring and chainstay (called *chain suck*)	1. dirty chain	clean chain	4
	2. bent chainring teeth	replace chainring	8
	3. chain too narrow	replace chain	4
	4. chain line off	adjust chain line	8
	5. stiff links in chain	free links, lube chain	4
chain jams in rear	1. maladjusted rear derailleur	adjust derailleur	5
	2. chain too wide	replace chain	4
	3. small cog not on spline	re-seat cogs	6
	4. poor frame clearance	return to dealer	15
chain skips	1. tight chain link	loosen tight link	4
	2. elongated (worn) chain	replace chain	4
	3. maladjusted derailleur	adjust derailleur	5
	4. worn rear cogs	replace cogs & chain	6, 4
	5. dirty or rusted chain	clean or replace chain	4
	6. bent rear derailleur	replace derailleur	5
	7. bent derailleur hanger	straighten hanger	15
	8. loose derailleur jockey wheel	tighten jockey wheel	5
	9. bent chain link	replace chain	4
	10. sticky rear shift cable	replace shift cable	5
chain slaps chainstay	1. chain too long	shorten chain	4
	2. weak rear derailleur spring	replace spring or derailleur	5
	3. terrain very bumpy	ignore noise; use lg chainring	n/a
derailleur hits spokes	1. maladjusted rear derailleur	adjust derailleur	5
	2. broken spoke	replace spoke	6
	3. bent rear derailleur	replace derailleur	5
	4. bent derailleur hanger	straighten or replace	15
knee pain	1. poor shoe cleat position	reposition cleat	9
	2. saddle too low or high	adjust saddle	10
	3. clip-in pedal has no float	get floating pedal	9
	4. foot rolled in or out	replace shoes or get orthotics	n/a
pain or fatigue when riding, particularly in the back, neck and arms	1. incorrect seat position	adjust seat position	10
	2. too much riding	build up miles gradually	
	3. incorrect stem length	replace stem	11
	4. poor frame fit	replace frame	15
pedal(s) move laterally clunk, click or twist while pedaling	1. loose crankarm	tighten crank bolt	8
	2. pedal loose in crank	tighten pedal to crank	9
	3. bent pedal axle	replace pedal or axle	9

SYMPTOM	LIKELY CAUSES	ACTION	CHAPTER
pedal(s)...	4. loose bottom bracket	adjust bottom bracket	8
(cont., see bottom	5. bent bottom bracket axle	replace bottom bracket or axle	8
of facing page)	6. bent crankarm	replace crankarm	8
	7. loose pedal bearings	adjust pedal bearings	9
pedal entry difficult	1. spring tension set high	reduce spring tension	9
(with clip-in pedals)	2. cleat guide loose or gone	tighten or replace	9
pedal release difficult	1. spring tension set high	reduce spring tension	9
(with clip-in pedals)	2. loose cleat on shoe	tighten cleat	9
	3. dry pedal spring pivot	oil spring pivots	9
	4. dirty pedals	clean and lube pedals	9
	5. bent pedal clips	replace pedals or clips	9
	6. dirty cleats	clean, lube cleats	9
pedal release too easy	1. release tension too low	increase release tension	9
(with clip-in pedals)	2. cleats worn out	replace cleats	9
rear shifting	1. maladjusted derailleur	adjust derailleur	5
working poorly	2. sticky or damaged cable	replace cable	5
	3. loose rear cogs	re-seat and tighten cogs	6
	4. worn rear cogs	replace cogs and chain	6, 4
	5. worn/damaged chain	replace chain	4
	6. see also *chain jams in rear* and *chain skips* above		
resistance	1. tire rubs frame or fork	adjust axle; true wheel	2, 6
while coasting	2. brake drags on rim	adjust brake	7
or pedaling	3. tire pressure too low	inflate tire	2, 6
	4. hub bearings too tight	adjust hubs	6
	5. hub bearings dirty/worn	overhaul hubs	6
	6. mud packed around tires	clean bike	2
resistance	1. bottom bracket too tight	adjust bottom bracket	8
while pedaling only	2. bottom bracket dirty/worn	overhaul bottom bracket	8
	3. chain dry/dirty/rusted	clean/lube or replace	4
	4. pedal bearings too tight	adjust pedal bearings	9
	5. pedal bearings dirty/worn	overhaul pedals	9
	6. bent chain ring rubs frame	straighten or replace	8
	7. true chainring rubs frame	adjust chain line	8
stiff steering	1. tight headset	adjust headset	11
tire bulged	1. broken casing threads	replace tire	6
	2. slipped tubular tire	re-glue tire and line up valve stem	6
tire pinch flats	1. insufficient pressure	pump tire higher	6
	2. tire diameter too small	replace with larger tire	6
tire valve-stem	1. tube slipped in tire	deflate and slide tire around rim	6
angled sharply	2. slipped tubular tire	re-glue tire and line up valve stem	6

STRANGE NOISES

Weird noises can be hard to locate; use this to assist in locating them.

SYMPTOM	LIKELY CAUSES	ACTION	CHAPTER
creaking noise	1. dry handlebar/stem joint	grease inside stem clamp	11
	2. loose seatpost	tighten seatpost	10
	3. loose shoe cleats	tighten cleats	9
	4. loose crankarm	tighten crankarm bolt	8
	5. cracked frame	replace frame	15
	6. dry, rusty seatpost	grease seatpost	10
	7. see *squeaking* below	see *squeaking* below	
clicking noise	1. cracked shoe cleats	replace cleats	9
	2. cracked shoe sole	replace shoes	9
	3. loose bottom bracket	tighten BB	8
	4. loose crankarm	tighten crankarm	8
	5. loose pedal	tighten pedal	9
chattering and vibration when braking	1. bent or dented rim	replace rim	13
	2. loose headset	adjust headset	11
	3. brake pads toed out	adjust brake pads	7
	4. wheel way out of round	true wheel	6
	5. greasy sections of rim	clean rim	6
	6. loose brake pivot bolts	tighten brake bolts	7
	7. rim worn through & ready to collapse	replace rim ASAP!	13
clunking from fork	1. headset loose	adjust headset	11
rubbing or scraping noise *when pedaling*	1. crossed chain	avoid extreme gears	5
	2. front derailleur rubbing	adjust front derailleur	5
	3. chain ring rubs frame	longer bottom bracket *or,*	8
		move bottom bracket over	8
rubbing, squealing or scraping noise *when coasting or pedaling*	1. tire dragging on frame	straighten wheel	2, 6
	2. tire dragging on fork	straighten wheel	2, 6
	3. brake dragging on rim	adjust brake	7
	4. dry hub dust seals	clean and lube dust seals	6
squeaking noise	1. dry hub or BB bearings	overhaul hubs or BB	6, 8
	2. dry pedal bushings	overhaul pedals	9
	3. squeaky saddle	replace saddle	10
	4. rusted or dry chain	lube or replace chain	4
squealing noise when braking	1. brake pads toed out	adjust brake pads	7
	2. greasy rims	clean rims and pads	7
	3. loose brake arms	tighten brake pivot bolt(s)	7
ticking noise when coasting	1. wheel magnet hits sensor	move computer sensor	12
	2. badly glued tubular	re-glue tire	6
ticking noise when braking	1. glue on rim sidewall	clean rim with solvent	6
	2. gouge in rim sidewall	sand rough spot	6
	3. high rim seam junction	ignore, or sand seam	6

APPENDIX B

gear chart

This gear table is based on a 700C x 28mm tire (671mm diameter). Your gear-development numbers may be slightly different if the diameter of the fully-inflated rear tire, with your weight on it, is not 671mm. Unless your bike has 650C, 24-inch, or some other non-standard-size wheels, these numbers will be very close.

If you want to have accurate gear development numbers for the tire you happen to have on at the time, at a certain inflation pressure, then measure the tire diameter very precisely with the procedure below. You can come up with your own gear chart by plugging the tire diameter into the following gear development formula, or by multiplying each number in this chart by the ratio of the tire diameter divided by 671mm (the tire diameter we used). Even easier, go to Tom Compton's interactive gear chart at:

www.analyticcycling.com/GearChart_Page.html

MEASURING TIRE DIAMETER

1. Sit on the bike with the tire pumped to your desired pressure.

2. Mark the spot on the rear rim that is at the bottom, and mark the floor adjacent to that spot.

3. Roll forward one wheel revolution, and mark the floor again where the mark on the rim is again at the bottom.

4. Measure the distance between the marks on the floor; this is the tire circumference at pressure with your weight on it.

5. Divide this number by π—3.14159—to get the diameter.

Note: *This roll-out procedure is also the method to measure the wheel size with which to calibrate your bike computer, except that it will be done on the front wheel with most computers (see Fig. 12.2).*

CHAINRING TEETH

COG TEETH	28	29	30	31	32	33	34	35	36	37	38	39	40	41
11	67.2	69.6	72.0	74.4	76.9	79.3	81.7	84.1	86.5	88.9	91.3	93.7	96.1	98.
12	61.6	63.8	66.0	68.2	70.4	72.6	74.8	77.1	79.3	81.5	83.7	85.9	88.1	90.
13	56.9	58.9	61.0	63.0	65.0	67.1	69.1	71.1	73.2	75.2	77.2	79.3	81.3	83.
14	52.8	54.7	56.6	58.5	60.4	62.3	64.2	66.0	67.9	69.8	71.7	73.6	75.5	77.
15	49.3	51.1	52.8	54.6	56.4	58.1	59.9	61.6	63.4	65.2	66.9	68.7	70.4	72.
16	46.2	47.9	49.5	51.2	52.8	54.5	56.1	57.8	59.4	61.1	62.7	64.4	66.0	67.
17	43.5	45.1	46.6	48.2	49.7	51.3	52.8	54.4	55.9	57.5	59.1	60.6	62.2	63.
18	41.1	42.6	44.0	45.5	47.0	48.4	49.9	51.4	52.8	54.3	55.8	57.2	58.7	60.
19	38.9	40.3	41.7	43.1	44.5	45.9	47.3	48.7	50.1	51.4	52.8	54.2	55.6	57.
20	37.0	38.3	39.6	40.9	42.3	43.6	44.9	46.2	47.6	48.9	50.2	51.5	52.8	54.
21	35.2	36.5	37.7	39.0	40.3	41.5	42.8	44.0	45.3	46.5	47.8	49.1	50.3	51.
22	33.6	34.8	36.0	37.2	38.4	39.6	40.8	42.0	43.2	44.4	45.6	46.8	48.0	49.
23	32.2	33.3	34.5	35.6	36.8	37.9	39.1	40.2	41.3	42.5	43.6	44.8	45.9	47.
24	30.8	31.9	33.0	34.1	35.2	36.3	37.4	38.5	39.6	40.7	41.8	42.9	44.0	45.
25	29.6	30.6	31.7	32.8	33.8	34.9	35.9	37.0	38.0	39.1	40.2	41.2	42.3	43.
26	28.4	29.5	30.5	31.5	32.5	33.5	34.5	35.6	36.6	37.6	38.6	39.6	40.6	41.
27	27.4	28.4	29.4	30.3	31.3	32.3	33.3	34.2	35.2	36.2	37.2	38.2	39.1	40
28	26.4	27.4	28.3	29.2	30.2	31.1	32.1	33.0	34.0	34.9	35.9	36.8	37.7	38

GEAR FORMULA:

Gear = (number of chainring teeth) x (tire diameter) ÷ (number of cog teeth)

If you want the gear in inches, put in the tire diameter in inches.

To find out how far you get with each pedal stroke (gear rollout), multiply the gear by π (3.14159).

gear chart

CHAINRING TEETH

GEAR INCHES

42	43	44	45	46	47	48	49	50	51	52	53	54	55
00.9	103.3	105.7	108.1	110.5	112.9	115.3	117.7	120.1	122.5	124.9	127.3	129.7	132.1
2.5	94.7	96.9	99.1	101.3	103.5	105.7	107.9	110.1	112.3	114.5	116.7	118.9	121.1
5.3	87.4	89.4	91.4	93.5	95.5	97.5	99.6	101.6	103.6	105.7	107.7	109.7	111.8
9.3	81.1	83.0	84.9	86.8	88.7	90.6	92.5	94.3	96.2	98.1	100.0	101.9	103.8
4.0	75.7	77.5	79.3	81.0	82.8	84.5	86.3	88.1	89.8	91.6	93.3	95.1	96.9
9.3	71.0	72.6	74.3	75.9	77.6	79.3	80.9	82.6	84.2	85.9	87.5	89.2	90.8
5.3	66.8	68.4	69.9	71.5	73.0	74.6	76.1	77.7	79.3	80.8	82.4	83.9	85.5
1.6	63.1	64.6	66.0	67.5	69.0	70.4	71.9	73.4	74.8	76.3	77.8	79.3	80.7
8.4	59.8	61.2	62.6	64.0	65.3	66.7	68.1	69.5	70.9	72.3	73.7	75.1	76.5
5.5	56.8	58.1	59.4	60.8	62.1	63.4	64.7	66.0	67.4	68.7	70.0	71.3	72.6
2.8	54.1	55.4	56.6	57.9	59.1	60.4	61.6	62.9	64.2	65.4	66.7	67.9	69.2
0.4	51.6	52.8	54.0	55.2	56.4	57.6	58.8	60.0	61.2	62.4	63.6	64.8	66.0
8.2	49.4	50.5	51.7	52.8	54.0	55.1	56.3	57.4	58.6	59.7	60.9	62.0	63.2
5.2	47.3	48.4	49.5	50.6	51.7	52.8	53.9	55.0	56.1	57.2	58.3	59.4	60.5
1.4	45.4	46.5	47.6	48.6	49.7	50.7	51.8	52.8	53.9	54.9	56.0	57.1	58.1
2.7	43.7	44.7	45.7	46.7	47.8	48.8	49.8	50.8	51.8	52.8	53.9	54.9	55.9
1.1	42.1	43.1	44.0	45.0	46.0	47.0	47.9	48.9	49.9	50.9	51.9	52.8	53.8
9.6	40.6	41.5	42.5	43.4	44.3	45.3	46.2	47.2	48.1	49.1	50.0	50.9	51.9

APPENDIX C

ROAD BIKE FITTING

If you are getting a new bike, get one that fits you properly. Fit should be the primary consideration when selecting a bike; you can adapt to heavier bikes and bikes not painted your favorite color, but your body will soon protest on one that doesn't fit. The simple need to protect your more sensitive parts should keep you away from a bike without sufficient standover clearance (Fig. C.1), but there are a lot of other factors to consider as well. Make certain that your bike has enough reach to ensure that you don't bang your knees on the handlebar, that your neck and back are not in agony after a long ride, and that your weight is distributed over the wheels evenly. And, if you are racing triathlon and time trials, aerodynamics and efficient positioning on aero' handlebars will be important. An improperly sized bike will cause you to ride with less efficiency and more discomfort. So, take some time and find out how you can pick the properly sized bike.

I've outlined two methods for finding your frame size. The first is a simple method of checking your fit to fully assembled bikes at a bike shop. The second is a bit more elaborate, since it involves taking body measurements. This more detailed approach will allow you to calculate the proper frame dimensions whether the bike is assembled or not.

C.1 **standover height and bottom-bracket height**

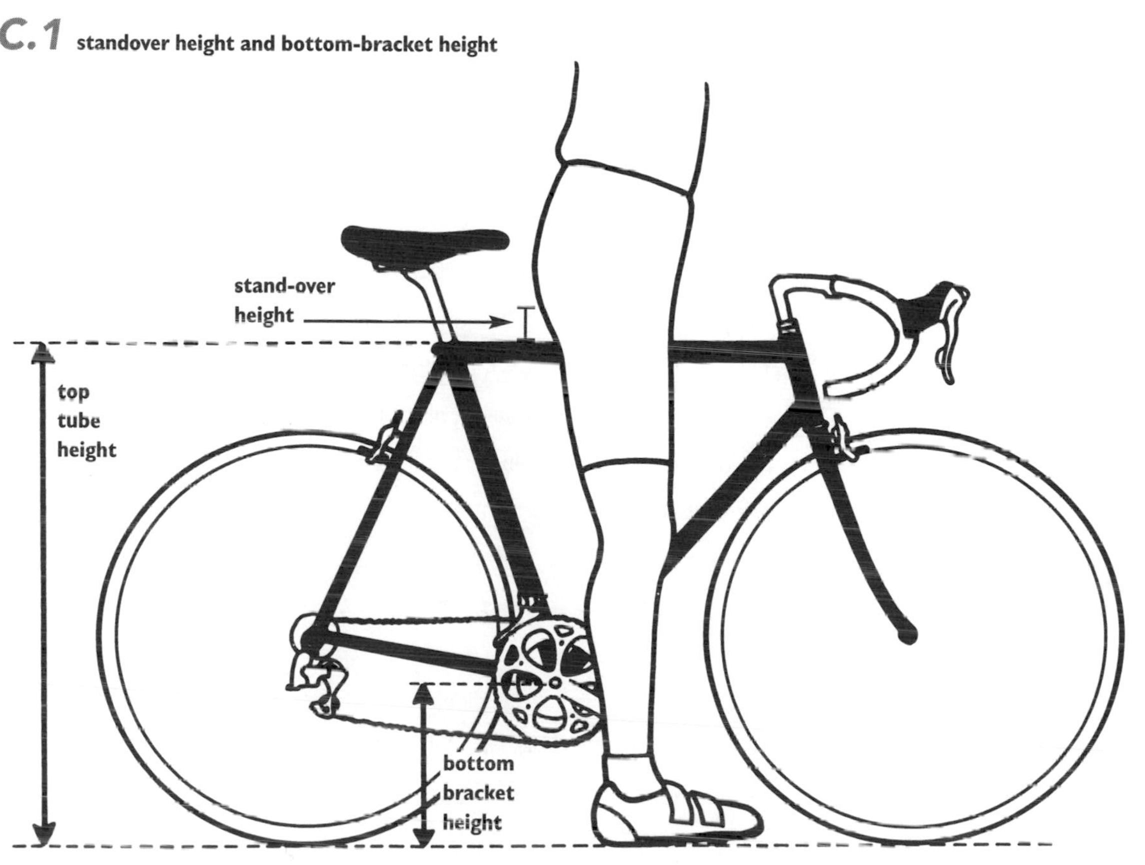

C-1: SELECTING THE SIZE OF A BUILT-UP BIKE

1. Standover height

Stand over the bike's top tube and lift the bike straight up until the top tube hits your crotch. The wheels should be at least 1 inch off of the ground to ensure that you can jump off of the bike safely without hitting your crotch. On a bike with sloping top tube, there is no maximum measurement. On a bike with a level top tube, unless the frame has been built with a head tube with extra extension above the top tube to lift the stem higher, you probably don't want any more than 3 or 4 inches of standover.

Note: *If you have 2 inches of standover clearance over one bike, do not assume that another bike with the same listed frame size will also offer you the same standover clearance. Manufacturers measure frame size using a variety of methods. They also may slope their top tubes differently and use different bottom bracket heights (Fig. C.1), all of which affect the final standover height.*

All manufacturers measure the frame size up the seat tube from the center of the bottom bracket, but the top of the measurement varies. Some manufacturers measure to the center of the top tube ("center-to-center" measurement), some measure to the top of the top tube ("center-to-top"), and others measure to the top of the seat tube (also called "center-to-top"), even though there is wide variation in the length of the seat post collar above the top tube. Obviously, each of these methods will have a different "frame size" for the same frame.

No matter how the frame size is measured, the standover height of a bike depends on the slope of the top tube. Most road bikes have level top tubes, but top tubes that slant up to the front are becoming increasingly more common, and standover clearance above a sloping tube is obviously a function of where you are standing. With an up-angled top tube, stand over it a few inches forward of the nose of the saddle, and then lift the bike up into your crotch to measure standover clearance.

Standover height is also a function of bottom bracket height above the ground, but there is normally not substantial variation between sizes and brands of road bikes.

Unless the manufacturer lists the standover height in its brochure and you know your inseam length, you need to actually stand over the bike.

Another note: *If you are short and cannot find a frame size small enough to get at least one inch of standover clearance, consider a bike with 650C (26-inch) wheels rather than 700C.*

2. Knee-to-handlebar clearance

Make sure your knee cannot hit the handlebar (Fig. C.2). Do this standing out of the saddle as well as seated and with the front wheel turned slightly, to make sure that the knee will not hit when you are in the most awkward pedaling position you might use.

3. Handlebar reach and drop

Ride the bike. See if the reach feels comfortable to you when holding the bars on the flat section adjacent the stem clamp, on top of the brake hoods, or in the drops. Make sure it is easy to grab the brake levers. Make sure your knees do not hit your elbows as you pedal (Fig. C.5). Make sure that the stem can be raised or lowered enough to achieve a comfortable handlebar height.

Note: *Threadless headsets allow very limited adjustment of stem height. Large changes in height require a change in stems.*

4. "Pedal overlap"

"Pedal overlap" is a misnomer, since you are actually interested in whether the toe, not the pedal,

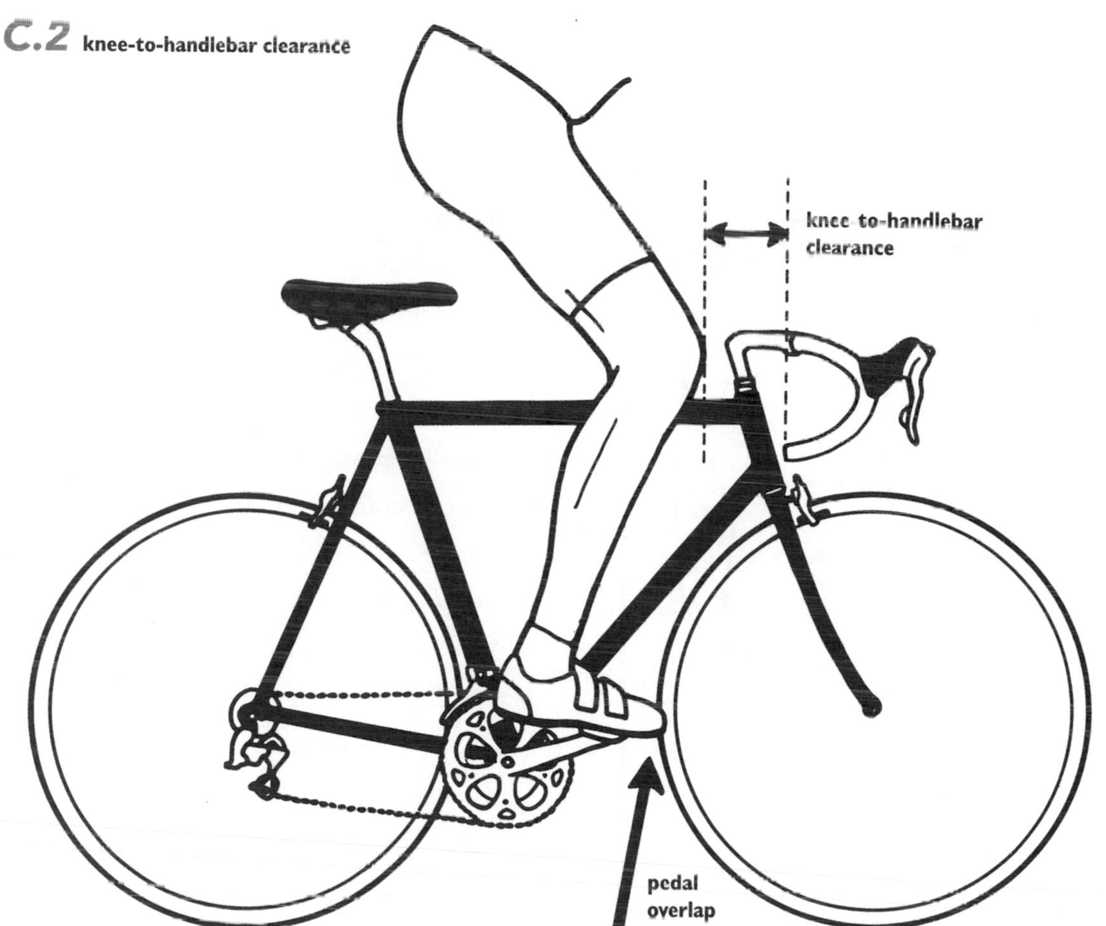

C.2 knee-to-handlebar clearance

can hit the front tire when turning sharply at low speeds. Sitting on the bike with the crankarms horizontal and the foot on the pedal, turn the handlebars and check that your toe does not hit the front tire (Fig. C.2). Toe overlap is to be avoided for any kind of slow-speed riding, since making a slow, tight turn in a parking lot can put you on your nose. Toe overlap it is not an issue for most riding, since the speeds are high enough on the road that turning the bike does not require turning the front wheel at enough of an angle to hit the foot.

C-2: CHOOSING A FRAME SIZE FROM BODY MEASUREMENTS

You will need a second person to assist you.

By taking three easy measurements (Fig. C.3), most people can get a very good frame fit. When designing a custom frame, I go through a more complex procedure than this, involving more measurements. For picking an off-the-shelf bike, the following method works well. You can download a measurement form to use for this at www.zinncycles.com.

1. Measure your inseam

Spread your stocking feet about 2 inches apart, and measure up from the floor to a broomstick held level and lifted firmly up into your crotch. You can also use a large book and slide it up a wall to keep the top edge horizontal—as you pull it up as hard as you can—into your crotch. You can mark the top of the book on the wall and measure up from the floor to the mark.

2. Measure your inseam-plus-torso length

Hold a pencil horizontally in your sternal notch, the U-shaped bone depression just below your Adam's Apple. Standing up straight in front of a

C.3 body measurements

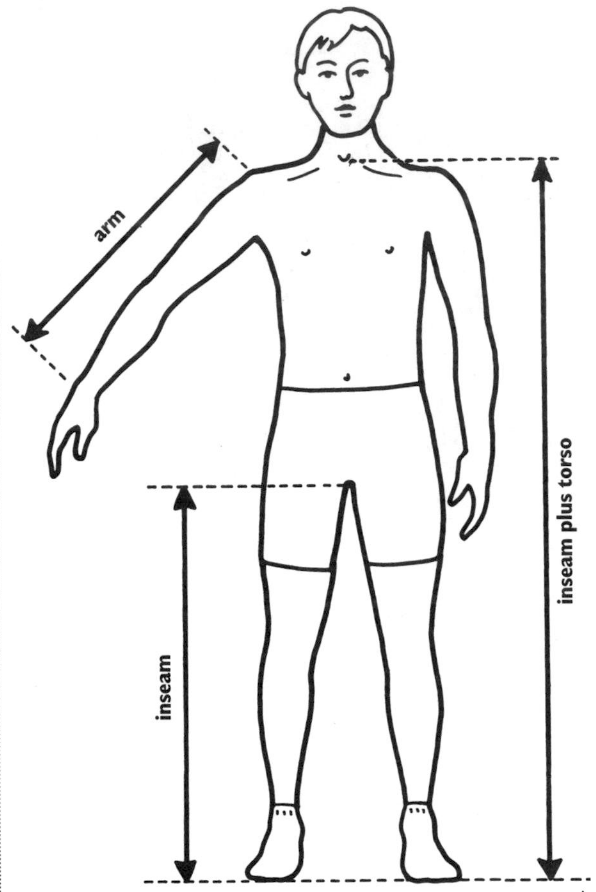

wall, mark the wall with the horizontal pencil. Measure up from the floor to the mark.

3. Measure your arm length

Hold your arm out from your side at a 45-degree angle with your elbow straight. Measure from the sharp bone point directly behind your shoulder joint to the wrist bone on your little finger side.

4. Find your frame size

Subtract 27.5 to 32cm (10.8 inches-12.6 inches) from your inseam length. This length is your frame size (also known as seat-tube length) measured along the seat tube from the center of the bottom bracket to the top of the top tube (Fig. C.4). If the frame you are interested in has a sloping top tube, you need a bike with a shorter seat tube. In the case of a sloping top tube, project a horizontal line back to the seat tube (or seatpost) from the top of the top tube at the center of its length (Fig. C.4). Mark the seat tube or seat post at this line. Measure from the center of the bottom bracket to this mark; this length should be 27.5-32cm less than your inseam measurement.

Also, if the bike has a bottom bracket higher than 27cm (10.6 inches), subtract the additional bottom-bracket height from the seat-tube length as well.

Generally, smaller riders will want to subtract close to 27.5cm from their inseam measurement, while taller riders will subtract closer to 32cm. Since an average bottom-bracket height on a road bike is 26.5cm, subtracting any less than 27.5cm could result in less than one inch (2.5cm) of standover clearance. But there is considerable range here. The top-tube length is more important than the frame size, and, if you have short torso and arms, you can use a small frame to get the right top-tube length, as long as you can raise your bars as high as you need them.

If you are short and cannot find a bike small enough for you to get at least an inch of standover clearance, consider one with 650C (26 inches) or even 24-inch wheels rather than 700C.

Note: *A step-through frame (i.e., "women's" frame, "mixte frame," or "girl's bike") having a steeply up-angled top tube meeting near the bottom bracket shell makes seat-tube length irrelevant for determining standover clearance. With a step-through bike, the only considerations will be horizontal and vertical reach to the bars.*

5. Find your top-tube length

To find your torso length, subtract your inseam measurement (found in Step 1) from your inseam-plus-torso measurement (found in Step 2). Add this torso length to your arm length measurement (found in Step 3). To find the top-tube length, multi-

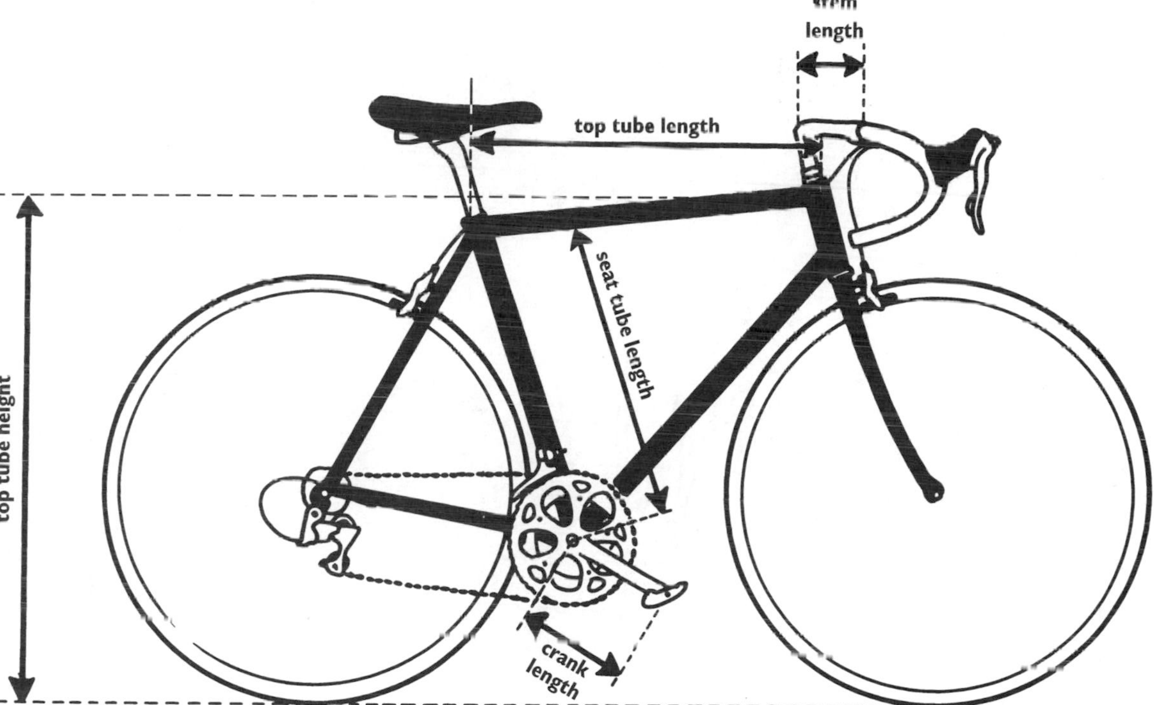

ply this arm-plus-torso measurement by a factor in the range between 0.47 and 0.485. If you are a casual rider, use 0.47; if you are a very aggressive rider, use 0.485, and, if you are in between, use a factor in between. This top-tube length is measured horizontally from the center of the seat tube to the center of the head tube (Fig. C.4).

But if this is a bike you plan to set up exclusively with aero' handlebars and race in draft-illegal triathlons or time trials, you will generally want a longer top tube. Use 0.495 as the multiplier to find the top tube in this case. If the seat angle on the bike you will be using for this purpose is not very steep—less than 75 degrees—you will likely need to add more length yet to the top tube. This would occur if you will be pushing your saddle all of the way forward or using a forward-offset seatpost to position yourself in a forward position. The forward-set saddle will consume much of your reach to the bars, so you will need more top-tube length to stretch out properly. The longer top tube will also insure a more even weight distribution over the wheels and prevent you from using such a long stem and bar that you will be hanging way out over the front of the bike with too much weight on the front wheel.

Note: *On a sloping-top-tube bike, the actual horizontal top-tube length is less than the length found by measuring along the top tube.*

6. Find your stem length

Multiply the arm-plus-torso length you found in step 5 by 0.09 to 0.11 to find the stem length. Again, a casual rider will multiply by 0.09 or so, while an aggressive rider will multiply by closer to 0.11. This is a starting stem length. Finalize the stem length (Fig. C.4) once you are sitting on the bike and see what feels best.

7. Determine crankarm length

Generally, road crankarms come in 2.5mm length increments (Fig C.4) from 165mm to

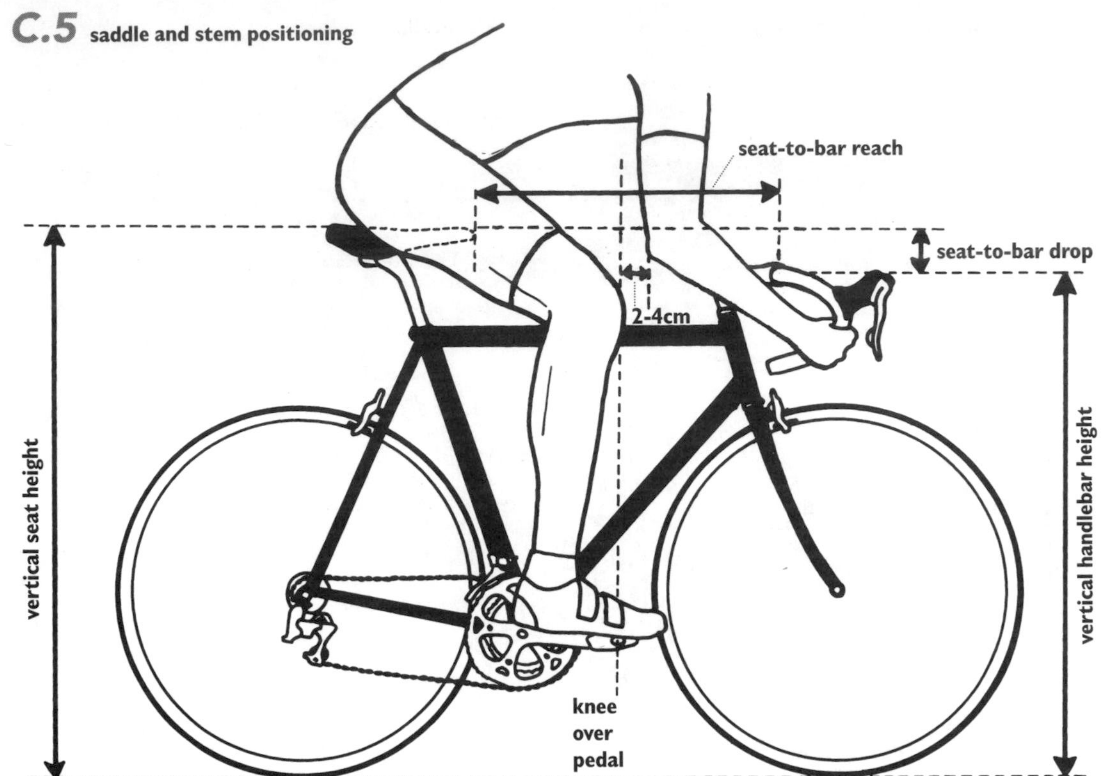

180mm—although 167.5mm is often hard to find. Longer than 175mm can usually only be found on high-end cranks, and Campagnolo no longer makes longer than 175mm in any model. It is possible to find 185mm and even 200mm and over from some small manufacturers.

Given that there is no consensus on ideal crank length, I will give you a simple selection method that works well for most people. If the frame size you determined in step four is less than 45cm, use 165mm cranks; if your frame is between 46 and 49cm, use 167.5s; 50-53, use 170cm; 54-57, use 172.5; 58-61, 175; 61-64, 177.5, and if your frame size is 65cm or bigger use 180mm or longer. If your riding is focused on time trialing, triathlon, or hill climbing, try 2.5mm longer than the recommendations above.

I have done numerous crank-length tests for *VeloNews*, and the results show that there is no one crank length that works for a given body size. It is worth experimenting to see what you like.

8. Choosing handlebar width and drop

Your handlebars should be the same width or slightly wider than the distance from the center of the top of one upper-arm bone—humerus—to the other. You can hold the front of the bar up to your shoulders and see if each side meets in the center of the top of each humerus or slightly overlaps the outside of your arms. That way, your arms will support your shoulders straight in line, and your chest will be able to open for efficient breathing.

If you are a small person, you will want a shallow drop bar, while a big person will want a deep drop.

If you have small hands, look for a bar with a bend specifically made to reduce the reach to an STI or ErgoPower brake lever.

C-3: POSITIONING OF SADDLE AND HANDLEBARS

The frame fit is only part of the equation. Except for the standover clearance, a good frame fit is relatively meaningless if the seat setback, seat height,

handlebar height, and handlebar reach are not set correctly for you.

1. Saddle height

When your foot is at the bottom of the stroke, lock your knee without rocking your hips. Do this sitting on your bike on a trainer with someone else observing. Your foot should be level, or the heel should be slightly higher than the ball of the foot. Another way to determine seat height is to take your inseam measurement (found in step 1 under "Choosing frame size from your body measurements", above) and multiply it by 1.09; this is the length from the center of the pedal spindle (when the pedal is down) to one of the points on the top of the saddle where your butt bones (ischial tuberosities) contact it. Adjust the seat height (Chapter 10) until you get it the proper height.

Note: *These two methods yield similar results, although the measurement-multiplying method is dependent on the thickness of your shoe sole and the pedal. Either method yields a biomechanically efficient pedaling position.*

2. Saddle setback

Sit on your bike on a stationary trainer with cranks horizontal and forward foot at the angle it is at that point when pedaling. Have a friend drop a plumb line from the front of your knee below your knee cap. You can use a heavy ring or washer tied to a string for the plumb line. The plumb line should bisect the pedal axle or pass up to 2cm behind it (Fig. C.5); you will need to lean the knee out to get the string to hang clear. A saddle positioned fore-aft in this manner encourages smooth pedaling at high rpm, while 2cm behind the pedal spindle encourages powerful seated climbing.

Slide the saddle back and forth on the seatpost (Chapter 10) until you achieve the desired fore-aft saddle position. Set the saddle level or very close to it. Re-check the seat height in Step 1 above, since fore-aft saddle movements affect seat-to-pedal distance as well.

For draft-illegal-triathlon and time-trial purposes, most riders using aero' bars will want to position their saddle considerably further forward than this, however. Being forward will allow the shoulders to drop low and out of the wind without constraining the hips and having the knees hit the chest—or swing outward to avoid hitting. If it is a frame built for triathlon and/or time trials, it will generally have a steep—maybe 76- to 78-degree—seat angle, making the forward seat position easy to accomplish. If not, you may need to get a forward-position seatpost, but this may make your reach to the bars too short or require such a long stem that you will be hanging dangerously far out over the front wheel. Set the fore-aft seat position so that you are not constricted at the hips when your shoulder joint is the same level as your hip joint. You may need to tip the saddle very slightly downward and even perhaps turn it a few degrees from straight ahead to find some more crotch comfort. Speed can be painful.

3. Handlebar height

Measure the handlebar height relative to the saddle height by measuring the vertical distance of the saddle and bar up from the floor (Fig. C.5). How much higher the saddle is than your bar, or vice versa, depends on flexibility, riding style, overall size, and type of riding you prefer.

Aggressive and/or tall riders will prefer to have their saddle 10cm or more higher than the bars. Shorter riders will want proportionately less drop, as will less aggressive riders. Generally, people beginning at road riding will like their bars high and can lower them as they gain flexibility and become more comfortable with the bike.

If in doubt, start with 4cm of drop and vary it from there. The higher the bar, the more weight is

C.6 aero' bar position

carried on your butt, and the more wind resistance you can expect. Change the bar height by raising or lowering the stem (Chapter 11), or by switching stems and/or bars.

Again, threadless headsets allow only limited stem-height adjustment without substitution of a differently angled stem.

For time trials and draft-illegal triathlons on flat or rolling terrain, you will want your aero' bar elbow pads low enough to get your back close to parallel with the ground (Fig. C.6). This will make significant aerodynamic difference, but it may take a while to get used to it, so you should work the handlebar height down gradually. Also, you may find a position that is this low impossible to maintain for an Ironman distance or other long event.

4. Setting handlebar reach

The reach from the saddle to the handlebar is also very dependent on personal preference. More aggressive riders will want a more stretched position than will casual riders. This length is subjective, and I usually need to look at the rider on the bike and get a feel for how they would be comfortable and efficient.

A useful starting place is to drop a plumb line from the back of your elbow with your arms bent in a comfortable riding position. This plane determined by your elbows and the plumb line should be 2-4cm horizontally ahead of each knee at the point in the pedal stroke when the crank arm is horizontal forward (Fig. C.5). The idea is to select a position you find comfortable and efficient; listen to what your body wants.

Vary the saddle-to-bar distance by changing stem length (Chapter 11), not by changing the seat fore-aft position, which is based on pedaling efficiency (Step 2 above) and not on reach.

On aero' bars, set the reach so that a plumb bob from your ear comes out over your elbow (Fig. C.6). This will position your upper arms to be angled slightly forward.

Note: *There is no single formula for determining han-*

dlebar reach and height. Using the all-too-common method of placing your elbow against the saddle and seeing if your fingertips reach the handlebar is close to useless. Similarly, the oft-suggested method of seeing if the handlebar obscures your vision of the front hub is not worth the brief time it takes to look, being dependent on elbow bend and front end geometry. Another method involving dropping a plumb bob from the rider's nose is dependent on the handlebar height and elbow bend and thus does not lend itself to a proscribed relationship for all riders.

5. Other settings for aero' handlebars

The elbow pads should be positioned for both comfort, and in the case of racing in time trials and draft-illegal triathlons on flat or rolling terrain, they should be placed close to each other as well.

And the further forward from your elbows the pads are, the more leverage you will have smashing the pads against on your forearms. Achieving pad support under the elbows can be accomplished by using aero' bars with the pads cantilevered back behind the bars—toward the rider—or by using a shorter stem and a longer aero' bar.

Narrow elbows makes a big difference in aerodynamic efficiency. Wind tunnel tests consistently show that narrowness of knees and elbows makes a very large difference. But if you can't find a comfortable position to breathe in and pull hard and handle the bike well with narrowly spaced elbow pads, move them out until you can.

The tilt of the aero' bar is a matter of personal preference. Wind tunnel tests have shown time and again that many different angles appear to be equally efficient aerodynamically. Start with a moderate up-angle to the bar, perhaps 5 or 10 degrees (Fig. C.6).

APPENDIX D

glossary

adjustable cup: The non-drive side cup in the bottom bracket. This cup is removed for maintenance of the bottom bracket spindle and bearings, and it adjusts the bearings. Term sometimes applied to top headset cup as well.

AheadSet: a style of headset that allows the use of a fork with a threadless steering tube. Also called "threadless headset."

Allen key (Allen wrench, hex key): a hexagonal wrench that fits inside the head of the bolt.

anchor bolt (cable anchor, cable-fixing bolt): a bolt securing a cable to a component.

axle: the shaft about which a part turns, usually on bearings or bushings.

axle overlock dimension: the length of a hub axle from dropout to dropout, referring to the distance from locknut face to locknut face.

ball bearing: a part consisting of steel balls running on a circular track that supports a shaft and allows it to spin freely; any of the steel balls from a ball bearing.

barrel adjuster: a threaded cable stop that allows for fine adjustment of cable tension. Barrel adjusters are commonly found on rear derailleurs, shift-cable stops and brake calipers.

BB: see "bottom bracket."

bearing: see "ball bearing."

bearing cup: see "cup."

bearing race: see "race."

binder bolt: a bolt clamping a seat post in a frame, a handlebar inside a stem, or a threadless steering tube inside a stem clamp.

bottom bracket (BB): the assembly that allows the crank to rotate. Generally the bottom bracket assembly includes bearings, an axle, a fixed cup, an adjustable cup, and sometimes a lockring.

bottom-bracket shell: the cylindrical housing at the bottom of a bicycle frame through which the bottom-bracket axle passes.

brake boss (brake post or pivot; cantilever boss, post, or pivot): a fork- or frame-mounted pivot for a brake arm.

brake bridge: the cross tube between the seatstays to which a rear road brake is bolted.

brake pad (brake block): a block of rubber or similar material used to slow the bike by creating friction on the rim or other braking surface.

brake post: (see "brake boss.")

brake shoe: the metal pad holder that holds the brake pad to the brake arm.

braze-on: a generic term for most metal frame attachments, even those welded or glued on.

brazing: a method commonly used to construct steel bicycle frames. Brazing involves the use of brass or silver solder to connect frame tubes and attach various "braze-on" items including brake bosses, cable guides and rack mounts to the frame.

bushing: a metal or plastic sleeve that acts as a simple bearing on pedals, suspension forks, suspension swing arms, and jockey wheels.

butted tubing: a common type of frame tubing with varying wall thicknesses. Butted tubing is designed to accommodate high stress points at the ends of the tube by being thicker there.

cable (inner wire): wound or braided wire strands used to operate brakes and derailleurs.

cable anchor: see "anchor bolt."

cable end: a cap on the end of a cable to keep it from fraying.

cable-fixing bolt: see "anchor bolt."

cable hanger: cable stop on a fork- or seatstay-arch used to stop the brake cable housing for a cantilever brake.

cable housing: a metal-reinforced exterior sheath through which a cable passes.

cable housing stop: see "cable stop."

cable-fixing bolt: an anchor bolt that attaches cables to brakes or derailleurs.

cable stop: a fitting on the frame, fork, or stem at which a cable-housing segment terminates.

cage: two guiding plates through which the chain travels. Both the front and rear derailleurs have cages. The cage on the rear also holds the jockey pulleys. Also: a water bottle holder.

cantilever boss: see "brake boss."

cantilever brake: a cable-operated rim brake that moves two opposing arms, pivoting on frame- or fork-mounted posts, toward the braking surface of the rim.

cantilever pivot: see "brake boss."

cantilever post: see "brake boss."

cartridge bearing: ball bearings encased in a cartridge consisting of steel inner and outer rings, ball retainers, and, sometimes, bearing covers.

cassette hub: a rear hub that has a built-in freewheel mechanism. Also: *freehub.*

chain: a series of metal links held together by pins and used to transmit energy from the crank to the rear wheel.

chain line: the imaginary line connecting the centerline between double chainrings (or the center of the middle chainring) with the middle of the cogset. This line should in theory be straight and parallel with the vertical plane passing through the center of the bicycle. This is measured as the distance from the center of the seat tube to the centerline between chainrings (or the center of the middle chainring).

chain link: a single unit of bicycle chain consisting of four plates with a roller on each end and in the center.

chainring: a multiple-tooth sprocket attached to the right crankarm.

chainstays: the tubes leading from the bottom bracket shell to the rear hub axle.

chain suck: the dragging of the chain by the chainring past the release point at the bottom of the chainring. The chain can be dragged upward and until it is jammed between the chainring and the chainstay.

chainring-nut spanner: a tool used to secure the chainring nuts while tightening the chainring bolts.

chain whip (chain wrench): a steel lever attached to two lengths of chain. This tool is used to remove the rear cogs on a freehub.

chase, wild goose: see "goose."

circlip (snap ring, Jesus clip): a C-shaped spring-steel ring that fits in a groove to retain parts.

clincher rim: a rim with a high sidewall with a "hook" facing inward to constrain the bead of a clincher tire.

clincher tire: a tire with a "bead," to hook into the rim sides. A separate inner tube is inserted inside the tire.

clip-in pedal (clipless pedal): a pedal that relies on spring-loaded clips to grip the rider's shoe, without the use of toe clips and straps.

clipless pedal: see "clip-in pedal."

cog: a sprocket attached to the rear hub.

compression damping: the diminishing of the speed of the compression of a spring on impact.

cone: a threaded conical nut that serves to hold a set of bearings in place and also provides a smooth surface upon which those bearings can roll.

crankarm: the lever attached at the bottom bracket spindle used to transmit a rider's energy to the chain.

crankarm-fixing bolt: the bolt attaching the crank to the bottom bracket spindle.

crankset: the assembly that includes a bottom bracket, two crankarms, chainring set and accompanying nuts and bolts.

cross three: a pattern used by wheel builders, that calls for each spoke to cross three others in its path from the hub to the rim.

cup: a concave bearing surface that a set of bearings roll in.

damper: a mechanism in a suspension fork or shock that provides damping of the spring's oscillation.

damping: the diminishing of the oscillation of a spring, as in a suspension fork or shock.

derailleur: a gear-changing device that allows a rider to move the chain from one cog or chainring to another.

derailleur hanger: a metal extension of the right rear dropout to which the rear derailleur attaches.

diamond frame: the traditional bicycle frame shape.

dish: a difference in spoke tension on the two sides of the rear wheel so that the rim is centered in the frame.

disc brake: a brake that stops the bike by squeezing brake pads against a circular disc attached to the wheel.

double: a two-chainring drivetrain setup (as opposed to a three-chainring, or "triple", drivetrain).

down tube: the tube that connects the head tube and bottom-bracket shell together.

drivetrain: the crankarms, chainrings, bottom bracket, front derailleur, chain, rear derailleur, and freewheel (or cassette).

drop: the vertical distance between the center of the bottom bracket and a horizontal line passing through the wheel hub centers.

dropouts: the slots in the fork and rear triangle where the wheel axles attach.

dual-pivot sidepull brake: a sidepull brake whose arms pivot at two points rather than one.

dust cap: a protective cap keeping dirt out of a part.

elastomer: a urethane spring used in suspension mechanisms.

ErgoPower: Campagnolo integrated road brake/shift lever.

ferrule: a cap for the end of cable housing.

fixed cup: the non-adjustable cup of the bottom bracket located on the drive side of the bottom bracket.

flange: the largest diameter of the hub where the spoke heads are anchored.

fork: the part that attaches the front wheel to the frame.

fork crown: the cross piece connecting the fork legs to the steering tube.

fork ends: see "dropouts."

fork rake (rake): the perpendicular offset distance of the front axle from an imaginary extension of the steering tube centerline (steering axis).

fork tips (fork ends): see "dropouts."

frame: the central structure of a bicycle to which all of the parts are attached.

freehub: see "cassette hub."

freewheel: a cluster of cogs that only engages in a clockwise direction, allowing a rider to stop pedaling as the bicycle is moving forward.

friction shifter: a traditional (non-indexed) shifter attached to the frame or handle bars. Cable tension is maintained by a combination of friction washers and bolts.

front triangle (main triangle): the head tube, top tube, down tube and seat tube of a bike frame.

"girl's" bike: see "step-through frame."

goose chase, wild: see "wild."

Grip Shift: a shifter that is integrated with the handle bar grip. The rider shifts gears by twisting the grip. See also "twist shifter."

hex key: see "Allen key."

headset: the cup, lock ring, and bearings that hold the fork to the frame and allow the fork to spin in the frame.

head tube: the front tube of the frame through which the steering tube of the fork passes. The head tube is attached to the top tube and down tube and holds the headset.

hub: the central part of a wheel to which the spokes are anchored and through which the wheel axle passes.

hub brake: a disc, drum or coaster brake that stops the wheel with friction applied to a braking surface attached to the hub.

hydraulic brake: a type of brake that uses oil pressure to move the brake pads against the braking surface.

index shifter: a shifter that clicks into fixed positions as it moves the derailleur from gear to gear.

inner wire: see "cable."

Jesus clip: see "circlip."

jockey wheel (jockey pulley): a circular cog-shaped-pulley attached to the rear derailleur used to guide, apply tension to, and laterally move the chain from rear cog to rear cog.

knobby tire: an all-terrain tire with a raised tread for traction.

link: (1) a pivoting steel hook on a V-brake arm that the cable-guide "noodle" hooks into. (2) see "chain link."

locknut: a nut that binds an adjacent nut to prevent it from turning. A locknut can serve to secure the bearing adjustment in a headset, hub or pedal.

lockring: a large, thin locknut. The outer ring that tightens the adjustable cup of a bottom bracket against the face of the bottom-bracket shell.

lock washer: a notched or toothed washer that serves to hold surrounding nuts and washers in position.

master link: a unique link different from all of the others used to connect a together.

Mektronic: Mavic electronic rear-derailleur system.

mixte frame: see "step-through frame."

mounting bolt: a bolt that mounts a part to a frame, fork, or component. (see also "pivot bolt.")

needle bearing: steel cylindrical cartridge with rod-shaped coaxial rollers.

nipple: a thin nut designed to receive the end of a spoke and seat in the holes of a rim.

noodle: curved cable-guide pipe on a V-brake arm which stops the cable housing and directs the cable to the cable anchor bolt on the opposite arm.

outer wire: see "cable housing."

outer wire stop: see "cable stop."

pedal: the platform connected to the crankarm on which the foot sits.

pedal overlap: contact of the toe with the front tire when in place on the pedal with the crankarm positioned horizontally forward.

pin spanner: a V-shaped wrench with an end pin at each of its two tips to fit into holes in a lockring.

pivot bolt: a bolt on which a brake or derailleur part pivots.

preload: see spring preload.

Presta valve: thin, metal tire valve that uses a locking nut to stop air flow from the tire.

quick release: (1) the tightening lever and shaft used to attach a wheel to the fork or rear dropouts without using axle nuts. (2) a quick-opening lever and shaft pinching the seat post inside the seat tube, in lieu of a wrench-operated bolt. (3) a quick cable-release on a brake. (4) a fixing mechanism that can be quickly opened and closed, as on a brake cable or wheel axle. (5) a fixing bolt that can be quickly opened and closed by a lever.

quill: the vertical tube of a stem which inserts into the fork steering tube. It has an expander wedge and bolt inside to secure the stem to the steering tube.

race: a ring-shaped surface on which the bearings roll freely.

Rapid-fire shifter: an indexing shifter manufactured by Shimano for use on mountain bikes with two separate levers operating each shift cable.

rear triangle: the rear portion of the bicycle frame, including the seat stays, the chain stays and the seat tube.

rebound damping: the diminishing of rebound speed of a spring.

rim: the outer hoop of a wheel to which the tire is attached.

saddle (seat): a platform, usually made of leather and/or plastic, upon which the rider sits.

saddle rails: the two metal rods supporting the saddle and to which the seatpost is clamped.

Schrader valve: a high-pressure air valve with a spring-loaded air-release pin inside. Schrader valves are found on some bicycle tubes and air-sprung suspension forks as well as on adjustable rear shocks and automobile tires and tubes.

sealed bearing: a bearing enclosed in an attempt to keep contaminants out. (See also "cartridge bearing.")

seat cluster: the intersection of the seat tube, top tube, and seat stays.

seat: see "saddle."

seat post: the tube inserted into the frame to which the saddle is secured.

sew-up tire: see "tubular tire."

sidepull brake: a road brake with two arms extending to the side engaged by a cable.

sidepull cantilever brake: see "V-brake."

skewer: a long rod; a hub quick-release; a shaft passing through a stack of elastomer bumpers in a suspension fork.

snapring: see "circlip."

spanner: wrench (British).

spider: a star-shaped piece of metal that connects the right crank arm to the chainrings.

spokes: wires that connect the hub to the rim of a wheel.

spring: an elastic contrivance, which, when compressed, returns to its original shape by virtue of its elasticity. In bicycle suspension applications, the spring used is normally either an elastic polymer cylinder, a coil of steel or titanium wire, or compressed air.

spring preload: the initial loading of a spring so part of its compression range is taken up prior to impact.

sprocket: a circular, multiple-toothed piece of metal that engages a chain. (See also: "cog" and "chain ring.")

standover clearance ("standover height"): the distance between the top tube of the bike and the rider's crotch when standing over the bicycle.

star nut ("Star-fangled nut"): a tanged nut that is forced down into the steering tube and anchors the stem bolt of a threadless headset.

steering axis: the imaginary line about which the fork rotates.

steering tube: the vertical tube on a fork that is attached to the fork crown and fits inside the head tube.

step-through frame ("women's frame"; "girl's bike"; "mixte frame"): a bicycle frame with a steeply up-angled top tube connecting the bottom of the seat tube to the top of the head tube. The frame design is intended to provide ease of stepping over the frame and ample standover clearance.

STI ("Shimano Total Integration"): Shimano integrated brake/shift lever.

straddle cable: short segment of cable connecting two brake arms together.

straddle-cable holder: see "yoke."

swingarm: the movable rear end of a rear-suspension frame.

TIG welding: electric-arc welding using a tungsten electrode (from which the arc jumps) surrounded by a stream of an inert gas (such as argon) to prevent oxidation of the hot weld.

threadless headset: see "AheadSet."

three cross: see "cross three."

thumb shifter: a thumb-operated shift lever attached on top of the handlebars.

top tube: the tube that connects the seat tube to the head tube.

triple: a term used to describe the three-chainring combination attached to the right crankarm.

tub: see "tubular tire."

tubular: see "tubular tire."

tubular rim: a rim for a tubular tire. A tubular rim is generally double-walled and concave on top. It is devoid of hook sides to constrain the beads of a clincher tire.

tubular tire: (also, "tubular," "sew-up," "tub"(British)), a tire without a bead. The tube is surrounded by the tire casing, which is sewed together on the bottom. A layer of cotton tape is usually glued over the stitching, and rim cement is applied to the base tape and the rim to bond the tire to the rim.

twist shifter: a cable-pulling derailleur-control handle surrounding the handlebar; it is twisted forward or back to cause the derailleur to shift. (see also "Grip Shift.")

U-brake: a brake consisting of two arms shaped like inverted L's affixed to posts on the frame or fork.

V-brake (sidepull cantilever): a cable-operated cantilever rim brake consisting of two vertical brake arms with a cable link and cable guide pipe on one arm and a cable anchor on the opposite arm.

welding: the process of melting one metal surface to another to join them.

wheel base: the horizontal distance between the two wheel axles.

wild goose chase: see "chase."

women's frame: see "step-through frame."

yoke: the part attaching the brake cable to the straddle cable on a cantilever or U-brake.

APPENDIX E

If you have a torque wrench or two (which I highly recommend), these are the standard tightening torques specified by the manufacturers for their products. When the manufacturer is not mentioned, it generally applies at least to Shimano and likely to many other companies that base torque specs on Shimano.

Divide these numbers by 12 to convert them to foot-pounds (ft-lbs). Multiply these numbers by 0.113 to convert to Newton-meters (N-m).

BRAKE ASSEMBLIES

brake-lever-to-handlebar-clamp bolt .52-69 inch-pounds
Campagnolo brake lever clamp bolt . . . . .89 inch-pounds
STI lever handlebar-clamp nut . . . . .50-70 inch-pounds
Campagnolo ErgoPower lever clamp bolt . . . . .71 inch-pounds
Mavic Mektronic lever clamp bolt .62-80 inch-pounds
brake-caliper mounting nut . . . . .69-87 inch-pounds
Campagnolo brake-caliper-mount nut . . . . .89 inch-pounds
brake cable fixing bolt . . . . .52-69 inch-pounds
Campagnolo brake cable fixing bolt . . . . .44 inch-pounds
brake pad mounting bolt . . . . .43-61 inch-pounds
Campagnolo brake pad mounting bolt . . . . .68 inch-pounds
STI lever-stud set screw . . . . .8 inch-pounds

DERAILLEUR AND SHIFTER ASSEMBLIES

front derailleur cable fixing bolt . . . . .44-60 inch-pounds
Campagnolo front derailleur cable fixing bolt . . . . .44 inch-pounds
front derailleur clamp bolt . . . . .44-60 inch-pounds
Campagnolo front derailleur clamp bolt . . . . .31 inch-pounds
Campagnolo front derailleur braze-on clamp bolt . . . . .62 inch-pounds
rear derailleur cable fixing bolt . . . . .44-60 inch-pounds
Campagnolo rear derailleur cable fixing bolt . . . . .53 inch-pounds
rear derailleur mounting bolt . . . . .70-86 inch-pounds
Mavic Mektronic rear derailleur mounting bolt . . . . .71-88 inch-pounds
Campagnolo rear derailleur mounting bolt . . . . .133 inch-pounds
rear derailleur pulley center bolts . . . . .27-34 inch-pounds
down-tube-shifter-boss cable stop bolt . . . . .13-18 inch-pounds
STI lever handlebar-clamp nut . . . . .50-70 inch-pounds
Campagnolo ErgoPower lever clamp bolt . . . . .71 inch-pounds
STI shift lever pivot bolt . . . . .70-85 inch-pounds
STI lever-stud set screw . . . . .8 inch-pounds

HUBS, CASSETTES, QUICK RELEASES

hub quick release lever closing .43-65 inch-pounds
bolt-on steel skewer . . . . .65 inch-pounds
bolt-on titanium skewer . . . . .85 inch-pounds
quick release axle locknut . . . . .87-217 inch-pounds
Campagnolo quick-release: to tighten . . . . .480 inch-pounds
Campagnolo quick-release: to release . . . . .144-300 inch-pounds

torque table

HUBS, CASSETTES, QUICK RELEASES (cont.)

freehub cassette body fixing bolt . . . . .305-434 inch-pounds
cassette cog lockring . . . . .261-434 inch-pounds
Campagnolo cassette cog lockring . . . . .442 inch-pounds
cassette lockring on Mavic freehub .354 inch-pounds

CRANK, BOTTOM BRACKET ASSEMBLIES

crank arm fixing bolt . . . . .305-435 inch-pounds
Campagnolo crank arm fixing bolt . . . . .283-336 inch-pounds
one-key-release retaining dust cap . . . . .44-60 inch-pounds
simple dust cap . . . . .30-40 inch-pounds
chainring fixing bolt . . . . .70-100 inch-pounds
Campagnolo chainring fixing bolt . . . . .96-120 inch-pounds
cartridge bottom bracket cups .435-608 inch-pounds
Campagnolo cartridge bottom-bracket cups . . . . .620 inch-pounds
standard bottom bracket fixed cup . . . . .609-695 inch-pounds
standard bottom bracket lockring . . . . .609-695 inch-pounds
pedal axle to crankarm . . . . .304 inch-pounds minimum
Campagnolo pedal axle to crankarm . . . . .354-398 inch-pounds

PEDALS

pedal axle cartridge unit into body . . . . .87-104 inch-pounds
pedal axle to crankarm . . . . .304 inch-pounds minimum
Campagnolo pedal axle to crankarm . . . . .354-398 inch-pounds
SPD-R pedal face plate screws . . . . .13 inch-pounds minimum
Speedplay X/1, X/2 axle Torx screw . . . . .35-40 inch-pounds
Speedplay X/3 axle locknut . . . . .35-40 inch-pounds
Campagnolo Record cartridge unit into body . . . . .115 inch-pounds
Campagnolo Chorus cartridge unit into body . . . . .115 inch-pounds
Campagnolo Veloce cartridge unit into body . . . . .89 inch-pounds
shoe cleat fixing bolt . . . . .43-52 inch-pounds

SEATS, STEMS, HEADSETS

seat post band-clamp bolt . . . . .174-347 inch-pounds
seat tube clamp binder bolt . . . . .106-140 inch-pounds
Campagnolo seat binder bolt . . . . .36-60 inch-pounds
Campagnolo seatpost clamp bolt . . . . .194 inch-pounds
stem handlebar clamping bolt .160-260 inch-pounds
3T Forge Ahead handlebar clamp bolt . . . . .159-177 inch-pounds
AheadSet stem clamp bolts . . . . .130 inch-pounds
Aheadset bearing preload . . . . .22 inch-pounds
stem expander bolt . . . . .174-260 inch-pounds
3T Forge Ahead wedge bolt .MAX 177 inch-pounds
Campagnolo headset locknut . . . . .300 inch-pounds

SUSPENSION FORKS

Rock Shox Ruby plunger bolt . . . . .60 inch-pounds

SHOES

shoe cleat fixing bolt . . . . .43-52 inch-pounds

INDEX

index

ILLUSTRATION INDEX

BIBLIOGRAPHY

Barnett, John. *Barnett's Manual: Analysis and Procedures for Bicycle Mechanics*. Brattleboro, VT: Vitesse Press, 1989, VeloPress, 1996

Brandt, Jobst. *The Bicycle Wheel*. Menlo Park, CA: Avocet, 1988

Compton, Tom, www.analyticcycling.com Web site, 1998

Dushan, Allan. *Surviving the Trail*, Tumbleweed Films, 1993

Editors of *Bicycling* and *Mountain Bike* magazines. *Bicycling Magazine's Complete Guide to Bicycle Maintenance and Repair*. Emmaus, PA: Rodale Press, 1994

Leslie, David. *The Mountain Bike Book*. London: Ward Lock, 1996

Lindorf, W. *Mountain Bike Repair and Maintenance*. London: Ward Lock, 1995

Muir, John and Gregg, Tosh. *How to Keep Your Volkswagen Alive: a Manual of Step by Step Procedures for the Complete Idiot*. Santa Fe, NM: John Muir Publications, 1969, 74, 75, 81, 85, 88, 90, 92, 94

Pirsig, Robert. *Zen and the Art of Motorcycle Maintenance*. New York, NY: William Morrow & Co., 1974

Schraner, Gerd. *The Art of Wheelbuilding*. Denver, CO: Buonpane, 1999

Stevenson, John, and Richards, Brant. *Mountain Bikes: Maintenance and Repair*. Mill Valley, CA: Bicycle Books, 1994

Taylor, Garrett, *Bicycle Wheelbuilding 101, a Video Lesson in the Art of Wheelbuilding*. Westwood, MA: Roxadog, 1994

Van der Plas, Robert. *The Bicycle Repair Book*. Mill Valley, CA: Bicycle Books, 1993

Van der Plas, Robert. *Mountain Bike Maintenance*. San Francisco: Bicycle Books, 1994

Zinn, Lennard, *Zinn & the Art of Mountain Bike Maintenance*. Boulder, CO: VeloPress, 1996, 1997

Zinn, Lennard, *Mountain Bike Performance Handbook*. Osceola, WI: MBI, 1998

Frame	Serial Number	
	Size	Date of purchase
Fork	Serial Number	
	Steerer tube length	Date of purchase
Stem	Size	Date of purchase
Handlebars	Size	Date of purchase
Shifters		Date of purchase
Brakes		Date of purchase
Pedals		Date of purchase
Cranks	Size	Date of purchase
Chainrings	Size	Date of purchase
Bottom bracket	Size	Date of purchase
Saddle		Date of purchase
Stem	Size	Date of purchase
Wheels	Spokes	Date of purchase

Other

Frame	Serial Number	
	Size	Date of purchase
Fork	Serial Number	
	Steerer tube length	Date of purchase
Stem	Size	Date of purchase
Handlebars	Size	Date of purchase
Shifters		Date of purchase
Brakes		Date of purchase
Pedals		Date of purchase
Cranks	Size	Date of purchase
Chainrings	Size	Date of purchase
Bottom bracket	Size	Date of purchase
Saddle		Date of purchase
Stem	Size	Date of purchase
Wheels	Spokes	Date of purchase

Other

Frame	Serial Number	
	Size	Date of purchase
Fork	Serial Number	
	Steerer tube length	Date of purchase
Stem	Size	Date of purchase
Handlebars	Size	Date of purchase
Shifters		Date of purchase
Brakes		Date of purchase
Pedals		Date of purchase
Cranks	Size	Date of purchase
Chainrings	Size	Date of purchase
Bottom bracket	Size	Date of purchase
Saddle		Date of purchase
Stem	Size	Date of purchase
Wheels	Spokes	Date of purchase

Other

Frame — Serial Number
Size — Date of purchase
Fork — Serial Number
Steerer tube length — Date of purchase
Stem — Size — Date of purchase
Handlebars — Size — Date of purchase
Shifters — Date of purchase
Brakes — Date of purchase
Pedals — Date of purchase
Cranks — Size — Date of purchase
Chainrings — Size — Date of purchase
Bottom bracket — Size — Date of purchase
Saddle — Date of purchase
Stem — Size — Date of purchase
Wheels — Spokes — Date of purchase

Other

OTHER BOOKS  FROM VELOPRESS

Cyclist's Training Bible *by Joe Friel*
Hailed as a major breakthrough in training for competitive cycling, this book helps take cyclists from where they are
to where they want to be — the podium. • 288 pp. • Photos, charts, diagrams • Paperback • **1-884737-21-8 •P-BIB $19.95**

Cyclo-cross *by Simon Burney*
Training and Technique
A must read for anyone brave enough to ride their road bike downhill through the mud. Expanded from the original to include mountain bike
conversion to cyclo-cross. • 200 pp. • Photos, charts, diagrams • Paperback **• 1-884737-20-X • P-CRS $19.95**

Off-Season Training for Cycling *by Edmund R. Burke, Ph.D.*
Get a jump on the competition with the newest training book from Ed Burke and VeloPress. Burke takes you through everything you need to know about winter training indoor workouts, weight training, cross-training, periodization and more. • 200 pp. • Paperback **• 1-884737-40-4 • P-OFF $14.95**

VeloNews Training Diary *by Joe Friel*
The world's most popular training diary for cyclists. Allows you to record every facet of training with plenty of room for notes. Non-dated, so you can start any time of the year. • 235 pp. • Spiral-bound **• 1-884737-42-0 • P-DIA $12.95**

Inside Triathlon Training Diary *by Joe Friel*
The best multisport diary available anywhere. Combines the best in quantitative and qualitative training notation. Designed to help you attain your best fitness ever. Non-dated, so you can start at any time of the year. • 235 pp. • Spiral-bound **•1-884737-41-2 •P-IDI $12.95**

Barnett's Manual *by John Barnett*
The most expensive bicycle maintenance manual in the world ... and worth every penny. Regarded by professionals world-wide as the final word in bicycle maintenance. • 950 pp. • Illustrations, diagrams, charts • Five-ring loose-leaf binder. **• 1-884737-16-1 •P-BNT $149.95**

Tales from the Toolbox *by Scott Parr and Rupert Guinness*
In his years as the Motorola team mechanic, Scott Parr saw it all. *Tales from the Toolbox* takes you inside the Motorola team van on the roads of Europe. Get the inside dirt on the pro peloton and the guys who really make it happen ... the mechanics, of course. • 168 pp. • Paperback **• 1-884737-39-0 • P-TFT $14.95**

Eddy Merckx *by Rik Vanwalleghem*
Discover the passion and fear that motivated the world's greatest cyclist. The man they called "the cannibal" is captured like never before in this lavish coffee-table book. • 216 pp. • 24 color & 165 B/W photos • Paperback **• 1-884737-22-6 • P-MPB $29.95**

John Wilcockson's World of Cycling
John Wilcockson, editor of *VeloNews*, has reported on every major bicycle race, including the Tour de France, for 30 years. His writing brings to life all the various facets of the fascinating sport of professional cycling and its leading racers and personalities. This book features 16 pages of color photos by Graham Watson, as well as stories on Greg LeMond, Lance Armstrong and many others. Essential reading for the cycling fan! • 336 pp. • 16 pages of color photos • Paperback **• 1-884737-50-1 •P-WOC $19.95**

The Athlete's Guide to Sponsorship *by Jennifer Drury and Cheri Elliott*
This concise, yet comprehensive step-by-step guide is for any athlete, team or sport event planner who is considering sponsorship. • **1-884737-45-5 •P-GUI $14.95**

The Giro d'Italia *by Dino Buzzati*
Coppi versus Bartali at the 1949 Tour of Italy
It was perhaps the most famous Giro of them all, pitting bitter arch-rivals Fausto Coppi and Gino Bartali as they battled it out on roads still marked by World War II. Buzzati's account is a true classic of cycling journalism that pulls the reader inside this famous race. Complete with maps and illustrations, as well as an introduction by VeloNews editor John Wilcockson. • Paperback • maps and illustrations **• 1-884737-51-X •P-GRO $16.95**

Zinn & the Art of Mountain Bike Maintenance *by Lennard Zinn*
Guides you through every aspect of mountain-bike maintenance, repair and troubleshooting in a succinct, idiot-proof format. • 288 pp. • illustrations • Paperback **• 1-884737-47-1 • P-ZYN $17.95**

Weight Training for Cyclists *by Eric Schmitz and Ken Doyle*
Written from the premise that optimum cycling performance demands total body strength, this book informs the serious cyclist on how to increase strength with weight training, as cycling alone cannot completely develop the muscle groups used while riding. • 160 pp. • 40 b/w photos • Paperback **• 1-884737-43-9 •P-WTC $14.95**

Complete Guide to Sports Nutrition *by Monique Ryan*
Monique Ryan's book has a wealth of cutting-edge information and concepts explained clearly. No other sports nutrition book places such a needed emphasis on menu and meal planning, food strategies, weight management, and other practical food-related topics. • 340 pp. • charts, graphs, tables • Paperback **• 1-884737-57-9 •P-NUT $16.95**

The Female Cyclist *by Gale Bernhardt*
Perfect for the woman who enjoys cycling for fitness and wants to improve her riding skills and achieve higher goals. Includes a special chapter on bike fit, as well as detailed programs for blending cycling and training, women's health and nutrition, and tips for making cycling more comfortable. Great information for male cyclists, too! • 240 pp. • Paperback **• 1-884737-58-7 •P-FEM $16.95**

please mail to
VeloPress
1830 N 55th St
Boulder CO
80301

or fax to
303/444-6788

or call toll-free
800/234-8356

or visit the Web at
www.velogear.com

VeloPress books are also available at your favorite bike shop or bookstore

Name ______________________

Street address ______________________

Phone ( )- ____________ **Fax ( ) -** ______________________

City ____________ **State** ____________ **Zip** ____________

☐ ☐ **credit card number** ______________________ **expiration date** ____________

PLEASE ENCLOSE PAYMENT WITH ORDER

QUANTITY	PRODUCT	PRODUCT TITLE	ISBN	RETAIL	AMOUNT
	P-BNT	Barnett's Manual	1-884737-16-1	$ 149.95	
	P-BIB	Cyclist's Training Bible	1-884737-21-8	19.95	
	P-CRS	Cyclo-Cross	1-884737-20-X	19.95	
	P-MPB	Eddy Merckx	1-884737-22-6	29.95	
	P-OFF	Off-Season Training	1-884737-40-4	14.95	
	P-BOX	Tales from the Tool Box	1-884737-39-0	14.95	
	P-MTW	Two Wheels	1-884737-11-0	12.95	
	P-IDI	Inside Triathlon Training Diary	1-884737-41-2	12.95	
	P-DIA	VeloNews Training Diary	1-884737-42-0	12.95	
	P-WOC	John Wilcockson's World of Cycling	1-884737-50-1	19.95	
	P-GUI	The Athlete's Guide to Sponsorship	1-884737-45-5	14.95	
	P-GRO	The Giro d'Italia	1-884737-51-X	16.95	
	P-ZYN	Zinn & the Art of Mountain Bike Maintenance	1-884737-47-1	17.95	
	P-WTC	Weight Training for Cyclists	1-884737-43-9	14.95	
	P-NUT	Complete Guide to Sports Nutrition	1-884737-57-9	16.95	
	P-FEM	The Female Cyclist	1-884737-58-7	16.95	
Total items ordered				SUB TOTAL	
		PLEASE ADD $3.95 SHIPPING PER ITEM ORDERED		SHIPPING	
				TOTAL	

ABOUT THE AUTHOR

Lennard Zinn is a bike racer, framebuilder and technical writer. He grew up cycling, skiing, running rivers and tinkering with mechanical devices in Los Alamos, New Mexico. After receiving a B.A. in physics from Colorado College, he became a member of the U.S. Olympic Development (road) Cycling Team. He went on to work in Tom Ritchey's framebuilding shop and has been producing custom road and mountain frames at Zinn Cycles since 1982.

Zinn has been writing for *VeloNews* since 1989 and is currently the senior technical writer for *VeloNews* and *Inside Triathlon* magazines. This is his fourth book; other titles by Zinn are *Zinn & the Art of Mountain Bike Maintenance* (VeloPress, 1996 and 1997), *Mountain Bike Performance Handbook* (MBI, 1998), and *Mountain Bike Owner's Manual* (VeloPress, 1998).

ABOUT THE ILLUSTRATOR

A former mechanic and bike racer, Todd Telander devotes most of his time now to artistic endeavors. In addition to drawing bicycle parts, he paints and draws wildlife for publishers, museums, design companies and individuals. Birds are his favorite subject, so he has included a little house sparrow.